THE HISTORY
OF ENGLAND

VOLUME V

THE HISTORY
OF ENGLAND

from the Invasion of Julius Caesar

to The Revolution in 1688

IN SIX VOLUMES

BY DAVID HUME, ESQ.

VOLUME V

Based on the Edition of 1778, with the Author's

Last Corrections and Improvements

Liberty Fund
Indianapolis

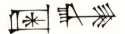

Foreword copyright © 1983 by William B. Todd. All rights reserved. All inquiries should be addressed to Liberty Fund, Inc., 8335 Allison Pointe Trail, Suite 300, Indianapolis, Indiana 46250-1684. This book was manufactured in the United States of America.

This Liberty Fund edition is based on the edition of 1778, containing the author's last corrections and improvements. The only two recorded sets of that edition in the United States were consulted. One is a complete set at the Humanities Research Center of the University of Texas at Austin. The other is an incomplete set in the Boston Public Library. The publisher acknowledges with thanks the cooperation of both institutions as well as the advice of Professors William B. Todd and David Levy.

Design by Martin Lubin/Betty Binns Graphics, New York, New York.
Editorial services provided by Harkavy Publishing Service, New York, New York.

Library of Congress Cataloging in Publication Data

Hume, David, 1711–1776.
    The history of England.

    "Based on the edition of 1778, with the author's last corrections and improvements."
    Reprint. Originally published: London: T. Cadell, 1778. With new foreword.
    1. Great Britain—History—To 1485. 2. Great Britain—History—Tudors, 1485–1603. 3. Great Britain—History—Stuarts, 1603–1714. I. Title.
DA30.H9 1983   942   82-25868
ISBN 0-86597-019-X (series)
ISBN 0-86597-020-3 (pbk. series)
ISBN 0-86597-032-7 (Volume V)
ISBN 0-86597-033-5 (Volume V pbk.)

16 17 18 19 20 C 8 7 6 5 4
16 17 18 19 20 P 10 9 8 7 6

CONTENTS

OF THE FIFTH VOLUME

A parliament – Return of Bristol – Rupture with Spain –
Treaty with France – Mansfeldt's expedition –
Death of the king – His character

PAGE 97

APPENDIX
TO THE
REIGN OF JAMES I

Civil government of England during
this period – Ecclesiastical government –
Manners – Finances – Navy – Commerce –
Manufactures – Colonies – Learning and arts

PAGE 124

L
CHARLES I

A parliament at Westminster –
At Oxford – Naval expedition against Spain –
Second parliament – Impeachment of Buckingham –
Violent measures of the court – War with France –
Expedition to the isle of Rhé

PAGE 156

L I

L I I

L I I I

THE HISTORY
OF ENGLAND

VOLUME V

XLV

JAMES I

---

*Introduction – James's first
transactions – State of Europe –
Rosni's negociations – Raleigh's conspiracy –
Hampton-court conference – A Parliament –
Peace with Spain*

THE CROWN OF ENGLAND was never transmitted from father to son with greater tranquillity, than it passed from the family of Tudor to that of Stuart. During the whole reign of Elizabeth, the eyes of men had been employed in search of her successor; and when old age made the prospect of her death more immediate, there appeared none but the king of Scots, who could advance any just claim or pretension to the throne. He was great grand-son of Margaret, elder daughter of Henry VII. and, on the failure of the male-line, his hereditary right remained unquestionable. If the religion of Mary queen of Scots, and the other prejudices contracted against her, had formed any considerable obstacle to her succession; these objections, being entirely personal, had no place with regard to her son. Men also considered, that, though the title, derived from blood, had been frequently violated since the Norman conquest, such licences had proceeded more from force or intrigue, than from any deliberate maxims of government. The lineal heir had still in the end prevailed; and both his exclusion and restoration had been commonly attended with such convulsions, as were sufficient to warn all prudent men not lightly to give way to such irregularities. If the will of Henry VIII. authorised by act of parliament, had tacitly excluded the Scottish line; the tyranny and caprices of that monarch had been so signal, that a settlement of this nature, unsupported by any just reason, had no authority with the people. Queen Elizabeth too, with her dying breath, had recognized the undoubted title of her kinsman James; and the whole nation seemed to dispose themselves with joy and pleasure for his reception. Though born and educated amidst a foreign and hostile people, men hoped, from his character of moderation and wisdom, that he would embrace the maxims of an English monarch; and the prudent foresaw greater advantages, resulting from a union with Scotland, than disadvantages from submitting to a prince of that nation. The alacrity, with which the English looked towards the successor, had appeared so evident to Elizabeth, that, concurring with other causes, it affected her with the deepest melancholy; and that wise princess, whose penetration and experience had given her the greatest insight into human affairs, had not yet sufficiently weighed the ingratitude of courtiers, and levity of the people.

As victory abroad, and tranquillity at home, had attended this princess, she left the nation in such flourishing circumstances, that her successor possessed every advantage, except that of comparison with her illustrious name, when he mounted the throne of *First trans- actions of this reign.* England. The king's journey from Edinburgh to London, immediately afforded to the inquisitive some circumstances of comparison, which even the natural partiality in favour of their new sovereign, could not interpret to his advantage. As he passed along, all ranks of men flocked about him, from every quarter; allured by interest or curiosity. Great were the rejoicings, and loud and hearty the acclamations which resounded from all sides; and every one could remember how the affability and popular manners of their queen displayed themselves, amidst such concourse and exultation of her subjects. But James, though sociable and familiar with his friends and courtiers, hated the bustle of a mixt multitude; and though far from disliking flattery, yet was he still fonder of tranquillity and ease. He issued therefore a proclamation, forbidding this resort of people, on pretence of the scarcity of provisions, and other inconveniencies, which, he said, would necessarily attend it.[a]

He was not, however, insensible to the great flow of affection, which appeared in his new subjects; and being himself of an affectionate temper, he seems to have been in haste to make them some return of kindness and good offices. To this motive, probably, we are to ascribe that profuseness of titles, which was observed in the beginning of his reign; when in six weeks time, after his entrance into the kingdom, he is computed to have bestowed knighthood on no less than 237 persons. If Elizabeth's frugality of honours, as well as of money, had formerly been repined at, it began now to be valued and esteemed: And every one was sensible, that the king, by his lavish and premature conferring of favours, had failed of obliging the persons, on whom he bestowed them. Titles of all kinds became so common, that they were scarcely marks of distinction; and being distributed, without choice or deliberation, to persons unknown to the prince, were regarded more as the proofs of facility and good-nature, than of any determined friendship or esteem.

A pasquinade was affixed to St. Paul's, in which an art was promised to be taught, very necessary to assist frail memories, in retaining the names of the new nobility.[b]

We may presume, that the English would have thrown less blame on the king's facility in bestowing favours, had these been confined entirely to their own nation, and had not been shared out, in too unequal proportions, to his old subjects. James, who, through his whole reign, was more guided by temper and inclination than by the rules of political prudence, had brought with him great numbers of his Scottish courtiers; whose impatience and importunity were apt, in many particulars, to impose on the easy nature of their master, and extort favours, of which, it is natural to imagine, his English subjects would loudly complain. The duke of Lenox, the earl of Marre, lord Hume, lord Kinloss, Sir George Hume, secretary Elphinstone,[c] were immediately added to the English privy council. Sir George Hume, whom he created earl of Dunbar, was his declared favourite as long as that nobleman lived, and was one of the wisest and most virtuous, though the least

[a] Kennet, p. 662.   [b] Wilson, in Kennet, p. 665.   [c] Ibid. p. 662.

powerful, of all those whom the king ever honoured with that distinction. Hay, some time after, was created Viscount Doncaster, then earl of Carlisle, and got an immense fortune from the crown; all of which he spent in a splendid and courtly manner. Ramsay obtained the title of Earl of Holderness; and many others, being raised, on a sudden, to the highest elevation, encreased, by their insolence, that envy, which naturally attended them, as strangers and ancient enemies.

It must, however, be owned, in justice to James, that he left almost all the chief offices in the hands of Elizabeth's ministers, and trusted the conduct of political concerns, both foreign and domestic, to his English subjects. Among these, secretary Cecil, created successively Lord Essindon, Viscount Cranborne, and Earl of Salisbury, was always regarded as his prime minister and chief counsellor. Though the capacity and penetration of this minister were sufficiently known, his favour with the king created surprize on the accession of that monarch. The secret correspondence into which he had entered with James, and which had sensibly contributed to the easy reception of that prince in England, laid the foundation of Cecil's credit; and while all his former associates, Sir Walter Raleigh, lord Grey, lord Cobham, were discountenanced on account of their animosity against Essex, as well as for other reasons, this minister was continued in employment, and treated with the greatest confidence and regard.

The capacity of James and his ministers in negociation was immediately put to trial, on the appearance of ambassadors from almost all the princes and states of Europe, in order to congratulate him on his accession, and to form with him new treaties and alliances. Beside ministers from Venice, Denmark, the Palatinate; Henry Frederic of Nassau, assisted by Barnevelt the Pensionary of Holland, was ambassador from the states of the United Provinces. Aremberg was sent by Archduke Albert; and Taxis was expected in a little time from Spain. But he who most excited the attention of the public, both on account of his own merit and that of his master, was the marquess of Rosni, afterwards duke of Sully, prime minister and favourite of Henry IV. of France.

State of Europe. When the dominions of the house of Austria devolved on Philip II. all Europe was struck with terror; lest the power of a family, which had been raised by fortune, should now be carried to an

CHAPTER XLV

immeasurable height, by the wisdom and conduct of this monarch. But never were apprehensions found in the event to be more groundless. Slow without prudence, ambitious without enterprize, false without deceiving any body, and refined without any true judgment; such was the character of Philip, and such the character, which, during his life-time, and after his death, he impressed on the Spanish councils. Revolted or depopulated provinces, discontented or indolent inhabitants, were the spectacles, which those dominions, lying in every climate of the globe, presented to Philip III. a weak prince, and to the duke of Lerma, a minister, weak and odious. But though military discipline, which still remained, was what alone gave some appearance of life and vigour to that languishing body; yet so great was the terror, produced by former power and ambition, that the reduction of the house of Austria was the object of men's vows, throughout all the states of Christendom. It was not perceived, that the French empire, now united in domestic peace, and governed by the most heroic and most amiable prince, that adorns modern history, was become, of itself, a sufficient counterpoise to the Spanish greatness. Perhaps, that prince himself did not perceive it, when he proposed, by his minister, a league with James, in conjunction with Venice, the United Provinces, and the northern crowns; in order to attack the Austrian dominions on every side, and depress the exorbitant power of that ambitious family.[d] But the genius of the English monarch was not equal to such vast enterprizes. The love of peace was his ruling passion; and it was his peculiar felicity, that the conjunctures of the times rendered the same object, which was agreeable to him, in the highest degree advantageous to his people.

Rosni's negociations.

The French ambassador, therefore, was obliged to depart from these extensive views, and to concert with James the means of providing for the safety of the United Provinces: Nor was this object altogether without its difficulties. The king, before his accession, had entertained scruples with regard to the revolt of the Low-Countries, and being commonly open and sincere,[e] he had, on many occasions, gone so far as to give to the Dutch the appellation of rebels:[f] But having conversed more fully with English

---

[d] Sully's Memoirs.   [e] La Boderie, vol. i. p. 120.   [f] Winwood, vol. ii. p. 55.

ministers and courtiers, he found their attachment to that republic so strong, and their opinion of common interest so established, that he was obliged to sacrifice to politics his sense of justice; a quality, which, even when erroneous, is respectable as well as rare in a monarch. He therefore agreed with Rosni to support secretly the states-general, in concert with the king of France; lest their weakness and despair should oblige them to submit to their old master. The articles of the treaty were few and simple. It was stipulated, that the two kings should allow the Dutch to levy forces in their respective dominions; and should underhand remit to that republic the sum of 1,400,000 livres a-year for the pay of these forces: That the whole sum should be advanced by the king of France; but that the third of it should be deducted from the debt due by him to queen Elizabeth. And if the Spaniards attacked either of the princes, they agreed to assist each other; Henry with a force of ten thousand men, James with that of six. This treaty, one of the wisest and most equitable concluded by James, during the course of his reign, was more the work of the prince himself, than any of his ministers.[g]

Raleigh's conspiracy.   Amidst the great tranquillity, both foreign and domestic, with which the nation was blest, nothing could be more surprising than the discovery of a conspiracy to subvert the government, and to fix on the throne Arabella Stuart, a near relation of the king's by the family of Lenox, and descended equally from Henry VII. Every thing remains still mysterious in this conspiracy; and history can give us no clue to unravel it. Watson and Clarke, two catholic priests, were accused of the plot: Lord Grey, a puritan: Lord Cobham, a thoughtless man, of no fixt principle: And Sir Walter Raleigh, suspected to be of that philosophical sect, who were then extremely rare in England, and who have since received the appellation of *free thinkers.* Together with these, Mr. Broke, brother to lord Cobham, Sir Griffin Markham, Mr. Copeley, Sir Edward Parham. What cement could unite men of such discordant principles in so dangerous a combination; what end they proposed, or what means proportioned to an undertaking of this nature, has never yet been explained, and cannot easily be imagined. As Raleigh, Grey, and Cobham were commonly believed, after the queen's

[g] Sully's Memoirs.

death, to have opposed proclaiming the king, till conditions should be made with him; they were upon that account extremely obnoxious to the court and ministry; and the people were apt, at first, to suspect, that the plot was merely a contrivance of secretary Cecil, to get rid of his old confederates, now become his most inveterate enemies. But the confession, as well as trial of the criminals, put the matter beyond doubt.[h] And though no one could find any marks of a concerted enterprize, it appeared, that men of furious and ambitious spirits, meeting frequently together, and believing all the world discontented like themselves, had entertained very criminal projects, and had even entered, some of them at least, into a correspondence with Aremberg, the Flemish ambassador, in order to give disturbance to the new settlement.

The two priests[i] and Broke[k] were executed: Cobham, Grey, and Markham were pardoned,[l] after they had laid their heads upon the block.[m] Raleigh too was reprieved, not pardoned; and he remained in confinement many years afterwards.

It appears from Sully's Memoirs, that Raleigh secretly offered his services to the French ambassador; and we may thence presume, that, meeting with a repulse from that quarter, he had recourse, for the same unwarrantable purposes, to the Flemish minister. Such a conjecture we are now enabled to form; but it must be confessed, that, on his trial, there appeared no proof of this transaction, nor indeed any circumstance which could justify his condemnation. He was accused by Cobham alone, in a sudden fit of passion, upon hearing, that Raleigh, when examined, had pointed out some circumstances, by which Cobham's guilt might be known and ascertained. This accusation Cobham afterwards retracted; and soon after, he retracted his retractation. Yet upon the written evidence of this single witness, a man of no honour or understanding, and so contradictory in his testimony; not confronted with Raleigh; not supported by any concurring circumstance; was that great man, contrary to all law and equity, found guilty by the jury. His name was at that time extremely odious in England; and every man was pleased to give sentence against the capital enemy of Essex, the favourite of the people.

[h] State Trials, p. 180. 2d edit. Winwood, vol. ii. p. 8, 11.   [i] November 29.
[k] December 5.   [l] December 9.   [m] Winwood, vol. ii. p. 11.

Sir Edward Coke, the famous lawyer, then attorney-general, managed the cause for the crown, and threw out on Raleigh such gross abuse, as may be deemed a great reflection, not only on his own memory, but even, in some degree, on the manners of the age. Traitor, monster, viper, and spider of hell, are the terms, which he employs against one of the most illustrious men of the kingdom, who was under trial for life and fortune, and who defended himself with temper, eloquence, and courage.[n]

1604. The next occupation of the king was entirely according to his heart's content. He was employed, in dictating magisterially to an assembly of divines concerning points of faith and discipline, and in receiving the applauses of these holy men for his superior zeal and learning. The religious disputes between the church and the puritans had induced him to call a conference at Hampton-court, on pretence of finding expedients, which might reconcile both parties.

Though the severities of Elizabeth towards the catholics had much weakened that party, whose genius was opposite to the prevailing spirit of the nation; like severities had had so little influence on the puritans, who were encouraged by that spirit, that no less than seven hundred and fifty clergymen of that party signed a petition to the king on his accession; and many more seemed willing to adhere to it.[o] They all hoped, that James, having received his education in Scotland, and having sometimes professed an attachment to the church, established there, would at least abate the rigour of the laws enacted in support of the ceremonies and against puritans; if he did not show more particular grace and encouragement to that sect. But the king's disposition had taken strongly a contrary biass. The more he knew the puritanical clergy, the less favour he bore to them. He had remarked in their Scottish brethren a violent turn towards republicanism, and a zealous attachment to civil liberty; principles nearly allied to that religious enthusiasm, with which they were actuated. He had found, that being mostly persons of low birth and mean education, the same lofty pretensions, which attended them in their familiar addresses to their Maker, of whom they believed themselves the peculiar

[n] State Trials, 1st edit. p. 176, 177, 182. [o] Fuller, book 10. Collier, vol. ii. p. 672.

CHAPTER XLV

favourites, induced them to use the utmost freedoms with their earthly sovereign. In both capacities, of monarch and of theologian, he had experienced the little complaisance, which they were disposed to show him; whilst they controuled his commands, disputed his tenets, and to his face, before the whole people, censured his conduct and behaviour. If he had submitted to the indignity of courting their favour, he treasured up, on that account, the stronger resentment against them, and was determined to make them feel, in their turn, the weight of his authority. Though he had often met with resistance and faction and obstinacy in the Scottish nobility, he retained no ill will to that order; or rather showed them favour and kindness in England, beyond what reason and sound policy could well justify: But the ascendant, which the presbyterian clergy had assumed over him, was what his monarchical pride could never thoroughly digest.[p]

He dreaded likewise the popularity, which attended this order of men in both kingdoms. As useless austerities and self-denial are imagined, in many religions, to render us acceptable to a benevolent Being, who created us solely for happiness, James remarked, that the rustic severity of these clergymen and of their whole sect had given them, in the eyes of the multitude, the appearance of sanctity and virtue. Strongly inclined himself to mirth and wine and sports of all kinds, he apprehended their censure for his manner of life, free and disengaged. And, being thus averse, from temper as well as policy, to the sect of puritans, he was resolved, if possible, to prevent its farther growth in England.

But it was the character of James's councils, throughout his whole reign, that they were more wise and equitable, in their end, than prudent and political, in the means. Though justly sensible, that no part of civil administration required greater care or a nicer judgment than the conduct of religious parties; he had not perceived, that, in the same proportion as this practical knowledge of theology is requisite, the speculative refinements in it are mean,

[p] James ventured to say in his Basilicon Doron, published while he was in Scotland: "I protest before the great God, and since I am here as upon my Testament, it is no place for me to lie in, that ye shall never find with any Highland or Borderer Thieves, greater ingratitude and more lies and vile perjuries, than with these fanatic spirits: And suffer not the principal of them to brook your land." *K. James's Works*, p. 161.

and even dangerous in a monarch. By entering zealously into frivolous disputes, James gave them an air of importance and dignity, which they could not otherwise have acquired; and being himself inlisted in the quarrel, he could no longer have recourse to contempt and ridicule, the only proper method of appeasing it. The church of England had not yet abandoned the rigid doctrines of grace and predestination: The puritans had not yet separated themselves from the church, nor openly renounced episcopacy. Though the spirit of the parties was considerably different, the only appearing subjects of dispute were concerning the cross in baptism, the ring in marriage, the use of the surplice, and the bowing at the name of Jesus. These were the mighty questions, which were solemnly agitated in the conference at Hampton-court between some bishops and dignified clergymen on the one hand, and some leaders of the puritanical party on the other; the king and his ministers being present.[q]

*Confer-
ence at
Hampton-
court.*

4th Jan.

The puritans were here so unreasonable as to complain of a partial and unfair management of the dispute; as if the search after truth were in any degree the object of such conferences, and a candid indifference, so rare even among private enquirers in *philosophical* questions, could ever be expected among princes and prelates, in a *theological* controversy. The king, it must be confessed, from the beginning of the conference, showed the strongest propensity to the established church, and frequently inculcated a maxim, which, though it has some foundation, is to be received with great limitations, NO BISHOP, NO KING. The bishops, in their turn, were very liberal of their praises towards the royal disputant; and the archbishop of Canterbury said, that *undoubtedly his majesty spake by the special assistance of God's spirit.*[r] A few alterations in the liturgy were agreed to, and both parties separated with mutual dissatisfaction.

It had frequently been the practice of the puritans to form certain assemblies, which they called *prophesyings;* where alternately, as moved by the spirit, they displayed their zeal in prayers and exhortations, and raised their own enthusiasm, as well as that of their audience, to the highest pitch, from that social contagion, which has so mighty an influence on holy fervours, and from the

---

[q] Fuller's Ecclesiast. History.   [r] Kennet, p. 665.

CHAPTER XLV

mutual emulation, which arose in those trials of religious eloquence. Such dangerous societies had been suppressed by Elizabeth; and the ministers in this conference moved the king for their
revival. But James sharply replied, *If you aim at a* Scottish *presbytery
it agrees as well with monarchy as God and the devil. There* Jack *and* Tom
and Will *and* Dick *shall meet and censure me and my council. Therefore
I reiterate my former speech:* Le Roi s'avisera. *Stay, I pray, for one seven
years before you demand; and then, if you find me grow pursie and fat, I
may perchance hearken unto you. For that government will keep me in
breath, and give me work enough.*[s] Such were the political considerations, which determined the king in his choice among religious
parties.

The next assembly, in which James displayed his learning and
eloquence, was one that showed more spirit of liberty than appeared among his bishops and theologians. The parliament was
now ready to assemble; being so long delayed on account of the
plague, which had broken out in London, and raged to such a
degree, that above 30,000 persons are computed to have died of it
in a year; though the city contained at that time little more than
150,000 inhabitants.

*A parlia-
ment.*

*19th
March.*

The speech which the king made on opening the parliament,
fully displays his character, and proves him to have possessed more
knowledge and better parts than prudence or any just sense of
decorum and propriety.[t] Though few productions of the age surpass this performance either in style or matter; it wants that majestic brevity and reserve, which becomes a king in his addresses to
the great council of the nation. It contains, however, a remarkable
stroke of candor, where he confesses his too great facility in yield-
ing to the solicitations of suitors:[u] A fault, which he promises to
correct, but which adhered to him, and distressed him, during the
whole course of his reign.

The first business, in which the commons were engaged, was of
the utmost importance to the preservation of their privileges; and
neither temper nor resolution were wanting in their conduct of it.

In the former periods of the English government, the house of
commons was of so small weight in the balance of the constitution,

[s] Fuller's Ecclesiast. History.   [t] K. James's Works, p. 484, 485, &c. Journ.
22d March, 1603. Kennet, p. 668.   [u] K. James's Works, p. 495, 496.

that little attention had been given, either by the crown, the people, or the house itself, to the choice and continuance of the members. It had been usual, after parliaments were prolonged beyond one session, for the chancellor to exert a discretionary authority, of issuing new writs to supply the place of any members, whom he judged incapable of attending, either on account of their employment, their sickness, or other impediment. This practice gave that minister, and consequently the prince, an unlimited power of modeling at pleasure the representatives of the nation; yet so little jealousy had it created, that the commons, of themselves, without any court influence or intrigue, and contrary to some former votes of their own, confirmed it in the twenty-third of Elizabeth.[w] At that time, though some members, whose places had been supplied on account of sickness, having now recovered their health, appeared in the house, and claimed their seat; such was the authority of the chancellor, that, merely out of respect to him, his sentence was adhered to, and the new members were continued in their places. Here a most dangerous prerogative was conferred on the crown: But to show the genius of that age, or rather the channels in which power then ran, the crown put very little value on this authority; insomuch that two days afterwards, the chancellor, of himself, resigned it back to the commons, and gave them power to judge of a particular vacancy in their house. And when the question, concerning the chancellor's new writs, was again brought on the carpet towards the end of the session, the commons were so little alarmed at the precedent, that, though they re-admitted some old members, whose seats had been vacated, on account of slight indispositions, yet they confirmed the chancellor's sentence, in instances where the distemper appeared to have been dangerous and incurable.[x] Nor did they proceed any farther, in vindication of their privileges, than to vote, *that during the sitting of parliament, there do not, at any time, any writ go out for chusing or returning any member without the warrant of the house.* In Elizabeth's reign we may remark, and the reigns preceding, sessions of parliament were not usually the twelfth part so long as the vacations; and during the latter, the chancellor's power, if he pleased to exert it, was

[w] Journ. January 19, 1580.   [x] Journ. March 18, 1580. See farther D'Ewes, p. 430.

CHAPTER XLV

confirmed, at least left, by this vote, as unlimited and unrestrained as ever.

In a subsequent parliament, the absolute authority of the queen was exerted in a manner still more open; and began for the first time to give alarm to the commons. New writs having been issued by the chancellor, when there was no vacancy, and a controversy arising upon that incident; the queen sent a message to the house, informing them, that it were impertinent for them to deal in such matters. These questions, she said, belonged only to the chancellor; and she had appointed him to confer with the judges, in order to settle all disputes with regard to elections. The commons had the courage, a few days after, to vote "That it was a most perilous precedent, where two knights of a county were duly elected, if any new writ should issue out for a second election, without order of the house itself; that the discussing and adjudging of this and such like differences belonged only to the house; and that there should be no message sent to the lord chancellor, not so much as to enquire what he had done in the matter, because it was conceived to be a matter derogatory to the power and privilege of the house."[y] This is the most considerable, and almost only instance of parliamentary liberty, which occurs during the reign of that princess.

Outlaws, whether on account of debts or crimes, had been declared by the judges,[z] incapable of enjoying a seat in the house, where they must themselves be lawgivers; but this opinion of the judges had been frequently over-ruled. I find, however, in the case of Vaughan,[a] who was questioned for an outlawry, that, having proved all his debts to have been contracted by suretiship, and to have been, most of them, honestly compounded, he was allowed, on account of these favourable circumstances, to keep his seat: Which plainly supposes, that, otherwise, it would have been vacated, on account of the outlawry.[b]

---

[y] D'Ewes, p. 397.   [z] 39 H. 6.   [a] Journ. Feb. 8, 1580.   [b] In a subsequent parliament, that of the 35th of the queen, the commons, after a great debate, expressly voted, that a person outlawed might be elected. D'Ewes, p. 518. But as the matter had been much contested, the king might think the vote of the house no law, and might esteem his own decision of more weight than theirs. We may also suppose, that he was not acquainted with this vote. Queen Elizabeth in her speech to her last parliament complained

When James summoned this parliament, he issued a proclamation;[c] in which, among many general advices, which, like a kind tutor, he bestowed on his people, he strictly enjoins them not to chuse any outlaw for their representative. And he adds; *If any person take upon him the place of knight, citizen, or burgess, not being duly elected, according to the laws and statutes in that behalf provided, and according to the purport, effect, and true meaning of this our proclamation, then every person so offending to be fined or imprisoned for the same.* A proclamation here was plainly put on the same footing with a law, and that in so delicate a point as the right of elections: Most alarming circumstances, had there not been reason to believe, that this measure, being entered into so early in the king's reign proceeded more from precipitation and mistake, than from any serious design of invading the privileges of parliament.[d]

Sir Francis Goodwin was chosen member for the county of Bucks; and his return, as usual, was made into chancery. The chancellor, pronouncing him an outlaw, vacated his seat, and issued writs for a new election.[e] Sir John Fortescue was chosen in his place by the county: But the first act of the house was to reverse the chancellor's sentence, and restore Sir Francis to his seat. At the king's suggestion, the lords desired a conference on the subject; but were absolutely refused by the commons, as the question entirely regarded their own privileges.[f] The commons, however, agreed to make a remonstrance to the king by the mouth of their speaker; in which they maintained that, though the returns were by form made into chancery, yet the sole right of judging with regard to elections belonged to the house itself, not to the chancellor.[g] James was not satisfied, and ordered a conference between

of their admitting outlaws, and represents that conduct of the house as a great abuse. [c] Jan. 11, 1604. Rymer, tom. xvi. p. 561. [d] The duke of Sully tells us, that it was a maxim of James, that no prince in the first year of his reign should begin any considerable undertaking. A maxim reasonable in itself, and very suitable to his cautious, not to say timid character. The facility, with which he departed from this pretension, is another proof, that his meaning was innocent. But had the privileges of parliament been at that time exactly ascertained, or royal power fully limited, could such an imagination ever have been entertained by him as to think, that his proclamation could regulate parliamentary elections? [e] Winwood, vol. ii. p. 18, 19. [f] Journ. 26th March, 1604. [g] Journ. 3d April, 1604.

the house and the judges, whose opinion in this case was opposite to that of the commons. This conference, he said, he commanded as an *absolute* king;[h] an epithet, we are apt to imagine, not very grateful to English ears, but one to which they had already been somewhat accustomed from the mouth of Elizabeth.[i] He added, *That all their privileges were derived from his grant, and hoped they would not turn them against him;*[k] a sentiment, which, from her conduct, it is certain, that princess had also entertained, and which was the reigning principle of her courtiers and ministers, and the spring of all her administration.

The commons were in some perplexity. Their eyes were now opened, and they saw the consequences of that power, which had been assumed by the chancellor, and to which their predecessors had, in some instances, blindly submitted. *By this course,* said a member, *the free election of the counties is taken away, and none shall be chosen but such as shall please the king and council. Let us, therefore, with fortitude, understanding, and sincerity, seek to maintain our privilege. This cannot be construed any contempt in us, but merely a maintenance of our common rights, which our ancestors have left us, and which it is just and fit for us to transmit to our posterity.*[l] Another said,[m] *This may be called a* quo warranto *to seize all our liberties. A chancellor,* added a third, *by this course may call a parliament consisting of what persons he pleases. Any suggestion, by any person, may be the cause of sending a new writ. It is come to this plain question, whether the chancery or parliament ought to have authority.*[n]

Notwithstanding this watchful spirit of liberty, which now appeared in the commons, their deference for majesty was so great, that they appointed a committee to confer with the judges before the king and council. There, the question of law began to appear, in James's eyes, a little more doubtful than he had hitherto imagined it; and in order to extricate himself with some honour, he proposed, that both Goodwin and Fortescue should be set aside, and a writ be issued, by warrant of the house, for a new election. Goodwin gave his consent; and the commons embraced the expedient; but in such a manner, that, while they showed their regard

---

[h] See note [A] at the end of the volume.   [i] Camden in Kennet, p. 375.
[k] Journ. 29th March, 5th April, 1604.   [l] Journ. 30th March, 1604.   [m] Id. ibid.   [n] Id. ibid.

for the king, they secured for the future the free possession of their seats, and the right, which they claimed, of judging solely in their own elections and returns.[o]

A power like this, so essential to the exercise of all their other powers, themselves so essential to public liberty, cannot fairly be deemed an encroachment in the commons; but must be regarded as an inherent privilege, happily rescued from that ambiguity, which the negligence of some former parliaments had thrown upon it.

At the same time, the commons, in the case of Sir Thomas Shirley, established their power of punishing, as well the persons at whose suit any member is arrested, as the officers, who either arrest or detain him. Their asserting of this privilege admits of the same reflection.[p]

About this period, the minds of men, throughout Europe, especially in England, seem to have undergone a general, but insensible revolution. Though letters had been revived in the preceding age, they were chiefly cultivated by those sedentary professions; nor had they, till now, begun to spread themselves, in any degree, among men of the world. Arts, both mechanical and liberal, were every day receiving great improvements. Navigation had extended itself over the whole globe. Travelling was secure and agreeable. And the general system of politics, in Europe, was become more enlarged and comprehensive.

In consequence of this universal fermentation, the ideas of men enlarged themselves on all sides; and the several constituent parts of the gothic governments, which seem to have lain long unactive, began, every where, to operate and encroach on each other. On the continent, where the necessity of discipline had begotten standing armies, the princes commonly established an unlimited authority, and overpowered, by force or intrigue, the liberties of the people. In England, the love of freedom, which, unless checked, flourishes extremely in all liberal natures, acquired new force, and was regulated by more enlarged views, suitably to that cultivated understanding, which became, every day, more common, among men of birth and education. A familiar acquaintance with the precious remains of antiquity excited in every generous breast a passion for a limited constitution, and begat an emulation

---

[o] See note [B] at the end of the volume.   [p] Journ. 6th and 7th May, 1604.

CHAPTER XLV

of those manly virtues, which the Greek and Roman authors, by such animating examples, as well as pathetic expressions, recommend to us. The severe though popular, government of Elizabeth had confined this rising spirit within very narrow bounds: But when a new and a foreign family succeeded to the throne, and a prince less dreaded and less beloved; symptoms immediately appeared of a more free and independent genius in the nation.

Happily this prince possessed neither sufficient capacity to perceive the alteration, nor sufficient art and vigour to check it in its early advances. Jealous of regal, because conscious of little personal authority, he had established within his own mind a speculative system of absolute government, which few of his subjects, he believed, and none but traitors and rebels, would make any scruple to admit. On which-ever side he cast his eye, everything concurred to encourage his prejudices. When he compared himself with the other hereditary sovereigns of Europe, he imagined, that, as he bore the same rank, he was entitled to equal prerogatives; not considering the innovations lately introduced by them, and the military force, by which their authority was supported. In England, that power, almost unlimited, which had been exercised for above a century, especially during the late reign, he ascribed solely to royal birth and title; not to the prudence and spirit of the monarchs, nor to the conjunctures of the times. Even the opposition, which he had struggled with in Scotland, encouraged him still farther in his favourite notions; while he there saw, that the same resistance, which opposed regal authority, violated all law and order, and made way, either for the ravages of a barbarous nobility, or for the more intolerable insolence of seditious preachers. In his own person, therefore, he thought all legal power to be centered, by an hereditary and a divine right: And this opinion might have proved dangerous, if not fatal, to liberty; had not the firmness of the persuasion, and its seeming evidence, induced him to trust solely to his right, without making the smallest provision either of force or politics, in order to support it.

Such were the opposite dispositions of parliament and prince, at the commencement of the Scottish line; dispositions just beginning to exist and to appear in the parliament,[q] but thoroughly established and openly avowed on the part of the prince.

[q] See note [C] at the end of the volume.

The spirit and judgment of the house of commons appeared, not only in defence of their own privileges, but also in their endeavour, though, at this time, in vain, to free trade from those shackles, which the high exerted prerogative, and even, in this respect, the ill-judged tyranny of Elizabeth, had imposed upon it.

James had already, of his own accord, called in and annulled all the numerous patents for monopolies, which had been granted by his predecessor, and which extremely fettered every species of domestic industry: But the exclusive companies still remained; another species of monopoly, by which almost all foreign trade, except that to France, was brought into the hands of a few rapacious engrossers, and all prospect of future improvement in commerce was for ever sacrificed to a little temporary advantage of the sovereign. These companies, though arbitrarily erected, had carried their privileges so far, that almost all the commerce of England was centered in London; and it appears, that the customs of that port amounted to 110,000-l. a-year, while those of all the kingdom beside yielded only seventeen thousand.[r] Nay, the whole trade of London was confined to about 200 citizens,[s] who were easily enabled, by combining among themselves, to fix whatever price they pleased both to the exports and imports of the nation. The committee, appointed to examine this enormous grievance, one of the greatest which we read of in English story, insist on it as a fact well known and avowed, however contrary to present received opinion, that shipping and seamen had sensibly decayed during all the preceding reign.[t] And though nothing be more common than complaints of the decay of trade even during the most flourishing periods; yet is this a consequence which might naturally result from such arbitrary establishments, at a time when the commerce of all the other nations of Europe, except that of Scotland, enjoyed full liberty and indulgence.

While the commons were thus attempting to give liberty to the trading part of the nation, they also endeavoured to free the landed property from the burthen of wardships,[u] and to remove

---

[r] Journ. 21 May, 1604.   [s] Id. ibid.   [t] A remonstrance from the trinity-house, in 1602, says, that in a little above twelve years, after 1588, the shipping and number of seamen in England decayed about a third. Anglesey's happy future state of England, p. 128, from Sir Julius Caesar's collections. See Journ. 21 May, 1604.   [u] Journ. 1 June, 1604.

CHAPTER XLV

those remains of the feudal tenures, under which the nation still laboured. A just regard was shown to the crown on the conduct of this affair; nor was the remedy, sought for, considered as a matter of right, but merely of grace and favour. The profit, which the king reaped both from wards and from respite of homage, was estimated; and it was intended to compound for these prerogatives by a secure and independent revenue. But after some debates in the house, and some conferences with the lords, the affair was found to contain more difficulties than could easily, at that time, be surmounted; and it was not then brought to any conclusion.

The same fate attended an attempt of a like nature, to free the nation from the burthen of purveyance. This prerogative had been much abused by the purveyors,[w] and the commons shewed some intention to offer the king fifty thousand pounds a-year for the abolition of it.

Another affair of the utmost consequence was brought before the parliament, where the commons shewed a greater spirit of independence than any true judgment of national interest. The union of the two kingdoms was zealously, and even impatiently urged by the king.[x] He justly regarded it as the peculiar felicity of his reign, that he had terminated the bloody animosities of these hostile nations, and had reduced the whole island under one government; enjoying tranquillity within itself, and security from all foreign invasions. He hoped, that, while his subjects of both kingdoms reflected on past disasters, besides regarding his person as infinitely precious, they would entertain the strongest desire of securing themselves against the return of like calamities, by a thorough union of laws, parliaments, and privileges. He considered not, that this very reflection operated, as yet, in a contrary manner, on men's prejudices, and kept alive that mutual hatred between the nations, which had been carried to the greatest extremities, and required time to allay it. The more urgent the king appeared in promoting so useful a measure, the more backward was the English parliament in concurring with him; while they ascribed his excessive zeal, to that partiality, in favour of his ancient subjects, of which they thought, that, on other occasions, they had reason to

---

[w] Journ. 30 April, 1604. [x] Journ. 21 April, 1 May, 1604. Parliamentary History, vol. v. p. 91.

complain. Their complaisance for the king, therefore, carried them no farther than to appoint forty-four English to meet with thirty-one Scottish commissioners, in order to deliberate concerning the terms of a union; but without any power of making advances towards the establishment of it.[y]

The same spirit of independence, and perhaps not better judgment, appeared in the house of commons, when the question of supply was brought before them, by some members, attached to the court. In vain was it urged, that, though the king received a supply, which had been voted to Elizabeth, and which had not been collected before her death; yet he found it burthened with a debt contracted by the queen, equal to the full amount of it: That peace was not yet thoroughly concluded with Spain, and that Ireland was still expensive to him: That on his journey from Scotland amidst such a concourse of people, and on that of the queen and royal family, he had expended considerable sums: And that, as the courtiers had looked for greater liberalities from the prince on his accession, and had imposed on his generous nature; so the prince, in his turn, would expect at the beginning, some mark of duty and attachment from his people and some consideration of his necessities. No impression was made on the house of commons by these topics; and the majority appeared fully determined to refuse all supply. The burthen of government, at that time, lay surprisingly light upon the people: And that very reason, which to us, at this distance, may seem a motive of generosity, was the real cause why the parliament was, on all occasions, so remarkably frugal and reserved. They were not, as yet, accustomed to open their purses in so liberal a manner as their successors, in order to supply the wants of their sovereign; and the smallest demand, however requisite, appeared in their eyes unreasonable and exorbitant. The commons seem also to have been desirous of reducing the crown to still farther necessities, by their refusing a bill, sent down to them by the lords, for entailing the crown lands for ever on the king's heirs and successors.[z] The dissipation, made by Elizabeth, had probably taught James the necessity of this law, and shewn them the advantage of refusing it.

[y] Journ. 7 June, 1604. Kennet, p. 673. [z] Parliamentary Hist. vol. v. p. 108.

CHAPTER XLV

In order to cover a disappointment with regard to supply, which might bear a bad construction both at home and abroad, James sent a message to the house,[a] in which he told them, that he desired no supply; and he was very forward in refusing what was never offered him. Soon after, he prorogued the parliament, not without discovering, in his speech, visible marks of dissatisfaction. Even so early in his reign, he saw reason to make public complaints of the restless and encroaching spirit of the puritanical party, and of the malevolence, with which they endeavoured to inspire the commons. Nor were his complaints without foundation, or the puritans without interest; since the commons, now finding themselves free from the arbitrary government of Elizabeth, made application for a conference with the lords, and presented a petition to the king; the purport of both which was to procure, in favour of the puritans, a relaxation of the ecclesiastical laws.[b] The use of the surplice and of the cross in baptism is there chiefly complained of; but the remedy seems to have been expected solely from the king's dispensing power.[c] In the papers, which contain this application and petition, we may also see proofs of the violent animosity of the commons against the catholics, together with the intolerating spirit of that assembly.[d]

7th July.

This summer, the peace with Spain was finally concluded, and was signed by the Spanish ministers at London.[e] In the conferences, previous to this treaty, the nations were found to have so few claims on each other, that, except on account of the support given by England to the Low-Country provinces, the war might appear to have been continued more on account of personal animosity between Philip and Elizabeth, than any contrariety of political interests between their subjects. Some articles in the treaty, which seemed prejudicial to the Dutch commonwealth, were never executed by the king; and as the Spaniards made no complaints on that head, it appeared, that, by secret agreement, the king had expressly reserved the power of sending assistance to the Hollanders.[f] The constable of Castile came into England to ratify the

Peace with Spain.
18th Aug.

---

[a] Journ. 26 June, 1604.   [b] La Boderie, the French ambassador, says, that the house of commons was composed mostly of puritans, vol. i. p. 81.
[c] Parliamentary History, vol. v. p. 98, 99, 100.   [d] See note [D] at the end of the volume.   [e] Rymer, tom. xvi. p. 585, &c.   [f] Winwood, vol. ii. p. 27, 330, *et alibi.* In this respect James's peace was more honourable than that

peace; and on the part of England, the earl of Hertford was sent into the Low-Countries for the same purpose, and the earl of Nottingham, high admiral, into Spain. The train of the latter was numerous and splendid; and the Spaniards, it is said, were extremely surprized, when they beheld the blooming countenances and graceful appearance of the English, whom their bigotry, inflamed by the priests, had represented as so many monsters and infernal demons.

Though England, by means of her naval force, was perfectly secure, during the later years of the Spanish war, James shewed an impatience to put an end to hostilities; and soon after his accession, before any terms of peace were concerted or even proposed by Spain, he recalled all the letters of marque,[g] which had been granted by queen Elizabeth. Archduke Albert had made some advances of a like nature,[h] which invited the king to take this friendly step. But what is remarkable; in James's proclamation for that purpose, he plainly supposes, that, as he had himself, while king of Scotland, always lived in amity with Spain, peace was attached to his person, and that merely by his accession to the crown of England, without any articles of treaty or agreement, he had ended the war between the kingdoms.[i] This ignorance of the law of nations may appear surprising in a prince, who was thirty-six years of age, and who had reigned from his infancy; did we not consider that a king of Scotland, who lives in close friendship with England, has few transactions to manage with foreign princes, and has little opportunity of acquiring experience. Unhappily for James, his timidity, his prejudices, his indolence, his love of amusement, particularly of hunting, to which he was much addicted, ever prevented him from making any progress in the knowledge or practice of foreign politics, and in a little time diminished that regard, which all the neighbouring nations had paid to England, during the reign of his predecessor.[k]

---

which Henry IV. himself made with Spain. This latter prince stipulated not to assist the Dutch; and the supplies, which he secretly sent them, were in direct contravention to the treaty. [g] 23d of June, 1603. [h] Grotii Annal, lib. 12. [i] See proclamations during the first seven years of K. James. Winwood, vol. ii. p. 65. [k] Memoirs de la Boderie, vol. i. p. 64, 181, 195, 217, 302. vol. ii. p. 244, 278.

XLVI

Gunpowder conspiracy –
A parliament – Truce betwixt Spain and
the United Provinces – A parliament – Death of
the French King – Arminianism –
State of Ireland

🏵 🏵 🏵

W E ARE NOW TO RELATE AN EVENT, one of the most memorable, that history has conveyed to posterity, and containing at once a singular proof both of the strength and weakness of
the human mind; its widest departure from morals, and most
steady attachment to religious prejudices. 'Tis the *Gunpowder treason* of which I speak; a fact as certain as it appears incredible.

The Roman catholics had expected great favour and in-   *Gunpowder*
dulgence on the accession of James, both as he was descended   *conspiracy.*
from Mary, whose life they believed to have been sacrificed to their
cause, and as he himself, in his early youth, was imagined to have
shown some partiality towards them; which nothing, they thought,
but interest and necessity had since restrained. It is pretended, that
he had even entered into positive engagements to tolerate their
religion, as soon as he should mount the throne of England;
whether their credulity had interpreted in this sense some obliging
expressions of the king's, or that he had employed such an artifice,
in order to render them favourable to his title.[l] Very soon they
discovered their mistake; and were at once surprized and enraged

---

[l] State Trials, vol. ii. p. 201, 202, 203. Winwood, vol. ii. p. 49.

to find James, on all occasions, express his intention of strictly
executing the laws enacted against them, and of persevering in all
the rigorous measures of Elizabeth. Catesby, a gentleman of good
parts and of an ancient family, first thought of a most extraordinary method of revenge; and he opened his intention to Piercy,
a descendent of the illustrious house of Northumberland. In one
of their conversations with regard to the distressed condition of the
catholics, Piercy having broken into a sally of passion, and mentioned assassinating the king; Catesby took the opportunity of
revealing to him a nobler and more extensive plan of treason,
which not only included a sure execution of vengeance, but afforded some hopes of restoring the catholic religion in England. In
vain, said he, would you put an end to the king's life: He has
children, who would succeed both to his crown and to his maxims
of government. In vain would you extinguish the whole royal
family: The nobility, the gentry, the parliament are all infected
with the same heresy, and could raise to the throne another prince
and another family, who, besides their hatred to our religion,
would be animated with revenge for the tragical death of their
predecessors. To serve any good purpose, we must destroy, at one
blow, the king, the royal family, the lords, the commons; and bury
all our enemies in one common ruin. Happily, they are all assembled on the first meeting of the parliament; and afford us the
opportunity of glorious and useful vengeance. Great preparations
will not be requisite. A few of us, combining, may run a mine below
the hall, in which they meet; and choosing the very moment when
the king harangues both houses, consign over to destruction these
determined foes to all piety and religion. Meanwhile, we ourselves
standing aloof, safe and unsuspected, shall triumph in being the
instruments of divine wrath, and shall behold with pleasure those
sacrilegious walls, in which were passed the edicts for proscribing
our church and butchering her children, tost into a thousand fragments; while their impious inhabitants, meditating perhaps still
new persecutions against us, pass from flames above to flames
below, there for ever to endure the torments due to their offences.[m]

[m] History of the Gunpowder Treason.

CHAPTER XLVI

Piercy was charmed with this project of Catesby; and they agreed to communicate the matter to a few more, and among the rest to Thomas Winter, whom they sent over to Flanders, in quest of Fawkes, an officer in the Spanish service, with whose zeal and courage they were all thoroughly acquainted. When they inlisted any new conspirator, in order to bind him to secrecy, they always, together with an oath, employed the Communion, the most sacred rite of their religion.″ And it is remarkable, that no one of these pious devotees ever entertained the least compunction with regard to the cruel massacre, which they projected, of whatever was great and eminent in the nation. Some of them only were startled by the reflection, that of necessity many catholics must be present; as spectators or attendants on the king, or as having seats in the house of peers: But Tesmond, a jesuit, and Garnet, superior of that order in England, removed these scruples, and shewed them how the interests of religion required, that the innocent should here be sacrificed with the guilty.

All this passed in the spring and summer of the year 1604; when the conspirators also hired a house in Piercy's name, adjoining to that in which the parliament was to assemble. Towards the end of that year they began their operations. That they might be less interrupted, and give less suspicion to the neighbourhood, they carried in store of provisions with them, and never desisted from their labour. Obstinate in their purpose, and confirmed by passion, by principle, and by mutual exhortation, they little feared death in comparison of a disappointment; and having provided arms, together with the instruments of their labour, they resolved there to perish in case of a discovery. Their perseverance advanced the work; and they soon pierced the wall, though three yards in *1605.* thickness; but on approaching the other side, they were somewhat startled at hearing a noise, which they knew not how to account for. Upon enquiry, they found, that it came from the vault below the house of lords; that a magazine of coals had been kept there; and that, as the coals were selling off, the vault would be let to the highest bidder. The opportunity was immediately seized; the place hired by Piercy; thirty-six barrels of powder lodged in it; the whole

″ State Trials, vol. i. p. 190, 198, 210.

covered up with faggots and billets; the doors of the cellar boldly flung open; and every body admitted, as if it contained nothing dangerous.

Confident of success, they now began to look forward, and to plan the remaining part of their project. The king, the queen, prince Henry, were all expected to be present at the opening of parliament. The Duke, by reason of his tender age, would be absent; and it was resolved, that Piercy should seize him, or assassinate him. The princess Elizabeth, a child likewise, was kept at Lord Harrington's house in Warwickshire; and Sir Everard Digby, Rookwood, Grant, being let into the conspiracy, engaged to assemble their friends, on pretence of a hunting match, and seizing that princess, immediately to proclaim her queen. So transported were they with rage against their adversaries, and so charmed with the prospect of revenge, that they forgot all care of their own safety; and trusting to the general confusion, which must result from so unexpected a blow, they foresaw not, that the fury of the people, now unrestrained by any authority, must have turned against them, and would probably have satiated itself, by an universal massacre of the catholics.

The day, so long wished for, now approached, on which the parliament was appointed to assemble. The dreadful secret, though communicated to above twenty persons, had been religiously kept, during the space of near a year and a half. No remorse, no pity, no fear of punishment, no hope of reward, had, as yet, induced any one conspirator, either to abandon the enterprize, or make a discovery of it. The holy fury had extinguished in their breast every other motive; and it was an indiscretion at last, proceeding chiefly from these very bigotted prejudices and partialities, which saved the nation.

Ten days before the meeting of parliament, Lord Monteagle, a catholic, son to Lord Morley, received the following letter, which had been delivered to his servant by an unknown hand. *My Lord, Out of the love I bear to some of your friends, I have a care of your preservation. Therefore I would advise you, as you tender your life, to devise some excuse to shift off your attendance at this parliament. For God and man have concurred to punish the wickedness of this time. And think not slightly of this advertisement; but retire yourself into your country, where you may expect the event in safety. For, though there be no appear-*

CHAPTER XLVI

ance of any stir, yet, I say, they will receive a terrible blow, this parliament,
and yet they shall not see who hurts them. This counsel is not to be con-
temned, because it may do you good, and can do you no harm: For the
danger is past, as soon as you have burned the letter. And I hope God will
give you the grace to make good use of it, unto whose holy protection I
commend you.[o]

Monteagle knew not what to make of this letter; and though
inclined to think it a foolish attempt to frighten and ridicule him,
he judged it safest to carry it to Lord Salisbury, secretary of state.
Though Salisbury too was inclined to pay little attention to it, he
thought proper to lay it before the king, who came to town a few
days after. To the king it appeared not so light a matter; and from
the serious earnest style of the letter, he conjectured, that it implied something dangerous and important. A *terrible blow,* and yet
the authors concealed; a danger so *sudden,* and yet so *great;* these
circumstances seemed all to denote some contrivance by gunpowder; and it was thought advisable to inspect all the vaults below
the houses of parliament. This care belonged to the earl of Suffolk,
Lord chamberlain; who purposely delayed the search, till the day
before the meeting of parliament. He remarked those great piles
of wood and faggots, which lay in the vault under the upper house;
and he cast his eye upon Fawkes, who stood in a dark corner, and
passed himself for Piercy's servant. That daring and determined
courage, which so much distinguished this conspirator, even
among those heroes in villany, was fully painted in his countenance, and was not passed unnoticed by the chamberlain.[p] Such a
quantity also of fuel, for the use of one who lived so little in town
as Piercy, appeared a little extraordinary;[q] and upon comparing all
circumstances, it was resolved that a more thorough inspection
should be made. About midnight, Sir Thomas Knevet, a justice of
peace, was sent with proper attendants; and before the door of the
vault, finding Fawkes, who had just finished all his preparations,
he immediately seized him, and turning over the faggots discovered the powder. The matches and every thing proper for setting
fire to the train were taken in Fawkes's pocket; who finding his
guilt now apparent, and seeing no refuge but in boldness and
despair, expressed the utmost regret, that he had lost the opportu-

[o] K. James's Works, p. 227.   [p] K. James's Works, p. 229.   [q] Id. Ibid.

nity, of firing the powder at once, and of sweetening his own death by that of his enemies.[r] Before the council, he displayed the same intrepid firmness, mixed even with scorn and disdain; refusing to discover his accomplices, and shewing no concern but for the failure of the enterprize.[s] This obstinacy lasted two or three days: But being confined to the Tower, left to reflect on his guilt and danger, and the rack being just shown to him; his courage, fatigued with so long an effort, and unsupported by hope or society, at last failed him; and he made a full discovery of all the conspirators.[t]

Catesby, Piercy, and the other criminals, who were in London, though they had heard of the alarm taken at the letter sent to Monteagle; though they had heard of the chamberlain's search; yet were resolved to persist to the utmost, and never abandon their hopes of success.[u] But at last, hearing that Fawkes was arrested, they hurried down to Warwickshire; where Sir Everard Digby, thinking himself assured, that success had attended his confederates, was already in arms, in order to seize the princess Elizabeth. She had escaped into Coventry; and they were obliged to put themselves on their defence against the country, who were raised from all quarters and armed, by the sheriff. The conspirators, with all their attendants, never exceeded the number of eighty persons; and being surrounded on every side, could no longer entertain hopes, either of prevailing or escaping. Having therefore confessed themselves, and received absolution, they boldly prepared for death, and resolved to sell their lives as dear as possible to the assailants. But even this miserable consolation was denied them. Some of their powder took fire, and disabled them for defence.[w] The people rushed in upon them. Piercy and Catesby were killed by one shot. Digby, Rookwood, Winter, and others, being taken prisoners, were tried, confessed their guilt, and died, as well as Garnet, by the hands of the executioner. Notwithstanding this horrid crime, the bigotted catholics were so devoted to Garnet, that they fancied miracles to be wrought by his blood;[x] and in Spain he was regarded as a martyr.[y]

---

[r] Ibid. p. 230.   [s] Winwood, vol. ii. p. 173.   [t] K. James's Works, p. 231.
[u] See note [E] at the end of the volume.   [w] State Trials, vol. i. p. 199.
Discourse of the manner, &c. p. 69, 70.   [x] Winwood, vol. ii. p. 300.
[y] Id. Ibid.

CHAPTER XLVI

Neither had the desperate fortune of the conspirators urged them to this enterprize, nor had the former profligacy of their lives prepared them for so great a crime. Before that audacious attempt, their conduct seems, in general, to be liable to no reproach. Catesby's character had entitled him to such regard, that Rookwood and Digby were seduced by their implicit trust in his judgement; and they declared, that, from the motive alone of friendship to him, they were ready, on any occasion to have sacrificed their lives.[z] Digby himself was as highly esteemed and beloved as any man in England; and he had been particularly honoured with the good opinion of Queen Elizabeth.[a] It was bigotted zeal alone, the most absurd of prejudices masqued with reason, the most criminal of passions covered with the appearance of duty, which seduced them into measures, that were fatal to themselves, and had so nearly proved fatal to their country.[b]

The Lords Mordaunt and Stourton, two catholics, were fined, the former 10,000 pounds, the latter 4,000, by the star-chamber; because their absence from parliament had begotten a suspicion of their being acquainted with the conspiracy. The earl of Northumberland was fined 30,000 pounds, and detained several years prisoner in the Tower; because, not to mention other grounds of suspicion, he had admitted Piercy into the number of gentlemen pensioners, without his taking the requisite oaths.[c]

The king, in his speech to the parliament, observed, that, though religion had engaged the conspirators in so criminal an attempt, yet ought we not to involve all the Roman catholics in the same guilt, or suppose them equally disposed to commit such enormous barbarities. Many holy men, he said, and our ancestors among the rest, had been seduced to concur with that church in her scholastic doctrines; who yet had never admitted her seditious principles, concerning the pope's power of dethroning kings, or sanctifying assassination. The wrath of Heaven is denounced

---

[z] State Trials, vol. i. p. 201. [a] Athen. Ox. vol. ii. fol. 254. [b] Digby, after his condemnation, said in a letter to his wife: "Now for my intention, let me tell you, that if I had thought there had been the least sin in the plot, I would not have been of it for all the world; and no other cause drew me, to hazard my fortune and life, but zeal to God's religion." He expresses his surprize to hear that any catholics had condemned it. *Digby's papers, published by secretary Coventry.* [c] Camden in Kennet, p. 692.

against crimes, but innocent error may obtain its favour; and nothing can be more hateful than the uncharitableness of the puritans, who condemn alike to eternal torments, even the most inoffensive partizans of popery. For his part, he added, that conspiracy, however atrocious, should never alter, in the least, his plan of government: While with one hand he punished guilt; with the other, he would still support and protect innocence.[d] After this speech, he prorogued the parliament, till the 22d of January.[e]

The moderation, and, I may say, magnanimity, of the king, immediately after so narrow an escape from a most detestable conspiracy, was no wise agreeable to his subjects. Their animosity against popery, even before this provocation, had risen to a great pitch; and it had perhaps been more prudent in James, by a little dissimulation, to have conformed himself to it. His theological learning, confirmed by disputation, had happily fixed his judgment in the protestant faith; yet was his heart a little byassed by the allurements of Rome, and he had been well pleased, if the making of some advances could have effected an union with that ancient mother-church. He strove to abate the acrimony of his own subjects against the religion of their fathers: He became himself the object of their dissidence and aversion. Whatever measures he embraced; in Scotland to introduce prelacy, in England to inforce the authority of the established church, and support its rites and ceremonies; were interpreted as so many steps towards popery; and were represented by the puritans as symptoms of idolatry and superstition. Ignorant of the consequences, or unwilling to sacrifice to politics his inclination, which he called his conscience, he persevered in the same measures, and gave trust and preferment, almost indifferently, to his catholic and protestant subjects. And finding his person, as well as his title, less obnoxious to the church of Rome, than those of Elizabeth, he gradually abated the rigour of those laws, which had been enacted against that church, and which were so acceptable to his bigotted subjects. But the effects of

1606.

---

[d] K. James's Works, p. 503, 504.   [e] The Parliament, this session, passed an act obliging every one to take the oath of allegiance: A very moderate test, since it decided no controverted points between the two religions, and only engaged the persons who took it to abjure the pope's power of dethroning kings. See K. James's Works, p. 250.

these dispositions on both sides became not very sensible, till towards the conclusion of his reign.

At this time, James seems to have possessed the affections even of his English subjects, and, in a tolerable degree, their esteem and regard. Hitherto their complaints were chiefly levelled against his too great constancy in his early friendships; a quality, which, had it been attended with more economy, the wise would have excused, and the candid would even, perhaps, have applauded. His parts, which were not despicable, and his learning, which was great, being highly extolled by his courtiers and gownmen, and not yet tried in the management of any delicate affairs, for which he was unfit, raised a high idea of him in the world; nor was it always through flattery or insincerity, that he received the title of the second Solomon. A report, which was suddenly spread about this time, of his being assassinated, visibly struck a great consternation into all orders of men.[f] The commons also abated, this session, somewhat of their excessive frugality, and granted him an aid, payable in four years, of three subsidies and six fifteenths, which, Sir Francis Bacon said in the house,[g] might amount to about four hundred thousand pounds: And for once the king and parliament parted in friendship and good humour. The hatred which the catholics so visibly bore him, gave him, at this time, an additional value in the eyes of his people. The only considerable point, in which the commons incurred his displeasure, was by discovering their constant goodwill to the puritans, in whose favour they desired a conference with the lords:[h] Which was rejected. *A parliament.*

The chief affair transacted next session, was the intended union of the two kingdoms.[i] Nothing could exceed the king's passion and zeal for this noble enterprize, but the parliament's prejudice and reluctance against it. There remain two excellent speeches in favour of the union, which it would not be improper to compare together; that of the king,[k] and that of Sir Francis Bacon. Those, who affect in every thing such an extreme contempt for James, will be surprised to find, that his discourse, both for good reasoning and elegant composition, approaches very near *November 18.*

[f] Kennet, p. 696.   [g] Journ. 20th May, 1606.   [h] Journ. 5th April, 1606.
[i] Kennet, p. 676.   [k] K. James's Works, p. 509.

that of a man, who was undoubtedly, at the time, one of the greatest geniuses in Europe. A few trivial indiscretions and indecorums may be said to characterize the harangue of the monarch, and mark it for his own. And in general, so open and avowed a declaration in favour of a measure, while he had taken no care, by any precaution or intrigue, to ensure success, may safely be pronounced an indiscretion. But the art of managing parliaments, by private interest or cabal, being found hitherto of little use or necessity, had not, as yet, become a part of English politics. In the common course of affairs, government could be conducted without their assistance; and when their concurrence became necessary to the measures of the crown, it was, generally speaking, except in times of great faction and discontent, obtained without much difficulty.

The king's influence seems to have rendered the Scottish parliament cordial in all the steps which they took towards the union. Though the advantages, which Scotland might hope from that measure, were more considerable; yet were the objections too, with regard to that kingdom, more striking and obvious. The benefit which must have resulted to England, both by accession of strength and security, was not despicable; and as the English were, by far the greater nation, and possessed the seat of government, the objections, either from the point of honour or from jealousy, could not reasonably have any place among them. The English parliament indeed seem to have been swayed merely by the vulgar motive of national antipathy. And they persisted so obstinately in their prejudices, that all the efforts for a thorough union and incorporation ended only in the abolition of the hostile laws, formerly enacted between the kingdoms.[l]

Some precipitate steps, which the king, a little after his accession, had taken, in order to promote his favourite project, had been here observed to do more injury than service. From his own authority, he had assumed the title of king of Great Britain; and

[l] The commons were even so averse to the union, that they had complained in the former session to the lords of the bishop of Bristol, for writing a book in favour of it, and the prelate was obliged to make submissions for this offence. The crime imputed to him seems to have consisted in his treating of a subject, which lay before the parliament. So little notion had they as yet of general liberty! See Parliamentary History, vol. v. p. 108, 109, 110.

had quartered the arms of Scotland, with those of England, in all coins, flags, and ensigns. He had also engaged the judges to make a declaration, that all those, who, after the union of the crowns, should be born in either kingdom, were, for that reason alone, naturalized in both. This was a nice question, and, according to the ideas of those times, susceptible of subtle reasoning on both sides. The king was the same: The parliaments were different. To render the people therefore the same, we must suppose, that the sovereign authority resided chiefly in the prince, and that these popular assemblies were rather instituted to assist with money and advice, than endowed with any controuling or active powers in the government. *It is evident,* says Bacon in his pleadings on this subject, *that all other commonwealths, monarchies only excepted, do subsist by a law precedent. For where authority is divided amongst many officers, and they not perpetual, but annual or temporary, and not to receive their authority but by election, and certain persons to have voices only in that election, and the like; these are busy and curious frames, which of necessity do presuppose a law precedent, written or unwritten, to guide and direct them: But in monarchies, especially hereditary, that is, when several families or lineages of people do submit themselves to one line, imperial or royal; the submission is more natural and simple; which afterwards, by law subsequent, is perfected, and made more formal: but that is grounded upon nature.*[m] It would seem from this reasoning, that the idea of a *hereditary, limited* monarchy, though implicitly supposed in many public transactions, had scarcely ever, as yet, been expressly formed by any English lawyer or politician.

Except the obstinacy of the parliament with regard to the union, and an attempt on the king's ecclesiastical jurisdiction,[n] most of their measures, during this session, were sufficiently respectful and obliging; though they still discover a vigilant spirit, and a careful attention towards national liberty. The votes also of the commons show, that the house contained a mixture of puritans, who had acquired great authority among them,[o] and who, together with religious prejudices, were continually suggesting ideas, more suitable to a popular than a monarchical form of

---

[m] Bacon's Works, vol. iv. p. 190, 191. Edit. 1730. [n] Journ. 2 December, 5 March, 1606, 25, 26 June, 1607. [o] Journ. 26 February, 4, 7 March, 1606. 2 May, 17 June, 1607.

government. The natural appetite for rule made the commons lend a willing ear to every doctrine, which tended to augment their own power and influence.

1607. A petition was moved in the lower house for a more rigorous execution of the laws against popish recusants, and an abatement towards protestant clergymen, who scrupled to observe the ceremonies. Both these points were equally unacceptable to the king; and he sent orders to the house to proceed no farther in that matter. The commons were inclined, at first, to consider these orders as a breach of privilege: But they soon acquiesced, when told, that this measure of the king's, was supported by many precedents, during the reign of Elizabeth.[p] Had they been always disposed to make the precedents of that reign the rule of their conduct, they needed never have had any quarrel with any of their monarchs.

5th of June. The complaints of Spanish depredations were very loud among the English merchants.[q] The lower house sent a message to the lords, desiring a conference with them, in order to their presenting a joint petition to the king on the subject. The lords took some time to deliberate on this message; because, they said, the matter was *weighty* and *rare*. It probably occurred to them, at first, that the parliament's interposing in affairs of state would appear unusual and extraordinary. And to show, that in this sentiment they were not guided by court influence; after they had deliberated, they agreed to the conference.

The house of commons began now to feel themselves of such importance, that on the motion of Sir Edwin Sandys, a member of great authority, they entered, for the first time, an order for the regular keeping of their journals.[r] When all business was finished, the king prorogued the parliament.

4th of July. About this time, there was an insurrection of the country people in Northamptonshire, headed by one Reynolds, a man of low condition. They went about destroying inclosures; but carefully avoided committing any other outrage. This insurrection was easily suppressed, and, though great lenity was used towards the rioters, yet were some of the ringleaders punished. The chief cause of that trivial commotion seems to have been, of itself, far from trivial. The practice still continued in England of disusing tillage,

[p] Journ. 16, 17 June, 1607. [q] Journ. 25 Feb, 1606. [r] Journ. 3 July, 1607.

CHAPTER XLVI

and throwing the land into inclosures for the sake of pasture. By this means, the kingdom was depopulated, at least, prevented from encreasing so much in people, as might have been expected from the daily encrease of industry and commerce.

Next year presents us with nothing memorable: But in the spring of the subsequent, after a long negociation, was concluded, by a truce of twelve years, that war, which for near half a century had been carried on with such fury between Spain and the states of the United Provinces. Never contest seemed, at first, more unequal: Never contest was finished with more honour to the weaker party. On the side of Spain were numbers, riches, authority, discipline: On the side of the revolted provinces were found the attachment to liberty and the enthusiasm of religion. By her naval enterprizes the republic maintained her armies; and joining peaceful industry to military valour, she was enabled, by her own force, to support herself, and gradually rely less on those neighbouring princes, who, from jealousy to Spain, were at first prompted to encourage her revolt. Long had the pride of that monarchy prevailed over her interest, and prevented her from hearkening to any terms of accommodation with her rebellious subjects. But finding all intercourse cut off between her provinces by the maritime force of the states, she at last agreed to treat with them as a free people, and solemnly to renounce all claim and pretension to their sovereignty.

This chief point being gained, the treaty was easily brought to a conclusion, under the joint mediation and guarantee of France and England. All exterior appearances of honour were paid equally to both crowns: But very different were the sentiments, which the states, as well as all Europe, entertained of the princes, who wore them. Frugality and vigour, the chief circumstances which procure regard among foreign nations, shone out as conspicuously in Henry as they were deficient in James. To a contempt of the English monarch, Henry seems to have added a considerable degree of jealousy and aversion, which were sentiments altogether without foundation. James was just and fair in all transactions with his allies,[s] but it appears from the memoirs of

1608.

1609.

Truce between Spain and the United Provinces.

March 30.

[s] The plan of accommodation which James recommended is found in Winwood, vol. ii. p. 429, 430; and is the same that was recommended by Henry, as we learn from Jeanin, tom. iii. p. 416, 417. It had long been imagined by historians from Jeanin's authority, that James had declared to the court

those times, that each side deemed him partial towards their adversary, and fancied, that he had entered into secret measures against them.[t] So little equity have men in their judgments of their own affairs; and so dangerous is that entire neutrality affected by the king of England!

1610.
Feb. 9.
A parliament.

The little concern, which James took in foreign affairs, renders the domestic occurrences, particularly those of parliament, the most interesting of his reign. A new session was held this spring; the king full of hopes of receiving supply; the commons, of circumscribing his prerogative. The earl of Salisbury, now created treasurer on the death of the earl of Dorset, laid open the king's necessities, first to the peers, then to a committee of the lower house.[u] He insisted on the unavoidable expence incurred, in supporting the navy, and in suppressing a late insurrection in Ireland: He mentioned three numerous courts, which the king was obliged to maintain, for himself, for the queen, and for the prince of Wales: He observed, that queen Elizabeth, though a single woman, had received very large supplies, in the years preceding her death, which alone were expensive to her: And he remarked, that, during her reign, she had alienated many of the crown lands; an expedient, which, though it supplied her present necessities, without laying burthens on her people, extremely multiplied the necessities of her successor. From all these causes he thought it nowise strange, that the king's income should fall short so great a sum as eighty-one thousand pounds of his stated and regular expence; without mentioning contingencies, which ought always to be esteemed a fourth of the yearly charges. And as the crown was now necessarily burthened with a great and urgent debt of 300,000 pounds, he thence inferred the absolute necessity of an immediate

March 21.

and large supply from the people. To all these reasons, which James likewise urged in a speech addressed to both houses, the commons remained inexorable. But not to shock the king with an absolute refusal, they granted him one subsidy and one fifteenth; which would scarcely amount to a hundred thousand pounds. And

---

of Spain that he would not support the Dutch in their pretensions to liberty and independence. But it has since been discovered by Winwood's Memorials, vol. ii. p. 456, 466, 469, 475, 476. that that report was founded on a lie of president Richardot's.   [t] Winwood, and Jeanin, *passim.*   [u] Journ. 17 Feb. 1609. Kennet, p. 681.

CHAPTER XLVI

James received the mortification of discovering, in vain, all his wants, and of begging aid of subjects, who had no reasonable indulgence or consideration for him.

Among the many causes of disgust and quarrel, which now daily and unavoidably multiplied between prince and parliament, this article of money is to be regarded as none of the least considerable. After the discovery and conquest of the West-Indies, gold and silver became every day more plentiful in England, as well as in the rest of Europe; and the price of all commodities and provisions rose to a height beyond what had been known, since the declension of the Roman empire. As the revenue of the crown rose not in proportion,[w] the prince was insensibly reduced to poverty amidst the general riches of his subjects, and required additional funds, in order to support the same magnificence and force, which had been maintained by former monarchs. But while money thus flowed into England, we may observe, that, at the same time, and probably from that very cause, arts and industry of all kinds received a mighty encrease; and elegance in every enjoyment of life became better known, and more cultivated among all ranks of people. The king's servants, both civil and military, his courtiers, his ministers, demanded more ample supplies from the impoverished prince, and were not contented with the same simplicity of living, which had satisfied their ancestors. The prince himself began to regard an encrease of pomp and splendor as requisite to support the dignity of his character, and to preserve the same superiority above his subjects, which his predecessors had enjoyed. Some equality too, and proportion to the other sovereigns of Europe, it was natural for him to desire; and as they had universally enlarged their revenue and multiplied their taxes, the king of England deemed it reasonable, that his subjects, who were generally as rich as theirs, should bear with patience some additional burthens and impositions.

Unhappily for the king, those very riches, with the encreasing knowledge of the age, bred opposite sentiments in his subjects; and begetting a spirit of freedom and independence, disposed them to pay little regard, either to the entreaties or menaces of

[w] Besides the great alienation of the crown-lands, the fee-farm rents never encreased, and the other lands were let on long leases and at a great undervalue, little or nothing above the old rent.

their sovereign. While the barons possessed their former immense property and extensive jurisdictions, they were apt, at every disgust, to endanger the monarch and throw the whole government into confusion: But this confusion often, in its turn, proved favourable to the monarch, and made the nation again submit to him, in order to re-establish justice and tranquillity. After the power of alienations, as well as the encrease of commerce had thrown the balance of property into the hands of the commons, the situation of affairs and the dispositions of men became susceptible of a more regular plan of liberty; and the laws were not supported singly by the authority of the sovereign. And though in that interval, after the decline of the peers and before the people had yet experienced their force, the princes assumed an exorbitant power, and had almost annihilated the constitution under the weight of their prerogative; as soon as the commons recovered from their lethargy, they seem to have been astonished at the danger, and were resolved to secure liberty by firmer barriers, than their ancestors had hitherto provided for it.

Had James possessed a very rigid frugality, he might have warded off this crisis somewhat longer; and waiting patiently for a favourable opportunity to encrease and fix his revenue, might have secured the extensive authority, transmitted to him. On the other hand, had the commons been inclined to act with more generosity and kindness towards their prince, they might probably have turned his necessities to good account, and have bribed him to depart peaceably from the more dangerous articles of his prerogative. But he was a foreigner, and ignorant of the arts of popularity; they were soured by religious prejudices and tenacious of their money: And, in this situation, it is no wonder, that, during this whole reign, we scarcely find an interval of mutual confidence and friendship between prince and parliament.

The king, by his prerogative alone, had, some years before, altered the rates of the customs, and had established higher impositions on several kinds of merchandize. This exercise of power will naturally, to us, appear arbitrary and illegal; yet, according to the principles and practices of that time, it might admit of some apology. The duties of tonnage and poundage were at first granted to the crown, by a vote of parliament, and for a limited time; and as the grant frequently expired and was renewed, there could not

then arise any doubt concerning the origin of the king's right to
levy these duties; and this imposition, like all others, was plainly
derived from the voluntary consent of the people. But as Henry V.
and all the succeeding sovereigns, had the revenue conferred on
them for life, the prince, so long in possession of these duties,
began gradually to consider them as his own proper right and
inheritance, and regarded the vote of parliament as a mere formality, which rather expressed the acquiescence of the people in
his prerogative, than bestowed any new gift of revenue upon him.

The parliament, when it first granted poundage to the crown,
had fixed no particular rates: The imposition was given as a shilling in a pound, or five *per cent* on all commodities: It was left to the
king himself, and the privy council, aided by the advice of such
merchants as they should think proper to consult, to fix the value
of goods, and thereby the rates of the customs: And as that value
had been settled before the discovery of the West-Indies, it was
become much inferior to the prices, which almost all commodities
bore in every market in Europe; and consequently, the customs on
many goods, though supposed to be five *per cent* was in reality
much inferior. The king, therefore, was naturally led to think, that
rates, which were now plainly false, ought to be corrected;[x] that a
valuation of commodities, fixed by one act of the privy council,
might be amended by another; that if his right to poundage were
inherent in the crown, he should also possess, of himself, the right
of correcting its inequalities; if this duty were granted by the people, he should at least support the spirit of the law, by fixing a new
and a juster valuation of all commodities. But besides this reasoning, which seems plausible, if not solid, the king was supported in
that act of power by direct precedents, some in the reign of Mary,
some in the beginning of Elizabeth.[y] Both these princesses had,
without consent of parliament, altered the rates of commodities;
and as their impositions had, all along, been submitted to without
a murmur, and still continued to be levied, the king had no reason
to apprehend, that a farther exertion of the same authority would
give any occasion of complaint. That less umbrage might be taken,
he was moderate in the new rates, which he established: The cus-

[x] Winwood, vol. ii. p. 438.   [y] Journ. 18th April, 5th and 10th May, 1614,
&c. 20th February, 1625. See also Sir John Davis's question concerning
impositions, p. 127, 128.

toms, during his whole reign, rose only from 127,000 pounds a-year to 190,000; though, besides the encrease of the rates, there was a sensible encrease of commerce and industry during that period: Every commodity, besides, which might serve to the subsistence of the people, or might be considered as a material of manufactures, was exempted from the new impositions of James:[z] But all this caution could not prevent the complaints of the commons. A spirit of liberty had now taken possession of the house: The leading members, men of an independent genius and large views, began to regulate their opinions, more by the future consequences which they foresaw, than by the former precedents which were set before them; and they less aspired at maintaining the ancient constitution, than at establishing a new one, and a freer, and a better. In their remonstrances to the king on this occasion, they observed it to be a general opinion. *That the reasons of that practice might be extended much farther, even to the utter ruin of the ancient liberty of the kingdom, and the subjects' right of property in their lands and goods.*[a] Though expressly forbidden by the king to touch his prerogative, they passed a bill abolishing these impositions; which was rejected by the house of lords.

In another address to the king, they objected to the practice of borrowing upon privy seals, and desired, that the subjects should not be forced to lend money to his majesty, or give a reason for their refusal. Some murmurs likewise were thrown out in the house against a new monopoly of the licence of wines.[b] It must be confessed, that forced loans and monopolies were established on many and ancient as well as recent precedents; though diametrically opposite to all the principles of a free government.[c]

The house likewise discovered some discontent against the king's proclamations. James told them, *That though he well knew, by the constitution and policy of the kingdom, that proclamations were not of equal force with laws; yet he thought it a duty incumbent on him, and a power inseparably annexed to the crown, to restrain and prevent such mischiefs and inconveniencies as he saw growing on the state, against which no certain law was extant, and which might tend to the great*

---

[z] Sir John Davis's question concerning impositions.   [a] Journ. 23 May, 1610.   [b] Parliament. Hist. vol. v. p. 241.   [c] See note [F] at the end of the volume.

detriment of the subject, if there should be no remedy provided till the meeting of a parliament. And this prerogative, he adds, *our progenitors have, in all times, used and enjoyed.*[d] The intervals between sessions, we may observe, were frequently so long, as to render it necessary for a prince to interpose by his prerogative. The legality of this exertion was established by uniform and undisputed practice; and was even acknowledged by lawyers, who made, however, this difference between laws and proclamations, that the authority of the former was perpetual, that of the latter expired with the sovereign who emitted them.[e] But what the authority could be, which bound the subject, yet was different from the authority of laws and inferior to it, seems inexplicable by any maxims of reason or politics: And in this instance, as in many others, it is easy to see, how inaccurate the English constitution was, before the parliament was enabled, by continued acquisitions or encroachments, to establish it on fixt principles of liberty.

Upon the settlement of the reformation, that extensive branch of power, which regards ecclesiastical matters, being then without an owner, seemed to belong to the first occupant; and Henry VIII. failed not immediately to seize it, and to exert it even to the utmost degree of tyranny. The possession of it was continued with Edward; and recovered by Elizabeth; and that ambitious princess was so remarkably jealous of this flower of her crown, that she severely reprimanded the parliament, if they ever presumed to intermeddle in these matters; and they were so over-awed by her authority, as to submit, and to ask pardon on these occasions. But James's parliaments were much less obsequious. They ventured to lift up their eyes, and to consider this prerogative. They there saw a large province of government, possessed by the king alone, and scarcely ever communicated with the parliament. They were sensible, that this province admitted not of any exact boundary or circumscription. They had felt, that the Roman pontiff, in former ages, under pretence of religion, was gradually making advances to usurp the whole civil power. They dreaded still more dangerous consequences from the claims of their own sovereign, who resided among them, and who, in many other respects, possessed such unlimited authority. They therefore deemed it absolutely neces-

---

[d] Parliament. Hist. vol. v. p. 250.   [e] Journ. 12 May, 1624.

sary to circumscribe this branch of prerogative, and accordingly, in the preceding session, they passed a bill against the establishment of any ecclesiastical canons without consent of parliament.[f] But the house of lords, as is usual, defended the barriers of the throne, and rejected the bill.

In this session, the commons, after passing anew the same bill, made remonstrances against the proceedings of the *high commission court*.[g] It required no great penetration to see the extreme danger to liberty, arising in a regal government, from such large discretionary powers, as were exercised by that court. But James refused compliance with the application of the commons. He was probably sensible, that, besides the diminution of his authority, many inconveniencies must necessarily result from the abolishing of all discretionary power in every magistrate; and that the laws, were they ever so carefully framed and digested, could not possibly provide against every contingency; much less, where they had not, as yet, attained a sufficient degree of accuracy and refinement.

But the business, which chiefly occupied the commons, during this session, was the abolition of wardships and purveyance; prerogatives, which had been more or less touched on, every session, during the whole reign of James. In this affair, the commons employed the proper means, which might intitle them to success: They offered the king a settled revenue as an equivalent for the powers, which he should part with; and the king was willing to hearken to terms. After much dispute, he agreed to give up these prerogatives for 200,000 pounds a-year, which they agreed to confer upon him.[h] And nothing remained, towards closing the bar-

[f] Journ. 2d, 11th December; 5th March, 1606.   [g] Parliament. Hist. vol. v. p. 247. Kennet, p. 681.   [h] We learn from Winwood's Memorials, vol. ii. p. 193. the reason assigned for this particular sum. "From thence my lord treasurer came to the price; and here he said, that the king would no more rise and fall like a merchant. That he would not have a flower of his crown (meaning the court of wards) so much tossed; that it was too dainty to be so handled: And then he said, that he must deliver the very countenance and character of the king's mind out of his own hand-writing: Which, before he read, he said he would acquaint us with a pleasant conceit of his majesty. As concerning the number of ninescore thousand pounds, which was our number; he could not affect, because nine was the number of the poets, who were always beggars, though they served so many muses; and eleven was the number of the apostles when the traitor, Judas, was away; and therefore might best be effected by his majesty. But there was a mean

gain, but that the commons should determine the funds, by which this sum should be levied. This session was too far advanced to bring so difficult a matter to a full conclusion; and though the parliament met again, towards the end of the year, and resumed the question, they were never able to terminate an affair, upon which they seemed so intent. The journals of that session are lost; and, as the historians of this reign are very negligent in relating parliamentary affairs, of whose importance they were not sufficiently apprised, we know not exactly the reason of this failure. It only appears, that the king was extremely dissatisfied with the conduct of the parliament, and soon after dissolved it. This was his first parliament, and it sat near seven years.

Amidst all these attacks, some more, some less violent, on royal prerogative, the king displayed, as openly as ever, all his exalted notions of monarchy and the authority of princes. Even in a speech to the parliament, where he begged for supply, and where he should naturally have used every art to ingratiate himself with that assembly, he expressed himself in these terms: "I conclude, then, the point, touching the power of kings, with this axiom of divinity, that, as to dispute *what God may do,* is blasphemy, but *what God wills,* that divines may lawfully and do ordinarily dispute and discuss; so is it sedition in subjects to dispute what a king may do in the height of his power. But just kings will ever be willing to declare what they will do, if they will not incur the curse of God. I will not be content, that my power be disputed upon; but I shall ever be willing to make the reason appear of my doings, and rule my actions according to *my* laws."[i] Notwithstanding the great extent of prerogative in that age, these expressions would probably give some offence. But we may observe, that, as the king's despotism was more speculative than practical, so the independency of the commons was, at this time, the reverse; and though strongly supported by their present situation as well as disposition, was too new and recent to be as yet founded on systematical principles and opinions.[k]

number, which might accord us both; and *that was ten:* Which, says my lord treasurer, is a sacred number; for so many were God's commandments, which tend to virtue and edification." If the commons really voted 20,000 pounds a-year more, on account of this *pleasant conceit* of the king and the treasurer, it was certainly the best paid wit, for its goodness, that ever was in the world. [i] K. James's Works, p. 531. [k] See note [G] at the end of the volume.

3d May.
Death
of the
French
king.

This year was distinguished by a memorable event, which gave great alarm and concern in England; the murder of the French monarch by the poinard of the fanatical Ravaillac. With his death, the glory of the French monarchy suffered an eclipse for some years; and as that kingdom fell under an administration weak and bigotted, factious and disorderly, the Austrian greatness began anew to appear formidable to Europe. In England, the antipathy to the catholics revived a little upon this tragical event; and some of the laws, which had formerly been enacted, in order to keep these religionists in awe, began now to be executed with greater rigour and severity.[l]

1611.

Though James's timidity and indolence fixed him, during most of his reign, in a very prudent inattention to foreign affairs, there happened, this year, an event in Europe of such mighty consequence as to rouze him from his lethargy, and summon up all his zeal and enterprize. A professor of divinity, named Vorstius, the

Arminian-
ism.

disciple of Arminius, was called from a German to a Dutch university; and as he differed from his Britannic Majesty in some nice questions concerning the intimate essence and secret decrees of God, he was considered as a dangerous rival in scholastic fame, and was, at last, obliged to yield to the legions of that royal doctor, whose syllogisms he might have refuted or eluded. If vigour was wanting in other incidents in James's reign, here he behaved even with haughtiness and insolence; and the states were obliged, after several remonstrances, to deprive Vorstius of his chair, and to banish him their dominions.[m] The king carried no farther his animosity against that professor; though he had very charitably hinted to the states, *That, as to the burning of Vorstius for his blasphemies and atheism, he left them to their own Christian wisdom, but surely never heretic better deserved the flames.*[n] It is to be remarked, that, at this period, all over Europe, except in Holland alone, the practice of burning heretics still prevailed, even in protestant countries; and instances were not wanting in England, during the reign of James.

To consider James in a more advantageous light, we must take a view of him as the legislator of Ireland; and most of the institutions, which he had framed for civilizing that kingdom, being

[l] Kennet, p. 684.   [m] Kennet, p. 715.   [n] K. James's Works, p. 355.

finished about this period, it may not here be improper to give some account of them, He frequently boasts of the management of Ireland as his master-piece; and it will appear, upon inquiry, that his vanity, in this particular, was not altogether without foundation.

After the subjection of Ireland by Elizabeth, the more difficult task still remained; to civilize the inhabitants, to reconcile them to laws and industry, and to render their subjection durable and useful to the crown of England. James proceeded in this work by a steady, regular, and well-concerted plan; and in the space of nine years, according to Sir John Davis, he made greater advances towards the reformation of that kingdom, than had been made in the 440 years, which had elapsed since the conquest was first attempted.[o]   *State of Ireland.*

It was previously necessary to abolish the Irish customs, which supplied the place of laws, and which were calculated to keep that people for ever in a state of barbarism and disorder.

By the *Brehon* law or custom, every crime, however enormous, was punished, not with death, but by a fine or pecuniary mulct, which was levied upon the criminal. Murder itself, as among all the ancient barbarous nations, was atoned for in this manner; and each man, according to his rank, had a different rate or value affixed to him, which, if any one were willing to pay, he needed not fear assassinating his enemy. This rate was called his *eric.* When Sir William Fitzwilliams being lord deputy, told Maguire, that he was to send a sheriff into Fermannah, which, a little before, had been made a county, and subjected to the English law; *Your sheriff,* said Maguire, *shall be welcome to me: But, let me know, beforehand, his* eric, *or the price of his head, that, if my people cut if off, I may levy the money upon the county.*[p] As for oppression, extortion, and other trespasses, so little were they regarded, that no penalty was affixed to them, and no redress for such offences could ever be obtained.

The customs of *Gavelkinde* and *Tanistry* were attended with the same absurdity in the distribution of property. The land, by the custom of Gavelkinde, was divided among all the males of the sept or family, both bastard and legitimate: And, after partition made, if any of the sept died, his portion was not shared out among his   *1612.*

[o] P. 259. edit. 1613.   [p] Sir John Davis, p. 166.

sons; but the chieftain, at his discretion, made a new partition of all the lands, belonging to that sept, and gave every one his share.[q] As no man, by reason of this custom, enjoyed the fixed property of any land; to build, to plant, to inclose, to cultivate, to improve, would have been so much lost labour.

The chieftains and the Tanists, though drawn from the principal families, were not hereditary, but were established by election, or more properly speaking, by force and violence. Their authority was almost absolute; and, notwithstanding that certain lands were assigned to the office, its chief profit resulted from exactions, dues, assessments, for which there was no fixed law, and which were levied at pleasure.[r] Hence arose that common byeword among the Irish, *That they dwelt westward of the law, which dwelt beyond the river of the Barrow:* Meaning the country, where the English inhabited, and which extended not beyond the compass of twenty miles, lying in the neighbourhood of Dublin.[s]

After abolishing these Irish customs, and substituting English law in their place, James, having taken all the natives under his protection, and declared them free citizens, proceeded to govern them by a regular administration, military as well as civil.

A small army was maintained, its discipline inspected, and its pay transmitted from England, in order to keep the soldiers from preying upon the country, as had been usual in former reigns. When Odoghartie raised an insurrection, a reinforcement was sent over, and the flames of that rebellion were immediately extinguished.

All minds being first quieted by a general indemnity;[t] circuits were established, justice administered, oppression banished, and crimes and disorders of every kind severely punished.[u] As the Irish had been universally engaged in the rebellion against Elizabeth, a resignation of all the rights, which had been formerly granted them to separate jurisdictions, was rigorously exacted; and no authority, but that of the king and the law, was permitted throughout the kingdom.[w]

A resignation of all private estates was even required; and when they were restored, the proprietors received them under such

[q] Sir John Davis, p. 167.   [r] Id. p. 173.   [s] Id. p. 237.   [t] Sir John Davis, p. 263.   [u] Id. p. 264, 265, &c.   [w] Id. p. 276.

CHAPTER XLVI

conditions as might prevent, for the future, all tyranny and oppression over the common people. The value of the dues, which
the nobles usually claimed from their vassals, was estimated at a
fixed sum, and all farther arbitrary exactions prohibited under
severe penalties.[x]

The whole province of Ulster having fallen to the crown by the
attainder of rebels, a company was established in London, for
planting new colonies in that fertile country: The property was
divided into moderate shares, the largest not exceeding 2000
acres: Tenants were brought over from England and Scotland:
The Irish were removed from the hills and fastnesses, and settled
in the open country: Husbandry and the arts were taught them:
A fixed habitation secured: Plunder and robbery punished: And,
by these means, Ulster, from being the most wild and disorderly
province of all Ireland, soon became the best cultivated and most
civilized.[y]

Such were the arts, by which James introduced humanity and
justice among the people, who had ever been buried in the most
profound barbarism. Noble cares! much superior to the vain and
criminal glory of conquests; but requiring ages of perseverance
and attention to perfect what had been so happily begun.

A laudable act of justice was, about this time, executed in England upon lord Sanquhir, a Scottish nobleman, who had been
guilty of the base assassination of Turner, a fencing-master. The
English nation, who were generally dissatisfied with the Scots,
were enraged at this crime, equally mean and atrocious; but James
appeased them, by preferring the severity of law to the intercession of the friends and family of the criminal.[z]

[x] Id. p. 278.   [y] Id. p. 280.   [z] Kennet, p. 688.

XLVII

Death of Prince Henry –
Marriage of the Princess Elizabeth
with the Palatine – Rise of Somerset –
His marriage – Overbury poisoned – Fall of
Somerset – Rise of Buckingham –
Cautionary towns delivered –
Affairs of Scotland

🏵 🏵 🏵

1612.

Nov. 6th.
Death of
Prince
Henry.

T HIS YEAR the sudden death of Henry, prince of Wales, diffused an universal grief throughout the nation. Though
youth and royal birth, both of them strong allurements, prepossess
men mightily in favour of the early age of princes; it is with peculiar fondness, that historians mention Henry: And, in every respect, his merit seems to have been extraordinary. He had not
reached his eighteenth year, and he already possessed more dignity in his behaviour, and commanded more respect, than his
father, with all his age, learning and experience. Neither his high
fortune, nor his youth, had seduced him into any irregular pleasures: Business and ambition seem to have been his sole passion.
His inclinations, as well as exercises, were martial. The French
ambassador, taking leave of him, and asking his commands for
France, found him employed in the exercise of the pike; *Tell your*
king, said he, *in what occupation you left me engaged.*[a] He had con-

[a] The French monarch had given particular orders to his ministers to

50

ceived great affection and esteem for the brave Sir Walter Raleigh. It was his saying, *Sure no king but my father would keep such a bird in a cage.*[b] He seems indeed to have nourished too violent a contempt for the king, on account of his pedantry and pusillanimity; and by that means struck in with the restless and martial spirit of the English nation. Had he lived, he had probably promoted the glory, perhaps not the felicity, of his people. The unhappy prepossession, which men commonly entertain in favour of ambition, courage, enterprize, and other warlike virtues, engages generous natures, who always love fame, into such pursuits as destroy their own peace, and that of the rest of mankind.

Violent reports were propagated, as if Henry had been carried off by poison; but the physicians, on opening his body, found no symptoms to confirm such an opinion.[c] The bold and criminal malignity of men's tongues and pens spared not even the king on the occasion. But that prince's character seems rather to have failed in the extreme of facility and humanity, than in that of cruelty and violence. His indulgence to Henry was great, and perhaps imprudent, by giving him a large and independent settlement, even in so early youth.

The marriage of the princess Elizabeth, with Frederic, Elector Palatine, was finished some time after the death of the prince, and served to dissipate the grief, which arose on that melancholy event. But this marriage, though celebrated with great joy and festivity, proved, itself, an unhappy event to the king, as well as to his son-in-law, and had ill consequences on the reputation and fortunes of both. The Elector, trusting to so great an alliance, engaged in enterprizes beyond his strength: And the king, not being able to support him in his distress, lost entirely, in the end of his life, what remained of the affections and esteem of his own subjects.

1613.

Febr. 14. Marriage of the Princess Elizabeth with the Palatine.

Except during sessions of parliament, the history of this reign may more properly be called the history of the court than that of the nation. An interesting object had, for some years, engaged the

Rise of Somerset.

cultivate the prince's friendship; who must soon, said he, have chief authority in England, where the king and queen are held in so little estimation. See Dep. de la Boderie, vol. i. p. 402, 415, vol. ii. p. 16, 349. [b] Coke's detection, p. 37. [c] Kennet, p. 690. Coke, p. 37. Welwood, p. 272.

attention of the court: It was a favourite, and one beloved by James with so profuse and unlimited an affection, as left no room for any rival or competitor. About the end of the year 1609, Robert Carre, a youth of twenty years of age, and of a good family in Scotland, arrived in London, after having passed some time in his travels. All his natural accomplishments consisted in good looks: All his acquired abilities, in an easy air and graceful demeanour. He had letters of recommendation to his countryman lord Hay; and that nobleman no sooner cast his eye upon him, than he discovered talents sufficient to entitle him immediately to make a great figure in the government. Apprized of the king's passion for youth, and beauty, and exterior appearance, he studied how matters might be so managed that this new object should make the strongest impression upon him. Without mentioning him at court, he assigned him the office, at a match of tilting, of presenting to the king his buckler and device; and hoped that he would attract the attention of the monarch. Fortune proved favourable to his design, by an incident, which bore, at first, a contrary aspect. When Carre was advancing to execute his office, his unruly horse flung him, and broke his leg in the king's presence. James approached him with pity and concern: Love and affection arose on the sight of his beauty and tender years; and the prince ordered him immediately to be lodged in the palace, and to be carefully attended. He himself, after the tilting, paid him a visit in his chamber, and frequently returned during his confinement. The ignorance and simplicity of the boy finished the conquest, begun by his exterior graces and accomplishments. Other princes have been fond of chusing their favourites from among the lower ranks of their subjects, and have reposed themselves on them with the more unreserved confidence and affection, because the object has been beholden to their bounty for every honour and acquisition: James was desirous that his favourite should also derive from him all his sense, experience, and knowledge. Highly conceited of his own wisdom, he pleased himself with the fancy, that this raw youth, by his lessons and instructions, would, in a little time, be equal to his sagest ministers, and be initiated into all the profound mysteries of government, on which he set so high a value. And as this kind of creation was more perfectly his own work than any other, he seems to have indulged

CHAPTER XLVII

an unlimited fondness for his minion, beyond even that which he bore to his own children. He soon knighted him, created him Viscount Rochester, gave him the garter, brought him into the privy-council, and, tho' at first without assigning him any particular office, bestowed on him the supreme direction of all his business and political concerns. Agreeable to this rapid advancement in confidence and honour, were the riches heaped upon the needy favourite; and while Salisbury and all the wisest ministers could scarcely find expedients sufficient to keep in motion the over-burthened machine of government, James, with unsparing hand, loaded with treasures this insignificant and useless pageant.[d]

It is said, that the king found his pupil so ill educated, as to be ignorant even of the lowest rudiments of the Latin tongue; and that the monarch, laying aside the sceptre, took the birch into his royal hand, and instructed him in the principles of grammar. During the intervals of this noble occupation, affairs of state would be introduced; and the stripling, by the ascendant which he had acquired, was now enabled to repay in political what he had received in grammatical instruction. Such scenes, and such incidents, are the more ridiculous, though the less odious, as the passion of James seems not to have contained in it any thing criminal or flagitious. History charges herself willingly with a relation of the great crimes, and still more with that of the great virtues of mankind; but she appears to fall from her dignity, when necessitated to dwell on such frivolous events and ignoble personages.

The favourite was not, at first, so intoxicated with advancement, as not to be sensible of his own ignorance and inexperience. He had recourse to the assistance and advice of a friend; and he was more fortunate in his choice, than is usual with such pampered minions. In Sir Thomas Overbury he met with a judicious and sincere counsellor, who, building all hopes of his own preferment on that of the young favourite, endeavoured to instil into him the principles of prudence and discretion. By zealously serving every body, Carre was taught to abate the envy, which might attend his sudden elevation: By shewing a preference for the English, he learned to escape the prejudices, which prevailed against his coun-

[d] Kennet, p. 685, 686, &c.

try. And so long as he was content to be ruled by Overbury's friendly counsels, he enjoyed, what is rare, the highest favour of the prince, without being hated by the people.

To complete the measure of courtly happiness, nought was wanting but a kind mistress; and, where high fortune concurred with all the graces of youth and beauty, this circumstance could not be difficult to attain. But it was here that the favourite met with that rock, on which all his fortunes were wrecked, and which plunged him for ever into an abyss of infamy, guilt, and misery.

No sooner had James mounted the throne of England, than he remembered his friendship for the unfortunate families of Howard and Devereux, who had suffered for their attachment to the cause of Mary and to his own. Having restored young Essex to his blood and dignity, and conferred the titles of Suffolk and Northampton on two brothers of the house of Norfolk, he sought the farther pleasure of uniting these families by the marriage of the earl of Essex with lady Frances Howard, daughter of the earl of Suffolk. She was only thirteen, he fourteen years of age; and it was thought proper, till both should attain the age of puberty, that he should go abroad, and pass some time in his travels.[e] He returned into England after four years absence, and was pleased to find his countess in the full lustre of beauty, and possessed of the love and admiration of the whole court. But, when the earl approached, and claimed the privileges of a husband, he met with nothing but symptoms of aversion and disgust, and a flat refusal of any farther familiarities. He applied to her parents, who constrained her to attend him into the country, and to partake of his bed: But nothing could overcome her rigid sullenness and obstinacy; and she still rose from his side, without having shared the nuptial pleasures. Disgusted with re-iterated denials, he at last gave over the pursuit, and separating himself from her, thenceforth abandoned her conduct to her own will and discretion.

Such coldness and aversion in lady Essex, arose not without an attachment to another object. The favourite had opened his addresses, and had been too successful in making impression on the tender heart of the young countess.[f] She imagined, that, so long as she refused the embraces of Essex, she never could be deemed his

---

[e] Kennet, p. 686.   [f] Idem, p. 687.

CHAPTER XLVII

wife, and that a separation and divorce might still open the way for a new marriage with her beloved Rochester.[g] Though their passion was so violent, and their opportunities of intercourse so frequent, that they had already indulged themselves in all the gratifications of love, they still lamented their unhappy fate, while the union between them was not entire and indissoluble. And the lover, as well as his mistress, was impatient, till their mutual ardour should be crowned by marriage.

So momentous an affair could not be concluded without consulting Overbury, with whom Rochester was accustomed to share all his secrets. While that faithful friend had considered his patron's attachment to the countess of Essex merely as an affair of gallantry, he had favoured its progress; and it was partly owing to the ingenious and passionate letters which he dictated, that Rochester had met with such success in his addresses. Like an experienced courtier, he thought, that a conquest of this nature would throw a lustre on the young favourite, and would tend still farther to endear him to James, who was charmed to hear of the amours of his court, and listened with attention to every tale of gallantry. But great was Overbury's alarm, when Rochester mentioned his design of marrying the Countess; and he used every method to dissuade his friend from so foolish an attempt. He represented, how invidious, how difficult an enterprize to procure her a divorce from her husband: How dangerous, how shameful, to take into his own bed a profligate woman, who, being married to a young nobleman of the first rank, had not scrupled to prostitute her character, and to bestow favours on the object of a capricious and momentary passion. And, in the zeal of friendship, he went so far as to threaten Rochester, that he would separate himself for ever from him, if he could so far forget his honour and his interest as to prosecute the intended marriage.[h]

Rochester had the weakness to reveal this conversation to the Countess of Essex; and when her rage and fury broke out against Overbury, he had also the weakness to enter into her vindictive projects, and to swear vengeance against his friend, for the utmost instance, which he could receive, of his faithful friendship. Some

[g] State Trials, vol. i. p. 228.   [h] State Trials, vol. i. p. 235, 236, 252. Franklyn, p. 14.

contrivance was necessary for the execution of their purpose. Rochester addressed himself to the king; and after complaining, that his own indulgence to Overbury had begotten in him a degree of arrogance, which was extremely disagreeable, he procured a commission for his embassy to Russia; which he represented as a retreat for his friend, both profitable and honourable. When consulted by Overbury, he earnestly dissuaded him from accepting this offer, and took on himself the office of satisfying the king, if he should be any wise displeased with the refusal.[i] To the king again, he aggravated the insolence of Overbury's conduct, and *April 21st.* obtained a warrant for committing him to the Tower, which James intended as a slight punishment for his disobedience. The lieutenant of the Tower was a creature of Rochester's and had lately been put into the office for this very purpose: He confined Overbury so strictly, that the unhappy prisoner was debarred the sight even of his nearest relations; and no communication of any kind was allowed with him, during near six months, which he lived in prison.

This obstacle being removed, the lovers pursued their purpose; and the king himself, forgetting the dignity of his character, and his friendship for the family of Essex, entered zealously into the project of procuring the Countess a divorce from her husband. Essex also embraced the opportunity of separating himself from a bad woman, by whom he was hated; and he was willing to favour their success by any honourable expedient. The pretence for a divorce was his incapacity to fulfil the conjugal duties; and he confessed, that, with regard to the Countess, he was conscious of such an infirmity, though he was not sensible of it with regard to any other woman. In her place too, it is said, a young virgin was substituted under a mask, to undergo the legal inspection by a jury of matrons. After such a trial, seconded by court-influence, and supported by the ridiculous opinion of fascination or witchcraft, the sentence of divorce was pronounced between the Earl of Essex and his Countess.[k] And, to crown the scene, the king, solicitous lest the lady should lose any rank by her new marriage, bestowed on his minion the title of Earl of Somerset.

Notwithstanding this success, the Countess of Somerset was not satisfied, till she should farther satiate her revenge on Overbury;

---

[i] State Trials, vol. i. p. 236, 237, &c.   [k] State Trials, vol. i. p. 223, 229, &c. Franklyn's Annals, p. 2, 3, &c.

CHAPTER XLVII

and she engaged her husband, as well as her uncle, the Earl of Northampton, in the atrocious design of taking him off secretly by poison. Fruitless attempts were re-iterated by weak poisons; but at last, they gave him one so sudden and violent, that the symptoms were apparent to every one, who approached him.[l] His interment was hurried on with the greatest precipitation; and, though a strong suspicion immediately prevailed in the public, the full proof of the crime was not brought to light, till some years after.

Overbury poisoned. 16th Sept.

The fatal catastrophe of Overbury encreased or begot the suspicion, that the prince of Wales had been carried off by poison, given him by Somerset. Men considered not, that the contrary inference was much juster. If Somerset was so great a novice in this detestable art, that, during the course of five months, a man, who was his prisoner, and attended by none but his emissaries, could not be dispatched but in so bungling a manner; how could it be imagined, that a young prince, living in his own court, surrounded by his own friends and domestics, could be exposed to Somerset's attempts, and be taken off by so subtile a poison, if such a one exist, as could elude the skill of the most experienced physicians?

The ablest minister that James ever possessed, the Earl of Salisbury, was dead:[m] Suffolk, a man of slender capacity, had succeeded him in his office: And it was now his task to supply, from an exhausted treasury, the profusion of James and of his young favourite. The title of baronet, invented by Salisbury, was sold; and two hundred patents of that species of knighthood, were disposed of for so many thousand pounds: Each rank of nobility had also its price affixed to it:[n] Privy seals were circulated to the amount of 200,000 pounds: Benevolences were exacted to the amount of 52,000 pounds:[o] And some monopolies of no great value, were erected. But all these expedients proved insufficient to supply the king's necessities; even though he began to enter into some schemes for retrenching his expences.[p] However small the hopes of success, a new parliament must be summoned, and this dangerous expedient, for such it was now become, once more be put to trial.

1614.
5th April.
A parliament.

When the commons were assembled, they discovered an extraordinary alarm, on account of the rumour, which was spread

---

[l] Kennet, p. 693. State Trials, vol. i. p. 233, 234, &c.   [m] 14th of May, 1612.
[n] Franklyn, p. 11, 33.   [o] Idem, p. 10.   [p] Idem, p. 49.

abroad concerning *undertakers.*[q] It was reported, that several persons, attached to the king, had entered into a confederacy; and having laid a regular plan for the new elections, had distributed their interest all over England, and had undertaken to secure a majority for the court. So ignorant were the commons, that they knew not this incident to be the first infallible symptom of any regular or established liberty. Had they been contented to follow the maxims of their predecessors, who, as the earl of Salisbury said to the last parliament, never, but thrice in six hundred years, refused a supply;[r] they needed not dread, that the crown should ever interest itself in their elections. Formerly, the kings even insisted, that none of their household should be elected members; and, though the charter was afterwards declared void, Henry VI. from his great favour to the city of York, conferred a peculiar privilege on its citizens, that they should be exempted from this trouble.[s] It is well known, that, in ancient times, a seat in the house being considered as a burthen, attended neither with honour nor profit, it was requisite for the counties and boroughs to pay fees to their representatives. About this time, a seat began to be regarded as an honour, and the country-gentlemen contended for it; though the practice of levying wages for the parliament men was not altogether discontinued. It was not till long after, when liberty was thoroughly established, and popular assemblies entered into every branch of public business, that the members began to join profit to honour, and the crown found it necessary to distribute among them all the considerable offices of the kingdom.

So little skill or so small means had the courtiers, in James's reign, for managing elections, that this house of commons showed rather a stronger spirit of liberty than the foregoing; and instead of entering upon the business of supply, as urged by the king, who made them several liberal offers of grace,[t] they immediately re-

[q] Parliam. Hist. vol. v. p. 286. Kennet, p. 696. Journ. 12 April, 2d May, 1614, &c. Franklyn, p. 48.   [r] Journ. 17 Feb. 1609. It appears, however, that Salisbury was somewhat mistaken in this fact: And if the kings were not oftener refused supply by the parliament, it was only because they would not often expose themselves to the hazard of being refused: But it is certain that English parliaments did anciently carry their frugality to an extreme, and seldom could be prevailed upon to give the necessary support to government.   [s] Coke's Institutes, part 4. chap. i. of charters of exemption.   [t] Journ. 11 April, 1614.

sumed the subject, which had been opened last parliament, and disputed his majesty's power of levying new customs and impositions, by the mere authority of his prerogative. It is remarkable, that, in their debates on this subject, the courtiers frequently pleaded, as a precedent, the example of all the other hereditary monarchs in Europe, and particularly mentioned the kings of France and Spain; nor was this reasoning received by the house, either with surprize or indignation.[u] The members of the opposite party, either contented themselves with denying the justness of the inference, or they disputed the truth of the observation.[w] And a patriot member in particular, Sir Roger Owen, even in arguing against the impositions, frankly allowed, that the king of England was endowed with as ample a power and prerogative as any prince in Christendom.[x] The nations on the continent, we may observe, enjoyed still, in that age, some small remains of liberty; and the English were possessed of little more.

The commons applied to the lords for a conference with regard to the new impositions. A speech of Neile, bishop of Lincoln, reflecting on the lower house, begat some altercation with the peers,[y] and the king seized the opportunity of dissolving immediately, with great indignation, a parliament, which had shown so *6th June.* firm a resolution of retrenching his prerogative, without communicating, in return, the smallest supply to his necessities. He carried his resentment so far as even to throw into prison some of the members, who had been the most forward in their opposition to his measures.[z] In vain did he plead, in excuse for this violence, the example of Elizabeth and other princes of the line of Tudor, as well as Plantagenet. The people and the parliament, without abandoning for ever all their liberties and privileges, could acquiesce in none of these precedents, how ancient and frequent soever. And were the authority of such precedents admitted, the utmost, that could be inferred is, that the constitution of England was, at that time, an inconsistent fabric, whose jarring and discordant parts must soon destroy each other, and from the dissolution of the old, beget some new form of civil government, more uniform and consistent.

[u] Journ. 21 May, 1614. [w] Journ. 12, 21 May, 1614. [x] Journ. 18 April, 1614. [y] See note [H] at the end of the volume. [z] Kennet, p. 696.

In the public and avowed conduct of the king and the house of commons, throughout this whole reign, there appears sufficient cause of quarrel and mutual disgust; yet are we not to imagine, that this was the sole foundation of that jealousy which prevailed between them. During debates in the house, it often happened, that a particular member, more ardent and zealous than the rest, would display the highest sentiments of liberty, which the commons contented themselves to hear with silence and seeming approbation; and the king, informed of these harangues, concluded the whole house to be infected with the same principles, and to be engaged in a combination, against his prerogative. The king, on the other hand, though he valued himself extremely on his king-craft, and perhaps was not altogether incapable of dissimulation, seems to have been very little endowed with the gift of secrecy; but openly, at his table, in all companies, inculcated those monarchical tenets, which he had so strongly imbibed. Before a numerous audience, he had expressed himself with great disparagement of the common law of England, and had given the preference, in the strongest terms, to the civil law: And for this indiscretion he found himself obliged to apologize, in a speech to the former parliament.[a] As a specimen of his usual liberty of talk, we may mention a story, though it passed some time after, which we meet with in the life of Waller, and which that poet used frequently to repeat. When Waller was young, he had the curiosity to go to court; and he stood in the circle, and saw James dine; where, among other company, there sat at table two bishops, Neile and Andrews. The king proposed aloud this question, Whether he might not take his subjects money, when he needed it, without all this formality of parliament? Neile replied, *God forbid you should not: For you are the breath of our nostrils.* Andrews declined answering, and said, he was not skilled in parliamentary cases: But upon the king's urging him, and saying he would admit of no evasion, the bishop replied pleasantly: *Why then I think your majesty may lawfully take my brother Neile's money: For he offers it.*[b]

1615.
Somerset's
fall.

The favourite had hitherto escaped the enquiry of justice; but he had not escaped that still voice, which can make itself be heard amidst all the hurry and flattery of a court, and astonishes the

[a] K. James's Works, p. 532.   [b] Preface to Waller's works.

CHAPTER XLVII

criminal with a just representation of his most secret enormities. Conscious of the murder of his friend, Somerset received small consolation from the enjoyments of love, or the utmost kindness and indulgence of his sovereign. The graces of his youth gradually disappeared, the gaiety of his manners was obscured, his politeness and obliging behaviour were changed into sullenness and silence. And the king, whose affection had been engaged by these superficial accomplishments, began to estrange himself from a man, who no longer contributed to his amusement.

The sagacious courtiers observed the first symptoms of this disgust: Somerset's enemies seized the opportunity, and offered a new minion to the king. George Villiers, a youth of one-and-twenty, younger brother of a good family, returned at this time from his travels, and was remarked for the advantages of a handsome person, genteel air, and fashionable apparel. At a comedy, he was purposely placed full in James's eye, and immediately engaged the attention, and, in the same instant, the affections of that monarch.[c] Ashamed of his sudden attachment, the king endeavoured, but in vain, to conceal the partiality, which he felt for the handsome stranger; and he employed all his profound politics to fix him in his service, without seeming to desire it. He declared his resolution not to confer any office on him, unless entreated by the queen; and he pretended, that it should only be in complaisance to her choice, he would agree to admit him near his person. The queen was immediately applied to; but she, well knowing the extreme, to which the king carried these attachments, refused, at first, to lend her countenance to this new passion. It was not till entreated by Abbot, archbishop of Canterbury, a decent prelate, and one much prejudiced against Somerset, that she would condescend to oblige her husband, by asking this favour of him.[d] And the king, thinking now that all appearances were fully saved, no longer constrained his affection, but immediately bestowed the office of cupbearer on young Villiers.

The whole court was thrown into parties between the two minions; while some endeavoured to advance the rising fortunes of Villiers, others deemed it safer to adhere to the established credit of Somerset. The king himself, divided between inclination and

[c] Franklyn, p. 50. Kennet, vol. ii. p. 698.   [d] Coke, p. 46, 47. Rush, vol. i. p. 456.

decorum, encreased the doubt and ambiguity of the courtiers; and the stern jealousy of the old favourite, who refused every advance of friendship from his rival, begat perpetual quarrels between their several partizans. But the discovery of Somerset's guilt in the murder of Overbury, at last decided the controversy, and exposed him to the ruin and infamy which he so well merited.

An apothecary's 'prentice, who had been employed in making up the poisons, having retired to Flushing, began to talk very freely of the whole secret; and the affair at last came to the ears of Trumbal, the king's envoy in the Low Countries. By his means, Sir Ralph Winwood, secretary of state, was informed; and he immediately carried the intelligence to James. The king, alarmed and astonished to find such enormous guilt in a man whom he had admitted into his bosom, sent for Sir Edward Coke, chief justice, and earnestly recommended to him the most rigorous and unbiassed scrutiny. This injunction was executed with great industry and severity: The whole labyrinth of guilt was carefully unravelled: The lesser criminals, Sir Jervis Elvis, lieutenant of the Tower, Franklin, Weston, Mrs. Turner, were first tried and condemned: Somerset and his countess were afterwards found guilty: Northampton's death, a little before, had saved him from a like fate.

It may not be unworthy of remark that Coke, in the trial of Mrs. Turner, told her, that she was guilty of the seven deadly sins: She was a whore, a bawd, a sorcerer, a witch, a papist, a felon, and a murderer.[e] And what may more surprize us, Bacon, then attorney-general, took care to observe, that poisoning was a popish trick.[f] Such were the bigotted prejudices which prevailed: Poisoning was not, of itself, sufficiently odious, if it were not represented as a branch of popery. Stowe tells us, that, when the king came to Newcastle, on his first entry into England, he gave liberty to all the prisoners, except those who were confined for treason, murder, and *papistry*. When one considers these circumstances, that furious bigotry of the catholics, which broke out in the gunpowder conspiracy, appears the less surprising.

All the accomplices in Overbury's murder received the punishment due to their crime: But the king bestowed a pardon on the

[e] State Trials, vol. i. p. 230.   [f] Ibid. vol. i. p. 242.

principals, Somerset and the countess. It must be confessed that James's fortitude had been highly laudable, had he persisted in his first intention of consigning over to severe justice all the criminals: But let us still beware of blaming him too harshly, if, on the approach of the fatal hour, he scrupled to deliver into the hands of the executioner, persons whom he had once favoured with his most tender affections. To soften the rigour of their fate, after some years' imprisonment, he restored them to their liberty, and conferred on them a pension, with which they retired, and languished out old age in infamy and obscurity. Their guilty loves were turned into the most deadly hatred; and they passed many years together in the same house, without any intercourse or correspondence with each other.[g]

Several historians,[h] in relating these events, have insisted much on the dissimulation of James's behaviour, when he delivered Somerset into the hands of the chief justice; on the insolent menaces of that criminal; on his peremptory refusal to stand a trial; and on the extreme anxiety of the king during the whole progress of this affair. Allowing all these circumstances to be true, of which some are suspicious, if not palpably false,[i] the great remains of tenderness, which James still felt for Somerset, may, perhaps, be sufficient to account for them. That favourite was high-spirited; and resolute rather to perish than live under the infamy to which he was exposed. James was sensible, that the pardoning of so great a criminal, which was of itself invidious, would become still more unpopular, if his obstinate and stubborn behaviour on his trial should augment the public hatred against him.[k] At least, the unreserved confidence, in which the king had indulged his favourite for several years, might render Somerset master of so many secrets, that it is impossible, without farther light, to assign the particular reason of that superiority, which, it is said, he appeared so much to assume.

The fall of Somerset, and his banishment from court, opened the way for Villiers to mount up at once to the full height of favour, of honours, and of riches. Had James's passion been governed by common rules of prudence, the office of cup-bearer would have

Rise of Bucking-ham.

[g] Kennet, p. 699.   [h] Coke, Weldon, &c.   [i] See Biog. Brit. article Coke, p. 1384.   [k] Bacon, vol. iv. p. 617.

attached Villiers to his person, and might well have contented one of his age and family; nor would any one, who was not cynically austere, have much censured the singularity of the king's choice in his friends and favourites. But such advancement was far inferior to the fortune, which he intended for his minion. In the course of a few years, he created him Viscount Villiers, Earl, Marquis, and Duke of Buckingham, knight of the garter, master of the horse, chief justice in Eyre, warden of the cinque ports, master of the king's bench office, steward of Westminster, constable of Windsor, and lord high admiral of England.[l] His mother obtained the title of Countess of Buckingham: His brother was created Viscount Purbeck; and a numerous train of needy relations were all pushed up into credit and authority. And thus the fond prince, while he meant to play the tutor to his favourite, and to train him up in the rules of prudence and politics, took an infallible method, by loading him with premature and exorbitant honours, to render him, for ever, rash, precipitate, and insolent.

1616.

A young minion to gratify with pleasure, a necessitous family to supply with riches, were enterprizes too great for the empty exchequer of James. In order to obtain a little money, the cautionary towns must be delivered up to the Dutch; a measure which has been severely blamed by almost all historians; and I may venture to affirm, that it has been censured much beyond its real weight and importance.

Caution-
ary towns
delivered.

When queen Elizabeth advanced money for the support of the infant republic; besides the view of securing herself against the power and ambition of Spain, she still reserved the prospect of re-imbursement; and she got consigned into her hands the three important fortresses of Flushing, the Brille, and Rammekins, as pledges for the money due to her. Indulgent to the necessitous condition of the states, she agreed that the debt should bear no interest; and she stipulated, that if ever England should make a separate peace with Spain, she should pay the troops, which garrisoned those fortresses.[m]

After the truce was concluded between Spain and the United Provinces, the States made an agreement with the king, that the

[l] Franklyn, p. 30. Clarendon, 8vo. edit. vol i. p. 10.   [m] Rymer, tom. xvi. p. 341. Winwood, vol. ii. p. 351.

debt, which then amounted to 800,000 pounds, should be discharged by yearly payments of 40,000 pounds; and as five years had elapsed, the debt was now reduced to 600,000 pounds, and in fifteen years more, if the truce were renewed, it would be finally extinguished.[n] But of this sum, 26,000 pounds a-year were expended on the pay of the garrisons: The remainder alone accrued to the king: And the States, weighing these circumstances, thought, that they made James a very advantageous offer, when they expressed their willingness, on the surrender of the cautionary towns, to pay him immediately 250,000 pounds, and to incorporate the English garrisons in their army. It occurred also to the king, that even the payment of the 40,000 pounds a-year was precarious, and depended on the accident that the truce should be renewed between Spain and the Republic: If war broke out, the maintenance of the garrisons lay upon England alone; a burthen very useless and too heavy for the slender revenues of that kingdom: That even during the truce, the Dutch, straitened by other expences, were far from being regular in their payments; and the garrisons were at present in danger of mutinying for want of subsistance: That the annual sum of 14,000 pounds, the whole saving on the Dutch payments, amounted, in fifteen years, to no more than 210,000 pounds; whereas 250,000 pounds were offered immediately, a larger sum, and if money be computed at ten per cent, the current interest, more than double the sum to which England was entitled:[o] That if James waited till the whole debt were discharged, the troops, which composed the garrisons, remained a burthen upon him, and could not be broken, without receiving some consideration for their past services: That the cautionary towns were only a temporary restraint upon the Hollanders; and in the present emergence, the conjunction of interest between England and the republic was so intimate as to render all other ties superfluous; and no reasonable measures for mutual support would be wanting from the Dutch, even though freed from the dependence of these garrisons. That the exchequer of

[n] Sir Dudley Carleton's letters, p. 27, 28.   [o] An annuity of 14,000 pounds during fifteen years, money being at 10 per cent, is worth on computation only 106,500 pounds; whereas the king received 250,000: Yet the bargain was good for the Dutch, as well as the king; because they were both of them freed from the maintenance of useless garrisons.

the republic was at present very low, insomuch that they found difficulty, now that the aids of France were withdrawn, to maintain themselves in that posture of defence, which was requisite during the truce with Spain: And that the Spaniards were perpetually insisting with the king on the restitution of these towns, as belonging to their crown; and no cordial alliance could ever be made with that nation, while they remained in the hands of the English.[p] These reasons, together with his urgent wants, induced the king to accept of Caron's offer; and he evacuated the cautionary towns, which held the States in a degree of subjection, and which an

6th June. ambitious and enterprizing prince would have regarded as his most valuable possessions. This is the date of the full liberty of the Dutch commonwealth.

1617.
Affairs of
Scotland.
When the crown of England devolved on James, it might have been foreseen by the Scottish nation, that the independence of their kingdom, the object for which their ancestors had shed so much blood, would now be lost; and that, if both states persevered in maintaining separate laws and parliaments, the weaker would more sensibly feel the subjection, than if it had been totally subdued by force of arms. But these views did not generally occur. The glory of having given a sovereign to their powerful enemy, the advantages of present peace and tranquillity, the riches acquired from the munificence of their master; these considerations secured their dutiful obedience to a prince, who daily gave such sensible proofs of his friendship and partiality towards them. Never had the authority of any king, who resided among them, been so firmly established as was that of James, even when absent; and as the administration had been hitherto conducted with great

May. order and tranquillity, there had happened no occurrence to draw thither our attention. But this summer, the king was resolved to pay a visit to his native country, in order to renew his ancient friendships and connexions, and to introduce that change of ecclesiastical discipline and government, on which he was extremely intent. The three chief points of this kind, which James proposed to accomplish by his journey to Scotland, were the enlarging of episcopal authority, the establishing of a few ceremonies in public

[p] Rushworth, vol. i. p. 3.

worship, and the fixing of a superiority in the civil above the ecclesiastical jurisdiction.

But it is an observation, suggested by all history, and by none more than by that of James and his successor, that the religious spirit, when it mingles with faction, contains in it something supernatural and unaccountable; and that, in its operations upon society, effects correspond less to their known causes than is found in any other circumstance of government. A reflection, which may, at once, afford a source of blame against such sovereigns as lightly innovate in so dangerous an article, and of apology for such, as being engaged in an enterprize of that nature, are disappointed of the expected event, and fail in their undertakings.

When the Scottish nation was first seized with that zeal for reformation, which, though it caused such disturbance during the time, has proved so salutary in the consequences; the preachers, assuming a character little inferior to the prophetic or apostolical, disdained all subjection to the spiritual rulers of the church, by whom their innovations were punished and opposed. The revenues of the dignified clergy, no longer considered as sacred, were either appropriated by the present possessors, or seized by the more powerful barons; and what remained, after mighty dilapidations, was, by act of parliament, annexed to the crown. The prelates, however, and abbots, maintained their temporal jurisdictions and their seats in parliament; and though laymen were sometimes endowed with ecclesiastical titles, the church, notwithstanding its frequent protestations to the contrary, was still supposed to be represented by those spiritual lords, in the states of the kingdom. After many struggles, the king, even before his accession to the throne of England, had acquired sufficient influence over the Scottish clergy, to extort from them an acknowledgment of the parliamentary jurisdiction of bishops; though attended with many precautions, in order to secure themselves against the spiritual encroachments of that order.[q] When king of England, he engaged them, though still with great reluctance on their part, to advance a step farther, and to receive the bishops as perpetual presidents or moderators in their ecclesiastical synods; re-iterating their pro-

[q] 1598.

testations against all spiritual jurisdiction of the prelates, and all controuling power over the presbyters.[r] And by such gradual innovations, the king flattered himself, that he should quietly introduce episcopal authority: But as his final scope was fully seen from the beginning, every new advance gave fresh occasion of discontent, and aggravated, instead of softening, the abhorrence entertained against the prelacy.

What rendered the king's aim more apparent, were the endeavours, which, at the same time, he used to introduce into Scotland some of the ceremonies of the church of England: The rest, it was easily foreseen, would soon follow. The fire of devotion, excited by novelty, and inflamed by opposition, had so possessed the minds of the Scottish reformers, that all rites and ornaments, and even order of worship, were disdainfully rejected as useless burthens; retarding the imagination in its rapturous ecstasies, and cramping the operations of that divine spirit, by which they supposed themselves to be animated. A mode of worship was established, the most naked and most simple imaginable; one that borrowed nothing from the senses; but reposed itself entirely on the contemplation of that divine Essence, which discovers itself to the understanding only. This species of devotion, so worthy of the supreme Being, but so little suitable to human frailty, was observed to occasion great disturbances in the breast, and in many respects to confound all rational principles of conduct and behaviour. The mind, straining for these extraordinary raptures, reaching them by short glances, sinking again under its own weakness, rejecting all exterior aid of pomp and ceremony, was so occupied in this inward life, that it fled from every intercourse of society, and from every chearful amusement, which could soften or humanize the character. It was obvious to all discerning eyes, and had not escaped the king's, that, by the prevalence of fanaticism, a gloomy and sullen disposition established itself among the people; a spirit, obstinate and dangerous; independent and disorderly; animated equally with a contempt of authority, and a hatred to every other mode of religion, particularly to the catholic. In order to mellow these humours, James endeavoured to infuse a small tincture of ceremony into the national worship, and to introduce such rites as

[r] 1606.

might, in some degree, occupy the mind, and please the senses, without departing too far from that simplicity, by which the reformation was distinguished. The finer arts too, though still rude in these northern kingdoms, were employed to adorn the churches; and the king's chapel, in which an organ was erected, and some pictures and statues displayed, was proposed as a model to the rest of the nation. But music was grating to the prejudiced ears of the Scottish clergy; sculpture and painting appeared instruments of idolatry; the surplice was a rag of popery; and every motion or gesture, prescribed by the liturgy, was a step towards that spiritual Babylon, so much the object of their horror and aversion. Every thing was deemed impious, but their own mystical comments on the Scriptures, which they idolized, and whose eastern prophetic style they employed in every common occurrence.

It will not be necessary to give a particular account of the ceremonies which the king was so intent to establish. Such institutions, for a time, are esteemed either too divine to have proceeded from any other being than the supreme Creator of the universe, or too diabolical to have been derived from any but an infernal demon. But no sooner is the mode of the controversy past, than they are universally discovered to be of so little importance as scarcely to be mentioned with decency amidst the ordinary course of human transactions. It suffices here to remark, that the rites introduced by James regarded the kneeling at the sacrament, private communion, private baptism, confirmation of children, and the observance of Christmas and other festivals.[s] The acts, establishing these ceremonies, were afterwards known by the name of the articles of Perth, from the place where they were ratified by the assembly.

A conformity of discipline and worship between the churches of England and Scotland, which was James's aim, he never could hope to establish, but by first procuring an acknowledgment to his own authority in all spiritual causes; and nothing could be more contrary to the practice as well as principles of the presbyterian clergy. The ecclesiastical courts possessed the power of pronouncing excommunication; and that sentence, besides the spiritual consequences supposed to follow from it, was attended with

---

[s] Franklyn, p. 25. Spotswood.

immediate effects of the most important nature. The person ex-
communicated was shunned by every one as profane and impious;
and his whole estate, during his life-time, and all his moveables, for
ever, were forfeited to the crown. Nor were the previous steps,
requisite before pronouncing this sentence, formal or regular, in
proportion to the weight of it. Without accuser, without summons,
without trial, any ecclesiastical court, however inferior, sometimes
pretended, in a summary manner, to denounce excommunication,
for any cause, and against any person, even though he lived not
within the bounds of their jurisdiction.[t] And, by this means, the
whole tyranny of the inquisition, though without its order, was
introduced into the kingdom.

But the clergy were not content with the unlimited jurisdiction,
which they exercised in ecclesiastical matters: They assumed a
censorial power over every part of administration; and, in all their
sermons, and even prayers, mingling politics with religion, they
inculcated the most seditious and most turbulent principles. Black,
minister of St. Andrews, went so far,[u] in a sermon, as to pronounce
all kings the devil's children; he gave the queen of England the
appellation of atheist; he said, that the treachery of the king's heart
was now fully discovered; and in his prayers for the queen he used
these words; *We must pray for her for the fashion's sake, but we have no
cause: She will never do us any good.* When summoned before the
privy council, he refused to answer to a civil court for any thing
delivered from the pulpit, even though the crime, of which he was
accused, was of a civil nature. The church adopted his cause. They
raised a sedition in Edinburgh.[w] The king, during some time, was
in the hands of the enraged populace; and it was not without
courage, as well as dexterity, that he was able to extricate himself.[x]
A few days after, a minister, preaching in the principal church of
that capital, said, that the king was possessed with a devil; and, that
one devil being expelled, seven worse had entered in his place.[y] To
which he added, that the subjects might lawfully rise, and take the
sword out of his hand. Scarcely, even during the darkest night of
papal superstition, are there found such instances of priestly encroachments, as the annals of Scotland present to us during that
period.

[t] Spotswood.   [u] 1596.   [w] 17 Dec. 1596.   [x] Spotswood.   [y] Ibid.

CHAPTER XLVII

By these extravagant stretches of power, and by the patient conduct of James, the church began to lose ground, even before the king's accession to the throne of England: But no sooner had that event taken place, than he made the Scottish clergy sensible, that he was become the sovereign of a great kingdom, which he governed with great authority. Though formerly he would have thought himself happy to have made a fair partition with them of the civil and ecclesiastical authority, he was now resolved to exert a supreme jurisdiction in church as well as state, and to put an end to their seditious practices. An assembly had been summoned at Aberdeen;[z] but, on account of his journey to London, he prorogued it to the year following. Some of the clergy, disavowing his ecclesiastical supremacy, met at the time first appointed, notwithstanding his prohibition. He threw them into prison. Such of them as submitted, and acknowledged their error, were pardoned. The rest were brought to their trial. They were condemned for high treason. The king gave them their lives; but banished them the kingdom. Six of them suffered this penalty.[a]

The general assembly was afterwards induced[b] to acknowledge the king's authority in summoning ecclesiastical courts, and to submit to the jurisdiction and visitation of the bishops. Even their favourite sentence of excommunication was declared invalid, unless confirmed by the ordinary. The king recommended to the inferior courts the members whom they should elect to this assembly; and every thing was conducted in it with little appearance of choice and liberty.[c]

By his own prerogative likewise, which he seems to have stretched on this occasion, the king erected a court of high commission,[d] in imitation of that which was established in England. The bishops and a few of the clergy, who had been summoned, willingly acknowledged this court; and it proceeded immediately upon business, as if its authority had been grounded on the full consent of the whole legislature.

But James reserved the final blow for the time when he should himself pay a visit to Scotland. He proposed to the parliament, which was then assembled, that they should enact, that, "whatever

13th June.

---

[z] July 1604.   [a] Spotswood.   [b] 6th June, 1610.   [c] Spotswood.   [d] 15th Feb. 1610.

his majesty should determine in the external government of the church, with the consent of the archbishops, bishops, and a competent number of the ministry, should have the force of "law."[e] What number should be deemed competent was not determined: And their nomination was left entirely to the king: So that his ecclesiastical authority, had this bill passed, would have been established in its full extent. Some of the clergy protested. They apprehended, they said, that the purity of their church would, by means of this new authority, be polluted with all the rites and liturgy of the church of England. James, dreading clamour and opposition, dropped the bill, which had already passed the lords of articles; and asserted, that the inherent prerogative of the crown contained more power than was recognized by it. Some time after, he called, at St. Andrews, a meeting of the bishops and thirty-six of the most eminent clergy. He there declared his resolution of exerting his prerogative, and of establishing, by his own authority, the few ceremonies, which he had recommended to them. They entreated him rather to summon a general assembly, and to gain their assent. An assembly was accordingly summoned to meet on the 25th of November ensuing.

10th
July.

Yet this assembly, which met after the king's departure from Scotland, eluded all his applications; and it was not till the subsequent year, that he was able to procure a vote for receiving his ceremonies. And through every step in this affair, in the parliament as well as in all the general assemblies, the nation betrayed the utmost reluctance to all these innovations; and nothing but James's importunity and authority had extorted a seeming consent, which was belied by the inward sentiments of all ranks of people. Even the few, over whom religious prejudices were not prevalent, thought national honour sacrificed by a servile imitation of the modes of worship practised in England. And every prudent man agreed in condemning the measures of the king, who, by an ill-timed zeal for insignificant ceremonies, had betrayed, though in an opposite manner, equal narrowness of mind with the persons, whom he treated with such contempt. It was judged, that, had not these dangerous humours been irritated by opposition; had they been allowed peaceably to evaporate; they

[e] Spotswood. Franklyn, p. 29.

would at last have subsided within the limits of law and civil authority. And that, as all fanatical religions naturally circumscribe to very narrow bounds the numbers and riches of the ecclesiastics; no sooner is their first fire spent, than they lose their credit over the people, and leave them under the natural and beneficent influence of their civil and moral obligations.

At the same time that James shocked, in so violent a manner, the religious principles of his Scottish subjects, he acted in opposition to those of his English. He had observed, in his progress through England, that a judaical observance of the Sunday, chiefly by means of the puritans, was every day gaining ground throughout the kingdom, and that the people, under colour of religion, were, contrary to former practice, debarred such sports and recreations as contributed both to their health and their amusement.*f* Festivals, which, in other nations and ages, are partly dedicated to public worship, partly to mirth and society, were here totally appropriated to the offices of religion, and served to nourish those sullen and gloomy contemplations, to which the people were, of themselves, so unfortunately subject. The king imagined, that it would be easy to infuse chearfulness into this dark spirit of devotion. He issued a proclamation to allow and encourage, after divine service, all kinds of lawful games and exercises; and, by his authority, he endeavoured to give sanction to a practice, which his subjects regarded as the utmost instance of profaneness and impiety.*g*

f Kennet, p. 709. *g* Franklyn, p. 31. To show how rigid the English, chiefly the puritans, were become in this particular, a bill was introduced into the house of commons, in the 18th of the king, for the more strict observance of the Sunday, which they affected to call the Sabbath. One Shepherd opposed this bill, objected to the appellation of Sabbath as puritanical, defended dancing by the example of David, and seems even to have justified sports on that day. For this profaneness he was expelled the house, by the suggestion of Mr. Pym. The house of Lords opposed so far this puritanical spirit of the commons, that they proposed, that the appellation of *Sabbath* should be changed into that of the *Lord's Day.* Journ. 15, 16 Feb. 1620. 28 May 1621. In Shepherd's sentence, his offence is said by the house to be great, exorbitant, unparalleled.

XLVIII

Sir Walter Raleigh's expedition –
His execution – Insurrections in Bohemia –
Loss of the Palatinate – Negociations with Spain –
A parliament – Parties – Fall of Bacon –
Rupture between the king and the commons –
Protestation of the commons

1618.
Sir Walter
Raleigh's
expedition.

A T THE TIME when Sir Walter Raleigh was first confined in the Tower, his violent and haughty temper had rendered him the most unpopular man in England; and his condemnation was chiefly owing to that public odium, under which he laboured. During the thirteen years imprisonment which he suffered, the sentiments of the nation were much changed with regard to him. Men had leisure to reflect on the hardship, not to say injustice, of his sentence; they pitied his active and enterprizing spirit, which languished in the rigours of confinement; they were struck with the extensive genius of the man, who, being educated amidst naval and military enterprizes, had surpassed in the pursuits of litera-ture even those of the most recluse and sedentary lives; and they admired his unbroken magnanimity, which, at his age and under his circumstances, could engage him to undertake and execute so great a work as his History of the World. To encrease these favour-able dispositions, on which he built the hopes of recovering his liberty, he spread the report of a golden mine, which he had discovered in Guiana, and which was sufficient, according to his

CHAPTER XLVIII

representation, not only to enrich all the adventurers, but to afford immense treasures to the nation. The king gave little credit to these mighty promises; both because he believed, that no such mine as the one described was any-where in nature, and because he considered Raleigh as a man of desperate fortunes, whose business it was, by any means, to procure his freedom, and to reinstate himself in credit and authority. Thinking, however, that he had already undergone sufficient punishment, he released him from the Tower; and when his vaunts of the golden mine had induced multitudes to engage with him, the king gave them permission to try the adventure, and, at their desire, he conferred on Raleigh authority over his fellow-adventurers. Though strongly solicited, he still refused to grant him a pardon, which seemed a natural consequence, when he was intrusted with power and command. But James declared himself still diffident of Raleigh's intentions; and he meant, he said, to reserve the former sentence, as a check upon his future behaviour.

Raleigh well knew, that it was far from the king's purpose to invade any of the Spanish settlements: He therefore firmly denied that Spain had planted any colonies on that part of the coast where his mine lay. When Gondomar, the ambassador of that nation, alarmed at his preparations, carried complaints to the king, Raleigh still protested the innocence of his intentions: And James assured Gondomar, that he durst not form any hostile attempt, but should pay with his head for so audacious an enterprize. The minister, however, concluding, that twelve armed vessels were not fitted out without some purpose of invasion, conveyed the intelligence to the court of Madrid, who immediately gave orders for arming and fortifying all their settlements, particularly those along the coast of Guiana.

When the courage and avarice of the Spaniards and Portuguese had discovered so many new worlds, they were resolved to shew themselves superior to the barbarous heathens whom they invaded, not only in arts and arms, but also in the justice of the quarrel: They applied to Alexander VI. who then filled the papal chair; and he generously bestowed on the Spaniards the whole western, and on the Portuguese the whole eastern part of the globe. The more scrupulous protestants, who acknowledged not the authority of the Roman pontiff, established the first discovery as the foundation of *their* title; and if a pirate or sea-adventurer of their nation had but erected a stick or stone on the coast, as a memorial of his taking possession, they concluded the whole continent to belong to them, and thought themselves intitled to expel or exterminate, as usurpers, the ancient possessors and inhabitants. It was in this manner that Sir Walter Raleigh, about twenty-three years before, had acquired to the crown of England a claim to the continent of Guiana, a region as large as the half of Europe; and though he had immediately left the coast, yet he pretended that the English title to the whole remained certain and indefeazable. But it had happened in the mean time, that the Spaniards, not knowing or not acknowledging this imaginary claim, had taken possession of a part of Guiana, had formed a settlement on the river Oronooko, had built a little town called St. Thomas, and were there working some mines of small value.

To this place Raleigh directly bent his course; and, remaining himself at the mouth of the river with five of the largest ships, he sent up the rest to St. Thomas, under the command of his son, and of captain Keymis, a person entirely devoted to him. The Spaniards, who had expected this invasion, fired on the English at their landing, were repulsed, and pursued into the town. Young Raleigh, to encourage his men, called out, *That this was the true mine, and none but fools looked for any other;* and advancing upon the Spaniards, received a shot, of which he immediately expired. This dismayed not Keymis and the others. They carried on the attack; got possession of the town, which they afterwards reduced to ashes; and found not in it any thing of value.

Raleigh did not pretend, that he had himself seen the mine, which he had engaged so many people to go in quest of: It was Keymis, he said, who had formerly discovered it, and had brought him that lump of ore, which promised such immense treasures. Yet Keymis, who owned that he was within two hours' march of the place, refused, on the most absurd pretences, to take any effectual step towards finding it; and he returned immediately to Raleigh, with the melancholy news of his son's death, and the ill success of the enterprize. Sensible to reproach, and dreading punishment for his behaviour, Keymis, in despair retired into his cabin, and put an end to his own life.

CHAPTER XLVIII

The other adventurers now concluded, that they were deceived by Raleigh; that he never had known of any such mine as he pretended to go in search of; that his intention had ever been to plunder St. Thomas; and having encouraged his company by the spoils of that place, to have thence proceeded to the invasion of the other Spanish settlements; that he expected to repair his ruined fortunes by such daring enterprizes; and that he trusted to the money he should acquire, for making his peace with England; or if that view failed him, that he purposed to retire into some other country, where his riches would secure his retreat.

The small acquisitions, gained by the sack of St. Thomas, discouraged Raleigh's companions from entering into these views; though there were many circumstances in the treaty and late transactions, between the nations, which might invite them to engage in such a piratical war against the Spaniards.

When England made peace with Spain, the example of Henry IV. was imitated, who, at the treaty of Vervins, finding a difficulty in adjusting all questions with regard to the Indian trade, had agreed to pass over that article in total silence. The Spaniards, having, all along, published severe edicts against the intercourse of any European nation with their colonies, interpreted this silence in their own favour, and considered it as a tacit acquiescence of England in the established laws of Spain. The English, on the contrary, pretended, that, as they had never been excluded by any treaty from commerce with any part of the king of Spain's dominions, it was still as lawful for them to trade with his settlements in either Indies, as with his European territories. In consequence of this ambiguity, many adventurers from England sailed to the Spanish Indies, and met with severe punishment, when caught; as they, on the other hand, often stole, and, when superior in power, forced a trade with the inhabitants, and resisted, nay sometimes plundered, the Spanish governors. Violences of this nature, which had been carried to a great height on both sides, it was agreed to bury in total oblivion; because of the difficulty, which was found, in remedying them, upon any fixed principles.

But as there appeared a great difference between private adventurers in single ships, and a fleet acting under a royal commission; Raleigh's companions thought it safest to return immediately to England, and carry him along with them to answer for his conduct. It appears, that he employed many artifices, first to engage them to attack the Spanish settlements, and, failing of that, to make his escape into France: But, all these proving unsuccessful, he was delivered into the king's hands, and strictly examined, as well as his fellow-adventurers, before the privy-council. The council, upon enquiry, found no difficulty in pronouncing, that the former suspicions, with regard to Raleigh's intentions, had been well grounded; that he had abused the king in the representations which he had made of his projected adventure; that, contrary to his instructions, he had acted in an offensive and hostile manner against his majesty's allies; and that he had wilfully burned and destroyed a town belonging to the king of Spain. He might have been tried, either by common law for this act of violence and piracy, or by martial law for breach of orders: But it was an established principle among lawyers,[h] that, as he lay under an actual attainder for high-treason, he could not be brought to a new trial for any other crime. To satisfy, therefore, the court of Spain, which raised the loudest complaints against him, the king made use of that power which he had purposely reserved in his own hands, and signed the warrant for his execution upon his former sentence.[i]

Raleigh, finding his fate inevitable, collected all his courage: And though he had formerly made use of many mean artifices, such as feigning madness, sickness, and a variety of diseases, in order to protract his examination, and procure his escape; he now resolved to act his part with bravery and resolution. *'Tis a sharp remedy,* he said, *but a sure one for all ills;* when he felt the edge of the ax, by which he was to be beheaded.[k] His harangue to the people was calm and eloquent; and he endeavoured to revenge himself, and to load his enemies with the public hatred, by strong asseverations of facts, which, to say the least, may be esteemed very doubtful.[l] With the utmost indifference, he laid his head upon the block, and received the fatal blow. And in his death, there ap-

29th Octob. Raleigh's execution.

---

[h] See this matter discussed in Bacon's letters, published by Dr. Birch, p. 181.
[i] See note [I] at the end of the volume.   [k] Franklyn, p. 32.   [l] He asserted in the most solemn manner, that he had no wise contributed to Essex's death: But the last letter in Murden's collection contains the strongest proof of the contrary.

CHAPTER XLVIII

peared the same great, but ill-regulated mind, which, during his life, had displayed itself in all his conduct and behaviour.

No measure of James's reign was attended with more public dissatisfaction than the punishment of Sir Walter Raleigh. To execute a sentence, which was originally so hard, which had been so long suspended, and which seemed to have been tacitly pardoned by conferring on him a new trust and commission, was deemed an instance of cruelty and injustice. To sacrifice, to a concealed enemy of England, the life of the only man in the nation, who had a high reputation for valour and military experience, was regarded as meanness and indiscretion: And the intimate connections, which the king was now entering into with Spain, being universally distasteful, rendered this proof of his complaisance still more invidious and unpopular.

James had entertained an opinion, which was peculiar to himself, and which had been adopted by none of his predecessors, that any alliance, below that of a great king, was unworthy of a prince of Wales; and he never would allow any princess but a daughter of France or Spain, to be mentioned as a match for his son.[m] This instance of pride, which really implies meanness, as if he could receive honour from any alliance, was so well known, that Spain had founded on it the hopes of governing, in the most important transactions, this monarch, so little celebrated for politics or prudence. During the life of Henry, the king of Spain had dropped some hints of bestowing on that prince his eldest daughter, whom he afterwards disposed of in marriage to the young king of France, Lewis XIII. At that time, the views of the Spaniards were to engage James into a neutrality with regard to the succession of Cleves, which was disputed between the protestant and popish line:[n] But the bait did not then take; and James, in consequence of his alliance with the Dutch, and with Henry IV. of France, marched[o] 4000 men, under the command of Sir Edward Cecil, who joined these two powers, and put the marquis of Brandenburgh and the Palatine of Newbourg, in possession of that duchy.

Gondomar was, at this time, the Spanish ambassador in England; a man whose flattery was the more artful, because covered

[m] Kennet, p. 703, 748.   [n] Rushworth, vol. i. p. 2.   [o] 1610.

with the appearance of frankness and sincerity; whose politics were the more dangerous, because disguised under the masque of mirth and pleasantry. He now made offer of the second daughter of Spain to prince Charles; and, that he might render the temptation irresistible to the necessitous monarch, he gave hopes of an immense fortune, which should attend the princess. The court of Spain, though determined to contract no alliance with a heretic,[p] entered into negociations with James, which they artfully protracted, and, amidst every disappointment, they still redoubled his hopes of success.[q] The transactions in Germany, so important to the Austrian greatness, became every day a new motive for this duplicity of conduct.

Insurrections in Bohemia.   In that great revolution of manners, which happened during the sixteenth and the seventeenth centuries, the only nations, who had the honourable, though often melancholy advantage, of making an effort for their expiring privileges, were such as, together with the principles of civil liberty, were animated with a zeal for religious parties and opinions. Besides the irresistible force of standing armies, the European princes possessed this advantage, that they were descended from the ancient royal families; that they continued the same appellations of magistrates, the same appearance of civil government; and restraining themselves by all the forms of legal administration, could insensibly impose the yoke on their unguarded subjects. Even the German nations, who formerly broke the Roman chains, and restored liberty to mankind, now lost their own liberty, and saw with grief the absolute authority of their princes firmly established among them. In their circumstances, nothing but a pious zeal, which disregards all motives of human prudence, could have made them entertain hopes of preserving any longer those privileges, which their ancestors, through so many ages, had transmitted to them.

As the house of Austria, throughout all her extensive dominions, had ever made religion the pretence for her usurpations, she now met with resistance from a like principle; and the catholic religion, as usual, had ranged itself on the side of monarchy; the protestant, on that of liberty. The states of Bohemia, having taken arms against the emperor Matthias, continued their revolt against his successor Ferdinand, and claimed the observance of all the

[p] La Boderie, vol. ii. p. 30.   [q] Franklyn, p. 71.

CHAPTER XLVIII

edicts enacted in favour of the new religion, together with the restoration of their ancient laws and constitution. The neighbouring principalities, Silesia, Moravia, Lusatia, Austria, even the kingdom of Hungary, took part in the quarrel; and throughout all these populous and martial provinces, the spirit of discord and civil war had universally diffused itself.[r]

Ferdinand II. who possessed more vigour and greater abilities, *1619.* though not more lenity and moderation, than are usual with the Austrian princes, strongly armed himself for the recovery of his authority; and besides employing the assistance of his subjects, who professed the ancient religion, he engaged on his side a powerful alliance of the neighbouring potentates. All the catholic princes of the empire had embraced his defence; even Saxony, the most powerful of the protestant: Poland had declared itself in his favour;[s] and, above all, the Spanish monarch, deeming his own interest closely connected with that of the younger branch of his family, prepared powerful succours from Italy, and from the Low-Countries; and he also advanced large sums for the support of Ferdinand and of the catholic religion.

The states of Bohemia, alarmed at these mighty preparations, began also to solicit foreign assistance; and, together with that support, which they obtained from the evangelical union in Germany, they endeavoured to establish connexions with greater princes. They cast their eyes on Frederic, elector Palatine. They considered, that, besides commanding no despicable force of his own, he was son-in-law to the king of England, and nephew to prince Maurice, whose authority was become almost absolute in the United Provinces. They hoped, that these princes, moved by the connexions of blood, as well as by the tie of their common religion, would interest themselves in all the fortunes of Frederic, and would promote his greatness. They therefore made him a tender of their crown, which they considered as elective; and the young Palatine, stimulated by ambition, without consulting either James[t] or Maurice, whose opposition he foresaw, immediately accepted the offer, and marched all his forces into Bohemia, in support of his new subjects.

The news of these events no sooner reached England, than the

[r] Rushworth, vol. i. p. 7, 8.   [s] Rushworth, vol. i. p. 13, 14.   [t] Franklyn, p. 49.

whole kingdom was on fire to engage in the quarrel. Scarcely was the ardour greater, with which all the states of Europe, in former ages, flew to rescue the holy land from the dominion of infidels. The nation was, as yet, sincerely attached to the blood of their monarchs, and they considered their connexion with the Palatine, who had married a daughter of England, as very close and intimate. And, when they heard of catholics carrying on wars and persecutions against protestants, they thought their own interest deeply concerned, and regarded their neutrality as a base desertion of the cause of God, and of his holy religion. In such a quarrel, they would gladly have marched to the opposite extremity of Europe, have plunged themselves into a chaos of German politics, and have expended all the blood and treasure of the nation, by maintaining a contest with the whole house of Austria, at the very time, and in the very place, in which it was the most potent, and almost irresistible.

But James, besides that his temper was too little enterprizing for such vast undertakings, was restrained by another motive, which had a mighty influence over him: He refused to patronize the revolt of subjects against their sovereign. From the very first he denied to his son-in-law the title of king of Bohemia:[u] He forbade him to be prayed for in the churches under that appellation: And though he owned, that he had nowise examined the pretensions, privileges, and constitution of the revolted states;[w] so exalted was his idea of the rights of kings, that he concluded subjects must ever be in the wrong, when they stood in opposition to those, who had acquired or assumed that majestic title. Thus, even in measures, founded on true politics, James intermixed so many narrow prejudices, as diminished his authority, and exposed him to the imputation of weakness and of error.

1620. Meanwhile, affairs every where hastened to a crisis. Ferdinand levied a great force under the command of the duke of Bavaria and the count of Bucquoy; and advanced upon his enemy in Bohemia. In the Low-Countries, Spinola collected a veteran army of thirty thousand men. When Edmonds, the king's resident at Brussels, made remonstrances to the archduke Albert, he was answered, that the orders for this armament had been transmitted to Spinola

[u] Rushworth, vol. i. p. 12, 13.   [w] Franklyn, p. 48.

CHAPTER XLVIII

from Madrid, and that he alone knew the secret destination of it. Spinola again told the minister, that his orders were still sealed; but, if Edmonds would accompany him in his march to Coblentz, he would there open them, and give him full satisfaction.[x] It was more easy to see his intentions, than to prevent their success. Almost at one time it was known in England, that Frederic, being defeated in the great and decisive battle of Prague, had fled with his family into Holland, and that Spinola had invaded the Palatinate, and, meeting with no resistance, except from some princes of the union, and from one English regiment of 2,400 men, commanded by the brave Sir Horace Vere,[y] had, in a little time, reduced the greater part of that principality.

Loss of the Palatinate.

High were now the murmurs and complaints against the king's neutrality and unactive disposition. The happiness and tranquillity of their own country became distasteful to the English, when they reflected on the grievances and distresses of their protestant brethren in Germany. They considered not, that their interposition in the wars of the continent, though agreeable to religious zeal, could not, at that time, be justified by any sound maxims of politics; that, however exorbitant the Austrian greatness, the danger was still too distant to give any just alarm to England; that mighty resistance would yet be made by so many potent and warlike princes and states in Germany, ere they would yield their neck to the yoke; that France, now engaged to contract a double alliance with the Austrian family, must necessarily be soon rouzed from her lethargy, and oppose the progress of so hated a rival; that in the farther advance of conquests, even the interests of the two branches of that ambitious family must interfere, and beget mutual jealousy and opposition; that a land-war, carried on at such a distance, would waste the blood and treasure of the English nation, without any hopes of success; that a sea-war, indeed, might be both safe and successful against Spain, but would not affect the enemy in such vital parts as to make them stop their career of success in Germany, and abandon all their acquisitions; and that the prospect of recovering the Palatinate being at present desperate, the affair was reduced to this simple question, whether peace and commerce

---

[x] Franklyn, p. 44. Rushworth, vol. i. p. 14.   [y] Ibid. p. 42, 43. Rushworth, vol. i. p. 15. Kennet, p. 723.

with Spain, or the uncertain hopes of plunder and of conquest in the Indies, were preferable? a question, which, at the beginning of the king's reign, had already been decided, and perhaps with reason, in favour of the former advantages.

Negocia-tions with Spain.

James might have defended his pacific measures by such plausible arguments: But these, though the chief, seem not to have been the sole motives which swayed him. He had entertained the notion, that, as his own justice and moderation had shone out so conspicuously throughout all these transactions, the whole house of Austria, though not awed by the power of England, would willingly, from mere respect to his virtue, submit themselves to so equitable an arbitration. He flattered himself, that, after he had formed an intimate connexion with the Spanish monarch, by means of his son's marriage, the restitution of the Palatinate might be procured, from the motive alone of friendship and personal attachment. He perceived not, that his unactive virtue, the more it was extolled, the greater disregard was it exposed to. He was not sensible, that the Spanish match was itself attended with such difficulties, that all his art of negociation would scarcely be able to surmount them; much less, that this match could in good policy be depended on, as the means of procuring such extraordinary advantages. His unwarlike disposition, encreased by age, rivetted him still faster in his errors, and determined him to seek the restoration of his son-in-law, by remonstrances and entreaties, by arguments and embassies, rather than by blood and violence. And the same defect of courage, which held him in awe of foreign nations, made him likewise afraid of shocking the prejudices of his own subjects, and kept him from openly avowing the measures, which he was determined to pursue. Or, perhaps, he hoped to turn these prejudices to account; and by their means, engage his people to furnish him with supplies, of which their excessive frugality had hitherto made them so sparing and reserved.[z]

He first tried the expedient of a benevolence or free-gift from individuals; pretending the urgency of the case, which would not admit of leisure for any other measure: But the jealousy of liberty was now rouzed, and the nation regarded these pretended benevolences as real extortions, contrary to law and dangerous to free-

A par-liament.

[z] Franklyn, p. 47. Rushworth, vol. i. p. 21.

dom, however authorized by ancient precedent. A parliament was found to be the only resource, which could furnish any large supplies; and writs were accordingly issued for summoning that great council of the nation.[a]

In this parliament, there appeared, at first, nothing but duty and submission on the part of the commons; and they seemed determined to sacrifice every thing, in order to maintain a good correspondence with their prince. They would allow no mention to be made of the new customs or impositions, which had been so eagerly disputed in the former parliament:[b] The imprisonment of the members of that parliament was here, by some, complained of; but, by the authority of the graver and more prudent part of the house, that grievance was buried in oblivion:[c] And being informed, that the king had remitted several considerable sums to the Palatine, the commons, without a negative, voted him two subsidies;[d] and that too, at the very beginning of the session, contrary to the maxims frequently adopted by their predecessors.

1621.
16th
June.

Afterwards, they proceeded, but in a very temperate manner, to the examination of grievances. They found, that patents had been granted to Sir Giles Mompesson and Sir Francis Michel, for licensing inns and ale-houses; that great sums of money had been exacted, under pretext of these licences; and that such inn-keepers as presumed to continue their business, without satisfying the rapacity of the patentees, had been severely punished by fine, imprisonment, and vexatious prosecutions.

The same persons had also procured a patent, which they shared with Sir Edward Villiers, brother to Buckingham, for the sole making of gold and silver thread and lace, and had obtained very extraordinary powers for preventing any rivalship in these manufactures: They were armed with authority to search for all goods, which might interfere with their patent; and even to punish, at their own will and discretion, the makers, importers, and venders of such commodities. Many had grievously suffered by this exorbitant jurisdiction; and the lace, which had been manufactured by the patentees, was universally found to be adulterated, and to be composed more of copper than of the precious metals.

[a] See note [J] at the end of the volume. [b] Journ. 5 Dec. 1621. [c] Journ. 12, 16 Feb. 1620. [d] Journ. 16 Feb. 1620.

These grievances the commons represented to the king; and they met with a very gracious and very cordial reception. He seemed even thankful for the information given him; and declared himself ashamed, that such abuses, unknowingly to him, had creeped into his administration. "I assure you," said he, "had I before heard these things complained of, I would have done the office of a just king, and out of parliament have punished them, as severely, and peradventure more, than you now intend to do."[e] A sentence was passed for the punishment of Michel and Mompesson.[f] It was executed on the former. The latter broke prison and escaped. Villiers was, at that time, sent purposely on a foreign employment; and his guilt being less enormous or less apparent than that of the others, he was the more easily protected by the credit of his brother, Buckingham.[g]

Bacon's fall.

Encouraged by this success, the commons carried their scrutiny, and still with a respectful hand, into other abuses of importance. The great seal was, at that time, in the hands of the celebrated Bacon, created Viscount St. Albans; a man universally admired for the greatness of his genius, and beloved for the courteousness and humanity of his behaviour. He was the great ornament of his age and nation; and nought was wanting to render him the ornament of human nature itself, but that strength of mind, which might check his intemperate desire of preferment, that could add nothing to his dignity, and might restrain his profuse inclination to expence, that could be requisite neither for his honour nor entertainment. His want of economy and his indulgence to servants had involved him in necessities; and, in order to supply his prodigality, he had been tempted to take bribes, by the title of presents, and that in a very open manner, from suitors in chancery. It appears, that it had been usual for former chancellors

[e] Franklyn, p. 51. Rushworth, p. 25. [f] Franklyn, p. 52. Rushworth, vol. i. p. 27. [g] Yelverton the attorney-general was accused by the commons for drawing the patents for these monopolies, and for supporting them. He apologized for himself, that he was forced by Buckingham, and that he supposed it to be the king's pleasure. The lords were so offended at these articles of defence, though necessary to the attorney-general, that they fined him 10,000 pounds to the king, 5000 to the duke. The fines, however, were afterwards remitted. Franklyn, p. 55. Rushworth, vol. i. p. 31, 32, &c.

CHAPTER XLVIII

to take presents; and it is pretended, that Bacon, who followed the same dangerous practice, had still, in the seat of justice, preserved the integrity of a judge, and had given just decrees against those very persons, from whom he had received the wages of iniquity. Complaints rose the louder on that account, and at last reached the house of commons, who sent up an impeachment against him to the peers. The chancellor, conscious of guilt, deprecated the vengeance of his judges, and endeavoured, by a general avowal, to escape the confusion of a stricter enquiry. The lords insisted on a particular confession of all his corruptions. He acknowledged twenty-eight articles; and was sentenced to pay a fine of 40,000 pounds, to be imprisoned in the Tower during the king's pleasure, to be for ever incapable of any office, place, or employment, and never again to sit in parliament, or come within the verge of the court.

This dreadful sentence, dreadful to a man of nice sensibility to honour, he survived five years; and being released in a little time from the Tower, his genius, yet unbroken, supported itself amidst involved circumstances and a depressed spirit, and shone out in literary productions, which have made his guilt or weaknesses be forgotten or overlooked by posterity. In consideration of his great merit, the king remitted his fine, as well as all the other parts of his sentence, conferred on him a large pension of 1800 pounds a-year, and employed every expedient to alleviate the weight of his age and misfortunes. And that great philosopher, at last, acknowledged with regret, that he had too long neglected the true ambition of a fine genius; and by plunging into business and affairs, which require much less capacity, but greater firmness of mind, than the pursuits of learning, had exposed himself to such grievous calamities.[h]

The commons had entertained the idea, that they were the great patrons of the people, and that the redress of all grievances must proceed from them; and to this principle they were chiefly beholden for the regard and consideration of the public. In the execution of this office, they now kept their ears open to com-

[h] It is thought, that appeals from chancery to the house of peers first came into practice, while Bacon held the great seal. Appeals, under the form of *writs of error,* had long before lain against the courts of law. Blackstone's Commentary, vol. iii. p. 454.

plaints of every kind; and they carried their researches into many grievances, which, though of no great importance, could not be touched on, without sensibly affecting the king and his ministers. The prerogative seemed every moment to be invaded; the king's authority, in every article, was disputed; and James, who was willing to correct the abuses of his power, would not submit to have his power itself questioned and denied. After the house, therefore, had sitten near six months, and had, as yet brought no considerable business to a full conclusion, the king resolved, under pretence of the advanced season, to interrupt their proceedings; and he sent them word, that he was determined, in a little time, to adjourn them till next winter. The commons made application to the lords, and desired them to join in a petition for delaying the adjournment; which was refused by the upper house. The king regarded this project of a joint petition as an attempt to force him from his measures: He thanked the peers for their refusal to concur in it, and told them, that, if it were their desire, he would delay the adjournment, but would not so far comply with the request of the lower house.[i] And thus, in these great national affairs, the same peevishness, which, in private altercations, often raises a quarrel from the smallest beginnings, produced a mutual coldness and disgust between the king and the commons.

Rupture between the king and the commons.

During the recess of parliament, the king used every measure to render himself popular with the nation, and to appease the rising ill-humour of their representatives. He had voluntarily offered the parliament to circumscribe his own prerogative, and to abrogate for the future his power of granting monopolies. He now recalled all the patents of that kind, and redressed every article of grievance, to the number of thirty-seven, which had ever been complained of in the house of commons.[k] But he gained not the end which he proposed. The disgust, which had appeared at parting, could not so suddenly be dispelled. He had likewise been so imprudent as to commit to prison Sir Edwin Sandys,[l] without any known cause, besides his activity and vigour in discharging his duty as member of parliament. And above all, the transactions in Germany were sufficient, when joined to the king's cautions, nego-

[i] Rushworth, vol. i. p. 35.   [k] Ibid. vol. i. p. 36. Kennet, p. 733.   [l] Journ. 1 Dec. 1621.

CHAPTER XLVIII

ciations, and delays, to inflame that jealousy of honour and religion, which prevailed throughout the nation.[m] This summer, the ban of the empire had been published against the elector Palatine; and the execution of it was committed to the duke of Bavaria.[n] The Upper Palatinate was, in a little time, conquered by that prince; and measures were taking in the empire for bestowing on him the electoral dignity, of which the Palatine was despoiled. Frederic now lived with his numerous family, in poverty and distress, either in Holland, or at Sedan with his uncle the duke of Bouillon. And throughout all the new conquests, in both the Palatinates, as well as in Bohemia, Austria, Lusatia, the progress of the Austrian arms was attended with rigours and severities, exercised against the professors of the reformed religion.

The zeal of the commons immediately moved them, upon their assembling, to take all these transactions into consideration. They framed a remonstrance, which they intended to carry to the king. They represented, that the enormous growth of the Austrian power threatened the liberties of Europe; that the progress of the catholic religion in England bred the most melancholy apprehensions, lest it should again acquire an ascendant in the kingdom; that the indulgence of his majesty towards the professors of that religion had encouraged their insolence and temerity; that the uncontrouled conquests, made by the Austrian family in Germany, raised mighty expectations in the English papists; but above all, that the prospect of the Spanish match elevated them so far as to hope for an entire toleration, if not the final re-establishment of their religion. The commons, therefore, entreated his majesty,

14th Nov.

[m] To show to what degree the nation was inflamed with regard to the Palatinate, there occurs a remarkable story this session. One Floyd, a prisoner in the Fleet, a catholic, had dropped some expressions, in private conversation, as if he were pleased with the misfortunes of the Palatine and his wife. The commons were in a flame; and pretending to be a court of judicature and of record, proceeded to condemn him to a severe punishment. The house of lords checked this encroachment; and what was extraordinary, considering the present humour of the lower house, the latter acquiesced in the sentiments of the peers. This is almost the only pretension of the English commons, in which they have not prevailed. Happily for the nation, they have been successful in almost all their other claims. See Parliamentary History, vol. v. p. 428, 429, &c. Journ. 4, 8, 12 May, 1621.   [n] Franklyn, p. 73.

that he would immediately undertake the defence of the Palatine, and maintain it by force of arms; that he would turn his sword against Spain, whose armies and treasures were the chief support of the catholic interest in Europe; that he would enter into no negociation for the marriage of his son but with a protestant princess; that the children of popish recusants should be taken from their parents, and be committed to the care of protestant teachers and schoolmasters; and that the fines and confiscations, to which the catholics were by law liable, should be levied with the utmost severity.[o]

By this *bold* step, unprecedented in England for many years, and scarcely ever heard of in peaceable times, the commons attacked at once all the king's favourite maxims of government; his cautious and pacific measures, his lenity towards the Romish religion, and his attachment to the Spanish alliance, from which he promised himself such mighty advantages. But what most disgusted him was, their seeming invasion of his prerogative, and their pretending, under colour of advice, to direct his conduct in such points, as had ever been acknowledged to belong solely to the management and direction of the sovereign. He was, at that time, absent at Newmarket; but as soon as he heard of the intended remonstrance of the commons, he wrote a letter to the speaker, in which he sharply rebuked the house for openly debating matters far above their reach and capacity, and he strictly forbade them to meddle with any thing that regarded his government or deep matters of state, and especially not to touch on his son's marriage with the daughter of Spain, nor to attack the honour of that king or any other of his friends and confederates. In order the more to intimidate them, he mentioned the imprisonment of Sir Edwin Sandys; and though he denied, that the confinement of that member had been owing to any offence committed in the house, he plainly told them, that he thought himself fully intitled to punish every misdemeanor in parliament, as well during its sitting as after its dissolution; and that he intended thenceforward to chastize any man, whose insolent behaviour there should minister occasion of offence.[p]

[o] Franklyn, p. 58, 59. Rushworth, vol. i. p. 40, 41. Kennet, p. 737.
[p] Franklyn, p. 60. Rushworth, vol. i. p. 43. Kennet, p. 741.

CHAPTER XLVIII

This *violent* letter, in which the king, though he here imitated former precedents, may be thought not to have acted altogether on the defensive, had the effect, which might naturally have been expected from it: The commons were inflamed, not terrified. Secure of their own popularity, and of the bent of the nation towards a war with the catholics abroad, and the persecution of popery at home, they little dreaded the menaces of a prince, who was unsupported by military force, and whose gentle temper would, of itself, so soon disarm his severity. In a new remonstrance, therefore, they still insisted on their former remonstrance and advice; and they maintained, though in respectful terms, that they were intitled to interpose with their counsel in all matters of government; that to possess entire freedom of speech, in their debates on public business, was their ancient and undoubted right, and an inheritance transmitted to them from their ancestors; and that, if any member abused this liberty, it belonged to the house alone, who were witnesses of his offence, to inflict a proper censure upon him.[q]

So *vigorous* an answer was nowise calculated to appease the king. It is said, when the approach of the committee, who were to present it, was notified to him, he ordered twelve chairs to be brought: For that there were so many kings a coming.[r] His answer was prompt and sharp. He told the house, that their remonstrance was more like a denunciation of war than an address of dutiful subjects; that their pretension to inquire into all state-affairs, without exception, was such a *plenipotence* as none of their ancestors, even during the reign of the weakest princes, had ever pretended to; that public transactions depended on a complication of views and intelligence, with which they were entirely unacquainted; that they could not better show their wisdom as well as duty, than by keeping within their proper[s] sphere; and that in any business, which depended on his prerogative, they had no title to interpose with their advice, except when he was pleased to desire it. And he concluded with these memorable words; *And though we cannot allow of your stile, in mentioning your ancient and undoubted right and inher-*

---

[q] Franklyn, p. 60. Rushworth, vol. i. p. 44. Kennet, p. 741.   [r] Kennet, p. 43.   [s] *Ne sutor ultra crepidam.* This expression is imagined to be insolent and disobliging: But it was a Latin proverb familiarly used on all occasions.

itance, but would rather have wished, that ye had said, that your privileges were derived from the grace and permission of our ancestors and us (for the most of them grew from precedents, which shews rather a toleration than inheritance); yet we are pleased to give you our royal assurance, that as long as you contain yourselves within the limits of your duty, we will be as careful to maintain and preserve your lawful liberties and privileges as ever any of our predecessors were, nay, as to preserve our own royal prerogative.[t]

This open pretension of the king's naturally gave great alarm to the house of commons. They saw their title to every privilege, if not plainly denied, yet considered, at least, as precarious. It might be forfeited by abuse, and they had already abused it. They thought proper, therefore, immediately to oppose pretension to pretension. They framed a protestation, in which they repeated all their former claims for freedom of speech, and an unbounded authority to interpose with their advice and counsel. And they asserted, *That the liberties, franchises, privileges, and jurisdictions of parliament, are the ancient and undoubted birth-right and inheritance of the subjects of England.*[u]

18th Dec.

Protesta-tion of the commons.

The king, informed of these encreasing heats and jealousies in the house, hurried to town. He sent immediately for the journals of the commons; and, with his own hand, before the council, he tore out this protestation;[w] and ordered his reasons to be inserted in the council-book. He was doubly displeased, he said, with the protestation of the lower house, on account of the manner of framing it, as well as of the matter which it contained. It was tumultuously voted, at a late hour, and in a thin house; and it was expressed in such general and ambiguous terms, as might serve for a foundation to the most enormous claims, and to the most un-warrantable usurpations upon his prerogative.[x]

The meeting of the house might have proved dangerous after so violent a breach. It was no longer possible, while men were in such a temper, to finish any business. The king, therefore, pro-rogued the parliament, and soon after dissolved it by proclama-tion; in which he also made an apology to the public for his whole conduct.

[t] Franklyn, p. 62, 63, 64. Rushworth, vol. i. p. 46, 47, &c. Kennet, p. 743.
[u] See note [K] at the end of the volume.   [w] Journ. 18 Dec. 1621.
[x] Franklyn, p. 65.

CHAPTER XLVIII

The leading members of the house, Sir Edward Coke and Sir Robert Philips, were committed to the Tower; Selden, Pym, and Mallory, to other prisons.[y] As a lighter punishment, Sir Dudley Digges, Sir Thomas Crew, Sir Nathaniel Rich, Sir James Perrot, joined in commission with others, were sent to Ireland, in order to execute some business.[z] The king, at that time, enjoyed, at least exercised, the prerogative of employing any man, even without his consent, in any branch of public service.

Sir John Savile, a powerful man in the house of commons, and a zealous opponent of the court, was made comptroller of the household, a privy counsellor, and soon after, a baron.[a] This event is memorable; as being the first instance, perhaps, in the whole history of England, of any king's advancing a man, on account of parliamentary interest, and of opposition to his measures. However irregular this practice, it will be regarded by political reasoners, as one of the most early and most infallible symptoms of a regular established liberty.

The king having thus, with so rash and indiscreet a hand, torn off that sacred veil, which had hitherto covered the English constitution, and which threw an obscurity upon it, so advantageous to royal prerogative, every man began to indulge himself in political reasonings and enquiries; and the same factions, which commenced in parliament, were propagated throughout the nation. In vain did James, by re-iterated proclamations, forbid the discoursing of state affairs.[b] Such proclamations, if they had any effect, served rather to inflame the curiosity of the public. And in every company or society, the late transactions became the subject of argument and debate.

All history, said the partizans of the court, as well as the history of England, justify the king's position with regard to the origin of popular privileges; and every reasonable man must allow, that, as monarchy is the most simple form of government, it must first have occurred to rude and uninstructed mankind. The other com-

[y] Franklyn, p. 66. Rushworth, vol. i. p. 55.   [z] Franklyn, p. 66. Rushworth, vol. i. p. 55.   [a] Kennet, p. 749.   [b] Franklyn, p. 56. Rushworth, vol. i. p. 21, 36, 55. The king also, in imitation of his predecessors, gave rules to preachers. Franklyn, p. 70. The pulpit was at that time much more dangerous than the press. Few people could read, and still fewer were in the practice of reading.

plicated and artificial additions were the successive invention of sovereigns and legislators; or, if they were obtruded on the prince by seditious subjects, their origin must appear, on that very account, still more precarious and unfavourable. In England, the authority of the king, in all the exterior forms of government and in the common style of law, appears totally absolute and sovereign; nor does the real spirit of the constitution, as it has ever discovered itself in practice, fall much short of these appearances. The parliament is created by his will; by his will it is dissolved. It is his will alone, though at the desire of both houses, which gives authority to laws. To all foreign nations, the majesty of the monarch seems to merit sole attention and regard. And no subject, who has exposed himself to royal indignation, can hope to live with safety in the kingdom; nor can he even leave it, according to law, without the consent of his master. If a magistrate, invironed with such power and splendor, should consider his authority as sacred, and regard himself as the anointed of heaven, his pretensions may bear a very favourable construction. Or, allowing them to be merely pious frauds, we need not be surprized, that the same stratagem which was practised by Minos, Numa, and the most celebrated legislators of antiquity, should now, in these restless and inquisitive times, be employed by the king of England. Subjects are not raised above that quality, though assembled in parliament. The same humble respect and deference is still due to their prince. Though he indulges them in the privilege of laying before him their domestic grievances, with which they are supposed to be best acquainted, this warrants not their bold intrusion into every province of government. And, to all judicious examiners, it must appear, "That the lines of duty are as much transgressed by a more independent and less respectful exercise of acknowledged powers, as by the usurpation of such as are new and unusual."

The lovers of liberty, throughout the nation, reasoned after a different manner. It is in vain, said they, that the king traces up the English government to its first origin, in order to represent the privileges of parliament as dependent and precarious: Prescription and the practice of so many ages, must, long ere this time, have given a sanction to these assemblies, even though they had been derived from an orgin no more dignified, than that which he assigns them. If the written records of the English nation, as

CHAPTER XLVIII

asserted, represent parliaments to have arisen from the consent of
monarchs, the principles of human nature, when we trace government a step higher, must show us, that monarchs themselves owe
all their authority to the voluntary submission of the people. But,
in fact, no age can be shown, when the English government was
altogether an unmixed monarchy: And if the privileges of the
nation have, at any period, been overpowered by violent irruptions
of foreign force or domestic usurpation; the generous spirit of
the people has ever seized the first opportunity of re-establishing
the ancient government and constitution. Though in the style of the
laws, and in the usual forms of administration, royal authority may
be represented as sacred and supreme; whatever is essential to the
exercise of sovereign and legislative power, must still be regarded
as equally divine and inviolable. Or, if any distinction be made in
this respect, the preference is surely due to those national councils,
by whose interposition the exorbitancies of tyrannical power are
restrained, and that sacred liberty is preserved, which heroic spirits, in all ages, have deemed more precious than life itself. Nor is
it sufficient to say, that the mild and equitable administration of
James, affords little occasion, or no occasion of complaint. How
moderate soever the exercise of his prerogative, how exact soever
his observance of the laws and constitution; "If he founds his
authority on arbitrary and dangerous principles, it is requisite to
watch him with the same care, and to oppose him with the same
vigour, as if he had indulged himself in all the excesses of cruelty
and tyranny."

Amidst these disputes, the wise and moderate in the nation
endeavoured to preserve, as much as possible, an equitable neutrality between the opposite parties; and the more they reflected
on the course of public affairs, the greater difficulty they found in
fixing just sentiments with regard to them. On the one hand, they
regarded the very rise of parties as a happy prognostic of the
establishment of liberty; nor could they ever expect to enjoy, in a
mixed government, so invaluable a blessing, without suffering that
inconvenience, which, in such governments, has ever attended it.
But, when they considered, on the other hand, the necessary aims
and pursuits of both parties, they were struck with apprehension
of the consequences, and could discover no feasible plan of accommodation between them. From long practice, the crown was now

possessed of so exorbitant a prerogative, that it was not sufficient for liberty to remain on the defensive, or endeavour to secure the little ground, which was left her: It was become necessary to carry on an offensive war, and to circumscribe, within more narrow, as well as more exact bounds, the authority of the sovereign. Upon such provocation, it could not but happen, that the prince, however just and moderate, would endeavour to repress his opponents; and, as he stood upon the very brink of arbitrary power, it was to be feared that he would, hastily and unknowingly, pass those limits, which were not precisely marked by the constitution. The turbulent government of England, ever fluctuating between privilege and prerogative, would afford a variety of precedents, which might be pleaded on both sides. In such delicate questions, the people must be divided: The arms of the state were still in their hands: A civil war must ensue; a civil war, where no party or both parties would justly bear the blame, and where the good and virtuous would scarcely know what vows to form; were it not that liberty, so necessary to the perfection of human society, would be sufficient to byass their affections towards the side of its defenders.

XLIX

Negociations with regard to the
marriage and the Palatinate – Character of
Buckingham – Prince's journey to Spain –
Marriage treaty broken – A parliament –
Return of Bristol – Rupture with Spain –
Treaty with France – Mansfeldt's
expedition – Death of the
king – His character

🌼 🌼 🌼

To WREST THE PALATINATE from the hands of the emperor
and the duke of Bavaria, must always have been regarded as
a difficult task for the power of England, conducted by so unwarlike a prince as James: It was plainly impossible, while the
breach subsisted between him and the commons. The king's negociations, therefore, had they been managed with ever so great
dexterity, must now carry less weight with them; and it was easy to
elude all his applications. When lord Digby, his ambassador to the
emperor, had desired a cessation of hostilities, he was referred to
the duke of Bavaria, who commanded the Austrian armies. The
duke of Bavaria told him, that it was entirely superfluous to form
any treaty for that purpose. *Hostilities are already ceased,* said he; *and
I doubt not but I shall be able to prevent their revival by keeping firm
possession of the Palatinate, till a final agreement shall be concluded*

*Negoci-
ations with
regard
to the
marriage
and the
Palatinate.*

97

between the contending parties.[c] Notwithstanding this insult, James endeavoured to resume with the emperor a treaty of accommodation; and he opened the negociations at Brussels, under the mediation of archduke Albert, and, after his death, which happened about this time, under that of the Infanta: When the conferences were entered upon, it was found, that the powers of these princes to determine in the controversy were not sufficient or satisfactory. Schwartzenbourg, the Imperial minister, was expected at London; and it was hoped that he would bring more ample authority: His commission referred entirely to the negociation at Brussels. It was not difficult for the king to perceive, that his applications were neglected by the emperor; but as he had no choice of any other expedient, and it seemed the interest of his son-in-law to keep alive his pretensions, he was still content to follow Ferdinand through all his shifts and evasions. Nor was he entirely discouraged, even when the Imperial diet at Ratisbon, by the influence, or rather authority of the emperor, though contrary to the protestation of Saxony and of all the protestant princes and cities, had transferred the electoral dignity from the Palatine to the duke of Bavaria.

Meanwhile, the efforts made by Frederic, for the recovery of his dominions, were vigorous. Three armies were levied in Germany by his authority, under three commanders, duke Christian of Brunswick, the prince of Baden-Dourlach, and count Mansfeldt. The two former generals were defeated by count Tilly and the Imperialists: The third though much inferior in force to his enemies, still maintained the war; but with no equal supplies of money either from the Palatine or the king of England. It was chiefly by pillage and free quarters in the Palatinate, that he subsisted his army. As the Austrians were regularly paid, they were kept in more exact discipline; and James justly became apprehensive, lest so unequal a contest, besides ravaging the Palatine's hereditary dominions, would end in the total alienation of the people's affections from their ancient sovereign, by whom they were plundered, and in an attachment to their new masters, by whom they were protected.[d] He persuaded therefore his son-in-law to disarm, under colour of duty and submission to the em-

[c] Franklyn, p. 57. Rushworth, vol. i. p. 38.   [d] Parl. Hist. vol. v. p. 484.

CHAPTER XLIX

peror: And accordingly, Mansfeldt was dismissed from the Palatine's service; and that famous general withdrew his army into the Low Countries, and there received a commission from the States of the United Provinces.

To shew how little account was made of James's negociations abroad, there is a pleasantry mentioned by all historians, which, for that reason, shall have place here. In a farce, acted at Brussels, a courier was introduced carrying the doleful news, that the Palatinate would soon be wrested from the house of Austria; so powerful were the succours, which, from all quarters, were hastening to the relief of the despoiled elector: the king of Denmark had agreed to contribute to his assistance a hundred thousand pickled herrings, the Dutch a hundred thousand butter-boxes, and the king of England a hundred thousand ambassadors. On other occasions, he was painted with a scabbard, but without a sword; or with a sword, which nobody could draw, though several were pulling at it.[e]

It was not from his negociations with the emperor or the duke of Bavaria, that James expected any success in his project of restoring the Palatine: His eyes were entirely turned towards Spain; and if he could effect his son's marriage with the Infanta, he doubted not, but that, after so intimate a conjunction, this other point could easily be obtained. The negociations of that court being commonly dilatory, it was not easy for a prince of so little penetration in business, to distinguish, whether the difficulties, which occurred, were real or affected; and he was surprized, after negociating five years on so simple a demand, that he was not more advanced than at the beginning. A dispensation from Rome was requisite for the marriage of the Infanta with a protestant prince; and the king of Spain, having undertaken to procure that dispensation, had thereby acquired the means of retarding at pleasure, or of forwarding the marriage, and at the same time of concealing entirely his artifices from the court of England.

In order to remove all obstacles, James dispatched Digby, soon after created earl of Bristol, as his ambassador to Philip IV. who had lately succeeded his father in the crown of Spain. He secretly employed Gage as his agent at Rome; and finding that the differ-

[e] Kennet, p. 749.

ence of religion was the principal, if not the sole difficulty, which retarded the marriage, he resolved to soften that objection as much as possible. He issued public orders for discharging all popish recusants who were imprisoned; and it was daily apprehended, that he would forbid, for the future, the execution of the penal laws enacted against them. For this step, so opposite to the rigid spirit of his subjects, he took care to apologize; and he even endeavoured to ascribe it to his great zeal for the reformed religion. He had been making applications, he said, to all foreign princes for some indulgence to the distressed protestants; and he was still answered by objections derived from the severity of the English laws against catholics.[f] It might indeed occur to him, that, if the extremity of religious zeal were ever to abate among christian sects, one of them must begin; and nothing would be more honourable for England, than to have led the way in sentiments so wise and moderate.

Not only the religious puritans murmured at this tolerating measure of the king: The lovers of civil liberty were alarmed at so important an exertion of prerogative. But, among other dangerous articles of authority, the kings of England were at that time possessed of the dispensing power; at least, were in the constant practice of exercising it. Besides, though the royal prerogative in civil matters was then extensive, the princes, during some late reigns, had been accustomed to assume a still greater in ecclesiastical. And the king failed not to represent the toleration of catholics as a measure entirely of that nature.

By James's concession in favour of the catholics, he attained his end. The same religious motives which had hitherto rendered the court of Madrid insincere in all the steps taken with regard to the marriage, were now the chief cause of promoting it. By its means, it was there hoped, the English catholics would for the future enjoy ease and indulgence; and the Infanta would be the happy instrument of procuring to the church some tranquillity, after the many severe persecutions, which it had hitherto undergone. The earl of Bristol, a minister of vigilance and penetration, and who had formerly opposed all alliance with catholics,[g] was now fully convinced of the sincerity of Spain; and he was ready to congratulate

[f] Franklyn, p. 69. Rushworth, vol. i. p. 63.　　[g] Rushworth, vol. i. p. 292.

CHAPTER XLIX

the king on the entire completion of his views and projects.[h] A
daughter of Spain, whom he represents as extremely accomplished, would soon, he said, arrive in England, and bring with her
an immense fortune of two millions of pieces of eight, or 600,000
pounds sterling; a sum four times greater than Spain had ever
before given with any princess, and almost equal to all the money,
which the parliament, during the whole course of this reign, had
hitherto granted to the king. But what was of more importance to
James's honour and happiness, Bristol considered this match as
an infallible prognostic of the Palatine's restoration; nor would
Philip, he thought, ever have bestowed his sister and so large a
fortune, under the prospect of entering next day into a war with
England. So exact was his intelligence, that the most secret counsels of the Spaniards, he boasts, had never escaped him;[i] and he
found that they had all along considered the marriage of the
Infanta and the restitution of the Palatinate as measures closely
connected, or altogether inseparable.[k] However little calculated
James's character to extort so vast a concession; however improper
the measures which he had pursued for attaining that end; the
ambassador could not withstand the plain evidence of facts, by
which Philip now demonstrated his sincerity. Perhaps too, like a
wise man, he considered, that reasons of state, which are supposed
solely to influence the councils of monarchs, are not always the
motives, which there predominate; that the milder views of gratitude, honour, friendship, generosity, are frequently able, among
princes as well as private persons, to counterbalance these selfish
considerations; that the justice and moderation of James had been
so conspicuous in all these transactions, his reliance on Spain, his
confidence in her friendship, that he had at last obtained the
cordial alliance of that nation, so celebrated for honour and fidelity. Or if politics must still be supposed the ruling motive of all
public measures, the maritime power of England was so considerable, and the Spanish dominions so divided, as might well induce
the council of Philip to think, that a sincere friendship with the

[h] Ibid. p. 69.   [i] Rushworth, vol. i. p. 272.   [k] We find by private letters
between Philip IV. and the Condé Olivarez, shown by the latter to Buckingham, that the marriage and the restitution of the Palatinate were always
considered by the court of Spain as inseparable. See Franklyn, p. 71, 72.
Rushworth, vol. i. p. 71, 280, 299, 300. Parl. Hist. vol. vi. p. 66.

masters of the sea could not be purchased by too great concessions.[l] And as James, during so many years, had been allured and
seduced by hopes and protestations, his people enraged by delays
and disappointments; it would probably occur, that there was now
no medium left between the most inveterate hatred and the most
intimate alliance between the nations. Not to mention, that, as a
new spirit began about this time to animate the councils of France,
the friendship of England became every day more necessary to the
greatness and security of the Spanish monarch.

All measures being, therefore, agreed on between the parties,
naught was wanting but the dispensation from Rome, which might
be considered as a mere formality.[m] The king justified by success,
now exulted in his pacific counsels, and boasted of his superior
sagacity and penetration; when all these flattering prospects were
blasted by the temerity of a man, whom he had fondly exalted from
a private condition, to be the bane of himself, of his family, and of
his people.

Character of Buckingham. Ever since the fall of Somerset, Buckingham had governed,
with an uncontrouled sway, both the court and nation; and could
James's eyes have been opened, he had now full opportunity of
observing how unfit his favourite was for the high station, to which
he was raised. Some accomplishments of a courtier he possessed:
Of every talent of a minister he was utterly destitute. Headlong in
his passions, and incapable equally of prudence and of dissimulation: Sincere from violence rather than candour; expensive
from profusion more than generosity: A warm friend, a furious
enemy; but without any choice of discernment in either: With
these qualities he had early and quickly mounted to the highest
rank; and partook at once of the insolence which attends a fortune
newly acquired, and the impetuosity which belongs to persons
born in high stations, and unacquainted with opposition.

1623. Among those who had experienced the arrogance of this over-
grown favourite, the prince of Wales himself had not been entirely
spared; and a great coldness, if not an enmity, had, for that reason,
taken place between them. Buckingham, desirous of an opportunity, which might connect him with the prince, and overcome his
aversion, and at the same time envious of the great credit acquired

[l] Franklyn, p. 72.   [m] Rushworth, vol. i. p. 66.

CHAPTER XLIX

by Bristol in the Spanish negociation, bethought himself of an expedient, by which he might at once gratify both these inclinations. He represented to Charles, that persons of his exalted station were peculiarly unfortunate in their marriage, the chief circumstance of life; and commonly received into their arms a bride, unknown to them, to whom they were unknown; not endeared by sympathy, not obliged by service; wooed by treaties alone, by negociations, by political interests: That however accomplished the Infanta, she must still consider herself as a melancholy victim of state, and could not but think with aversion of that day, when she was to enter the bed of a stranger; and passing into a foreign country and a new family, bid adieu for ever to her father's house and to her native land: That it was in the prince's power to soften all these rigours, and lay such an obligation on her, as would attach the most indifferent temper, as would warm the coldest affections: That his journey to Madrid would be an unexpected gallantry, which would equal all the fictions of Spanish romance, and suiting the amorous and enterprising character of that nation, must immediately introduce him to the princess under the agreeable character of a devoted lover and daring adventurer: That the negociations with regard to the Palatinate, which had hitherto languished in the hands of ministers, would quickly be terminated by so illustrious an agent, seconded by the mediation and intreaties of the grateful infanta: That Spanish generosity, moved by that unexampled trust and confidence, would make concessions beyond what could be expected from political views and considerations: And that he would quickly return to the king with the glory of having re-established the unhappy Palatine, by the same enterprize, which procured him the affections and the person of the Spanish princess."

The mind of the young prince, replete with candor, was inflamed by these generous and romantic ideas, suggested by Buckingham. He agreed to make application to the king for his approbation. They chose the moment of his kindest and most jovial humour; and more by the earnestness which they expressed, than by the force of their reasons, they obtained a hasty and unguarded consent of their undertaking. And having engaged his promise to

" Clarendon, vol. i. p. 11, 12.

keep their purpose secret, they left him, in order to make preparations for the journey.

No sooner was the king alone, than his temper, more cautious than sanguine, suggested very different views of the matter, and represented every difficulty and danger, which could occur. He reflected, that, however the world might pardon this sally of youth in the prince, they would never forgive himself, who, at his years, and after his experience, could entrust his only son, the heir of his crown, the prop of his age, to the discretion of foreigners, without so much as providing the frail security of a safe conduct in his favour: That if the Spanish monarch were sincere in his professions, a few months must finish the treaty of marriage, and bring the Infanta into England; if he were not sincere, the folly was still more egregious of committing the prince into his hands: That Philip, when possessed of so invaluable a pledge, might well rise in his demands, and impose harder conditions of treaty: And that the temerity of the enterprize was so apparent, that the event, how prosperous soever, could not justify it; and if disastrous, it would render himself infamous to his people, and ridiculous to all posterity.[o]

Tormented with these reflections, as soon as the prince and Buckingham returned for their dispatches, he informed them of all the reasons, which had determined him to change his resolution; and he begged them to desist from so foolish an adventure. The prince received the disappointment with sorrowful submission and silent tears: Buckingham presumed to speak in an imperious tone, which he had ever experienced to be prevalent over his too easy master. He told the king, that nobody for the future would believe any thing he said, when he retracted so soon the promise so solemnly given; that he plainly discerned this change of resolution to proceed from another breach of his word, in communicating the matter to some rascal, who had furnished him with those pitiful reasons which he had alleged, and he doubted not but he should hereafter know who his counsellor had been; and that if he receded from what he had promised, it would be such a disobligation to the prince, who had now set his heart upon the journey, after his majesty's approbation, that he could never forget it, nor forgive any man who had been the cause of it.[p]

[o] Clarendon, vol. i. p. 14.   [p] Ibid. vol. i. p. 16.

CHAPTER XLIX

The king, with great earnestness, fortified by many oaths, made his apology, by denying that he had communicated the matter to any; and finding himself assailed, as well by the boisterous importunities of Buckingham, as by the warm intreaties of his son, whose applications had hitherto, on other occasions, been always dutiful, never earnest; he had again the weakness to assent to their purposed journey. It was agreed that Sir Francis Cottington alone, the prince's secretary, and Endymion Porter, gentleman of his bed-chamber, should accompany them; and the former being at that time in the anti-chamber, he was immediately called in by the king's orders.

James told Cottington, that he had always been an honest man, and therfore he was now to trust him in an affair of the highest importance, which he was not, upon his life, to disclose to any man whatever. "Cottington," added he, "here is baby Charles and Stenny," (these ridiculous appellations he usually gave to the prince and Buckingham) "who have a great mind to go post into Spain, and fetch home the Infanta: They will have but two more in their company, and have chosen you for one. What think you of the journey?" Sir Francis, who was a prudent man, and had resided some years in Spain as the king's agent, was struck with all the obvious objections to such an enterprize, and scrupled not to declare them. The king threw himself upon his bed, and cried, *I told you this before;* and fell into a new passion and new lamentations, complaining that he was undone, and should lose baby Charles.

The prince showed by his countenance, that he was extremely dissatisfied with Cottington's discourse; but Buckingham broke into an open passion against him. The king, he told him, asked him only of the journey, and of the manner of travelling; particulars, of which he might be a competent judge, having gone the road so often by post; but that he, without being called to it, had the presumption to give his advice upon matters of state and against his master, which he should repent as long as he lived. A thousand other reproaches he added, which put the poor king into a new agony in behalf of a servant, who, he foresaw, would suffer for answering him honestly. Upon which he said with some emotion: *Nay, by God, Stenny, you are much to blame for using him so: He answered me directly to the question which I asked him, and very honestly and wisely; and yet, you know, he said no more than I told you before he was called in.* However, after all this passion on both sides, James renewed his consent; and proper directions were given for the journey. Nor was he now at any loss to discover, that the whole intrigue was originally contrived by Buckingham, as well as pursued violently by his spirit and impetuosity.

These circumstances, which so well characterise the persons, seem to have been related by Cottington to lord Clarendon, from whom they are here transcribed; and though minute, are not undeserving of a place in history.

The prince and Buckingham, with their two attendants, and Sir Richard Graham, master of horse to Buckingham, passed disguised and undiscovered through France; and they even ventured into a court-ball at Paris, where Charles saw the princess Henrietta, whom he afterwards espoused, and who was at that time in the bloom of youth and beauty. In eleven days after their departure from London, they arrived at Madrid; and surprized every-body by a step so unusual among great princes. The Spanish monarch immediately paid Charles a visit, expressed the utmost gratitude for the confidence reposed in him, and made warm protestations of a correspondent confidence and friendship. By the most studied civilities, he showed the respect which he bore to his royal guest. He gave him a golden key, which opened all his apartments, that the prince might, without any introduction, have access to him at all hours: He took the left hand of him on every occasion, except in the apartments assigned to Charles; for there, he said, the prince was at home: Charles was introduced into the palace with the same pomp and ceremony that attends the kings of Spain on their coronation: The council received public orders to obey him as the king himself: Olivarez too, though a grandee of Spain, who has the right of being covered before his own king, would not put on his hat in the prince's presence:[q] All the prisons of Spain were thrown open, and all the prisoners received their freedom, as if the event, the most honourable and most fortunate, had happened to the monarchy.[r] And every sumptuary law with regard to apparel was suspended during Charles's residence in Spain. The Infanta, however, was only shown to her lover in public, the Spanish ideas of decency being so strict, as not to allow of any farther intercourse, till the arrival of the dispensation.[s]

7th March. The prince's journey to Spain.

[q] Franklyn, p. 73.   [r] Idem, p. 74.   [s] Rushworth, vol. i. p. 77.

CHAPTER XLIX

The point of honour was carried so far by that generous people, that no attempt was made, on account of the advantage which
they had acquired, of imposing any harder conditions of treaty:
Their pious zeal only prompted them, on one occasion, to desire
more concessions in the religious articles; but, upon the opposition
of Bristol, accompanied with some reproaches, they immediately
desisted; The Pope, however, hearing of the prince's arrival in
Madrid, tacked some new clauses to the dispensation;[t] and it became necessary to transmit the articles to London, that the king
might ratify them. This treaty, which was made public, consisted
of several articles, chiefly regarding the exercise of the catholic
religion by the Infanta and her household. Nothing could reasonably be found fault with, except one article, in which the king
promised, that the children should be educated by the princess, till
ten years of age. This condition could not be insisted on, but with
a view of seasoning their minds with catholic principles; and
though so tender an age seemed a sufficient security against theological prejudices, yet the same reason, which made the pope in-
sert that article, should have induced the king to reject it.

Besides the public treaty, there were separate articles, privately
sworn to by the king; in which he promised to suspend the penal
laws enacted against catholics, to procure a repeal of them in
parliament, and to grant a toleration for the exercise of the catholic religion in private houses.[u] Great murmurs, we may believe,
would have arisen against these articles, had they been made
known to the public; since we find it to have been imputed as an
enormous crime to the prince, that, having received, about this
time, a very civil letter from the pope, he was induced to return a
very civil answer.[w]

Meanwhile Gregory XV. who granted the dispensation died;
and Urban VIII. was chosen in his place. Upon this event, the
nuncio refused to deliver the dispensation, till it should be
renewed by Urban; and that crafty pontiff delayed sending a
new dispensation, in hopes, that, during the prince's residence in
Spain, some expedient might be fallen upon to effect his conversion. The king of England, as well as the prince, became im-

[t] Idem, vol. i. p. 84. [u] Franklyn, p. 80. Rushworth, vol. i. p. 89. Kennet,
p. 769. [w] Rushworth, vol. i. p. 82. Franklyn, p. 77.

patient. On the first hint, Charles obtained permission to return; and Philip graced his departure with all the circumstances of elaborate civility and respect, which had attended his reception. He even erected a pillar, on the spot where they took leave of each other, as a monument of mutual friendship; and the prince, having sworn to the observance of all the articles, entered on his journey, and embarked on board the English fleet at St. Andero.

The character of Charles, composed of decency, reserve, modesty, sobriety; virtues so agreeable to the manners of the Spaniards; the unparalleled confidence, which he had reposed in their nation; the romantic gallantry, which he had practised towards the princess; all these circumstances, joined to his youth and advantageous figure, had endeared him to the whole court of Madrid, and had impressed the most favourable ideas of him.[x] But, in the same proportion, that the prince was beloved and esteemed, was Buckingham despised and hated. His behaviour, composed of English familiarity, and French vivacity; his sallies of passion, his indecent freedoms with the prince, his dissolute pleasures, his arrogant, impetuous temper, which he neither could, nor cared to disguise; qualities like these, could, most of them, be esteemed no where, but to the Spaniards were the objects of peculiar aversion.[y] They could not conceal their surprize, that such a youth could intrude into a negotiation, now conducted to a period, by so accomplished a minister as Bristol, and could assume to himself all the merit of it. They lamented the Infanta's fate, who must be approached by a man, whose temerity seemed to respect no laws, divine or human.[z] And when they observed, that he had the imprudence to insult the Condé duke of Olivarez, their prime minister; every one, who was ambitious of paying court to the Spanish, became desirous of showing a contempt for the English favourite.

The duke of Buckingham told Olivarez, that his own attachment to the Spanish nation and to the king of Spain was extreme; that he would contribute to every measure, which could cement the friendship between England and them; and that his peculiar ambition would be to facilitate the prince's marriage with the Infanta. But, he added, with a sincerity equally insolent and indis-

<hr>

[x] Franklyn, p. 80. Rushworth, vol. i. p. 103.   [y] Ibid. vol. i. p. 101.
[z] Clarendon, vol. i. p. 36.

CHAPTER XLIX

creet, *With regard to you, Sir, in particular, you must not consider me as your friend, but must ever expect from me all possible enmity and opposition.* The Condé duke replied, with a becoming dignity, that he very willingly accepted of what was proffered him: And on these terms the favourites parted.[a]

Buckingham, sensible how odious he was become to the Spaniards, and dreading the influence, which that nation would naturally acquire after the arrival of the Infanta, resolved to employ all his credit, in order to prevent the marriage. By what arguments he could engage the prince to offer such an insult to the Spanish nation, from whom he had met with such generous treatment, by what colours he could disguise the ingratitude, and imprudence of such a measure; these are totally unknown to us. We may only conjecture, that the many unavoidable causes of delay, which had so long prevented the arrival of the dispensation, had afforded to Buckingham a pretence for throwing on the Spaniards the imputation of insincerity in the whole treaty. It also appears, that his impetuous and domineering character had acquired, what it ever after maintained, a total ascendant over the gentle and modest temper of Charles; and, when the prince left Madrid, he was firmly determined, notwithstanding all his professions, to break off the treaty with Spain.

It is not likely, that Buckingham prevailed so easily with James to abandon a project, which, during so many years, had been the object of all his wishes, and which he had now unexpectedly conducted to a happy period.[b] A rupture with Spain, the loss of two millions, were prospects little agreeable to this pacific and indigent monarch. But finding his only son bent against a match, which had always been opposed by his people and his parliament, he yielded to difficulties, which he had not courage or strength of mind sufficient to overcome. The prince therefore, and Buckingham, on their arrival at London, assumed entirely the direction of the negotiation; and it was their business to seek for pretences, by which they could give a colour to their intended breach of treaty.

Though the restitution of the Palatinate had ever been considered by James as a natural or necessary consequence of the Span-

---

[a] Rushworth, vol. i. p. 103. Clarendon, vol. i. p. 37.   [b] *Hacket's Life of Williams.*

ish alliance, he had always forbidden his ministers to insist on it as a preliminary article to the conclusion of the marriage treaty. He considered, that this principality was now in the hands of the emperor and the duke of Bavaria; and that it was no longer in the king of Spain's power, by a single stroke of his pen, to restore it to its ancient master. The strict alliance of Spain with these princes would engage Philip, he thought, to soften so disagreeable a demand by every art of negociation; and many articles must of necessity be adjusted, before such an important point could be effected. It was sufficient, in James's opinion, if the sincerity of the Spanish court could, for the present, be ascertained; and, dreading farther delays of the marriage, so long wished for, he was resolved to trust the Palatine's full restoration to the event of future counsels and deliberations.[c]

This whole system of negotiation, Buckingham now reversed; and he overturned every supposition, upon which the treaty had hitherto been conducted. After many fruitless artifices were employed to delay or prevent the espousals, Bristol received positive orders not to deliver the proxy, which had been left in his hands, or to finish the marriage, till security were given for the full restitution of the Palatinate.[d] Philip understood this language. He had been acquainted with the disgust received by Buckingham; and deeming him a man capable of sacrificing, to his own ungovernable passions, the greatest interests of his master and of his country, he had expected, that the unbounded credit of that favourite would be employed to embroil the two nations. Determined, however, to throw the blame of the rupture entirely on the English, he delivered into Bristol's hand a written promise, by which he bound himself to procure the restoration of the Palatine, either by persuasion, or by every other possible means; and, when he found that this concession gave no satisfaction, he ordered the Infanta to lay aside the title of princess of Wales, which she bore after the arrival of the dispensation from Rome, and to drop the study of the English language.[e] And thinking that such rash counsels, as now governed the court of England, would not stop at the breach of the marriage treaty, he ordered preparations for war immediately to be made, throughout all his dominions.[f]

Marriage treaty broken.

---

[c] Parl. Hist. vol. vi. p. 57.   [d] Rushworth, vol. i. p. 105. Kennet, p. 776.
[e] Franklyn, p. 80. Rushworth, vol. i. p. 112.   [f] Rushworth, vol. i. p. 114.

CHAPTER XLIX

Thus James, having, by means inexplicable from the ordinary rules of politics, conducted, so near an honourable period, the marriage of his son and the restoration of his son-in-law, failed at last of his purpose, by means equally unaccountable.

But, though the expedients, already used by Buckingham, were sufficiently inglorious, both for himself and for the nation; it was necessary for him, ere he could fully effect his purpose, to employ artifices still more dishonourable.

The king, having broken with Spain, was obliged to concert new measures; and, without the assistance of parliament, no effectual step of any kind could be taken. The benevolence, which, during the interval, had been rigorously exacted for recovering the Palatinate, though levied for so popular an end, had procured to the king less money than ill-will from his subjects.[g] Whatever discouragements, therefore, he might receive from his ill agreement with former parliaments, there was a necessity of summoning once more this assembly: and, it might be hoped, that the Spanish alliance, which gave such umbrage, being abandoned, the commons would now be better satisfied with the king's administration. In his speech to the houses, James dropped some hints of his causes of complaint against Spain; and he graciously condescended to ask the advice of parliament, which he had ever before rejected, with regard to the conduct of so important an affair as his son's marriage.[h] Buckingham delivered, to a committee of lords and commons, a long narrative, which he pretended to be true and complete, of every step taken in the negociations with Philip: But partly by the suppression of some facts, partly by the false colouring laid on others, this narrative was calculated entirely to mislead the parliament, and to throw on the court of Spain the reproach of artifice and insincerity. He said, that, after many years' negotiation, the king found not himself any nearer his purpose; and that Bristol had never brought the treaty beyond general

1624.

A parliament.

29th Feb.

---

[g] To show by what violent measures benevolences were usually raised, Johnstone tells us, in his *Rerum Britannicarum historia*, that Barnes, a citizen of London, was the first who refused to contribute anything; upon which, the treasurer sent him word, that he must immediately prepare himself to carry by post a dispatch into Ireland. The citizen was glad to make his peace by paying a hundred pounds; and no one durst afterwards refuse the benevolence required. See farther, Coke, p. 80. [h] Franklyn, p. 79. Rushworth, vol. i. p. 115. Kennet, p. 778.

professions and declarations: That the prince, doubting the good intentions of Spain, resolved at last to take a journey to Madrid, and put the matter to the utmost trial: That he there found such artificial dealing as made him conclude all the steps taken towards the marriage to be false and deceitful: That the restitution of the Palatinate, which had ever been regarded by the king as an essential preliminary, was not seriously intended by Spain: And that, after enduring much bad usage, the prince was obliged to return to England, without any hopes, either of obtaining the Infanta, or of restoring the Elector Palatine.[i]

This narrative, which, considering the importance of the occasion, and the solemnity of that assembly, to which it was delivered, deserves great blame, was yet vouched for truth by the prince of Wales, who was present; and the king himself lent it, indirectly, his authority, by telling the parliament, that it was by his orders Buckingham laid the whole affair before them. The conduct of these princes it is difficult fully to excuse. It is in vain to plead the youth and inexperience of Charles; unless his inexperience and youth, as is probable,[k] if not certain, really led him into error, and made him swallow all the falsities of Buckingham. And though the king was here hurried from his own measures by the impetuosity of others; nothing should have induced him to prostitute his character, and seem to vouch the impostures, at least false colourings, of his favourite, of which he had so good reason to entertain a suspicion.[l]

Buckingham's narrative, however artfully disguised, contained so many contradictory circumstances as were sufficient to open the eyes of all reasonable men; but it concurred so well with the passions and prejudices of the parliament, that no scruple was made of immediately adopting it.[m] Charmed with having obtained at length the opportunity, so long wished for, of going to war with papists, they little thought of future consequences; but immediately advised the king to break off both treaties with Spain, as well that which regarded the marriage, as that for the restitution of the

---

[i] Franklyn, p. 89, 90, 91, &c. Rushworth, vol. i. p. 119, 120, &c. Parl. Hist. vol. vi. p. 20, 21, &c.   [k] See note [L] at the end of the volume.   [l] It must, however, be confessed, that the king afterwards warned the house not to take Buckingham's narrative for his, though it was laid before them by his order. Parl. Hist. vol. vi. p. 104. James was probably ashamed to have been carried so far by his favourite.   [m] Parl. Hist. vol. vi. p. 75.

Palatinate." The people, ever greedy of war, till they suffer by it, displayed their triumph at these violent measures by public bonfires and rejoicings, and by insults on the Spanish ministers. Buckingham was now the favourite of the public and of the parliament. Sir Edward Coke, in the house of commons, called him the Saviour of the nation." Every place resounded with his praises. And he himself, intoxicated by a popularity, which he enjoyed so little time, and which he so ill deserved, violated all duty to his indulgent master, and entered into cabals with the puritanical members, who had ever opposed the royal authority. He even encouraged schemes for abolishing the order of bishops, and selling the dean and chapter lands, in order to defray the expences of a Spanish war. And the king, though he still entertained projects for temporizing, and for forming an accommodation with Spain, was so borne down by the torrent of popular prejudices, conducted and encreased by Buckingham, that he was at last obliged, in a speech to parliament, to declare in favour of hostile measures, if they would engage to support him." Doubts of their sincerity in this respect; doubts which the event showed not to be ill grounded; had probably been one cause of his former pacific and dilatory measures.

In his speech on this occasion, the king began with lamenting his own unhappiness, that, having so long valued himself on the epithet of the pacific monarch, he should now, in his old age, be obliged to exchange the blessings of peace for the inevitable calamities of war. He represented to them the immense and continued expence, requisite for military armaments; and besides supplies, from time to time, as they should become necessary, he demanded a vote of six subsidies and twelve fifteenths, as a proper stock before the commencement of hostilities. He told them of his intolerable debts, chiefly contracted by the sums remitted to the Palatine;" but he added, that he did not insist on any supply for his own relief, and that it was sufficient for him, if the honour and security of the public were provided for. To remove all suspicion, he, who had ever strenuously maintained his prerogative, and who

" Franklyn, p. 98. Rushworth, vol. i. p. 128. Parl. Hist. vol. vi. p. 103.
° Clarendon, vol. i. p. 6.   ᵖ Franklyn, p. 94, 95. Rushworth, vol. i. p. 129, 130.   ᵠ See note [M] at the end of the volume.

had even extended it into some points esteemed doubtful, now made an imprudent concession, of which the consequences might have proved fatal to royal authority: He voluntarily offered, that the money voted should be paid to a committee of parliament, and should be issued by them, without being intrusted to his management.[r] The commons willingly accepted of this concession, so unusual in an English monarch; they voted him only three subsidies and three fifteenths:[s] and they took no notice of the complaints, which he made, of his own wants and necessities.

Advantage was also taken of the present good agreement between the king and parliament, in order to pass the bill against monopolies, which had formerly been encouraged by the king, but which had failed by the rupture between him and the last house of commons. This bill was conceived in such terms as to render it merely declaratory; and all monopolies were condemned, as contrary to law and to the known liberties of the people. It was there supposed, that every subject of England had entire power to dispose of his own actions, provided he did no injury to any of his fellow-subjects; and that no prerogative of the king, no power of any magistrate, nothing but the authority alone of laws, could restrain that unlimited freedom. The full prosecution of this noble principle into all its natural consequences, has at last, through many contests, produced that singular and happy government, which we enjoy at present.[t]

The house of commons also corroborated, by a new precedent, the important power of impeachment, which, two years before, they had exercised, in the case of chancellor Bacon, and which had lain dormant for near two centuries, except when they served as instruments of royal vengeance. The earl of Middlesex had been raised, by Buckingham's interest, from the rank of a London merchant, to be treasurer of England; and, by his activity and address, seemed not unworthy of that preferment. But, as he incurred the displeasure of his patron, by scrupling or refusing some demands of money, during the prince's residence in Spain, that favourite vowed revenge, and employed all his credit among the commons to procure an impeachment of the treasurer. The king was ex-

---

[r] Rushworth, vol. i. p. 137.   [s] Less than 300,000 pounds.   [t] See note [N] at the end of the volume.

CHAPTER XLIX

tremely dissatisfied with this measure, and prophesied to the prince and duke, that they would live to have their fill of parliamentary prosecutions.[u] In a speech to the parliament, he endeavoured to apologize for Middlesex, and to soften the accusation against him.[w] The charge, however, was still maintained by the commons; and the treasurer was found guilty by the peers, though the misdemeanors, proved against him, were neither numerous nor important. The accepting of two presents of five hundred pounds a-piece, for passing two patents, was the article of greatest weight. His sentence was, to be fined 50,000 pounds for the king's use, and to suffer all the other penalties formerly inflicted upon Bacon. The fine was afterwards remitted by the prince, when he mounted the throne.

This session, an address was also made, very disagreeable to the king, craving the severe execution of the laws against catholics. His answer was gracious and condescending;[x] though he declared against persecution, as being an improper measure for the suppression of any religion, according to the received maxim, *That the blood of the martyrs was the seed of the church.* He also condemned an entire indulgence of the catholics; and seemed to represent a middle course, as the most humane and most politic. He went so far as even to affirm, with an oath, that he never had entertained any thoughts of granting a toleration to these religionists.[y] The liberty of exercising their worship in private houses, which he had secretly agreed to in the Spanish treaty, did not appear to him deserving that name; and it was probably by means of this explication, he thought that he had saved his honour. And as Buckingham, in his narrative,[z] confessed, that the king had agreed to a temporary suspension of the penal laws against the catholics, which he distinguished from a toleration, a term at that time extremely odious, James naturally deemed his meaning to be sufficiently explained, and feared not any reproach of falsehood or duplicity, on account *29th May.* of this asseveration. After all these transactions, the parliament was prorogued by the king, who let fall some hints, though in gentle terms, of the sense which he entertained of their unkindness, in not supplying his necessities.[a]

[u] Clarendon, vol. i. p. 23.   [w] Parl. Hist. vol. vi. p. 19.   [x] Franklyn, p. 101, 102.   [y] See farther, Franklyn, p. 87.   [z] Parl. Hist. vol. vi. p. 37. [a] Franklyn, p. 103.

James, unable to resist so strong a combination as that of his people, his parliament, his son, and his favourite, had been compelled to embrace measures, for which, from temper as well as judgment, he had ever entertained a most settled aversion. Though he dissembled his resentment, he began to estrange himself from Buckingham, to whom he ascribed all those violent counsels, and whom he considered as the author, both of the prince's journey to Spain, and of the breach of the marriage treaty. The arrival of Bristol he impatiently longed for; and it was by the assistance of that minister, whose wisdom he respected, and whose views he approved, that he hoped in time to extricate himself from his present difficulties.

Return of Bristol. During the prince's abode in Spain, that able negociator had ever opposed, though unsuccessfully, to the impetuous measures suggested by Buckingham, his own wise and well tempered counsels. After Charles's departure, he still, upon the first appearance of a change of resolution, interposed his advice, and strenuously insisted on the sincerity of the Spaniards in the conduct of the treaty, as well as the advantages, which England must reap from the completion of it. Enraged to find, that his successful labours should be rendered abortive by the levities and caprices of an insolent minion, he would understand no hints; and nothing but express orders from his master could engage him to make that demand, which, he was sensible, must put a final period to the treaty. He was not therefore surprised to hear, that Buckingham had declared himself his open enemy, and, on all occasions, had thrown out many violent reflections against him.

Nothing could be of greater consequence to Buckingham, than to keep Bristol at a distance both from the king and the parliament; lest the power of truth, enforced by so well-informed a speaker, should open scenes, which were but suspected by the former, and of which the latter had as yet entertained no manner of jealousy. He applied therefore to James, whose weakness, disguised to himself under the appearance of finesse and dissimulation, was now become absolutely incurable. A warrant for sending Bristol to the Tower was issued immediately upon his arrival in England;[b] and though he was soon released from confinement, yet orders were carried him from the king, to retire to his country

[b] Rushworth, vol. i. p. 145.

CHAPTER XLIX

seat, and to abstain from all attendance in parliament. He obeyed; but loudly demanded an opportunity of justifying himself, and of laying his whole conduct before his master. On all occasions, he protested his innocence, and threw on his enemy the blame of every miscarriage. Buckingham, and, at his instigation, the prince, declared, that they would be reconciled to Bristol, if he would but acknowledge his errors and ill-conduct: But the spirited nobleman, jealous of his honour, refused to buy favour at so high a price. James had the equity to say, that the insisting on that condition was a strain of unexampled tyranny: But Buckingham scrupled not to assert, with his usual presumption, that neither the king, the prince, nor himself, were as yet satisfied of Bristol's innocence.[c]

While the attachment of the prince to Buckingham, while the timidity of James, or the shame of changing his favourite, kept the whole court in awe; the Spanish ambassador, Inoiosa, endeavoured to open the king's eyes, and to cure his fears, by instilling greater fears into him. He privately slipped into his hand a paper, and gave him a signal to read it alone. He there told him, that he was as much a prisoner at London as ever Francis I. was at Madrid; that the prince and Buckingham had conspired together, and had the whole court at their devotion; that cabals among the popular leaders in parliament were carrying on to the extreme prejudice of his authority; that the project was to confine him to some of his hunting seats, and to commit the whole administration to Charles; and that it was necessary for him, by one vigorous effort, to vindicate his authority, and to punish those who had so long and so much abused his friendship and beneficence.[d]

What credit James gave to this representation does not appear. He only discovered some faint symptoms, which he instantly retracted, of dissatisfaction with Buckingham. All his public measures, and all the alliances into which he entered, were founded on the system of enmity to the Austrian family, and of war to be carried on for the recovery of the Palatinate.

Rupture with Spain.

The states of the United Provinces were, at this time, governed by Maurice; and that aspiring prince, sensible that his credit would languish during peace, had, on the expiration of the twelve years'

[c] Id. vol. i. p. 259.   [d] Rushworth, vol. i. p. 144. Hacket's Life of Williams. Coke, p. 107.

truce, renewed the war with the Spanish monarchy. His great capacity in the military art would have compensated the inferiority of his forces, had not the Spanish armies been commanded by Spinola, a general equally renowned for conduct, and more celebrated for enterprize and activity. In such a situation, nothing could be more welcome to the republic than the prospect of a rupture between James and the catholic king; and they flattered themselves, as well from the natural union of interests between them and England, as from the influence of the present conjuncture, that powerful succours would soon march to their relief. Accordingly, an army of six thousand men was levied in England, and sent over to Holland, commanded by four young noblemen, Essex, Oxford, Southampton, and Willoughby, who were ambitious of distinguishing themselves in so popular a cause, and of acquiring military experience under so renowned a captain as Maurice.

Treaty with France. It might reasonably have been expected, that, as religious zeal had made the recovery of the Palatinate appear a point of such vast importance in England; the same effect must have been produced in France, by the force merely of political views and considerations. While that principality remained in the hands of the house of Austria, the French dominions were surrounded on all sides by the possessions of that ambitious family, and might be invaded by superior forces from every quarter. It concerned the king of France, therefore, to prevent the peaceable establishment of the emperor in his new conquests; and both by the situation and greater power of his state, he was much better enabled than James to give succour to the distressed Palatine.[e] But though these views escaped not Louis, nor cardinal Richlieu, who now began to acquire an ascendant in the French court; that minister was determined to pave the way for his enterprizes by first subduing the Hugonots, and thence to proceed, by mature counsels, to humble the house of Austria. The prospect, however, of a conjunction with England was presently embraced, and all imaginable encouragement was given to every proposal for conciliating a marriage between Charles and the princess Henrietta.

Notwithstanding the sensible experience, which James might have acquired of the unsurmountable antipathy, entertained by

[e] See Collection of State Papers by the Earl of Clarendon, p. 393.

CHAPTER XLIX

his subjects, against all alliance with catholics, he still persevered in the opinion, that his son would be degraded by receiving into his bed a princess of less than royal extraction. After the rupture, therefore, with Spain, nothing remained but an alliance with France; and to that court he immediately applied himself.[f] The same allurements had not here place, which had so long entangled him in the Spanish negociation: The portion promised was much inferior; and the peaceable restoration of the Palatine could not thence be expected. But James was afraid lest his son should be altogether disappointed of a bride; and therefore, as soon as the French king demanded, for the honour of his crown, the same terms which had been granted to the Spanish, he was prevailed with to comply. And as the prince, during his abode in Spain, had given a verbal promise to allow the Infanta the education of her children till the age of thirteen, this article was here inserted in the treaty; and to that imprudence is generally imputed the present distressed condition of his posterity. The court of England, however, it must be confessed, always pretended, even in their memorials to the French court, that all the favourable conditions granted to the catholics, were inserted in the marriage treaty merely to please the pope, and that their strict execution was, by an agreement with France, secretly dispensed with.[g]

As much as the conclusion of the marriage treaty was acceptable to the king, as much were all the military enterprizes disagreeable, both from the extreme difficulty of the undertaking in which he was engaged, and from his own incapacity for such a scene of action.

During the Spanish negociation, Heidelberg and Manheim had been taken by the Imperial forces; and Frankendale, though the garrison was entirely English, was closely besieged by them. After reiterated remonstrances from James, Spain interposed, and procured a suspension of arms during eighteen months. But as Frankendale was the only place of Frederic's ancient dominions, which was still in his hands, Ferdinand, desirous of withdrawing his forces from the Palatinate, and of leaving that state in security, was unwilling that so important a fortress should remain in the possession of the enemy. To compromise all differences, it was agreed to sequestrate it in the hands of the Infanta as a neutral person; upon

[f] Rushworth, vol. i. p. 152. [g] See note [O] at the end of the volume.

condition that, after the expiration of the truce, it should be delivered to Frederic; though peace should not, at that time, be concluded between him and Ferdinand.[h] After the unexpected rupture with Spain, the Infanta, when James demanded the execution of the treaty, offered him peaceable possession of Frankendale, and even promised a safe conduct for the garrison through the Spanish Netherlands: But there was some territory of the empire interposed between her state and the Palatinate; and for passage over that territory, no terms were stipulated.[i] By this chicane, which certainly had not been employed, if amity with Spain had been preserved, the Palatine was totally dispossessed of his patrimonial dominions.

The English nation, however, and James's warlike council, were not discouraged. It was still determined to reconquer the Palatinate; a state lying in the midst of Germany, possessed entirely by the Emperor and duke of Bavaria, surrounded by potent enemies, and cut off from all communication with England. Count *Mansfeldt* was taken into pay; and an English army of 12,000 foot and 200 horse was levied by a general press throughout the kingdom. During the negociation with France, vast promises had been made, though in general terms, by the French ministry; not only that a free passage should be granted to the English troops, but that powerful succours should also join them in their march towards the Palatinate. In England, all these professions were hastily interpreted to be positive engagements. The troops under Mansfeldt's command were embarked at Dover; but, upon sailing over to Calais, found no orders yet arrived for their admission. After waiting in vain during some time, they were obliged to sail towards Zealand; where it had also been neglected to concert proper measures for their disembarkation; and some scruples arose among the States on account of the scarcity of provisions. Meanwhile, a pestilential distemper creeped in among the English forces, so long cooped up in narrow vessels. Half the army died while on board; and the other half, weakened by sickness, appeared too small a body to march into the Palatinate.[k] And thus ended this ill-concerted and fruitless expedition; the only disaster which hap-

*Mans-
feldt's
expedition.*

December.

1625.

---

[h] Rushworth, vol. i. p. 74.   [i] Idem, ibid. p. 151.   [k] Franklyn, p. 104. Rushworth, vol. i. p. 154. Dugdale, p. 24.

pened to England, during the prosperous and pacific reign of James.

That reign was now drawing towards a conclusion. With peace, so successfully cultivated, and so passionately loved by this monarch, his life also terminated. This spring he was seized with a tertian ague; and, when encouraged by his courtiers with the common proverb, that such a distemper, during that season, was health for a king, he replied, that the proverb was meant of a young king. After some fits, he found himself extremely weakened, and sent for the prince, whom he exhorted to bear a tender affection for his wife, but to preserve a constancy in religion; to protect the church of England; and to extend his care towards the unhappy family of the Palatine.[l] With decency and courage, he prepared himself for his end; and he expired on the 27th of March, after a reign over England of twenty-two years and some days; and in the fifty-ninth year of his age. His reign over Scotland was almost of equal duration with his life. In all history, it would be difficult to find a reign less illustrious, yet more unspotted and unblemished than that of James in both kingdoms. *Death of the king.*

No prince, so little enterprising and so inoffensive, was ever so much exposed to the opposite extremes of calumny and flattery, of satire and panegyric. And the factions, which began in his time, being still continued, have made his character be as much disputed to this day, as is commonly that of princes who are our contemporaries. Many virtues, however, it must be owned, he was possessed of; but scarce any of them pure, or free from the contagion of the neighbouring vices. His generosity bordered on profusion, his learning on pedantry, his pacific disposition on pusillanimity, his wisdom on cunning, his friendship on light fancy and boyish fondness. While he imagined that he was only maintaining his own authority, he may perhaps be suspected, in a few of his actions, and still more of his pretensions, to have somewhat encroached on the liberties of his people: While he endeavoured, by an exact neutrality, to acquire the good will of all his neighbours, he was able to preserve fully the esteem and regard of none. His capacity was considerable; but fitter to discourse on general maxims than to conduct any intricate business: His intentions were just; but more *His character.*

[l] Rushworth, vol. i. p. 155.

adapted to the conduct of private life, than to the government of kingdoms. Aukward in his person, and ungainly in his manners, he was ill qualified to command respect; partial and undiscerning in his affections, he was little fitted to acquire general love. Of a feeble temper more than of a frail judgment: Exposed to our ridicule from his vanity; but exempt from our hatred by his freedom from pride and arrogance. And upon the whole, it may be pronounced of his character, that all his qualities were sullied with weakness and embellished by humanity. Of political courage he certainly was destitute; and thence chiefly is derived the strong prejudice, which prevails against his personal bravery: An inference, however, which must be owned, from general experience, to be extremely fallacious.

He was only once married, to Anne of Denmark, who died on the 3d of March 1619, in the forty-fifth year of her age; a woman eminent neither for her vices nor her virtues. She loved shows and expensive amusements; but possessed little taste in her pleasures. A great comet appeared about the time of her death; and the vulgar esteemed it the prognostic of that event. So considerable in their eyes are even the most insignificant princes.

He left only one son, Charles, then in the twenty-fifth year of his age; and one daughter, Elizabeth, married to the elector Palatine. She was aged twenty-nine years. Those alone remained of six legitimate children born to him. He never had any illegitimate; and he never discovered any tendency, even the smallest, towards a passion for any mistress.

The archbishops of Canterbury during this reign were, Whytgift, who died in 1604; Bancroft, in 1610; Abbot, who survived the king. The chancellors, lord Ellesmore, who resigned in 1617; Bacon was first lord keeper till 1619; then was created chancellor, and was displaced in 1621; Williams, bishop of Lincoln, was created lord keeper in his place. The high treasurers were the earl of Dorset, who died in 1609; the earl of Salisbury, in 1612; the earl of Suffolk fined and displaced for bribery in 1618; lord Mandeville, resigned in 1621; the earl of Middlesex, displaced in 1624; the earl of Marlborough succeeded. The lord admirals were, the earl of Nottingham, who resigned in 1618; the earl, afterwards duke of Buckingham. The secretaries of state were, the earl of

CHAPTER XLIX

Salisbury, Sir Ralph Winwood, Nanton, Calvert, lord Conway, Sir Albertus Moreton.

The numbers of the house of lords, in the first parliament of this reign, were seventy-eight temporal peers. The numbers in the first parliament of Charles were ninety-seven. Consequently James, during that period, created nineteen new peerages above those that expired.

The house of commons, in the first parliament of this reign, consisted of four hundred and sixty-seven members. It appears, that four boroughs revived their charters, which they had formerly neglected. And as the first parliament of Charles consisted of four hundred and ninety-four members, we may infer that James created ten new boroughs.

APPENDIX TO THE
REIGN OF JAMES I*

*Civil government of England
during this period – Ecclesiastical
government – Manners – Finances – Navy –
Commerce – Manufactures – Colonies –
Learning and arts*

🌼 🌼 🌼

IT MAY NOT BE IMPROPER, at this period, to make a pause: and to take a survey of the state of the kingdom, with regard to government, manners, finances, arms, trade, learning. Where a just notion is not formed of these particulars, history can be little instructive, and often will not be intelligible.

Civil government of England.

We may safely pronounce, that the English government, at the accession of the Scottish line, was much more arbitrary, than it is at present; the prerogative less limited, the liberties of the subject less accurately defined and secured. Without mentioning other particulars, the courts alone of high commission and star-chamber were sufficient to lay the whole kingdom at the mercy of the prince.

The court of high commission had been erected by Elizabeth, in consequence of an act of parliament, passed in the beginning of

---

* This history of the house of Stuart was written and published by the author before the history of the house of Tudor. Hence it happens that some passages, particularly in the present Appendix, may seem to be repetitions of what was formerly delivered in the reign of Elizabeth. The author, in order to obviate this objection, has cancelled some few passages in the foregoing chapters.

APPENDIX IV

her reign: By this act, it was thought proper, during the great revolution of religion, to arm the sovereign with full powers, in order to discourage and suppress opposition. All appeals from the inferior ecclesiastical courts were carried before the high commission; and, of consequence, the whole life and doctrine of the clergy lay directly under its inspection. Every breach of the act of uniformity, every refusal of the ceremonies, was cognizable in this court; and during the reign of Elizabeth, had been punished by deprivation, by fine, confiscation, and imprisonment. James contented himself with the gentler penalty of deprivation; nor was that punishment inflicted with rigour on every offender. Archbishop Spotswood tells us, that he was informed by Bancroft, the primate, several years after the king's accession, that not above forty-five clergymen had then been deprived. All the catholics too were liable to be punished by this court, if they exercised any act of their religion, or sent abroad their children or other relations, to receive that education, which they could not procure them in their own country. Popish priests were thrown into prison, and might be delivered over to the law, which punished them with death; though that severity had been sparingly exercised by Elizabeth, and never almost by James. In a word, that liberty of conscience, which we so highly and so justly value at present, was totally suppressed; and no exercise of any religion, but the established, was permitted throughout the kingdom. Any word or writing, which tended towards heresy or schism, was punishable by the high commissioners or any three of them: They alone were judges what expressions had that tendency: They proceeded not by information, but upon rumour, suspicion, or according to their discretion: They administered an oath, by which the party cited before them, was bound to answer any question, which should be propounded to him: Whoever refused this oath, though he pleaded ever so justly, that he might thereby be brought to accuse himself or his dearest friend, was punishable by imprisonment: And in short, an inquisitorial tribunal, with all its terrors and iniquities, was erected in the kingdom. Full discretionary powers were bestowed with regard to the enquiry, trial, sentence, and penalty inflicted; excepting only that corporal punishments were restrained by that patent of the prince, which erected the court, not by the act of parliament, which empowered him. By reason of the uncertain limits, which separate ecclesiastical from civil causes, all accusations of adultery and incest were tried by the court of high commission; and every complaint of wives against their husbands was there examined and discussed.[m] On like pretences, every cause which regarded conscience, that is, every cause, could have been brought under their jurisdiction.

But there was a sufficient reason, why the king would not be solicitous to stretch the jurisdiction of this court: The star-chamber possessed the same authority in civil matters; and its methods of proceeding were equally arbitrary and unlimited. The origin of this court was derived from the most remote antiquity;[n] though it is pretended, that its power had first been carried to the greatest height by Henry VII. In all times, however, it is confessed, it enjoyed authority; and at no time was its authority circumscribed, or method of proceeding directed, by any law or statute.

We have had already, or shall have sufficient occasion, during the course of this history, to mention the dispensing power, the power of imprisonment, of exacting loans[o] and benevolence, of pressing and quartering soldiers, of altering the customs, of erecting monopolies. These branches of power, if not directly opposite to the principles of all free government, must, at least, be acknowledged dangerous to freedom in a monarchical constitution, where an eternal jealousy must be preserved against the sovereign, and no discretionary powers must ever be entrusted to him, by which the property or personal liberty of any subject can be affected. The kings of England, however, had almost constantly exercised these powers; and if, on any occasion, the prince had been obliged to submit to laws enacted against them, he had ever, in practice, eluded these laws, and returned to the same arbitrary administration. During almost three centuries before the accession of James, the regal authority, in all these particulars, had never once been called in question.

---

[m] Rymer, tom. xvii. p. 200.   [n] Rushworth, vol. ii. p. 473. In Chambers's case it was the unanimous opinion of the court of King's Bench, that the court of star-chamber was not derived from the statute of Henry VII. but was a court many years before, and one of the most high and honourable courts of justice. See Coke's rep. term. Mich. 5 Car. I. See further Camden's Brit. vol. i. introd. p. 254. Edit. of Gibson.   [o] During several centuries, no reign had passed without some forced loans from the subject.

APPENDIX IV

We may also observe, that the principles in general which prevailed during that age, were so favourable to monarchy, that they bestowed on it an authority almost absolute and unlimited, sacred and indefeasible.

The meetings of parliament were so precarious; their sessions so short, compared to the vacations; that, when men's eyes were turned upwards in search of sovereign power, the prince alone was apt to strike them as the only permanent magistrate, invested with the whole majesty and authority of the state. The great complaisance too of parliaments, during so long a period, had extremely degraded and obscured those assemblies; and as all instances of opposition to prerogative must have been drawn from a remote age, they were unknown to a great many, and had the less authority even with those, who were acquainted with them. These examples, besides, of liberty had commonly, in ancient times, been accompanied with such circumstances of violence, convulsion, civil war, and disorder, that they presented but a disagreeable idea to the inquisitive part of the people, and afforded small inducement to renew such dismal scenes. By a great many, therefore, monarchy, simple and unmixed, was conceived to be the government of England; and those popular assemblies were supposed to form only the ornament of the fabric, without being, in any degree, essential to its being and existence.[p] The prerogative of the crown was represented by lawyers as something real and durable; like those eternal essences of the schools, which no time or force could alter. The sanction of religion was, by divines, called in aid; and the monarch of heaven was supposed to be interested in supporting the authority of his earthly vicegerent. And though it is pretended, that these doctrines were more openly inculcated and more strenuously insisted on during the reign of the Stuarts, they were not then invented; and were only found by the court to be more necessary at that period, by reason of the opposite doctrines, which *began* to be promulgated by the puritanical party.[q]

In consequence of these exalted ideas of kingly authority, the prerogative, besides the articles of jurisdiction, founded on precedent, was, by many supposed to possess an inexhaustible fund of

---

[p] See note [P] at the end of the volume.   [q] See note [Q] at the end of the volume.

latent powers, which might be exerted on any emergence. In every government, necessity, when real, supersedes all laws, and levels all limitations: But, in the English government, convenience alone was conceived to authorize any extraordinary act of regal power, and to render it obligatory on the people. Hence the strict obedience required to proclamations, during all periods of the English history; and, if James has incurred blame on account of his edicts, it is only because he too frequently issued them at a time, when they began to be less regarded, not because he first assumed or extended to an unusual degree that exercise of authority. Of his maxims in a parallel case, the following is a pretty remarkable instance.

Queen Elizabeth had appointed commissioners for the inspection of prisons, and had bestowed on them full discretionary powers to adjust all differences between prisoners and their creditors, to compound debts, and to give liberty to such debtors as they found honest, and insolvent. From the uncertain and undefined nature of the English constitution, doubts sprang up in many, that this commission was contrary to law; and it was represented in that light to James. He forebore therefore renewing the commission, till the fifteenth of his reign; when complaints rose so high, with regard to the abuses practised in prisons, that he thought himself obliged to overcome his scruples, and to appoint new commissioners, invested with the same discretionary powers which Elizabeth had formerly conferred.[r]

Upon the whole, we must conceive that monarchy, on the accession of the house of Stuart, was possessed of a very extensive authority: An authority, in the judgment of all, not exactly limited; in the judgment of some, not limitable. But, at the same time, this authority was founded merely on the opinion of the people, influenced by ancient precedent and example. It was not supported either by money or by force of arms. And, for this reason, we need not wonder, that the princes of that line were so extremely jealous of their prerogative; being sensible, that, when those claims were ravished from them, they possessed no influence, by which they could maintain their dignity, or support the laws. By the changes, which have since been introduced, the liberty and independence of

[r] Rymer, tom. xviii. p. 117, 594.

individuals has been rendered much more full, intire, and secure; that of the public more uncertain and precarious. And it seems a necessary, though perhaps a melancholy truth, that, in every government, the magistrate must either possess a large revenue and a military force, or enjoy some discretionary powers, in order to execute the laws, and support his own authority.

We have had occasion to remark, in so many instances, the bigotry which prevailed in that age, that we can look for no toleration among the different sects. Two Arians, under the title of heretics, were punished by fire during this period; and no one reign, since the reformation, had been free from like barbarities. Stowe says, that these Arians were offered their pardon at the stake, if they would merit it by a recantation. A madman, who called himself the Holy Ghost, was, without any indulgence for his frenzy, condemned to the same punishment. Twenty pounds a month could, by law, be levied on every one, who frequented not the established worship. This rigorous law, however, had one indulgent clause, that the fines exacted should not exceed two-thirds of the yearly income of the person. It had been usual for Elizabeth to allow those penalties to run on for several years; and to levy them all at once, to the utter ruin of such catholics as had incurred her displeasure. James was more humane in this, as in every other respect. The Puritans formed a sect, which secretly lurked in the church, but pretended not to any separate worship or discipline. An attempt of that kind would have been universally regarded as the most unpardonable enormity. And had the king been disposed to grant the Puritans a full toleration for a separate exercise of their religion, it is certain, from the spirit of the times, that this sect itself would have despised and hated him for it, and would have reproached him with lukewarmness and indifference in the cause of religion. They maintained, that they themselves were the only pure church; that their principles and practices ought to be established by law; and that no others ought to be tolerated. It may be questioned, therefore, whether the administration at this time could with propriety deserve the appellation of persecutors with regard to the Puritans. Such of the clergy, indeed, as refused to comply with the legal ceremonies, were deprived of their livings, and sometimes, in Elizabeth's reign, were otherwise punished: And ought any man to accept of an office or benefice in an estab-

Ecclesiastical government.

lishment, while he declines compliance with the fixed and known rules of that establishment? But Puritans were never punished for frequenting separate congregations; because there were none such in the kingdom; and no protestant ever assumed or pretended to the right of erecting them. The greatest well-wishers of the puritanical sect would have condemned a practice, which in that age was universally, by statesmen and ecclesiastics, philosophers and zealots, regarded as subversive of civil society. Even so great a reasoner as lord Bacon, thought that uniformity in religion was absolutely necessary to the support of government, and that no toleration could with safety be given to sectaries.[s] Nothing but the imputation of idolatry, which was thrown on the catholic religion, could justify, in the eyes of the Puritans themselves, the schism made by the Hugonots and other protestants, who lived in popish countries.

In all former ages, not wholly excepting even those of Greece and Rome, religious sects and heresies and schisms, had been esteemed dangerous, if not pernicious to civil government, and were regarded as the source of faction, and private combination, and opposition to the laws.[t] The magistrate, therefore, applied himself directly to the cure of this evil as of every other; and very naturally attempted, by penal statutes, to suppress those separate communities, and punish the obstinate innovators. But it was found by fatal experience, and after spilling an ocean of blood in those theological quarrels, that the evil was of a peculiar nature, and was both enflamed by violent remedies, and diffused itself more rapidly throughout the whole society. Hence, though late, arose the paradoxical principle and salutary practice of toleration.

The liberty of the press was incompatible with such maxims and such principles of government, as then prevailed, and was therefore quite unknown in that age. Besides employing the two terrible courts of star-chamber and high commission, whose powers were unlimited; Queen Elizabeth exerted her authority by restraints upon the press. She passed a decree in her court of star-chamber, that is, by her own will and pleasure, forbidding any book to be printed in any place but in London, Oxford, and Cambridge:[u] And another, in which she prohibited, under severe pen-

---

[s] See his essay *De unitate ecclesiae.*   [t] See Cicero de legibus.   [u] 28th of Elizabeth. See State Trials. Sir Robert Knightly, vol. vii. edit. 1.

APPENDIX IV

alties, the publishing of any book or pamphlet *against the form or meaning of any restraint or ordinance, contained, or to be contained, in any statute or laws of this realm, or in any injunction made or set forth by her majesty or her privy-council, or against the true sense or meaning of any letters patent, commissions or prohibitions under the great seal of England.*[w] James extended the same penalties to the importing of such books from abroad.[x] And to render these edicts more effectual, he afterwards inhibited the printing of any book without a licence from the archbishop of Canterbury, the archbishop of York, the bishop of London, or the vice-chancellor of one of the universities, or of some person appointed by them.[y]

In tracing the coherence among the systems of modern theology, we may observe, that the doctrine of absolute decrees has ever been intimately connected with the enthusiastic spirit; as that doctrine affords the highest subject of joy, triumph, and security to the supposed elect, and exalts them, by infinite degrees, above the rest of mankind. All the first reformers adopted these principles; and the Jansenists too, a fanatical sect in France, not to mention the Mahometans in Asia, have ever embraced them. As the Lutheran establishments were subjected to episcopal jurisdiction, their enthusiastic genius gradually decayed, and men had leisure to perceive the absurdity of supposing God to punish, by infinite torments, what he himself, from all eternity, had unchangeably decreed. The king, though, at this time, his Calvinistic education had rivetted him in the doctrine of absolute decrees, yet, being a zealous partizan of episcopacy, was insensibly engaged, towards the end of his reign, to favour the milder theology of Arminius. Even in so great a doctor, the genius of the religion prevailed over its speculative tenets; and with him, the whole clergy gradually dropped the more rigid principles of absolute reprobation and unconditional decrees. Some noise was, at first, made about these innovations; but being drowned in the fury of factions and civil wars which ensued, the scholastic arguments made an insignificant figure amidst those violent disputes about civil and ecclesiastical power, with which the nation was agitated. And at the restoration, the church, though she still retained her old subscriptions and articles of faith, was found to have totally changed her speculative doctrines, and to have embraced tenets

[w] Rymer, tom. xvii. p. 522. [x] Id. ibid. [y] Rymer, tom. xvii. p. 616.

more suitable to the genius of her discipline and worship, without its being possible to assign the precise period, in which the alteration was produced.

It may be worth observing, that James, from his great desire to promote controversial divinity, erected a college at Chelsea for the entertainment of twenty persons, who should be entirely employed in refuting the papists and puritans.[z] All the efforts of the great Bacon could not procure an establishment for the cultivation of natural philosophy: Even to this day, no society has been instituted for the polishing and fixing of our language. The only encouragement, which the sovereign in England has ever given to any thing, that has the appearance of science, was this short-lived establishment of James; an institution quite superfluous, considering the unhappy propension, which, at that time, so universally possessed the nation for polemical theology.

Manners.   The manners of the nation were agreeable to the monarchical government, which prevailed; and contained not that strange mixture, which, at present, distinguishes England from all other countries. Such violent extremes were then unknown, of industry and debauchery, frugality and profusion, civility and rusticity, fanaticism and scepticism. Candour, sincerity, modesty are the only qualities, which the English of that age possessed in common with the present.

High pride of family then prevailed; and it was by a dignity and stateliness of behaviour, that the gentry and nobility distinguished themselves from the common people. Great riches, acquired by commerce, were more rare, and had not, as yet been able to confound all ranks of men, and render money the chief foundation of distinction. Much ceremony took place in the common intercourse of life, and little familiarity was indulged by the great. The advantages, which result from opulence, are so solid and real, that those who are possessed of them need not dread the near approaches of their inferiors. The distinctions of birth and title, being more empty and imaginary, soon vanish upon familiar access and acquaintance.

The expences of the great consisted in pomp and show, and a numerous retinue, rather than in convenience and true pleasure.

[z] Kennet, p. 685. Camden's Brit. vol. i. p. 370. Gibson's edit.

APPENDIX IV

The earl of Nottingham, in his embassy to Spain, was attended by 500 persons: The earl of Hertford, in that to Brussels, carried 300 gentlemen along with him. Lord Bacon has remarked, that the English nobility, in his time, maintained a larger retinue of servants than the nobility of any other nation, except, perhaps, the Polanders.[a]

Civil honours, which now hold the first place, were, at that time, subordinate to the military. The young gentry and nobility were fond of distinguishing themselves by arms. The fury of duels too prevailed more than at any time before or since.[b] This was the turn, that the romantic chivalry, for which the nation was formerly so renowned, had lately taken.

Liberty of commerce between the sexes was indulged; but without any licentiousness of manners. The court was very little an exception to this observation. James had rather entertained an aversion and contempt for the females; nor were those young courtiers, of whom he was so fond, able to break through the established manners of the nation.

The first sedan chair, seen in England, was in this reign, and was used by the duke of Buckingham; to the great indignation of the people, who exclaimed, that he was employing his fellow-creatures to do the service of beasts.

The country life prevails at present in England beyond any cultivated nation of Europe; but it was then much more generally embraced by all the gentry. The encrease of arts, pleasures, and social commerce was just beginning to produce an inclination for the softer and more civilized life of the city. James discouraged, as much as possible, this alteration of manners. "He was wont to be very earnest," as lord Bacon tells us, "with the country gentlemen to go from London to their country seats. And sometimes he would say thus to them: *Gentlemen, at London, you are like ships in a sea, which show like nothing; but, in your country villages, you are like ships in a river, which look like great things.*"[c]

He was not content with reproof and exhortation. As queen Elizabeth had perceived, with regret, the encrease of London, and had restrained all new buildings by proclamation; James, who

---

[a] Essays De profer. fin. imp. [b] Franklyn, p. 5. See also Lord Herbert's Memoirs. [c] Apophthegms.

found that these edicts were not exactly obeyed, frequently renewed them; though a strict execution seems still to have been
wanting. He also issued reiterated proclamations, in imitation of
his predecessor; containing severe menaces against the gentry,
who lived in town.[d] This policy is contrary to that, which has ever
been practised by all princes, who studied the encrease of their
authority. To allure the nobility to court; to engage them in expensive pleasures or employments, which dissipate their fortune;
to encrease their subjection to ministers by attendance; to weaken
their authority in the provinces by absence: These have been the
common arts of arbitrary government. But James, besides that he
had certainly laid no plan for extending his power, had no money
to support a splendid court, or bestow on a numerous retinue of
gentry and nobility. He thought too, that, by their living together,
they became more sensible of their own strength, and were apt to
indulge too curious researches into matters of government. To
remedy the present evil, he was desirous of dispersing them into
their country-seats; where, he hoped, they would bear a more
submissive reverence to his authority, and receive less support
from each other. But the contrary effect soon followed. The riches,
amassed during their residence at home, rendered them independant. The influence, acquired by hospitality, made them formidable. They would not be led by the court: They could not be
driven: And thus the system of the English government received
a total and a sudden alteration in the course of less than forty years.

The first rise of commerce and the arts had contributed, in
preceding reigns, to scatter those immense fortunes of the barons,
which rendered them so formidable both to king and people. The
farther progress of these advantages began, during this reign, to
ruin the small proprietors of land;[e] and, by both events, the gentry,
or that rank which composed the house of commons, enlarged
their power and authority. The early improvements in luxury were
seized by the greater nobles, whose fortunes, placing them above
frugality, or even calculation, were soon dissipated in expensive
pleasures. These improvements reached at last all men of property; and those of slender fortunes, who, at that time, were often
men of family, imitating those of a rank immediately above them,

[d] Rymer, tom. xvii. p. 632.   [e] Cabbala, p. 224. first edit.

reduced themselves to poverty. Their lands, coming to sale, swelled the estates of those, who possessed riches sufficient for the fashionable expences; but who were not exempted from some care and attention to their domestic economy.

The gentry also of that age were engaged in no expence, except that of country hospitality. No taxes were levied, no wars waged, no attendance at court expected, no bribery or profusion required at elections.[f] Could human nature ever reach happiness, the condition of the English gentry, under so mild and benign a prince, might merit that appellation.

The amount of the king's revenue, as it stood in 1617, is thus stated.[g] Of crown lands, 80,000 pounds a year; by customs and new impositions, near 190,000; by wards and other various branches of revenue, beside purveyance, 180,000. The whole amounting to 450,000. The king's ordinary disbursements, by the same account, are said to exceed this sum thirty-six thousand pounds.[h] All the extraordinary sums, which James had raised by subsidies, loans, sale of lands, sale of the title of baronet, money paid by the states, and by the king of France's benevolences, &c. were, in the whole, about two millions two hundred thousand pounds. Of which the sale of lands afforded seven hundred and seventy-five thousand pounds. The extraordinary disbursements of the king amounted to two millions; beside above four hundred thousand pounds given in presents. Upon the whole, a sufficient reason appears, partly from necessary expences, partly for want of a rigid economy, why the king, even early in his reign, was deeply involved in debt, and found great difficulty to support the government.

Farmers, not commissioners, levied the customs. It seems, indeed, requisite, that the former method should always be tried before the latter; though a preferable one. When men's own interest is concerned, they fall upon a hundred expedients to prevent

Finances.

---

[f] Men seem then to have been ambitious of representing the counties, but careless of the boroughs. A seat in the house was, in itself, of small importance: But the former became a point of honour among the gentlemen. Journ. 10 Feb. 1620. Towns, which had formerly neglected their right of sending members, now began to claim it. Journ. 26 Feb. 1623. [g] An abstract, or brief declaration of his Majesty's revenue, with the assignations and defalcations upon the same. [h] The excess was formerly greater, as appears by Salisbury's account. See chap. 2.

frauds in the merchants; and these the public may afterwards imitate, in establishing proper rules for its officers.

The customs were supposed to amount to five *per cent* of the value, and were levied upon exports, as well as imports. Nay, the imposition upon exports, by James's additions, is said to amount, in some few instances, to twenty-five *per cent.* This practice, so hurtful to industry, prevails still in France, Spain, and most countries of Europe. The customs in 1604, yielded 127,000 pounds a-year:[i] They rose to 190,000 towards the end of the reign.

Interest, during this reign, was at ten *per cent* till 1624, when it was reduced to eight. This high interest is an indication of the great profits and small progress of commerce.

The extraordinary supplies granted by parliament, during this whole reign, amounted not to more than 630,000 pounds; which, divided among twenty-one years, makes 30,000 pounds a-year. I do not include those supplies, amounting to 300,000 pounds, which were given to the king by his last parliament. These were paid in to their own commissioners; and the expences of the Spanish war were much more than sufficient to exhaust them. The distressed family of the Palatine was a great burthen on James, during part of his reign. The king, it is pretended, possessed not frugality, proportioned to the extreme narrowness of his revenue. Splendid equipages, however, he did not affect, nor costly furniture, nor a luxurious table, nor prodigal mistresses. His buildings too were not sumptuous; though the Banqueting-house must not be forgotten, as a monument which does honour to his reign. Hunting was his chief amusement, the cheapest pleasure in which a king can indulge himself. His expences were the effects of liberality, rather than of luxury.

One day, it is said, while he was standing amidst some of his courtiers, a porter passed by, loaded with money, which he was carrying to the treasury. The king observed, that Rich, afterwards earl of Holland, one of his handsome agreeable favourites, whispered something to one standing near him. Upon enquiry, he found, that Rich had said, *how happy would that money make me!* Without hesitation, James bestowed it all upon him, though it amounted to 3000 pounds. He added, *You think yourself very happy*

[i] Journ. 21 May, 1604.

in obtaining so large a sum; but I am more happy, in having an opportunity of obliging a worthy man, whom I love. The generosity of James was more the result of a benign humour or light fancy, than of reason or judgment. The objects of it were such as could render themselves agreeable to him in his loose hours; not such as were endowed with great merit, or who possessed talents or popularity, which could strengthen his interest with the public.

The same advantage, we may remark, over the people, which the crown formerly reaped from that interval between the fall of the peers and rise of the commons, was now possessed by the people against the crown, during the continuance of a like interval. The sovereign had already lost that independant revenue, by which he could subsist without regular supplies from parliament; and he had not yet acquired the means of influencing those assemblies. The effects of this situation, which commenced with the accession of the house of Stuart, soon rose to a great height, and were more or less propagated throughout all the reigns of that unhappy family.

Subsidies and fifteenths are frequently mentioned by historians; but neither the amount of these taxes, nor the method of levying them, had been well explained. It appears, that the fifteenths formerly corresponded to the name, and were that proportionable part of the moveables.[k] But a valuation having been made, in the reign of Edward III. that valuation was always adhered to, and each town paid unalterably a particular sum, which the inhabitants themselves assessed upon their fellow-citizens. The same tax in corporate towns was called a tenth; because, there, it was, at first, a tenth of the moveables. The whole amount of a tenth and a fifteenth throughout the kingdom, or a fifteenth, as it is often more concisely called, was about 29,000 pounds.[l] The amount of a subsidy was not invariable, like that of a fifteenth. In the eighth of Elizabeth, a subsidy amounted to 120,000 pounds: In the fortieth, it was not above 78,000.[m] It afterwards fell to 70,000; and was continually decreasing.[n] The reason is easily collected from the method of levying it. We may learn from the subsidy bills,[o] that one

---

[k] Coke's Inst. book iv. chap. i. of fifteenths, quinzins.   [l] Id. subsidies temporary.   [m] Journ. 11 July, 1610.   [n] Coke's Inst. book iv. chap. i. subsidies temporary.   [o] See Statutes at large.

subsidy was given for four shillings in the pound on land, and two
shillings and eight pence on moveables throughout the counties;
a considerable tax, had it been strictly levied. But this was only the
ancient state of a subsidy. During the reign of James, there was not
paid the twentieth part of that sum. The tax was so far personal,
that a man paid only in the county where he lived, though he
should possess estates in other counties; and the assessors formed
a loose estimation of his property, and rated him accordingly. To
preserve, however, some rule in the estimation, it seems to have
been the practice to keep an eye to former assessments, and to rate
every man according as his ancestors, or men of such an estimated
property, were accustomed to pay. This was a sufficient reason,
why subsidies could not encrease, notwithstanding the great encrease of money and rise of rents. But there was an evident reason,
why they continually decreased. The favour, as is natural to suppose, ran always against the crown; especially during the latter end
of Elizabeth, when subsidies became numerous and frequent, and
the sums levied were considerable, compared to former supplies.
The assessors, though accustomed to have an eye to ancient esti-
mations, were not bound to observe any such rule; but might rate
anew any person, according to his present income. When rents
fell, or parts of an estate were sold off, the proprietor was sure to
represent these losses, and obtain a diminution of his subsidy; but
where rents rose, or new lands were purchased, he kept his own
secret, and paid no more than formerly. The advantage, therefore
of every change was taken against the crown; and the crown could
obtain the advantage of none. And to make the matter worse, the
alterations, which happened in property during this age, were, in
general unfavourable to the crown. The small proprietors, or
twenty pound men, went continually to decay; and when their
estates were swallowed up by a greater, the new purchaser encreased not his subsidy. So loose indeed is the whole method of
rating subsidies, that the wonder was not how the tax should continually diminish; but how it yielded any revenue at all. It became
at last so unequal and uncertain, that the parliament was obliged
to change it into a land tax.

The price of corn, during this reign, and that of the other
necessaries of life, was no lower, or was rather higher, than at
present. By a proclamation of James, establishing public maga-

zines, whenever wheat fell below thirty-two shillings a-quarter, rye below eighteen, barley below sixteen, the commissioners were empowered to purchase corn for the magazines.^{p} These prices then are to be regarded as low; though they would rather pass for high by our present estimation. The usual bread of the poor was at this time made of barley.^{q} The best wool, during the greater part of James's reign, was at thirty-three shillings a tod:^{r} At present, it is not above two-thirds of that value; though it is to be presumed, that our exports in woollen goods are somewhat encreased. The finer manufactures too, by the progress of arts and industry have rather diminished in price, notwithstanding the great encrease of money. In Shakespeare, the hostess tells Falstaff, that the shirts she bought him were holland at eight shillings a-yard; a high price at this day, even supposing, what is not probable, that the best holland at that time was equal in goodness to the best that can now be purchased. In like manner, a yard of velvet, about the middle of Elizabeth's reign, was valued at two and twenty shillings. It appears, from Dr. Birch's life of prince Henry,^{s} that that prince, by contract with his butcher, payed near a groat a-pound throughout the year, for all the beef and mutton used in his family. Besides, we must consider, that the general turn of that age, which no laws could prevent, was the converting of arable land into pasture: A certain proof that the latter was found more profitable, and consequently that all butcher's meat, as well as bread, was rather higher than at present. We have a regulation of the market with regard to poultry and some other articles, very early in Charles I.'s reign;^{t} and the prices are high. A turkey cock four shillings and sixpence, a turkey hen three shillings, a pheasant cock six, a pheasant hen five, a partridge one shilling, a goose two, a capon two and sixpence, a pullet one and sixpence, a rabbit eight pence, a dozen of pigeons six shillings.^{u} We must consider, that London at present is more than three times more populous than it was at that time: A circumstance, which much encreases the price of poultry, and of

---

^{p} Rymer, tom. xvii. p. 526. To the same purpose, see also 21 Jac. vi. cap. 28.
^{q} Rymer, tom. xx. p. 157. ^{r} See a compendium or dialogue inserted in the Memoirs of Wool, chap. 23. ^{s} P. 449. ^{t} Rymer, tom. xix. p. 511. ^{u} We may judge of the great grievance of purveyance by this circumstance, that the purveyors often gave but sixpence for a dozen of pigeons, and two pence for a fowl. Journ. 25 May, 1626.

every thing that cannot conveniently be brought from a distance: Not to mention, that these regulations by authority are always calculated to diminish, never to encrease the market prices. The contractors for victualing the navy were allowed by government eight pence a-day for the diet of each man, when in harbour, seven pence halfpenny when at sea;[w] which would suffice at present. The chief difference in expence between that age and the present consists in the imaginary wants of men, which have since extremely multiplied. These[x] are the principal reasons, why James's revenue would go farther than the same money in our time; though the difference is not near so great as is usually imagined.

Arms. The public was entirely free from the danger and expence of a standing army. While James was vaunting his divine vicegerency, and boasting of his high prerogative, he possessed not so much as a single regiment of guards to maintain his extensive claims: A sufficient proof, that he sincerely believed his pretensions to be well grounded, and a strong presumption, that they were at least built on what were then deemed plausible arguments. The militia of England, amounting to 160,000 men,[y] was the sole defence of the kingdom. It is pretended, that they were kept in good order during this reign.[z] The city of London procured officers, who had served abroad, and who taught the trained bands their exercises in Artillery garden; a practice which had been discontinued since 1588. All the counties of England, in emulation of the capital, were fond of showing a well-ordered and well-appointed militia. It appeared, that the natural propensity of men towards military shows and exercises will go far, with a little attention in the sovereign, towards exciting and supporting this spirit in any nation. The very boys, at this time, in mimickry of their elders, inlisted themselves voluntarily into companies, elected officers, and practised the discipline, of which the models were every day exposed to their view.[a] Sir Edward Harwood, in a memorial composed at the beginning of the subsequent reign, says, that England was so unprovided with horses fit for war, that 2000 men could not possibly be mounted

---

[w] Rymer, tom. xvii. p. 441. et seq.   [x] This volume was writ above twenty years before the present edition of 1778. In that short period, prices have perhaps risen more, than during the preceding hundred and fifty. [y] Journ. 1 March, 1623.   [z] Stowe. See also Sir Walter Raleigh of the prerogatives of parliament, and Johnstoni hist. lib. xviii.   [a] Stowe.

throughout the whole kingdom.[b] At present, the breed of horses is so much improved, that almost all those which are employed, either in the plough, waggon, or coach, would be fit for that purpose.

The disorders of Ireland obliged James to keep up some forces there, and put him to great expence. The common pay of a private man in the infantry was eight pence a-day, a lieutenant two shillings, an ensign eighteen pence.[c] The armies in Europe were not near so numerous, during that age; and the private men, we may observe, were drawn from a better rank than at present, and approaching nearer to that of the officers.

In the year 1583, there was a general review made of all the men in England, capable of bearing arms; and these were found to amount to 1,172,000 men, according to Raleigh.[d] It is impossible to warrant the exactness of this computation; or rather, we may fairly presume it to be somewhat inaccurate. But if it approached near the truth, England has probably, since that time, encreased in populousness. The growth of London, in riches and beauty, as well as in numbers of inhabitants, has been prodigious. From 1600, it doubled every forty years;[e] and consequently, in 1680, it contained four times as many inhabitants, as at the beginning of the century. It has ever been the center of all the trade in the kingdom; and almost the only town that affords society and amusement. The affection, which the English bear to a country life, makes the provincial towns be little frequented by the gentry. Nothing but the allurements of the capital, which is favoured by the residence of the king, and by being the seat of government, and of all the courts of justice, can prevail over their passion for their rural villas.

London, at this time, was almost entirely built of wood, and in every respect was certainly a very ugly city. The earl of Arundel first introduced the general practice of brick buildings.[f]

The navy of England was esteemed formidable in Elizabeth's time, yet it consisted only of thirty-three ships besides pinnaces:[g]   *Navy.*

[b] In the Harleyan miscellany, vol. iv. p. 255.   [c] Rymer, tom. xvi. p. 717. [d] Of the invention of shipping. This number is much superior to that contained in Murden, and that delivered by Sir Edward Coke to the house of commons; and is more likely.   [e] Sir William Petty.   [f] Sir Edward Walker's political discourses, p. 270.   [g] Coke's Inst. book iv. chap. 1. Consultation in parliament for the navy.

And the largest of these would not equal our fourth rates at present. Raleigh advises never to build a ship of war above 600 tons.[h] James was not negligent of the navy. In five years preceding 1623, he built ten new ships, and expended fifty thousand pounds a-year on the fleet, beside the value of thirty-six thousand pounds in timber, which he annually gave from the royal forests.[i] The largest ship that ever had come from the English docks, was built during this reign. She was only 1400 tons, and carried sixty-four guns.[k] The merchant ships, in cases of necessity, were instantly converted into ships of war. The king affirmed to the parliament, that the navy had never before been in so good a condition.[l]

Commerce. Every session of parliament, during this reign, we meet with grievous lamentations concerning the decay of trade and the growth of popery: Such violent propensity have men to complain of the present times, and to entertain discontent against their fortune and condition. The king himself was deceived by these popular complaints, and was at a loss to account for the total want of money, which he heard so much exaggerated.[m] It may, however, be affirmed, that, during no preceding period of English history, was there a more sensible encrease, than during the reign of this monarch, of all the advantages which distinguish a flourishing people. Not only the peace which he maintained, was favourable to industry and commerce: His turn of mind inclined him to promote the peaceful arts: And trade being as yet in its infancy, all additions to it must have been the more evident to every eye, which was not blinded by melancholy prejudices.[n]

By an account,[o] which seems judicious and accurate, it appears, that all the seamen, employed in the merchant service, amounted to 10,000 men, which probably exceeds not the fifth part of their present number. Sir Thomas Overbury says, that the Dutch possessed three times more shipping than the English, but that their ships were of inferior burden to those of the latter.[p] Sir William

---

[h] By Raleigh's account, in his discourse of the first invention of shipping the fleet in the twenty-fourth of the queen, consisted only of thirteen ships, and were augmented afterwards eleven. He probably reckoned some to be pinnaces, which Coke called ships.   [i] Journ. 11 March, 1623. Sir William Monson makes the number amount only to nine new ships, p. 253. [k] Stowe.   [l] Parl. Hist. vol. vi. p. 94.   [m] Rymer, tom. xvii. p. 413.   [n] See note [R] at the end of the volume.   [o] The trade's encrease in the Harleyan Misc. vol. iii.   [p] Remarks on his travels, Harl. misc. vol. ii. p. 349.

APPENDIX IV

Monson computed the English naval power to be little or nothing inferior to the Dutch,[q] which is surely an exaggeration. The Dutch at this time traded to England with 600 ships; England to Holland with sixty only.[r]

A catalogue of the manufactures, for which the English were *Manufac-* then eminent, would appear very contemptible, in comparison of *tures.* those which flourish among them at present. Almost all the more elaborate and curious arts were only cultivated abroad, particularly in Italy, Holland, and the Netherlands. Ship building and the founding of iron cannon were the sole, in which the English excelled. They seem, indeed, to have possessed alone the secret of the latter; and great complaints were made every parliament against the exportation of English ordnance.

Nine tenths of the commerce of the kingdom consisted in woollen goods.[s] Wool, however, was allowed to be exported, till the 19th of the king. Its exportation was then forbidden by proclamation; though that edict was never strictly executed. Most of the cloth was exported raw, and was dyed and dressed by the Dutch; who gained, it is pretended, 700,000 pounds a-year by this manufacture.[t] A proclamation, issued by the king, against exporting cloth in that condition, had succeeded so ill, during one year, by the refusal of the Dutch to buy the dressed cloth, that great murmurs arose against it; and this measure was retracted by the king, and complained of by the nation, as if it had been the most impolitic in the world. It seems indeed to have been premature.

In so little credit was the fine English cloth even at home, that the king was obliged to seek expedients, by which he might engage the people of fashion to wear it.[u] The manufacture of fine linen was totally unknown in the kingdom.[w]

The company of merchant-adventurers, by their patent, possessed the sole commerce of woollen goods, though the staple commodity of the kingdom. An attempt, made during the reign of Elizabeth, to lay open this important trade, had been attended with

[q] Naval Tracts, p. 329, 350.   [r] Raleigh's observations.   [s] Journ. 26th May, 1621.   [t] Journ. 20 May, 1614. Raleigh, in his observations, computes the loss at 400,000 pounds to the nation. There are about 80,000 undressed cloths, says he, exported yearly. He computes, besides, that about 100,000 pounds a-year had been lost by kersies; not to mention other articles. The account of 200,000 cloths a-year exported in Elizabeth's reign seems to be exaggerated.   [u] Rymer, tom. xvii. p. 415.   [w] Id. ibid.

bad consequences for a time, by a conspiracy of the merchant-adventurers, not to make any purchases of cloth; and the queen immediately restored them their patent.

It was the groundless fear of a like accident, that enslaved the nation to those exclusive companies, which confined so much every branch of commerce and industry. The parliament, however, annulled, in the third of the king, the patent of the Spanish company; and the trade to Spain, which was, at first, very insignificant, soon became the most considerable in the kingdom. It is strange, that they were not thence encouraged to abolish all the other companies, and that they went no farther than obliging them to enlarge their bottom, and to facilitate the admission of new adventurers.

A board of trade was erected by the king in 1622.[x] One of the reasons assigned in the commission, is to remedy the low price of wool, which begat complaints of the decay of the woollen manufactory. It is more probable, however, that this fall of prices proceeded from the encrease of wool. The king likewise recommends it to the commissioners to enquire and examine, whether a greater freedom of trade and an exemption from the restraint of exclusive companies, would not be beneficial. Men were then fettered by their own prejudices; and the king was justly afraid of embracing a bold measure, whose consequences might be uncertain. The digesting of a navigation act, of a like nature with the famous one executed afterwards by the republican parliament, is likewise recommended to the commissioners. The arbitrary powers, then commonly assumed by the privy-council, appear evidently through the whole tenor of the commission.

The silk manufacture had no footing in England: But, by James's direction, mulberry-trees were planted, and silk-worms introduced.[y] The climate seems unfavourable to the success of this project. The planting of hops encreased much in England during this reign.

Greenland is thought to have been discovered about this period; and the whale fishery was carried on with success: But the industry of the Dutch, in spite of all opposition, soon deprived the English of this source of riches. A company was erected for the

---

[x] Rymer, tom. xvii. p. 410.   [y] Stowe.

APPENDIX IV

discovery of the north-west passage; and many fruitless attempts were made for that purpose. In such noble projects, despair ought never to be admitted, till the absolute impossibility of success be fully ascertained.

The passage to the East-Indies had been opened to the English during the reign of Elizabeth; but the trade to those parts was not entirely established till this reign, when the East-India company received a new patent, enlarged their stock to 1,500,000 pounds,[z] and fitted out several ships on these adventures. In 1609 they built a vessel of 1200 ton, the largest merchant-ship that England had ever known. She was unfortunate, and perished by shipwreck. In 1611, a large ship of the company, assisted by a pinnace, maintained five several engagements with a squadron of Portuguese, and gained a complete victory over forces much superior. During the following years the Dutch company was guilty of great injuries towards the English, in expelling many of their factors, and destroying their settlements: But these violences were resented with a proper spirit by the court of England. A naval force was equipped under the earl of Oxford,[a] and lay in wait for the return of the Dutch East-India fleet. By reason of cross winds, Oxford failed of his purpose, and the Dutch escaped. Sometime after, one rich ship was taken by vice-admiral Merwin; and it was stipulated by the Dutch to pay 70,000 pounds to the English company, in consideration of the losses which that company had sustained.[b] But neither this stipulation, nor the fear of reprisals, nor the sense of that friendship which subsisted between England and the States, could restrain the avidity of the Dutch company, or render them equitable in their proceedings towards their allies. Impatient to have the sole possession of the spice-trade, which the English then shared with them, they assumed a jurisdiction over a factory of the latter in the island of Amboyna; and on very improbable, and even absurd pretences, seized all the factors with their families, and put them to death with the most inhuman tortures. This dismal news arrived in England at the time when James, by the prejudices of his subjects and the intrigues of his favourite, was constrained to make a breach with Spain; and he was obliged, after some remonstrances, to acquiesce in this indignity from a state, whose alliance

[z] Journ. 26th Nov. 1621.　[a] In 1622.　[b] Johnstoni hist. lib. 19.

was now become necessary to him. It is remarkable, that the nation, almost without a murmur, submitted to this injury from their protestant confederates; an injury, which, besides the horrid enormity of the action, was of much deeper importance to national interest, than all those which they were so impatient to resent from the house of Austria.

The exports of England from Christmas 1612 to Christmas 1613 are computed at 2,487,435 pounds: The imports at 2,141,151: So that the balance in favour of England was 346,284.[c] But in 1622 the exports were 2,320,436 pounds; the imports 2,619,315; which makes a balance of 298,879 pounds against England.[d] The coinage of England from 1599 to 1619 amounted to 4,779,314 pounds, 13 shillings and 4 pence:[e] A proof that the balance in the main was considerably in favour of the kingdom. As the annual imports and exports together rose to near five millions, and the customs never yielded so much as 200,000 pounds a-year, of which tonnage made a part, it appears, that the new rates, affixed by James, did not, on the whole, amount to one shilling in the pound, and consequently were still inferior to the intention of the original grant of parliament. The East-India company usually carried out a third of their cargo in commodities.[f] The trade to Turkey was one of the most gainful to the nation.[g] It appears that copper halfpence and farthings began to be coined in this reign.[h] Tradesmen had commonly carried on their retail business chiefly by means of leaden tokens. The small silver penny was soon lost, and at this time was no where to be found.

Colonies. What chiefly renders the reign of James memorable, is the commencement of the English colonies in America; colonies established on the noblest footing that has been known in any age or nation. The Spaniards, being the first discoverers of the new world, immediately took possession of the precious mines which they found there; and, by the allurement of great riches, they were tempted to depopulate their own country as well as that which they conquered; and added the vice of sloth to those of avidity and barbarity, which had attended their adventurers in those re-

[c] Misselden's Circle of Commerce, p. 121. [d] Id. ibid. [e] Happy future State of England, p. 78. [f] Munn's Discourse on the East-India Trade. [g] Munn's Discourse on the East-India Trade, p. 17. [h] Anderson, vol. i. p. 477.

APPENDIX IV

nowned enterprizes. That fine coast was entirely neglected, which reaches from St. Augustine to Cape Breton, and which lies in all the temperate climates, is watered by noble rivers, and offers a fertile soil, but nothing more, to the industrious planter. Peopled gradually from England by the necessitous and indigent, who, at home, encreased neither wealth nor populousness, the colonies, which were planted along that tract, have promoted the navigation, encouraged the industry, and even perhaps multiplied the inhabitants of their mother-country. The spirit of independency, which was reviving in England, here shone forth in its full lustre, and received new accession from the aspiring character of those, who, being discontented with the established church and monarchy, had sought for freedom amidst those savage desarts.

Queen Elizabeth had done little more than given a name to the continent of Virginia; and, after her planting one feeble colony, which quickly decayed, that country was entirely abandoned. But when peace put an end to the military enterprizes against Spain, and left ambitious spirits no hopes of making any longer such rapid advances towards honour and fortune, the nation began to second the pacific intentions of its monarch, and to seek a surer, though slower expedient, for acquiring riches and glory. In 1606, Newport carried over a colony, and began a settlement; which the company, erected by patent for that purpose in London and Bristol, took care to supply with yearly recruits of provisions, utensils, and new inhabitants. About 1609, Argal discovered a more direct and shorter passage to Virginia, and left the tract of the ancient navigators, who had first directed their course southwards to the tropic, sailed westward by means of the trade-winds, and then turned northward, till they reached the English settlements. The same year, five hundred persons under Sir Thomas Gates and Sir George Somers were embarked for Virginia. Somers's ship, meeting with a tempest, was driven into the Bermudas, and laid the foundation of a settlement in those islands. Lord Delawar afterwards undertook the government of the English colonies: But notwithstanding all his care, seconded by supplies from James, and by money raised from the first lottery ever known in the kingdom, such difficulties attended the settlement of these countries, that, in 1614, there were not alive more than 400 men, of all that had been sent thither. After supplying themselves with provisions more immediately necessary for the support of life, the new planters began the cultivating of tobacco; and James, notwithstanding his antipathy to that drug, which he affirmed to be pernicious to men's morals as well as their health,[i] gave them permission to enter it in England; and he inhibited by proclamation all importation of it from Spain.[k] By degrees, new colonies were established in that continent, and gave new names to the places where they settled, leaving that of Virginia to the province first planted. The island of Barbadoes was also planted in this reign.

Speculative reasoners, during that age, raised many objections to the planting of those remote colonies; and foretold, that, after draining their mother-country of inhabitants, they would soon shake off her yoke, and erect an independent government in America: But time has shewn, that the views, entertained by those who encouraged such generous undertakings, were more just and solid. A mild government and great naval force have preserved, and may still preserve during some time, the dominion of England over her colonies. And such advantages have commerce and navigation reaped from these establishments, that more than a fourth of the English shipping is at present computed to be employed in carrying on the traffic with the American settlements.

Agriculture was anciently very imperfect in England. The sudden transitions, so often mentioned by historians, from the lowest to the highest price of grain, and the prodigious inequality of its value in different years, are sufficient proofs, that the produce depended entirely on the seasons, and that art had as yet done nothing to fence against the injuries of the heavens. During this reign, considerable improvements were made, as in most arts, so in this, the most beneficial of any. A numerous catalogue might be formed of books and pamphlets, treating of husbandry, which were written about this time. The nation, however, was still dependent on foreigners for daily bread; and though its exportation of grain now forms a considerable branch of its commerce, notwithstanding its probable encrease of people, there was, in that period, a regular importation from the Baltic as well as from France; and if it ever stopped, the bad consequences were sensibly felt by the nation. Sir Walter Raleigh in his observations computes,

[i] Rymer, tom. xvii. p. 621.   [k] Rymer, tom. xviii. p. 621, 633.

that two millions went out at one time for corn. It was not till the fifth of Elizabeth, that the exportation of corn had been allowed in England; and Camden observes, that agriculture, from that moment, received new life and vigour.

The endeavours of James, or, more properly speaking, those of the nation, for promoting trade, were attended with greater success than those for the encouragement of learning. Though the age was by no means destitute of eminent writers, a very bad taste in general prevailed during that period; and the monarch himself was not a little infected with it.

On the origin of letters among the Greeks, the genius of poets and orators, as might naturally be expected, was distinguished by an amiable simplicity, which, whatever rudeness may sometimes attend it, is so fitted to express the genuine movements of nature and passion, that the compositions possessed of it must ever appear valuable to the discerning part of mankind. The glaring figures of discourse, the pointed antithesis, the unnatural conceit, the jingle of words; such false ornaments were not employed by early writers; not because they were rejected, but because they scarcely ever occurred to them. An easy, unforced strain of sentiment runs through their compositions; though at the same time we may observe, that, amidst the most elegant simplicity of thought and expression, one is sometimes surprised to meet with a poor conceit, which had presented itself unsought for, and which the author had not acquired critical observation enough to condemn.[1] A bad taste seizes with avidity these frivolous beauties, and even perhaps a good taste, ere surfeited by them: They multiply every day more and more in the fashionable compositions: Nature and good sense are neglected: Laboured ornaments studied and admired: And a total degeneracy of style and language prepares the

Learning and arts.

---

[1] The name of Polynices, one of Oedipus's sons, means in the original *much quarrelling.* In the altercations between the two brothers, in Aeschylus, Sophocles, and Euripides, this conceit is employed; and it is remarkable, that so poor a conundrum could not be rejected by any of these three poets, so justly celebrated for their taste and simplicity. What could Shakespeare have done worse? Terence has his *inceptio est amentium, non amantium.* Many similar instances will occur to the learned. It is well known that Aristotle treats very seriously of puns, divides them into several classes, and recommends the use of them to orators.

way for barbarism and ignorance. Hence the Asiatic manner was found to depart so much from the simple purity of Athens: Hence that tinsel eloquence, which is observable in many of the Roman writers, from which Cicero himself is not wholly exempted, and which so much prevails in Ovid, Seneca, Lucan, Martial, and the Plinys.

On the revival of letters, when the judgment of the public is yet raw and unformed, this false glister catches the eye, and leaves no room, either in eloquence or poetry, for the durable beauties of solid sense and lively passion. The reigning genius is then diametrically opposite to that which prevails on the first origin of arts. The Italian writers, it is evident, even the most celebrated, have not reached the proper simplicity of thought and composition; and in Petrarch, Tasso, Guarini, frivolous witticisms and forced conceits are but too predominant. The period, during which letters were cultivated in Italy, was so short as scarcely to allow leisure for correcting this adulterated relish.

The more early French writers are liable to the same reproach. Voiture, Balzac, even Corneille, have too much affected those ambitious ornaments, of which the Italians in general, and the least pure of the ancients supplied them with so many models. And it was not till late, that observation and reflection gave rise to a more natural turn of thought and composition among that elegant people.

A like character may be extended to the first English writers; such as flourished during the reigns of Elizabeth and James, and even till long afterwards. Learning, on its revival in this island, was attired in the same unnatural garb, which it wore at the time of its decay among the Greeks and Romans. And, what may be regarded as a misfortune, the English writers were possessed of great genius before they were endowed with any degree of taste, and by that means gave a kind of sanction to those forced turns and sentiments, which they so much affected. Their distorted conceptions and expressions are attended with such vigour of mind, that we admire the imagination which produced them, as much as we blame the want of judgment which gave them admittance. To enter into an exact criticism of the writers of that age, would exceed our present purpose. A short character of the most eminent, delivered with the same freedom which history exercises

APPENDIX IV

over kings and ministers, may not be improper. The national pre-possessions, which prevail, will perhaps render the former liberty not the least perilous for an author.

If Shakespeare be considered as a MAN, born in a rude age, and educated in the lowest manner, without any instruction, either from the world or from books, he may be regarded as a prodigy: If represented as a POET, capable of furnishing a proper entertainment to a refined or intelligent audience, we must abate much of this eulogy. In his compositions, we regret, that many irregularities, and even absurdities, should so frequently disfigure the animated and passionate scenes intermixed with them; and at the same time, we perhaps admire the more those beauties, on account of their being surrounded with such deformities. A striking peculiarity of sentiment, adapted to a singular character, he frequently hits, as it were by inspiration; but a reasonable propriety of thought he cannot, for any time, uphold. Nervous and picturesque expressions, as well as descriptions, abound in him; but it is in vain we look either for purity or simplicity of diction. His total ignorance of all theatrical art and conduct, however material a defect; yet, as it affects the spectator rather than the reader, we can more easily excuse, than that want of taste which often prevails in his productions, and which gives way, only by intervals, to the irradiations of genius. A great and fertile genius he certainly possessed, and one enriched equally with a tragic and comic vein; but, he ought to be cited as a proof, how dangerous it is to rely on these advantages alone for attaining an excellence in the finer arts.[m] And there may even remain a suspicion, that we over-rate, if possible, the greatness of his genius; in the same manner as bodies often appear more gigantic, on account of their being disproportioned and mishapen. He died in 1616, aged 53 years.

Johnson possessed all the learning which was wanting to Shakespeare, and wanted all the genius of which the other was possessed. Both of them were equally deficient in taste and elegance, in harmony and correctness. A servile copyist of the ancients, Johnson translated into bad English the beautiful passages of the Greek and Roman authors, without accommodating them to the manners of his age and country. His merit has been totally eclipsed by that of

[m] *Invenire etiam barbari solent, disponere et ornare non nisi eruditus.* Plin.

Shakespeare, whose rude genius prevailed over the rude art of his cotemporary. The English theatre has ever since taken a strong tincture of Shakespeare's spirit and character; and thence it has proceeded, that the nation has undergone, from all it's neighbours, the reproach of barbarism, from which it's valuable productions in some other parts of learning would otherwise have exempted it. Johnson had a pension of a hundred marks from the king, which Charles afterwards augmented to a hundred pounds. He died in 1637, aged 63.

Fairfax has translated Tasso with an elegance and ease, and, at the same time, with an exactness, which, for that age, are surprising. Each line in the original is faithfully rendered by a correspondent line in the translation. Harrington's translation of Ariosto is not likewise without its merit. It is to be regretted, that these poets should have imitated the Italians in their stanza, which has a prolixity and uniformity in it, that displeases in long performances. They had otherwise, as well as Spencer, who went before them, contributed much to the polishing and refining of the English versification.

In Donne's satires, when carefully inspected, there appear some flashes of wit and ingenuity; but these totally suffocated and buried by the harshest and most uncouth expression, that is anywhere to be met with.

If the poetry of the English was so rude and imperfect during that age, we may reasonably expect that their prose would be liable to still greater objections. Though the latter appears the more easy, as it is the more natural method of composition; it has ever in practice been found the more rare and difficult; and there scarcely is an instance, in any language, that it has reached a degree of perfection, before the refinement of poetical numbers and expression. English prose, during the reign of James, was written with little regard to the rules of grammar, and with a total disregard to the elegance and harmony of the period. Stuffed with Latin sentences and quotations, it likewise imitated those inversions, which, however forcible and graceful in the ancient languages, are entirely contrary to the idiom of the English. I shall indeed venture to affirm, that, whatever uncouth phrases and expressions occur in old books, they were chiefly owing to the unformed taste of the author; and that the language, spoken in the courts of Elizabeth and James, was very little different from that which we meet with at present in good company. Of this opinion, the little scraps of speeches which are found in the parliamentary journals, and which carry an air so opposite to the laboured orations, seem to be a sufficient proof; and there want not productions of that age, which, being written by men who were not authors by profession, retain a very natural manner, and may give us some idea of the language which prevailed among men of the world. I shall particularly mention Sir John Davis's discovery, Throgmorton's, Essex's, and Nevil's letters. In a more early period, Cavendish's life of cardinal Wolsey, the pieces that remain of bishop Gardiner, and Anne Boleyn's letter to the king, differ little or nothing from the language of our time.

The great glory of literature in this island, during the reign of James, was lord Bacon. Most of his performances were composed in Latin; though he possessed neither the elegance of that, nor of his native tongue. If we consider the variety of talents displayed by this man; as a public speaker, a man of business, a wit, a courtier, a companion, an author, a philosopher; he is justly the object of great admiration. If we consider him merely as an author and philosopher, the light in which we view him at present, though very estimable, he was yet inferior to his cotemporary Galileo, perhaps even to Kepler. Bacon pointed out at a distance the road to true philosophy: Galileo both pointed it out to others, and made himself considerable advances in it. The Englishman was ignorant of geometry: The Florentine revived that science, excelled in it, and was the first that applied it, together with experiment, to natural philosophy. The former rejected, with the most positive disdain, the system of Copernicus: The latter fortified it with new proofs, derived both from reason and the senses. Bacon's style is stiff and rigid: His wit, though often brilliant, is also often unnatural and far-fetched; and he seems to be the original of those pointed similies and long-spun allegories, which so much distinguish the English authors: Galileo is a lively and agreeable, though somewhat a prolix writer. But Italy, not united in any single government, and perhaps satiated with that literary glory, which it has possessed both in ancient and modern times, has too much neglected the renown which it has acquired by giving birth to so great a man. That national spirit, which prevails among the

English, and which forms their great happiness, is the cause why they bestow on all their eminent writers, and on Bacon among the rest, such praises and acclamations, as may often appear partial and excessive. He died in 1626, in the 66th year of his age.

If the reader of Raleigh's history can have the patience to wade through the Jewish and Rabbinical learning which compose the half of the volume, he will find, when he comes to the Greek and Roman story, that his pains are not unrewarded. Raleigh is the best model of that ancient style, which some writers would affect to revive at present. He was beheaded in 1618, aged 66 years.

Camden's history of queen Elizabeth may be esteemed good composition, both for style and matter. It is written with simplicity of expression, very rare in that age, and with a regard to truth. It would not perhaps be too much to affirm, that it is among the best historical productions which have yet been composed by any Englishman. It is well known that the English have not much excelled in that kind of literature. He died in 1623, aged 73 years.

We shall mention the king himself at the end of these English writers; because that is *his* place, when considered as an author. It may safely be affirmed, that the mediocrity of James's talents in literature, joined to the great change in national taste, is one cause of that contempt, under which his memory labours, and which is often carried by party-writers to a great extreme. It is remarkable, how different from ours were the sentiments of the ancients with regard to learning. Of the first twenty Roman emperors, counting from Cesar to Severus, above the half were authors; and though few of them seem to have been eminent in that profession, it is always remarked to their praise, that, by their example, they encouraged literature. Not to mention Germanicus, and his daughter Agrippina, persons so nearly allied to the throne, the greater part of the classic writers, whose works remain, were men of the highest quality. As every human advantage is attended with inconveniences, the change of men's ideas in this particular may probably be ascribed to the invention of printing; which has rendered books so common, that even men of slender fortunes can have access to them.

That James was but a middling writer may be allowed: That he was a contemptible one can by no means be admitted. Whoever will read his Basilicon Doron, particularly the two last books, the true

APPENDIX IV

law of free monarchies, his answer to cardinal Perron, and almost all his speeches and messages to parliament, will confess him to have possessed no mean genius. If he wrote concerning witches and apparitions; who, in that age, did not admit the reality of these fictitious beings? If he has composed a commentary on the Revelations, and proved the pope to be Antichrist; may not a similar reproach be extended to the famous Napier; and even to Newton, at a time when learning was much more advanced than during the reign of James? From the grossness of its superstitions, we may infer the ignorance of an age; but never should pronounce concerning the folly of an individual, from his admitting popular errors, consecrated by the appearance of religion.

Such a superiority do the pursuits of literature possess above every other occupation, that even he, who attains but a mediocrity in them, merits the pre-eminence above those that excel the most in the common and vulgar professions. The speaker of the house of commons is usually an eminent lawyer; yet the harangue of his Majesty will always be found much superior to that of the speaker, in every parliament during this reign.

Every science, as well as polite literature, must be considered as being yet in its infancy. Scholastic learning and polemical divinity retarded the growth of all true knowledge. Sir Henry Saville, in the preamble of that deed by which he annexed a salary to the mathematical and astronomical professors in Oxford, says, that geometry was almost totally abandoned and unknown in England.[n] The best learning of that age was the study of the ancients. Casaubon, eminent for this species of knowledge, was invited over from France by James, and encouraged by a pension of 300 a-year, as well as by church preferments.[o] The famous Antonio di Dominis, archbishop of Spalato, no despicable philosopher, came likewise into England, and afforded great triumph to the nation, by their gaining so considerable a proselyte from the papists. But the mortification followed soon after: The archbishop, though advanced to some ecclesiastical preferments,[p] received not encouragement sufficient to satisfy his ambition: He made his escape into Italy, where he died in confinement.

[n] Rymer, tom. xvii. p. 217.   [o] Ibid. p. 709.   [p] Rymer, tom. xvii. p. 95.

L

CHARLES I

A parliament at Westminster –
At Oxford – Naval expedition against Spain –
Second parliament – Impeachment of
Buckingham – Violent measures of the court –
War with France – Expedition
to the isle of Rhé

❀ ❀ ❀

1625.
27th
March.

N O SOONER HAD CHARLES taken into his hands the reins of government, than he showed an impatience to assemble the great council of the nation; and he would gladly, for the sake of dispatch, have called together the same parliament, which had sitten under his father, and which lay at that time under prorogation. But being told that this measure would appear unusual, he issued writs for summoning a new parliament on the 7th of May; and it was not without regret that the arrival of the princess Henrietta, whom he had espoused by proxy, obliged him to delay, by repeated prorogations, their meeting till the eighteenth of June, when they assembled at Westminster for the dispatch of business. The young prince, unexperienced and impolitic, regarded as sincere all the praises and caresses, with which he had been loaded, while active in procuring the rupture with the house of Austria. And besides that he laboured under great necessities, he hastened with alacrity to a period, when he might receive the most undoubted testimony of the dutiful attachment of his subjects. His discourse to the parliament was full of simplicity and

A parlia-
ment at
Westmin-
ster.
18th
June.

CHAPTER L

cordiality. He lightly mentioned the occasion which he had for supply.[q] He employed no intrigue to influence the suffrages of the members. He would not even allow the officers of the crown, who had seats in the house to mention any particular sum, which might be expected by him. Secure of the affections of the commons, he was resolved, that their bounty should be intirely their own deed; unasked, unsolicited; the genuine fruit of sincere confidence and regard.

The house of commons accordingly took into consideration the business of supply. They knew, that all the money granted by the last parliament had been expended on naval and military armaments; and that great anticipations were likewise made on the revenues of the crown. They were not ignorant, that Charles was loaded with a large debt, contracted by his father, who had borrowed money both from his own subjects and from foreign princes. They had learned by experience, that the public revenue could with difficulty maintain the dignity of the crown, even under the ordinary charges of government. They were sensible, that the present war was, very lately, the result of their own importunate applications and intreaties, and that they had solemnly engaged to support their sovereign in the management of it. They were acquainted with the difficulty of military enterprizes, directed against the whole house of Austria; against the king of Spain, possessed of the greatest riches and most extensive dominions of any prince in Europe; against the emperor Ferdinand, hitherto the most fortunate monarch of his age, who had subdued and astonished Germany by the rapidity of his victories. Deep impressions they saw, must be made by the English sword, and a vigorous offensive war be waged against these mighty potentates, ere they would resign a principality, which they had now fully subdued, and which they held in secure possession, by its being surrounded with all their other territories.

To answer, therefore, all these great and important ends; to satisfy their young king in the first request which he made them; to prove their sense of the many royal virtues, particularly economy, with which Charles was endued; the house of commons, conducted by the wisest and ablest senators that had ever flour-

[q] Rushworth, vol. i. p. 171. Parl. Hist. vol. vi. p. 346. Franklyn, p. 108.

ished in England, thought proper to confer on the king a supply of two subsidies, amounting to 112,000 pounds.[r]

This measure, which discovers rather a cruel mockery of Charles, than any serious design of supporting him, appears so extraordinary, when considered in all its circumstances, that it naturally summons up our attention, and raises an enquiry concerning the causes of a conduct, unprecedented in an English parliament. So numerous an assembly, composed of persons of various dispositions, was not, it is probable, wholly influenced by the same motives; and few declared openly their true reason. We shall, therefore, approach nearer to the truth, if we mention all the views, which the present conjuncture could suggest to them.

It is not to be doubted, but spleen and ill-will against the duke of Buckingham had an influence with many. So vast and rapid a fortune, so little merited, could not fail to excite public envy; and, however men's hatred might have been suspended for a moment, while the duke's conduct seemed to gratify their passions and their prejudices, it was impossible for him long to preserve the affections of the people. His influence over the modesty of Charles exceeded even that which he had acquired over the weakness of James; nor was any public measure conducted but by his council and direction. His vehement temper prompted him to raise suddenly, to the highest elevation, his flatterers and dependents: And upon the least occasion of displeasure, he threw them down with equal impetuosity and violence. Implacable in his hatred; fickle in his friendships: All men were either regarded as his enemies, or dreaded soon to become such. The whole power of the kingdom was grasped by his insatiable hand; while he both engrossed the intire confidence of his master, and held, invested in his single person, the most considerable offices of the crown.

However the ill-humour of the commons might have been encreased by these considerations, we are not to suppose them the sole motives. The last parliament of James, amidst all their joy and festivity, had given him a supply very disproportioned to his demand and to the occasion. And, as every house of commons, which was elected during forty years, succeeded to all the passions and

---

[r] A subsidy was now fallen to about 56,000 pounds. Cabbala, p. 224. first edit.

CHAPTER L

principles of their predecessors; we ought rather to account for this obstinacy from the general situation of the kingdom during that whole period, than from any circumstances, which attended this particular conjuncture.

The nation was very little accustomed at that time to the burthen of taxes, and had never opened their purses in any degree for supporting their sovereign. Even Elizabeth, notwithstanding her vigour and frugality, and the necessary wars in which she was engaged, had reason to complain of the commons in this particular; nor could the authority of that princess, which was otherwise almost absolute, ever extort from them the requisite supplies. Habits, more than reason, we find, in every thing, to be the governing principle of mankind. In this view likewise the sinking of the value of subsidies must be considered as a loss to the king. The parliament swayed by custom would not augment their number in the same proportion.

The puritanical party, though disguised, had a great authority over the kingdom; and many of the leaders among the commons had secretly embraced the rigid tenets of that sect. All these were disgusted with the court, both by the prevalence of the principles of civil liberty essential to their party; and on account of the restraint, under which they were held by the established hierarchy. In order to fortify himself against the resentment of James, Buckingham had affected popularity, and entered into the cabals of the puritans: But, being secure of the confidence of Charles he had since abandoned this party; and, on that account, was the more exposed to their hatred and resentment. Though the religious schemes of many of the puritans, when explained, appear pretty frivolous, we are not thence to imagine, that they were pursued by none but persons of weak understandings. Some men of the greatest parts and most extensive knowledge, that the nation, at this time, produced, could not enjoy any peace of mind; because obliged to hear prayers offered up to the Divinity, by a priest covered with a white linen vestment.

The match with France and the articles in favour of catholics, which were suspected to be in the treaty, were likewise causes of disgust to this whole party: Though it must be remarked, that the connections with that crown were much less obnoxious to the protestants, and less agreeable to the catholics, than the alliance formerly projected with Spain, and were therefore received rather with pleasure than dissatisfaction.

To all these causes we must yet add another, of considerable moment. The house of commons, we may observe, was almost entirely governed by a set of men of the most uncommon capacity and the largest views: Men, who were now formed into a regular party, and united, as well by fixed aims and projects, as by the hardships which some of them had undergone in prosecution of them. Among these we may mention the names of Sir Edward Coke, Sir Edwin Sandys, Sir Robert Philips, Sir Francis Seymour, Sir Dudley Digges, Sir John Elliot, Sir Thomas Wentworth, Mr. Selden, and Mr. Pym. Animated with a warm regard to liberty, these generous patriots saw with regret an unbounded power exercised by the crown, and were resolved to seize the opportunity, which the king's necessities offered them, of reducing the prerogative within more reasonable compass. Though their ancestors had blindly given way to practices and precedents favourable to kingly power, and had been able, notwithstanding, to preserve some small remains of liberty; it would be impossible, they thought, when all these pretensions were methodized and prosecuted by the encreasing knowledge of the age, to maintain any shadow of popular government, in opposition to such unlimited authority in the sovereign. It was necessary to fix a choice: Either to abandon entirely the privileges of the people, or to secure them by firmer and more precise barriers than the constitution had hitherto provided for them. In this dilemma, men of such aspiring geniuses and such independent fortunes could not long deliberate: They boldly embraced the side of freedom, and resolved to grant no supplies to their necessitous prince, without extorting concessions in favour of civil liberty. The end, they esteemed beneficent and noble: The means, regular and constitutional. To grant or refuse supplies was the undoubted privilege of the commons. And as all human governments, particularly those of a mixed frame, are in continual fluctuation; it was as natural, in their opinion, and allowable, for popular assemblies to take advantage of favourable incidents, in order to secure the subject; as for monarchs, in order to extend their own authority. With pleasure they beheld the king involved in a foreign war, which rendered him every day more dependent on the parliament; while at the same

CHAPTER L

time the situation of the kingdom, even without any military preparations, gave it sufficient security against all invasion from foreigners. Perhaps too, it had partly proceeded from expectations of this nature, that the popular leaders had been so urgent for a rupture with Spain; nor is it credible, that religious zeal could so far have blinded all of them as to make them discover, in such a measure, any appearance of necessity, or any hopes of success.

But, however natural all these sentiments might appear to the country-party, it is not to be imagined, that Charles would entertain the same ideas. Strongly prejudiced in favour of the duke, whom he had heard so highly extolled in parliament, he could not conjecture the cause of so sudden an alteration in their opinions. And when the war, which they themselves had so earnestly solicited, was at last commenced, the immediate desertion of their sovereign could not but seem very unaccountable. Even though no farther motive had been suspected, the refusal of supply in such circumstances, would naturally to him appear cruel and deceitful: But when he perceived, that this measure proceeded from an intention of encroaching on his authority, he failed not to regard these aims as highly criminal and traitorous. Those lofty ideas of monarchical power, which were very commonly adopted during that age, and to which the ambiguous nature of the English constitution gave so plausible an appearance, were firmly rivetted in Charles; and however moderate his temper, the natural and unavoidable prepossessions of self-love, joined to the late uniform precedents in favour of prerogative, had made him regard his political tenets as certain and uncontroverted. Taught to consider even the antient laws and constitution more as lines to direct his conduct than barriers to withstand his power; a conspiracy to erect new ramparts, in order to straiten his authority, appeared but one degree removed from open sedition and rebellion. So atrocious in his eyes was such a design, that he seems even unwilling to impute it to the commons: And, tho' he was constrained to adjourn the parliament by reason of the plague, which at that time raged in London; he immediately re-assembled them at Oxford, and made a new attempt to gain from them some supplies in such an urgent necessity. *11th July. 1st August.*

Charles now found himself obliged to depart from that delicacy, which he had formerly maintained. By himself or his minis- *Parliament at Oxford.*

ters, he entered into a particular detail, both of the alliances which he had formed, and of the military operations which he had projected.[s] He told the parliament, that, by a promise of subsidies, he had engaged the king of Denmark to take part in the war; that this monarch intended to enter Germany by the north, and to rouze to arms those princes, who impatiently longed for an opportunity of asserting the liberty of the empire; that Mansfeldt had undertaken to penetrate with an English army into the Palatinate, and by that quarter to excite the members of the evangelical union; that the states must be supported in the unequal warfare which they maintained with Spain; that no less a sum than 700,000 pounds a year had been found, by computation, requisite for all these purposes; that the maintenance of the fleet and the defence of Ireland demanded an annual expence of 400,000 pounds; that he himself had already exhausted and anticipated, in the public service, his whole revenue, and had scarcely left sufficient for the daily subsistence of himself and his family;[t] that on his accession to the crown, he found a debt of above 300,000 pounds, contracted by his father, in support of the Palatine; and that, while prince of Wales, he had himself contracted debts, notwithstanding his great frugality, to the amount of 70,000 pounds, which he had expended entirely on naval and military armaments. After mentioning all these facts, the king even condescended to use entreaties. He said, that this request was the first that he had ever made them; that he was young and in the commencement of his reign; and, if he now met with kind and dutiful usage, it would endear to him the use of parliaments, and would for ever preserve an entire harmony between him and his people.[u]

To these reasons the commons remained inexorable. Notwithstanding that the king's measures, on the supposition of a foreign war, which they had constantly demanded, were altogether unexceptionable, they obstinately refused any farther aid. Some members favourable to the court, having insisted on an addition of two fifteenths to the former supply, even this pittance was refused;[w] though it was known, that a fleet and army were lying at Portsmouth, in great want of pay and provisions; and that Buck-

[s] Dugdale, p. 25, 26.   [t] Parl. Hist. vol. vi. p. 396.   [u] Rush. vol. i. p. 177, 178, &c. Parl. Hist. vol. vi. p. 399. Franklyn, p. 108, 109. Journ. 10 Aug. 1625.   [w] Rush. vol. i. p. 190.

ingham the admiral, and the treasurer of the navy, had advanced on their own credit near a hundred thousand pounds for the sea-service.[x] Besides all their other motives, the house of commons had made a discovery, which, as they wanted but a pretence for their refusal, inflamed them against the court and against the duke of Buckingham.

When James deserted the Spanish alliance, and courted that of France, he had promised to furnish Lewis, who was entirely destitute of naval force, with one ship of war together with seven armed vessels, hired from the merchants. These the French court had pretended they would employ against the Genoese, who, being firm and useful allies to the Spanish monarchy, were naturally regarded with an evil eye, both by the king of France and of England. When these vessels, by Charles's orders, arrived at Diepe, there arose a strong suspicion, that they were to serve against Rochelle. The sailors were inflamed. That race of men, who are at present both careless and ignorant in all matters of religion, were at that time only ignorant. They drew up a remonstrance to Pennington, their commander; and signing all their names in a circle, lest he should discover the ringleaders, they laid it under his prayer-book. Pennington declared, that he would rather be hanged in England for disobedience, than fight against his brother protestants in France. The whole squadron sailed immediately to the Downs. There they received new orders from Buckingham, lord admiral, to return to Diepe. As the duke knew, that authority alone would not suffice, he employed much art and many subtleties to engage them to obedience; and a rumor, which was spread, that peace had been concluded between the French king and the Hugonots, assisted him in his purpose. When they arrived at Diepe, they found that they had been deceived. Sir Ferdinando Gorges, who commanded one of the vessels, broke thro' and returned to England. All the officers and sailors of all the other ships, notwithstanding great offers made them by the French, immediately deserted. One gunner alone preferred duty towards his king to the cause of religion; and he was afterwards killed in charging a cannon before Rochelle.[y] The care, which historians have taken

---

[x] Parl. Hist. vol. vi. p. 390.   [y] Franklyn, p. 109. Rush. vol. i. p. 175, 176, &c. 325, 326, &c.

to record this frivolous event, proves with what pleasure the news was received by the nation.

The house of commons, when informed of these transactions, showed the same attachment with the sailors for the protestant religion; nor was their zeal much better guided by reason and sound policy. It was not considered, that it was highly probable the king and the duke themselves had here been deceived by the artifices of France, nor had they any hostile intention against the Hugonots; that, were it otherwise, yet might their measures be justified by the most obvious and most received maxims of civil policy; that, if the force of Spain were really so exorbitant as the commons imagined, the French monarch was the only prince that could oppose its progress, and preserve the balance of Europe; that his power was at present fettered by the Hugonots, who, being possessed of many privileges and even of fortified towns, formed an empire within his empire, and kept him in perpetual jealousy and inquietude; that an insurrection had been at that time, wantonly and voluntarily, formed by their leaders, who, being disgusted in some court-intrigue, took advantage of the never-failing pretence of religion, in order to cover their rebellion; that the Dutch, influenced by these views, had ordered a squadron of twenty ships to join the French fleet, employed against the inhabitants of Rochelle;[z] that the Spanish monarch, sensible of the same consequences, secretly supported the protestants in France; and that all princes had ever sacrificed to reasons of state the interests of their religion in foreign countries. All these obvious considerations had no influence. Great murmurs and discontents still prevailed in parliament. The Hugonots, though they had no ground of complaint against the French court, were thought to be as much entitled to assistance from England, as if they had taken arms in defence of their liberties and religion against the persecuting rage of the catholics. And it plainly appears from this incident, as well as from many others, that, of all European nations, the British were at that time, and till long after, the most under the influence of that religious spirit, which tends rather to inflame bigotry than encrease peace and mutual charity.

[z] Journ. 18 April, 1626.

CHAPTER L

On this occasion, the commons renewed their eternal complaints against the growth of popery, which was ever the chief of
their grievances, and now their only one.[a] They demanded a strict
execution of the penal laws against the catholics, and remonstrated
against some late pardons, granted to priests.[b] They attacked Montague, one of the king's chaplains, on account of a moderate book,
which he had lately published, and which, to their great disgust,
saved virtuous catholics, as well as other Christians, from eternal
torments.[c] Charles gave them a gracious and a compliant answer to
all their remonstrances. He was however, in his heart, extremely
averse to these furious measures. Though a determined protestant, by principle as well as inclination, he had entertained no
violent horror against popery; and a little humanity, he thought,
was due by the nation to the religion of their ancestors. That
degree of liberty, which is now indulged to catholics, though a
party much more obnoxious than during the reign of the Stuarts,
it suited neither with Charles's sentiments, nor the humour of the
age, to allow them. An abatement of the more rigorous laws was
all he intended; and his engagements with France, notwithstanding that their regular execution had never been promised or expected, required of him some indulgence. But so unfortunate was
this prince, that no measure, embraced during his whole reign, was
ever attended with more unhappy and more fatal consequences.

The extreme rage against popery was a sure characteristic of
puritanism. The house of commons discovered other infallible
symptoms of the prevalence of that party. They petitioned the
king for replacing such able clergy as had been silenced for want
of conformity to the ceremonies.[d] They also enacted laws for the
strict observance of Sunday, which the Puritans affected to call the
Sabbath, and which they sanctified by the most melancholy indolence.[e] It is to be remarked, that the different appellations of this
festival were at that time known symbols of the different parties.

The king, finding that the parliament was resolved to grant him
no supply, and would furnish him with nothing but empty pro-

---

[a] Franklyn, p. 3, &c.   [b] Parl. Hist. vol. vi. p. 374. Journ. 1 Aug. 1625.
[c] Parl. Hist. vol. vi. p. 353. Journ. 7 July, 1625.   [d] Rush. vol. i. p. 281.
[e] 1 Car. I. cap. 1. Journ. 21 June, 1625.

testations of duty,[f] or disagreeable complaints of grievances; took advantage of the plague,[g] which began to appear at Oxford, and on that pretence, immediately dissolved them. By finishing the session with a dissolution, instead of a prorogation, he sufficiently expressed his displeasure at their conduct.

August 12.

To supply the want of parliamentary aids, Charles issued privy seals for borrowing money from his subjects.[h] The advantage reaped by this expedient was a small compensation for the disgust which it occasioned. By means, however, of that supply, and by other expedients, he was, though with difficulty, enabled to equip

October 1.

Naval expedition against Spain.

his fleet. It consisted of eighty vessels, great and small; and carried on board an army of 10,000 men. Sir Edward Cecil, lately created Viscount Wimbleton, was entrusted with the command. He sailed immediately for Cadiz, and found the bay full of Spanish ships of great value. He either neglected to attack these ships, or attempted it preposterously. The army was landed, and a fort taken: But the undisciplined soldiers, finding store of wine, could not be restrained from the utmost excesses. Farther stay appearing fruitless, they were reimbarked; and the fleet put to sea with an intention of intercepting the Spanish galleons. But the plague hav-

November.

ing seized the seamen and soldiers, they were obliged to abandon all hopes of this prize, and return to England. Loud complaints were made against the court for entrusting so important a command to a man like Cecil, whom, though he possessed great experience, the people, judging by the event, esteemed of slender capacity.[i]

1626.

Charles, having failed of so rich a prize, was obliged again to have recourse to a parliament. Though the ill success of his enterprizes diminished his authority, and showed every day more plainly the imprudence of the Spanish war; though the encrease of his necessities rendered him more dependent, and more exposed

---

[f] Franklyn, p. 113. Rushworth, vol. i. p. 190. [g] The plague was really so violent, that it had been moved in the house, at the beginning of the session, to petition the king to adjourn them. Journ. 21 June, 1625. So it was impossible to enter upon grievances, even if there had been any. The only business of the parliament was to give supply, which was so much wanted by the king, in order to carry on the war in which they had engaged him. [h] Rush. vol. i. p. 192. Parl. Hist. vol. vi. p. 407. [i] Franklyn, p. 113. Rushworth, vol. i. p. 196.

to the encroachments of the commons; he was resolved to try once more that regular and constitutional expedient for supply. Perhaps too, a little political art, which at that time he practised, was much trusted to. He had named four popular leaders, sheriffs of counties; Sir Edward Coke, Sir Robert Philips, Sir Thomas Wentworth, and Sir Francis Seymour; and, though the question had been formerly much contested,[k] he thought that he had by that means incapacitated them from being elected members. But his intention being so evident, rather put the commons more upon their guard. Enow of patriots still remained to keep up the ill humour of the house; and men needed but little instruction or rhetoric to recommend to them practices, which encreased their own importance and consideration. The weakness of the court also could not more evidently appear, than by its being reduced to use so ineffectual an expedient, in order to obtain an influence over the commons.

Second parliament.

The views, therefore, of the last parliament were immediately adopted; as if the same men had been every where elected, and no time had intervened since their meeting. When the king laid before the house his necessities, and asked for supply, they immediately voted him three subsidies and three fifteenths; and though they afterwards added one subsidy more, the sum was little proportioned to the greatness of the occasion, and ill fitted to promote those views of success and glory, for which the young prince, in his first enterprize, so ardently longed. But this circumstance was not the most disagreeable one. The supply was only voted by the commons. The passing of that vote into a law was reserved till the end of the session.[l] A condition was thereby made, in a very undisguised manner, with their sovereign. Under colour of redressing grievances, which, during this short reign, could not be very numerous; they were to proceed in regulating and controuling every part of government, which displeased them: And if the king either cut them short in this undertaking, or refused compliance with their demands, he must not expect any supply from the commons. Great dissatisfaction was expressed by Charles at a treat-

February 6.

---

[k] It is always an express clause in the writ of summons, that no sheriff shall be chosen, but the contrary practice had often prevailed. D'Ewes, p. 38. Yet still great doubts were entertained on this head. See Journ. 9 April, 1614.
[l] Journ. 27 March, 1626.

ment, which he deemed so harsh and undutiful.[m] But his urgent necessities obliged him to submit; and he waited with patience, observing to what side they would turn themselves.

Impeach-
ment of
Bucking-
ham.

The duke of Buckingham, formerly obnoxious to the public, became every day more unpopular, by the symptoms which appeared both of his want of temper and prudence, and of the uncontrouled ascendant, which he had acquired over his master.[n] Two violent attacks he was obliged this session to sustain; one from the earl of Bristol, another from the house of commons.

As long as James lived, Bristol, secure of the concealed favour of that monarch, had expressed all duty and obedience; in expectation that an opportunity would offer of re-instating himself in his former credit and authority. Even after Charles's accession, he despaired not. He submitted to the king's commands of remaining at his country-seat, and of absenting himself from parliament. Many trials he made to regain the good opinion of his master; but finding them all fruitless, and observing Charles to be entirely governed by Buckingham, his implacable enemy, he resolved no longer to keep any measures with the court. A new spirit, he saw, and a new power arising in the nation; and to these he was determined for the future to trust for his security and protection.

When the parliament was summoned, Charles, by a stretch of prerogative, had given orders that no writ, as is customary, should be sent to Bristol.[o] That nobleman applied to the house of lords by petition; and craved their good offices with the king for obtaining what was his due as a peer of the realm. His writ was sent him; but accompanied with a letter from the lord keeper, Coventry, commanding him, in the king's name, to absent himself from parliament. This letter Bristol conveyed to the lords, and asked advice how to proceed in so delicate a situation.[p] The king's prohibition was withdrawn, and Bristol took his seat. Provoked at these repeated instances of rigour, which the court denominated contumacy, Charles ordered his attorney-general to enter an accusa-

[m] Parliamentary History, vol. vi. p. 449. Rushworth, vol. i. p. 224.   [n] His credit with the king had given him such influence, that he had no less than twenty proxies granted him this parliament by so many peers; which occasioned a vote, that no peer should have above two proxies. The earl of Leicester in 1585 had once ten proxies. D'Ewes, p. 314.   [o] Rushworth, vol. i. p. 236.   [p] Ibid. vol. i. p. 237. Franklyn, p. 120, &c.

tion of high treason against him. By way of recrimination, Bristol accused Buckingham of high treason. Both the earl's defence of himself and accusation of the duke remain;[q] and together with some original letters still extant, contain the fullest and most authentic account of all the negociations with the house of Austria. From the whole, the great inprudence of the duke evidently appears, and the sway of his ungovernable passions; but it would be difficult to collect thence any action, which in the eye of the law could be deemed a crime; much less could subject him to the penalty of treason.

The impeachment of the commons was still less dangerous to the duke, were it estimated by the standard of law and equity. The house, after having voted, upon some queries of Dr. Turner's, *that common fame was a sufficient ground of accusation by the commons,*[r] proceeded to frame regular articles against Buckingham. They accused him, of having united many offices in his person; of having bought two of them; of neglecting to guard the seas, insomuch that many merchant-ships had fallen into the hands of the enemy; of delivering ships to the French king, in order to serve against the Hugonots; of being employed in the sale of honours and offices; of accepting extensive grants from the crown; of procuring many titles of honour for his kindred; and of administering physic to the late king without acquainting his physicians. All these articles appear, from comparing the accusation and reply, to be either frivolous, or false, or both.[s] The only charge, which could be regarded as important, was, that he had extorted a sum of ten thousand pounds from the East-India company, and that he had confiscated some goods belonging to French merchants, on pretence of their being the property of Spanish. The impeachment never came to a full determination; so that it is difficult for us to give a decisive opinion with regard to these articles: But it must be confessed, that the duke's answer in these particulars, as in all the rest, is so clear and satisfactory, that it is impossible to refuse our assent to it.[t] His faults and blemishes were in many respects very great; but rapacity and avarice were vices, with which he was entirely unacquainted.

---

[q] Rushworth, vol. i. p. 256, 262, 263, &c. Franklyn, p. 123, &c.
[r] Rushworth, vol. i. p. 217. Whitlocke, p. 5. [s] Rushworth, vol. i. p. 306, &c. 375, &c. Journ. 25 March, 1626. [t] Whitlocke, p. 7.

It is remarkable, that the commons, though so much at a loss to find articles of charge against Buckingham, never adopted Bristol's accusation, or impeached the duke for his conduct in the Spanish treaty, the most blameable circumstance in his whole life. He had reason to believe the Spaniards sincere in their professions; yet, in order to gratify his private passions, he had hurried his master and his country into a war pernicious to the interests of both. But so rivetted throughout the nation were the prejudices with regard to Spanish deceit and falsehood, that very few of the commons seem as yet to have been convinced that they had been seduced by Buckingham's narrative: A certain proof that a discovery of this nature was not, as is imagined by several historians, the cause of so sudden and surprising a variation in the measures of the parliament.[u]

While the commons were thus warmly engaged against Buckingham, the king seemed desirous of embracing every opportunity, by which he could express a contempt and disregard for them. No one was at that time sufficiently sensible of the great weight, which the commons bore in the balance of the constitution. The history of England had never hitherto afforded one instance, where any great movement or revolution had proceeded from the lower house. And as their rank, both considered in a body and as individuals, was but the second in the kingdom; nothing less than fatal experience could engage the English princes to pay a due regard to the inclinations of that formidable assembly.

The earl of Suffolk, chancellor of the university of Cambridge, dying about this time, Buckingham, though lying under impeachment, was yet, by means of court-interest, chosen in his place. The commons resented and loudly complained of this affront; and the more to enrage them, the king himself wrote a letter to the university, extolling the duke, and giving them thanks for his election.[w]

The lord keeper, in the king's name, expressly commanded the house not to meddle with his minister and servant, Buckingham; and ordered them to finish, in a few days, the bill, which they had begun for the subsidies, and to make some addition to them; otherwise they must not expect to sit any longer.[x] And though these

---

[u] See note [S] at the end of the volume.   [w] Rushworth, vol. i. p. 371.
[x] Parl. Hist. vol. vi. p. 444.

CHAPTER L

harsh commands were endeavoured to be explained and mollified, a few days after, by a speech of Buckingham's,[y] they failed not to leave a disagreeable impression behind them.

Besides a more stately stile, which Charles in general affected to this parliament than to the last, he went so far, in a message, as to threaten the commons, that, if they did not furnish him with supplies, he should be obliged to try *new counsels*. This language was sufficiently clear: Yet, lest any ambiguity should remain, Sir Dudley Carleton, vice-chamberlain, took care to explain it. "I pray you consider," said he, "what these new counsels are or may be. I fear to declare those that I conceive. In all Christian kingdoms, you know that parliaments were in use anciently, by which those kingdoms were governed in a most flourishing manner; until the monarchs began to know their own strength, and, seeing the turbulent spirit of their parliaments, at length they, by little and little, began to stand on their prerogatives, and at last overthrew the parliaments, throughout Christendom, except here only with us.—Let us be careful then to preserve the king's good opinion of parliaments, which bringeth such happiness to this nation, and makes us envied of all others, while there is this sweetness between his majesty and the commons; lest we lose the repute of a free people by our turbulency in parliament."[z] These imprudent suggestions rather gave warning than struck terror. A precarious liberty, the commons thought, which was to be preserved by unlimited complaisance, was no liberty at all. And it was necessary, while yet in their power, to secure the constitution by such invincible barriers, that no king or minister should ever, for the future, dare to speak such a language to any parliament, or even entertain such a project against them.

Two members of the house, Sir Dudley Digges and Sir John Elliott, who had been employed as managers of the impeachment against the duke, were thrown into prison.[a] The commons immediately declared, that they would proceed no farther upon business, till they had satisfaction in their privileges. Charles alledged, as the reason of this measure, certain seditious expressions, which, he said, had, in their accusation of the duke, dropped from these

[y] Id. ibid. p. 451. Rushworth, vol. i. p. 225. Franklyn, p. 118.
[z] Rushworth, vol. i. p. 359. Whitlocke, p. 6.   [a] Rushworth, vol. i. p. 356.

members. Upon enquiry, it appeared, that no such expression had been used.[b] The members were released, and the king reaped no other benefit from this attempt than to exasperate the house still farther, and to show some degree of precipitancy and indiscretion.

Moved by this example, the house of peers were rouzed from their inactivity; and claimed liberty for the earl of Arundel, who had been lately confined in the Tower. After many fruitless evasions, the king, though somewhat ungracefully, was at last obliged to comply.[c] And in this incident, it sufficiently appeared, that the lords, how little soever inclined to popular courses, were not wanting in a just sense of their own dignity.

The ill humour of the commons, thus wantonly irritated by the court, and finding no gratification in the legal impeachment of Buckingham, sought other objects, on which it might exert itself. The never-failing cry of popery here served them in stead. They again claimed the execution of the penal laws against catholics; and they presented to the king a list of persons, entrusted with offices, most of them insignificant, who were either convicted or suspected recusants.[d] In this particular, they had, perhaps, some reason to blame the king's conduct. He had promised to the last house of commons a redress of this religious grievance: But he was apt, in imitation of his father, to imagine, that the parliament, when they failed of supplying his necessities, had, on their part, freed him from the obligation of a strict performance. A new odium, likewise, by these representations, was attempted to be thrown upon Buckingham. His mother, who had great influence over him, was a professed catholic; his wife was not free from suspicion: And the indulgence given to catholics was of course supposed to proceed entirely from his credit and authority. So violent was the bigotry of the times, that it was thought a sufficient reason for disqualifying any one from holding an office, that his wife, or relations, or companions, were papists, though he himself were a conformist.[e]

It is remarkable, that persecution was here chiefly pushed on by laymen; and that the church was willing to have granted more

---

[b] Id. ibid. p. 358, 361. Franklyn, p. 180. [c] Rushworth, vol. i. p. 363, 364, &c. Franklyn, p. 181. [d] Franklyn, p. 195. Rushworth. [e] See the list in Franklyn and Rushworth.

CHAPTER L

liberty than would be allowed by the commons. The reconciling
doctrines likewise of Montague failed not anew to meet with severe
censures from that zealous assembly.[f]

The next attack, made by the commons, had it prevailed, would
have proved decisive. They were preparing a remonstrance
against the levying of tonnage and poundage without consent of
parliament. This article, together with the new impositions laid
on merchandize by James, constituted near half of the crown-
revenues; and by depriving the king of these resources, they would
have reduced him to total subjection and dependence. While they
retained such a pledge, besides the supply already promised, they
were sure that nothing could be refused them. Though after can-
vassing the matter near three months, they found themselves utterly incapable of fixing any legal crime upon the duke, they regarded him as an unable and perhaps a dangerous minister; and
they intended to present a petition, which would then have been
equivalent to a command, for removing him from his majesty's
person and councils.[g]

The king was alarmed at the yoke which he saw prepared for
him. Buckingham's sole guilt, he thought, was the being his friend
and favourite.[h] All the other complaints against him were mere
pretences. A little before he was the idol of the people. No new
crime had since been discovered. After the most diligent enquiry,
prompted by the greatest malice, the smallest appearance of guilt
could not be fixed upon him. What idea, he asked, must all mankind entertain of his honour, should he sacrifice his innocent
friend to pecuniary considerations? What farther authority should
he retain in the nation, were he capable, in the beginning of his
reign, to give, in so signal an instance, such matter of triumph to
his enemies, and discouragement to his adherents? To-day, the
commons pretend to wrest his minister from him. To-morrow,
they will attack some branch of his prerogative. By their remonstrances, and promises, and protestations, they had engaged the
crown in a war. As soon as they saw a retreat impossible, without
waiting for new incidents, without covering themselves with
new pretences, they immediately deserted him, and refused him

[f] Rushworth, vol. i. p. 209. [g] Rushworth, vol. i. p. 400. Franklyn, p. 199.
[h] Franklyn, p. 178.

all reasonable supply. It was evident, that they desired nothing so much as to see him plunged in inextricable difficulties, of which they intended to take advantage. To such deep perfidy, to such unbounded usurpations, it was necessary to oppose a proper firmness and resolution. All encroachments on supreme power could only be resisted successfully on the first attempt. The sovereign authority was, with some difficulty, reduced from its ancient and legal height; but when once pushed downwards, it soon became contemptible, and would easily, by the continuance of the same effort, now encouraged by success, be carried to the lowest extremity.

Prompted by these plausible motives, Charles was determined immediately to dissolve the parliament. When this resolution was known, the house of peers, whose compliant behaviour entitled them to some authority with him, endeavoured to interpose;[i] and they petitioned him, that he would allow the parliament to sit some time longer. *Not a moment longer,* cried the king hastily;[k] and he soon after ended the session by a dissolution.

As this measure was foreseen, the commons took care to finish and disperse their remonstrance, which they intended as a justification of their conduct to the people. The king likewise, on his part, published a declaration, in which he gave the reasons of his disagreement with the parliament, and of their sudden dissolution, before they had time to conclude any one act.[l] These papers furnished the partizans on both sides with ample matter of apology or of recrimination. But all impartial men judged, "*That* the commons, though they had not as yet violated any law, yet, by their unpliableness and independence, were insensibly changing, perhaps improving, the spirit and genius, while they preserved the forms of the constitution: And *that* the king was acting altogether without any plan; running on in a road surrounded on all sides with the most dangerous precipices, and concerting no proper measures, either for submitting to the obstinacy of the commons, or for subduing it."

15th June.

After a breach with the parliament, which seemed so difficult to repair, the only rational counsel, which Charles could pursue,

---

[i] Rushworth, vol. i. p. 398.   [k] Sanderson's Life of Charles I. p. 58.
[l] Franklyn, p. 203, &c. Parl. Hist. vol. vii. p. 300.

CHAPTER L

was immediately to conclude a peace with Spain, and to render himself, as far as possible, independant of his people, who discovered so little inclination to support him, or rather who seem to have formed a determined resolution to abridge his authority. Nothing could be more easy in the execution than this measure, nor more agreeable to his own and to national interest. But, besides the treaties and engagements, which he had entered into with Holland and Denmark, the king's thoughts were at this time averse to pacific counsels. There are two circumstances in Charles's character, seemingly incompatible, which attended him during the whole course of his reign, and were in part the cause of his misfortunes: He was very steady and even obstinate in his purpose; and he was easily governed, by reason of his facility, and of his deference to men much inferior to himself both in morals and understanding. His great ends he inflexibly maintained: But the means of attaining them, he readily received from his ministers and favourites, though not always fortunate in his choice. The violent, impetuous Buckingham, inflamed with a desire of revenge for injuries which he himself had committed, and animated with a love of glory which he had not talents to merit, had at this time, notwithstanding his profuse licentious life, acquired an invincible ascendant over the virtuous and gentle temper of the king.

The *new counsel,* which Charles had mentioned to the parliament, were now to be tried, in order to supply his necessities. Had he possessed any military force, on which he could rely, it is not improbable, that he had at once taken off the mask, and governed without any regard to parliamentary privileges: So high an idea had he received of kingly prerogative, and so contemptible a notion of the rights of those popular assemblies, from which, he very naturally thought, he had met with such ill usage. But his army was new levied, ill paid, and worse disciplined; no-wise superior to the militia, who were much more numerous, and who were in a great measure under the influence of the country-gentlemen. It behoved him, therefore, to proceed cautiously, and to cover his enterprizes under the pretence of ancient precedents, which, considering the great authority commonly enjoyed by his predecessors, could not be wanting to him.

A commission was openly granted to compound with the catholics, and agree for dispensing with the penal laws enacted against

Violent measures of the court.

them.[m] By this expedient, the king both filled his coffers, and gratified his inclination of giving indulgence to these religionists: But he could not have employed any branch of prerogative, which would have been more disagreeable, or would have appeared more exceptionable, to his protestant subjects.

From the nobility, he desired assistance: From the city, he required a loan of 100,000 pounds. The former contributed slowly: But the latter, covering themselves under many pretences and excuses, gave him at last a flat refusal.[n]

In order to equip a fleet, a distribution, by order of council, was made to all the maritime towns; and each of them was required, with the assistance of the adjacent counties, to arm so many vessels as were appointed them.[o] The city of London was rated at twenty ships. This is the first appearance, in Charles's reign, of shipmoney; a taxation which had once been imposed by Elizabeth, but which afterwards, when carried some steps farther by Charles, created such violent discontents.

Of some, loans were required:[p] To others the way of benevolence was proposed: Methods supported by precedent, but always invidious even in times more submissive and compliant. In the most absolute governments, such expedients would be regarded as irregular and unequal.

These counsels for supply were conducted with some moderation; till news arrived, that a great battle was fought between the king of Denmark and count Tilly, the imperial general; in which the former was totally defeated. Money now, more than ever, became necessary, in order to repair so great a breach in the alliance, and to support a prince, who was so nearly allied to Charles, and who had been engaged in the war chiefly by the intrigues, solicitations, and promises of the English monarch. After some deliberation, an act of council was passed; importing, that as the urgency of affairs admitted not the way of parliament, the most speedy, equal, and convenient method of supply was by a GENERAL LOAN from the subject, according as every man was assessed in the rolls of the last subsidy. That precise sum was required, which each would have paid, had the vote of four sub-

25th Aug.

---

[m] Rushworth, vol. i. p. 413. Whitlocke, p. 7. [n] Rushworth, vol. i. p. 415. Franklyn, p. 206. [o] Rushworth ut supra. [p] Rushworth, vol. i. p. 416.

CHAPTER L

sidies passed into a law: But care was taken to inform the people, that the sums exacted were not to be called subsidies, but loans.[q] Had any doubt remained, whether forced loans, however authorized by precedent, and even by statute, were a violation of liberty, and must, by necessary consequence, render all parliaments superfluous; this was the proper expedient for opening the eyes of the whole nation. The example of Henry VIII. who had once, in his arbitrary reign, practised a like method of levying a regular supply, was generally deemed a very insufficient authority.

The commissioners appointed to levy these loans, among other articles of secret instruction, were enjoined, "If any shall refuse to lend, and shall make delays or excuses, and persist in his obstinacy, that they examine him upon oath, whether he has been dealt with to deny or refuse to lend, or make an excuse for not lending? Who has dealt with him, and what speeches or persuasions were used to that purpose? And that they also shall charge every such person, in his majesty's name, upon his allegiance, not to disclose to any one what his answer was."[r] So violent an inquisitorial power, so impracticable an attempt at secrecy, were the objects of indignation, and even, in some degree, of ridicule.

That religious prejudices might support civil authority, sermons were preached by Sibthorpe and Manwaring, in favour of the general loan; and the court industriously spread them over the kingdom. Passive obedience was there recommended in its full extent, the whole authority of the state was represented as belonging to the king alone, and all limitations of law and a constitution were rejected as seditious and impious.[s] So openly was this doctrine espoused by the court, that Archbishop Abbot, a popular and virtuous prelate, was, because he refused to license Sibthorpe's sermon, suspended from the exercise of his office, banished from London, and confined to one of his country-seats.[t] Abbot's principles of liberty, and his opposition to Buckingham, had always rendered him very ungracious at court, and had acquired him the character of a puritan. For it is remarkable, that this party made the privileges of the nation as much a part of their religion, as the church-party did the prerogatives of the crown; and nothing

[q] Ibid. p. 418. Whitlocke, p. 8.　[r] Rushworth, vol. i. p. 419. Franklyn, p. 207.　[s] Rushworth, vol. i. p. 422. Franklyn, p. 208.　[t] Rushworth, vol. i. p. 431.

tended farther to recommend among the people, who always take opinions in the lump, the whole system and all the principles of the former sect. The king soon found, by fatal experience, that this engine of religion, which with so little necessity was introduced into politics, falling under more fortunate management, was played with the most terrible success against him.

While the king, instigated by anger and necessity, thus employed the whole extent of his prerogative, the spirit of the people was far from being subdued. Throughout England, many refused these loans; some were even active in encouraging their neighbours to insist upon their common rights and privileges. By warrant of the council, *these* were thrown into prison.[u] Most of them with patience submitted to confinement, or applied by petition to the king, who commonly released them. Five gentlemen alone, Sir Thomas Darnel, Sir John Corbet, Sir Walter Earl, Sir John Heveningham, and Sir Edmond Hambden, had spirit enough, at their own hazard and expence, to defend the public liberties, and to demand releasement, not as a favour from the court, but as their due, by the laws of their country.[w] No particular cause was assigned of their commitment. The special command alone of the king and council was pleaded. And it was asserted, that, by law, this was not sufficient reason for refusing bail or releasement to the prisoners.

This question was brought to a solemn trial, before the king's bench; and the whole kingdom was attentive to the issue of a cause, which was of much greater consequence than the event of many battles.

By the debates on this subject, it appeared, beyond controversy, to the nation, that their ancestors had been so jealous of personal liberty, as to secure it against arbitrary power, in the crown, by six[x] several statutes, and by an article[y] of the GREAT CHARTER itself, the most sacred foundation of the laws and constitution. But the kings of England, who had not been able to prevent the enacting of these laws, had sufficient authority, when the tide of liberty was spent, to obstruct their regular execution; and they deemed it superfluous, to attempt the formal repeal of statutes which they

[u] Rushworth, vol. i. p. 429. Franklyn, p. 210. [w] Rushworth, vol. i. p. 458. Franklyn, p. 224. Whitlocke, p. 8. [x] 25 Edw. III. cap. 4. 28 Edw. III. cap. 3. 37 Edw. III. cap. 18. 38 Edw. III. cap. 9. 42 Edw. III. cap. 3. 1 Richard II. cap. 12. [y] Chap. 29.

CHAPTER L

found so many expedients and pretences to elude. Turbulent and seditious times frequently occurred, when the safety of the people absolutely required the confinement of factious leaders; and by the genius of the old constitution, the prince, of himself, was accustomed to assume every branch of prerogative, which was found necessary for the preservation of public peace and of his own authority. Expediency, at other times, would cover itself under the appearance of necessity; and, in proportion as precedents multiplied, the will alone of the sovereign was sufficient to supply the place of expediency, of which he constituted himself the sole judge. In an age and nation where the power of a turbulent nobility prevailed, and where the king had no settled military force, the only means, that could maintain public peace, was the exertion of such prompt and discretionary powers in the crown; and the public itself had become so sensible of the necessity, that those ancient laws in favour of personal liberty, while often violated, had never been challenged or revived, during the course of near three centuries. Though rebellious subjects had frequently, in the open field, resisted the king's authority; no person had been found so bold, while confined and at mercy, as to set himself in opposition to regal power, and to claim the protection of the constitution, against the will of the sovereign. It was not till this age, when the spirit of liberty was universally diffused, when the principles of government were nearly reduced to a system, when the tempers of men, more civilized, seemed less to require those violent exertions of prerogative, that these five gentlemen above-mentioned, by a noble effort, ventured, in this national cause, to bring the question to a final determination. And the king was astonished to observe, that a power, exercised by his predecessors almost without interruption, was found, upon trial, to be directly opposite to the clearest laws, and supported by few undoubted precedents in courts of judicature. These had scarcely, in any instance, refused bail upon commitments by special command of the king; because the persons committed had seldom or never dared to demand it; at least, to insist on their demand.

Sir Randolf Crew, chief justice, had been displaced, as unfit for the purposes of the court: Sir Nicholas Hyde, esteemed more obsequious, had obtained that high office: Yet the judges, by his direction, went no farther than to remand the gentlemen to

1627.

prison, and refuse the bail which was offered.[z] Heathe, the attorney-general, insisted, that the court, in imitation of the judges in the 34th of Elizabeth,[a] should enter a general judgement that no bail could be granted, upon a commitment by the king or council.[b] But the judges wisely declined complying. The nation, they saw, was already, to the last degree, exasperated. In the present disposition of men's minds, universal complaints prevailed, as if the kingdom were reduced to slavery. And the most invidious prerogative of the crown, it was said, that of imprisoning the subject, is here openly, and solemnly, and in numerous instances, exercised for the most invidious purpose; in order to extort loans, or rather subsidies, without consent of parliament.

But this was not the only hardship, of which, the nation then thought, they had reason to complain. The army, which had made the fruitless expedition to Cadiz, was dispersed throughout the kingdom; and money was levied upon the counties, for the payment of their quarters.[c]

The soldiers were billetted upon private houses, contrary to custom, which required, that, in all ordinary cases, they should be quartered in inns and public houses.[d]

Those, who had refused or delayed the loan, were sure to be loaded with a great number of these dangerous and disorderly guests.

Many too, of low condition, who had shown a refractory disposition, were pressed into the service, and inlisted in the fleet or army.[e] Sir Peter Hayman, for the same reason, was dispatched on an errand to the Palatinate.[f] Glanville, an eminent lawyer, had been obliged, during the former interval of parliament, to accept of an office in the navy.[g]

The soldiers, ill-paid and undisciplined, committed many crimes and outrages; and much encreased the public discontents. To prevent these disorders, martial law, so requisite to the support of discipline, was exercised upon the soldiers. By a contradiction, which is natural, when the people are exasperated, the outrages of

---

[z] Rushworth, vol. i. p. 462.   [a] State Trials, vol. vii. p. 147.   [b] State Trials, ibid. p. 161.   [c] Rushworth, vol. i. p. 419.   [d] Ibid.   [e] Ibid. p. 422.   [f] Ibid. p. 431.   [g] Parl. Hist. vol. vii. p. 310.

CHAPTER L

the army were complained of; the remedy was thought still more intolerable.[h] Though the expediency, if we are not rather to say, the necessity of martial law, had formerly been deemed, of itself, a sufficient ground for establishing it; men, now become more jealous of liberty, and more refined reasoners in questions of government, regarded, as illegal and arbitrary, every exercise of authority, which was not supported by express statute, or uninterrupted precedent.

It may safely be affirmed, that, except a few courtiers or ecclesiastics, all men were displeased with this high exertion of prerogative, and this new spirit of administration. Though ancient precedents were pleaded in favour of the king's measures; a considerable difference, upon comparison, was observed between the cases. Acts of power, however irregular, might casually, and at intervals, be exercised by a prince, for the sake of dispatch or expediency; and yet liberty still subsist, in some tolerable degree, under his administration. But where all these were reduced into a system, were exerted without interruption, were studiously sought for, in order to supply the place of laws, and subdue the refractory spirit of the nation; it was necessary to find some speedy remedy, or finally to abandon all hopes of preserving the freedom of the constitution. Nor did moderate men esteem the provocation, which the king had received, though great, sufficient to warrant all these violent measures. The commons, as yet, had no wise invaded his authority: They had only exercised, as best pleased them, their own privileges. Was he justifiable, because, from one house of parliament, he had met with harsh and unkind treatment, to make, in revenge, an invasion on the rights and liberties of the whole nation?

But great was at this time the surprize of all men, when Charles, baffled in every attempt against the Austrian dominions, embroiled with his own subjects, unsupplied with any treasure but what he extorted by the most invidious and most dangerous measures; as if the half of Europe, now his enemy, were not sufficient for the exercise of military prowess; wantonly attacked France, the other great kingdom in his neighbourhood, and engaged at once

War with France.

[h] Rushworth, vol. i. p. 419. Whitlocke, p. 7.

in war against these two powers, whose interests were hitherto deemed so incompatible, that they could never, it was thought, agree either in the same friendships or enmities. All authentic memoirs, both foreign and domestic, ascribe to Buckingham's counsels this war with France, and represent him, as actuated by motives, which would appear incredible, were we not acquainted with the violence and temerity of his character.

The three great monarchies of Europe were at this time ruled by young princes, Philip, Louis, and Charles, who were nearly of the same age, and who had resigned the government of themselves, and of their kingdoms, to their creatures and ministers, Olivarez, Richelieu, and Buckingham. The people, whom the moderate temper or narrow genius of their princes, would have allowed to remain for ever in tranquillity, were strongly agitated by the emulation and jealousy of the ministers. Above all, the towering spirit of Richelieu, incapable of rest, promised an active age, and gave indications of great revolutions throughout all Europe.

This man had no sooner, by suppleness and intrigue, gotten possession of the reins of government, than he formed, at once, three mighty projects; to subdue the turbulent spirits of the great, to reduce the rebellious hugonots, and to curb the encroaching power of the house of Austria. Undaunted and implacable, prudent and active, he braved all the opposition of the French princes and nobles in the prosecution of his vengeance; he discovered and dissipated all their secret cabals and conspiracies. His sovereign himself he held in subjection, while he exalted the throne. The people, while they lost their liberties, acquired, by means of his administration, learning, order, discipline, and renown. That confused and inaccurate genius of government, of which France partook in common with other European kingdoms, he changed into a simple monarchy; at the very time, when the incapacity of Buckingham encouraged the free spirit of the commons to establish in England a regular system of liberty.

However unequal the comparison between these ministers, Buckingham had entertained a mighty jealousy against Richelieu; a jealousy not founded on rivalship of power and politics, but of love and gallantry; where the duke was as much superior to the cardinal, as he was inferior in every other particular.

CHAPTER L

At the time, when Charles married by proxy the princess Henrietta, the duke of Buckingham had been sent to France, in order to grace the nuptials, and conduct the new queen into England. The eyes of the French court were directed by curiosity towards that man, who had enjoyed the unlimited favour of two successive monarchs, and who, from a private station, had mounted, in the earliest youth, to the absolute government of three kingdoms. The beauty of his person, the gracefulness of his air, the splendor of his equipage, his fine taste in dress, festivals, and carousals, corresponded to the prepossessions entertained in his favour: The affability of his behaviour, the gaiety of his manners, the magnificence of his expence, encreased still farther the general admiration which was paid him. All business being already concerted, the time was entirely spent in mirth and entertainments; and, during those splendid scenes, among that gay people, the duke found himself in a situation, where he was perfectly qualified to excel.[i] But his great success at Paris proved as fatal as his former failure at Madrid. Encouraged by the smiles of the court, he dared to carry his ambitious addresses to the queen herself; and he failed not to make impression on a heart not undisposed to the tender passions. That attachment, at least, of the mind, which appears so delicious, and is so dangerous, seems to have been encouraged by the princess; and the duke presumed so far on her good graces, that, after his departure, he secretly returned upon some pretence, and, paying a visit to the queen, was dismissed with a reproof, which savoured more of kindness than of anger.[k]

Information of this correspondence was soon carried to Richelieu. The vigilance of that minister was here farther rouzed by jealousy. He too, either from vanity or politics, had ventured to pay his addresses to the queen. But a priest, past middle age, of a severe character, and occupied in the most extensive plans of ambition or vengeance, was but an unequal match in that contest, for a young courtier, entirely disposed to gaiety and gallantry. The cardinal's disappointment strongly inclined him to counter-work the amorous projects of his rival. When the duke was making preparations for a new embassy to Paris, a message was sent him

[i] Clarendon, vol. i. p. 38.   [k] Memoirs de Mad. de Motteville.

from Lewis, that he must not think of such a journey. In a romantic passion, he swore, *That he would see the queen, in spite of all the power of France;* and, from that moment, he determined to engage England in a war with that kingdom.[l]

He first took advantage of some quarrels, excited by the queen of England's attendants; and he persuaded Charles to dismiss, at once, all her French servants, contrary to the articles of the marriage treaty.[m] He encouraged the English ships of war and privateers to seize vessels belonging to French merchants; and *these* he forthwith condemned as prizes, by a sentence of the court of admiralty. But finding that all these injuries produced only remonstrances and embassies, or at most reprisals, on the part of France; he resolved to second the intrigues of the duke of Soubize; and to undertake at once a military expedition against that kingdom.

Soubize, who, with his brother, the duke of Rohan, was the leader of the hugonot faction, was at that time in London, and strongly solicited Charles to embrace the protection of these distressed religionists. He represented, that after the inhabitants of Rochelle had been repressed by the combined squadrons of England and Holland, after peace was concluded with the French king under Charles's mediation, the ambitious cardinal was still meditating the destruction of the hugonots; that preparations were silently making in every province of France for the suppression of their religion; that forts were erected in order to bridle Rochelle, the most considerable bulwark of the protestants; that the reformed in France cast their eyes on Charles as the head of their faith, and considered him as a prince engaged by interest, as well as inclination, to support them; that so long as their party subsisted, Charles might rely on their attachment as much as on that of his own subjects; but if their liberties were once ravished from them, the power of France, freed from this impediment, would soon become formidable to England, and to all the neighbouring nations.

Though Charles probably bore but small favour to the hugonots, who so much resembled the puritans in discipline and worship, in religion and politics; he yet allowed himself to be gained by these arguments, inforced by the solicitations of Buckingham.

[l] Clarendon, vol. i. p. 38.   [m] Rushworth, vol. i. p. 423, 424.

CHAPTER L

A fleet of a hundred sail, and an army of 7000 men, were fitted out for the invasion of France, and both of them entrusted to the command of the duke, who was altogether unacquainted both with land and sea service. The fleet appeared before Rochelle: but so ill-concerted were Buckingham's measures, that the inhabitants of that city shut their gates, and refused to admit allies, of whose coming they were not previously informed.[n] All his military operations showed equal incapacity and inexperience. Instead of attacking Oleron, a fertile island and defenceless, he bent his course to the isle of Rhé, which was well garrisoned and fortified: Having landed his men, though with some loss, he followed not the blow, but allowed Toiras, the French governor, five days respite; during which St. Martin was victualled and provided for a siege.[o] He left behind him the small fort of Prie, which could at first have made no manner of resistance: Though resolved to starve St. Martin, he guarded the sea negligently, and allowed provisions and ammunition to be thrown into it: Despairing to reduce it by famine, he attacked it without having made any breach, and rashly threw away the lives of the soldiers: Having found that a French army had stolen over in small divisions, and had landed at Prie, the fort which he had at first overlooked, he began to think of a retreat; but made it so unskilfully, that it was equivalent to a total rout: He was the last of the army, that embarked; and he returned to England, having lost two thirds of his land forces; totally discredited both as an admiral and a general; and bringing no praise with him, but the vulgar one of courage and personal bravery.

9th July. Expedition to the Isle of Rhé.

Octob. 28.

The duke of Rohan, who had taken arms as soon as Buckingham appeared upon the coast, discovered the dangerous spirit of the sect, without being able to do any mischief: The inhabitants of Rochelle, who had at last been induced to join the English, hastened the vengeance of their master, exhausted their provisions in supplying their allies, and were threatened with an immediate siege. Such were the fruits of Buckingham's expedition against France.

[n] Rushworth, vol. i. p. 426.   [o] Whitlocke, p. 8. Sir Philip Warwick, p. 25.

LI

Third parliament – Petition of right –
Prorogation – Death of Buckingham –
New session of parliament –
Tonnage and poundage –
Arminianism – Dissolution
of the parliament

🌰 🌰 🌰

1628.   THERE WAS REASON to apprehend some disorder or insurrection from the discontents, which prevailed among the
people in England. Their liberties, they believed, were ravished
from them; illegal taxes extorted; their commerce which had met
with a severe check from the Spanish, was totally annihilated by the
French war; those military honours transmitted to them from their
ancestors, had received a grievous stain, by two unsuccessful
and ill-conducted expeditions; scarce an illustrious family but
mourned, from the last of them, the loss of a son or brother;
greater calamities were dreaded from the war with these powerful
monarchies, concurring with the internal disorders, under which
the nation laboured. And these ills were ascribed, not to the refractory disposition of the two former parliaments, to which they were
partly owing; but solely to Charles's obstinacy, in adhering to the
counsels of Buckingham; a man nowise intitled, by his birth, age,
services, or merit, to that unlimited confidence, reposed in him. To
be sacrificed to the interest, policy, and ambition of the great, is so
much the common lot of the people, that they may appear unrea-

sonable, who would pretend to complain of it: But to be the victim of the frivolous gallantry of a favourite, and of his boyish caprices, seemed the object of peculiar indignation.

In this situation, it may be imagined, the king and the duke dreaded, above all things, the assembling of a parliament: But, so little foresight had they possessed in their enterprizing schemes, that they found themselves under an absolute necessity of embracing that expedient. The money levied, or rather extorted, under colour of prerogative, had come in very slowly, and had left such ill-humour in the nation, that it appeared dangerous to renew the experiment. The absolute necessity of supply, it was hoped, would engage the commons to forget all past injuries; and, having experienced the ill effects of former obstinacy, they would probably assemble with a resolution of making some reasonable compliances. The more to soften them, it was concerted, by Sir Robert Cotton's advice,[p] that Buckingham should be the first person, that proposed in council the calling of a new parliament. Having laid in this stock of merit, he expected, that all his former misdemeanors would be overlooked and forgiven, and that, instead of a tyrant and oppressor, he should be regarded as the first patriot in the nation. *Third parliament.*

The views of the popular leaders were much more judicious and profound. When the commons assembled, they appeared to be men of the same independent spirit with their predecessors, and possessed of such riches, that their property was computed to surpass three times that of the house of peers;[q] they were deputed by boroughs and counties, inflamed, all of them, by the late violations of liberty; many of the members themselves had been cast into prison, and had suffered by the measures of the court; yet, notwithstanding these circumstances, which might prompt them to embrace violent resolutions, they entered upon business with perfect temper and decorum. They considered, that the king, disgusted at these popular assemblies, and little prepossessed in favour of their privileges, wanted but a fair pretence for breaking with them, and would seize the first opportunity offered by any incident or any undutiful behaviour of the members. He fairly told them, in his first speech, that, "If they should not do their duties, *March 17.*

---

[p] Franklyn, p. 230.   [q] Sanderson, p. 106. Walker, p. 339.

in contributing to the necessities of the state, he must, in discharge of his conscience, use those other means, which God had put into his hands, in order to save that which the follies of some particular men may otherwise put in danger. Take not this for a threatening," added the king, "for I scorn to threaten any but my equals; but as an admonition from him, who, by nature and duty, has most care of your preservation and prosperity."[r] The lord keeper, by the king's direction, subjoined, "This way of parliamentary supplies, as his majesty told you, he hath chosen, not as the only way, but as the fittest; not because he is destitute of others, but because it is most agreeable to the goodness of his own most gracious disposition, and to the desire and weal of his people. If this be deferred, necessity and the sword of the enemy make way for the others. Remember his majesty's admonition, I say, remember it."[s] From these avowed maxims, the commons foresaw, that, if the least handle were afforded, the king would immediately dissolve them, and would thenceforward deem himself justified for violating, in a manner still more open, all the ancient forms of the constitution. No remedy could then be looked for, but from insurrections and civil war, of which the issue would be extremely uncertain, and which must, in all events, prove calamitous to the nation. To correct the late disorders in the administration required some new laws, which would, no doubt, appear harsh to a prince, so enamoured of his prerogative; and it was requisite to temper, by the decency and moderation of their debates, the rigour, which must necessarily attend their determinations. Nothing can give us a higher idea of the capacity of those men, who now guided the commons, and of the great authority, which they had acquired, than the forming and executing of so judicious and so difficult a plan of operations.

The decency, however, which the popular leaders had prescribed to themselves, and recommended to others, hindered them not from making the loudest and most vigorous complaints against the grievances, under which the nation had lately laboured. Sir Francis Seymour said, "This is the great council of the kingdom, and here with certainty, if not here only, his majesty may see, as in a true glass, the state of the kingdom. We are called hither by his

---

[r] Rushworth, vol. i. p. 477. Franklyn, p. 233. [s] Rushworth, vol. i. p. 479. Franklyn, p. 234.

writs, in order to give him faithful counsel; such as may stand with his honour: And this we must do without flattery. We are also sent hither by the people, in order to deliver their just grievances: And this we must do without fear. Let us not act like Cambyses's judges, who, when their approbation was demanded by the prince to some illegal measure, said, that, *Though there was a written law, the Persian kings might follow their own will and pleasure.* This was base flattery, fitter for our reproof than our imitation; and as fear, so flattery, taketh away the judgment. For my part, I shall shun both; and speak my mind with as much duty, as any man, to his majesty, without neglecting the public.

"But how can we express our affections, while we retain our fears; or speak of giving, till we know whether we have any thing to give. For, if his majesty may be persuaded to take what he will, what need we give?

"That this hath been done, appeareth by the billeting of soldiers, a thing nowise advantageous to the king's service, and a burthen to the commonwealth: By the imprisonment of gentlemen for refusing the loan, who, if they had done the contrary for fear, had been as blameable as the projectors of that oppressive measure. To countenance these proceedings, hath it not been preached in the pulpit, or rather prated, that *All we have is the king's by divine right?* But when preachers forsake their own calling, and turn ignorant statesmen; we see how willing they are to exchange a good conscience for a bishopric.

"He, I must confess, is no good subject, who would not, willingly and chearfully, lay down his life, when that sacrifice may promote the interests of his sovereign, and the good of the commonwealth. But he is not a good subject, he is a slave, who will allow his goods to be taken from him against his will, and his liberty against the laws of the kingdom. By opposing these practices, we shall but tread in the steps of our forefathers, who still preferred the public before their private interest, nay, before their very lives. It will in us be a wrong done to ourselves, to our posterities, to our consciences, if we forego this claim and pretension."[1]

"I read of a custom," said Sir Robert Philips, "among the old Romans, that, once every year, they held a solemn festival, in which their slaves had liberty, without exception, to speak what

[1] Franklyn, p. 243. Rushworth, vol. i. p. 499.

they pleased, in order to ease their afflicted minds; and, on the conclusion of the festival, the slaves severally returned to their former servitudes.

"This institution may, with some distinction, well set forth our present state and condition. After the revolution of some time, and the grievous sufferance of many violent oppressions, we have now, at last, as those slaves, obtained, for a day, some liberty of speech: But shall not, I trust, be hereafter slaves: For we are born free. Yet, what new illegal burthens our estates and persons have groaned under, my heart yearns to think of, my tongue faulters to utter.—

"The grievances, by which we are oppressed, I draw under two heads; acts of power against law, and the judgments of lawyers against our liberty."

Having mentioned three illegal judgments, passed within his memory; that by which the Scots, born after James's accession, were admitted to all the privileges of English subjects; that by which the new impositions had been warranted; and the late one, by which arbitrary imprisonments were authorized; he thus proceeded.

"I can live, though another, who has no right, be put to live along with me; nay, I can live, though burthened with impositions, beyond what at present I labour under: But to have my liberty, which is the soul of my life, ravished from me; to have my person pent up in a jail, without relief by law, and to be so adjudged,—O, improvident ancestors! O, unwise forefathers! to be so curious in providing for the quiet possession of our lands, and the liberties of parliament; and, at the same time, to neglect our personal liberty, and let us lie in prison, and that during pleasure, without redress or remedy! If this be law, why do we talk of liberties? Why trouble ourselves with disputes about a constitution, franchises, property of goods, and the like? What may any man call his own, if not the liberty of his person?

"I am weary of treading these ways; and therefore conclude to have a select committee, in order to frame a petition to his majesty for redress of these grievances. And this petition being read, examined, and approved, may be delivered to the king; of whose gracious answer we have no cause to doubt, our desires being so reasonable, our intentions so loyal, and the manner so dutiful. Neither need we fear, that this is the critical parliament, as has

CHAPTER LI

been insinuated; or that this is the way to distraction: But assure ourselves of a happy issue. Then shall the king, as he calls us his great council, find us his true council, and own us his good council."[u]

The same topics were enforced by Sir Thomas Wentworth. After mentioning projectors and ill ministers of state, "These," said he, "have introduced a privy-council, ravishing, at once, the spheres of all ancient government; destroying all liberty; imprisoning us without bail or bond. They have taken from us— What shall I say? Indeed, what have they left us? By tearing up the roots of all property, they have taken from us every means of supplying the king, and of ingratiating ourselves by voluntary proofs of our duty and attachment towards him.

"To the making whole all these breaches, I shall apply myself; and, to all these diseases, shall propound a remedy. By one and the same thing, have the king and the people been hurt, and by the same must they be cured. We must vindicate: What? New things? No: Our ancient, legal, and vital liberties; by reinforcing the laws, enacted by our ancestors; by setting such a stamp upon them, that no licentious spirit shall dare henceforth to invade them. And shall we think this a way to break a parliament? No: Our desires are modest and just. I speak both for the interest of king and people. If we enjoy not these rights, it will be impossible for us to relieve him. Let us never, therefore, doubt of a favourable reception from his goodness."[w]

These sentiments were unanimously embraced by the whole house. Even the court party pretended not to plead, in defence of the late measures, any thing but the necessity to which the king had been reduced, by the obstinacy of the two former parliaments. A vote, therefore, was passed without opposition, against arbitrary imprisonments and forced loans.[x] And the spirit of liberty having obtained some contentment by this exertion, the reiterated messages of the king, who pressed for supply, were attended to with more temper. Five subsidies were voted him; with which, though much inferior to his wants, he declared himself well satisfied; and even tears of affection started in his eye, when he was informed of

[u] Franklyn, p. 245. Parl. Hist. vol. vii. p. 363. Rushworth, vol. i. p. 502.
[w] Franklyn, p. 243. Rushworth, vol. i. p. 500.   [x] Franklyn, p. 251. Rushworth, vol. i. p. 513. Whitlocke, p. 9.

this concession. The duke's approbation too was mentioned by secretary Coke; but the conjunction of a subject with the sovereign was ill received by the house.[y] Though disgusted with the king, the jealousy, which they felt for his honour, was more sensible than that, which his unbounded confidence in the duke would allow even himself to entertain.

The supply, though voted, was not, as yet, passed into a law; and the commons resolved to employ the interval, in providing some barriers to their rights and liberties so lately violated. They knew, that their own vote, declaring the illegality of the former measures, had not, of itself, sufficient authority to secure the constitution against future invasion. Some act to that purpose must receive the sanction of the whole legislature; and they appointed a committee to prepare the model of so important a law. By collecting into one effort all the dangerous and oppressive claims of his prerogative, Charles had exposed them to the hazard of one assault; and had farther, by presenting a nearer view of the consequences attending them, rouzed the independent genius of the commons. Forced loans, benevolences, taxes without consent of parliament, arbitrary imprisonments, the billeting of soldiers, martial law; these were the grievances complained of, and against these an eternal remedy was to be provided. The commons pretended not, as they affirmed, to any unusual powers or privileges: They aimed only at securing those which had been transmitted them from their ancestors: And their law they resolved to call a *Petition of right.* PETITION OF RIGHT; as implying that it contained a corroboration or explanation of the ancient constitution, not any infringement of royal prerogative, or acquisition of new liberties.

While the committee was employed in framing the petition of right, the favourers of each party, both in parliament and throughout the nation, were engaged in disputes about this bill, which, in all likelihood, was to form a memorable aera in the English government.

That the statutes, said the partizans of the commons, which secure English liberty, are not become obsolete, appears hence, that the English have ever been free, and have ever been governed by law and a limited constitution. Privileges in particular, which are founded on the GREAT CHARTER, must always remain in force,

[y] Rushworth, vol. i. p. 526. Whitlocke, p. 9.

because derived from a source of never-failing authority; regarded in all ages, as the most sacred contract between king and people. Such attention was paid to this charter by our generous ancestors, that they got the confirmation of it re-iterated thirty several times; and even secured it by a rule, which, though vulgarly received, seems in the execution impracticable. They have established it as a maxim, *That even a statute, which should be enacted in contradiction to any article of that charter, cannot have force or validity.* But with regard to that important article, which secures personal liberty; so far from attempting, at any time, any legal infringement of it, they have corroborated it by six statutes, and put it out of all doubt and controversy. If in practice it has often been violated, abuses can never come in the place of rules; nor can any rights or legal powers be derived from injury and injustice. But the title of the subject to personal liberty not only is founded on ancient, and therefore the more sacred laws: It is confirmed by the whole ANALOGY of the government and constitution. A free monarchy in which every individual is a slave, is a glaring contradiction; and it is requisite, where the laws assign privileges to the different orders of the state, that it likewise secure the independence of the members. If any difference could be made in this particular, it were better to abandon even life or property to the arbitrary will of the prince; nor would such immediate danger ensue, from that concession, to the laws and to the privileges of the people. To bereave of his life a man not condemned by any legal trial, is so egregious an exercise of tyranny, that it must at once shock the natural humanity of princes, and convey an alarm throughout the whole commonwealth. To confiscate a man's fortune, besides its being a most atrocious act of violence, exposes the monarch so much to the imputation of avarice and rapacity, that it will seldom be attempted in any civilized government. But confinement, though a less striking, is no less severe a punishment; nor is there any spirit, so erect and independent, as not to be broken by the long continuance of the silent and inglorious sufferings of a jail. The power of imprisonment, therefore, being the most natural and potent engine of arbitrary government, it is absolutely necessary to remove it from a government which is free and legal.

The partizans of the court reasoned after a different manner. The true rule of government, said they, during any period, is that to which the people, from time immemorial, have been accustomed and to which they naturally pay a prompt obedience. A practice which has ever struck their senses, and of which they have seen and heard innumerable precedents, has an authority with them much superior to that which attends maxims, derived from antiquated statutes and mouldy records. In vain do the lawyers establish it as a principle, that a statute can never be abrogated by opposite custom; but requires to be expressly repealed by a contrary statute: While they pretend to inculcate an axiom, peculiar to English jurisprudence, they violate the most established principles of human nature; and even, by necessary consequence, reason in contradiction to law itself, which they would represent as so sacred and inviolable. A law, to have any authority, must be derived from a legislature, which has right. And whence do all legislatures derive their right but from long custom and established practice? If a statute, contrary to public good, has, at any time, been rashly voted and assented to, either from the violence of faction, or the inexperience of senates and princes; it cannot be more effectually abrogated, than by a train of contrary precedents, which prove, that, by common consent, it has been tacitly set aside, as inconvenient and impracticable. Such has been the case with all those statutes enacted during turbulent times, in order to limit royal prerogative, and cramp the sovereign in his protection of the public, and his execution of the laws. But above all branches of prerogative, that which is most necessary to be preserved, is the power of imprisonment. Faction and discontent, like diseases, frequently arise in every political body; and during these disorders, it is by the salutary exercise alone of this discretionary power, that rebellious and civil wars can be prevented. To circumscribe this power, is to destroy its nature: Entirely to abrogate it, is impracticable; and the attempt itself must prove dangerous, if not pernicious to the public. The supreme magistrate, in critical and turbulent times, will never, agreeably either to prudence or duty, allow the state to perish, while there remains a remedy, which, how irregular soever, it is still in his power to apply. And if, moved by a regard to public good, he employs any exercise of power condemned by recent and express statute, how greedily, in such dangerous times, will factious leaders seize this pretence of throwing on his government the imputation of tyranny and despotism? Were the alternative quite necessary, it were surely much better for human society to be deprived of liberty than to be destitute of government.

CHAPTER LI

Impartial reasoners will confess, that the subject is not, on both sides, without its difficulties. Where a general and rigid law is enacted against arbitrary imprisonment, it would appear, that government cannot, in times of sedition and faction, be conducted but by temporary suspensions of the law; and such an expedient was never thought of during the age of Charles. The meetings of parliament were too precarious, and their determinations might be too dilatory, to serve in cases of urgent necessity. Nor was it then conceived, that the king did not possess of himself sufficient power for the security and protection of his people, or that the authority of these popular assemblies was ever to become so absolute, that the prince must always conform himself to it, and could never have any occasion to guard against *their* practices, as well as against those of his other subjects.

Though the house of lords was not insensible to the reasons urged in favour of the pretensions of the commons, they deemed the arguments, pleaded in favour of the crown, still more cogent and convincing. That assembly seems, during this whole period, to have acted, in the main, a reasonable and a moderate part; and if their bias inclined a little too much, as is natural, to the side of monarchy, they were far from entertaining any design of sacrificing to arbitrary will the liberties and privileges of the nation. Ashley, the king's serjeant, having asserted, in a pleading before the peers, that the king must sometimes govern by acts of state as well as by law; this position gave such offence, that he was immediately committed to prison, and was not released but upon his recantation and submission.[z] Being, however, afraid, lest the commons should go too far in their projected petition, the peers proposed a plan of one more moderate, which they recommended to the consideration of the other house. It consisted merely in a general declaration, that the great charter and the six statutes, conceived to be explanations of it, stand still in force, to all intents and purposes; that, in consequence of the charter and the statutes, and by the tenor of the ancient customs and laws of the realm, every subject has a fundamental property in his goods, and a fundamental liberty of his person; that this property and liberty are as entire at present as during any former period of the English government; that in all common cases, the common law ought to

[z] Whitlocke, p. 10.

be the standard of proceedings: "And in case, that, for the security of his majesty's person, the general safety of his people, or the peaceable government of the kingdom, the king shall find just cause, for reasons of state, to imprison or restrain any man's person; he was petitioned graciously to declare, that, within a *convenient* time, he shall and will express the cause of the commitment or restraint, either general or special, and upon a cause so expressed, will leave the prisoner immediately to be tried according to the common law of the land."[a]

Archbishop Abbot was employed by the lords to recommend, in a conference, this plan of a petition to the house of commons. The prelate, as was, no doubt, foreseen from his known principles, was not extremely urgent in his applications; and the lower house was fully convinced, that the general declarations signified nothing, and that the latter clause left their liberties rather in a worse condition than before. They proceeded, therefore, with great zeal, in framing the model of a petition, which should contain expressions, more precise, and more favourable to public freedom.

The king could easily see the consequence of these proceedings. Though he had offered at the beginning of the session, to give his consent to any law for the security of the rights and liberties of the people; he had not expected that such inroads would be made on his prerogative. In order, therefore, to divert the commons from their intention, he sent a message, wherein he acknowledged past errors, and promised, that, hereafter, there should be no just cause of complaint. And he added, "That the affairs of the kingdom press him so, that he could not continue the session above a week or two longer: And if the house be not ready, by that time, to do what is fit for themselves, it shall be their own fault."[b] On a subsequent occasion, he asked them, "Why demand explanations, if you doubt not the performance of the statutes, according to their true meaning. Explanations will hazard an encroachment upon the prerogative. And it may well be said, What need a new law to confirm an old, if you repose confidence in the declarations, which his majesty made to both houses?"[c] The truth is, the great charter and the old statutes were sufficiently clear in

---

[a] State Trials, vol. vii. p. 187. Rushworth, vol. i. p. 546.　[b] State Trials, vol. vii. p. 193.　[c] State Trials, vol. vii. p. 196. Rushworth, vol. i. p. 556.

CHAPTER LI

favour of personal liberty: But as all kings of England had ever, in cases of necessity or expediency, been accustomed, at intervals, to elude them, and as Charles, in a complication of instances, had lately violated them; the commons judged it requisite to enact a new law, which might not be eluded or violated, by any interpretation, construction, or contrary precedent. Nor was it sufficient, they thought, that the king promised to return into the way of his predecessors. His predecessors, in all times, had enjoyed too much discretionary power; and by his recent abuse of it, the whole world had reason to see the necessity of entirely retrenching it.

The king still persevered in his endeavours to elude the petition. He sent a letter to the house of lords, in which he went so far as to make a particular declaration, "That neither he nor his privy-council shall or will, at any time hereafter, commit or command to prison, or otherwise restrain, any man for not lending money, or for any other cause, which, in his conscience, he thought not to concern the public good, and the safety of king and people." And he farther declared, "That he never would be guilty of so base an action as to pretend any cause, of whose truth he was not fully satisfied."[d] But this promise, though enforced to the commons by the recommendation of the upper house, made no more impression than all the former messages.

Among the other evasions of the king, we may reckon the proposal of the house of peers, to subjoin, to the intended petition of right, the following clause. "We humbly present this petition to your majesty, not only with a care of preserving our own liberties, but with due regard to leave entire that *sovereign power,* with which your majesty is entrusted for the protection, safety and happiness of your people."[e] Less penetration, than was possessed by the leaders of the house of commons, could easily discover how captious this clause was, and how much it was calculated to elude the whole force of the petition.

These obstacles, therefore, being surmounted, the petition of right passed the commons, and was sent to the upper house.[f] The peers, who were probably well pleased in secret, that all their

[d] State Trials, vol. vii. p. 198. Rushworth, vol. i. p. 560. Parl. Hist. vol. viii. p. 111. [e] State Trials, vol. vii. p. 199. Rushworth, vol. i. p. 561. Parl. Hist. vol. viii. p. 116. Whitlocke, p. 10. [f] See note [T] at the end of the volume.

solicitations had been eluded by the commons, quickly passed the petition without any material alteration; and nothing but the royal assent was wanting to give it the force of a law. The king accordingly came to the house of peers; sent for the commons; and, being seated in his chair of state, the petition was read to him. Great was now the astonishment of all men, when, instead of the usual concise, and clear form, by which a bill is either confirmed or rejected, Charles said, in answer to the petition, "The king willeth, that right be done according to the laws and customs of the realm, and that the statutes be put into execution; that his subjects may have no cause to complain of any wrong or oppression, contrary to their just rights and liberties, to the preservation whereof he holds himself in conscience as much obliged as of his own prerogative."[g]

It is surprising, that Charles, who had seen so many instances of the jealousy of the commons, who had himself so much roused that jealousy by his frequent evasive messages during this session, could imagine that they would rest satisfied with an answer so vague and undeterminate. It was evident, that the unusual form alone of the answer must excite their attention; that the disappointment must inflame their anger; and that therefore it was necessary, as the petition seemed to bear hard on royal prerogative, to come early to some fixed resolution, either gracefully to comply with it, or courageously to reject it.

It happened as might have been forseen. The commons returned in very ill humour. Usually, when in that disposition, their zeal for religion, and their enmity against the unfortunate catholics, ran extremely high. But they had already, in the beginning of the session, presented their petition of religion, and had received a satisfactory answer; though they expected, that the execution of the laws against papists would, for the future, be no more exact and rigid, than they had hitherto found it. To give vent to their present indignation, they fell with their utmost force, on Dr. Manwaring.

There is nothing, which tends more to excuse, if not to justify, the extreme rigour of the commons towards Charles, than his open encouragement and avowal of such general principles, as were altogether incompatible with a limited government. Manwaring

[g] State Trials, vol. vii. p. 212. Rushworth, vol. i. p. 590.

had preached a sermon, which the commons found, upon enquiry, to be printed by special command of the king;[h] and, when this sermon was looked into, it contained doctrines subversive of all civil liberty. It taught, that, though property was commonly lodged in the subject, yet, whenever any exigency required supply, all property was transferred to the sovereign; that the consent of parliament was not necessary for the imposition of taxes; and that the divine laws required compliance with every demand, how irregular soever, which the prince should make upon his subjects.[i] For these doctrines the commons impeached Manwaring. The sentence, pronounced upon him by the peers, was, that he should be imprisoned during the pleasure of the house, be fined a thousand pounds to the king, make submission and acknowledgment for his offence, be suspended during three years, be incapable of holding any ecclesiastical dignity or secular office, and that his book be called in and burnt.[k]

It may be worthy of notice, that no sooner was the session ended, than this man, so justly obnoxious to both houses, received a pardon, and was promoted to a living of considerable value.[l] Some years after, he was raised to the see of St. Asaph. If the republican spirit of the commons encreased, beyond all reasonable bounds, the monarchical spirit of the court, this latter, carried to so high a pitch, tended still farther to augment the former. And thus extremes were every where affected, and the just medium was gradually deserted by all men.

From Manwaring, the house of commons proceeded to censure the conduct of Buckingham, whose name hitherto, they had cautiously foreborn to mention.[m] In vain did the king send them a message, in which he told them, that the session was drawing near to a conclusion; and desired, that they would not enter upon new business, nor cast any aspersions on his government and ministry.[n] Though the court endeavoured to explain and soften this message by a subsequent message;[o] as Charles was apt hastily to correct any hasty step, which he had taken; it served rather to inflame than

[h] Parl. Hist. vol. viii. p. 206.   [i] Rushworth, vol. i. p. 585, 594. Parl. Hist. vol. viii. p. 168, 169, 170, &c. Welwood, p. 44.   [k] Rushworth, vol. i. p. 65. Parl. Hist. vol. viii. p. 212.   [l] Rushworth, vol. i. p. 635. Whitlocke, p. 11. [m] Rushworth, vol. i. p. 607.   [n] Ibid. vol. i. p. 605.   [o] Ibid. vol. i. p. 610. Parl. Hist. vol. viii. p. 197.

appease the commons: As if the method of their proceedings had here been prescribed to them. It was foreseen, that a great tempest was ready to burst on the duke; and in order to divert it, the king thought proper, upon a joint application of the lords and commons,[p] to endeavour giving them satisfaction, with regard to the petition of right. He came, therefore, to the house of peers, and pronouncing the usual form of words, *Let it be law as is desired,* gave full sanction and authority to the petition. The acclamations, with which the house resounded, and the universal joy diffused over the nation, showed how much this petition had been the object of all men's vows and expectations.[q]

It may be affirmed, without any exaggeration, that the king's assent to the petition of right produced such a change in the government, as was almost equivalent to a revolution; and by circumscribing, in so many articles, the royal prerogative, gave additional security to the liberties of the subject. Yet were the commons far from being satisfied with this important concession. Their ill humour had been so much irritated by the king's frequent evasions and delays, that it could not be presently appeased by an assent, which he allowed to be so reluctantly extorted from him. Perhaps too, the popular leaders, implacable and artful, saw the opportunity favourable; and turning against the king those very weapons, with which he had furnished them, resolved to pursue the victory. The bill, however, for five subsidies, which had been formerly voted, immediately passed the house; because the granting of that supply was, in a manner, tacitly contracted for, upon the royal assent to the petition; and had faith been here violated, no farther confidence could have subsisted between king and parliament. Having made this concession, the commons continued to carry their scrutiny into every part of government. In some particulars, their industry was laudable; in some, it may be liable to censure.

A little after writs were issued for summoning this parliament, a commission had been granted to Sir Thomas Coventry lord keeper, the earl of Marlborough, treasurer, the earl of Manchester, president of the council, the earl of Worcester, privy seal, the duke of Buckingham, high admiral, and all the considerable

[p] Rushworth, vol. i. p. 613. Journ. 7 June, 1628. Parl. Hist. vol. viii. p. 201.
[q] Rushworth, vol. i. p. 613.

CHAPTER LI

officers of the crown, in the whole thirty-three. By this commission, which from the number of persons named in it could be no secret, the commissioners were empowered to meet, and to concert among themselves the methods of levying money by impositions, or otherwise; *Where form and circumstance,* as expressed in the commission, *must be dispensed with, rather than the substance be lost or hazarded[r]* In other words, this was a scheme for finding expedients, which might raise the prerogative to the greatest height, and render parliaments entirely useless. The commons applied for cancelling the commission;[s] and were, no doubt, desirous that all the world should conclude the king's principles to be extremely arbitrary, and should observe what little regard he was disposed to pay to the liberties and privileges of his people.

A commission had likewise been granted, and some money remitted, in order to raise a thousand German horse, and transport them into England. These were supposed to be levied, in order to support the projected impositions or excises; tho' the number seems insufficient for such a purpose.[t] The house took notice of this design in severe terms: And no measure, surely, could be projected more generally odious to the whole nation. It must, however, be confessed, that the king was so far right, that he had, now at last, fallen on the only effectual method for supporting his prerogative. But at the same time, he should have been sensible, that, till provided with a sufficient military force, all his attempts, in opposition to the rising spirit of the nation, must, in the end, prove wholly fruitless; and that the higher he screwed up the springs of government, while he had so little real power to retain them in that forced situation, with more fatal violence must they fly out, when any accident occurred to restore them to their natural action.

The commons next resumed their censure of Buckingham's conduct and behaviour, against whom they were implacable. They agreed to present a remonstrance to the king, in which they recapitulated all national grievances and misfortunes, and omitted no circumstance, which could render the whole administration despicable and odious. The compositions with catholics, they said, amounted to no less than a toleration, hateful to God, full of

---

[r] Rush. vol. i. p. 614. Parl. Hist. vol. viii. p. 214.   [s] Journ. 13 June, 1628.

dishonour and disprofit to his majesty, and of extreme scandal and grief to his good people: They took notice of the violations of liberty above-mentioned, against which the petition of right seems to have provided a sufficient remedy: They mentioned the decay of trade, the unsuccessful expeditions to Cadiz and the isle of Rhé, the encouragement given to Arminians, the commission for transporting German horse, that for levying illegal impositions; and all these grievances they ascribed solely to the ill conduct of the duke of Buckingham." This remonstrance was, perhaps, not the less provoking to Charles, because, joined to the extreme acrimony of the subject, there were preserved in it, as in most of the remonstrances of that age, an affected civility and submission in the language. And as it was the first return, which he met with for his late beneficial concessions, and for his sacrifices of prerogative, the greatest by far ever made by an English sovereign, nothing could be more the object of just and natural indignation.

It was not without good grounds, that the commons were so fierce and assuming. Though they had already granted the king the supply of five subsidies, they still retained a pledge in their hands, which, they thought, ensured them success in all their applications. Tonnage and poundage had not yet been granted by parliament; and the commons had artfully, this session, concealed their intention of invading that branch of revenue, till the royal assent had been obtained to the petition of right, which they justly deemed of such importance. They then openly asserted, that the levying of tonnage and poundage without consent of parliament, *Proro-gation. 26th June.* was a palpable violation of the ancient liberties of the people, and an open infringement of the petition of right, so lately granted." The king, in order to prevent the finishing and presenting this remonstrance, came suddenly to the parliament, and ended this session by a prorogation.*

Being freed, for some time, from the embarrassment of this assembly, Charles began to look towards foreign wars, where all his efforts were equally unsuccessful, as in his domestic government. The earl of Denbigh, brother-in-law to Buckingham, was dispatched to the relief of Rochelle, now closely besieged by land, and

^t Rush. vol. i. p. 612.   ^u Rush. vol. i. p. 619. Parl. Hist. vol. viii. 219, 220, &c.   ^w Rush. vol. i. p. 628. Journ. 18, 20 June, 1628.   ^x Journ. 26 June, 1628.

threatened with a blockade by sea: But he returned without effecting any thing; and having declined to attack the enemy's fleet, he brought on the English arms the imputation either of cowardice or ill conduct. In order to repair this dishonour, the duke went to Portsmouth, where he had prepared a considerable fleet and army, on which all the subsidies given by parliament, had been expended. This supply had very much disappointed the king's expectations. The same mutinous spirit, which prevailed in the house of commons, had diffused itself over the nation; and the commissioners, appointed for making the assessments, had connived at all frauds, which might diminish the supply, and reduce the crown to still greater necessities. This national discontent, communicated to a desperate enthusiast, soon broke out in an event, which may be considered as remarkable.

There was one Felton, of a good family, but of an ardent, melancholic temper, who had served under the duke, in the station of lieutenant. His captain being killed in the retreat at the isle of Rhé, Felton had applied for the company; and when disappointed, he threw up his commission, and retired in discontent from the army. While private resentment was boiling in his sullen, unsociable mind, he heard the nation resound with complaints against the duke; and he met with the remonstrance of the commons, in which his enemy was represented as the cause of every national grievance, and as the great enemy of the public. Religious fanaticism farther inflamed these vindictive reflections; and he fancied, that he should do heaven acceptable service, if, at one blow, he dispatched this dangerous foe to religion and to his country.[y] Full of these dark views he secretly arrived at Portsmouth, at the same time with the duke, and watched for an opportunity of effecting his bloody purpose.

Buckingham had been engaged in conversation with Soubize and other French gentlemen; and a difference of sentiment having arisen, the dispute, though conducted with temper and decency, had produced some of those vehement gesticulations and lively exertions of voice, in which that nation, more than the English, are apt to indulge themselves. The conversation being finished, the duke drew towards the door; and in that passage, turning himself

[y] May's Hist. of the Parliament, p. 10.

to speak to Sir Thomas Fryar, a colonel in the army, he was, on the sudden, over Sir Thomas's shoulder, struck upon the breast with a knife. Without uttering other words than *The villain has killed me;* in the same moment, pulling out the knife, he breathed his last.

Death of Buckingham.

No man had seen the blow, nor the person who gave it; but in the confusion, every one made his own conjecture; and all agreed, that the murder had been committed by the French gentlemen, whose angry tone of voice had been heard, while their words had not been understood by the bystanders. In the hurry of revenge, they had instantly been put to death, had they not been saved by some of more temper and judgement, who, though they had the same opinion of their guilt, thought proper to reserve them for a judicial trial and examination.

Near the door, there was found a hat, in the inside of which was sewed a paper, containing four or five lines of that remonstrance of the commons, which declared Buckingham an enemy to the kingdom; and under these lines was a short ejaculation, or attempt towards a prayer. It was easily concluded that this hat belonged to the assassin: But the difficulty still remained *Who that person should be?* For the writing discovered not the name, and whoever he was, it was natural to believe, that he had already fled far enough not to be found without a hat.

In this hurry, a man without a hat was seen walking very composedly before the door. One crying out, *Here is the fellow, who killed the duke;* every body ran to ask, *Which is he?* The man very sedately answered, *I am he.* The more furious immediately rushed upon him with drawn swords: Others, more deliberate, defended and protected him: He himself, with open arms, calmly and chearfully exposed his breast to the swords of the most enraged; being willing to fall a sudden sacrifice to their anger, rather than be reserved for that public justice, which, he knew, must be executed upon him.

He was now known to be that Felton, who had served in the army. Being carried into a private room, it was thought proper so far to dissemble as to tell him, that Buckingham was only grievously wounded, but not without hopes of recovery. Felton smiled and told them, that the duke, he knew full well, had received a blow, which had terminated all their hopes. When asked, at whose instigation he had performed that horrid deed? He replyed, that they needed not to trouble themselves in that enquiry; that no man living had credit enough with him to have disposed him to such an action; that he had not even entrusted his purpose to any one; that the resolution proceeded only from himself, and the impulse of his own conscience; and that his motives would appear, if his hat were found: For that, believing he should perish in the attempt, he had there taken care to explain them.[z]

When the king was informed of this assassination, he received the news in public with an unmoved and undisturbed countenance; and the courtiers, who studied his looks, concluded, that secretly he was not displeased to be rid of a minster, so generally odious to the nation.[a] But Charles's command of himself proceeded entirely from the gravity and composure of his temper. He was still, as much as ever, attached to his favourite; and, during his whole life, he retained an affection for Buckingham's friends, and a prejudice against his enemies. He urged, too, that Felton should be put to the question, in order to extort from him a discovery of his accomplices: But the judges declared, that, though that practice had formerly been very usual, it was altogether illegal. So much more exact reasoners, with regard to law, had they become, from the jealous scruples of the house of commons.

Meanwhile the distress of Rochelle had risen to the utmost extremity. That vast genius of Richlieu, which made him form the greatest enterprizes, led him to attempt their execution, by means equally great and extraordinary. In order to deprive Rochelle of all succour, he had dared to project the throwing across the harbour a mole of a mile's extent in that boisterous ocean; and having executed his project, he now held the town closely blockaded on all sides. The inhabitants, though pressed with the greatest rigours of famine, still refused to submit; being supported, partly by the lectures of their zealous preachers, partly by the daily hopes of relief from England. After Buckingham's death, the command of the fleet and army was conferred on the earl of Lindesey; who, arriving before Rochelle, made some attempts to break through the mole, and force his way into the harbour: But by the delays of the English, that work was now fully finished and fortified; and the Rochellers, finding their last hopes to fail them, were reduced to surrender at discretion, even in sight of the English admiral. Of

18th October.

[z] Clarendon, vol. i. p. 27, 28.   [a] Warwick, p. 34.

fifteen thousand persons, shut up in the city, four thousand alone survived the fatigues and famine, which they had undergone.[b]

This was the first necessary step towards the prosperity of France. Foreign enemies, as well as domestic factions, being deprived of this resource, that kingdom began now to shine forth in its full splendour. By a steddy prosecution of wise plans, both of war and policy, it gradually gained an ascendant over the rival power of Spain; and every order of the state, and every sect, were reduced to pay submission to the lawful authority of the sovereign. The victory, however, over the Hugonots was, at first, pushed by the French king with great moderation. A toleration was still continued to them; the only avowed and open toleration, which, at that time, was granted in any European kingdom.

1629.

The failure of an enterprize, in which the English nation, from religious sympathy, so much interested themselves, could not but diminish the king's authority in the parliament during the approaching session: But the commons, when assembled, found many other causes of complaint. Buckingham's conduct and character, with some had afforded a reason, with others a pretence, for discontent against public measures: But after his death, there wanted not new reasons and new pretences, for general dissatisfaction. Manwaring's pardon and promotion were taken notice of: Sibthorpe and Cosins, two clergymen, who, for like reasons, were no less obnoxious to the commons, had met with like favour from the king: Montague, who had been censured for moderation towards the catholics, the greatest of crimes, had been created bishop of Chichester. They found, likewise, upon enquiry, that all the copies of the petition of right, which were dispersed, had, by the king's orders, annexed to them the first answer, which had given so little satisfaction to the commons:[c] An expedient, by which Charles endeavoured to persuade the people, that he had nowise receded from his former claims and pretensions, particularly with regard to the levying of tonnage and poundage. Selden also complained in the house, that one Savage, contrary to the petition of right, had been punished with the loss of his ears, by a discretionary or arbitrary sentence of the star-chamber.[d] So apt were

20 January. New session of parliament.

---

[b] Rush. vol. i. p. 636.   [c] State Trials, vol. vii. p. 216. Rush. vol. i. p. 643.
[d] State Trials, vol. vii. p. 216. Parl. Hist. vol. viii. p. 246.

CHAPTER LI

they on their part, to stretch the petition into such consequences as might deprive the crown of powers, which, from immemorial custom, were supposed inherent in it.

But the great article, on which the house of commons broke with the king, and which finally created in Charles a disgust to all parliaments, was their claim with regard to tonnage and poundage. On this occasion, therefore, it is necessary to give an account of the controversy. *Tonnage and poundage.*

The duty of tonnage and poundage, in more ancient times, had been commonly a temporary grant of parliament; but it had been conferred on Henry V. and all the succeeding princes, during life, in order to enable them to maintain a naval force for the defence of the kingdom. The necessity of levying this duty had been so apparent, that each king had ever claimed it from the moment of his accession; and the first parliament of each reign had usually by vote conferred on the prince what they found him already in possession of. Agreeably to the inaccurate genius of the old constitution, this abuse, however considerable, had never been perceived nor remedied; though nothing could have been easier than for the parliament to have prevented it.[e] By granting this duty to each prince, during his own life, and, for a year after his demise, to the successor, all inconveniencies had been obviated; and yet the duty had never, for a moment, been levied without proper authority. But contrivances of that nature were not thought of during those rude ages: And as so complicated and jealous a government as the English cannot subsist without many such refinements; it is easy to see, how favourable every inaccuracy must formerly have proved to royal authority, which, on all emergencies, was obliged to supply, by discretionary power, the great deficiency of the laws.

The parliament did not grant the duty of tonnage and poundage to Henry VIII. till the sixth of his reign: Yet this prince, who had not then raised his power to its greatest height, continued, during that whole time, to levy the imposition: The parliament, in their very grant, blame the merchants, who had neglected to make payment to the crown; and though one expression of that bill may seem ambiguous, they employ the plainest terms in calling tonnage and poundage the king's due, even before that duty was

[e] Parl. Hist. vol. viii. p. 339, 340.

conferred on him by parliamentary authority.[f] Four reigns, and above a whole century, had since elapsed; and this revenue had still been levied before it was voted by parliament. So long had the inaccuracy continued, without being remarked or corrected!

During that short interval, which passed, between Charles's accession and his first parliament, he had followed the example of his predecessors; and no fault was found with his conduct in this particular. But what was most remarkable in the proceedings of that house of commons, and what proved beyond controversy, that they had seriously formed a plan for reducing their prince to subjection, was, that, instead of granting this supply during the king's life-time, as it had been enjoyed by all his immediate predecessors, they voted it only for a year; and, after that should be elapsed, reserved to themselves the power of renewing or refusing the same concession.[g] But the house of peers, who saw, that this duty was now become more necessary than ever to supply the growing necessities of the crown, and who did not approve of this encroaching spirit in the commons, rejected the bill; and the dissolution of that parliament followed so soon after, that no attempt seems to have been made for obtaining tonnage and poundage in any other form.[h]

Charles, meanwhile, continued still to levy this duty by his own authority; and the nation was so accustomed to that exertion of royal power, that no scruple was at first entertained of submitting to it. But the succeeding parliament excited doubts in every one. The commons took there some steps towards declaring it illegal to levy tonnage and poundage without consent of parliament; and they openly showed their intention of employing this engine, in order to extort from the crown concessions of the most important nature. But Charles was not yet sufficiently tamed to compliance; and the abrupt dissolution of that parliament, as above related, put an end, for the time, to their farther pretensions.

The following interval, between the second and third parliament, was distinguished by so many exertions of prerogative, that men had little leisure to attend to the affair of tonnage and pound-

---

[f] 6 Henry VIII. cap. 14.   [g] Journ. 5 July, 1625.   [h] See note [U] at the end of the volume.

CHAPTER LI

age, where the abuse of power in the crown might seem to be of a more disputable nature. But after the commons, during the precedent session, had remedied all these grievances by means of their petition of right, which they deemed so necessary; they afterwards proceeded to take the matter into consideration, and they showed the same intention, as formerly, of exacting, in return for the grant of this revenue, very large compliances on the part of the crown. Their sudden prorogation prevented them from bringing their pretensions to a full conclusion.

When Charles opened this session, he had foreseen, that the same controversy would arise; and he therefore took care, very early, among many mild and reconciling expressions, to inform the commons, "That he had not taken these duties as appertaining to his hereditary prerogative; but that it ever was, and still is, his meaning to enjoy them as a gift of his people: And that, if he had hitherto levied tonnage and poundage, he pretended to justify himself only by the necessity of so doing, not by any right which he assumed."[i] This concession, which probably arose from the king's moderate temper, now freed from the impulse of Buckingham's violent counsels, might have satisfied the commons, had they entertained no other view than that of ascertaining their own powers and privileges. But they carried their pretensions much higher. They insisted, as a necessary preliminary, that the king should once entirely desist from levying these duties; after which, they were to take it into consideration, how far they would restore him to the possession of a revenue, of which he had clearly divested himself. But besides that this extreme rigour had never been exercised towards any of his predecessors, and many obvious inconveniencies must follow from the intermission of the customs; there were other reasons, which deterred Charles from complying with so hard a condition. It was probable, that the commons might renew their former project of making this revenue only temporary, and thereby reducing their prince to perpetual dependence; they certainly would cut off the new impositions, which Mary and Elizabeth, but especially James, had levied, and which formed no despicable part of the public revenue; and they openly declared,

[i] Rushworth, vol. i. p. 644. Parl. Hist. vol. viii. p. 256, 346.

that they had, at present, many important pretensions, chiefly with regard to religion; and if compliance were refused, no supply must be expected from the commons.

It is easy to see in what an inextricable labyrinth Charles was now involved. By his own concessions, by the general principles of the English government, and by the form of every bill, which had granted this duty, tonnage and poundage was derived entirely from the free gift of the people; and, consequently, might be withdrawn at their pleasure. If unreasonable in their refusal, they still refused nothing but what was their own. If public necessity required this supply, it might be thought also to require the king's compliance with those conditions, which were the price of obtaining it. Though the motive for granting it had been the enabling of the king to guard the seas; it did not follow, that, because he guarded the seas, he was therefore entitled to this revenue, without farther formality: Since the people had still reserved to themselves the right of judging how far that service merited such a supply. But Charles, notwithstanding his public declaration, was far from assenting to this conclusion, in its full extent. The plain consequence, he saw, of all these rigours, and refinements, and inferences, was, that he, without any public necessity, and without any fault of his own, must of a sudden, even from his accession, become a magistrate of a very different nature from any of his predecessors, and must fall into a total dependence on subjects, over whom former kings, especially those immediately preceding, had exercised an authority almost unlimited. Entangled in a chain of consequences, which he could not easily break, he was inclined to go higher, and rather deny the first principle, than admit of conclusions, which to him appeared so absurd and unreasonable. Agreeably to the ideas hitherto entertained both by natives and foreigners, the monarch he esteemed the essence and soul of the English government; and whatever other power pretended to annihilate or even abridge the royal authority, must necessarily, he thought, either in its nature or exercise, be deemed no better than a usurpation. Willing to preserve the ancient harmony of the constitution, he had ever intended to comply, as far as he *easily* could, with the ancient forms of administration: But when these forms appeared to him, by the inveterate obstinacy of the commons, to have no other tendency than to disturb that harmony, and to

CHAPTER LI

introduce a new constitution; he concluded, that, in this violent situation, what was subordinate must necessarily yield to what was principal, and the privileges of the people, for a time, give place to royal prerogative. From the rank of a monarch, to be degraded into a slave of his insolent, ungrateful subjects, seemed, of all indignities, the greatest; and nothing, in his judgment, could exceed the humiliation attending such a state, but the meanness of tamely submitting to it, without making some efforts to preserve the authority transmitted to him by his predecessors.

Though these were the king's reflections and resolutions before the parliament assembled, he did not immediately break with them, upon their delay in voting him this supply. He thought, that he could better justify any strong measure, which he might afterwards be obliged to take, if he allowed them to carry to the utmost extremities their attacks upon his government and prerogative.[k] He contented himself, for the present, with soliciting the house by messages and speeches. But the commons, instead of hearkening to his solicitations, proceeded to carry their scrutiny into his management of religion,[l] which was the only grievance, to which, in their opinion, they had not as yet, by their petition of right, applied a sufficient remedy.

It was not possible, that this century, so fertile in religious sects and disputes, could escape the controversy concerning fatalism and free-will, which, being strongly interwoven both with philosophy and theology, had, in all ages, thrown every school and every church into such inextricable doubt and perplexity. The first reformers in England, as in other European countries, had embraced the most rigid tenets of predestination and absolute decrees, and had composed, upon that system, all the articles of their religious creed. But these principles having met with opposition from Arminius and his sectaries, the controversy was soon brought into this island, and began here to diffuse itself. The Arminians, finding more encouragement from the superstitious spirit of the church than from the fanaticism of the puritans, gradually incorporated themselves with the former; and some of that sect, by the indulgence of James and Charles, had attained the highest preferments in the hierarchy. But their success with the public had not

Arminian-ism.

___

[k] Rushworth, vol. i. p. 642.   [l] Idem, ibid. p. 651. Whitlocke, p. 12.

been altogether answerable to that which they met with in the church and the court. Throughout the nation, they still lay under the reproach of innovation and heresy. The commons now levelled against them their formidable censures, and made them the objects of daily invective and declamation. Their protectors were stigmatized; their tenets canvassed; their views represented as dangerous and pernicious. To impartial spectators surely, if any such had been at that time in England, it must have given great entertainment, to see a popular assembly, enflamed with faction and enthusiasm, pretend to discuss questions, to which the greatest philosophers, in the tranquillity of retreat, had never hitherto been able to find any satisfactory solution.

Amidst that complication of disputes, in which men were then involved, we may observe, that the appellation *puritan* stood for three parties, which, though commonly united, were yet actuated by very different views and motives. There were the political puritans, who maintained the highest principles of civil liberty; the puritans in discipline, who were averse to the ceremonies and episcopal government of the church; and the doctrinal puritans, who rigidly defended the speculative system of the first reformers. In opposition to all these stood the court party, the hierarchy, and the Arminians; only with this distinction, that the latter sect, being introduced a few years before, did not as yet comprehend all those who were favourable to the church and to monarchy. But, as the controversies on every subject grew daily warmer, men united themselves more intimately with their friends, and separated themselves wider from their antagonists; and the distinction gradually became quite uniform and regular.

This house of commons, which, like all the preceding, during the reigns of James and Charles, and even of Elizabeth, was much governed by the puritanical party, thought that they could not better serve their cause, than by branding and punishing the Arminian sect, which, introducing an innovation in the church, were the least favoured and least powerful of all their antagonists. From this measure, it was easily foreseen, that, besides gratifying the animosity of the doctrinal puritans, both the puritans in discipline and those in politics would reap considerable advantages. Laud, Neile, Montague, and other bishops, who were the chief supporters of episcopal government, and the most zealous partizans of the

CHAPTER LI

discipline and ceremonies of the church, were all supposed to be tainted with Arminianism. The same men and their disciples were the strenuous preachers of passive obedience, and of entire submission to princes; and if these could once be censured, and be expelled the church and court, it was concluded, that the hierarchy would receive a mortal blow, the ceremonies be less rigidly insisted on, and the king, deprived of his most faithful friends, be obliged to abate those high claims of prerogative, on which at present he insisted.

But Charles, besides a view of the political consequences, which must result from a compliance with such pretensions, was strongly determined, from principles of piety and conscience, to oppose them. Neither the dissipation incident to youth, nor the pleasures attending a high fortune, had been able to prevent this virtuous prince from embracing the most sincere sentiments of religion; and that character, which, in that religious age, should have been of infinite advantage to him, proved in the end the chief cause of his ruin: Merely because the religion, adopted by him, was not of that precise mode and sect, which *began* to prevail among his subjects. His piety, though remote from popery, had a tincture of superstition in it; and, being averse to the gloomy spirit of the puritans, was represented by them as tending towards the abominations of antichrist. Laud also had unfortunately acquired a great ascendant over him: And as all those prelates, obnoxious to the commons, were regarded as his chief friends and most favoured courtiers; he was resolved not to disarm and dishonour himself, by abandoning them to the resentment of his enemies. Being totally unprovided with military force, and finding a refractory independent spirit to prevail among the people; the most solid basis of his authority, he thought, consisted in the support, which he received from the hierarchy.

In the debates of the commons, which are transmitted to us, it is easy to discern so early some sparks of that enthusiastic fire, which afterwards set the whole nation in combustion. One Rouse made use of an allusion, which, though familiar, seems to have been borrowed from the writings of lord Bacon.[m] "If a man meet a dog alone," said he, "the dog is fearful, though ever so fierce by

---

[m] Essay of Atheism.   [n] Rushworth, vol. i. p. 646. Parl. Hist. vol. viii. p. 260.

nature: But, if the dog have his master with him, he will set upon that man, from whom he fled before. This shows, that lower natures, being backed by higher, encrease in courage and strength, and certainly man, being backed with Omnipotency, is a kind of omnipotent creature. All things are possible to him that believes; and where all things are possible, there is a kind of omnipotency. Wherefore, let it be the unanimous consent and resolution of us all to make a vow and covenant henceforth to hold fast our God and our religion; and then shall we henceforth expect with certainty happiness in this world."[n]

Oliver Cromwell, at that time a young man of no account in the nation, is mentioned in these debates, as complaining of one, who, he was told, preached flat popery.[o] It is amusing to observe the first words of this fanatical hypocrite correspond so exactly to his character.

The enquiries and debates concerning tonnage and poundage went hand in hand with these theological or metaphysical controversies. The officers of the custom-house were summoned before the commons, to give an account by what authority they had seized the goods of merchants, who had refused to pay these duties: The barons of the exchequer were questioned concerning their decrees on that head.[p] One of the sheriffs of London was committed to the Tower for his activity in supporting the officers of the custom-house: The goods of Rolles, a merchant, and member of the house, being seized for his refusal to pay the duties, complaints were made of this violence, as if it were a breach of privilege:[q] Charles supported his officers in all these measures; and the quarrel grew every day higher between him and the commons.[r] Mention was made in the house of impeaching Sir Richard Weston, the treasurer;[s] and the king began to entertain thoughts of finishing the session by a dissolution.

Sir John Elliot framed a remonstrance against levying tonnage and poundage without consent of parliament, and offered it to the clerk to read. It was refused. He read it himself. The question being then called for, the speaker, Sir John Finch, said, *That he had*

---

[o] Rushworth, vol. i. p. 655. Parl. Hist. vol. viii. p. 289. [p] Rushworth, vol. i. p. 654. Parl. Hist. vol. viii. p. 301. [q] Rushworth, vol. i. p. 653. [r] Ibid. p. 658. [s] Parl. Hist. vol. viii. p. 326.

CHAPTER LI

a command from the king to adjourn, and to put no question.[t] Upon
which he rose and left the chair. The whole house was in an
uproar. The speaker was pushed back into the chair, and forcibly
held in it by Hollis and Valentine; till a short remonstrance was
framed, and was passed by acclamation rather than by vote. Papists
and Arminians were there declared capital enemies to the commonwealth. Those, who levied tonnage and poundage, were
branded with the same epithet. And even the merchants who
should voluntarily pay these duties, were denominated betrayers
of English liberty, and public enemies. The doors being locked, the
gentleman usher of the house of lords, who was sent by the king,
could not get admittance till this remonstrance was finished. By
the king's order, he took the mace from the table, which ended
their proceedings.[u] And a few days after the parliament was
dissolved.

Dissolution of the parliament. March 10.

The discontents of the nation ran high, on account of this
violent rupture between the king and parliament. These discontents Charles inflamed by his affectation of a severity, which he
had not power, nor probably inclination, to carry to extremities.
Sir Miles Hobart, Sir Peter Heyman, Selden, Coriton, Long,
Strode, were committed to prison, on account of the last tumult in
the house, which was called sedition.[w] With great difficulty, and
after several delays, they were released; and the law was generally
supposed to be wrested, in order to prolong their imprisonment.
Sir John Elliot, Hollis, and Valentine, were summoned to their
trial in the king's bench, for seditious speeches and behaviour in
parliament; but refusing to answer before an inferior court for
their conduct, as members of a superior, they were condemned to
be imprisoned during the king's pleasure, to find sureties for their
good behaviour, and to be fined, the two former a thousand
pounds a-piece, the latter five hundred.[x] This sentence, procured

---

[t] The king's power of adjourning as well as proroguing the parliament, was
and is never questioned. In the 19th of the late king, the judges determined, that the adjournment by the king kept the parliament *in statu quo*
until the next sitting; but that then no committees were to meet: But if the
adjournment be by the house, then the committees and other matters do
continue. Parl. Hist vol. v. p. 466.   [u] Rushworth, vol. i. p. 660. Whitlocke,
p. 12.   [w] Rushworth, vol. i. p. 661, 681. Parl. Hist. vol. viii. p. 354. May,
p. 13.   [x] Rushworth, vol. i. p. 684, 691.

by the influence of the crown, served only to show the king's disregard to the privileges of parliament, and to acquire an immense stock of popularity to the sufferers, who had so bravely, in opposition to arbitrary power, defended the liberties of their native country. The commons of England, though an immense body, and possessed of the greater part of national property, were naturally somewhat defenceless; because of their personal equality and their want of leaders: But the king's severity, if these prosecutions deserve the name, here pointed out leaders to them, whose resentment was inflamed, and whose courage was no-wise daunted, by the hardships, which they had undergone in so honourable a cause.

So much did these prisoners glory in their sufferings, that, though they were promised liberty on that condition, they would not condescend even to present a petition to the king, expressing their sorrow for having offended him.[y] They unanimously refused to find sureties for their good behaviour; and disdained to accept of deliverance on such easy terms. Nay, Hollis was so industrious to continue his meritorious distress, that, when one offered to bail him, he would not yield to the rule of court, and be himself bound with his friend. Even Long, who had actually found sureties in the chief justice's chamber, declared in court, that his sureties should no longer continue.[z] Yet because Sir John Elliot happened to die while in custody, a great clamour was raised against the administration; and he was universally regarded as a martyr to the liberties of England.[a]

[y] Whitlocke, p. 13.   [z] Kennet, vol. iii. p. 49.   [a] Rushworth, vol. v. p. 440.

LII

Peace with France – Peace with Spain – State of the court and ministry – Character of the queen – Strafford – Laud – Innovations in the church – Irregular levies of money – Severities in the star-chamber and high commission – Ship money – Trial of Hambden

⚜ ⚜ ⚜

THERE NOW OPENS to us a new scene. Charles, naturally disgusted with parliaments, who, he found, were determined to proceed against him with unmitigated rigour, both in invading his prerogative, and refusing him all supply, resolved not to call any more, till he should see greater indications of a compliant disposition in the nation. Having lost his great favourite, Buckingham, he became his own minister; and never afterwards reposed in any one such unlimited confidence. As he chiefly follows his own genius and disposition, his measures are henceforth less rash and hasty; though the general tenor of his administration still wants somewhat of being entirely legal, and perhaps more of being entirely prudent.

We shall endeavour to exhibit a just idea of the events which followed for some years; so far as they regard foreign affairs, the state of the court, and the government of the nation. The incidents are neither numerous nor illustrious; but the knowledge of them is necessary for understanding the subsequent transactions, which are so memorable.

Charles, destitute of all supply, was necessarily reduced to embrace a measure, which ought to have been the result of reason and sound policy: He made peace with the two crowns, against which he had hitherto waged a war, entered into without necessity, and conducted without glory. Notwithstanding the distracted and helpless condition of England, no attempt was made either by France or Spain, to invade their enemy; nor did they entertain any farther project, than to defend themselves against the feeble and ill-concerted expeditions of that kingdom. Pleased that the jealousies and quarrels between king and parliament had disarmed so formidable a power, they carefully avoided any enterprize, which might rouze either the terror or anger of the English, and dispose them to domestic union and submission. The endeavours to regain the good-will of the nation were carried so far by the king of Spain, that he generously released and sent home all the English prisoners taken in the expedition against Cadiz. The example was *Peace with* imitated by France, after the retreat of the English from the isle of *France and* Rhé. When princes were in such dispositions, and had so few *Spain.* pretensions on each other, it could not be difficult to conclude a peace. The treaty was first signed with France.[b] The situation of the king's affairs did not entitle him to demand any conditions for the Hugonots, and they were abandoned to the will of their sov-*14th April.* ereign. Peace was afterwards concluded with Spain; where no conditions were made in favour of the Palatine, except that Spain *1630.* promised in general to use their good offices for his restoration.[c] *5th Nov.* The influence of these two wars on domestic affairs, and on the dispositions of king and people, was of the utmost consequence: But no alteration was made by them on the foreign interests of the kingdom.

Nothing more happy can be imagined than the situation, in which England then stood with regard to foreign affairs. Europe was divided between the rival families of Bourbon and Austria, whose opposite interests, and still more their mutual jealousies, secured the tranquillity of this island. Their forces were so nearly

---

[b] Rushworth, vol. ii. p. 23, 24.   [c] Idem ibid. p. 75. Whitlocke, p. 14.

CHAPTER LII

counterpoised, that no apprehensions were entertained of any event, which could suddenly disturb the balance of power between them. The Spanish monarch, deemed the most powerful, lay at greatest distance: and the English, by that means, possessed the advantage of being engaged by political motives into a more intimate union and confederacy with the neighbouring potentate. The dispersed situation of the Spanish dominions rendered the naval power of England formidable to them, and kept that empire in continual dependence. France, more vigorous and more compact, was every day rising in policy and discipline; and reached at last an equality of power with the house of Austria: But her progress, slow and gradual, left it still in the power of England, by a timely interposition to check her superiority. And thus Charles, could he have avoided all dissentions with his own subjects, was in a situation to make himself be courted and respected by every power in Europe; and, what has scarcely ever since been attained by the princes of this island, he could either be active with dignity, or neutral with security.

A neutrality was embraced by the king; and, during the rest of his reign, he seems to have little regarded foreign affairs, except so far as he was engaged by honour, and by friendship for his sister and the Palatine, to endeavour the procuring of some relief for that unhappy family. He joined his good offices to those of France, and mediated a peace between the kings of Sweden and Poland, in hopes of engaging the former to embrace the protection of the oppressed protestants in the empire. This was the famed Gustavus, whose heroic genius, seconded by the wisest policy, made him in a little time the most distinguished monarch of the age, and rendered his country, formerly unknown and neglected, of great weight in the balance of Europe. To encourage and assist him in his projected invasion of Germany, Charles agreed to furnish him with six thousand men; but, that he might preserve the appearance of neutrality, he made use of the marquis of Hamilton's name.[d] That nobleman entered into an engagement with Gustavus; and enlisting these troops in England and Scotland at Charles's expence, he landed them in the Elbe. The decisive battle of Leipsic was fought soon after; where the conduct of Tilly and

[d] Rushworth, vol. i. p. 46, 53, 62, 83.

the valour of the Imperialists were overcome by the superior conduct of Gustavus and the superior valour of the Swedes. What remained of this hero's life was one continued series of victory, for which he was less beholden to fortune, than to those personal endowments, which he derived from nature and from industry. That rapid progress of conquest, which we so much admire in ancient history, was here renewed in modern annals; and without that cause, to which, in former ages, it had ever been owing. Military nations were not now engaged against an undisciplined and unwarlike people; nor heroes set in opposition to cowards. The veteran troops of Ferdinand, conducted by the most celebrated generals of the age, were foiled in every encounter, and all Germany was over-run in an instant by the victorious Swede. But by this extraordinary and unexpected success of his ally, Charles failed of the purpose, for which he framed the alliance. Gustavus, elated by prosperity, began to form more extensive plans of ambition; and in freeing Germany from the yoke of Ferdinand, he intended to reduce it to subjection under his own. He refused to restore the Palatine to his principality, except on conditions, which would have kept him in total dependence.[e] And thus the negociation was protracted; till the battle of Lutzen, where the Swedish monarch perished in the midst of a complete victory, which he obtained over his enemies.

We have carried on these transactions a few years beyond the present period, that we might not be obliged to return to them; nor be henceforth interrupted in our account of Charles's court and kingdoms.

State of the court and ministry.

When we consider Charles as presiding in his court, as associating with his family, it is difficult to imagine a character at once more respectable and more amiable. A kind husband, an indulgent father, a gentle master, a stedfast friend; to all these eulogies, his conduct in private life fully intitled him. As a monarch too, in the exterior qualities, he excelled; in the essential, he was not defective. His address and manner, though perhaps inclining a little towards stateliness and formality, in the main corresponded to his high rank, and gave grace to that reserve and gravity, which were natural to him. The moderation and equity, which shone forth in

[e] Franklyn, vol. i. p. 415.

CHAPTER LII

his temper, *seemed* to secure him against rash and dangerous enterprizes: The good sense, which he displayed in his discourse and
conversation, *seemed* to warrant his success in every reasonable
undertaking. Other endowments likewise he had attained, which,
in a private gentleman, would have been highly ornamental, and
which, in a great monarch, might have proved extremely useful to
his people. He was possessed of an excellent taste in all the fine
arts; and the love of painting was in some degree his favourite
passion. Learned beyond what is common in princes, he was a
good judge of writing in others, and enjoyed, himself, no mean
talent in composition. In any other age or nation, this monarch
had been secure of a prosperous and a happy reign. But the high
idea of his own authority, which he had imbibed, made him incapable of giving way to the spirit of liberty, which *began* to prevail
among his subjects. His politics were not supported by such vigour
and foresight as might enable him to subdue their pretensions, and
maintain his prerogative at the high pitch, to which it had been
raised by his predecessors. And above all, the spirit of enthusiasm,
being universally diffused, disappointed all the views of human
prudence, and disturbed the operation of every motive, which
usually influences society.

But the misfortunes, arising from these causes, were yet remote. Charles now enjoyed himself in the full exercise of his authority, in a social intercourse with his friends and courtiers, and
in a moderate use of those pleasures, which he most affected.

After the death of Buckingham, who had somewhat alienated *Character*
Charles from the queen, she is to be considered as his chief friend *of the*
and favourite. That rustic contempt of the fair sex, which James *queen.*
affected, and which, banishing them from his court, made it resemble more a fair or an exchange, than the seat of a great prince,
was very wide of the disposition of this monarch. But though full
of complaisance to the whole sex, Charles reserved all his passion
for his consort, to whom he attached himself with unshaken fidelity and confidence. By her sense and spirit, as well as by her
beauty, she justified the fondness of her husband; though it is
allowed, that, being somewhat of a passionate temper, she precipitated him into hasty and imprudent measures. Her religion, likewise, to which she was much addicted, must be regarded as a great
misfortune; since it augmented the jealousy, which prevailed

against the court, and engaged her to procure for the catholics some indulgences, which were generally distasteful to the nation.[f]

In the former situation of the English government, when the sovereign was in a great measure independent of his subjects, the king chose his ministers, either from personal favour, or from an opinion of their abilities; without any regard to their parliamentary interest or talents. It has since been the maxim of princes, wherever popular leaders encroach too much on royal authority, to confer offices on them; in expectation that they will afterwards become more careful not to diminish that power, which has become their own. These politics were now embraced by Charles; a sure proof that a secret revolution had happened in the constitution, and had necessitated the prince to adopt new maxims of government.[g] But the views of the king were at this time so repugnant to those of the puritans, that the leaders, whom he gained, lost, from that moment, all interest with their party, and were even pursued as traitors, with implacable hatred and resent-

Strafford. ment. This was the case with Sir Thomas Wentworth, whom the king created, first a baron, then a viscount, and afterwards earl of Strafford; made him president of the council of York; and deputy of Ireland; and regarded him as his chief minister and counsellor. By his eminent talents and abilities, Strafford merited all the confidence, which his master reposed in him: His character was stately and austere; more fitted to procure esteem than love: His fidelity to the king was unshaken; but as he now employed all his counsels to support the prerogative, which he had formerly bent all his endeavours to diminish, his virtue seems not to have been entirely pure, but to have been susceptible of strong impressions from private interest and ambition. Sir Dudley Digges was about the same time created master of the rolls: Noy, attorney-general: Littleton, solicitor-general. All these had likewise been parliamentary leaders; and were men eminent in their profession.[h]

Laud. In all ecclesiastical affairs, and even in many civil, Laud, bishop of London, had great influence over the king. This man was virtuous, if severity of manners alone and abstinence from pleasure, could deserve that name. He was learned, if polemical knowledge

---

[f] May, p. 21. [g] Sir Edw. Walker, p. 328. [h] Whitlocke, p. 13. May, p. 20.

CHAPTER LII

could intitle him to that praise. He was disinterested, but with unceasing industry he studied to exalt the priestly and prelatical character, which was his own. His zeal was unrelenting in the cause of religion; that is, in imposing, by rigorous measures, his own tenets and pious ceremonies on the obstinate puritans, who had profanely dared to oppose him. In prosecution of his holy purposes, he overlooked every human consideration; or, in other words, the heat and indiscretion of his temper made him neglect the views of prudence and rules of good manners. He was in this respect happy, that all his enemies were also imagined by him the declared enemies to loyalty and true piety, and that every exercise of his anger, by that means, became in his eyes a merit and a virtue. This was the man who acquired so great an ascendant over Charles, and who led him, by the facility of his temper, into a conduct, which proved so fatal to himself and to his kingdoms.

The humour of the nation ran at that time into the extreme opposite to superstition; and it was with difficulty that the ancient ceremonies, to which men had been accustomed, and which had been sanctified by the practice of the first reformers, could be retained in divine service: Yet was this the time which Laud chose for the introduction of new ceremonies and observances. Besides that these were sure to displease as innovations, there lay, in the opinion of the public, another very forcible objection against them. Laud, and the other prelates who embraced his measures, were generally well-instructed in sacred antiquity, and had adopted many of those religious sentiments, which prevailed during the fourth and fifth centuries; when the Christian church, as is well known, was already sunk into those superstitions, which were afterwards continued and augmented by the policy of Rome. The revival, therefore, of the ideas and practices of that age, could not fail of giving the English faith and liturgy some resemblance to the catholic superstition, which the kingdom in general, and the puritans in particular, held in the greatest horror and detestation. Men also were apt to think, that without some secret purpose, such insignificant observances would not be imposed with such unrelenting zeal on the refractory nation; and that Laud's scheme was to lead back the English, by gradual steps, to the religion of their ancestors. They considered not, that the very insignificancy of these ceremonies recommended them to the superstitious prel-

Innovations in the church.

ate, and made them appear the more peculiarly sacred and religious, as they could serve to no other purpose. Nor was the resemblance to the Romish ritual any objection, but rather a merit, with Laud and his brethren; who bore a much greater kindness to the mother-church, as they called her, than to the sectaries and presbyterians, and frequently recommended her as a true Christian church; an appellation which they refused, or at least scrupled to give to the others. So openly were these tenets espoused, that not only the discontented puritans believed the church of England to be relapsing fast into Romish superstition: The court of Rome itself entertained hopes of regaining its authority in this island; and, in order to forward Laud's supposed good intentions, an offer was twice made him, in private, of a cardinal's hat, which he declined accepting.[k] His answer was, as he says himself, *That something dwelt within him, which would not suffer his compliance, till Rome were other than it is.*[l]

A court lady, daughter of the earl of Devonshire, having turned catholic, was asked by Laud the reasons of her conversion. *'Tis chiefly,* said she, *because I hate to travel in a crowd.* The meaning of this expression being demanded, she replied, *I perceive your grace and many others are making haste to Rome; and therefore, in order to prevent my being crowded, I have gone before you.* It must be confessed, that though Laud deserved not the appellation of papist, the genius of his religion was, though in a less degree, the same with that of the Romish: The same profound respect was exacted to the sacerdotal character, the same submission required to the creeds and decrees of synods and councils, the same pomp and ceremony was affected in worship, and the same superstitious regard to days, postures, meats, and vestments. No wonder, therefore, that this prelate was, every-where, among the puritans, regarded with horror, as the forerunner of antichrist.

As a specimen of the new ceremonies, to which Laud sacrificed his own quiet and that of the nation, it may not be amiss to relate those, which, he was accused of employing in the consecration of St. Catherine's church, and which were the object of such general scandal and offence.

On the bishop's approach to the west door of the church, a loud

---

[i] May, p. 25. [k] Rushworth, vol. ii. p. 190. Welwood, p. 61. [l] Rushworth, vol. iii. p. 1327. Whitlocke, p. 97.

CHAPTER LII

voice cried, *Open, Open, ye everlasting doors, that the king of glory may enter in!* Immediately the doors of the church flew open, and the bishop entered. Falling upon his knees, with eyes elevated and arms expanded, he uttered these words: *This place is holy; the ground is holy: In the name of the Father, Son, and Holy Ghost, I pronounce it holy.*

Going towards the chancel, he several times took up from the floor some of the dust, and threw it in the air. When he approached, with his attendants, near to the communion-table, he bowed frequently towards it: And on their return, they went round the church repeating as they marched along, some of the psalms: And then said a form of prayer, which concluded with these words: *We consecrate this church, and separate it unto thee as holy ground, not to be profaned any more to common uses.*

After this, the bishop, standing near the communion-table, solemnly pronounced many imprecations upon such as should afterwards pollute that holy place by musters of soldiers, or keeping in it profane law courts, or carrying burthens through it. On the conclusion of every curse he bowed towards the east, and cried, *Let all the people say, Amen.*

The imprecations being all so piously finished, there were poured out a number of blessings upon such as had any hand in framing and building that sacred and beautiful edifice, and on such as had given, or should hereafter give to it, any chalices, plate, ornaments, or utensils. At every benediction, he in like manner bowed towards the east, and cried, *Let all the people say, Amen.*

The sermon followed; after which, the bishop consecrated and administered the sacrament in the following manner:

As he approached the communion table, he made many lowly reverences: And coming up to that part of the table where the bread and wine lay, he bowed seven times. After the reading of many prayers, he approached the sacramental elements, and gently lifted up the corner of the napkin, in which the bread, was placed. When he beheld the bread, he suddenly let fall the napkin, drew back a step or two, bowed three several times towards the bread; then he drew nigh again, opened the napkin, and bowed as before.

Next, he laid his hand on the cup, which had a cover upon it, and was filled with wine. He let go the cup, fell back, and bowed thrice toward it. He approached again; and lifting up the cover, peeped into the cup. Seeing the wine, he let fall the cover, started back, and bowed as before. Then he received the sacrament, and gave it to others. And many prayers being said, the solemnity of the consecration ended. The walls and floor and roof of the fabric were then supposed to be sufficiently holy.*

Orders were given, and rigorously insisted on, that the communion-table should be removed from the middle of the area, where it hitherto stood in all churches, except in cathedrals.* It was placed at the east end, railed in, and denominated an Altar; as the clergyman, who officiated, received commonly the appellation of PRIEST. It is not easy to imagine the discontents excited by this innovation, and the suspicions which it gave rise to.

The kneeling at the altar, and the using of copes, a species of embroidered vestment, in administring the sacrament, were also known to be great objects of scandal, as being popish practices: But the opposition rather encreased than abated the zeal of the prelate, for the introduction of these habits and ceremonies.

All kinds of ornament, especially pictures, were necessary for supporting that mechanical devotion, which was purposed to be raised in this model of religion: But as these had been so much employed by the church of Rome, and had given rise to so much superstition, or what the puritans called idolatry; it was impossible to introduce them into English churches, without exciting general murmurs and complaints. But Laud, possessed of present authority, persisted in his purpose, and made several attempts towards acquiring these ornaments. Some of the pictures, introduced by him, were also found, upon enquiry, to be the very same that might be met with in the mass-book. The crucifix too, that eternal consolation of all pious catholics, and terror to all sound protestants, was not forgotten on this occasion.*

It was much remarked, that Sherfield, the recorder of Salisbury, was tried in the star-chamber, for having broken, contrary to the bishop of Salisbury's express injunctions, a painted window of St. Edmond's church in that city. He boasted, that he had destroyed these monuments of idolatry: But for this effort of his zeal, he was fined 500 pounds, removed from his office, condemned

---

m Rushworth, vol. ii. p. 76, 77. Welwood, p. 275. Franklyn, p. 386.
n Rushworth, vol. ii. p. 207. Whitlocke, p. 24.   *o* Rushworth, vol. ii. p. 272, 273.

CHAPTER LII

to make a public acknowledgment, and be bound to his good behaviour.[p]

Not only such of the clergy, as neglected to observe every ceremony, were suspended and deprived by the high-commission court: Oaths were, by many of the bishops, imposed on the church-wardens; and they were sworn to inform against any one, who acted contrary to the ecclesiastical canons.[q] Such a measure, though practised during the reign of Elizabeth, gave much offence; as resembling too nearly the practice of the Romish inquisition.

To show the greater alienation from the churches reformed after the presbyterian model, Laud advised, that the discipline and worship of the church should be imposed on the English regiments and trading companies abroad.[r] All foreigners of the Dutch and Walloon congregations were commanded to attend the established church; and indulgence was granted to none after the children of the first denizens.[s] Scudamore too, the king's ambassador at Paris, had orders to withdraw himself from the communion of the hugonots. Even men of sense were apt to blame this conduct, not only because it gave offence in England, but because, in foreign countries, it lost the crown the advantage of being considered as the head and support of the reformation.[t]

On pretence of pacifying disputes, orders were issued from the council, forbidding on both sides, all preaching and printing with regard to the controverted points of predestination and free-will. But it was complained of, and probably with reason, that the impartiality was altogether confined to the orders, and that the execution of them was only meant against the calvinists.

In return for Charles's indulgence towards the church, Laud and his followers took care to magnify, on every occasion, the regal authority, and to treat, with the utmost disdain or detestation, all puritanical pretensions to a free and independent constitution. But while these prelates were so liberal in raising the crown at the expence of public liberty, they made no scruple of encroaching

---

[p] Ibid, p. 152. State Trials, vol. v. p. 46. Franklyn, p. 410, 411, 412.
[q] Rushworth, vol. ii. p. 186.   [r] Ibid. p. 249. Franklyn, p. 451.
[s] Rushworth, vol. ii. p. 272.   [t] State papers collected by the earl of Clarendon, p. 338.

themselves, on the royal rights the most incontestible; in order to exalt the hierarchy, and procure to their own order dominion and independence. All the doctrines which the Romish church had borrowed from some of the fathers, and which freed the spiritual from subordination to the civil power, were now adopted by the church of England, and interwoven with her political and religious tenets. A divine and apostolical charter was insisted on, preferably to a legal and parliamentary one." The sacerdotal character was magnified as sacred and indefeizable: All right to spiritual authority, or even to private judgment in spiritual subjects, was refused to profane laymen: Ecclesiastical courts were held by the bishops in their own name, without any notice taken of the king's authority: And Charles, though extremely jealous of every claim in popular assemblies, seemed rather to encourage than repress those encroachments of his clergy. Having felt many sensible inconveniences from the independent spirit of parliaments, he attached himself entirely to those who professed a devoted obedience to his crown and person; nor did he foresee, that the ecclesiastical power, which he exalted, not admitting of any precise boundary, might in time become more dangerous to public peace, and no less fatal to royal prerogative than the other.

So early as the coronation, Laud was the person, according to general opinion, that introduced a novelty, which, though overlooked by Charles, made a deep impression on many of the byestanders. After the usual ceremonies, these words were recited to the king. "Stand and hold fast, from henceforth, the place to which you have been heir by the succession of your forefathers, being now delivered to you by the authority of Almighty God, and by the hands of us and all the bishops and servants of God. And, as you see the clergy to come nearer the altar than others, so remember, that, in all places convenient, you give them greater honour; that the Mediator of God and man may establish you on the kingly throne, to be a mediator betwixt the clergy and the laity; and that you may reign for ever with Jesus Christ, the King of kings, and Lord of lords."[w]

The principles, which exalted prerogative, were not entertained by the king merely as soft and agreeable to his royal ears: They were also put in practice during the time that he ruled with-

---

" Whitlocke, p. 22.   [w] Franklyn, p. 114. Rushworth, vol. i. p. 201.

CHAPTER LII

out parliaments. Though frugal and regular in his expence, he wanted money for the support of government; and he levied it, either by the revival of obsolete laws, or by violations, some more open, some more disguised, of the privileges of the nation. Though humane and gentle in his temper, he gave way to a few severities in the star-chamber and high-commission, which seemed necessary, in order to support the present mode of administration, and repress the rising spirit of liberty throughout the kingdom. Under these two heads may be reduced all the remarkable transactions of this reign, during some years: For, in peaceable and prosperous times, where a neutrality in foreign affairs is observed, scarcely any thing is remarkable, but what is, in some degree, blamed, or blameable. And, lest the hope of relief or protection from parliament might encourage opposition, Charles issued a proclamation in which he declared, "That, whereas, for several ill ends, the calling again of a parliament is divulged; though his majesty has shown, by frequent meetings with his people, his love to the use of parliaments: Yet the late abuse having, for the present, driven him unwillingly out of that course; he will account it presumption for any one to prescribe to him any time for the calling of that assembly."[x] This was generally construed as a declaration, that, during this reign, no more parliaments were intended to be summoned. And every measure of the king's confirmed a suspicion, so disagreeable to the generality of the people.

Tonnage and poundage continued to be levied by the royal authority alone. The former additional impositions were still exacted. Even new impositions were laid on several kinds of merchandize.[z]

Irregular levies of money.

The custom-house officers received orders from the council to enter in to any house, warehouse, or cellar; to search any trunk or chest; and to break any bulk whatever; in default of the payment of customs.[a]

In order to exercise the militia, and to keep them in good order, each county, by an edict of the council, was assessed in a certain sum, for maintaining a muster-master, appointed for that service.[b]

Compositions were openly made with recusants, and the pop-

[x] Parl. Hist. vol. viii. p. 389. Rush. vol. ii. p. 3.   [y] Clarendon, vol. i. p. 4. May, p. 14.   [z] Rush. vol. ii. p. 8. May, p. 16.   [a] Rush. vol. ii. p. 9.   [b] Rush. vol. ii. p. 10.

ish religion became a regular part of the revenue. This was all the persecution which it underwent during the reign of Charles.[c]

A commission was granted for compounding with such as were possessed of crown-lands upon defective titles; and, on this pretence, some money was exacted from the people.[d]

There was a law of Edward II.,[e] That whoever was possessed of twenty pounds a year in land, should be obliged, when summoned, to appear and to receive the order of knighthood. Twenty pounds, at that time, partly by the change of denomination, partly by that in the value of money, were equivalent to 200 in the seventeenth century; and it seemed just, that the king should not strictly insist on the letter of the law, and oblige people of so small revenue to accept of that expensive honour. Edward VI.,[f] and queen Elizabeth[g] who had both of them made use of this expedient for raising money, had summoned only those who were possessed of forty pounds a year and upwards to receive knighthood, or compound for their neglect; and Charles imitated their example, in granting the same indulgence. Commissioners were appointed for fixing the rates of composition; and instructions were given to these commissioners, not to accept of a less sum than would have been due by the party, upon a tax of three subsidies and a half.[h] Nothing proves more plainly, how ill-disposed the people were to the measures of the crown, than to observe, that they loudly complained of an expedient, founded on positive statute, and warranted by such recent precedents. The law was pretended to be obsolete; though only one reign had intervened since the last execution of it.

Severities of the star-chamber and high commission. Barnard, lecturer of St. Sepulchre's, London, used this expression in his prayer before sermon; *Lord, open the eyes of the queen's majesty, that she may see Jesus Christ, whom she has pierced with her infidelity, superstition, and idolatry.* He was questioned in the high-commission court for this insult on the queen; but, upon his submission, dismissed.[i] Leighton who had written libels against the king, the queen, the bishops, and the whole administration, was condemned by a very severe, if not a cruel, sentence; but the

---

[c] Idem, ibid. p. 11, 12, 13, 247.   [d] Idem, ibid. p. 49.   [e] *Statutum de militibus.*   [f] Rymer, tom. xv. p. 124.   [g] Idem, 493, 504.   [h] Rush. vol. ii. p. 70, 71, 72. May, p. 16.   [i] Rushworth, vol. ii. p. 32.

execution of it was suspended for some time, in expectation of his submission.[k] All the severities, indeed, of this reign were exercised against those who triumphed in their sufferings, who courted persecution, and braved authority: And, on that account, their punishment may be deemed the more just, but the less prudent. To have neglected them entirely, had it been consistent with order and public safety, had been the wisest measure, that could have been embraced; as perhaps it had been the most severe punishment, that could have been inflicted on these zealots.

In order to gratify the clergy with a magnificent fabric, sub- *1631.* scriptions were set on foot, for repairing and rebuilding St. Paul's; and the king, by his countenance and example, encouraged this laudable undertaking.[l] By order of the privy-council, St. Gregory's church was removed, as an impediment to the project of extending and beautifying the cathedral. Some houses and shops likewise were pulled down; and compensation was made to the owners.[m] As there was no immediate prospect of assembling a parliament, such acts of power in the king became necessary; and in no former age would the people have entertained any scruple with regard to them. It must be remarked, that the Puritans were extremely averse to the raising of this ornament to the capital. It savoured, as they pretended, of popish superstition.

A stamp duty was imposed on cards: A new tax, which, of itself, was liable to no objection; but appeared of dangerous consequence, when considered as arbitrary and illegal.[n]

Monopolies were revived; an oppressive method of levying money, being unlimited as well as destructive of industry. The last parliament of James, which abolished monopolies, had left an equitable exception in favour of new inventions; and on pretence of these, and of erecting new companies and corporations, was this grievance now renewed. The manufacture of soap was given to a company who paid a sum for their patent.[o] Leather, salt, and many other commodities, even down to linen rags, were likewise put under restrictions.

It is affirmed by Clarendon, that so little benefit was reaped

[k] Kennet's complete hist. vol. iii. p. 60. Whitlocke, p. 15.   [l] Idem, p. 17.
[m] Rushworth, vol. ii. p. 88, 89, 90. 207, 462, 718.   [n] Idem, ibid. p. 103.
[o] Rushworth, vol. ii. p. 136, 142, 189, 252.

from these projects, that of 200,000 pounds thereby levied on the people, scarcely 1500 came into the king's coffers. Though we ought not to suspect the noble historian of exaggerations to the disadvantage of Charles's measures; this fact, it must be owned, appears somewhat incredible. The same author adds, that the king's intention was to teach his subjects how unthrifty a thing it was to refuse reasonable supplies to the crown. An imprudent project! to offend a whole nation, under the view of punishment; and to hope, by acts of violence, to break their refractory spirits, without being possessed of any force to prevent resistance.

1632.   The council of York had been first erected, after a rebellion, by a patent from Henry VIII. without any authority of parliament; and this exercise of power, like many others, was indulged to that arbitrary monarch. This council had long acted chiefly as a criminal court; but, besides some innovations, introduced by James, Charles thought proper, some time after Wentworth was made president, to extend its powers, and to give it a large civil jurisdiction, and that, in some respects, discretionary.[p] It is not improbable, that the king's intention was only to prevent inconveniencies, which arose from the bringing of every cause, from the most distant parts of the kingdom, into Westminster-hall: But the consequence, in the mean time, of this measure, was the putting of all the northern counties out of the protection of ordinary law, and subjecting them to an authority somewhat arbitrary. Some irregular acts of that council were, this year, complained of.[q]

1633.   The court of star-chamber extended its authority; and it was matter of complaint, that it encroached upon the jurisdiction of the other courts; imposing heavy fines and inflicting severe punishment, beyond the usual course of justice. Sir David Foulis was fined 5000 pounds, chiefly because he had dissuaded a friend from compounding with the commissioners of knighthood.[r]

Prynne, a barrister of Lincoln's-Inn, had written an enormous quarto of a thousand pages, which he called *Histrio-Mastyx*. Its professed purpose was to decry stage-plays, comedies, interludes, music, dancing; but the author likewise took occasion to declaim against hunting, public festivals, Christmas-keeping, bonfires, and Maypoles. His zeal against all these levities, he says, was first

[p] Rushworth, vol. ii. p. 158, 159, &c. Franklyn, p. 412.   [q] Rushworth, vol. ii. p. 202, 203.   [r] Ibid. vol. ii. p. 215, 216, &c.

moved, by observing, that plays sold better than the choicest sermons, and that they were frequently printed on finer paper than
the Bible itself. Besides, that the players were often papists, and
desperately wicked; the play-houses, he affirms, are Satan's cha-
pels, and play-haunters little better than incarnate devils; and so
many steps in a dance, so many paces to hell. The chief crime of
Nero he represents to have been, his frequenting and acting of
plays; and those, who nobly conspired his death, were principally
moved to it, as he affirms, by their indignation at that enormity.
The rest of his thousand pages is of a like strain. He had obtained
a licence from archbishop Abbot's chaplain; yet was he indicted in
the star-chamber as a libeller. It was thought somewhat hard, that
general invectives against plays should be interpreted into satires
against the king and queen, merely because they frequented these
amusements, and because the queen sometimes acted a part in
pastorals and interludes, which were represented at court. The
author, it must be owned, had, in plainer terms, blamed the hierarchy, the ceremonies, the innovations in religious worship, and
the new superstitions, introduced by Laud;[s] and this probably,
together with the obstinacy and petulance of his behaviour before
the star-chamber, was the reason why his sentence was so severe.
He was condemned to be put from the bar; to stand on the pillory
in two places, Westminster and Cheapside; to lose both his ears,
one in each place; to pay 5000 pounds, fine to the king; and to be
imprisoned during life.[t]

This same Prynne was a great hero among the Puritans; and it
was chiefly with a view of mortifying that sect, that, though of an
honourable profession, he was condemned by the star-chamber to
so ignominious a punishment. The thorough-paced Puritans were
distinguishable by the sourness and austerity of their manners,
and by their aversion to all pleasure and society.[u] To inspire them
with better humour, was certainly, both for their own sake and that

---

[s] The music in the churches, he affirmed not to be the noise of men, but a
bleating of brute beasts; choiristers bellow the tenor, as it were oxen; bark
a counterpart, as it were a kennel of dogs; roar out a treble, as it were a sort
of bulls; and grunt out a base, as it were a number of hogs: Christmas, as
it is kept, is the devil's Christmas; and Prynne employed a great number of
pages to persuade men to affect the name of *Puritan,* as if Christ had been
a Puritan; and so he saith in his Index. Rush. vol. ii. p. 223.   [t] Rush. vol.
ii. p. 220, 221, &c.   [u] Dugdale, p. 2.

of the public, a laudable intention in the court; but whether pillories, fines, and prisons, were proper expedients for that purpose, may admit of some question.

Another expedient which the king tried, in order to infuse chearfulness into the national devotion, was not much more successful. He renewed his father's edict for allowing sports and recreations on Sunday to such as attended public worship; and he ordered his proclamation for that pupose to be publicly read by the clergy after divine service.[w] Those who were puritanically affected, refused obedience, and were punished by suspension or deprivation. The differences between the sects were before sufficiently great; nor was it necessary to widen them farther by these inventions.

Some encouragement and protection, which the king and the bishops gave to wakes, church-ales, bride-ales, and other chearful festivals of the common people, were the objects of like scandal to the Puritans.[x]

June 12. This year, Charles made a journey to Scotland, attended by the court, in order to hold a parliament there, and to pass through the ceremony of his coronation. The nobility and gentry of both kingdoms rivaled each other, in expressing all duty and respect to the king, and in showing mutual friendship and regard to each other. No one could have suspected, from exterior appearances, that such dreadful scenes were approaching.

One chief article of business (for it deserves the name), which the king transacted in this parliament, was, besides obtaining some supply, to procure authority for ordering the habits of clergymen.[y] The act did not pass without opposition and difficulty. The dreadful surplice was before men's eyes; and they apprehended, with some reason, that, under sanction of this law, it would soon be introduced among them. Though the king believed, that his prerogative intitled him to a power, in general, of directing whatever belonged to the exterior government of the church; this was deemed a matter of too great importance to be ordered without the sanction of a particular statute.

Immediately after the king's return to England, he heard of

[w] Rush. vol. ii. p. 193, 459. Whitlocke, p. 16, 17. Franklyn, p. 437.   [x] Rush. vol. ii. p. 191, 192. May, p. 2.   [y] Rush. ibid. p. 183.

CHAPTER LII

archbishop Abbot's death: And, without delay, he conferred that dignity on his favourite, Laud; who, by this accession of authority, was now enabled to maintain ecclesiastical discipline with greater rigour, and to aggravate the general discontent of the nation.

Laud obtained the bishopric of London for his friend, Juxon; and, about a year after the death of Sir Richard Weston, created earl of Portland, had interest enough to engage the king to make that prelate high treasurer. Juxon was a person of great integrity, mildness, and humanity, and endued with a good understanding.[z] Yet did this last promotion give general offence. His birth and character were deemed too obscure for a man raised to one of the highest offices of the crown. And the clergy, it was thought, were already too much elated by former instances of the king's attachment to them, and needed not this farther encouragement to assume dominion over the laity.[a] The Puritans, likewise, were much dissatisfied with Juxon, notwithstanding his eminent virtues; because he was a lover of profane field-sports, and hunting.

Ship-money was now introduced. The first writs of this kind had been directed to sea-port towns only: But ship-money was at this time levied on the whole kingdom; and each country was rated at a particular sum, which was afterwards assessed upon individuals.[b] The amount of the whole tax was very moderate, little exceeding 200,000 pounds: It was levied upon the people with equality: The money was entirely expended on the navy, to the great honour and advantage of the kingdom: As England had no military force, while all the other powers of Europe were strongly armed, a fleet seemed absolutely necessary for her security: And it was obvious, that a navy must be built and equipped at leisure, during peace; nor could it possibly be fitted out on a sudden emergence, when the danger became urgent: Yet all these considerations could not reconcile the people to the imposition. It was entirely arbitrary: By the same right any other tax might be imposed: And men thought a powerful fleet, though very desirable, both for the credit and safety of the kingdom, but an unequal recompence for their liberties, which, they apprehended, were thus sacrificed to the obtaining of it.

1634.
Ship-money.

___

[z] Whitlocke, p. 23. Clarendon, vol. i. p. 99. [a] Clarendon, vol. i. p. 97. May, p. 23. [b] Rushworth, vol. ii. p. 257, 258, &c.

England, it must be owned, was, in this respect, unhappy in its present situation, that the king had entertained a very different idea of the constitution, from that which *began,* in general, to prevail among his subjects. He did not regard national privileges as so sacred and inviolable, that nothing but the most extreme necessity could justify an infringement of them. He considered himself as the supreme magistrate, to whose care heaven, by his birth-right, had committed his people, whose duty it was to provide for their security and happiness, and who was vested with ample discretionary powers for that salutary purpose. If the observance of ancient laws and customs was consistent with the present convenience of government, he thought himself obliged to comply with that rule; as the easiest, the safest, and what procured the most prompt and willing obedience. But when a change of circumstances, especially if derived from the obstinacy of the people, required a new plan of administration; national privileges, he thought, must yield to supreme power; nor could any order of the state oppose any right to the will of the sovereign, directed to the good of the public.[c] That these principles of government were derived from the uniform tenor of the English laws, it would be rash to affirm. The fluctuating nature of the constitution, the impatient humour of the people, and the variety of events, had, no doubt, in different ages, produced exceptions and contradictions. These observations alone may be established on both sides, *that* the appearances were sufficiently strong in favour of the king to apologize for his following such maxims; and *that* public liberty must be so precarious under this exorbitant prerogative, as to render an opposition not only excuseable, but laudable, in the people.[d]

Some laws had been enacted, during the reign of Henry VII. against depopulation, or the converting of arable lands into pasture. By a decree of the star-chamber, Sir Anthony Roper was fined 4000 pounds for an offence of that nature.[e] This severe sentence was intended to terrify others into composition; and above 30,000 pounds were levied by that expedient.[f] Like compositions, or, in default of them, heavy fines, were required for

---

[c] Rushworth, vol. iv. p. 535, 542.   [d] See note [V] at the end of the volume.
[e] Rushworth, vol. ii. p. 270. Vol. iii. App. p. 106.   [f] Idem, vol. iii. p. 333.
Franklyn, p. 478.

CHAPTER LII

encroachments on the king's forests; whose bounds, by decrees deemed arbitrary, were extended much beyond what was usual.[g] The bounds of one forest, that of Rockingham were encreased from six miles to sixty.[h] The same refractory humour, which made the people refuse to the king voluntary supplies, disposed them, with better reason, to murmur against these irregular methods of taxation.

Morley was fined 10,000 pounds, for reviling, challenging, and striking, in the court of Whitehall, Sir George Theobald, one of the king's servants.[i] This fine was thought exorbitant; but whether it was compounded, as was usual in fines imposed by the star-chamber, we are not informed.

Allison had reported, that the archbishop of York had incurred the king's displeasure, by asking a limited toleration for the catholics, and an allowance to build some churches for the exercise of their religion. For this slander against the archbishop, he was condemned in the star-chamber to be fined 1000 pounds, to be committed to prison, to be bound to his good behaviour during life, to be whipped, and to be set on the pillory at Westminster, and in three other towns in England. Robins, who had been an accomplice in the guilt, was condemned by a sentence equally severe.[k] Such events are rather to be considered as rare and detached incidents, collected by the severe scrutiny of historians, than as proofs of the prevailing genius of the king's administration, which seems to have been more gentle and equitable than that of most of his predecessors: There were on the whole only five or six such instances of rigour during the course of fifteen years, which elapsed before the meeting of the long parliament. And it is also certain, that scandal against the great, though seldom prosecuted at present, is, however, in the eye of the law, a great crime, and subjects the offender to very heavy penalties.

There are other instances of the high respect paid to the nobility and to the great in that age; when the powers of monarchy, though disputed, still maintained themselves in their pristine vigour. Clarendon[l] tells us a pleasant incident to this purpose: A waterman, belonging to a man of quality, having a squabble with

[g] May, p. 16. [h] Strafford's letters and dispatches, vol. ii. p. 117. [i] Rushworth, vol. ii. p. 270. [k] Ibid. p. 269. [l] Life of Clarendon, vol. i. p. 72.

a citizen about his fare, showed his badge, the crest of his master, which happened to be a swan; and thence insisted on better treatment from the citizen. But the other replied carelessly, that he did not trouble his head about that goose. For this offence, he was summoned before the marshal's court; was fined, as having opprobriously defamed the nobleman's crest, by calling the swan a goose; and was in effect reduced to beggary.

Sir Richard Granvile had thought himself ill used by the earl of Suffolk in a law-suit; and he was accused before the star-chamber of having said of that nobleman, that he was a base lord. The evidence against him was somewhat lame; yet for this slight offence, insufficiently proved, he was condemned to pay a fine of 8000 pounds; one half to the earl, the other to the king.[m]

Sir George Markham, following a chace where lord Darcy's huntsman was exercising his hounds, kept closer to the dogs than was thought proper by the huntsman, who, besides other rudeness, gave him foul language, which Sir George returned with a stroke of his whip. The fellow threatened to complain to his master: The knight replied, If his master should justify such insolence, he would serve him in the same manner, or words to that effect. Sir George was summoned before the star-chamber, and fined 10,000 pounds. *So fine a thing was it in those days to be a lord!* —A natural reflection of lord Lansdown's, in relating this incident.[n] The people, in vindicating their liberties from the authority of the crown, threw off also the yoke of the nobility. It is proper to remark, that this last incident happened early in the reign of James. The present practice of the star-chamber was far from being an innovation; though the present dispositions of the people made them repine more at this servitude.

1635. Charles had imitated the example of Elizabeth and James, and had issued proclamations forbidding the landed gentlemen and the nobility to live idly in London, and ordering them to retire to their country-seats.[o] For disobedience to this edict, many were indicted by the attorney-general, and were fined in the star-

---

[m] Lord Lansdown, p. 514. [n] Lord Lansdown, p. 515. This story is told differently in Hobart's Reports, p. 120. It there appears, that Markham was fined only 500 pounds, and very deservedly: For he gave the lie and wrote a challenge to lord Darcy. James was anxious to discourage the practice of duelling, which was then very prevalent. [o] Rushworth, vol. ii. p. 144.

chamber.[p] This occasioned discontents; and the sentences were complained of, as illegal. But if proclamations had authority, of which nobody pretended to doubt, must they not be put in execution? In no instance, I must confess, does it more evidently appear, what confused and uncertain ideas were, during that age, entertained concerning the English constitution.

Ray, having exported fullers-earth, contrary to the king's proclamation, was, besides the pillory, condemned in the star-chamber to a fine of 2000 pounds.[q] Like fines were levied on Terry, Eman, and others, for disobeying a proclamation which forbad the exportation of gold.[r] In order to account for the subsequent convulsions, even these incidents are not to be overlooked, as frivolous or contemptible. Such severities were afterwards magnified into the greatest enormities.

There remains a proclamation of this year, prohibiting hackney coaches from standing in the street.[s] We are told, that there were not above twenty coaches of that kind in London. There are, at present, near eight hundred.

The effects of ship-money began now to appear. A formidable *1636.* fleet of sixty sail, the greatest that England had ever known, was equipped under the earl of Northumberland, who had orders to attack the herring-busses of the Dutch, which fished in what were called the British seas. The Dutch were content to pay 30,000 pounds for a licence during this year. They openly denied, however, the claim of dominion in the seas, beyond the friths, bays, and shores; and it may be questioned whether the laws of nations warrant any farther pretensions.

This year the king sent a squadron against Sallee; and with the assistance of the emperor of Morocco, destroyed that receptacle of pyrates, by whom the English commerce and even the English coasts had long been infested.

Burton a divine, and Bastwick a physician, were tried in the *1637.* star-chamber for seditious and schismatical libels, and were condemned to the same punishment that had been inflicted on Prynne. Prynne himself was tried for a new offence; and, together with another fine of 5000 pounds, was condemned to lose what

[p] Idem ibid. p. 288.   [q] Rushworth, vol. ii. p. 348.   [r] Idem ibid. p. 350.
[s] Idem ibid. p. 316.

remained of his ears. Besides, that these writers had attacked, with great severity, and even an intemperate zeal, the ceremonies, rites, and government of the church; the very answers, which they gave in to the court, were so full of contumacy and of invectives against the prelates, that no lawyer could be prevailed on to sign them.[t] The rigors, however, which they underwent, being so unworthy men of their profession, gave general offence; and the patience, or rather alacrity, with which they suffered, encreased still farther the indignation of the public.[u] The severity of the star-chamber, which was generally ascribed to Laud's passionate disposition, was, perhaps, in itself, somewhat blameable; but will naturally, to us, appear enormous, who enjoy, in the utmost latitude, that liberty of the press, which is esteemed so necessary in every monarchy, confined by strict legal limitations. But as these limitations were not regularly fixed during the age of Charles, nor at any time before; so was this liberty totally unknown, and was generally deemed, as well as religious toleration, incompatible with all good government. No age or nation, among the moderns, had ever set an example of such an indulgence: And it seems unreasonable to judge of the measures, embraced during one period, by the maxims, which prevail in another.

Burton, in his book where he complained of innovations, mentioned among others, that a certain Wednesday had been appointed for a fast, and that the fast was ordered to be celebrated without any sermons.[w] The intention, as he pretended, of that novelty, was, by the example of a fast without sermons, to suppress all the Wednesday's lectures in London. It is observable, that the church of Rome and that of England, being, both of them, lovers of form and ceremony and order, are more friends to prayer than preaching; while the puritanical sectaries, who find that the latter method of address, being directed to a numerous audience present and visible, is more inflaming and animating, have always regarded it as the chief part of divine service. Such circumstances, though minute, it may not be improper to transmit to posterity; that those, who are curious of tracing the history of the human

[t] Rushworth, vol. ii. p. 381, 382, &c. State Trials, vol. v. p. 66. [u] State Trials, vol. v. p. 80. [w] Ibid. p. 74. Franklyn, p. 839.

CHAPTER LII

mind, may remark, how far its several singularities coincide in different ages.

Certain zealots had erected themselves into a society for buying in of impropriations, and transferring them to the church; and great sums of money had been bequeathed to the society for these purposes. But it was soon observed, that the only use, which they made of their funds, was, to establish lectures in all the considerable churches; men, who, without being subjected to episcopal authority, employed themselves entirely in preaching and spreading the fire of puritanism. Laud took care, by a decree, which was passed in the court of exchequer, and which was much complained of, to abolish this society, and to stop their progress.[x] It was, however, still observed, that, throughout England, the lectures were all of them puritanically affected; and from them the clergymen, who contented themselves with reading prayers and homilies to the people, commonly received the reproachful appellation of *dumb dogs.*

The puritans, restrained in England, shipped themselves off for America, and laid there the foundations of a government, which possessed all the liberty, both civil and religious, of which they found themselves bereaved in their native country. But their enemies, unwilling that they should any where enjoy ease and contentment, and dreading, perhaps, the dangerous consequences of so disaffected a colony, prevailed on the king to issue a proclamation, debarring these devotees access even into those inhospitable deserts.[y] Eight ships, lying in the Thames, and ready to sail, were detained by order of the council; and in these were embarked Sir Arthur Hazelrig, John Hambden, John Pym, and Oliver Cromwel,[z] who had resolved for ever to abandon their native country, and fly to the other extremity of the globe; where

---

[x] Rushworth, vol. ii. p. 150, 151. Whitlocke, p. 15. History of the life and sufferings of Laud, p. 211, 212.　[y] Rush. vol. ii. p. 409. 418.　[z] Mather's History of New England, book i. Dugdale. Bates. Hutchinson's Hist. of Massachuset's Bay, vol. i. p. 42. This last quoted author puts the fact beyond controversy. And it is a curious fact, as well with regard to the characters of the men, as of the times. Can any one doubt, that the ensuing quarrel was almost entirely theological not political? What might be expected of the populace, when such was the character of the most enlightened leaders?

they might enjoy lectures and discourses of any length or form which pleased them. The king had afterwards full leisure to repent this exercise of his authority.

The bishop of Norwich, by rigorously insisting on uniformity, had banished many industrious tradesmen from that city, and chaced them into Holland.[a] The Dutch began to be more intent on commerce than on orthodoxy; and thought, that the knowledge of useful arts and obedience to the laws formed a good citizen; though attended with errors in subjects, where it is not allowable for human nature to expect any positive truth or certainty.

Complaints about this time were made, that the petition of right was, in some instances, violated, and that, upon a commitment by the king and council, bail or releasement had been refused to Jennings, Pargiter, and Danvers.[b]

Williams, bishop of Lincoln, a man of spirit and learning, a popular prelate, and who had been lord keeper, was fined 10,000 pounds by the star-chamber, committed to the Tower during the king's pleasure, and suspended from his office. This severe sentence was founded on frivolous pretences, and was more ascribed to Laud's vengeance, than to any guilt of the bishop.[c] Laud, however, had owed his first promotion to the good offices of that prelate with king James. But so implacable was the haughty primate, that he raised up a new prosecution against Williams, on the strangest pretence imaginable. In order to levy the fine above-mentioned, some officers had been sent to seize all the furniture and books of his episcopal palace of Lincoln; and in rummaging the house, they found in a corner some neglected letters, which had been thrown bye as useless. These letters were written by one Osbaldistone, a schoolmaster, and were directed to Williams. Mention was there made of *a little great man;* and in another passage, the same person was denominated *a little urchin.* By inferences and constructions, these epithets were applied to Laud; and on no better foundation was Williams tried anew, as having received scandalous letters, and not discovering that private correspondence. For this offence, another fine of 8000 pounds was levied on him: Osbaldistone was likewise brought to trial, and condemned to pay a fine of 5000 pounds, and to have his ears nailed to the pillory

---

[a] May, p. 82.   [b] Rush. vol. ii. p. 414.   [c] Rushworth, vol. ii. p. 416, &c.

CHAPTER LII

before his own school. He saved himself by flight; and left a note in his study, wherein he said, "That he was gone beyond Canterbury."[d]

These prosecutions of Williams seem to have been the most iniquitous measure, pursued by the court during the time that the use of parliaments was suspended. Williams had been indebted for all his fortune to the favour of James; but having quarreled, first with Buckingham, then with Laud, he threw himself into the country party; and with great firmness and vigour opposed all the measures of the king. A creature of the court to become its obstinate enemy, a bishop to countenance puritans; these circumstances excited indignation, and engaged the ministers in those severe measures. Not to mention, what some writers relate, that, before the sentence was pronounced against him, Williams was offered a pardon upon his submission, which he refused to make. The court was apt to think, that so refractory a spirit must by any expedient be broken and subdued.

In a former trial, which Williams underwent.[e] (for these were not the first) there was mentioned, in court, a story, which, as it discovers the genius of parties, may be worth relating. Sir John Lambe urging him to prosecute the puritans, the prelate asked, what sort of people these same puritans were? Sir John replied, "That to the world they seemed to be such as would not swear, whore, or be drunk; but they would lye, cozen, and deceive: That they would frequently hear two sermons a-day, and repeat them too, and that sometimes they would fast all day long." This character must be conceived to be satirical; yet, it may be allowed, that that sect was more averse to such irregularities as proceed from the excess of gaiety and pleasure, than to those enormities, which are the most destructive of society. The former were opposite to the very genius and spirit of their religion; the latter were only a transgression of its precepts: And it was not difficult for a gloomy enthusiast to convince himself, that a strict observance of the one would atone for any violation of the other.

In 1632, the treasurer, Portland, had insisted with the vintners, that they should submit to a tax of a penny a quart, upon all the wine, which they retailed. But they rejected the demand. In order

[d]Ibid. p. 803, &c. Whitlocke, p. 25.   [e] Rushworth, vol. ii. p. 416.

to punish them, a decree, suddenly, without much enquiry or examination passed in the star-chamber, prohibiting them to sell or dress victuals in their houses./ Two years after, they were questioned for the breach of this decree; and in order to avoid punishment, they agreed to lend the king six thousand pounds. Being threatened, during the subsequent years, with fines and prosecutions, they at last compounded the matter, and submitted to pay half of that duty, which was at first demanded of them.*g* It required little foresight to perceive, that the king's right of issuing proclamations must, if prosecuted, draw on a power of taxation.

Lilburne was accused before the star-chamber, of publishing and dispersing seditious pamphlets. He was ordered to be examined; but refused to take the oath, usual in that court, that he would answer interrogatories, even though they might lead him to accuse himself. For this contempt, as it was interpreted, he was condemned to be whipped, pilloried, and imprisoned. While he was whipped at the cart, and stood on the pillory, he harangued the populace, and declaimed violently against the tyranny of bishops. From his pockets also he scattered pamphlets, said to be seditious; because they attacked the hierarchy. The star-chamber, which was sitting at that very time, ordered him immediately to be gagged. He ceased not, however, though both gagged and pilloried, to stamp with his foot and gesticulate, in order to show the people, that, if he had it in his power, he would still harangue them. This behaviour gave fresh provocation to the star-chamber; and they condemned him to be imprisoned in a dungeon, and to be loaded with irons.*h* It was found difficult to break the spirits of men, who placed both their honour and their conscience in suffering.

The jealousy of the church appeared in another instance less tragical. Archy, the king's fool, who, by his office, had the privilege of jesting on his master, and the whole court, happened unluckily to try his wit upon Laud, who was too sacred a person to be played with. News having arrived from Scotland of the first commotions excited by the liturgy, Archy seeing the primate pass by, called to him, *Who's fool, now, my lord?* For this offence, Archy was ordered,

/ Rush. vol. ii. p. 197. *g* Idem. ibid. p. 451. *h* Ibid. p. 465, 466, 467.

by sentence of the council, to have his coat pulled over his head, and to be dismissed the king's service.[i]

Here is another instance of that rigorous subjection, in which all men were held by Laud. Some young gentlemen of Lincoln's-inn, heated by their cups, having drunk confusion to the archbishop, were at his instigation cited before the star-chamber. They applied to the earl of Dorset for protection. *Who bears witness against you?* said Dorset, *One of the drawers*, they said. *Where did he stand, when you were supposed to drink this health?* subjoined the earl. *He was at the door*, they replied, *going out of the room. Tush!* cried he, *the drawer was mistaken: You drank confusion to the archbishop of Canterbury's enemies; and the fellow was gone before you pronounced the last word.* This hint supplied the young gentlemen with a new method of defence: And being advised by Dorset to behave with great humility and great submission to the primate; the modesty of their carriage, the ingenuity of their apology, with the patronage of that noble lord, saved them from any severer punishment than a reproof and admonition, with which they were dismissed.[k]

This year, John Hambden acquired, by his spirit and courage, universal popularity throughout the nation, and has merited great renown with posterity, for the bold stand which he made, in defence of the laws and liberties of his country. After the imposing of ship-money, Charles, in order to discourage all opposition, had proposed this question to the judges; "Whether, in a case of necessity, for the defence of the kingdom, he might not impose this taxation? and whether he were not sole judge of the necessity?" These guardians of law and liberty replied, with great complaisance, "That in a case of necessity he might impose that taxation, and that he was sole judge of the necessity."[l] Hambden had been rated at twenty shillings for an estate, which he possessed in the county of Buckingham: Yet notwithstanding this declared opinion of the judge, notwithstanding the great power, and sometimes rigorous maxims of the crown, notwithstanding the small prospect of relief from parliament; he resolved, rather than tamely submit to so illegal an imposition, to stand a legal prosecution, and expose himself to all the indignation of the court. The case was

---

[i] Rush. vol. ii. p. 470. Welwood, p. 278.   [k] Rush. vol. iii. p. 180.   [l] Rush. vol. ii. p. 355. Whitlocke, p. 24.

argued during twelve days, in the exchequer chamber, before all the judges of England; and the nation regarded, with the utmost anxiety, every circumstance of this celebrated trial. The event was easily foreseen: But the principles, and reasonings, and behaviour of the parties, engaged in the trial, were much canvassed and enquired into; and nothing could equal the favour paid to the one side, except the hatred which attended the other.

It was urged by Hambden's council, and by his partizans in the nation, that the plea of necessity was in vain introduced into a trial of law; since it was the nature of necessity to abolish all law, and, by irresistible violence, to dissolve all the weaker and more artificial ties of human society. Not only the prince, in cases of extreme distress, is exempted from the ordinary rules of administration: All orders of men are then levelled; and any individual may consult the public safety by any expedient, which his situation enables him to employ. But to produce so violent an effect, and so hazardous to every community, an ordinary danger or difficulty is not sufficient; much less, a necessity, which is merely factitious and pretended. Where the peril is urgent and extreme, it will be palpable to every member of the society; and though all ancient rules of government are in that case abrogated, men will readily, of themselves, submit to that irregular authority, which is exerted for their preservation. But what is there in common between such suppositions, and the present condition of the nation? England enjoys a profound peace with all her neighbours: And what is more, all her neighbours are engaged in furious and bloody wars among themselves, and by their mutual enmities farther ensure her tranquillity. The very writs themselves, which are issued for the levying of ship-money, contradict the supposition of necessity, and pretend only that the seas are infested with pirates; a slight and temporary inconvenience, which may well await a legal supply from parliament. The writs likewise allow several months for equipping the ships; which proves a very calm and deliberate species of necessity, and one that admits of delay much beyond the forty days requisite for summoning that assembly. It is strange too, that an extreme necessity which is always apparent, and usually comes to a sudden crisis, should now have continued, without interruption, for near four years, and should have remained, during so long a time, invisible to the whole kingdom. And as to the pretension, that the king is sole judge of the necessity; what is this but to subject all

CHAPTER LII

the privileges of the nation to his arbitrary will and pleasure? To expect that the public will be convinced by such reasoning, must aggravate the general indignation; by adding, to violence against men's persons and their property, so cruel a mockery of their understanding.

In vain are precedents of ancient writs produced: These writs, when examined, are only found to require the sea-ports, sometimes at their own charge, sometimes at the charge of the counties, to send their ships for the defence of the nation. Even the prerogative, which empowered the crown to issue such writs, is abolished, and its exercise almost entirely discontinued, from the time of Edward III.;[m] and all the authority, which remained, or was afterwards exercised, was to press ships into the public service, to be paid for by the public. How wide are these precedents from a power of obliging the people, at their own charge, to build new ships, to victual and pay them, for the public; nay, to furnish money to the crown for that purpose? What security either against the farther extension of this claim, or against diverting to other purposes the public money, so levied? The plea of necessity would warrant any other taxation as well as that of ship-money: Wherever any difficulty shall occur, the administration, instead of endeavouring to elude or overcome it, by gentle and prudent measures, will instantly represent it as a reason for infringing all ancient laws and institutions: And if such maxims and such practices prevail; what has become of national liberty? What authority is left to the great charter, to the statutes, and to that very petition of right, which, in the present reign, had been so solemnly enacted by the concurrence of the whole legislature?

The defenceless condition of the kingdom while unprovided with a navy; the inability of the king, from his established revenues, with the utmost care and frugality, to equip and maintain one; the impossibility of obtaining, on reasonable terms, any voluntary supply from parliament: All these are reasons of state, not topics of law. If these reasons appear to the king so urgent as to dispense with the legal rules of government; let him enforce his edicts, by his court of star-chamber, the proper instrument of irregular and absolute power; not prostitute the character of his judges by a decree, which is not, and cannot possibly be legal. By

[m] State Trials, vol. v. p. 545, 255.

this means the boundaries, at least, will be kept more distinct between ordinary law and extraordinary exertions of prerogative; and men will know, that the national constitution is only suspended during a present and difficult emergence, but has not undergone a total and fundamental alteration.

Notwithstanding these reasons, the prejudiced judges, four[n] excepted, gave sentence in favour of the crown. Hambden, however, obtained by the trial the end, for which he had so generously sacrificed his safety and his quiet: The people were rouzed from their lethargy, and became sensible of the danger, to which their liberties were exposed. These national questions were canvassed in every company; and the more they were examined, the more evidently did it appear to many, that liberty was totally subverted, and an unusual and arbitrary authority exercised over the kingdom. Slavish principles, they said, concur with illegal practices; ecclesiastical tyranny gives aid to civil usurpation; iniquitous taxes are supported by arbitrary punishments; and all the privileges of the nation, transmitted through so many ages, secured by so many laws, and purchased by the blood of so many heroes and patriots, now lye prostrate at the feet of the monarch. What though public peace and national industry encreased the commerce and opulence of the kingdom? This advantage was temporary, and due alone, not to any encouragement given by the crown, but to the spirit of the English, the remains of their ancient freedom. What though the personal character of the king, amidst all his misguided counsels, might merit indulgence, or even praise? He was but one man; and the privileges of the people, the inheritance of millions, were too valuable to be sacrificed to his prejudices and mistakes. Such, or more severe, were the sentiments promoted by a great party in the nation: No excuse on the king's part, or alleviation, how reasonable soever, could be harkened to or admitted: And to redress these grievances, a parliament was impatiently longed for; or any other incident, however calamitous, that might secure the people against those oppressions, which they felt, or the greater ills, which they apprehended, from the combined encroachments of church and state.

[n] See State Trials: Article Ship-money, which contains the speeches of four judges in favour of Hambden.

LIII

Discontents in Scotland –
Introduction of the canons and liturgy –
A tumult at Edinburgh – The covenant – A general
assembly – Episcopacy abolished – War –
A pacification – Renewal of
the war – Fourth English
parliament – Dissolution – Discontents
in England – Rout at Newburn –
Treaty at Rippon – Great
council of the peers

⚜ ⚜ ⚜

THE GRIEVANCES, under which the English laboured, when considered in themselves, without regard to the constitution, scarcely deserve the name; nor were they either burthensome on the people's properties, or anywise shocking to the natural humanity of mankind. Even the imposition of ship-money, independent of the consequences, was a great and evident advantage to the public; by the judicious use, which the king made of the money levied by that expedient. And though it was justly apprehended, that such precedents, if patiently submitted to, would end in a total disuse of parliaments, and in the establishment of arbitrary authority; Charles dreaded no opposition from the people, who are not commonly much affected with consequences, and require some striking motive, to engage them in a resistance of established

1637.

government. All ecclesiastical affairs were settled by law and uninterrupted precedent; and the church was become a considerable barrier to the power, both legal and illegal, of the crown. Peace too, industry, commerce, opulence; nay, even justice and lenity of administration, notwithstanding some very few exceptions: All these were enjoyed by the people; and every other blessing of government, except liberty, or rather the present exercise of liberty, and its proper security.° It seemed probable, therefore, that affairs might long have continued on the same footing in England, had it not been for the neighbourhood of Scotland; a country more turbulent, and less disposed to submission and obedience. It was thence the commotions first arose; and it is therefore time for us to return thither, and to give an account of the state of affairs in that kingdom.

Discontents in Scotland. Though the pacific, and not unskilful government of James, and the great authority, which he had acquired, had much allayed the feuds among the great families, and had established law and order throughout the kingdom; the Scotish nobility were still possessed of the chief power and influence over the people. Their property was extensive; their hereditary jurisdictions and the feudal tenures encreased their authority; and the attachment of the gentry to the heads of families established a kind of voluntary servitude under the chieftains. Besides that long absence had much loosened the king's connections with the nobility, who resided chiefly at their country-seats; they were, in general, at this time, though from slight causes, much disgusted with the court. Charles, from the natural piety or superstition of his temper, was extremely attached to the ecclesiastics: And as it is natural for men to persuade themselves, that their interest coincides with their inclination; he had established it as a fixed maxim of policy, to encrease the power and authority of that order. The prelates, he thought, established regularity and discipline among the clergy; the clergy inculcated obedience and loyalty among the people: And as that rank of men had no separate authority, and no dependence but on the crown; the royal power, it would seem, might, with the greater safety, be entrusted in their hands. Many of the prelates, therefore, were raised to the chief dignities of the

° Clarendon, p. 74, 75. May, p. 18. Warwick, p. 62.

state:[p] Spotswood, archbishop of St. Andrews, was created chancellor: Nine of the bishops were privy counsellors: The bishop of
Ross aspired to the office of treasurer: Some of the prelates possessed places in the exchequer: And it was even endeavoured to
revive the first institution of the college of justice, and to share
equally between the clergy and laity the whole judicial authority.[q]
These advantages, possessed by the church, and which the bishops
did not always enjoy with suitable modesty, disgusted the haughty
nobility, who, deeming themselves much superior in rank and
quality to this new order of men, were displeased to find themselves inferior in power and influence. Interest joined itself to
ambition; and begat a jealousy, lest the episcopal sees, which, at
the reformation, had been pillaged by the nobles, should again be
enriched at the expence of that order. By a most useful and beneficial law, the impropriations had already been ravished from the
great men: Competent salaries had been assigned to the impoverished clergy from the tythes of each parish: And what remained,
the proprietor of the land was impowered to purchase at a low
valuation?[r] The king likewise, warranted by ancient law and practice, had declared for a general resumption of all crownlands,
alienated by his predecessors; and though he took no step towards
the execution of this project, the very pretension to such power
had excited jealousy and discontent.[s]

Notwithstanding the tender regard which Charles bore to the
whole church, he had been able, in Scotland, to acquire only the
affection of the superior rank among the clergy. The ministers, in
general, equalled, if not exceeded the nobility, in their prejudices
against the court, against the prelates, and against episcopal authority.[t] Though the establishment of the hierarchy might seem
advantageous to the inferior clergy, both as it erected dignities, to
which all of them might aspire, and as it bestowed a lustre on the
whole body, and allured men of family into it; these views had no
influence on the Scottish ecclesiastics. In the present disposition of
men's minds, there was another circumstance, which drew consideration, and counterbalanced power and riches, the usual founda-

[p]Rushworth, vol. ii. p. 386. May, p. 29.   [q] Guthry's Memoirs, p. 14.
Burnet's Mem. p. 29, 30.   [r] King's Declaration, p. 7. Franklyn, p. 611.
[s] King's Declaration, p. 6.   [t] Burnet, Mem. p. 29, 30.

tions of distinction among men; and that was, the fervour of piety, and the rhetoric, however barbarous, of religious lectures and discourses. Checked by the prelates in the licence of preaching, the clergy regarded episcopal jurisdiction both as a tyranny and an usurpation, and maintained a parity among ecclesiastics to be a divine privilege, which no human law could alter or infringe. While such ideas prevailed, the most moderate exercise of authority would have given disgust; much more, that extensive power, which the king's indulgence encouraged the prelates to assume. The jurisdiction of presbyteries, synods, and other democratical courts, was, in a manner, abolished by the bishops; and the general assembly itself had not been summoned for several years.[u] A new oath was arbitrarily imposed on intrants, by which they swore to observe the articles of Perth, and submit to the liturgy and canons. And in a word, the whole system of church government, during a course of thirty years, had been changed by means of the innovations, introduced by James and Charles.

The people, under the influence of the nobility and clergy, could not fail to partake of the discontents, which prevailed among these two orders; and where real grounds of complaint were wanting, they greedily laid hold of imaginary ones. The same horror against popery, with which the English puritans were possessed, was observable among the populace in Scotland; and among these, as being more uncultivated and uncivilized, seemed rather to be inflamed into a higher degree of ferocity. The genius of religion, which prevailed in the court and among the prelates, was of an opposite nature; and having some affinity to the Romish worship, led them to mollify, as much as possible, these severe prejudices, and to speak of the catholics in more charitable language, and with more reconciling expressions. From this foundation, a panic fear of popery was easily raised; and every new ceremony or ornament, introduced into divine service, was part of that great mystery of iniquity, which, from the encouragement of the king and the bishops, was to overspread the nation.[w] The few innovations, which James had made, were considered as preparatives to this grand design; and the farther alterations, attempted by Charles, were represented as a plain declaration of his intentions. Through the

[u] May, p. 29.   [w] Burnet's Mem. p. 29, 30, 31.

CHAPTER LIII

whole course of this reign, nothing had more fatal influence, in both kingdoms, than this groundless apprehension, which, with so much industry, was propagated, and with so much credulity, was embraced, by all ranks of men.

Amidst these dangerous complaints and terrors of religious innovation, the civil and ecclesiastical liberties of the nation were imagined, and with some reason, not to be altogether free from invasion.

The establishment of the high-commission by James, without any authority of law, seemed a considerable encroachment of the crown; and erected the most dangerous and arbitrary of all courts, by a method equally dangerous and arbitrary. All the steps towards the settlement of episcopacy had indeed been taken with consent of parliament: The articles of Perth were confirmed in 1621: In 1633, the king had obtained a general ratification of every ecclesiastical establishment: But these laws had less authority with the nation, as they were known to have passed contrary to the sentiments even of those who voted for them, and were in reality extorted by the authority and importunity of the sovereign. The means, however, which both James and Charles had employed, in order to influence the parliament, were entirely regular; and no reasonable pretence had been afforded for representing these laws as null or invalid.

But there prevailed among the greater part of the nation another principle, of the most important and most dangerous nature, and which, if admitted, destroyed entirely the validity of all such statutes. The ecclesiastical authority was supposed totally independent of the civil; and no act of parliament, nothing but the consent of the church itself, was represented as sufficient ground for the introduction of any change in religious worship or discipline. And though James had obtained the vote of assemblies for receiving episcopacy and his new rites; it must be confessed, that such irregularities had prevailed in constituting these ecclesiastical courts, and such violence in conducting them, that there were some grounds for denying the authority of all their acts. Charles, sensible that an extorted consent, attended with such invidious circumstances, would rather be prejudicial to his measures, had wholly laid aside the use of assemblies, and was resolved, in conjunction with the bishops, to govern the church by an authority, to which he thought himself fully intitled, and which he believed inherent in the crown.

The king's great aim was to compleat the work, so happily begun by his father; to establish discipline upon a regular system of canons, to introduce a liturgy into public worship, and to render the ecclesiastical government of all his kingdoms regular and uniform. Some views of policy might move him to this undertaking: But his chief motives were derived from principles of zeal and conscience.

Introduction of the canons and liturgy.
The canons for establishing ecclesiastical jurisdiction were promulgated in 1635; and were received by the nation, though without much appearing opposition, yet with great inward apprehension and discontent. Men felt displeasure, at seeing the royal authority highly exalted by them, and represented as absolute and uncontroulable. They saw these speculative principles reduced to practice, and a whole body of ecclesiastical laws established without any previous consent either of church or state.[x] They dreaded, lest, by a parity of reason, like arbitrary authority, from like pretences and principles, would be assumed in civil matters: They remarked, that the delicate boundaries, which separate church and state, were already passed, and many civil ordinances established by the canons, under colour of ecclesiastical institutions: And they were apt to deride the negligence, with which these important edicts had been compiled; when they found, that the new liturgy or service-book was every where, under severe penalties, enjoined by them, though it had not yet been composed or published.[y] It was, however, soon expected; and in the reception of it, as the people are always most affected by what is external and exposed to the senses, it was apprehended, that the chief difficulty would consist.

The liturgy, which the king, from his own authority, imposed on Scotland, was copied from that of England: But lest a servile imitation might shock the pride of his ancient kingdom, a few alterations, in order to save appearances, were made in it; and in that shape it was transmitted to the bishops at Edinburgh.[z] But the Scots had universally entertained a notion, that, though riches and worldly glory had been shared out to them with a sparing hand,

[x] Clarendon, vol. i. p. 106.   [y] Idem, ibid. p. 105.   [z] King's Decl. p. 18. May, p. 32.

CHAPTER LIII

they could boast of spiritual treasures more abundant and more genuine, than were enjoyed by any nation under heaven. Even their southern neighbours, they thought, though separated from Rome, still retained a great tincture of the primitive pollution; and their liturgy was represented as a species of mass, though with some less show and embroidery.[a] Great prejudices, therefore, were entertained against it, even considered in itself; much more, when regarded as a preparative, which was soon to introduce into Scotland all the abominations of popery. And as the very few alterations, which distinguished the new liturgy from the English, seemed to approach nearer to the doctrine of the real presence; this circumstance was deemed an undoubted confirmation of every suspicion, with which the people were possessed.[b]

Easter-day was, by proclamation, appointed for the first reading of the service in Edinburgh: But in order to judge more surely of men's dispositions, the council delayed the matter till the 23d of July; and they even gave notice, the Sunday before, of their intention to commence the use of the new liturgy. As no considerable symptoms of discontent appeared, they thought that they might safely proceed in their purpose;[c] and accordingly, in the cathedral church of St. Giles, the dean of Edinburgh, arrayed in his surplice, began the service; the bishop himself and many of the privy-council being present. But no sooner had the dean opened the book, than a multitude of the meanest sort, most of them women, clapping their hands, cursing, and crying out, *A pope! a pope! antichrist! stone him!* raised such a tumult, that it was impossible to proceed with the service. The bishop, mounting the pulpit, in order to appease the populace, had a stool thrown at him: The council was insulted: And it was with difficulty, that the magistrates were able, partly by authority, partly by force, to expel the rabble, and to shut the doors against them. The tumult, however, still continued without: Stones were thrown at the doors and windows: And when the service was ended, the bishop, going home, was attacked, and narrowly escaped from the hands of the enraged multitude. In the afternoon, the privy-seal, because he carried the

Tumult at Edinburgh.

---

[a] King's Decl. p. 20. [b] Burnet's Mem. p. 31. Rushworth, vol. ii. p. 396. May, p. 31. [c] King's Decl. p. 22. Clarendon, vol. i. p. 108. Rushworth, vol. ii. p. 387.

bishop in his coach, was so pelted with stones, and hooted at with execrations, and pressed upon by the eager populace, that, if his servants, with drawn swords, had not kept them off, the bishop's life had been exposed to the utmost danger.[d]

Though it was violently suspected, that the low populace, who alone appeared, had been instigated by some of higher condition, yet no proof of it could be produced; and every one spake with disapprobation of the licentiousness of the giddy multitude.[e] It was not thought safe, however, to hazard a new insult by any new attempt to read the liturgy; and the people seemed, for the time, to be appeased and satisfied. But it being known, that the king still persevered in his intentions of imposing that mode of worship, men fortified themselves still farther in their prejudices against it; and great multitudes resorted to Edinburgh, in order to oppose the introduction of so hated a novelty.[f] It was not long before they broke out in the most violent disorder. The bishop of Galloway was attacked in the streets, and chased into the chamber, where the privy-council was sitting. The council itself was besieged and violently attacked: The town-council met with the same fate: And nothing could have saved the lives of all of them, but their application to some popular lords, who protected them, and dispersed the multitude. In this sedition, the actors were of some better condition than in the former; though nobody of rank seemed, as yet, to countenance them.[g]

All men, however, began to unite and to encourage each other, in opposition to the religious innovations introduced into the kingdom. Petitions to the council were signed and presented by persons of the highest quality: The women took part, and, as was usual, with violence: The clergy, every where, loudly declaimed against popery and the liturgy, which they represented as the same: The pulpits resounded with vehement invectives against antichrist: and the populace, who first opposed the service, was often compared to Balaam's ass, an animal, in itself, stupid and senseless, but whose mouth had been opened by the Lord, to the admiration of the whole world.[h] In short, fanaticism mingling with

[d] King's Decl. p. 23, 24, 25. Rushworth, vol. ii. p. 388. [e] King's Decl. p. 26, 30. Clarendon, vol. i. p. 109. [f] King's Decl. p. 32. Rushworth, vol. ii. p. 400. [g] King's Decl. p. 35, 36, &c. Rushworth, vol. ii. p. 404. [h] King's Decl. p. 31.

faction, private interest with the spirit of liberty, symptoms appeared, on all hands, of the most dangerous insurrection and disorder.

The primate, a man of wisdom and prudence, who was all along averse to the introduction of the liturgy, represented to the king the state of the nation: The earl of Traquaire, the treasurer, set out for London, in order to lay the matter more fully before him: Every circumstance, whether the condition of England or of Scotland were considered, should have engaged him to desist from so hazardous an attempt: Yet was Charles inflexible. In his whole conduct of this affair, there appear no marks of the good sense, with which he was endowed: A lively instance of that species of character, so frequently to be met with; where there are sound parts and judgment in every discourse and opinion; in many actions, indiscretion and imprudence. Men's views of things are the result of their understanding alone: Their conduct is regulated by their understanding, their temper, and their passions.

To so violent a combination of a whole kingdom, Charles had nothing to oppose but a proclamation; in which he pardoned all past offences, and exhorted the people to be more obedient for the future, and to submit peaceably to the use of the liturgy. This proclamation was instantly encountered with a public protestation, presented by the earl of Hume and lord Lindesey: And this was the first time, that men of quality had appeared in any violent act of opposition.[i] But this proved a crisis. The insurrection, which had been advancing by a gradual and slow progress, now blazed up at once. No disorder, however, attended it. On the contrary, a new order immediately took place. Four *tables,* as they were called, were formed in Edinburgh. One consisted of nobility, another of gentry, a third of ministers, a fourth of burgesses. The table of gentry was divided into many subordinate tables, according to their different counties. In the hands of the four tables, the whole authority of the kingdom was placed. Orders were issued by them, and every where obeyed, with the utmost regularity.[k] And among the first acts of their government was the production of the Covenant.

1638.
19th
Feb.

[i] King's Decl. p. 47, 48, &c. Guthry, p. 28. May, p. 37. [k] Clarendon, vol. i. p. 111. Rushworth, vol. ii. p. 734.

This famous covenant consisted first of a renunciation of popery, formerly signed by James in his youth, and composed of many invectives, fitted to inflame the minds of men against their fellow creatures, whom heaven has enjoined them to cherish and to love. There followed a bond of union, by which the subscribers obliged themselves to resist religious innovations, and to defend each other against all opposition whatsoever: And all this, for the greater glory of God, and the greater honour and advantage of their king and country.[l] The people, without distinction of rank or condition, of age or sex, flocked to the subscription of this covenant: Few, in their judgment, disapproved of it; and still fewer durst openly condemn it. The king's ministers and counsellors themselves were, most of them, seized by the general contagion. And none but rebels to God, and traitors to their country, it was thought, would withdraw themselves from so salutary and so pious a combination.

The treacherous, the cruel, the unrelenting Philip, accompanied with all the terrors of a Spanish inquisition, was scarcely, during the preceding century, opposed in the Low Countries with more determined fury, than was now, by the Scots, the mild, the humane Charles, attended with his inoffensive liturgy.

June. The king began to apprehend the consequences. He sent the marquis of Hamilton, as commissioner, with authority to treat with the covenanters. He required the covenant to be renounced and recalled: And he thought, that on his part he had made very satisfactory concessions, when he offered to suspend the canons and the liturgy, till, in a fair and legal way, they could be received; and so to model the high commission, that it should no longer give offence to his subjects.[m] Such general declarations could not well give content to any, much less to those who carried so much higher their pretensions. The covenanters found themselves seconded by the zeal of the whole nation. Above sixty thousand people were assembled in a tumultuous manner in Edinburgh and the neighbourhood. Charles possessed no regular forces in either of his kingdoms. And the discontents in England, though secret, were believed so violent, that the king, it was thought, would find it very difficult to employ in such a cause the power of that kingdom. The

[l] King's Decl. p. 57, 58. Rushworth, vol. ii. p. 734. May, p. 38.
[m] Rushworth, vol. ii. p. 754, &c.

more, therefore, the popular leaders in Scotland considered their situation, the less apprehension did they entertain of royal power, and the more rigorously did they insist on entire satisfaction. In answer to Hamilton's demand of renouncing the covenant, they plainly told him, that they would sooner renounce their baptism." And the clergy invited the commissioner himself to subscribe it; by informing him; "With what peace and comfort it had filled the hearts of all God's people; what resolutions and beginnings of reformation of manners were sensibly perceived in all parts of the nation, above any measure they had ever before found or could have expected; how great glory the Lord had received thereby; and what confidence they had, that God would make Scotland a blessed kingdom."*o*

Hamilton returned to London: Made another fruitless journey, with new concessions, to Edinburgh: Returned again to London; and was immediately sent back with still more satisfactory concessions. The king was now willing entirely to abolish the canons, the liturgy, and the high commission court. He was even resolved to limit extremely the power of the bishops, and was content, if, on any terms, he could retain that order in the church of Scotland.*p* And to ensure all these gracious offers, he gave Hamilton authority to summon first an assembly, then a parliament, where every national grievance might be redressed and remedied. These successive concessions of the king, which yet came still short of the rising demands of the malcontents, discovered his own weakness, encouraged their insolence, and gave no satisfaction. The offer, however, of an assembly and a parliament, in which they expected to be entirely masters, was willingly embraced by the covenanters.

17th Sept.

Charles, perceiving what advantage his enemies had reaped from their covenant, resolved to have a covenant on his side; and he ordered one to be drawn up for that purpose. It consisted of the same violent renunciation of popery above-mentioned; which, though the king did not approve of it, he thought it safest to adopt, in order to remove all the suspicions entertained against him. As the covenanters, in their bond of mutual defence against all opposition, had been careful not to except the king; Charles had formed

---

" King's Decl. p. 87.   *o* Ibid. p. 88. Rushworth, vol. ii. p. 751.   *p* King's Decl. p. 137. Rushworth, vol. ii. p. 762.

. a bond, which was annexed to this renunciation, and which expressed the duty and loyalty of the subscribers to his majesty.[q] But the covenanters, perceiving, that this new covenant was only meant to weaken and divide them, received it with the utmost scorn and detestation. And without delay they proceeded to model the future assembly, from which such great atchievements were expected.[r]

A general assembly. The genius of that religion, which prevailed in Scotland, and which, every day, was secretly gaining ground in England, was far from inculcating deference and submission to the ecclesiastics, merely as such: Or rather, by nourishing in every individual, the highest raptures and ecstasies of devotion, it consecrated, in a manner, every individual, and in his own eyes, bestowed a character on him, much superior to what forms and ceremonious institutions could alone confer. The clergy of Scotland, though such tumult was excited about religious worship and discipline, were both poor, and in small numbers; nor are they, in general, to be considered, at least in the beginning, as the ringleaders of the sedition, which was raised on their account. On the contrary, the laity, apprehending, from several instances, which occurred, a spirit of moderation in that order, resolved to domineer entirely in the assembly, which was summoned, and to hurry on the ecclesiastics by the same furious zeal, with which they were themselves transported.[s]

It had been usual, before the establishment of prelacy, for each presbytery to send to the assembly, besides two or three ministers, one lay-commissioner;[t] and, as all the boroughs and universities sent likewise commissioners, the lay-members, in that ecclesiastical court, nearly equalled the ecclesiastics. Not only this institution, which James, apprehensive of zeal in the laity, had abolished, was now revived by the covenanters: They also introduced an innovation, which served still farther to reduce the clergy to subjection. By an edict of the tables, whose authority was supreme, an elder from each parish was ordered to attend the presbytery, and to give

---

[q] King's Decl. p. 140, &c. [r] Rushworth, vol. ii. p. 772. [s] King's Decl. p. 188, 189. Rushworth, vol. ii. p. 761. [t] A presbytery in Scotland is an inferior ecclesiastical court, the same that was afterwards called a Classis in England, and is composed of the clergy of the neighbouring parishes to the number commonly of between twelve and twenty.

his vote in the choice both of the commissioners and ministers, who should be deputed to the assembly. As it is not usual for the ministers, who are put in the list of candidates, to claim a vote, all the elections, by that means, fell into the hands of the laity: The most furious of all ranks were chosen: And the more to overawe the clergy, a new device was fallen upon, of chusing, to every commissioner, four or five lay-assessors, who, though they could have no vote, might yet interpose with their advice and authority in the assembly.[u]

The assembly met at Glasgow: And, besides a great concourse of the people, all the nobility and gentry of any family or interest were present, either as members, assessors, or spectators; and it was apparent, that the resolutions, taken by the covenanters, could here meet with no manner of opposition. A firm determination had been entered into of utterly abolishing episcopacy; and as a preparative to it, there was laid before the presbytery of Edinburgh, and solemnly read in all the churches of the kingdom, an accusation against the bishops, as guilty, all of them, of heresy, simony, bribery, perjury, cheating, incest, adultery, fornication, common swearing, drunkenness, gaming, breach of the sabbath, and every other crime that had occurred to the accusers.[w] The bishops sent a protest, declining the authority of the assembly; the commissioner too protested against that court, as illegally constituted and elected; and, in his majesty's name, dissolved it. This measure was foreseen, and little regarded. The court still continued to sit, and to finish their business.[x] All the acts of assembly, since the accession of James to the crown of England, were, upon pretty reasonable grounds, declared null and invalid. The acts of parliament, which affected ecclesiastical affairs, were supposed, on that very account, to have no manner of authority. And thus episcopacy, the high commission, the articles of Perth, the canons, and the liturgy, were abolished and declared unlawful: And the whole fabric, which James and Charles, in a long course of years, had been rearing with so much care and policy, fell at once to the ground. The covenant likewise was ordered to be signed by every one, under pain of excommunication.[y]

Episcopacy abolished.

[u] King's Decl. p. 190, 191, 290. Guthry, p. 39. &c.   [w] King's Decl. p. 218. Rushworth, vol. ii. p. 787.   [x] May, p. 44.   [y] King's Decl. p. 317.

The independency of the ecclesiastical upon the civil power was the old presbyterian principle, which had been zealously adopted at the reformation, and which, though James and Charles had obliged the church publickly to disclaim it, had secretly been adhered to by all ranks of people. It was commonly asked, whether Christ or the king were superior? And as the answer seemed obvious, it was inferred, that the assembly, being Christ's council, was superior, in all spiritual matters, to the parliament, which was only the king's. But as the covenanters were sensible, that this consequence, though it seemed to them irrefragable, would not be assented to by the king; it became necessary to maintain their religious tenets by military force, and not to trust entirely to supernatural assistance, of which, however, they held themselves well assured. They cast their eyes on all sides, abroad and at home, whence ever they could expect any aid or support.

After France and Holland had entered into a league against Spain, and framed a treaty of partition, by which they were to conquer and to divide between them the Low Country provinces, England was invited to preserve a neutrality between the contending parties, while the French and Dutch should attack the maritime towns of Flanders. But the king replied to d'Estrades, the French ambassador, who opened the proposal, that he had a squadron ready, and would cross the seas, if necessary, with an army of 15,000 men, in order to prevent these projected conquests.[z] This answer, which proves, that Charles, though he expressed his mind with an imprudent candour, had, at last, acquired a just idea of national interest, irritated cardinal Richlieu; and in revenge, that politic and enterprizing minister carefully fomented the first commotions in Scotland, and secretly supplied the covenanters with money and arms, in order to encourage them in their opposition against their sovereign.

But the chief resource of the Scottish malcontents, was in themselves, and in their own vigour and abilities. No regular established commonwealth could take juster measures, or execute them with greater promptitude, than did this tumultuous combination, inflamed with bigotry for religious trifles, and faction without a reasonable object. The whole kingdom was, in a manner, engaged;

---

[z] Mem. d'Estrades, vol. i.

and the men of greatest abilities soon acquired the ascendant, which their family interest enabled them to maintain. The earl of Argyle, though he long seemed to temporize, had, at last, embraced the covenant; and he became the chief leader of that party: A man equally supple and inflexible, cautious and determined, and entirely qualified to make a figure during a factious and turbulent period. The earls of Rothes; Cassils, Montrose, Lothian, the lords Lindesey, Loudon, Yester, Balmerino, distinguished themselves in that party. Many Scotch officers had acquired reputation in the German wars, particularly under Gustavus; and these were *War.* invited over to assist their country in her present necessity. The command was entrusted to Lesley, a soldier of experience and abilities. Forces were regularly inlisted and disciplined. Arms were commissioned and imported from foreign countries. A few castles, which belonged to the king, being unprovided with victuals, ammunition, and garrisons, were soon seized. And the whole country, except a small part, where the marquis of Huntley still adhered to the king, being in the hands of the covenanters, was, in a very little time, put in a tolerable posture of defence.[a]

The fortifications of Leith were begun and carried on with great rapidity. Besides the inferior sort, and those who laboured for pay, incredible numbers of volunteers, even noblemen and gentlemen, put their hand to the work, and deemed the most abject employment to be dignified by the sanctity of the cause. Women too, of rank and condition, forgetting the delicacy of their sex, and the decorum of their character, were intermingled with the lowest rabble; and carried on their shoulders the rubbish, requisite for completing the fortifications.[b]

We must not omit another auxiliary of the covenanters, and no inconsiderable one; a prophetess, who was much followed and admired by all ranks of people. Her name was Michelson, a woman full of whimsies, partly hysterical, partly religious; and inflamed with a zealous concern for the ecclesiastical discipline of the presbyterians. She spoke at certain times only, and had often interruptions of days and weeks: But when she began to renew her ecstasies, warning of the happy event was conveyed over the whole country, thousands crowded about her house, and every word,

[a] May, p. 49.　[b] Guthry's Memoirs, p. 46.

which she uttered, was received with veneration, as the most sacred oracles. The covenant was her perpetual theme. The true, genuine covenant, she said, was ratified in heaven: The king's covenant was an invention of Satan: When she spoke of Christ, she usually gave him the name of the covenanting Jesus. Rollo, a popular preacher, and zealous covenanter, was her great favourite; and payed her, on his part, no less veneration. Being desired by the spectators to pray with her, and speak to her; he answered, "That he durst not, and that it would be ill manners in him to speak, while his master, Christ, was speaking in her."[c]

Charles had agreed to reduce episcopal authority so much, that it would no longer have been of any service to support the crown; and this sacrifice of his own interests he was willing to make, in order to attain public peace and tranquillity. But he could not consent entirely to abolish an order, which he thought as essential to the being of a christian church, as his Scottish subjects deemed it incompatible with that sacred institution. This narrowness of mind, if we would be impartial, we must either blame or excuse equally on both sides; and thereby anticipate, by a little reflection, that judgment, which time, by introducing new subjects of controversy, will undoubtedly render quite familiar to posterity.

So great was Charles's aversion to violent and sanguinary measures, and so strong his affection to his native kingdom, that, it is probable, the contest in his breast would be nearly equal between these laudable passions, and his attachment to the hierarchy. The latter affection, however, prevailed for the time, and made him hasten those military preparations, which he had projected for subduing the refractory spirit of the Scottish nation. By regular œconomy, he had not only payed all the debts contracted during the Spanish and French wars; but had amassed a sum of two hundred thousand pounds, which he reserved for any sudden exigency. The queen had great interest with the catholics, both from the sympathy of religion, and from the favours and indulgences, which she had been able to procure to them. She now employed her credit, and persuaded them, that it was reasonable to give large contributions, as a mark of their duty to the king, during this urgent necessity.[d] A considerable supply was obtained

[c] King's Declaration at large, p. 227. Burnet's Memoirs of Hamilton.
[d] Rush. vol. iii. p. 1329. Franklyn, p. 767.

CHAPTER LIII

by this means; to the great scandal of the puritans, who were offended at seeing the king on such good terms with the papists, and repined, that others should give what they themselves were disposed to refuse him.

Charles's fleet was formidable and well supplied. Having put 5000 land forces on board, he entrusted it to the marquis of Hamilton, who had orders to sail to the frith of Forth, and to cause a diversion in the forces of the malcontents. An army was levied of near 20,000 foot, and above 3000 horse, and was put under the command of the earl of Arundel, a nobleman of great family, but celebrated neither for military nor political abilities. The earl of Essex, a man of strict honour and extremely popular, especially among the soldiery, was appointed lieutenant-general: The earl of Holland was general of the horse. The king himself joined the army, and he summoned all the peers of England to attend him. The whole had the appearance of a splendid court, rather than of a military armament; and in this situation, carrying more show than real force with it, the camp arrived at Berwic.[e]

29th May.

The Scottish army was as numerous as that of the king, but inferior in cavalry. The officers had more reputation and experience; and the soldiers, though undisciplined and ill armed, were animated, as well by the national aversion to England and the dread of becoming a province to their old enemy, as by an unsurmountable fervour of religion. The pulpits had extremely assisted the officers in levying recruits, and had thundered out anathemas against all those *who went not out to assist the Lord against the mighty.*[f] Yet so prudent were the leaders of the malcontents, that they immediately sent submissive messages to the king, and craved to be admitted to a treaty.

Charles knew that the force of the covenanters was considerable, their spirits high, their zeal furious; and that, as they were not yet daunted by any ill success, no reasonable terms could be expected from them. With regard therefore to a treaty, great difficulties occurred on both sides. Should he submit to the pretensions of the malcontents; besides that the prelacy must be sacrificed to their religious prejudices; such a check would be given to royal authority, which had, very lately, and with much difficulty, been thoroughly established in Scotland, that he must expect, ever after,

---

[e] Clarendon, vol. i. p. 115, 116, 117.   [f] Burnet's Memoirs of Hamilton.

to retain, in that kingdom, no more than the appearance of majesty. The great men, having proved, by so sensible a trial, the impotence of law and prerogative, would return to their former licenciousness: The preachers would retain their innate arrogance: And the people, unprotected by justice, would recognize no other authority, than that which they found to domineer over them. England also, it was much to be feared, would imitate so bad an example; and having already a strong propensity towards republican and puritanical factions, would expect, by the same seditious practices, to attain the same indulgence. To advance so far, without bringing the rebels to a total submission, at least to reasonable concessions, was to promise them, in all future time, an impunity for rebellion.

On the other hand, Charles considered that Scotland was never before, under any of his ancestors, so united, and so animated in its own defence; yet had often been able to foil or elude the force of England, combined heartily in one cause, and enured by long practice to the use of arms. How much greater difficulty should he find, at present, to subdue, by violence, a people, inflamed with religious prejudices; while he could only oppose to them a nation, enervated by long peace, and lukewarm in his service; or what was more to be dreaded, many of them engaged in the same party with the rebels.[g] Should the war be only protracted beyond a campaign; (and who could expect to finish it in that period?) his treasures would fail him; and, for supply, he must have recourse to an English parliament, which, by fatal experience, he had ever found more ready to encroach on the prerogatives, than to supply the necessities, of the crown. And what if he receive a defeat from the rebel army? This misfortune was far from being impossible. They were engaged in a national cause, and strongly actuated by mistaken principles. His army was retained entirely by pay, and looked on the quarrel with the same indifference, which naturally belongs to mercenary troops, without possessing the discipline, by which such troops are commonly distinguished. And the consequences of a defeat, while Scotland was enraged and England discontented, were so dreadful, that no motive should persuade him to hazard it.

[g] Rush. vol. iii. p. 936.

CHAPTER LIII

It is evident, that Charles had fallen into such a situation, that, which ever side he embraced, his errors must be dangerous: No wonder, therefore, he was in great perplexity. But he did worse, than embrace the worst side: For, properly speaking, he embraced no side at all. He concluded a sudden pacification, in which it was stipulated, that he should withdraw his fleet and army; that, within eight and forty hours, the Scots should dismiss their forces; that the king's forts should be restored to him; his authority be acknowledged; and a general assembly and a parliament be immediately summoned, in order to compose all differences.[h] What were the *reasons*, which engaged the king to admit such strange articles of peace, it is in vain to enquire: For there scarcely could be any. The *causes* of that event may admit of a more easy explication.

The malcontents had been very industrious, in representing to the English the grievances, under which Scotland laboured, and the ill counsels, which had been suggested to their sovereign. Their liberties, they said, were invaded: The prerogatives of the crown extended beyond all former precedent: Illegal courts erected: The hierarchy exalted at the expence of national privileges: And so many new superstitions introduced by the haughty tyrannical prelates, as begat a just suspicion that a project was seriously formed for the restoration of popery. The king's conduct, surely, in Scotland, had been, in every thing, except in establishing the ecclesiastical canons, more legal than in England; yet was there such a general resemblance, in the complaints of both kingdoms, that the English readily assented to all the representations of the Scottish malcontents, and believed that nation to have been driven, by oppression, into the violent counsels, which they had embraced. So far, therefore, from being willing to second the king in subduing the free spirit of the Scots; they rather pitied that unhappy people, who had been pushed to those extremities: And they thought, that the example of such neighbours, as well as their assistance, might, some time, be advantageous to England, and encourage her to recover, by a vigorous effort, her violated laws and liberties. The gentry and nobility, who, without attachment to the court, without command in the army; attended in great numbers the English camp, greedily seized, and propagated,

[h] Ibid. p. 945.

and gave authority to these sentiments: A retreat, very little honourable, which the earl of Holland, with a considerable detachment of the English forces, had made before a detachment of the
Scottish, caused all these humours to blaze up at once: And the
king, whose character was not sufficiently vigorous or decisive, and
who was apt, from facility, to embrace hasty counsels, suddenly
assented to a measure, which was recommended by all about him,
and which favoured his natural propension towards the misguided
subjects of his native kingdom.[i]

Charles, having so far advanced in pacific measures, ought,
with a steady resolution, to have prosecuted them, and have submitted to every tolerable condition, demanded by the assembly and
parliament; nor should he have recommenced hostilities, but on
account of such enormous and unexpected pretensions, as would
have justified his cause, if possible, to the whole English nation. So
far, indeed, he adopted this plan, that he agreed, not only to
confirm his former concessions, of abrogating the canons, the
liturgy, the high commission, and the articles of Perth; but also to
abolish the order itself of bishops, for which he had so zealously
contended.[k] But this concession was gained by the utmost violence,
which he could impose on his disposition and prejudices: He even
secretly retained an intention of seizing favourable opportunities,
in order to recover the ground, which he had lost.[l] And one step
farther he could not prevail with himself to advance. The assembly, when it met, payed no deference to the king's prepossessions,
but gave full indulgence to their own. They voted episcopacy to be
unlawful in the church of Scotland: He was willing to allow it
contrary to the constitutions of that church. They stigmatised the
liturgy and canons, as popish: He agreed simply to abolish them.
They denominated the high commission, tyranny: He was content
to set it aside.[m] The parliament, which sat after the assembly,
advanced pretensions, which tended to diminish the civil power of
the monarch; and what probably affected Charles still more, they
were proceeding to ratify the acts of assembly, when,[n] by the king's
instructions, Traquaire, the commissioner, prorogued them. And

*Aug.
17th.*

*War
renewed.*

[i] Clarendon, vol. i. p. 122, 123. May, p. 46.   [k]Rush. vol. iii. p. 946.
[l] Burnet's Memoirs, p. 154. Rush. vol. iii. p. 951.   [m] Idem, ibid. p. 958, &c.
[n] Rush. vol. iii. p. 955.

CHAPTER LIII

on account of these claims, which might have been foreseen, was the war renewed; with great advantages on the side of the covenanters, and disadvantages on that of the king.

No sooner had Charles concluded the pacification without conditions, than the necessity of his affairs, and his want of money, obliged him to disband his army; and as the soldiers had been held together solely by mercenary views, it was not possible, without great trouble, and expence, and loss of time, again to assemble them. The more prudent covenanters had concluded, that their pretensions being so contrary to the interests, and still more to the inclinations of the king, it was likely, that they should again be obliged to support their cause by arms; and they were therefore careful, in dismissing their troops, to preserve nothing but the appearance of a pacific disposition. The officers had orders to be ready on the first summons: The soldiers were warned not to think the nation secure from an English invasion: And the religious zeal, which animated all ranks of men, made them immediately fly to their standards as soon as the trumpet was sounded by their spiritual and temporal leaders. The credit, which, in their last expedition, they had acquired, by obliging their sovereign to depart from all his pretensions, gave courage to every one, in undertaking this new enterprize.[o]

The king, with great difficulty, found means to draw together an army: But soon discovered, that, all savings being gone, and great debts contracted, his revenue would be insufficient to support them. An English parliament, therefore, formerly so unkind and intractable, must now, after above eleven years' intermission, after the king had tried many irregular methods of taxation, after multiplied disgusts given to the puritanical party, be summoned to assemble, amidst the most pressing necessities of the crown.

1640. April 13th.

4th English parliament.

As the king resolved to try, whether this house of commons would be more compliant than their predecessors, and grant him supply on any reasonable terms; the time, appointed for the meeting of parliament, was late, and very near the time allotted for opening the campaign against the Scots. After the past experience of their ill-humour, and of their encroaching disposition, he thought that he could not, in prudence, trust them with a long

[o] Clarendon, vol. i. p. 125. Rush. vol. iii. p. 1023.

session, till he had seen some better proofs of their good intentions: The urgency of the occasion, and the little time allowed for debate, were reasons which he reserved against the malcontents in the house: And an incident had happened, which, he believed, had now furnished him with still more cogent arguments.

The earl of Traquaire had intercepted a letter, written to the king of France by the Scottish malcontents; and had conveyed this letter to the king. Charles, partly repenting of the large concessions made to the Scots, partly disgusted at their fresh insolence and pretensions, seized this opportunity of breaking with them. He had thrown into the Tower lord Loudon, commissioner from the covenanters; one of the persons who had signed the treasonable letter.[p] And he now laid the matter before the parliament, whom he hoped to inflame by the resentment, and alarm by the danger, of this application to a foreign power. By the mouth of the lord keeper, Finch, he discovered his wants, and informed them, that he had been able to assemble his army, and to subsist them, not by any revenue which he possessed, but by means of a large debt of above 300,000 pounds, which he had contracted, and for which he had given security upon the crown-lands. He represented, that it was necessary to grant supplies for the immediate and urgent demands of his military armaments: That the season was far advanced, the time precious, and none of it must be lost in deliberation: That though his coffers were empty, they had not been exhausted by unnecessary pomp, or sumptuous buildings, or any other kind of magnificence: That whatever supplies had been levied on his subjects, had been employed for their advantage and preservation, and like vapours rising out of the earth, and gathered into a cloud, had fallen in sweet and refreshing showers on the same fields, from which they had, at first, been exhaled: That though he desired such immediate assistance as might prevent, for the time, a total disorder in the government, he was far from any intention of precluding them from their right to enquire into the state of the kingdom, and to offer him petitions for the redress of their grievances: That as much as was possible of this season should afterwards be allowed them for that purpose: That as he expected only such supply at present as the current service neces-

[p] Clarendon, vol. i. p. 129. Rush. vol. iii. p. 956. May, p. 56.

sarily required, it would be requisite to assemble them again next winter, when they should have full leisure to conclude whatever business had, this session, been left imperfect and unfinished: That the parliament of Ireland had twice put such trust in his good intentions as to grant him, in the beginning of the session, a large supply, and had ever experienced good effects, from the confidence reposed in him: And that, in every circumstance, his people should find his conduct suitable to a just, pious, and gracious king, and such as was calculated to promote an entire harmony between prince and parliament.[q]

However plausible these topics, they made small impression on the house of commons. By some illegal, and several suspicious measures of the crown, and by the courageous opposition, which particular persons, amidst dangers and hardships, had made to them; the minds of men, throughout the nation, had taken such a turn as to ascribe every honour to the refractory opposers of the king and the ministers. These were the only patriots, the only lovers of their country, the only heroes, and, perhaps too, the only true Christians. A reasonable compliance with the court was slavish dependance; a regard to the king, servile flattery; a confidence in his promises, shameful prostitution. This general cast of thought, which has, more or less, prevailed in England, during near a century and a half, and which has been the cause of much good and much ill in public affairs, never predominated more than during the reign of Charles. The present house of commons, being entirely composed of country-gentlemen, who came into parliament with all their native prejudices about them, and whom the crown had no means of influencing, could not fail to contain a majority of these stubborn patriots.

Affairs likewise, by means of the Scottish insurrection, and the general discontents in England, were drawing so near to a crisis, that the leaders of the house, sagacious and penetrating, began to foresee the consequences, and to hope, that the time, so long wished for, was now come, when royal authority must fall into a total subordination under popular assemblies, and when public liberty must acquire a full ascendant. By reducing the crown to necessities, they had hitherto found, that the king had been

[q] Rush. vol. iii. p. 1114.

pushed into violent counsels, which had served extremely the purposes of his adversaries: And by multiplying these necessities, it
was foreseen, that his prerogative, undermined on all sides, must,
at last, be overthrown, and be no longer dangerous to the privileges of the people. Whatever, therefore, tended to compose the
differences between king and parliament, and to preserve the government uniformly in its present channel, was zealously opposed
by these popular leaders; and their past conduct and sufferings
gave them credit sufficient to effect all their purposes.

The house of commons, moved by these and many other obvious reasons, instead of taking notice of the king's complaints
against his Scottish subjects, or his applications for supply, entered
immediately upon grievances; and a speech, which Pym made
them on that subject, was much more hearkened to, than that
which the lord keeper had delivered to them in the name of their
sovereign. The subject of Pym's harangue has been sufficiently
explained above; where we gave an account of all the grievances,
imaginary in the church, more real in the state, of which the nation, at that time, so loudly complained.[r] The house began with
examining the behaviour of the speaker the last day of the former
parliament; when he refused, on account of the king's command,
to put the question: And they declared it a breach of privilege.
They proceeded next to enquire into the imprisonment and prosecution of Sir John Elliot, Hollis, and Valentine:[s] The affair of
ship-money was canvassed: And plentiful subject of enquiry was
suggested on all hands. Grievances were regularly classed under
three heads; those with regard to privileges of parliament, to the
property of the subject, and to religion.[t] The king, seeing a large
and inexhaustible field opened, pressed them again for supply;
and finding his message ineffectual, he came to the house of peers,
and desired their good offices with the commons. The peers were
sensible of the king's urgent necessities; and thought, that supply,
on this occasion, ought, both in reason and in decency, to go before
grievances. They ventured to represent their sense of the matter
to the commons; but their intercession did harm. The commons
had always claimed, as their peculiar province, the granting of

[r] Clarendon, vol. i. p. 133. Rush. vol. iii. p. 1131. May, p. 60.　[s] Rush. vol.
iii. p. 1136.　[t] Idem, ibid. p. 1147.

supplies; and, though the peers had here gone no farther than offering advice, the lower house immediately thought proper to vote so unprecedented an interposition to be a breach of privilege." Charles, in order to bring the matter of supply to some issue, solicited the house by new messages: And finding, that ship-money gave great alarm and disgust; besides informing them, that he never intended to make a constant revenue of it, that all the money levied had been regularly, with other great sums, expended on equipping the navy; he now went so far as to offer them a total abolition of that obnoxious claim, by any law, which the commons should think proper to present to him. In return, he only asked, for his necessities, a supply of twelve subsidies, about six hundred thousand pounds, and that payable in three years; but, at the same time, he let them know, that, considering the situation of his affairs, a delay would be equivalent to a denial." The king, though the majority was against him, never had more friends in any house of commons; and the debate was carried on for two days, with great zeal and warmth on both sides.

It was urged by the partizans of the court, that the happiest occasion, which the fondest wishes could suggest, was now presented, for removing all disgusts and jealousies between king and people, and for reconciling their sovereign, for ever, to the use of parliaments. That if they, on their part, laid aside all enormous claims and pretensions, and provided, in a reasonable manner, for the public necessities; they needed entertain no suspicion of any insatiable ambition or illegal usurpation in the crown. That though due regard had not always been paid, during this reign, to the rights of the people, yet no invasion of them had been altogether deliberate and voluntary; much less, the result of wanton tyranny and injustice; and still less, of a formed design to subvert the constitution. That to repose a reasonable confidence in the king, and generously to supply his present wants, which proceeded neither from prodigality nor misconduct, would be the true means of gaining on his generous nature, and extorting, by a gentle violence, such concessions as were requisite for the establishment of public liberty. That he had promised, not only on the word of a

---

" Clarendon, vol. i. p. 134.   " Clarendon, vol. i. p. 135. Rush. vol. iii. p. 1154.

prince, but also on that of a gentleman (the expression which he had been pleased to use) that, after the supply was granted, the parliament should still have liberty to continue their deliberations: Could it be suspected, that any man, any prince, much less such a one, whose word was, as yet, sacred and inviolate, would, for so small a motive, forfeit his honour, and, with it, all future trust and confidence, by breaking a promise, so public and so solemn? That even if the parliament should be deceived in reposing this confidence in him, they neither lost any thing, nor incurred any danger; since it was evidently necessary, for the security of public peace, to supply him with money, in order to suppress the Scottish rebellion. That he had so far suited his first demands to their prejudices, that he only asked a supply for a few months, and was willing, after so short a trust from them, to fall again into dependance, and to trust them for his farther support and subsistence. That if he now seemed to desire something farther, he also made them, in return, a considerable offer, and was willing, for the future, to depend on them for a revenue, which was quite necessary for public honour and security. That the nature of the English constitution supposed a mutual confidence between king and parliament: And if they should refuse it on their part, especially with circumstances of such outrage and indignity; what could be expected but a total dissolution of government, and violent factions, followed by the most dangerous convulsions and intestine disorders?

In opposition to these arguments, it was urged by the malcontent party, that the court had discovered, on their part, but few symptoms of that mutual confidence to which they now so kindly invited the commons. That eleven years intermission of parliaments, the longest that was to be found in the English annals, was a sufficient indication of the jealousy entertained against the people; or rather of designs formed for the suppression of all their liberties and privileges. That the ministers might well plead necessity, nor could any thing, indeed, be a stronger proof of some invincible necessity, than their embracing a measure, for which they had conceived so violent an aversion, as the assembling of an English parliament. That this necessity, however, was purely ministerial, not national; And if the same grievances, ecclesiastical and civil, under which this nation itself laboured, had pushed the Scots to extremities; was it requisite, that the English should forge their own chains, by imposing chains on their unhappy neighbours? That the ancient practice of parliament was to give grievances the precedency of supply; and this order, so carefully observed by their ancestors, was founded on a jealousy inherent in the constitution, and was never interpreted as any peculiar diffidence of the present sovereign. That a practice, which had been upheld, during times the most favourable to liberty, could not, in common prudence, be departed from, where such undeniable reasons for suspicion had been afforded. That it was ridiculous to plead the advanced season, and the urgent occasion for supply; when it plainly appeared, that, in order to afford a pretence for this topic, and to seduce the commons, great political contrivance had been employed. That the writs for elections were issued early in the winter; and if the meeting of parliament had not purposely been delayed, till so near the commencement of military operations, there had been leisure sufficient to have redressed all national grievances, and to have proceeded afterwards to an examination of the king's occasion for supply. That the intention of so gross an artifice was to engage the commons, under pretence of necessity, to violate the regular order of parliament; and a precedent of that kind being once established, no enquiry into public measures would afterwards be permitted. That scarcely any argument, more unfavourable, could be pleaded for supply, than an offer to abolish ship-money; a taxation, the most illegal and the most dangerous, that had ever, in any reign, been imposed upon the nation. And that, by bargaining for the remission of that duty, the commons would, in a manner, ratify the authority, by which it had been levied; at least, give encouragement for advancing new pretensions of a like nature, in hopes of resigning them on like advantageous conditions.

These reasons, joined to so many occasions of ill humour, seemed to sway with the greater number: But to make the matter worse, Sir Harry Vane, the secretary, told the commons, without any authority from the king, that nothing less than twelve subsidies would be accepted as a compensation for the abolition of ship-money. This assertion, proceeding from the indiscretion, if we are not rather to call it the treachery, of Vane, displeased the house, by showing a stiffness and rigidity in the king, which, in a claim so ill grounded, was deemed inexcusable.[x] We are informed likewise, that some men, who were thought to understand the state of the nation, affirmed in the house, that the amount of twelve subsidies was a greater sum than could be found in all England. Such were the happy ignorance and inexperience of those times, with regard to taxes![y]

The king was in great doubt and perplexity. He saw, that his friends in the house were out-numbered by his enemies, and that the same counsels were still prevalent, which had ever bred such opposition and disturbance. Instead of hoping, that any supply would be granted him, to carry on war against the Scots, whom the majority of the house regarded as their best friends and firmest allies; he expected every day, that they would present him an address for making peace with those rebels. And if the house met again, a vote, he was informed, would certainly pass, to blast his revenue of ship-money; and thereby renew all the opposition, which, with so much difficulty, he had surmounted, in levying that taxation. Where great evils lie on all sides, it is difficult to follow the best counsel; nor is it any wonder, that the king, whose capacity was not equal to situations of such extreme delicacy, should hastily *Dissolution.* have formed and executed the resolution of dissolving this parliament: A measure, however, of which he soon after repented, and which the subsequent events, more than any convincing reason, inclined every one to condemn. The last parliament, which ended with such rigour and violence, had yet, at first, covered their intentions with greater appearance of moderation than this parliament had hitherto assumed.

An abrupt and violent dissolution naturally excites discontents among the people, who usually put entire confidence in their representatives, and expect from them the redress of all grievances. As if there were not already sufficient grounds of complaint, the king persevered still in those counsels, which, from experience, he might have been sensible, were so dangerous and unpopular. Bellasis and Sir John Hotham were summoned before the council; and refusing to give any account of their conduct in parliament, were committed to prison. All the petitions and complaints, which had been sent to the committee of religion, were demanded from

---

[x] Clarendon, vol. i. p. 138.   [y] Clarendon, vol. i. p. 136.

CHAPTER LIII

Crew, chairman of that committee; and on his refusal to deliver them, he was sent to the Tower. The studies and even the pockets of the earl of Warwic and lord Broke, before the expiration of privilege, were searched, in expectation of finding treasonable papers. These acts of authority were interpreted, with some appearance of reason, to be invasions on the right of national assemblies.[z] But the king, after the first provocation which he met with, never sufficiently respected the privileges of parliament; and, by his example, he farther confirmed their resolution, when they should acquire power, to pay like disregard to the prerogatives of the crown.

Though the parliament was dissolved, the convocation was still allowed to sit; a practice, of which, since the reformation, there were but few instances,[a] and which was for that reason supposed by many to be irregular. Besides granting to the king a supply from the spirituality, and framing many canons, the convocation, jealous of like innovations, with those which had taken place in Scotland, imposed an oath on the clergy, and the graduates in the universities, by which every one swore to maintain the established government of the church by archbishops, bishops, deans, chapters, &c.[b] These steps, in the present discontented humour of the nation, were commonly deemed illegal; because not ratified by consent of parliament, in whom all authority was now supposed to be centered. And nothing, besides, could afford more subject of ridicule, than an oath, which contained an *et cætera* in the midst of it.

The people, who generally abhorred the convocation as much as they revered the parliament, could scarcely be restrained from insulting and abusing this assembly; and the king was obliged to give them guards, in order to protect them.[c] An attack too was made during the night upon Laud, in his palace of Lambeth, by above 500 persons; and he found it necessary to fortify himself for his defence.[d] A multitude, consisting of two thousand sectaries, entered St. Paul's, where the high commission then sat; tore down

Discontents in England.

---

[z] Rush. vol. iii. p. 1167. May, p. 61. [a] There was one in 1586, See History of Archbishop Laud, p. 80. The authority of the convocation was indeed, in most respects, independent of the parliament, and there was no reason, which required the one to be dissolved upon the dissolution of the other. [b] Whitlocke, p. 33. [c] Whitlocke, p. 33. [d] Dugdale, p. 62. Clarendon, vol. i. p. 143.

the benches; and cried out, *No bishop, no high commission.*[e] All these instances of discontent were presages of some great revolution; had the court possessed sufficient skill to discern the danger, or sufficient power to provide against it.

In this disposition of men's minds, it was in vain that the king issued a declaration, in order to convince his people of the necessity, which he lay under, of dissolving the last parliament.[f] The chief topic, on which he insisted, was, that the commons imitated the bad example of all their predecessors of late years, in making continual encroachments on his authority, in censuring his whole administration and conduct, in discussing every circumstance of public government, and in their indirect bargaining and contracting with their king for supply; as if nothing ought to be given him but what he should purchase, either by quitting somewhat of his royal prerogative, or by diminishing and lessening his standing revenue. These practices, he said, were contrary to the maxims of their ancestors; and these practices were totally incompatible with monarchy.[g]

The king, disappointed of parliamentary subsidies, was obliged to have recourse to other expedients, in order to supply his urgent necessities. The ecclesiastical subsidies served him in some stead; and it seemed but just, that the clergy should contribute to a war, which was, in a great measure, of their own raising.[h] He borrowed money from his ministers and courtiers; and so much was he beloved among them, that above 300,000 pounds were subscribed in a few days: Though nothing surely could be more disagreeable to a prince, full of dignity, than to be a burthen on his friends, instead of being a support to them. Some attempts were made towards forcing a loan from the citizens; but still repelled by the spirit of liberty, which was now become unconquerable.[i] A loan of 40,000 pounds was extorted from the Spanish merchants, who had bullion in the Tower, exposed to the attempts of the king. Coat and conduct-money for the soldiery was levied on the counties; an ancient practice,[k] but supposed to be abolished by the petition of right. All the pepper was bought from the East-India company upon trust, and sold, at a great discount, for ready money.[l] A

---

[e] Dugdale, p. 65.   [f] Rushworth, vol. iii. p. 1166.   [g] See note [W] at the end of the volume.   [h] May, p. 48.   [i] Rush. vol. iii. p. 1181.   [k] Idem, vol. i. p. 168.   [l] May, p. 63.

scheme was proposed for coining two or three hundred thousand pounds of base money.[m] Such were the extremities to which Charles was reduced. The fresh difficulties, which, amidst the present distresses, were, every day, raised, with regard to the payment of ship-money, obliged him to exert continual acts of authority, augmented the discontents of the people, and encreased his indigence and necessities.[n]

The present expedients, however, enabled the king, though with great difficulty, to march his army, consisting of 19,000 foot, and 2000 horse.[o] The earl of Northumberland was appointed general: The earl of Strafford, who was called over from Ireland, lieutenant-general: Lord Conway, general of the horse. A small fleet was thought sufficient to serve the purposes of this expedition.

So great are the effects of zeal and unanimity, that the Scottish army, though somewhat superior, were sooner ready than the king's; and they marched to the borders of England. To engage them to proceed, besides their general knowledge of the secret discontents of that kingdom, lord Saville had forged a letter, in the name of six noblemen the most considerable of England, by which the Scots were invited to assist their neighbours, in procuring a redress of grievances.[p] Notwithstanding these warlike preparations and hostile attempts, the covenanters still preserved the most pathetic and most submissive language; and entered England, they said, with no other view, than to obtain access to the king's presence, and lay their humble petition at his royal feet. At Newburn upon Tyne, they were opposed by a detachment of 4,500 men under Conway, who seemed resolute to dispute with them the passage of the river. The Scots first entreated them, with great civility, not to stop them in their march to their gracious sovereign; and then attacked them with great bravery, killed several, and chased the rest from their ground. Such a panic seized the whole English army, that the forces at Newcastle fled immediately to Durham; and not yet thinking themselves safe, they deserted that town, and retreated into Yorkshire.[q]

The Scots took possession of Newcastle; and though suf-

20th Aug.

28th Aug.
Rout at
Newburn.

---

[m] Rush. vol. iii. p. 1216. May, p. 63. [n] Rush. vol. iii. p. 1173, 1182, 1184, 1199, 1200, 1203, 1204. [o] Rush. vol. iii. p. 1279. [p] Nalson, vol. ii. p. 427. [q] Clarendon, vol. i. p. 143.

ficiently elated with their victory, they preserved exact discipline, and persevered in their resolution of paying for every thing, in order still to maintain the appearance of an amicable correspondence with England. They also dispatched messengers to the king, who was arrived at York; and they took care, after the advantage, which they had obtained, to redouble their expressions of loyalty, duty, and submission to his person, and they even made apologies, full of sorrow and contrition, for their late victory.[r]

Charles was in a very distressed condition. The nation was universally and highly discontented. The army was discouraged, and began likewise to be discontented, both from the contagion of general disgust, and as an excuse for their misbehaviour, which they were desirous of representing rather as want of will than of courage to fight. The treasury too was quite exhausted, and every expedient for supply had been tried to the uttermost. No event had happened, but what might have been forseen as necessary, at least, as very probable; yet such was the king's situation, that no provision could be made, nor was even any resolution taken, against such an exigency.

Treaty at Rippon. In order to prevent the advance of the Scots upon him, the king agreed to a treaty, and named sixteen English noblemen, who met with eleven Scottish commissioners at Rippon. The earls of Hertford, Bedford, Salisbury, Warwick, Essex, Holland, Bristol, and Berkshire, the lords Kimbolton, Wharton, Dunsmore, Paget, Broke, Saville, Paulet, and Howard of Escric, were chosen by the king; all of them popular men, and consequently supposed no-wise averse to the Scottish invasion, or unacceptable to that nation.[s]

An address arrived from the city of London, petitioning for a parliament; the great point to which all men's projects at this time tended.[t] Twelve noblemen presented a petition to the same purpose.[u] But the king contented himself with summoning a great council of the peers at York; a measure, which had formerly been taken in cases of sudden emergency, but which, at present, could serve to little purpose. Perhaps, the king, who dreaded, above all

[r] Rush. vol. iii. p. 1255.   [s] Clarendon, vol. i. p. 155.   [t] Rush. vol. iii. p. 1263.   [u] Clarendon, vol. i. p. 146. Rush. vol. iii. p. 1260. May, p. 66. Warwick, p. 151.

things, the house of commons; and who expected no supply from them on any reasonable terms, thought, that, in his present distresses, he might be enabled to levy supplies by the authority of the peers alone. But the employing, so long, the plea of a necessity, which appeared distant and doubtful, rendered it impossible for him to avail himself of a necessity, which was now at last become real, urgent, and inevitable.

By Northumberland's sickness the command of the army had devolved on Strafford. This nobleman possessed more vigour of mind than the king or any of the council. He advised Charles rather to put all to hazard, than submit to such unworthy terms as were likely to be imposed upon him. The loss sustained at Newburn, he said, was inconsiderable; and though a panic had for the time seized the army, that event was nothing strange among new levied troops; and the Scots, being in the same condition, would, no doubt, be liable, in their turn, to a like accident. His opinion, therefore, was, that the king should push forward, and attack the Scots, and bring the affair to a quick decision; and, if he were ever so unsuccessful, nothing worse could befal him, than what, from his inactivity, he would certainly be exposed to.[w] To show how easy it would be to execute this project, he ordered an assault to be made on some quarters of the Scots, and he gained an advantage over them. No cessation of arms had, as yet, been agreed to, during the treaty at Rippon; yet great clamour prevailed, on account of this act of hostility. And when it was known that the officer, who conducted the attack, was a papist, a violent outcry was raised against the king, for employing that hated sect, in the murder of his protestant subjects.[x]

It may be worthy of remark that several mutinies had arisen among the English troops, when marching to join the army; and some officers had been murdered, merely on suspicion of their being papists.[y] The petition of right had abolished all martial law; and by an inconvenience, which naturally attended the plan, as yet new and unformed, of regular and rigid liberty, it was found absolutely impossible for the generals to govern the army, by all the authority, which the king could legally confer upon them. The

[w] Nalson, vol. ii. p. 5.   [x] Clarendon, vol. i. p. 159.   [y] Rush. vol. iii. p. 1190, 1191, 1192, &c. May, p. 64.

lawyers had declared, that martial law could not be exercised, except in the very presence of an enemy; and because it had been found necessary to execute a mutineer, the generals thought it adviseable, for their own safety, to apply for a pardon from the crown. This weakness, however, was carefully concealed from the army; and lord Conway said, that, if any lawyer were so imprudent as to discover the secret to the soldiers, it would be necessary instantly to refute him, and to hang the lawyer himself, by sentence of a court-martial.[z]

An army new levied, undisciplined, frightened, seditious, ill-paid, and governed by no proper authority, was very unfit for withstanding a victorious and high-spirited enemy, and retaining in subjection a discontented and zealous nation.

24th Sept. Great council of the peers.

Charles, in despair of being able to stem the torrent, at last determined to yield to it: And as he foresaw, that the great council of the peers would advise him to call a parliament, he told them, in his first speech, that he had already taken this resolution. He informed them likewise, that the queen, in a letter, which she had written to him, had very earnestly recommended that measure. This good prince, who was extremely attached to his consort, and who passionately wished to render her popular in the nation, forgot not, amidst all his distress, the interests of his domestic tenderness.[a]

In order to subsist both armies (for the king was obliged, in order to save the northern counties, to pay his enemies) Charles wrote to the city, desiring a loan of 200,000 pounds. And the peers at York, whose authority was now much greater than that of their sovereign, joined in the same request.[b] So low was this prince already fallen, in the eyes of his own subjects!

As many difficulties occurred in the negociation with the Scots, it was proposed to transfer the treaty from Rippon to London: A proposal willingly embraced by that nation, who were now sure of treating with advantage, in a place, where the king, they foresaw, would be, in a manner, a prisoner, in the midst of his implacable enemies, and their determined friends.[c]

---

[z] Rush. vol. iii. p. 1199. [a] Clarendon, vol. i. p. 154. Rush. vol. iii. p. 1275.
[b] Rush. vol. iii. p. 1279. [c] Ibid. p. 1305.

LIV

Meeting of the long parliament –
Strafford and Laud impeached – Finch and
Windebank fly – Great authority of the commons –
The bishops attacked – Tonnage and poundage –
Triennial bill – Strafford's trial –
Bill of attainder – Execution
of Strafford – High-commission and star-chamber
abolished – King's journey to Scotland

🌿 🌿 🌿

THE CAUSES OF DISGUST, which, for above thirty years, had daily been multiplying in England, were now come to full maturity, and threatened the kingdom with some great revolution or convulsion. The uncertain and undefined limits of prerogative and privilege had been eagerly disputed during that whole period; and in every controversy between prince and people, the question, however doubtful, had always been decided, by each party, in favour of its own pretensions. Too lightly, perhaps, moved by the appearance of necessity, the king had even assumed powers incompatible with the principles of limited government, and had rendered it impossible for his most zealous partizans entirely to justify his conduct, except by topics so unpopular, that they were more fitted, in the present disposition of men's minds, to inflame, than appease, the general discontent. Those great supports of public authority, law and religion, had likewise, by the unbounded compliance of judges and prelates, lost much of their influence over the people; or rather had in a great measure gone over to the side of faction, and authorized the spirit of opposition and rebellion. The nobility, also, whom the king had no means of retaining by offices and preferments suitable to their rank, had been seized with the general discontent, and unwarily threw themselves into the scale, which already began too much to preponderate. Sensible of some encroachments, which had been made by royal authority, men entertained no jealousy of the commons, whose enterprizes, for the acquisition of power, had ever been covered with the appearance of public good, and had hitherto gone no farther than some disappointed efforts and endeavours. The progress of the Scottish malcontents reduced the crown to an entire dependence for supply: Their union with the popular party in England brought great accession of authority to the latter: The near prospect of success roused all latent murmurs and pretensions, which had hitherto been held in such violent constraint: And the torrent of general inclination and opinion ran so strongly against the court, that the king was in no situation to refuse any reasonable demands of the popular leaders, either for defining or limiting the powers of his prerogative. Even many exorbitant claims, in his present situation, would probably be made, and must necessarily be complied with.

The triumph of the malcontents over the church was not yet so immediate or certain. Though the political and religious puritans mutually lent assistance to each other, there were many who joined the former, yet declined all connexion with the latter. The hierarchy had been established in England ever since the reformation: The Romish church, in all ages, had carefully maintained that form of ecclesiastical government: The ancient fathers too bore testimony to episcopal jurisdiction: And though parity may seem at first to have had place among Christian pastors, the period, during which it prevailed, was so short, that few undisputed traces of it remained in history. The bishops and their more zealous partizans inferred thence the divine indefeizable right of prelacy: Others regarded that institution as venerable and useful: And, if the love of novelty led some to adopt the new rites and discipline of the puritans, the reverence to antiquity retained many in their attachment to the liturgy and government of the church. It be-

CHAPTER LIV

hoved, therefore, the zealous innovators in parliament to proceed with some caution and reserve. By promoting all measures which reduced the powers of the crown, they hoped to disarm the king, whom they justly regarded, from principle, inclination, and policy, to be the determined patron of the hierarchy. By declaiming against the supposed encroachments and tyranny of the prelates, they endeavoured to carry the nation, from a hatred of their persons, to an opposition against their office and character. And when men were inlisted in party, it would not be difficult, they thought, to lead them by degrees into many measures, for which they formerly entertained the greatest aversion. Though the new sectaries composed not, at first, the majority of the nation, they were inflamed, as is usual among innovators, with extreme zeal for their opinions. Their unsurmountable passion, disguised to themselves, as well as to others, under the appearance of holy fervours, was well qualified to make proselytes, and to seize the minds of the ignorant multitude. And one furious enthusiast was able, by his active industry, to surmount the indolent efforts of many sober and reasonable antagonists.

When the nation, therefore, was so generally discontented, and little suspicion was entertained of any design to subvert the church and monarchy; no wonder, that almost all elections ran in favour of those, who, by their high pretensions to piety and patriotism, had encouraged the national prejudices. It is a usual compliment to regard the king's inclination in the choice of a speaker; and Charles had intended to advance Gardiner, recorder of London, to that important trust: But so little interest did the crown, at that time, possess in the nation, that Gardiner was disappointed of his election, not only in London, but in every other place where it was attempted: And the king was obliged to make the choice of speaker fall on Lenthal, a lawyer of some character, but not sufficiently qualified for so high and difficult an office.[d]

The eager expectations of men with regard to a parliament, summoned at so critical a juncture, and during such general discontents; a parliament, which, from the situation of public affairs, could not be abruptly dissolved, and which was to execute every thing left unfinished by former parliaments; these motives, so

Meeting of the long parliament. Nov. 3.

[d] Clarendon, vol. i. p. 169.

important and interesting, engaged the attendance of all the members; and the house of commons was never observed to be, from the beginning, so full and numerous. Without any interval, therefore, they entered upon business, and by unanimous consent they immediately struck a blow, which may, in a manner, be regarded as decisive.

The earl of Strafford was considered as chief minister, both on account of the credit which he possessed with his master, and of his own great and uncommon vigour and capacity. By a concurrence of accidents, this man laboured under the severe hatred of all the three nations, which composed the British monarchy. The Scots, whose authority now ran extremely high, looked on him as the capital enemy of their country, and one whose counsels and influence they had most reason to apprehend. He had engaged the parliament of Ireland to advance large subsidies, in order to support a war against them: He had levied an army of 9000 men, with which he had menaced all their western coast: He had obliged the Scots, who lived under his government, to renounce the covenant, their national idol: He had in Ireland proclaimed the Scottish covenanters rebels and traitors, even before the king had issued any such declaration against them in England: And he had ever dissuaded his master against the late treaty and suspension of arms, which he regarded as dangerous and dishonourable. So avowed and violent were the Scots in their resentment of all these measures, that they had refused to send commissioners to treat at York, as was at first proposed; because, they said, the lieutenant of Ireland, their capital enemy, being general of the king's forces, had there the chief command and authority.

Strafford, first as deputy, then as lord lieutenant, had governed Ireland during eight years with great vigilance, activity, and prudence, but with very little popularity. In a nation so averse to the English government and religion, these very virtues were sufficient to draw on him the public hatred. The manners too and character of this great man, though to all full of courtesy, and to his friends full of affection, were, at bottom, haughty, rigid, and severe. His authority and influence, during the time of his government, had been unlimited; but no sooner did adversity seize him, than the concealed aversion of the nation blazed up at once, and the Irish parliament used every expedient to aggravate the charge against him.

CHAPTER LIV

The universal discontent, which prevailed in England against the court, was all pointed towards the earl of Strafford; though without any particular reason, but because he was the minister of state, whom the king most favoured and most trusted. His extraction was honourable, his paternal fortune considerable: Yet envy attended his sudden and great elevation. And his former associates in popular counsels, finding that he owed his advancement to the desertion of their cause, represented him as the great apostate of the commonwealth, whom it behoved them to sacrifice, as a victim to public justice.

Strafford, sensible of the load of popular prejudices under which he laboured, would gladly have declined attendance in parliament; and he begged the king's permission to withdraw himself to his government of Ireland, at least to remain at the head of the army in Yorkshire; where many opportunities, he hoped, would offer, by reason of his distance, to elude the attacks of his enemies. But Charles, who had entire confidence in the earl's capacity, thought, that his counsels would be extremely useful during the critical session which approached. And when Strafford still insisted on the danger of his appearing amidst so many enraged enemies, the king, little apprehensive that his own authority was so suddenly to expire, promised him protection, and assured him, that not a hair of his head should be touched by the parliament.[e]

No sooner was Stafford's arrival known, than a concerted attack was made upon him in the house of commons. Pym, in a long, studied discourse, divided into many heads after his manner, enumerated all the grievances, under which the nation laboured; and, from a complication of such oppressions, inferred, that a deliberate plan had been formed of changing entirely the frame of government, and subverting the ancient laws and liberties of the kingdom.[f] Could any thing, he said, encrease our indignation against so enormous and criminal a project, it would be to find, that, during the reign of the best of princes, the constitution had been endangered by the worst of ministers, and that the virtues of the king had been seduced by wicked and pernicious counsel. We must enquire, added he, from what fountain these waters of bitterness flow; and though doubtless many evil counsellors will be found to have contributed their endeavours, yet there is one who challenges

11th Nov.

Strafford impeached.

[e] Whitlocke, p. 36.   [f] Id. ibid.

the infamous pre-eminence, and who, by his courage, enterprize, and capacity, is intitled to the first place among these betrayers of their country. He is the earl of Strafford, lieutenant of Ireland, and president of the council of York, who, in both places, and in all other provinces, where he has been entrusted with authority, has raised ample monuments of tyranny, and will appear, from a survey of his actions, to be the chief promoter of every arbitrary counsel. Some instances of imperious expressions, as well as actions, were given by Pym; who afterwards entered into a more personal attack of that minister, and endeavoured to expose his whole character and manners. The austere genius of Strafford, occupied in the pursuits of ambition, had not rendered his breast altogether inaccessible to the tender passions, or secured him from the dominion of the fair; and in that sullen age, when the irregularities of pleasure were more reproachful than the most odious crimes, these weaknesses were thought worthy of being mentioned, together with his treasons, before so great an assembly. And upon the whole, the orator concluded, that it belonged to the house to provide a remedy proportionable to the disease, and to prevent the farther mischiefs justly to be apprehended from the influence, which this man had acquired over the measures and counsels of their sovereign.[g]

Sir John Clotworthy an Irish gentleman, Sir John Hotham of Yorkshire, and many others, entered into the same topics: And after several hours spent in bitter invective, when the doors were locked, in order to prevent all discovery of their purpose; it was moved, in consequence of the resolution secretly taken, that Strafford should immediately be impeached of high treason. This motion was received with universal approbation; nor was there, in all the debate, one person that offered to stop the torrent by any testimony in favour of the earl's conduct. Lord Falkland alone, though known to be his enemy, modestly desired the house to consider, whether it would not better suit the gravity of their proceedings, first to digest, by a committee, many of those particulars, which had been mentioned, before they sent up an accusation against him. It was ingenuously answered by Pym, that such a delay might probably blast all their hopes, and put it out of their

[g] Clarendon, vol. i. p. 172.

power to proceed any farther in the prosecution: That when Strafford should learn, that so many of his enormities were discovered, his conscience would dictate his condemnation; and so great was his power and credit, he would immediately procure the dissolution of the parliament, or attempt some other desperate measure for his own preservation: That the commons were only accusers, not judges; and it was the province of the peers to determine, whether such a complication of enormous crimes, in one person, did not amount to the highest crime known by the law.[h] Without farther debate, the impeachment was voted: Pym was chosen to carry it up to the lords: Most of the house accompanied him on so agreeable an errand: And Strafford, who had just entered the house of peers, and who little expected so speedy a prosecution, was immediately, upon this general charge; ordered into custody, with several symptoms of violent prejudice in his judges, as well as in his prosecutors.

In the enquiry concerning grievances and in the censure of past measures, Laud could not long escape the severe scrutiny of the commons; who were led too, in their accusation of that prelate, as well by their prejudices against his whole order, as by the extreme antipathy, which his intemperate zeal had drawn upon him. After a deliberation, which scarcely lasted half an hour, an impeachment of high treason was voted against this subject, the first, both in rank and in favour, throughout the kingdom. Though this incident, considering the example of Strafford's impeachment and the present disposition of the nation and parliament, needed be no surprize to him; yet was he betrayed into some passion, when the accusation was presented. *The commons themselves,* he said, *though his accusers, did not believe him guilty of the crimes with which they charged him:* An indiscretion, which, next day, upon more mature deliberation, he desired leave to retract; but so little favourable were the peers, that they refused him this advantage or indulgence. Laud also was immediately, upon this general charge, sequestered from parliament, and committed to custody.[i]

The capital article, insisted on against these two great men, was the design which the commons supposed to have been formed of

Laud impeached.

[h] Clarendon, vol. i. p. 174.   [i] Clarendon, vol. i. p. 177. Whitlocke, p. 38. Rushworth, vol. iii. p. 1365.

subverting the laws and constitution of England, and introducing arbitrary and unlimited authority into the kingdom. Of all the king's ministers, no one was so obnoxious in this respect as the lord keeper, Finch. He it was, who, being speaker in the king's third parliament, had left the chair, and refused to put the question, when ordered by the house. The extrajudicial opinion of the judges in the case of ship-money had been procured by his intrigues, persuasions, and even menaces. In all unpopular and illegal measures, he was ever most active; and he was even believed to have declared publicly, that, while he was keeper, an order of council should always with him be equivalent to a law. To appease the rising displeasure of the commons, he desired to be heard at their bar. He prostrated himself with all humility before them; but this submission availed him nothing. An impeachment was resolved on; and in order to escape their fury, he thought proper

Lord keeper Finch flies.

secretly to withdraw, and retire into Holland. As he was not esteemed equal to Strafford, or even to Laud, either in capacity or in fidelity to his master; it was generally believed, that his escape had been connived at by the popular leaders.[k] His impeachment, however, in his absence, was carried up to the house of peers.

Sir Francis Windebank, the secretary, was a creature of Laud's; a sufficient reason for his being extremely obnoxious to the commons. He was secretly suspected too of the crime of popery; and it was known, that, from complaisance to the queen, and indeed in compliance with the king's maxims of government, he had granted many indulgences to catholics, and had signed warrants for the pardon of priests, and their delivery from confinement. Grimstone, a popular member, called him, in the house, the very

Secretary Windebank flies.

pander and broker to the whore of Babylon.[l] Finding that the scrutiny of the commons was pointing towards him, and being sensible that England was no longer a place of safety for men of his character, he suddenly made his escape into France.[m]

Thus, in a few weeks, this house of commons, not opposed, or rather seconded by the peers, had produced such a revolution in the government, that the two most powerful and most favoured ministers of the king were thrown into the Tower, and daily ex-

[k] Clarendon, vol. i. p. 177. Whitlocke, p. 38. Rushworth, vol. i. p. 129. 136.
[l] Rushworth, vol. v. p. 122.   [m] Clarendon, vol. i. p. 178. Whitlocke, p. 37.

pected to be tried for their life: Two other ministers had, by flight alone, saved themselves from a like fate: All the king's servants saw that no protection could be given them by their master: A new jurisdiction was erected in the nation; and before that tribunal all those trembled, who had before exulted most in their credit and authority.

What rendered the power of the commons more formidable, was, the extreme prudence with which it was conducted. Not content with the authority, which they had acquired by attacking these great ministers, they were resolved to render the most considerable bodies of the nation obnoxious to them. Though the idol of the people, they determined to fortify themselves likewise with terrors, and to overawe those who might still be inclined to support the falling ruins of monarchy.

Great authority of the commons.

During the late military operations, several powers had been exercised by the lieutenants and deputy-lieutenants of counties: And these powers, though necessary for the defence of the nation, and even warranted by all former precedent, yet not being authorized by statute, were now voted to be illegal; and the persons who had assumed them, declared *delinquents*. This term was newly come into vogue, and expressed a degree and species of guilt not exactly known or ascertained. In consequence of that determination, many of the nobility and prime gentry of the nation, while only exerting, as they justly thought, the legal powers of magistracy, unexpectedly found themselves involved in the crime of delinquency. And the commons reaped this multiplied advantage by their vote: They disarmed the crown; they established the maxims of rigid law and liberty; and they spread the terror of their own authority.[n]

The writs for ship-money had been directed to the sheriffs, who were required, and even obliged under severe penalties, to assess the sums upon individuals, and to levy them by their authority: Yet were all the sheriffs, and all those who had been employed in that illegal service, voted, by a very rigorous sentence, to be delinquents. The king, by the maxims of law, could do no wrong: His ministers and servants, of whatever degree, in case of any violation of the constitution, were alone culpable.[o]

[n] Clarendon, vol. i. p. 176.   [o] Clarendon, vol. i. p. 176.

All the farmers and officers of the customs, who had been employed during so many years, in levying tonnage and poundage and the new impositions, were likewise declared criminals, and were afterwards glad to compound for a pardon by paying a fine of 150,000 pounds.

Every discretionary or arbitrary sentence of the star-chamber and high commission; courts, which, from their very constitution, were arbitrary, underwent a severe scrutiny: And all those, who had concurred in such sentences, were voted to be liable to the penalties of law.[p] No minister of the king, no member of the council, but found himself exposed by this decision.

The judges, who had given their vote against Hambden in the trial of ship-money, were accused before the peers, and obliged to find surety for their appearance. Berkeley, a judge of the King's Bench, was seized by order of the house, even when sitting in his tribunal; and all men saw with astonishment the irresistible authority of their jurisdiction.[q]

The sanction of the lords and commons, as well as that of the king, was declared necessary for the confirmation of ecclesiastical canons.[r] And this judgment, it must be confessed, however reasonable, at least useful, it would have been difficult to justify by any precedent.[s] But the present was no time for question or dispute. That decision, which abolished all legislative power except that of parliament, was requisite for completing the new plan of liberty, and rendering it quite uniform and systematical. Almost all the bench of bishops, and the most considerable of the inferior clergy, who had voted in the late convocation, found themselves exposed, by these new principles, to the imputation of delinquency.[t]

The most unpopular of all Charles's measures, and the least justifiable, was the revival of monopolies, so solemnly abolished, after reiterated endeavours, by a recent act of parliament. Sensible

---

[p] Ibid. p. 177. [q] Whitlocke, p. 39. [r] Nalson, vol. i. p. 678. [s] An act of parliament, 25 Hen. VIII. cap. 19. allowed the convocation with the king's consent to make canons. By the famous act of submission to that prince, the clergy bound themselves to enact no canons without the king's consent. The parliament was never mentioned nor thought of. Such pretensions as the commons advanced at present, would, in any former age, have been deemed strange usurpations. [t] Clarendon, vol. i. p. 206. Whitlocke, p. 37. Rush. vol. v. p. 235. 359. Nalson, vol. i. p. 807.

CHAPTER LIV

of this unhappy measure, the king had, of himself, recalled, during the time of his first expedition against Scotland, many of these oppressive patents; and the rest were now annulled by authority of parliament, and every one who was concerned in them, declared delinquents. The commons carried so far their detestation of this odious measure, that they assumed a power which had formerly been seldom practised,[u] and they expelled all their members who were monopolists or projectors: An artifice, by which, besides encreasing their own privileges, they weakened still farther the very small party, which the king secretly retained in the house. Mildmay, a notorious monopolist, yet having associated himself with the ruling party, was still allowed to keep his seat. In all questions indeed of elections, no steddy rule of decision was observed; and nothing farther was regarded than the affections and attachments of the parties.[w] Men's passions were too much heated to be shocked with any instance of injustice, which served ends so popular as those which were pursued by this house of commons.

The whole sovereign power being thus in a manner transferred to the commons, and the government, without any seeming violence or disorder, being changed, in a moment, from a monarchy almost absolute, to a pure democracy; the popular leaders seemed willing for some time to suspend their active vigour, and to consolidate their authority, ere they proceeded to any violent exercise of it. Every day produced some new harangue on past grievances. The detestation of former usurpations, was farther enlivened: The jealousy of liberty rouzed: And agreeably to the spirit of free government, no less indignation was excited, by the view of a violated constitution, than by the ravages of the most enormous tyranny.

This was the time, when genius and capacity of all kinds, freed from the restraint of authority, and nourished by unbounded hopes and projects, began to exert themselves, and be distinguished by the public. Then was celebrated the sagacity of Pym, more fitted for use than ornament; matured, not chilled, by his advanced age and long experience: Then was displayed the mighty ambition of Hambden, taught disguise, not moderation, from

[u] Lord Clarendon says it was entirely new; but there are instances of it in the reign of Elizabeth. D'Ewes. p. 296, 352. There are also instances in the reign of James.   [w] Clarendon, vol. i. p. 176.

former constraint; supported by courage, conducted by prudence, embellished by modesty; but whether founded in a love of power or zeal for liberty, is still, from his untimely end, left doubtful and uncertain: Then too were known the dark, ardent, and dangerous character of St. John; the impetuous spirit of Hollis, violent and sincere, open and entire in his enmities and in his friendships; the enthusiastic genius of young Vane, extravagant in the ends which he pursued, sagacious and profound in the means which he employed; incited by the appearances of religion, negligent of the duties of morality.

So little apology would be received for past measures, so contagious the general spirit of discontent, that even men of the most moderate tempers, and the most attached to the church and monarchy, exerted themselves with the utmost vigour in the redress of grievances, and in prosecuting the authors of them. The lively and animated Digby displayed his eloquence on this occasion, the firm and undaunted Capel, the modest and candid Palmer. In this list too of patriot royalists are found the virtuous names of Hyde and Falkland. Though in their ultimate views and intentions, these men differed widely from the former; in their present actions and discourses, an entire concurrence and unanimity was observed.

By the daily harangues and invectives against illegal usurpations, not only the house of commons inflamed themselves with the highest animosity against the court: The nation caught new fire from the popular leaders, and seemed now to have made the first discovery of the many supposed disorders in the government. While the law, in several instances, seemed to be violated, they went no farther than some secret and calm murmurs; but mounted up into rage and fury, as soon as the constitution was thought to be restored to its former integrity and vigour. The capital especially, being the seat of parliament, was highly animated with the spirit of mutiny and dissaffection. Tumults were daily raised; seditious assemblies encouraged; and every man, neglecting his own business, was wholly intent on the defence of liberty and religion. By stronger contagion, the popular affections were communicated from breast to breast, in this place of general rendezvous and society.

The harangues of members, now first published and dispersed, kept alive the discontents against the king's administration. The

CHAPTER LIV

pulpits, delivered over to puritanical preachers and lecturers, whom the commons arbitrarily settled in all the considerable churches, resounded with faction and fanaticism. Vengeance was fully taken for the long silence and constraint, in which, by the authority of Laud and the high commission, these preachers had been retained. The press, freed from all fear or reserve, swarmed with productions, dangerous by their seditious zeal and calumny, more than by any art or eloquence of composition. Noise and fury, cant and hypocrisy, formed the sole rhetoric, which, during this tumult of various prejudices and passions, could be heard or attended to.

The sentence, which had been executed against Prynne, Bastwic, and Burton, now suffered a revisal from parliament. These libellers, far from being tamed by the rigorous punishments, which they had undergone, showed still a disposition of repeating their offence; and the ministers were afraid, lest new satires should issue from their prisons, and still farther inflame the prevailing discontents. By an order, therefore, of council, they had been carried to remote prisons; Bastwic to Scilly, Prynne to Jersey, Burton to Guernsey; all access to them was denied; and the use of books, and of pen, ink, and paper, was refused them. The sentence for these additional punishments was immediately reversed, in an arbitrary manner by the commons: Even the first sentence, upon examination, was declared illegal: and the judges, who passed it, were ordered to make reparation to the sufferers.[x] When the prisoners landed in England, they were received and entertained with the highest demonstrations of affection, were attended by a mighty confluence of company, their charges were borne with great magnificence, and liberal presents bestowed on them. On their approach to any town, all the inhabitants crowded to receive them, and welcomed their reception with shouts and acclamations. Their train still encreased, as they drew nigh to London. Some miles from the city, the zealots of their party met them in great multitudes, and attended their triumphant entrance: Boughs were carried in this tumultuous procession; the roads were strewed with flowers; and amidst the highest exultations of joy, were intermingled loud and virulent invectives against the prelates, who had

[x] Nalson, vol. i. p. 783. May, p. 79.

so cruelly persecuted such godly personages.[y] The more ignoble these men were, the more sensible was the insult upon royal authority, and the more dangerous was the spirit of disaffection and mutiny, which it discovered among the people.

Lilburne, Leighton, and every one that had been punished for seditious libels during the preceding administration, now recovered their liberty, and were decreed damages from the judges and ministers of justice.[z]

Not only the present disposition of the nation ensured impunity to all libellers: A new method of framing and dispersing libels was invented by the leaders of popular discontent. Petitions to parliament were drawn, craving redress against particular grievances; and when a sufficient number of subscriptions were procured, the petitions were presented to the commons, and immediately published. These petitions became secret bonds of association among the subscribers, and seemed to give undoubted sanction and authority to the complaints, which they contained.

It is pretended by historians favourable to the royal cause,[a] and is even asserted by the king himself in a declaration,[b] that a most disingenuous or rather criminal practice prevailed, in conducting many of these addresses. A petition was first framed; moderate, reasonable, such as men of character willingly subscribed. The names were afterwards torn off, and affixed to another petition, which served better the purposes of the popular faction. We may judge of the wild fury which prevailed throughout the nation, when so scandalous an imposture, which affected such numbers of people, could be openly practised, without drawing infamy and ruin upon the managers.

So many grievances were offered, both by the members, and by petitions without-doors, that the house was divided into above forty committees, charged, each of them, with the examination of some particular violation of law and liberty, which had been complained of. Besides the general committees of religion, trade, privileges, laws; many subdivisions of these were framed, and a strict scrutiny was every where carried on. It is to be remarked, that,

---

[y] Clarendon, vol. i. p. 199, 200, &c. Nalson, vol. i. p. 570. May, p. 80.
[z] Rush. vol. v. p. 228. Nalson, vol. i. p. 800.   [a] Dugdale. Clarendon, vol. i. p. 203.   [b] Husb. Col. p. 536.

CHAPTER LIV

before the beginning of this century, when the commons assumed less influence and authority, complaints of grievances were usually presented to the house, by any members who had had particular opportunity of observing them. These general committees, which were a kind of inquisitorial courts, had not then been established; and we find, that the king, in a former declaration,^c complains loudly of this innovation, so little favourable to royal authority. But never was so much multiplied, as at present, the use of these committees; and the commons, though themselves the greatest innovators, employed the usual artifice of complaining against innovations, and pretending to recover the ancient and established government.

From the reports of their committees, the house daily passed votes, which mortified and astonished the court, and inflamed and animated the nation. Ship-money was declared illegal and arbitrary; the sentence against Hambden cancelled; the court of York abolished; compositions for knighthood stigmatized; the enlargement of the forests condemned; patents for monopolies annulled; and every late measure of administration treated with reproach and obloquy. To day, a sentence of the star-chamber was exclaimed against: To morrow, a decree of the high commission. Every discretionary act of council was represented as arbitrary and tyrannical; and the general inference was still inculcated, that a formed design had been laid to subvert the laws and constitution of the kingdom.

From necessity, the king remained entirely passive during all these violent operations. The few servants, who continued faithful to him, were seized with astonishment at the rapid progress made by the commons in power and popularity, and were glad, by their unactive and inoffensive behaviour, to compound for impunity. The torrent rising to so dreadful and unexpected a height, despair seized all those, who from interest or habit, were most attached to monarchy. And as for those, who maintained their duty to the king, merely from their regard to the constitution, they seemed by their concurrence to swell that inundation, which began already to deluge every thing. "You have taken the whole machine of govern-

---

^c Published on dissolving the third parliament. See Parl. Hist. vol. viii. p. 347.

ment in pieces," said Charles in a discourse to the parliament; "a practice frequent with skilful artists, when they desire to clear the wheels from any rust, which may have grown upon them. The engine," continued he, "may again be restored to its former use and motions, provided it be put up entire; so as not a pin of it be wanting." But this was far from the intention of the commons. The machine they thought, with some reason, was incumbered with many wheels and springs, which retarded and crossed its operations, and destroyed its utility. Happy! had they proceeded with moderation, and been contented, in their present plenitude of power, to remove such parts only as might justly be deemed superfluous and incongruous.

In order to maintain that high authority, which they had acquired, the commons, besides confounding and overawing their opponents, judged it requisite to inspire courage into their friends and adherents; particularly into the Scots, and the religious puritans, to whose assistance and good offices they were already so much beholden.

No sooner were the Scots masters of the·northern counties, than they laid aside their first professions, which they had not indeed means to support, of paying for every thing; and in order to prevent the destructive expedient of plunder and free quarters, the country consented to give them a regular contribution of 850 pounds a day, in full of their subsistence.[d] The parliament, that they might relieve the northern counties from so grievous a burden, agreed to remit pay to the Scottish, as well as to the English army; and because subsidies would be levied too slowly for so urgent an occasion, money was borrowed from the citizens upon the security of particular members. Two subsidies, a very small sum,[e] were at first voted; and as the intention of this supply was to indemnify the members, who, by their private, had supported public credit, this pretence was immediately laid hold of, and the money was ordered to be paid, not into the treasury, but to commissioners appointed by parliament: A practice, which, as it diminished the authority of the crown, was willingly embraced, and was afterwards continued by the commons, with regard to every

[d] Rushworth, vol. iii. p. 1295.   [e] It appears, that a subsidy was now fallen to 50,000 pounds.

branch of revenue, which they granted to the king. The invasion of the Scots had evidently been the cause of assembling the parliament: The presence of their army reduced the king to that total subjection, in which he was now held: The commons, for this reason, openly professed their intention of retaining these invaders, till all their own enemies should be suppressed, and all their purposes effected. *We cannot yet spare the Scots,* said Strode plainly in the house; *the sons of Zeruiah are still too strong for us:*[f] An allusion to a passage of scripture, according to the mode of that age. Eighty thousand pounds a month were requisite for the subsistence of the two armies; a sum much greater than the subject had ever been accustomed, in any former period, to pay to the public. And though several subsidies, together with a poll-tax, were from time to time voted to answer the charge; the commons still took care to be in debt, in order to render the continuance of the session the more necessary.

The Scots being such useful allies to the malcontent party in England, no wonder they were courted with the most unlimited complaisance and the most important services. The king having, in his first speech, called them *rebels,* observed, that he had given great offence to the parliament; and he was immediately obliged to soften, and even retract the expression. The Scottish commissioners, of whom the most considerable were the earl of Rothes and lord Loudon, found every advantage in conducting their treaty; yet made no haste in bringing it to an issue. They were lodged in the city, and kept an intimate correspondence, as well with the magistrates, who were extremely disaffected, as with the popular leaders in both houses. St. Antholine's church was assigned them for their devotions; and their chaplains, here, began openly to practise the presbyterian form of worship, which, except in foreign languages, had never hitherto been allowed any indulgence or toleration. So violent was the general propensity towards this new religion, that multitudes of all ranks crowded to the church. Those, who were so happy as to find access early in the morning, kept their places the whole day: Those, who were excluded, clung to the doors or windows, in hopes of catching, at least, some distant murmur or broken phrases of the holy rhet-

[f] Dugdale, p. 71.

oric.[g] All the eloquence of parliament, now well refined from pedantry, animated with the spirit of liberty, and employed in the most important interests, was not attended to with such insatiable avidity, as were these lectures, delivered with ridiculous cant, and a provincial accent, full of barbarism and of ignorance.

The most effectual expedient for paying court to the zealous Scots was to promote the presbyterian discipline and worship throughout England and to this innovation, the popular leaders among the commons, as well as their more devoted partizans, were, of themselves, sufficiently inclined. The puritanical party, whose progress, though secret, had hitherto been gradual in the kingdom, taking advantage of the present disorders, began openly to profess their tenets, and to make furious attacks on the established religion. The prevalence of that sect in the parliament discovered itself, from the beginning, by insensible, but decisive symptoms. Marshall and Burgess, two puritanical clergymen, were chosen to preach before them, and entertained them with discourses seven hours in length.[h] It being the custom of the house always to take the sacrament before they enter upon business, they ordered, as a necessary preliminary, that the communion table should be removed from the east end of St. Margaret's into the middle of the area.[i] The name of the *spiritual lords* was commonly left out in acts of parliament; and the laws ran in the name of king, lords, and commons. The clerk of the upper house, in reading bills, turned his back on the bench of bishops; nor was his insolence ever taken notice of. On a day appointed for a solemn fast and humiliation, all the orders of temporal peers, contrary to former practice, in going to church, took place of the spiritual; and lord Spencer remarked, that the humiliation, that day, seemed confined alone to the prelates.

The bishops attacked. Every meeting of the commons produced some vehement harangue against the usurpations of the bishops, against the high commission, against the late convocation, against the new canons. So disgusted were all lovers of civil liberty at the doctrines promoted by the clergy, that these invectives were received without controul; and no distinction, at first, appeared between such as

[g] Clarendon, vol. i. p. 189.   [h] Nalson, vol. i. p. 530, 533.   [i] Idem, ibid. p. 537.

desired only to repress the exorbitancies of the hierarchy, and such as pretended totally to annihilate episcopal jurisdiction. Encouraged by these favourable appearances, petitions against the church were framed in different parts of the kingdom. The epithet of the ignorant and vicious priesthood was commonly applied to all churchmen, addicted to the established discipline and worship; though the episcopal clergy in England, during that age, seem to have been, as they are at present, sufficiently learned and exemplary. An address against episcopacy was presented by twelve clergymen to the committee of religion, and pretended to be signed by many hundreds of the puritanical persuasion. But what made most noise was the city petition for a total alteration of church government; a petition, to which 15,000 subscriptions were annexed, and which was presented by Alderman Pennington, the city-member.[k] It is remarkable, that, among the many ecclesiastical abuses there complained of, an allowance, given by the licencers of books, to publish a translation of Ovid's Art of Love, is not forgotten by these rustic censors.[l]

Notwithstanding the favourable disposition of the people, the leaders in the house resolved to proceed with caution. They introduced a bill for prohibiting all clergymen the exercise of any civil office. As a consequence, the bishops were to be deprived of their seats in the house of peers; a measure not unacceptable to the zealous friends of liberty, who observed, with regret, the devoted attachment of that order to the will of the monarch. But when this bill was presented to the peers, it was rejected by a great majority:[m] The first check which the commons had received in their popular career, and a prognostic of what they might afterwards expect from the upper house, whose inclinations and interests could never be totally separated from the throne. But to show how little they were discouraged, the puritans immediately brought in another bill for the total abolition of episcopacy; though they thought proper to let that bill sleep at present, in expectation of a more favourable opportunity of reviving it.[n]

Among other acts of regal executive power, which the commons were every day assuming, they issued orders for demolishing

[k] Clarendon, vol. i. p. 203. Whitlocke, p. 37. Nalson, vol. i. p. 666. [l] Rush. vol. v. p. 171. [m] Clarendon, vol. i. p. 237. [n] Idem, ibid. p. 237.

all images, altars, crucifixes. The zealous Sir Robert Harley, to whom the execution of these orders was committed, removed all crosses even out of streets and markets; and from his abhorrence of that superstitious figure, would not any where allow one piece of wood or stone to lie over another at right angles.[o]

The bishop of Ely and other clergymen were attacked on account of innovations.[p] Cozens, who had long been obnoxious, was exposed to new censures. This clergyman, who was dean of Peterborough, was extremely zealous for ecclesiastical ceremonies: And so far from permitting the communicants to break the sacramental bread with their fingers; a privilege on which the puritans strenuously insisted; he would not so much as allow it to be cut with an ordinary household instrument. A consecrated knife must perform that sacred office, and must never afterwards be profaned by any vulgar service.[q]

Cozens likewise was accused of having said, *The king has no more authority in ecclesiastical matters, than the boy who rubs my horse's heels.*[r] The expression was violent: But it is certain, that all those high churchmen, who were so industrious in reducing the laity to submission, were extremely fond of their own privileges and independency, and were desirous of exempting the mitre from all subjection to the crown.

A committee was elected by the lower house as a court of inquisition upon the clergy, and was commonly denominated the committee of *scandalous ministers.* The politicians among the commons were apprized of the great importance of the pulpit for guiding the people; the bigots were enraged against the prelatical clergy; and both of them knew that no established government could be overthrown by strictly observing the principles of justice, equity, or clemency. The proceedings, therefore, of this famous committee, which continued for several years, were cruel and arbitrary, and made great havoc both on the church and the universities. They began with harassing, imprisoning, and molesting the clergy; and ended with sequestrating and ejecting them. In order to join contumely to cruelty, they gave the sufferers the epithet of *scandalous,* and endeavoured to render them as odious as they were

---

[o] Whitlocke, p. 45.   [p] Rushworth, vol. v. p. 351.   [q] Ibid. p. 203.   [r] Parl. Hist. vol. vii. p. 282. Rushworth, vol. v. p. 209.

miserable.[s] The greatest vices, however, which they could reproach to a great part of them, were, bowing at the name of
Jesus, placing the communion table in the east, reading the king's
orders for sports on Sunday, and other practices, which the
established government, both in church and state, had strictly
enjoined them.

It may be worth observing, that all historians, who lived near
that age, or what perhaps is more decisive, all authors, who have
casually made mention of those public transactions, still represent
the civil disorders and convulsions, as proceeding from religious
controversy, and consider the political disputes about power and
liberty as entirely subordinate to the other. It is true, had the king
been able to support government, and at the same time, to abstain
from all invasion of national privileges, it seems not probable, that
the puritans ever could have acquired such authority as to overturn the whole constitution: Yet so entire was the subjection, into
which Charles was now fallen, that, had not the wound been poisoned by the infusion of theological hatred, it must have admitted
of an easy remedy. Disuse of parliaments, imprisonments and
prosecution of members, ship-money, an arbitrary administration; these were loudly complained of: But the grievances, which
tended chiefly to inflame the parliament and nation, especially the
latter, were, the surplice, the rails placed about the altar, the bows
exacted on approaching it, the liturgy, the breach of the sabbath,
embroidered copes, lawn sleeves, the use of the ring in marriage,
and of the cross in baptism. On account of these, were the popular
leaders content to throw the government into such violent convulsions; and to the disgrace of that age and of this island, it must
be acknowledged, that the disorders in Scotland entirely, and those
in England mostly, proceeded from so mean and contemptible an
origin.[t]

---

[s] Clarendon, vol. i. p. 199. Whitlocke, p. 122. May, p. 81.   [t] Lord Clarendon, vol. i. p. 233, says, that the parliamentary party were not agreed
about the entire abolition of episcopacy: They were only the *root and branch
men,* as they were called, who insisted on that measure. But those who
were willing to retain bishops, insisted on reducing their authority to a low
ebb; as well as on abolishing the ceremonies of worship and vestments of
the clergy. The controversy, therefore between the parties was almost
wholly theological, and that of the most frivolous and ridiculous kind.

Some persons, partial to the patriots of this age, have ventured to put them in a balance with the most illustrious characters of antiquity; and mentioned the names of Pym, Hambden, Vane, as a just parallel to those of Cato, Brutus, Cassius. Profound capacity, indeed, undaunted courage, extensive enterprize; in these particulars, perhaps the Roman do not much surpass the English worthies: But what a difference, when the discourse, conduct, conversation, and private as well as public behaviour, of both are inspected! Compare only one circumstance, and consider its consequences. The leisure of those noble ancients was totally employed in the study of Grecian eloquence and philosophy; in the cultivation of polite letters and civilized society: The whole discourse and language of the moderns were polluted with mysterious jargon, and full of the lowest and most vulgar hypocrisy.

The laws, as they stood at present, protected the church; but they exposed the catholics to the utmost rage of the puritans; and these unhappy religionists, so obnoxious to the prevailing sect, could not hope to remain long unmolested. The voluntary contribution, which they had made, in order to assist the king in his war against the Scottish covenanters, was enquired into, and represented as the greatest enormity.[u] By an address from the commons, all officers of that religion were removed from the army, and application was made to the king for seizing two thirds of the lands of recusants; a proportion to which, by law, he was intitled, but which he had always allowed them to possess upon easy compositions. The execution of the severe and bloody laws against priests was insisted on: And one Goodman, a jesuit, who was found in prison, was condemned to a capital punishment. Charles, however, agreeably to his usual principles, scrupled to sign the warrant for his execution; and the commons expressed great resentment on the occasion.[w] There remains a singular petition of Goodman, begging to be hanged, rather than prove a source of contention between the king and his people.[x] He escaped with his life; but it seems more probable, that he was overlooked, amidst affairs of greater consequence, than that such unrelenting hatred would be softened by any consideration of his courage and generosity.

[u] Rushworth, vol. v. p. 160.   [w] Idem, ibid. p. 158, 159. Nalson, vol. i. p. 739.   [x] Rushworth, vol. v. p. 166. Nalson, vol. i. p. 749.

CHAPTER LIV

For some years, Con, a Scotchman; afterwards, Rosetti, an Italian, had openly resided at London, and frequented the court, as vested with a commission from the Pope. The queen's zeal and her authority with her husband had been the cause of this imprudence, so offensive to the nation.[y] But the spirit of bigotry now rose too high to permit any longer such indulgences.[z]

Hayward, a justice of peace, having been wounded, when employed in the exercise of his office, by one James, a catholic madman, this enormity was ascribed to the popery, not to the phrenzy, of the assassin; and great alarms seized the nation and parliament.[a] An universal conspiracy of the papists was supposed to have taken place; and every man for some days, imagined that he had a sword at his throat. Though some persons of family and distinction were still attached to the catholic superstition; it is certain that the numbers of that sect did not amount to the fortieth part of the nation: And the frequent panics, to which men, during this period, were so subject on account of the catholics, were less the effects of fear, than of extreme rage and aversion entertained against them.

The queen mother of France, having been forced into banishment by some court-intrigues, had retired into England; and expected shelter, amidst her present distresses, in the dominions of her daughter and son-in-law. But though she behaved in the most inoffensive manner, she was insulted by the populace on account of her religion; and was even threatened with worse treatment. The earl of Holland, lieutenant of Middlesex, had ordered a hundred musqueteers to guard her; but finding that they had imbibed the same prejudices with the rest of their countrymen, and were unwillingly employed in such a service, he laid the case before the house of peers: For the king's authority was now entirely annihilated. He represented the indignity of the action, that so great a princess, mother to the king of France and to the queens

---

[y] It is now known from the Clarendon papers, that the king had also an authorized agent who resided at Rome. His name was Bret, and his chief business was to negociate with the pope concerning indulgences to the catholics, and to engage the catholics in return to be good and loyal subjects. But this whole matter, though very innocent, was most carefully kept secret. The king says, that he believed Bret to be as much his as any papist could be. See p. 348, 354. [z] Rushworth, vol. v. p. 301. [a] Clarendon, vol. i. p. 249. Rushworth, vol. v. p. 57.

of Spain and England, should be affronted by the multitude. He observed the indelible reproach, which would fall upon the nation, if that unfortunate queen should suffer any violence from the misguided zeal of the people. He urged the sacred rights of hospitality, due to every one, much more to a person in distress, of so high a rank, with whom the nation was so nearly connected. The peers thought proper to communicate the matter to the commons, whose authority over the people was absolute. The commons agreed to the necessity of protecting the queen mother; but at the same time prayed, that she might be desired to depart the kingdom; "For the quieting those jealousies in the hearts of his majesty's well-affected subjects, occasioned by some ill instruments about that queen's person, by the flowing of priests and papists to her house, and by the use and practice of the idolatry of the mass, and exercise of other superstitious services of the Romish church, to the great scandal of true religion."[b]

Charles, in the former part of his reign, had endeavoured to overcome the intractable and encroaching spirit of the commons, by a perseverance in his own measures, by a stately dignity of behaviour, and by maintaining, at their utmost height, and even perhaps stretching beyond former precedent, the rights of his prerogative. Finding by experience how unsuccessful those measures had proved, and observing the low condition to which he was now reduced, he resolved to alter his whole conduct, and to regain the confidence of his people, by pliableness, by concessions, and by a total conformity to their inclinations and prejudices. It may safely be averred, that this new extreme, into which the king, for want of proper counsel or support was fallen, became no less dangerous to the constitution, and pernicious to public peace, than the other, in which he had so long and so unfortunately persevered.

Tonnage and poundage. The pretensions with regard to tonnage and poundage were revived, and with certain assurance of success, by the commons.[c] The levying of these duties, as formerly, without consent of parlia-

---

[b] Rushworth, vol. v. p. 267.   [c] It appears not, that the commons, though now entirely masters, abolished the new impositions of James, against which they had formerly so loudly complained: A certain proof that the rates of customs, settled by that prince, were in most instances just, and proportioned to the new price of commodities. They seem rather to have been low. See Journ. 10th Aug. 1625.

ment, and even encreasing them at pleasure, was such an incongruity in a free constitution, where the people, by their fundamental privileges, cannot be taxed but by their own consent, as could no longer be endured by these jealous patrons of liberty. In the preamble, therefore, to the bill, by which the commons granted these duties to the king, they took care, in the strongest and most positive terms, to assert their own right of bestowing this gift, and to divest the crown of all independent title of assuming it. And that they might encrease, or rather finally fix, the entire dependence and subjection of the king, they voted these duties only for two months; and afterwards, from time to time, renewed their grant for very short periods.[d] Charles, in order to show that he entertained no intention ever again to separate himself from his parliament, passed this important bill; without any scruple or hesitation.[e]

With regard to the bill for triennial parliaments, he made a little difficulty. By an old statute, passed during the reign of Edward III. it had been enacted, that parliaments should be held once every year, or more frequently, if necessary: But as no provision had been made in case of failure, and no precise method pointed out for execution; this statute had been considered merely as a general declaration, and was dispensed with at pleasure. The defect was supplied by those vigilant patriots, who now assumed the reins of government. It was enacted, that if the chancellor, who was first bound under severe penalties, failed to issue writs by the third of September in every third year, any twelve or more of the peers should be impowered to exert this authority: In default of the peers, that the sheriffs, mayors, bailiffs, &c. should summon the voters: And in their default, that the voters themselves should meet and proceed to the election of members, in the same manner as if writs had been regularly issued from the crown. Nor could the parliament, after it was assembled, be adjourned, prorogued, or dissolved, without their own consent, during the space of fifty days. By this bill, some of the noblest and most valuable prerog-

Triennial bill.

---

[d] It was an instruction given by the house to the committee which framed one of these bills, to take care that the rates upon exportation may be as light as possible; and upon importation as heavy as trade will bear: A proof that the nature of commerce began now to be understood. Journ. 1 June, 1641. [e] Clarendon, vol. i. p. 208.

atives of the crown were retrenched; but at the same time, nothing could be more necessary than such a statute, for completing a regular plan of law and liberty. A great reluctance to assemble parliaments must be expected in the king; where these assemblies, as of late, establish it as a maxim to carry their scrutiny into every part of government. During long intermissions of parliament, grievances and abuses, as was found by recent experience, would naturally creep in; and it would even become necessary for the king and council to exert a great discretionary authority, and, by acts of state, to supply, in every emergence, the legislative power, whose meeting was so uncertain and precarious. Charles, finding that nothing less would satisfy his parliament and people, at last gave his assent to this bill, which produced so great an innovation in the constitution.[f] Solemn thanks were presented him by both houses. Great rejoicings were expressed both in the city and throughout the nation. And mighty professions were every-where made of gratitude and mutual returns of supply and confidence. This concession of the king, it must be owned, was not entirely voluntary: It was of a nature too important to be voluntary. The sole inference, which his partizans were intitled to draw from the submissions so frankly made to present necessity, was, that he had certainly adopted a new plan of government, and for the future, was resolved, by every indulgence, to acquire the confidence and affections of his people.

Charles thought, that what concessions were made to the public were of little consequence, if no gratifications were bestowed on individuals, who had acquired the direction of public counsels and determinations. A change of ministers, as well as of measures, was therefore resolved on. In one day several new privy-counsellors were sworn; the earls of Hertford, Bedford, Essex, Bristol; the lords Say, Saville, Kimbolton: Within a few days after, was admitted the earl of Warwic.[g] All these noblemen were of the popular party; and some of them afterwards, when matters were pushed to extremities by the commons, proved the greatest support of monarchy.

[f] Clarendon, vol. i. p. 209. Whitlocke, p. 39. Rushworth, vol. v. p. 189.
[g] Clarendon, vol. i. p. 195.

Juxon, bishop of London, who had never desired the treasurer's staff, now earnestly solicited for leave to resign it, and retire to the care of that turbulent diocese, committed to him. The king gave his consent; and it is remarkable, that, during all the severe enquiries carried on against the conduct of ministers and prelates, the mild and prudent virtues of this man, who bore both these invidious characters, remained unmolested.[h] It was intended, that Bedford, a popular man, of great authority, as well as wisdom and moderation, should succeed Juxon: But that nobleman, unfortunately both for king and people, died about this very time. By some promotions, place was made for St. John, who was created solicitor-general. Hollis was to be made secretary of state, in the room of Windebank, who had fled: Pym, chancellor of the exchequer, in the room of lord Cottington, who had resigned: Lord Say, master of the wards, in the room of the same nobleman: The earl of Essex, governor; and Hambden, tutor to the prince.[i]

What retarded the execution of these projected changes, was the difficulty of satisfying all those, who from their activity and authority in parliament, had pretensions for offices, and who still had it in their power to embarrass and distress the public measures. Their associates too in popularity, whom the king intended to distinguish by his favour, were unwilling to undergo the reproach of having driven a separate bargain, and of sacrificing, to their own ambitious views, the cause of the nation. And as they were sensible that they must owe their preferment entirely to their weight and consideration in parliament, they were most of them resolved still to adhere to that assembly, and both to promote its authority, and to preserve their own credit in it. On all occasions, they had no other advice to give the king, than to allow himself to be directed by his great council, or, in other words, to resign himself passively to their guidance and government. And Charles found, that, instead of acquiring friends by the honours and offices which he should bestow, he should only arm his enemies with more power to hurt him.

The end, on which the king was most intent in changing ministers, was, to save the life of the earl of Strafford, and to mollify, by

[h] Warwick, p. 95.   [i] Clarendon, vol. i. p. 210, 211.

these indulgences, the rage of his most furious prosecutors. But so high was that nobleman's reputation for experience and capacity, that all the new counsellors and intended ministers plainly saw, that, if he escaped their vengeance, he must return into favour and authority; and they regarded his death as the only security which they could have, both for the establishment of their present power, and for success in their future enterprizes. His impeachment, therefore, was pushed on with the utmost vigour; and, after long and solemn preparations, was brought to a final issue.

Strafford's *trial.* Immediately after Strafford was sequestered from parliament, and confined in the Tower, a committee of thirteen was chosen by the lower house, and entrusted with the office of preparing a charge against him. These, joined to a small committee of lords, were vested with authority to examine all witnesses, to call for every paper, and to use any means of scrutiny, with regard to any part of the earl's behaviour and conduct.[k] After so general and unbounded an inquisition, exercised by such powerful and implacable enemies; a man must have been very cautious or very innocent, not to afford, during the whole course of his life, some matter of accusation, against him.

This committee, by direction from both houses, took an oath of secrecy; a practice very unusual, and which gave them the appearance of conspirators, more than ministers of justice.[l] But the intention of this strictness was to render it more difficult for the earl to elude their search, or prepare for his justification.

Application was made to the king, that he would allow this committee to examine privy-counsellors with regard to opinions delivered at the board: A concession which Charles unwarily made, and which thenceforth banished all mutual confidence from the deliberations of council; where every man is supposed to have entire freedom, without fear of future punishment or enquiry, of proposing any expedient, questioning any opinion, or supporting any argument.[m]

Sir George Ratcliffe, the earl's intimate friend and confident, was accused of high treason, sent for from Ireland, and committed to close custody. As no charge ever appeared or was prosecuted

[k] Clarendon, vol. i. p. 192.   [l] Whitlocke, p. 37.   [m] Clarendon, vol. i. p. 193.

CHAPTER LIV

against him, it is impossible to give a more charitable interpretation to this measure, than that the commons thereby intended to deprive Strafford, in his present distress, of the assistance of his best friend, who was most enabled, by his testimony, to justify the innocence of his patron's conduct and behaviour.[n]

When intelligence arrived in Ireland of the plans laid for Strafford's ruin, the Irish house of commons, though they had very lately bestowed ample praises on his administration, entered into all the violent counsels against him, and prepared a representation of the miserable state, into which, by his misconduct, they supposed the kingdom to be fallen. They sent over a committee to London, to assist in the prosecution of their unfortunate governor; and by intimations from this committee, who entered into close confederacy with the popular leaders in England, was every measure of the Irish parliament governed and directed. Impeachments, which were never prosecuted, were carried up against Sir Richard Bolton the chancellor, Sir Gerard Louther chief justice, and Bramhall bishop of Derry.[o] This step, which was an exact counterpart to the proceedings in England, served also the same purposes: It deprived the king of the ministers whom he most trusted; it discouraged and terrified all the other ministers; and it prevented those persons, who were best acquainted with Strafford's counsels, from giving evidence in his favour before the English parliament.

The bishops, being forbidden by the ancient canons to assist in   *1641.* trials for life, and being unwilling, by any opposition, to irritate the commons, who were already much prejudiced against them, thought proper, of themselves, to withdraw.[p] The commons also voted, that the new-created peers ought to have no voice in this trial; because the accusation being agreed to, while they were commoners, their consent to it was implied with that of all the commons of England. Notwithstanding this decision, which was meant only to deprive Strafford of so many friends, lord Seymour, and some others, still continued to keep their seat; nor was their right to it any farther questioned.[q]

To bestow the greater solemnity on this important trial, scaf-

---

[n] Idem, vol. i. p. 214.   [o] Rush. vol. v. p. 214.   [p] Clarendon, vol. i. p. 216.
[q] Idem, ibid.

folds were erected in Westminster-hall; where both houses sat, the one as accusers, the other as judges. Besides the chair of state, a close gallery was prepared for the king and queen, who attended during the whole trial.[r]

An accusation, carried on by the united effort of three kingdoms, against one man, unprotected by power, unassisted by council, discountenanced by authority, was likely to prove a very unequal contest: Yet such were the capacity, genius, presence of mind, displayed by this magnanimous statesman, that, while argument and reason and law had any place, he obtained an undisputed victory. And he perished at last, overwhelmed and still unsubdued, by the open violence of his fierce and unrelenting antagonists.

March 22. The articles of impeachment against Strafford are twenty-eight in number; and regard his conduct, as president of the council of York, as deputy or lieutenant of Ireland, and as counsellor or commander in England. But though four months were employed by the managers in framing the accusation, and all Strafford's answers were extempory; it appears from comparison, not only that he was free from the crime of treason, of which there is not the least appearance, but that his conduct, making allowance for human infirmities, exposed to such severe scrutiny, was innocent, and even laudable.

The powers of the northern council, while he was president, had been extended, by the king's instructions, beyond what formerly had been practised: But that court being, at first, instituted by a stretch of royal prerogative, it had been usual for the prince to vary his instructions; and the largest authority, committed to it, was altogether as legal as the most moderate and most limited. Nor was it reasonable to conclude, that Strafford had used any art to procure those extensive powers; since he never once sat as president, or exercised one act of jurisdiction, after he was invested with the authority so much complained of.[s]

In the government of Ireland, his administration had been equally promotive of his master's interest, and that of the subjects committed to his care. A large debt he had paid off: He had left a

---

[r] Whitlocke, p. 40. Rush. vol. iv. p. 41. May, p. 90.   [s] Rushworth, vol. iv. p. 145.

considerable sum in the exchequer: The revenue, which never before answered the charges of government, was now raised to be equal to them.[t] A small standing army, formerly kept in no order, was augmented, and was governed by exact discipline: And a great force was there raised and paid, for the support of the king's authority against the Scottish covenanters.

Industry, and all the arts of peace, were introduced among that rude people: The shipping of the kingdom augmented a hundred fold:[u] The customs tripled upon the same rates:[w] The exports double in value to the imports: Manufactures, particularly that of linen, introduced and promoted.[x] Agriculture, by means of the English and Scottish plantations, gradually advancing: The protestant religion encouraged, without the persecution or discontent of the catholics.

The springs of authority he had enforced without overstraining them. Discretionary acts of jurisdiction, indeed, he had often exerted, by holding courts-martial, billetting soldiers, deciding causes upon paper-petitions before the council, issuing proclamations, and punishing their infraction. But discretionary authority, during that age, was usually exercised even in England. In Ireland, it was still more requisite, among a rude people, not yet thoroughly subdued, averse to the religion and manners of their conquerors, ready on all occasions to relapse into rebellion and disorder. While the managers of the commons demanded, every moment, that the deputy's conduct should be examined by the line of rigid law and severe principles; he appealed still to the practice of all former deputies, and to the uncontroulable necessity of his situation.

So great was his art of managing elections, and balancing parties, that he had engaged the Irish parliament to vote whatever was necessary, both for the payment of former debts, and for support of the new-levied army; nor had he ever been reduced to the illegal expedients practiced in England, for the supply of public necessities. No imputation of rapacity could justly lie against his administration. Some instances of imperious expressions and even actions may be met with. The case of lord Mountnorris, of all those which

[t] Rush. vol. iv. p. 120, 247. Warwick, p. 115.   [u] Nalson, vol. ii. p. 45.
[w] Rush. vol. iv. p. 124.   [x] Warwick, p. 115.

were collected with so much industry, is the most flagrant and the least excusable.

It had been reported at the table of lord chancellor Loftus, that Annesley, one of the deputy's attendants, in moving a stool, had sorely hurt his master's foot, who was at that time afflicted with the gout. *Perhaps,* said Mountnorris, who was present at table, *it was done in revenge of that public affront which my lord deputy formerly put upon him:* BUT HE HAS A BROTHER, WHO WOULD NOT HAVE TAKEN SUCH A REVENGE. This casual, and seemingly innocent, at least ambiguous, expression, was reported to Strafford; who, on pretence that such a suggestion might prompt Annesley to avenge himself in another manner, ordered Mountnorris, who was an officer, to be tried by a court-martial for mutiny and sedition against his general. The court, which consisted of the chief officers of the army, found the crime to be capital, and condemned that nobleman to lose his head.[y]

In vain did Strafford plead in his own defence against this article of impeachment, that the sentence of Mountnorris was the deed, and that too unanimous, of the court; not the act of the deputy; that he spake not to a member of the court, nor voted in the cause, but sat uncovered as a party, and then immediately withdrew, to leave them to their freedom; that sensible of the iniquity of the sentence, he procured his majesty's free pardon to Mountnorris; and that he did not even keep that nobleman a moment in suspence with regard to his fate, but instantly told him, that he himself would sooner lose his right hand than execute such a sentence, nor was his lordship's life in any danger. In vain did Strafford's friends add, as a further apology, that Mountnorris was a man of an infamous character, who paid court, by the lowest adulation, to all deputies, while present; and blackened their character, by the vilest calumnies, when recalled: And that Strafford, expecting like treatment, had used this expedient for no other purpose than to subdue the petulant spirit of the man. These excuses alleviate the guilt; but there still remains enough to prove, that the mind of the deputy, though great and firm, had been not a little debauched by the riot of absolute power, and uncontrouled authority.

[y] Rush. vol. iv. p. 187.

CHAPTER LIV

When Strafford was called over to England, he found every thing falling into such confusion, by the open rebellion of the Scots, and the secret discontents of the English, that, if he had counselled or executed any violent measure, he might perhaps have been able to apologize for his conduct, from the great law of necessity, which admits not, while the necessity is extreme, of any scruple, ceremony, or delay.[z] But in fact, no illegal advice or action was proved against him; and the whole amount of his guilt, during this period, was some peevish, or at most imperious expressions, which, amidst such desperate extremities, and during a bad state of health, had unhappily fallen from him.

If Strafford's apology was, in the main, so satisfactory, when he pleaded to each particular article of the charge, his victory was still more decisive, when he brought the whole together, and repelled the imputation of treason; the crime which the commons would infer from the full view of his conduct and behaviour. Of all species of guilt, the law of England had, with the most scrupulous exactness, defined that of treason, because on the side it was found most necessary to protect the subject against the violence of the king and of his ministers. In the famous statute of Edward III. all the kinds of treason are enumerated, and every other crime, besides such as are there expressly mentioned, is carefully excluded from that appellation. But with regard to this guilt, *An endeavour to subvert the fundamental laws*, the statute of treasons is totally silent: And arbitrarily to introduce it into the fatal catalogue, is itself a subversion of all law; and, under colour of defending liberty, reverses a statute the best calculated for the security of liberty, that had ever been enacted by an English parliament.

As this species of treason, discovered by the commons, is entirely new and unknown to the laws; so is the species of proof, by which they pretend to fix that guilt upon the prisoner. They have invented a kind of *accumulative or constructive* evidence, by which many actions either totally innocent in themselves, or criminal in a much inferior degree, shall, when united, amount to treason, and subject the person to the highest penalties inflicted by the law. A hasty and unguarded word, a rash and passionate action, assisted by the malevolent fancy of the accuser, and tortured by doubt-

[z] Rush. vol. iv. 559.

ful constructions, is transmuted into the deepest guilt; and the lives and fortunes of the whole nation, no longer protected by justice, are subjected to arbitrary will and pleasure.

"Where has this species of guilt lain so long concealed?" said Strafford in conclusion: "Where has this fire been so long buried, during so many centuries, that no smoke should appear, till it burst out at once, to consume me and my children? Better it were to live under no law at all, and by the maxims of cautious prudence, to conform ourselves the best we can, to the arbitrary will of a master; than fancy we have a law on which we can rely, and find at last, that this law shall inflict a punishment precedent to the promulgation, and try us by maxims unheard of till the very moment of the prosecution. If I sail on the Thames, and split my vessel on an anchor; in case there be no buoy to give warning, the party shall pay me damages: But, if the anchor be marked out, then is the striking on it at my own peril. Where is the mark set upon this crime? Where the token by which I should discover it? It has lain concealed, under water; and no human prudence, no human innocence, could save me from the destruction, with which I am at present threatened.

"It is now full two hundred and forty years since treasons were defined; and so long has it been, since any man was touched to this extent, upon this crime, before myself. We have lived, my lords, happily to ourselves at home: We have lived gloriously abroad to the world: Let us be content with what our fathers have left us: Let not our ambition carry us to be more learned than they were, in these killing and destructive arts. Great wisdom it will be in your lordships, and just providence, for yourselves, for your posterities, for the whole kingdom, to cast from you, into the fire, these bloody and mysterious volumes of arbitrary and constructive treasons, as the primitive christians did their books of curious arts, and betake yourselves to the plain letter of the statute, which tells you where the crime is, and points out to you the path by which you may avoid it.

"Let us not, to our own destruction, awake those sleeping lions, by rattling up a company of old records, which have lain for so many ages, by the wall, forgotten and neglected. To all my afflictions, add not this, my lords, the most severe of any; that I, for my other sins, not for my treasons, be the means of introducing a precedent, so pernicious to the laws and liberties of my native country.

"However these gentlemen at the bar say they speak for the commonwealth; and they believe so: Yet, under favour, it is I who, in this particular, speak for the commonwealth. Precedents, like those which are endeavoured to be established against me, must draw along such inconveniences and miseries, that, in a few years, the kingdom will be in the condition expressed in a statute of Henry IV.; and no man shall know by what rule to govern his words and actions.

"Impose not, my lords, difficulties insurmountable upon ministers of state, nor disable them from serving with chearfulness their king and country. If you examine them, and under such severe penalties, by every grain, by every little weight; the scrutiny will be intolerable. The public affairs of the kingdom must be left waste; and no wise man, who has any honour or fortune to lose, will ever engage himself in such dreadful, such unknown perils.

"My lords, I have now troubled your lordships a great deal longer than I should have done. Were it not for the interest of these pledges, which a saint in heaven, left me, I should be loth"—Here he pointed to his children, and his weeping stopped him.—"What I forfeit for myself, it is nothing: But, I confess, that my indiscretion should forfeit for them, it wounds me very deeply. You will be pleased to pardon my infirmity: Something I should have said; but I see I shall not be able, and therefore I shall leave it.

"And now, my lords, I thank God, I have been, by his blessing, sufficiently instructed in the extreme vanity of all temporary enjoyments, compared to the importance of our eternal duration. And so, my lords, even so, with all humility, and with all tranquillity of mind, I submit, clearly and freely, to your judgments: And whether that righteous doom shall be to life or death, I shall repose myself, full of gratitude and confidence, in the arms of the great Author of my existence."[a]

Certainly, says Whitlocke[b] with his usual candor, *never any man acted such a part, on such a theatre, with more wisdom, constancy, and eloquence, with greater reason, judgment, and temper, and with a better*

---

[a] Rush. vol. iv. p. 659, &c. [b] Page 41.

grace in all his words and actions, than did this great and excellent person;
and he moved the hearts of all his auditors, some few excepted, to remorse
and pity. It is remarkable, that the historian, who expresses himself
in these terms, was himself chairman of that committee, which
conducted the impeachment against this unfortunate statesman.
The accusation and defence lasted eighteen days. The managers
divided the several articles among them, and attacked the prisoner
with all the weight of authority, with all the vehemence of rhetoric,
with all the accuracy of long preparation. Strafford was obliged to
speak with deference and reserve towards his most inveterate enemies, the commons, the Scottish nation, and the Irish parliament.
He took only a very short time, on each article, to recollect himself:
Yet he alone, without assistance, mixing modesty and humility
with firmness and vigour, made such a defence that the commons
saw it impossible, by a legal prosecution, ever to obtain a sentence
against him.

But the death of Strafford was too important a stroke of party
to be left unattempted by any expedient, however extraordinary.
Besides the great genius and authority of that minister, he had
threatened some of the popular leaders with an impeachment;
and, had he not, himself, been suddenly prevented by the impeachment of the commons, he had, that very day, it was thought,
charged Pym, Hambden, and others, with treason, for having invited the Scots to invade England. A bill of attainder was therefore
brought into the lower house immediately after finishing these
pleadings; and preparatory to it, a new proof of the earl's guilt was
produced, in order to remove such scruples as might be entertained with regard to a method of proceeding so unusual and
irregular.

Sir Henry Vane, secretary, had taken some notes of a debate in
council, after the dissolution of the last parliament; and being at a
distance, he had sent the keys of his cabinet, as was pretended, to
his son, Sir Henry, in order to search for some papers, which were
necessary for completing a marriage-settlement. Young Vane, falling upon this paper of notes, deemed the matter of the utmost
importance; and immediately communicated it to Pym, who now
produced the paper before the house of commons. The question
before the council was: *Offensive or defensive war with the Scots.* The
king proposes this difficulty, "But how can I undertake offensive

war, if I have no more money?" The answer ascribed to Strafford was in these words: "Borrow of the city a hundred thousand pounds: Go on vigorously to levy ship-money. Your majesty having tried the affections of your people, you are absolved and loose from all rules of government, and may do what power will admit. Your majesty, having tried all ways, shall be acquitted before God and man. And you have an army in Ireland, which you may employ to reduce this kingdom to obedience: For I am confident the Scots cannot hold out five months." There followed some counsels of Laud and Cottington equally violent, with regard to the king's being absolved from all rules of government.[c]

This paper, with all the circumstances of its discovery and communication, was pretended to be equivalent to two witnesses, and to be an unanswerable proof of those pernicious counsels of Strafford, which tended to the subversion of the laws and constitution. It was replied by Strafford and his friends, That old Vane was his most inveterate and declared enemy; and if the secretary himself, as was by far most probable, had willingly delivered to his son this paper of notes, to be communicated to Pym, this implied such a breach of oaths and of trust as rendered him totally unworthy of all credit. That the secretary's deposition was at first exceedingly dubious: Upon two examinations, he could not remember any such words: Even the third time, his testimony was not positive, but imported only, that Strafford had spoken such or such-like words: And words may be very like in sound, and differ much in sense; nor ought the lives of men to depend upon grammatical criticisms of any expressions, much less of those which had been delivered by the speaker without premeditation, and committed by the hearer, for any time, however short, to the uncertain record of memory. That, in the present case, changing *This kingdom* into *That kingdom*, a very slight alteration! the earl's discourse could regard nothing but Scotland, and implies no advice unworthy of an English counsellor. That even retaining the expression, *This kingdom*, the words may fairly be understood of Scotland, which alone was the kingdom that the debate regarded, and which alone had thrown off allegiance, and could be reduced to obedience. That it could be proved, as well by the evidence of all the king's ministers,

[c] Clarendon, vol. i. p. 223, 229, 230, &c. Whitlocke, p. 41. May, p. 93.

as by the known disposition of the forces, that the intention never was to land the Irish army in England, but in Scotland. That of six other counsellors present, Laud and Windebank could give no evidence; Northumberland, Hamilton, Cottington, and Juxon, could recollect no such expression; and the advice was too remarkable to be easily forgotten. That it was no-wise probable such a desperate counsel would be openly delivered at the board, and before Northumberland, a person of that high rank, and whose attachments to the court were so much weaker than his connections with the country. That though Northumberland, and he alone, had recollected some such expression, as that *Of being absolved from rules of government;* yet, in such desperate extremities as those into which the king and kingdom were then fallen, a maxim of that nature, allowing it to be delivered by Strafford, may be defended, upon principles the most favourable to law and liberty. And that nothing could be more iniquitous, than to extract an accusation of treason from an opinion simply proposed at the council-table; where all freedom of debate ought to be permitted, and where it was not unusual for the members, in order to draw forth the sentiments of others, to propose counsels very remote from their own secret advice and judgment.[d]

Bill of attainder

The evidence of Secretary Vane, though exposed to such unsurmountable objections, was the real cause of Strafford's unhappy fate; and made the bill of attainder pass the commons with no greater opposition than that of fifty-nine dissenting votes. But there remained two other branches of the legislature, the king and the lords, whose assent was requisite; and these, if left to their free judgment, it was easily foreseen, would reject the bill without scruple or deliberation. To overcome this difficulty, the popular leaders employed expedients, for which they were beholden, partly to their own industry, partly to the indiscretion of their adversaries.

Next Sunday after the bill passed the commons, the puritanical pulpits resounded with declamations concerning the necessity of executing justice upon great delinquents.[e] The populace took the alarm. About six thousand men, armed with swords and cudgels, flocked from the city, and surrounded the houses of parliament.[f] The names of the fifty-nine commoners, who had voted against

[d] Rushworth, vol. iv. p. 560. [e] Whitlocke, p. 43. [f] Idem ibid.

CHAPTER LIV

the bill of attainder, were posted up under the title of *Straffordians, and betrayers of their country.* These were exposed to all the insults of the ungovernable multitude. When any of the lords passed, the cry for *Justice* against Strafford resounded in their ears: And such as were suspected of friendship to that obnoxious minister, were sure to meet with menaces, not unaccompanied with symptoms of the most desperate resolutions in the furious populace.[g]

Complaints in the house of commons being made against these violences as the most flagrant breach of privilege, the ruling members, by their affected coolness and indifference, showed plainly, that the popular tumults were not disagreeable to them.[h] But a new discovery, made about this time, served to throw every thing into still greater flame and combustion.

Some principal officers, Piercy, Jermyn, ONeale, Goring, Wilmot, Pollard, Ashburnham, partly attached to the court, partly disgusted with the parliament, had formed a plan of engaging into the king's service the English army, whom they observed to be displeased at some marks of preference given by the commons to the Scots. For this purpose, they entered into an association, took an oath of secrecy, and kept a close correspondence with some of the king's servants. The form of a petition to the king and parliament was concerted; and it was intended to get this petition subscribed by the army. The petitioners there represent the great and unexampled concessions made by the king for the security of public peace and liberty; the endless demands of certain insatiable and turbulent spirits, whom nothing less will content than a total subversion of the ancient constitution; the frequent tumults which these factious malcontents had excited, and which endangered the liberty of parliament. To prevent these mischiefs, the army offered to come up and guard that assembly. "So shall the nation," as they express themselves in the conclusion, "not only be vindicated from preceding innovations, but be secured from the future, which are threatened, and which are likely to produce more dangerous effects than the former."[i] The draught of this petition being conveyed to the king, he was prevailed on, somewhat imprudently, to countersign it himself as a mark of his approbation. But as several

[g] Clarendon, vol. i. p. 232, 256. Rush. vol v. p. 248, 1279. [h] Whitlocke, ut supra. [i] Clarendon, vol. i. p. 247. Whitlocke, p. 43.

difficulties occurred, the project was laid aside two months before any public discovery was made of it.

It was Goring who betrayed the secret to the popular leaders. The alarm may easily be imagined, which this intelligence conveyed. Petitions from the military to the civil power are always looked on as disguised, or rather undisguised commands; and are of a nature widely different from petitions presented by any other rank of men. Pym opened the matter in the house.[k] On the first intimation of a discovery, Piercy concealed himself, and Jermyn withdrew beyond sea. This farther confirmed the suspicion of a dangerous conspiracy. Goring delivered his evidence before the house: Piercy wrote a letter to his brother, Northumberland, confessing most of the particulars.[l] Both their testimonies agree with regard to the oath of secrecy; and as this circumstance had been denied by Pollard, Ashburnham, and Wilmot, in all their examination, it was regarded as a new proof of some desperate resolutions, which had been taken.

To convey more quickly the terror and indignation at this plot, the commons voted, that a protestation should be signed by all the members. It was sent up to the lords, and signed by all of them, except Southampton and Robarts. Orders were given by the commons alone, without other authority, that it should be subscribed by the whole nation. The protestation was in itself very inoffensive, even insignificant; and contained nothing but general declarations, that the subscribers would defend their religion and liberties.[m] But it tended to encrease the popular panic, and intimated, what was more expressly declared in the preamble, that these blessings were now exposed to the utmost peril.

Alarms were every day given of new conspiracies:[n] In Lancashire, great multitudes of papists were assembling: Secret meetings were held by them in caves and under-ground in Surrey: They had entered into a plot to blow up the river with gun-powder, in order to drown the city:[o] Provisions of arms were making beyond sea: Sometimes France, sometimes Denmark, was forming designs against the kingdom: And the populace, who are always terrified

[k] Rush. vol. v. p. 240.   [l] Idem, ibid. p. 255.   [m] Clarendon, vol. i. p. 252. Rush. vol. v. p. 241. Warwick, p. 180.   [n] Dugdale, p. 69. Franklyn, p. 901. [o] Sir Edw. Walker, p. 349.

CHAPTER LIV

with present, and enraged with distant dangers, were still farther animated in their demands of justice against the unfortunate Strafford.

The king came to the house of lords: And though he expressed his resolution, for which he offered them any security, never again to employ Strafford in any branch of public business; he professed himself totally dissatisfied with regard to the circumstance of treason, and on that account declared his difficulty in giving his assent to the bill of attainder.[p] The commons took fire, and voted it a breach of privilege for the king to take notice of any bill; depending before the houses. Charles did not perceive that his attachment to Strafford was the chief motive for the bill; and that, the greater proofs he gave of anxious concern for this minister, the more inevitable did he render his destruction.

About eighty peers had constantly attended Strafford's trial; but such apprehensions were entertained on account of the popular tumults, that only forty-five were present when the bill of attainder was brought into the house. Yet of these, nineteen had the courage to vote against it;[q] A certain proof, that, if entire freedom had been allowed, the bill had been rejected by a great majority.

In carrying up the bill to the lords, St. John, the solicitor-general, advanced two topics, well suited to the fury of the times; that, though the testimony against Strafford were not clear, yet, in this way of bill, private satisfaction to each man's conscience was sufficient, even should no evidence at all be produced; and that the earl had no title to plead law, because he had broken the law. It is true, added he, we give law to hares and deer; for they are beasts of chace. But it was never accounted either cruel or unfair to destroy foxes or wolves, where-ever they can be found; for they are beasts of prey.[r]

After popular violence had prevailed over the lords, the same battery was next applied to force the king's assent. The populace flocked about Whitehall, and accompanied their demand of justice with the loudest clamours and most open menaces. Rumours of conspiracies against the parliament were anew spread abroad: In-

[p] Rushworth, vol. v. p. 239.　[q] Whitlocke, p. 43.　[r] Clarendon, vol. i. p. 232.

vasions and insurrections talked of: And the whole nation was raised into such a ferment, as threatened some great and imminent convulsion. On which-ever side the king cast his eyes, he saw no resource of security. All his servants, consulting their own safety, rather than their master's honour, declined interposing with their advice between him and his parliament. The queen, terrified with the appearance of so mighty a danger, and bearing formerly no good will to Strafford, was in tears, and pressed him to satisfy his people in this demand, which, it was hoped, would finally content them. Juxon alone, whose courage was not inferior to his other virtues, ventured to advise him, if, in his conscience, he did not approve of the bill, by no means to assent to it.[s]

Strafford, hearing of Charles's irresolution and anxiety, took a very extraordinary step: He wrote a letter, in which he entreated the king, for the sake of public peace, to put an end to his unfortunate, however innocent, life, and to quiet the tumultuous people by granting them the request, for which they were so importunate.[t] "In this," added he, "my consent will more acquit you to God than all the world can do besides. To a willing man there is no injury. And as, by God's grace, I forgive all the world with a calmness and meekness, of infinite contentment to my dislodging soul; so, Sir, to you, I can resign the life of this world with all imaginable chearfulness, in the just acknowledgment of your exceeding favours." Perhaps, Strafford hoped, that this unusual instance of generosity would engage the king still more strenuously to protect him: Perhaps he gave his life for lost; and finding himself in the hands of his enemies, and observing that Balfour, the lieutenant of the Tower, was devoted to the popular party;[u] he absolutely despaired of ever escaping the multiplied dangers, with which he was every way environed. We might ascribe this step to a noble effort of disinterestedness, not unworthy the great mind of Strafford; if the measure which he advised had not been, in the event, as pernicious to his master, as it was immediately fatal to himself.[w]

[s] Ibid. p. 257. Warwick, p. 160. [t] Clarendon, vol. i. p. 258. Rush. vol. v. p. 251. [u] Whitlocke, p. 44. Franklyn, p. 896. [w] See note [X] at the end of the volume.

CHAPTER LIV

After the most violent anxiety and doubt, Charles at last granted a commission to four noblemen to give the royal assent, in his name, to the bill: Flattering himself, probably, in this extremity of distress, that, as neither his will consented to the deed, nor was his hand immediately engaged in it, he was the more free from all the guilt which attended it. These commissioners he empowered, at the same time, to give his assent to the bill which rendered the parliament perpetual.

The commons, from policy, rather than necessity, had embraced the expedient of paying the two armies by borrowing money from the city; and these loans they had repaid afterwards by taxes levied upon the people. The citizens, either of themselves or by suggestion, began to start difficulties, with regard to a farther loan which was demanded. We make no scruple of trusting the parliament, said they, were we certain, that the parliament were to continue till our repayment. But, in the present precarious situation of affairs, what security can be given us for our money? In pretence of obviating this objection, a bill was suddenly brought into the house, and passed with great unanimity and rapidity, that the parliament should not be dissolved, prorogued, or adjourned, without their own consent. It was hurried in like manner through the house of peers; and was instantly carried to the king for his assent. Charles, in the agony of grief, shame, and remorse, for Strafford's doom, perceived not that this other bill was of still more fatal consequence to his authority; and rendered the power of his enemies perpetual, as it was already uncontroulable.[x] In comparison of the bill of attainder, by which he deemed himself an accomplice in his friend's murder, this concession made no figure in his eyes:[y] A circumstance, which, if it lessen our idea of his resolution or penetration, serves to prove the integrity of his heart, and the goodness of his disposition. It is indeed certain, that strong compunction for his consent to Strafford's execution attended this unfortunate prince during the remainder of his life: and even at his own fatal end, the memory of this guilt, with great sorrow and remorse, recurred upon him. All men were so sensible of the

[x] Clarendon, vol. i. p. 261, 262. Rushworth, vol. v. p. 264.   [y] See note [Y] at the end of the volume.

extreme violence which was done him, that he suffered the less, both in character and interest, from this unhappy measure; and though he abandoned his best friend, yet was he still able to preserve, in some degree, the attachment of all his adherents.

Secretary Carleton was sent by the king to inform Strafford of the final resolution, which necessity had extorted from him. The earl seemed surprised, and, starting up, exclaimed in the words of Scripture, *Put not your trust in princes, nor in the sons of men: For in them there is no salvation.*[z] He was soon able, however, to collect his courage; and he prepared himself to suffer the fatal sentence. Only three days' interval was allowed him. The king, who made a new effort in his behalf, and sent, by the hands of the young prince, a letter addressed to the peers, in which he entreated them to confer with the commons about a mitigation of Strafford's sentence, and begged at least for some delay, was refused in both requests.[a]

Execution of Strafford. Strafford, in passing from his apartment to Tower-hill, where the scaffold was erected, stopped under Laud's windows, with whom he had long lived in intimate friendship; and intreated the assistance of his prayers, in those awful moments which were approaching: The aged primate dissolved in tears; and having pronounced, with a broken voice, a tender blessing on his departing friend, sunk into the arms of his attendants.[b] Strafford, still superior to his fate, moved on with an elated countenance, and with an air even of greater dignity than what usually attended him. He wanted that consolation, which commonly supports those who perish by the stroke of injustice and oppression: He was not buoyed up by glory, nor by the affectionate compassion of the spectators: Yet his mind, erect and undaunted, found resources within itself, and maintained its unbroken resolution, amidst the terrors of death, and the triumphant exultations of his misguided enemies. His discourse on the scaffold was full of decency and courage. "He feared," he said, "that the omen was bad for the intended reformation of the state, that it commenced with the shedding of innocent blood." Having bid a last adieu to his brother and friends who attended him, and having sent a blessing to his nearer relations who were absent; "And now," said he, "I have

[z] Whitlocke, p. 44.   [a] Rush. vol. v. p. 265.   [b] Nalson, vol. ii. p. 198.

nigh done! One stroke will make my wife a widow, my dear children fatherless, deprive my poor servants of their indulgent master, and separate me from my affectionate brother and all my friends! But let God be to you and them all in all!" Going to disrobe, and prepare himself for the block, "I thank God," said he, "that I am nowise afraid of death, nor am daunted with any terrors; but do as chearfully lay down my head at this time, as ever I did when going to repose!" With one blow was a period put to his life by the executioner.[c]

Thus perished, in the 49th year of his age, the earl of Strafford, one of the most eminent personages that has appeared in England. Though his death was loudly demanded as a satisfaction to justice, and an atonement for the many violations of the constitution; it may safely be affirmed, that the sentence, by which he fell, was an enormity greater than the worst of those, which his implacable enemies prosecuted with so much cruel industry. The people, in their rage, had totally mistaken the proper object of their resentment. All the necessities, or, more properly speaking, the difficulties, by which the king had been induced to use violent expedients for raising supply, were the result of measures previous to Strafford's favour; and if they arose from ill conduct, he, at least, was entirely innocent. Even those violent expedients themselves, which occasioned the complaint that the constitution was subverted, had been, all of them, conducted, so far as appeared, without his counsel or assistance. And whatever his private advice might be,[d] this salutary maxim he failed not, often and publicly, to inculcate in the king's presence, that, if any inevitable necessity ever obliged the sovereign to violate the laws, this licence ought to be practised with extreme reserve, and, as soon as possible, a just atonement be made to the constitution, for any injury which it might sustain from such dangerous precedents.[e] This first parliament after the restoration reversed the bill of attainder; and even a few weeks after Strafford's execution, this very parliament remitted to his children the more severe consequences of his sentence:

---

[c] Rushworth, vol. v. p. 267.   [d] That Strafford was secretly no enemy to arbitrary counsel, appears from some of his letters and dispatches, particularly, vol. ii. p. 60. where he seems to wish that a standing army were established.   [e] Rushworth, vol. iv. p. 567, 568, 569, 570.

As if conscious of the violence, with which the prosecution had been conducted.

In vain did Charles expect, as a return for so many instances of unbounded compliance, that the parliament would at last show him some indulgence, and would cordially fall into that unanimity, to which, at the expence of his own power, and of his friend's life, he so earnestly courted them. All his concessions were poisoned by their suspicion of his want of cordiality; and the supposed attempt to engage the army against them, served with many as a confirmation of this jealousy. It was natural for the king to seek some resource, while all the world seemed to desert him, or combine against him; and this probably was the utmost of the embryo scheme which was formed with regard to the army. But the popular leaders still insisted, that a desperate plot was laid to bring up the forces immediately, and offer violence to the parliament: A design of which Piercy's evidence acquits the king, and which the near neighbourhood of the Scottish army seems to render absolutely impracticable.*f* By means, however, of these suspicions, was the same implacable spirit still kept alive; and the commons, without giving the king any satisfaction in the settlement of his revenue, proceeded to carry their inroads, with great vigour, into his now defenceless prerogative.*g*

High commission and star-chamber abolished. The two ruling passions of this parliament, were zeal for liberty, and an aversion to the church; and to both of these, nothing could appear more exceptionable, than the court of high commission, whose institution rendered it entirely arbitrary, and assigned to it the defence of the ecclesiastical establishment. The star-chamber also was a court, which exerted high discretionary powers; and had no precise rule or limit, either with regard to the causes which came under its jurisdiction, or the decisions which it formed. A bill unanimously passed the houses to abolish these two

---

f The project of bringing up the army to London, according to Piercy, was proposed to the king; but he rejected it as foolish: Because the Scots, who were in arms, and lying in their neighbourhood, must be at London as soon as the English army. This reason is so solid and convincing, that it leaves no room to doubt of the veracity of Piercy's evidence; and consequently acquits the king of this terrible plot of bringing up the army, which made such a noise at the time, and was a pretence for so many violences.   *g* Clarendon, vol. i. p. 266.

CHAPTER LIV

courts; and, in them, to annihilate the principal and most dangerous articles of the king's prerogative. By the same bill, the jurisdiction of the council was regulated, and its authority abridged.[h]
Charles hesitated before he gave his assent. But finding that he
had gone too far to retreat, and that he possessed no resource in
case of a rupture, he at last affixed the royal sanction to this
excellent bill. But to show the parliament, that he was sufficiently
apprised of the importance of his grant, he observed to them, that
this statute altered in a great measure the fundamental laws, ecclesiastical and civil, which many of his predecessors had established.[i]

By removing the star-chamber, the king's power of binding the
people by his proclamations, was indirectly abolished; and that
important branch of prerogative, the strong symbol of arbitrary
power, and unintelligible in a limited constitution, being at last
removed, left the system of government more consistent and uniform. The star-chamber alone was accustomed to punish in-
fractions of the king's edicts: But as no courts of judicature now
remained, except those in Westminster-hall, which take cognizance only of common and statute law, the king may thenceforth
issue proclamations, but no man is bound to obey them. It must,
however, be confessed, that the experiment here made by the
parliament, was not a little rash and adventurous. No government,
at that time, appeared in the world, nor is perhaps to be found in
the records of any history, which subsisted without the mixture of
some arbitrary authority, committed to some magistrate; and it
might reasonably, beforehand, appear doubtful, whether human
society could ever reach that state of perfection, as to support itself
with no other controul than the general and rigid maxims of law
and equity. But the parliament justly thought, that the king was
too eminent a magistrate to be trusted with discretionary power,
which he might so easily turn to the destruction of liberty. And
in the event it has hitherto been found, that, though some sensible inconveniences arise from the maxim of adhering strictly to
law, yet the advantages overbalance them, and should render the
English grateful to the memory of their ancestors, who, after

[h] Idem, ibid. p. 283, 284. Whitlocke, p. 47. Rushworth, vol. iii.
p. 1383, 1384. [i] Rushworth, vol. v. p. 307.

repeated contests, at last established that noble, though dangerous, principle.

At the request of the parliament, Charles, instead of the patents
during pleasure, gave all the judges patents during their good
behaviour:[k] A circumstance of the greatest moment towards securing their independency, and barring the entrance of arbitrary
power into the ordinary courts of judicature.

The marshal's court, which took cognizance of offensive words,
and was not thought sufficiently limited by law, was also, for that
reason, abolished.[l] The stannary courts, which exercised jurisdiction over the miners, being liable to a like objection, underwent a
like fate. The abolition of the council of the north and the council
of Wales followed from the same principles. The authority of the
clerk of the market, who had a general inspection over the weights
and measures throughout the kingdom, was transferred to the
mayors, sheriffs, and ordinary magistrates.

In short, if we take a survey of the transactions of this memorable parliament, during the first period of its operations, we shall
find, that, excepting Strafford's attainder, which was a complication of cruel iniquity, their merits, in other respects, so much
outweigh their mistakes, as to entitle them to praise from all lovers
of liberty. Not only were former abuses remedied, and grievances
redressed: Great provision, for the future, was made by law against
the return of like complaints. And if the means, by which they
obtained such advantages, savour often of artifice, sometimes of
violence; it is to be considered, that revolutions of government
cannot be effected by the mere force of argument and reasoning:
And that factions being once excited, men can neither so firmly
regulate the tempers of others, nor their own, as to ensure themselves against all exorbitancies.

The parliament now came to a pause. The king had promised
his Scottish subjects, that he would this summer pay them a visit,
in order to settle their government; and though the English parliament was very importunate with him, that he should lay aside that
journey; they could not prevail with him so much as to delay it. As
he must necessarily in his journey have passed through the troops
of both nations, the commons seem to have entertained great

*8th of
Aug.
King's
journey to
Scotland.*

[k] May, p. 107.   [l] Nalson, vol. i. p. 778.

CHAPTER LIV

jealousy on that account, and to have now hurried on, as much as they formerly delayed, the disbanding of the armies. The arrears therefore of the Scots were fully paid them; and those of the English in part. The Scots returned home, and the English were separated into their several counties, and dismissed.

After this the parliament adjourned to the 20th of October; *9th of* and a committee of both houses, a thing unprecedented, was ap- *Sept.* pointed to sit during the recess, with very ample powers.[m] Pym was elected chairman of the committee of the lower house. Farther attempts were made by the parliament, while it sat, and even by the commons alone, for assuming sovereign executive powers, and publishing their ordinances, as they called them, instead of laws. The committee too, on their part, was ready to imitate the example.

A small committee of both houses was appointed to attend the king into Scotland, in order, as was pretended, to see that the articles of pacification were executed; but really to be spies upon him, and extend still farther the ideas of parliamentary authority, as well as eclipse the majesty of the king. The earl of Bedford, lord Howard, Sir Philip Stapleton, Sir William Armyne, Fiennes, and Hambden, were the persons chosen.[n]

Endeavours were used, before Charles's departure, to have a protector of the kingdom appointed, with a power to pass laws without having recourse to the king. So little regard was now paid to royal authority, or to the established constitution of the kingdom.

Amidst the great variety of affairs, which occurred during this busy period, we have almost overlooked the marriage of the princess Mary with William prince of Orange. The king concluded not this alliance without communicating his intentions to the parliament, who received the proposal with satisfaction.[o] This was the commencement of the connections with the family of Orange: Connections, which were afterwards attended with the most important consequences, both to the kingdom and to the house of Stuart.

[m] Rushworth, vol. v. p. 387.   [n] Ibid. p. 376.   [o] Whitlocke, p. 38.

LV

Settlement of Scotland – Conspiracy in
Ireland – Insurrection and massacre – Meeting
of the English parliament – The remonstrance –
Reasons on both sides – Impeachment of
the bishops – Accusation of the
five members – Tumults – King leaves
London – Arrives in York –
Preparations for civil war

THE SCOTS, who began these fatal commotions, thought, that they had finished a very perilous undertaking, much to their profit and reputation. Besides the large pay voted them for lying in good quarters during a twelvemonth, the English parliament had conferred on them a present of 300,000 pounds for their brotherly assistance.[p] In the articles of pacification, they were declared to have ever been good subjects; and their military expeditions were approved of, as enterprizes calculated and intended for his majesty's honour and advantage. To carry farther the triumph over their sovereign, these terms, so ignominious to him, were ordered by a vote of parliament, to be read in all churches, upon a day of thanksgiving, appointed for the national pacification:[q] All their claims for the restriction of prerogative, were agreed to be

---

[p] Nalson, vol. i. p. 747. May, p. 104.   [q] Rushworth, vol. v. p. 365. Clarendon, vol. ii. p. 293.

CHAPTER LV

ratified: And what they more valued than all these advantages; they had a near prospect of spreading the presbyterian discipline in England and Ireland, from the seeds, which they had scattered, of their religious principles. Never did refined Athens so exult in diffusing the sciences and liberal arts over a savage world; never did generous Rome so please herself in the view of law and order established by her victorious arms; as the Scots now rejoiced, in communicating their barbarous zeal and theological fervour, to the neighbouring nations.

Charles, despoiled in England of a considerable part of his authority, and dreading still farther encroachments upon him, arrived in Scotland, with an intention of abdicating almost entirely the small share of power, which *there* remained to him, and of giving full satisfaction, if possible, to his restless subjects in that kingdom. *Aug. 14. Settlement of Scotland.*

The lords of articles were an ancient institution in the Scottish parliament. They were constituted after this manner. The temporal lords chose eight bishops: The bishops elected eight temporal lords: These sixteen named eight commissioners of counties, and eight burgesses: And without the previous consent of the thirty-two, who were denominated lords of articles, no motion could be made in parliament. As the bishops were entirely devoted to the court, it is evident, that all the lords of articles, by necessary consequence, depended on the king's nomination; and the prince, besides one negative after the bills had passed through parliament, possessed indirectly another before their introduction; a prerogative of much greater consequence than the former. The bench of bishops being now abolished, the parliament laid hold of the opportunity, and totally set aside the lords of articles: And till this important point was obtained, the nation, properly speaking, could not be said to enjoy any regular freedom.[r]

It is remarkable, that, notwithstanding this institution, to which there was no parallel in England, the royal authority was always deemed much lower in Scotland than in the former kingdom. Bacon represents it as one advantage to be expected from the union, that the too extensive prerogative of England would be abridged by the example of Scotland, and the too narrow prerog-

[r] Burnet, Mem.

ative of Scotland be enlarged from the imitation of England. The English were, at that time, a civilized people, and obedient to the laws: But among the Scots, it was of little consequence how the laws were framed, or by whom voted, while the exorbitant aristocracy had it so much in their power to prevent their regular execution.

The peers and commons formed only one house in the Scottish parliament: And as it had been the practice of James, continued by Charles, to grace English gentlemen with Scottish titles, all the determinations of parliament it was to be feared, would in time depend upon the prince, by means of these votes of foreigners, who had no interest or property in the nation. It was therefore a law, deserving approbation, that no man should be created a Scotch peer, who possessed not 10,000 marks (above 500 pounds) of annual rent in the kingdom.[s]

A law for triennial parliaments was likewise passed; and it was ordained, that the last act of every parliament should be to appoint the time and place for holding the parliament next ensuing.[t]

The king was deprived of that power, formerly exercised, of issuing proclamations, which enjoined obedience, under the penalty of treason: A prerogative, which invested him with the whole legislative authority, even in matters of the highest importance.[u]

So far was laudable: But the most fatal blow given to royal authority, and what in a manner dethroned the prince, was the article, that no member of the privy council, in whose hands, during the king's absence, the whole administration lay, no officer of state, none of the judges, should be appointed but by advice and approbation of parliament. Charles even agreed to deprive of their seats, four judges who had adhered to his interests; and their place was supplied by others more agreeable to the ruling party. Several of the covenanters were also sworn of the privy council. And all the ministers of state, counsellors, and judges, were, by law, to hold their places during life or good behaviour.[w]

The king, while in Scotland, conformed himself entirely to the established church; and assisted with great gravity, at the long prayers and longer sermons, with which the presbyterians endeavoured to regale him. He bestowed pensions and preferments

[s] Burnet, Mem.　[t] Idem, ibid.　[u] Idem, ibid.　[w] Burnet, Mem.

CHAPTER LV

on Henderson, Gillespy, and other popular preachers; and practised every art to soften, if not to gain, his greatest enemies. The
earl of Argyle was created a marquis, lord Loudon an earl, Lesley
was dignified with the title of earl of Leven.[x] His friends, he was
obliged, for the present, to neglect and overlook: Some of them
were disgusted: And his enemies were not reconciled; but ascribed
all his caresses and favours to artifice and necessity.

Argyle and Hamilton, being seized with an apprehension real
or pretended, that the earl of Crawfurd and others meant to assassinate them, left the parliament suddenly, and retired into the
country: But upon invitation and assurances, returned in a few
days. This event, which had neither cause nor effect that was
visible, nor purpose, nor consequence, was commonly denominated the *incident*. But though the incident had no effect in Scotland; what was not expected, it was attended with consequences in
England. The English parliament, which was now assembled, being willing to awaken the people's tenderness by exciting their *October*
fears, immediately took the alarm; as if the malignants, so they *20.*
called the king's party, had laid a plot at once to murder them and
all the godly in both kingdoms. They applied, therefore, to Essex,
whom the king had left general in the south of England; and he
ordered a guard to attend them.[y]

But while the king was employed in pacifying the commotions
in Scotland, and was preparing to return to England, in order to
apply himself to the same salutary work in that kingdom; he received intelligence of a dangerous rebellion broken out in Ireland,
with circumstances of the utmost horror, bloodshed, and devas-
tation. On every side, this unfortunate prince was pursued with
murmurs, discontent, faction, and civil wars; and the fire, from all
quarters, even by the most independent accidents, at once blazed
up about him.

The great plan of James, in the administration of Ireland, continued by Charles, was, by justice and peace to reconcile that turbulent people to the authority of laws, and, introducing art and
industry among them, to cure them of that sloth and barbarism, to
which they had ever been subject. In order to serve both these

[x] Clarendon, vol. ii. p. 309. [y] Whitlocke, p. 40. Dugdale, p. 72. Burnet's
Memoirs of the House of Hamilton, p. 184, 185. Clarendon, p. 299.

purposes, and at the same time secure the dominion of Ireland to the English crown, great colonies of British had been carried over, and, being intermixed with the Irish, had every where introduced a new face of things into that country. During a peace of near forty years, the inveterate quarrels between the nations seemed, in a great measure, to be obliterated; and though much of the landed property, forfeited by rebellion, had been conferred on the new planters, a more than equal return had been made, by their instructing the natives in tillage, building, manufactures, and all the civilized arts of life.[z] This had been the course of things during the successive administrations of Chichester, Grandison, Falkland, and, above all, of Strafford. Under the government of this latter nobleman, the pacific plans, now come to greater maturity, and forwarded by his vigour and industry, seemed to have operated with full success, and to have bestowed, at last, on that savage country, the face of a European settlement.

After Strafford fell a victim to popular rage, the humours excited in Ireland by that great event, could not suddenly be composed, but continued to produce the greatest innovations in the government.

The British protestants, transplanted into Ireland, having, every moment before their eyes, all the horrors of popery, had naturally been carried into the opposite extreme, and had universally adopted the highest principles and practices of the puritans. Monarchy, as well as the hierarchy, was become odious to them; and every method of limiting the authority of the crown, and detaching themselves from the king of England, was greedily adopted and pursued. They considered not, that, as they scarcely-formed the sixth part of the people, and were secretly obnoxious to the ancient inhabitants; their only method of supporting themselves was by maintaining royal authority, and preserving a great dependance on their mother-country. The English commons, likewise, in their furious prosecution of Strafford, had overlooked the most obvious consequences; and, while they imputed to him, as a crime, every discretionary act of authority, they despoiled all succeeding governors of that power, by which alone the Irish could be retained in subjection. And so strong was the current for popular government

[z] Sir John Temple's Irish Rebellion, p. 12.

in all the three kingdoms, that the most established maxims of policy were every where abandoned, in order to gratify this ruling passion.

Charles, unable to resist, had been obliged to yield to the Irish, as to the Scottish and English parliaments; and found too, that their encroachments still rose in proportion to his concessions. Those subsidies, which themselves had voted, they reduced, by a subsequent vote, to a fourth part: The court of high commission was determined to be a grievance: Martial law abolished: The jurisdiction of the council annihilated: Proclamations and acts of state declared of no authority: Every order or institution, which depended on monarchy, was invaded; and the prince was despoiled of all his prerogative, without the least pretext of any violence or illegality in his administration.

The standing army of Ireland was usually about 3000 men; but in order to assist the king in suppressing the Scottish covenanters, Strafford had raised 8000 more, and had incorporated with them a thousand men, drawn from the old army; a necessary expedient for bestowing order and discipline on the new levied soldiers. The private men in this army were all catholics; but the officers, both commission and non-commission, were protestants, and could entirely be depended on by Charles. The English commons entertained the greatest apprehensions on account of this army; and never ceased soliciting the king, till he agreed to break it: Nor would they consent to any proposal for augmenting the standing army to 5000 men; a number which the king deemed necessary for retaining Ireland in obedience.

Charles, thinking it dangerous, that 8000 men accustomed to idleness, and trained to the use of arms, should be dispersed among a nation so turbulent and unsettled, agreed with the Spanish ambassador to have them transported into Flanders, and enlisted in his master's service. The English commons, pretending apprehensions, lest regular bodies of troops, disciplined in the Low Countries, should prove still more dangerous, showed some aversion to this expedient; and the king reduced his allowance to 4000 men. But when the Spaniards had hired ships for transporting these troops, and the men were ready to embark; the commons, willing to show their power, and not displeased with an opportunity of curbing and affronting the king, prohibited every one from furnishing vessels for that service. And thus the project, formed by Charles, of freeing the country from these men, was unfortunately disappointed.[a]

The old Irish remarked all these false steps of the English, and resolved to take advantage of them. Tho' their animosity against that nation, for want of an occasion to exert itself, seemed to be extinguished, it was only composed into a temporary and deceitful tranquillity.[b] Their interests, both with regard to *property* and *religion,* secretly stimulated them to a revolt. No individual of any sept, according to the ancient customs, had the property of any particular estate; but as the whole sept had a title to a whole territory, they ignorantly preferred this barbarous community before the more secure and narrower possessions assigned them by the English. An indulgence, amounting almost to a toleration, had been given to the catholic religion: But so long as the churches and the ecclesiastical revenues were kept from the priests, and they were obliged to endure the neighbourhood of profane heretics, being themselves discontented, they continually endeavoured to retard any cordial reconciliation between the English and the Irish nations.

Conspiracy in Ireland. There was a gentleman called Roger More, who, though of a narrow fortune, was descended from an ancient Irish family, and was much celebrated among his countrymen for valour and capacity. This man first formed the project of expelling the English, and asserting the independency of his native country.[c] He secretly went from chieftain to chieftain, and rouzed up every latent principle of discontent. He maintained a close correspondence with lord Maguire and Sir Phelim ONeale, the most powerful of the old Irish. By conversation, by letters, by his emissaries, he represented to his countrymen the motives of a revolt. He observed to them, that, by the rebellion of the Scots, and factions of the English, the king's authority in Britain was reduced to so low a condition, that he never could exert himself with any vigour, in maintaining the English dominion over Ireland; that the catholics, in the Irish house of commons, assisted by the protestants, had so diminished the royal prerogative and the power of the lieutenant, as would

---

[a] Clarendon, vol. i. p. 281. Rushworth, vol. v. p. 381. Dugdale, p. 75. May, book ii. p. 3.   [b] Temple, p. 14.   [c] Nalson, vol. ii. p. 543.

much facilitate the conducting, to its desired effect, any conspiracy or combination, which could be formed; that the Scots having so successfully thrown off dependence on the crown of England, and assumed the government into their own hands, had set an example to the Irish, who had so much greater oppressions to complain of; that the English planters, who had expelled them their possessions, suppressed their religion, and bereaved them of their liberties, were but a handful in comparison of the natives; that they lived in the most supine security, interspersed with their numerous enemies, trusting to the protection of a small army, which was itself scattered in inconsiderable divisions throughout the whole kingdom; that a great body of men, disciplined by the government, were now thrown loose, and were ready for any daring or desperate enterprize; that though the catholics had hitherto enjoyed, in some tolerable measure, the exercise of their religion, from the moderation of their indulgent prince, they must henceforth expect, that the government will be conducted by other maxims and other principles; that the puritanical parliament, having at length subdued their sovereign, would no doubt, as soon as they had consolidated their authority, extend their ambitious enterprizes to Ireland, and make the catholics in that kingdom feel the same furious persecution, to which their brethren in England were at present exposed; and that a revolt in the Irish, tending only to vindicate their native liberty against the violence of foreign invaders, could never, at any time, be deemed rebellion; much less during the present confusions, when their prince was, in a manner, a prisoner, and obedience must be paid, not to him, but to those who had traiterously usurped his lawful authority.[d]

By these considerations, More engaged all the heads of the native Irish into the conspiracy. The English of the pale, as they were called, or the old English planters, being all catholics, it was hoped, would afterwards join the party, which restored their religion to its ancient splendor and authority. The intention was, that Sir Phelim ONeale and the other conspirators should begin an insurrection on one day, throughout the provinces, and should attack all the English settlements; and that, on the same day, lord Maguire and Roger More should surprize the castle of Dublin. The

[d] Temple, p. 72, 73, 78. Dugdale, p. 73.

commencement of the revolt was fixed on the approach of winter; that there might be more difficulty in transporting forces from England. Succours to themselves and supplies of arms they expected from France, in consequence of a promise made them by cardinal Richelieu. And many Irish officers, who served in the Spanish troops, had engaged to join them, as soon as they saw an insurrection entered upon by their catholic brethren. News, which every day arrived from England, of the fury expressed by the commons against all papists, struck fresh terror into the Irish nation, and both stimulated the conspirators to execute their fatal purpose, and gave them assured hopes of the concurrence of all their countrymen.[e]

Such propensity to a revolt was discovered in all the Irish, that it was deemed unnecessary, as it was dangerous, to entrust the secret to many hands; and the appointed day drew nigh, nor had any discovery been yet made to the government. The king, indeed, had received information from his ambassadors, that something was in agitation among the Irish in foreign parts; but though he gave warning to the administration in Ireland, the intelligence was entirely neglected.[f] Secret rumours, likewise, were heard of some approaching conspiracy; but no attention was paid to them. The earl of Leicester, whom the king had appointed lieutenant, remained in London. The two justices, Sir William Parsons and Sir John Borlace, were men of small abilities; and, by an inconvenience, common to all factious times, owed their advancement to nothing but their zeal for the party, by whom every thing was now governed. Tranquil from their ignorance and inexperience, these men indulged themselves in the most profound repose, on the very brink of destruction.

But they were awakened from their security, on the very day before that which was appointed for the commencement of hostilities. The castle of Dublin, by which the capital was commanded, contained arms for 10,000 men, with thirty-five pieces of cannon, and a proportionable quantity of ammunition: Yet was this important place guarded, and that too without any care, by no greater force than fifty men. Maguire and More were already in town with a numerous band of their partizans: Others were ex-

[e] Dugdale, p. 74.   [f] Rushworth, vol. v. p. 408. Nalson, vol. ii. p. 565.

pected that night: And, next morning, they were to enter upon, what they esteemed the easiest of all enterprizes, the surprizal of the castle. Oconolly, an Irishman, but a protestant, betrayed the conspiracy to Parsons.[g] The justices and council fled immediately for safety, into the castle, and re-inforced the guards. The alarm was conveyed to the city, and all the protestants prepared for defence. More escaped: Maguire was taken; and Mahone, one of the conspirators, being likewise seized, first discovered to the justices, the project of a general insurrection, and redoubled the apprehensions, which already were universally diffused throughout Dublin.[h]

But though Oconolly's discovery saved the castle from a surprize, the confession extorted from Mahone, came too late to prevent the intended insurrection. ONeal and his confederates had already taken arms in Ulster. The Irish, every where intermingled with the English, needed but a hint from their leaders and priests to begin hostilities against a people whom they hated on account of their religion, and envied for their riches and prosperity.[i] The houses, cattle, goods, of the unwary English were first seized. Those, who heard of the commotions in their neighborhood, instead of deserting their habitations, and assembling for mutual protection, remained at home, in hopes of defending their property; and fell thus separately into the hands of their enemies.[k] After rapacity had fully exerted itself, cruelty, and the most barbarous, that ever, in any nation, was known or heard of, begin its operations. An universal massacre commenced of the English, now defenceless, and passively resigned to their inhuman foes. No age, no sex, no condition was spared. The wife weeping for her butchered husband, and embracing her helpless children, was pierced with them, and perished by the same stroke.[l] The old, the young, the vigorous, the infirm, underwent a like fate, and were confounded in one common ruin. In vain did flight save from the first assault: Destruction was, every where, let loose, and met the hunted victims at every turn. In vain was recourse had to relations, to companions, to friends: All connexions were dissolved, and

Irish insurrection and massacre.

---

[g] Rush, vol. v. p. 399. Nalson, vol. ii. p. 520. May, book ii. p. 6. [h] Temple, p. 17, 18, 19, 20. Rush. vol. v. p. 400. [i] Temple, p. 39, 40, 79. [k] Temple, p. 42. [l] Temple, p. 40.

death was dealt by that hand, from which protection was implored and expected. Without provocation, without opposition, the astonished English, living in profound peace, and full security, were massacred by their nearest neighbours, with whom they had long upheld a continued intercourse of kindness and good offices.[m]

But death was the lightest punishment, inflicted by those rebels: All the tortures which wanton cruelty could devise, all the lingering pains of body, the anguish of mind, the agonies of despair, could not satiate revenge excited without injury, and cruelty derived from no cause. To enter into particulars would shock the least delicate humanity. Such enormities, though attested by undoubted evidence, appear almost incredible. Depraved nature, even perverted religion, encouraged by the utmost licence, reach not to such a pitch of ferocity; unless the pity, inherent in human breasts, be destroyed by that contagion of example, which transports men beyond all the usual motives of conduct and behaviour.

The weaker sex themselves, naturally tender to their own sufferings, and compassionate to those of others, here emulated their more robust companions, in the practice of every cruelty.[n] Even children, taught by the example, and encouraged by the exhortation, of their parents, essayed their feeble blows on the dead carcasses of defenceless children of the English.[o] The very avarice of the Irish was not a sufficient restraint to their cruelty. Such was their frenzy, that the cattle, which they had seized, and by rapine made their own, yet, because they bore the name of English, were wantonly slaughtered, or, when covered with wounds, turned loose into the woods or desarts.[p]

The stately buildings or commodious habitations of the planters, as if upbraiding the sloth and ignorance of the natives, were consumed with fire, or laid level with the ground. And where the miserable owners, shut up in their houses, and preparing for defence, perished in the flames, together with their wives and children, a double triumph was afforded to their insulting foes.[q]

If any where a number assembled together, and, assuming courage from despair, were resolved to sweeten death by revenge

---

[m] Temple, p. 39, 40.   [n] Temple, p. 96, 101. Rush. vol. v. p. 415.
[o] Temple, p. 100.   [p] Idem, p. 84.   [q] Temple, p. 99. 106. Rush. vol. v. p. 414.

on their assassins; they were disarmed by capitulations, and promises of safety, confirmed by the most solemn oaths. But no sooner had they surrendered, than the rebels, with perfidy equal to their cruelty, made them share the fate of their unhappy countrymen.[r] .

Others, more ingenious still in their barbarity, tempted their prisoners, by the fond love of life, to embrue their hands in the blood of friends, brothers, parents; and having thus rendered them accomplices in guilt, gave them that death, which they sought to shun by deserving it.[s]

Amidst all these enormities, the sacred name of Religion resounded on every side; not to stop the hands of these murderers, but to enforce their blows, and to steel their hearts against every movement of human or social sympathy. The English, as heretics, abhorred of God, and detestable to all holy men, were marked out by the priests for slaughter; and, of all actions, to rid the world of these declared enemies to catholic faith and piety, was represented as the most meritorious.[t] Nature, which, in that rude people, was sufficiently inclined to atrocious deeds, was farther stimulated by precept; and national prejudices empoisoned by those aversions, more deadly and incurable, which arose from an enraged superstition. While death finished the sufferings of each victim, the bigotted assassins, with joy and exultation, still echoed in his expiring ears, that these agonies were but the commencement of torments, infinite and eternal.[u]

Such were the barbarities, by which Sir Phelim ONeale and the Irish in Ulster signalized their rebellion: An event, memorable in the annals of human kind, and worthy to be held in perpetual detestation and abhorrence. The generous nature of More was shocked at the recital of such enormous cruelties. He flew to ONeale's camp; but found, that his authority, which was sufficient to excite the Irish to an insurrection, was too feeble to restrain their inhumanity. Soon after, he abandoned a cause, polluted by so many crimes; and he retired into Flanders. Sir Phelim, recommended by the greatness of his family, and perhaps too, by the unrestrained brutality of his nature, though without any courage or capacity, acquired the entire ascendant over the northern reb-

---

[r] Whitlocke, p. 47. Rush. vol. v. p. 416.   [s] Temple, p. 100.   [t] Idem, p. 85, 106.   [u] Temple, p. 94, 107, 108. Rushworth, vol. v. p. 407.

els.[w] The English colonies were totally annihilated in the open country of Ulster: The Scots, at first, met with more favourable treatment. In order to engage them to a passive neutrality, the Irish pretended to distinguish between the British nations; and claiming friendship and consanguinity with the Scots, extended not over them the fury of their massacres. Many of them found an opportunity to fly the country: Others retired into places of security, and prepared themselves for defence: And by this means, the Scottish planters, most of them at least, escaped with their lives.[x]

From Ulster, the flames of rebellion diffused themselves, in an instant, over the other three provinces of Ireland. In all places death and slaughter were not uncommon; though the Irish, in these other provinces, pretended to act with moderation and humanity. But cruel and barbarous was their humanity! Not content with expelling the English their houses, with despoiling them of their goodly manors, with wasting their cultivated fields; they stripped them of their very cloaths, and turned them out, naked and defenceless, to all the severities of the season.[y] The heavens themselves, as if conspiring against that unhappy people were armed with cold and tempest, unusual to the climate, and executed what the merciless sword had left unfinished.[z] The roads were covered with crowds of naked English, hastening towards Dublin and the other cities, which yet remained in the hands of their countrymen. The feeble age of children, the tender sex of women, soon sunk under the multiplied rigours of cold and hunger. Here, the husband, bidding a final adieu to his expiring family, envied them for fate, which he himself expected so soon to share: There, the son, having long supported his aged parent, with reluctance obeyed his last commands, and abandoning him in this uttermost distress, reserved himself to the hopes of avenging that death, which all his efforts could not prevent or delay. The astonishing greatness of the calamity deprived the sufferers of any relief from the view of companions in affliction. With silent tears, or lamentable cries, they hurried on through the hostile territories; and found every heart, which was not steeled by native barbar-

[w] Temple, p. 44.   [x] Idem, p. 41. Rush. vol. i. p. 416.   [y] Temple, p. 42.   [z] Idem, p. 64.

ity, guarded by the more implacable furies of mistaken piety and religion.[a]

The saving of Dublin preserved in Ireland the remains of the English name. The gates of that city, though timorously opened, received the wretched supplicants, and presented to the view a scene of human misery, beyond what any eye had ever before beheld.[b] Compassion seized the amazed inhabitants, aggravated with the fear of like calamities; while they observed the numerous foes, without and within, which every where environed them, and reflected on the weak resources, by which they were themselves supported. The more vigorous of the unhappy fugitives, to the number of three thousand, were inlisted into three regiments: The rest were distributed into the houses; and all care was taken, by diet and warmth, to recruit their feeble and torpid limbs. Diseases of unknown name and species, derived from these multiplied distresses, seized many of them, and put a speedy period to their lives: Others, having now leisure to reflect on their mighty loss of friends and fortune, cursed that being which they had saved. Abandoning themselves to despair, refusing all succour, they expired; without other consolation, than that of receiving among their countrymen, the honours of a grave, which, to their slaughtered companions, had been denied by the inhuman barbarians.[c]

By some computations, those, who perished by all these cruelties, are supposed to be a hundred and fifty, or two hundred thousand: By the most moderate, and probably the most reasonable account, they are made to amount to 40,000; if this estimation itself be not, as is usual in such cases, somewhat exaggerated.

The justices ordered to Dublin all the bodies of the army, which were not surrounded by the rebels; and they assembled a force of 1500 veterans. They soon inlisted, and armed from the magazines above 4000 men more. They dispatched a body of 600 men to throw relief into Tredah, besieged by the Irish. But these troops, attacked by the enemy, were seized with a panic, and were most of them put to the sword. Their arms, falling into the hands of the Irish, supplied them with what they most wanted.[d] The justices, willing to foment the rebellion, in a view of profiting by the multi-

[a] Temple, p. 88.   [b] Idem, p. 62.   [c] Idem, p. 43, 62.   [d] Nalson, vol. ii. p. 905.

plyed forfeitures, henceforth thought of nothing more than providing for their own present security and that of the capital. The earl of Ormond, their general, remonstrated against such timid, not to say, base and interested counsels; but was obliged to submit to authority.

The English of the pale, who probably were not, at first, in the secret, pretended to blame the insurrection, and to detest the barbarity, with which it was accompanied.[e] By their protestations and declarations, they engaged the justices to supply them with arms, which they promised to employ in defence of the government.[f] But in a little time, the interests of religion were found more prevalent over them than regard and duty to their mother country. They chose lord Gormanstone their leader; and, joining the old Irish, rivaled them in every act of violence towards the English protestants. Besides many smaller bodies, dispersed over the kingdom, the principal army of the rebels amounted to twenty thousand men, and threatened Dublin with an immediate siege.[g]

Both the English and Irish rebels conspired in one imposture, with which they seduced many of their deluded countrymen: They pretended authority from the king and queen, but chiefly from the latter, for their insurrection; and they affirmed, that the cause of their taking arms was to vindicate royal prerogative, now invaded by the puritanical parliament.[h] Sir Phelim ONeale, having found a royal patent in lord Caufield's house, whom he had murdered, tore off the seal, and affixed it to a commission, which he had forged for himself.[i]

The king received an account of this insurrection by a messenger, dispatched from the north of Ireland. He immediately communicated his intelligence to the Scottish parliament. He expected, that the mighty zeal, expressed by the Scots for the protestant religion, would immediately engage them to fly to its defence, where it was so violently invaded: He hoped, that their horror against popery, a religion, which now appeared in its most horrible aspect, would second all his exhortations: He had observed with what alacrity they had twice run to arms, and assem-

---

[e] Temple, p. 33. Rushworth, vol. v. p. 402.   [f] Temple, p. 60. Borlase Hist. p. 28.   [g] Whitlocke, p. 49.   [h] Rush. vol. v. p. 400, 401.   [i] Idem, ibid. p. 402.

CHAPTER LV

bled troops in opposition to the rights of their sovereign: He saw
with how much greater facility they could now collect forces, which
had been very lately disbanded, and which had been so long enured to military discipline. The cries of their affrighted and distressed brethren in Ireland, he promised himself, would power-
fully incite them to send over succours, which could arrive so
quickly, and aid them with such promptitude in this uttermost
distress. But the zeal of the Scots, as is usual among religious sects,
was very feeble, when not stimulated either by faction or by interest. They now considered themselves entirely as a republic, and
made no account of the authority of their prince, which they had
utterly annihilated. Conceiving hopes from the present distresses
of Ireland, they resolved to make an advantageous bargain for the
succours, with which they should supply their neighbouring nation. And they cast their eye towards the English parliament, with
whom they were already so closely connected, and who could alone
fulfil any articles, which might be agreed on. Except dispatching a
small body to support the Scottish colonies in Ulster, they would,
therefore, go no farther at present, than sending commissioners to
London, in order to treat with that power, to whom the sovereign
authority was now in reality transferred.[k]

The king too, sensible of his utter inability to subdue the Irish
rebels, found himself obliged, in this exigency, to have recourse to
the English parliament, and depend on their assistance for supply.
After communicating to them the intelligence, which he had received, he informed them, that the insurrection was not, in his
opinion, the result of any rash enterprize, but of a formed conspiracy against the crown of England. To their care and wisdom,
therefore, he said, he committed the conduct and prosecution of
the war, which, in a cause so important to national and religious
interests, must of necessity be immediately entered upon, and
vigorously pursued.[l]

The English parliament was now assembled; and discovered, in
every vote, the same dispositions, in which they had separated.
The exalting of their own authority, the diminishing of the king's,
were still the objects pursued by the majority. Every attempt,
which had been made to gain the popular leaders, and by offices

Meeting of the English parliament.

---

[k] Rush. vol. v. p. 407.   [l] Clarendon, vol. ii. p. 301.

to attach them to the crown, had failed of success, either for want of skill in conducting it, or by reason of the slender preferments, which it was then in the king's power to confer. The ambitious and enterprising patriots disdained to accept, in detail, of a precarious power; while they deemed it so easy, by one bold and vigorous assault, to possess themselves for ever of the entire sovereignty. Sensible that the measures, which they had hitherto pursued, rendered them extremely obnoxious to the king; were many of them in themselves exceptionable; some of them, strictly speaking, illegal; they resolved to seek their own security, as well as greatness, by enlarging popular authority in England. The great necessities, to which the king was reduced; the violent prejudices, which generally, throughout the nation, prevailed against him; his facility in making the most important concessions; the example of the Scots, whose encroachments had totally subverted monarchy: All these circumstances farther instigated the commons in their invasion of royal prerogative. And the danger, to which the constitution seemed to have been so lately exposed, persuaded many, that it never could be sufficiently secured, but by the entire abolition of that authority, which had invaded it.

But this project, it had not been in the power, scarcely in the intention, of the popular leaders to execute, had it not been for the passion, which seized the nation for presbyterian discipline, and for the wild enthusiasm, which at that time accompanied it. The licence, which the parliament had bestowed on this spirit, by checking ecclesiastical authority; the countenance and encouragement, with which they had honoured it; had already diffused its influence to a wonderful degree: And all orders of men had drunk deep of the intoxicating poison. In every discourse or conversation, this mode of religion entered; in all business, it had a share; every elegant pleasure or amusement, it utterly annihilated; many vices or corruptions of mind, it promoted; even diseases and bodily distempers were not totally exempted from it; and it became requisite, we are told, for all physicians to be expert in the spiritual profession, and, by theological consideration, to allay those religious terrors, with which their patients were so generally haunted. Learning itself, which tends so much to enlarge the mind, and humanize the temper, rather served on this occasion to exalt that epidemical frenzy which prevailed. Rude as yet, and imperfect, it

CHAPTER LV

supplied the dismal fanaticism with a variety of views, founded it on some coherency of system, enriched it with different figures of elocution; advantages with which a people, totally ignorant and barbarous, had been happily unacquainted.

From policy, at first, and inclination, now from necessity, the king attached himself extremely to the hierarchy: For like reasons, his enemies were determined, by one and the same effort, to over-power the church and monarchy.

While the commons were in this disposition, the Irish rebellion was the event, which tended most to promote the views, in which all their measures terminated. A horror against the papists, how-ever innocent, they had constantly encouraged; a terror from the conspiracies of that sect, however improbable, they had at all times endeavoured to excite. Here was broken out a rebellion, dreadful and unexpected; accompanied with circumstances the most de-testable, of which there ever was any record; And what was the peculiar guilt of the Irish catholics, it was no difficult matter, in the present disposition of men's minds, to attribute to that whole sect, who were already so much the object of general abhorrence. Ac-customed, in all invectives, to join the prelatical party with the papists, the people immediately supposed this insurrection to be the result of their united counsels. And when they heard, that the Irish rebels pleaded the king's commission for all their acts of violence; bigotry, ever credulous and malignant, assented without scruple to that gross imposture, and loaded the unhappy prince with the whole enormity of a contrivance so barbarous and in-human.[m]

By the difficulties and distresses of the crown, the commons, who possessed alone the power of supply, had aggrandized them-selves; and it seemed a peculiar happiness, that the Irish rebellion had succeeded, at so critical a juncture, to the pacification of Scot-land. That expression of the king's, by which he committed to them the care of Ireland, they immediately laid hold of, and inter-preted in the most unlimited sense. They had, on other occasions, been gradually encroaching on the executive power of the crown, which forms its principal and most natural branch of authority; but, with regard to Ireland, they at once assumed it, fully and

[m] See note [Z] at the end of the volume.

entirely, as if delivered over to them by a regular gift or assignment. And to this usurpation the king was obliged passively to submit; both because of his inability to resist, and lest he should still more expose himself to the reproach of favouring the progress of that odious rebellion.

The project of introducing farther innovations in England being once formed by the leaders among the commons, it became a necessary consequence, that their operations with regard to Ireland should, all of them, be considered as subordinate to the former, on whose success, when once undertaken, their own grandeur, security, and even being, must entirely depend. While they pretended the utmost zeal against the Irish insurrection, they took no steps towards its suppression, but such as likewise tended to give them the superiority in those commotions, which, they foresaw, must so soon be excited in England.[n] The extreme contempt, entertained for the natives in Ireland, made the popular leaders believe, that it would be easy at any time to suppress their rebellion, and recover that kingdom: Nor were they willing to lose, by too hasty success, the advantage, which that rebellion would afford them in their projected encroachments on the prerogative. By assuming the total management of the war, they acquired the courtship and dependence of every one, who had any connexion with Ireland, or who was desirous of inlisting in these military enterprizes: They levied money under pretence of the Irish expedition; but reserved it for purposes, which concerned them more nearly: They took arms from the king's magazines; but still kept them with a secret intention of employing them against himself: Whatever law they deemed necessary for aggrandizing themselves, was voted, under colour of enabling them to recover Ireland; and if Charles with-held the royal assent, his refusal was imputed to those pernicious counsels, which had at first excited the popish rebellion, and which still threatened total destruction to the protestant interest throughout all his dominions.[o] And though no forces were for a long time sent over to Ireland, and very little money remitted, during the extreme distress of that kingdom; so strong was the people's attachment to the commons, that the fault

[n] Clarendon, vol. ii. p. 435. Sir Ed. Walker, p. 6.   [o] Nalson, vol. ii. p. 618. Clarendon, vol. iv. p. 590.

was never imputed to those pious zealots, whose votes breathed nothing but death and destruction to the Irish rebels.

To make the attack on royal authority by regular approaches, it was thought proper to frame a general remonstrance of the state of the nation; and accordingly the committee, which, at the first meeting of parliament, had been chosen for that purpose, and which had hitherto made no progress in their work, received fresh injunctions to finish that undertaking.

The committee brought into the house that remonstrance, which has become so memorable, and which was soon afterwards attended with such important consequences. It was not addressed to the king; but was openly declared to be an appeal to the people. The harshness of the matter was equalled by the severity of the language. It consists of many gross falsehoods, intermingled with some evident truths: Malignant insinuations are joined to open invectives: Loud complaints of the past, accompanied with jealous prognostications of the future. Whatever unfortunate, whatever invidious, whatever suspicious measure, had been embraced by the king from the commencement of his reign, is insisted on and aggravated with merciless rhetoric: The unsuccessful expeditions to Cadiz and the isle of Rhé, are mentioned: The sending of ships to France for the suppression of the hugonots: The forced loans: The illegal confinement of men for not obeying illegal commands: The violent dissolution of four parliaments: The arbitrary government which always succeeded: The questioning, fining, and imprisoning of members for their conduct in the house: The levying of taxes without consent of the commons: The introducing of superstitious innovations into the church, without authority of law: In short, every thing, which, either with or without reason, had given offence, during the course of fifteen years, from the accession of the king to the calling of the present parliament. And, though all these grievances had been already redressed, and even laws enacted for future security against their return, the praise of these advantages was ascribed, not to the king, but to the parliament, who had extorted his consent to such salutary statutes. Their own merits too, they asserted, towards the king, were no less eminent, than towards the people. Though they had seized his whole revenue, rendered it totally precarious, and made even their temporary supplies be paid to their own commissioners, who were

The remonstrance.

independent of him; they pretended, that they had liberally supported him in his necessities. By an insult still more egregious, the very giving of money to the Scots, for levying war against their sovereign, they represented as an instance of their duty towards him. And all their grievances, they said, which amounted to no less than a total subversion of the constitution, proceeded entirely from the formed combination of a popish faction, who had ever swayed the king's counsels, who had endeavoured, by an uninterrupted effort, to introduce their superstition into England and Scotland, and who had now, at last, excited an open and bloody rebellion in Ireland.[p]

This remonstrance, so full of acrimony and violence, was a plain signal for some farther attacks intended on royal prerogative, and a declaration, that the concessions, already made, however important, were not to be regarded as satisfactory. What pretensions would be advanced, how unprecedented, how unlimited, were easily imagined; and nothing less was foreseen, whatever ancient names might be preserved, than an abolition, almost total, of the monarchical government of England. The opposition, therefore, which the remonstrance met with in the house of commons, was great. For above fourteen hours, the debate was warmly managed; and from the weariness of the king's party, which probably consisted chiefly of the elderly people, and men of cool spirits, *22nd Nov.* the vote was at last carried by a small majority of eleven.[q] Some time after, the remonstrance was ordered to be printed and published, without being carried up to the house of peers, for their assent and concurrence.

Reasons on both sides. When this remonstrance was dispersed, it excited every-where the same violent controversy, which attended it when introduced into the house of commons. This parliament, said the partizans of that assembly, have at length profited by the fatal example of their predecessors; and are resolved, that the fabric, which they have generously undertaken to rear for the protection of liberty, shall not be left to future ages insecure and imperfect. At the time when the petition of right, that requisite vindication of a violated constitution, was extorted from the unwilling prince; who but imagined,

[p] Rush. vol. v. p. 438. Nalson, vol. ii. p. 694.   [q] Whitlocke, p. 40. Dugdale, p. 71. Nalson, vol. ii. p. 668.

CHAPTER LV

that liberty was at last secured, and that the laws would thenceforth maintain themselves in opposition to arbitrary authority? But what was the event? A *right* was indeed acquired to the people, or rather their ancient right was more exactly defined: But as the *power* of invading it still remained in the prince, no sooner did an opportunity offer, than he totally disregarded all laws and preceding engagements, and made his will and pleasure the sole rule of government. Those lofty ideas of monarchical authority, which he has derived from his early education, which are united in his mind with the irresistible illusions of self-love, which are corroborated by his mistaken principles of religion, it is in vain to hope, that, in his more advanced age, he will sincerely renounce, from any subsequent reflection or experience. Such conversions, if ever they happen, are extremely rare; but to expect, that they will be derived from necessity, from the jealousy and resentment of antagonists, from blame, from reproach, from opposition, must be the result of the fondest and most blind credulity. These violences, however necessary, are sure to irritate a prince against limitations so cruelly imposed upon him; and each concession, which he is constrained to make, is regarded as a temporary tribute paid to faction and sedition, and is secretly attended with a resolution of seizing every favourable opportunity to retract it. Nor should we imagine, that opportunities of that kind will not offer in the course of human affairs. Governments, especially those of a mixed kind, are in continual fluctuation: The humours of the people change perpetually from one extreme to another: And no resolution can be more wise, as well as more just, than that of employing the present advantages against the king, who had formerly pushed much less tempting ones to the utmost extremities against his people and his parliament. It is to be feared, that, if the religious rage, which has seized the multitude, be allowed to evaporate, they will quickly return to the ancient ecclesiastical establishment; and, with it, embrace those principles of slavery, which it inculcates with such zeal on its submissive proselytes. Those patriots, who are now the public idols, may then become the objects of general detestation; and equal shouts of joy attend their ignominious execution, with those which second their present advantages and triumphs. Nor ought the apprehension of such an event to be regarded in them as a selfish consideration: In their safety is involved the security of the laws:

The patrons of the constitution cannot suffer without a fatal blow to the constitution: And it is but justice in the public to protect, at any hazard, those who have so generously exposed themselves to the utmost hazard for the public interest. What though monarchy, the ancient government of England, be impaired, during these contests, in many of its former prerogatives: The laws will flourish the more by its decay; and it is happy, allowing that matters are really carried beyond the bounds of moderation, that the current at least runs towards liberty, and that the error is on that side, which is safest for the general interests of mankind and society.

The best arguments of the royalists against a farther attack on the prerogative were founded more on opposite ideas, which they had formed of the past events of this reign, than on opposite principles of government. Some invasions, they said, and those too of moment, had undoubtedly been made on national privileges: But were we to look for the cause of these violences, we should never find it to consist in the wanton tyranny and injustice of the prince, not even in his ambition or immoderate appetite for authority. The hostilities with Spain, in which the king, on his accession, found himself engaged, however imprudent and unnecessary, had proceeded from the advice, and even importunity of the parliament; who deserted him immediately after they had embarked him in those warlike measures. A young prince, jealous of honour, was naturally afraid of being soiled in his first enterprize, and had not as yet attained such maturity of counsel, as to perceive that his greatest honour lay in preserving the laws inviolate, and gaining the full confidence of his people. The rigour of the subsequent parliaments had been extreme with regard to many articles, particularly tonnage and poundage; and had reduced the king to an absolute necessity, if he would preserve entire the royal prerogative, of levying those duties by his own authority, and of breaking through the forms, in order to maintain the spirit, of the constitution. Having once made so perilous a step, he was naturally induced to continue, and to consult the public interest, by imposing ship-money, and other moderate, though irregular, burthens and taxations. A sure proof, that he had formed no system for enslaving his people is, that the chief object of his government has been to raise a naval, not a military force; a project useful, honourable, nay indispensibly requisite, and in spite of his great

CHAPTER LV

necessities, brought almost to a happy conclusion. It is now full time to free him from all these necessities, and to apply cordials and lenitives, after those severities, which have already had their full course against him. Never was sovereign blessed with more moderation of temper, with more justice, more humanity, more honour, or a more gentle disposition. What pity that such a prince should so long have been harassed with rigours, suspicions, calumnies, complaints, incroachments; and been forced from that path, in which the rectitude of his principles would have inclined him to have constantly trod! If some few instances are found of violations made on the petition of right, which he himself had granted; there is an easier and more natural way for preventing the return of like inconveniencies, than by a total abolition of royal authority. Let the revenue be settled, suitably to the ancient dignity and splendor of the crown; let the public necessities be fully supplied; let the remaining articles of prerogative be left untouched; and the king, as he has already lost the power, will lay aside the will, of invading the constitution. From what quarter can jealousies now arise? What farther security can be desired or expected? The king's preceding concessions, so far from being insufficient for public security, have rather erred on the other extreme; and, by depriving him of all power of self-defence, are the real cause why the commons are emboldened to raise pretensions hitherto unheard of in the kingdom, and to subvert the whole system of the constitution. But would they be content with moderate advantages, is it not evident, that, besides other important concessions, the present parliament may be continued, till the government be accustomed to the new track, and every part be restored to full harmony and concord? By the triennial act a perpetual succession of parliaments is established, as everlasting guardians to the laws, while the king possesses no independent power or military force, by which he can be supported in his invasion of them. No danger remains, but what is inseparable from all free constitutions, and what forms the very essence of their freedom: The danger of a change in the people's disposition, and of general disgust, contracted against popular privileges. To prevent such an evil, no expedient is more proper, than to contain ourselves within the bounds of moderation, and to consider, that all extremes, naturally and infallibly, beget each other. In the same manner as the past usurpations of the crown, however excusable on account of the necessity or provocations whence they arose, have excited an immeasurable appetite for liberty; let us beware, lest our encroachments, by introducing anarchy, make the people seek shelter under the peaceable and despotic rule of a monarch. Authority, as well as liberty, is requisite to government; and is even requisite to the support of liberty itself, by maintaining the laws, which can alone regulate and protect it. What madness, while every thing is so happily settled under ancient forms and institutions, now more exactly poised and adjusted, to try the hazardous experiment of a new constitution, and renounce the mature wisdom of our ancestors for the crude whimsies of turbulent innovators! Besides the certain and inconceivable mischiefs of civil war; are not the perils apparent, which the delicate frame of liberty must inevitably sustain amidst the furious shock of arms? Whichever side prevails, *she* can scarcely hope to remain inviolate, and may suffer no less, or rather greater injuries from the boundless pretensions of forces engaged in her cause, than from the invasion of enraged troops, inlisted on the side of monarchy.

Nov. 25.   The king, upon his return from Scotland, was received in London with the shouts and acclamations of the people, and with every demonstration of regard and affection.[r] Sir Richard Gournay, lord mayor, a man of moderation and authority, had promoted these favourable dispositions, and had engaged the populace, who so lately insulted the king, and who so soon after made furious war upon him, to give him these marks of their dutiful attachment. But all the pleasure, which Charles reaped from this joyous reception, was soon damped by the remonstrance of the commons, which was presented him, together with a petition of a like strain. The bad counsels, which he followed, are there complained of; his concurrence in the Irish rebellion plainly insinuated; the scheme, laid for the introduction of popery and superstition, inveighed against; and, as a remedy for all these evils, he is desired to entrust every office and command to persons, in whom his parliament should have cause to confide.[s] By this phrase, which is so often repeated in all the memorials and addresses of that time, the commons meant themselves and their adherents.

As soon as the remonstrance of the commons was published,

[r] Rushworth, vol. v. p. 429.   [s] Idem, ibid. p. 437. Nalson, vol. ii. p. 692.

the king dispersed an answer to it. In this contest, he lay under great disadvantages. Not only the ears of the people were extremely prejudiced against him; the best topics, upon which he could justify, at least apologize for his former conduct, were such as it was not safe or prudent for him at this time to employ. So high was the national idolatry towards parliaments, that to blame the past conduct of these assemblies, would have been very ill received by the generality of the people. So loud were the complaints against regal usurpations, that, had the king asserted the prerogative of supplying, by his own authority, the deficiencies in government, arising from the obstinacy of the commons, he would have encreased the clamours, with which the whole nation already resounded. Charles, therefore, contented himself, with observing, in general, that even during that period, so much complained of, the people enjoyed a great measure of happiness, not only comparatively, in respect of their neighbours, but even in respect of those times, which were justly accounted the most fortunate. He made warm protestations of sincerity in the reformed religion; he promised indulgence to tender consciences with regard to the ceremonies of the church; he mentioned his great concessions to national liberty; he blamed the infamous libels every-where dispersed against his person and the national religion; he complained of the general reproaches thrown out in the remonstrance, with regard to ill counsels, though he had protected no minister from parliamentary justice, retained no unpopular servant, and conferred offices on no one, who enjoyed not a high character and estimation in the public. "If, notwithstanding this," he adds, "any malignant party shall take heart, and be willing to sacrifice the peace and happiness of their country to their own sinister ends and ambition, under whatever pretence of religion and conscience; if they shall endeavour to lessen my reputation and interest, and to weaken my lawful power and authority; if they shall attempt, by discountenancing the present laws, to loosen the bands of government, that all disorder and confusion may break in upon us; I doubt not but God, in his good time, will discover them to me, and that the wisdom and courage of my high court of parliament will join with me in their suppression and punishment."[t] Nothing shows more evidently the hard situation, in which Charles was

[t] Nalson, vol. ii. p. 748.

placed, than to observe, that he was obliged to confine himself within the limits of civility towards subjects, who had transgressed all bounds of regard, and even of good manners, in the treatment of their sovereign.

The first instance of those parliamentary encroachments, which Charles was now to look for, was, the bill for pressing soldiers to the service of Ireland. This bill quickly passed the lower house. In the preamble, the king's power of pressing, a power exercised during all former times, was declared illegal, and contrary to the liberty of the subject. By a necessary consequence, the prerogative, which the crown had ever assumed, of obliging men to accept of any branch of public service, was abolished and annihilated: A prerogative, it must be owned, not very compatible with a limited monarchy. In order to elude this law, the king offered to raise 10,000 volunteers for the Irish service: But the commons were afraid lest such an army should be too much at his devotion. Charles, still unwilling to submit to so considerable a diminution of power, came to the house of peers, and offered to pass the law without the preamble; by which means, he said, that ill-timed question with regard to the prerogative would for the present be avoided, and the pretensions of each party be left entire. Both houses took fire at this measure, which, from a similar instance, while the bill of attainder against Strafford was in dependence, Charles might foresee, would be received with resentment. The lords, as well as commons, passed a vote, declaring it to be a high breach of privilege for the king to take notice of any bill, which was in agitation in either of the houses, or to express his sentiments with regard to it, before it be presented to him for his assent in a parliamentary manner. The king was obliged to compose all matters by an apology."

The general question, we may observe, with regard to privileges of parliament, has always been, and still continues, one of the greatest mysteries in the English constitution; and, in some respects, notwithstanding the accurate genius of that government, these privileges are at present as undetermined as were formerly the prerogatives of the crown. Such privileges as are founded on

" Rushworth, vol. v. p. 457, 458, &c. Clarendon, vol. ii. p. 327. Nalson, vol. ii. p. 738, 750, 751, &c.

long precedent cannot be controverted: But though it were certain, that former kings had not in any instance taken notice of bills lying before the houses (which yet appears to have been very common) it follows not, merely from their never exerting such a power, that they had renounced it, or never were possessed of it. Such privileges also as are essential to all free assemblies which deliberate, they may be allowed to assume, whatever precedents may prevail: But though the king's interposition, by an offer or advice, does in some degree overawe or restrain liberty; it may be doubted, whether it imposes such evident violence as to entitle the parliament, without any other authority or concession, to claim the privilege of excluding it. But this was the favourable time for extending privileges; and had none more exorbitant or unreasonable been challenged, few bad consequences had followed. The establishment of this rule, it is certain, contributes to the order and regularity, as well as freedom, of parliamentary proceedings.

The interposition of peers in the election of commoners was likewise about this time declared a breach of privilege; and continues ever since to be condemned by votes of the commons, and universally practiced throughout the nation.

Every measure pursued by the commons, and, still more, every attempt made by their partizans, were full of the most inveterate hatred against the hierarchy, and showed a determined resolution of subverting the whole ecclesiastical establishment. Besides numberless vexations and persecutions, which the clergy underwent from the arbitrary power of the lower house; the peers, while the king was in Scotland, having passed an order for the observance of the laws with regard to public worship, the commons assumed such authority, that, by a vote alone of their house, they suspended those laws, though enacted by the whole legislature: And they particularly forbade bowing at the name of Jesus; a practice which gave them the highest scandal, and which was one of their capital objections against the established religion.[w] They complained of the king's filling five vacant sees, and considered it as an insult upon them, that he should complete and strengthen an order, which they intended soon entirely to abolish.[x] They had accused

[w] Rushworth, vol. v. p. 385, 386. Nalson, vol. ii. p. 482.   [x] Nalson, vol. ii. p. 511.

thirteen bishops of high treason, for enacting canons without consent of parliament,[y] though, from the foundation of the monarchy, no other method had ever been practised: And they now
insisted, that the peers, upon this general accusation, should sequester those bishops from their seats in parliament, and commit
them to prison. Their bill for taking away the bishops' votes had
last winter been rejected by the peers: But they again introduced
the same bill, though no prorogation had intervened; and they
endeavoured, by some minute alterations, to elude that rule of
parliament, which opposed them. And when they sent up this bill
to the lords, they made a demand, the most absurd in the world,
that the bishops, being all of them parties, should be refused a vote
with regard to that question.[z] After the resolution was once formed
by the commons, of invading the established government of
church and state, it could not be expected, that their proceedings,
in such a violent attempt, would thenceforth be altogether regular
and equitable: But it must be confessed, that, in their attack on the
hierarchy, they still more openly passed all bounds of moderation;
as supposing, no doubt, that the sacredness of the cause would
sufficiently atone for employing means the most irregular and
unprecedented. This principle, which prevails so much among
zealots, never displayed itself so openly as during the transactions
of this whole period.

But, notwithstanding these efforts of the commons, they could
not expect the concurrence of the upper house, either to this law,
or to any other, which they should introduce for the farther limitation of royal authority. The majority of the peers adhered to the
king, and plainly foresaw the depression of nobility, as a necessary
consequence of popular usurpations on the crown. The insolence,
indeed, of the commons, and their haughty treatment of the lords,
had already risen to a great height, and gave sufficient warning to
their future attempts upon that order. They muttered somewhat
of their regret that they should be obliged to save the kingdom
alone, and that the house of peers would have no part in the
honour. Nay, they went so far as openly to tell the lords, "That they
themselves were the representative body of the whole kingdom,
and that the peers were nothing but individuals, who held their
seats in a particular capacity: And therefore, if their lordships will

[y] Rush. vol. v. p. 359.   [z] Clarendon, vol. ii. p. 304.

not consent to the passing of acts necessary for the preservation of the people, the commons, together with such of the lords as are more sensible of the danger, must join together, and represent the matter to his majesty."[a] So violent was the democratical, enthusiastic spirit diffused throughout the nation, that a total confusion of all rank and order was justly to be apprehended; and the wonder was not, that the majority of the nobles should seek shelter under the throne, but that any of them should venture to desert it. But the tide of popularity seized many, and carried them wide of the most established maxims of civil policy. Among the opponents of the king are ranked the earl of Northumberland, lord admiral, a man of the first family and fortune, and endowed with that dignified pride, which so well became his rank and station: The earl of Essex, who inherited all his father's popularity, and having, from his early youth, sought renown in arms, united to a middling capacity that rigid inflexibility of honour, which forms the proper ornament of a nobleman and a soldier: Lord Kimbolton, soon after Earl of Manchester, a person distinguished by humanity, generosity, affability, and every amiable virtue. These men, finding that their credit ran high with the nation, ventured to encourage those popular disorders, which, they vainly imagined, they possessed authority sufficient to regulate and controul.

In order to obtain a majority in the upper house, the commons had recourse to the populace, who, on other occasions, had done them such important service. Amidst the greatest security, they affected continual fears of destruction to themselves and the nation, and seemed to quake at every breath or rumour of danger. They again, excited the people by never-ceasing enquiries after conspiracies, by reports of insurrections, by feigned intelligence of invasions from abroad, by discoveries of dangerous combinations at home among papists and their adherents. When Charles dismissed the guard, which they had ordered during his absence, they complained; and, upon his promising them a new guard, under the command of the earl of Lindesey, they absolutely refused the offer, and were well pleased to insinuate, by this instance of jealousy, that their danger chiefly arose from the king himself.[b] They ordered halberts to be brought into the hall where they assembled,

---

[a] Clarendon, vol. ii. p. 415.   [b] Journ. 30th Nov. 1641. Nalson, vol. ii. p. 688.

and thus armed themselves against those conspiracies, with which, they pretended, they were hourly threatened. All stories of plots, however ridiculous, were willingly attended to, and were dispersed among the multitude, to whose capacity they were well adapted. Beale, a taylor, informed the commons, that, walking in the fields, he had hearkened to the discourse of certain persons, unknown to him, and had heard them talk of a most dangerous conspiracy. A hundred and eight ruffians, as he learned, had been appointed to murder a hundred and eight lords and commoners, and were promised rewards for these assassinations, ten pounds for each lord, forty shillings for each commoner. Upon this notable intelligence, orders were issued for seizing priests and jesuits, a conference was desired with the lords, and the deputy-lieutenants of some suspected counties were ordered to put the people in a posture of defence.[c]

The pulpits likewise were called in aid, and resounded with the dangers, which threatened religion, from the desperate attempts of papists and malignants. Multitudes flocked towards Westminster, and insulted the prelates and such of the lords as adhered to the crown. The peers voted a declaration against those tumults, and sent it to the lower house; but these refused their concurrence.[d] Some seditious apprentices, being seized and committed to prison, immediately received their liberty; by an order of the commons.[e] The sheriffs and justices having appointed constables with strong watches to guard the parliament; the commons sent for the constables, and required them to discharge the watches, convened the justices, voted their orders a breach of privilege, and sent one of them to the Tower.[f] Encouraged by these intimations of their pleasure, the populace crouded about Whitehall, and threw out insolent menaces against Charles himself. Several reduced officers and young gentlemen of the inns of court, during this time of disorder and danger, offered their service to the king. Between them and the populace there passed frequent skirmishes, which ended not without bloodshed. By way of reproach, these gentlemen gave the rabble the appellation of ROUNDHEADS; on account

---

[c] Nalson, vol. ii. p. 646. Journ. 16th Nov. 1641. Dugdale, p. 77.
[d] Rushworth, part iii. vol. i. p. 710.   [e] Nalson, vol. ii. p. 784, 792.   [f] Ibid. p. 792. Journ. 27, 28, and 29th of December 1641.

CHAPTER LV

of the short cropt hair which they wore: These called the others CAVALIERS. And thus the nation, which was before sufficiently provided with religious as well as civil causes of quarrel, was also supplied with party-names, under which the factions might rendezvous and signalize their mutual hatred.[g]

Meanwhile the tumults still continued, and even encreased about Westminster and Whitehall. The cry incessantly resounded against *bishops and rotten-hearted lords.*[h] The former especially, being distinguishable by their habit, and being the object of violent hatred to all the sectaries, were exposed to the most dangerous insults.[i] Williams, now created archbishop of York, having been abused by the populace, hastily called a meeting of his brethren. By his advice, a protestation was drawn and addressed to the king and the house of lords. The bishops there set forth, that though they had an undoubted right to sit and vote in parliament, yet in coming thither, they had been menaced, assaulted, affronted, by the unruly multitude, and could no longer with safety attend their duty in the house. For this reason they protested against all laws, votes, and resolutions, as null and invalid, which should pass during the time of their constrained absence. This protestation, which, though just and legal, was certainly ill-timed, was signed by twelve bishops, and communicated to the king, who hastily approved of it. As soon as it was presented to the lords, that house desired a conference with the commons, whom they informed of this unexpected protestation. The opportunity was seized with joy and triumph. An impeachment of high treason was immediately sent up against the bishops, as endeavouring to subvert the fundamental laws, and to invalidate the authority of the legislature.[k] They were, on the first demand, sequestered from parliament, and committed to custody. No man, in either house, ventured to speak a word in their vindication; so much displeased was every one at the egregious imprudence, of which they had been guilty. One person alone said, that he did not believe them guilty of high treason; but that they were stark mad, and therefore desired they might be sent to bedlam.[l]

Decemb. 27.

Impeachment of the bishops.

---

[g] Clarendon, vol. ii. p. 339.   [h] Idem, ibid. p. 336.   [i] Dugdale, p. 78.
[k] Whitlocke, p. 51. Rushworth, vol. v. p. 466. Nalson, vol. ii. p. 794.
[l] Clarendon, vol. ii. p. 355.

A few days after, the king was betrayed into another indiscretion, much more fatal: An indiscretion, to which all the ensuing
disorders and civil wars ought immediately and directly to be ascribed. This was the impeachment of lord Kimbolton and the five
members.

When the commons employed, in their remonstrance, language so severe and indecent, they had not been actuated entirely
by insolence and passion: Their views were more solid and profound. They considered, that, in a violent attempt, such as an
invasion of the ancient constitution, the more leisure was afforded
the people to reflect, the less would they be inclined to second that
rash and dangerous enterprize; that the peers would certainly
refuse their concurrence, nor were there any hopes of prevailing
on them, but by instigating the populace to tumult and disorder;
that the employing of such odious means for so invidious an end,
would, at long-run, lose them all their popularity, and turn the tide
of favour to the contrary party; and that, if the king only remained
in tranquillity, and cautiously eluded the first violence of the tempest, he would, in the end, certainly prevail, and be able at least to
preserve the ancient laws and constitution. They were therefore
resolved, if possible, to excite him to some violent passion; in hopes
that he would commit indiscretions, of which they might make
advantage.

It was not long before they succeeded beyond their fondest
wishes. Charles was enraged to find that all his concessions but
encreased their demands; that the people, who were returning to
a sense of duty towards him, were again roused to sedition and
tumults; that the blackest calumnies were propagated against him,
and even the Irish massacre ascribed to his counsels and machina-
tions; and that a method of address was adopted not only unsuitable towards so great a prince, but which no private gentleman
could bear without resentment. When he considered all these in-
creasing acts of insolence in the commons, he was apt to ascribe
them, in a great measure, to his own indolence and facility. The
queen and the ladies of the court farther stimulated his passion,
and represented, that, if he exerted the vigour, and displayed the
majesty of a monarch, the daring usurpations of his subjects would
shrink before him. Lord Digby, a man of fine parts, but full of
levity, and hurried on by precipitate passions, suggested like coun-

CHAPTER LV

sels; and Charles, who, though commonly moderate in his temper, was ever disposed to hasty resolutions, gave way to the fatal importunity of his friends and servants.[m]

Herbert, attorney general, appeared in the house of peers, and, in his majesty's name, entered an accusation of high treason against lord Kimbolton and five commoners, Hollis, Sir Arthur Hazlerig, Hambden, Pym, and Strode. The articles were, That they had traiterously endeavoured to subvert the fundamental laws and government of the kingdom, to deprive the king of his regal power, and to impose on his subjects an arbitrary and tyrannical authority; that they had endeavoured, by many foul aspersions on his majesty and his government, to alienate the affections of his people, and make him odious to them; that they had attempted to draw his late army to disobedience of his royal commands, and to side with them in their traiterous designs; that they had invited and encouraged a foreign power to invade the kingdom; that they had aimed at subverting the rights and very being of parliament; that in order to complete their traiterous designs, they had endeavoured, as far as in them lay, by force and terror, to compel the parliament to join with them, and, to that end, had actually raised and countenanced tumults against the king and parliament; and that they had traiterously conspired to levy and actually had levied, war against the king."

Accusations of the five members.

The whole world stood amazed at this important accusation, so suddenly entered upon, without concert, deliberation, or reflection. Some of these articles of accusation, men said, to judge by appearance, seem to be common between the impeached members and the parliament; nor did these persons appear any farther active in the enterprizes, of which they were accused, than so far as they concurred with the majority in their votes and speeches. Though proofs, might, perhaps, be produced, of their privately inviting the Scots to invade England; how could such an attempt be considered as treason, after the act of oblivion which had passed, and after that both houses, with the king's concurrence, had voted that nation three hundred thousand pounds for their brotherly assistance? While the house of peers are scarcely able to

[m] Clarendon, vol. ii. p. 360.   [n] Whitlocke, p. 50. Rushworth, vol. v. p. 473. Nalson, vol. ii. p. 811. Franklyn, p. 906.

maintain their independency, or to reject the bills sent them by the commons; will they ever be permitted by the populace, supposing them inclined, to pass a sentence, which must totally subdue the lower house, and put an end to their ambitious undertakings? These five members, at least Pym, Hambden, and Hollis, are the very heads of the popular party; and if these be taken off, what fate must be expected by their followers, who are many of them accomplices in the same treason? The punishment of leaders is ever the last triumph over a broken and routed party; but surely was never before attempted, in opposition to a faction, during the full tide of its power and success.

But men had not leisure to wonder at the indiscretion of this measure: Their astonishment was excited by new attempts, still more precipitate and imprudent. A serjeant at arms, in the king's name, demanded of the house the five members; and was sent back without any positive answer. Messengers were employed to search for them, and arrest them. Their trunks, chambers, and studies, were sealed, and locked. The house voted all these acts of violence to be breaches of privilege, and commanded every one to defend the liberty of the members.[o] The king, irritated by all this opposition, resolved next day to come in person to the house, with an intention to demand, perhaps seize in their presence, the persons whom he had accused.

This resolution was discovered to the countess of Carlisle, sister of Northumberland, a lady of spirit, wit, and intrigue.[p] She privately sent intelligence to the five members; and they had time to withdraw, a moment before the king entered. He was accompanied by his ordinary retinue to the number of above two hundred, armed as usual, some with halberts, some with walking swords. The king left them at the door, and he himself advanced alone through the hall; while all the members rose to receive him. The speaker withdrew from his chair, and the king took possession of it. The speech, which he made, was as follows; "Gentlemen, I am sorry for this occasion of coming to you. Yesterday, I sent a serjeant at arms, to demand some, who, by my order, were accused of high treason. Instead of obedience, I received a message. I must

[o] Whitlocke, p. 50. Rushworth, vol. v. p. 474, 475.   [p] Whitlocke, p. 51. Warwick, p. 204.

here declare to you, that, though no king, that ever was in England, could be more careful of your privileges than I shall be, yet in cases of treason no person has privilege. Therefore, am I come to tell you, that I must have these men wheresoever I can find them. Well, since I see all the birds are flown, I do expect that you will send them to me as soon as they return. But I assure you, on the word of a king, I never did intend any force, but shall proceed against them in a fair and legal way: For I never meant any other. And now since I see I cannot do what I came for, I think this is no unfit occasion to repeat what I have said formerly, that whatever I have done in favour and to the good of my subjects, I do intend to maintain it."[q]

When the king was looking around for the accused members he asked the speaker, who stood below, whether any of these persons were in the house? The speaker, falling on his knee, prudently replied: "I have, Sir, neither eyes to see, nor tongue to speak in this place, but as the house is pleased to direct me, whose servant I am. And I humbly ask pardon, that I cannot give any other answer to what your majesty is pleased to demand of me."[r]

The commons were in the utmost disorder; and, when the king was departing, some members cried aloud, so as he might hear them, *Privilege! privilege!* And the house immediately adjourned till next day.[s]

That evening, the accused members, to show the greater apprehension, removed into the city, which was their fortress. The citizens were the whole night, in arms. Some people, who were appointed for that purpose, or perhaps actuated by their own terrors, ran from gate to gate, crying out, that the cavaliers were coming to burn the city, and that the king himself was at their head.

Next morning Charles sent to the mayor, and ordered him to call a common-council immediately. About ten o'clock, he himself, attended only by three or four lords, went to Guildhall. He told the common-council, that he was sorry to hear of the apprehensions entertained of him; that he was come to them without any guard, in order to show how much he relied on their affections; and that he had accused certain men of high-treason, against whom he

[q] Whitlocke, p. 50   [r] Whitlocke, p. 50. May, book ii. p. 20.   [s] Whitlocke, p. 51.

would proceed in a legal way, and therefore presumed that they would not meet with protection in the city. After many other gracious expressions, he told one of the sheriffs; who of the two was thought the least inclined to his service, that he would dine with him. He departed the hall without receiving the applause, which he expected. In passing through the streets, he heard the cry, *Privilege of parliament! privilege of parliament!* resounding from all quarters. One of the populace, more insolent that the rest, drew nigh to his coach, and called out with a loud voice, *To your tents, O Israel!* the words employed by the mutinous Israelites, when they abandoned Rehoboam, their rash and ill-counselled sovereign.[t]

When the house of commons met, they affected the greatest dismay; and adjourning themselves for some days, ordered a committee to sit in merchant-taylors hall in the city. The committee made an exact enquiry into all circumstances attending the king's entry into the house: Every passionate speech, every menacing gesture of any, even the meanest, of his attendants, was recorded and aggravated. An intention of offering violence to the parliament, of seizing the accused members in the very house, and of murdering all who should make resistance, was inferred. And that unparalleled breach of privilege, so it was called, was still ascribed to the counsel of papists and their adherents. This expression, which then recurred every moment in speeches and memorials, and which, at present, is so apt to excite laughter in the reader, begat at that time the deepest and most real consternation throughout the kingdom.

A letter was pretended to be intercepted, and was communicated to the committee, who pretended to lay great stress upon it. One catholic there congratulates another on the accusation of the members; and represents that incident as a branch of the same pious contrivance, which had excited the Irish insurrection, and by which the profane heretics would soon be exterminated in England.[u]

The house again met; and, after confirming the votes of their committee, instantly adjourned, as if exposed to the most eminent perils from the violence of their enemies. This practice they continued for some time. When the people, by these affected panics,

[t] Rush. vol. v. p. 470. Clarendon, vol. ii. p. 361. [u] Nalson, vol. ii. p. 836.

CHAPTER LV

were wrought up to a sufficient degree of rage and terror, it was thought proper, that the accused members should, with a triumphant and military procession, take their seats in the house. The river was covered with boats, and other vessels, laden with small pieces of ordnance, and prepared for fight. Skippon, whom the parliament had appointed, by their own authority, major-general of the city-militia,[w] conducted the members, at the head of this tumultuary army, to Westminster-hall. And when the populace, by land and by water, passed Whitehall, they still asked with insulting shouts, *What was become of the king and his cavaliers? And whither are they fled?*[x]

Tumults.

The king, apprehensive of danger from the enraged multitude, had retired to Hampton-court, deserted by all the world, and overwhelmed with grief, shame, and remorse, for the fatal measures, into which he had been hurried. His distressed situation he could no longer ascribe to the rigors of destiny, or the malignity of enemies: His own precipitancy and indiscretion must bear the blame of whatever disasters should henceforth befal him. The most faithful of his adherents, between sorrow and indignation, were confounded with reflections on what had happened, and what was likely to follow. Seeing every prospect blasted, faction triumphant, the discontented populace inflamed to a degree of fury, they utterly despaired of success, in a cause, to whose ruin friends and enemies seemed equally to conspire.

King leaves London.

The prudence of the king, in his conduct of this affair, nobody pretended to justify. The legality of his proceedings met with many and just apologies; though generally offered to unwilling ears. No maxim of law, it was said, is more established or more universally allowed, than that privilege of parliament extends not to treason, felony, or breach of peace; nor has either house, during former ages, ever pretended, in any of those cases, to interpose in behalf of its members. Though some inconveniencies should result from the observance of this maxim; that would not be sufficient, without other authority, to abolish a principle established by uninterrupted precedent, and founded on the tacit consent of the whole legislature. 'But what are the inconveniencies so much

[w] Nalson, vol. ii. p. 833. [x] Whitlocke, p. 52. Dugdale, p. 82. Clarendon, vol. ii. p. 380.

dreaded? The king, on pretence of treason, may seize any members of the opposite faction, and, for a time, gain to his partizans the majority of voices. But if he seize only a few; will he not lose more friends, by such a gross artifice, than he confines enemies?' If he seize a great number; is not this expedient force, open and barefaced? And what remedy, at all times, against such force, but to oppose to it a force, which is superior? Even allowing that the king intended to employ violence, not authority, for seizing the members; though at that time, and ever afterwards, he positively asserted the contrary; yet will his conduct admit of excuse. That the hall, where the parliament assembles, is an inviolable sanctuary, was never yet pretended. And if the commons complain of the affront offered them, by an attempt to arrest their members in their very presence; the blame must lie entirely on themselves, who had formerly refused compliance with the king's message, when he peaceably demanded these members. The sovereign is the great executor of the laws; and his presence was here legally employed, both in order to prevent opposition, and to protect the house against those insults which their disobedience had so well merited.

Charles knew to how little purpose he should urge these reasons against the present fury of the commons. He proposed, therefore, by a message, that they would agree upon a legal method, by which he might carry on his prosecution against the members, lest farther misunderstandings happen with regard to privilege. They desired him to lay the grounds of accusation before the house; and pretended that they must first judge, whether it were proper to give up their members to a legal trial. The king then informed them, that he would wave, for the present, all prosecution: By successive messages, he afterwards offered a pardon to the members; offered to concur in any law that should acquit or secure them; offered any reparation to the house for the breach of privilege, of which, he acknowledged, they had reason to complain.' They were resolved to accept of no satisfaction, unless he would discover his advisers in that illegal measure: A condition, to which, they knew, that, without rendering himself for ever vile and contemptible, he could not possibly submit. Meanwhile, they continued to thunder against the violation of parliamentary privi-

---

' Dugdale, p. 84. Rushworth, vol. v. p. 484, 488, 492, &c.

leges, and, by their violent outcries, to inflame the whole nation. The secret reason of their displeasure, however obvious, they carefully concealed. In the king's accusation of the members, they plainly saw his judgment of late parliamentary proceedings; and every adherent of the ruling faction dreaded the same fate, should royal authority be re-established in its ancient lustre. By the most unhappy conduct, Charles, while he extremely augmented, in his opponents, the will, had also encreased the ability, of hurting him.

The more to excite the people, whose dispositions were already very seditious, the expedient of petitioning was renewed. A petition from the county of Buckingham was presented to the house by six thousand subscribers who promised to live and die in defence of the privileges of parliament.[z] The city of London, the county of Essex, that of Hertford, Surrey, Berks, imitated the example. A petition from the apprentices was graciously received.[a] Nay, one was encouraged from the porters; whose numbers amounted, as they said, to fifteen thousand.[b] The address of that great body contained the same articles with all the others; the privileges of parliament, the danger of religion, the rebellion of Ireland, the decay of trade. The porters farther desired, that justice might be done upon offenders, as the atrociousness of their crimes had deserved. And they added, *That if such remedies were any longer suspended, they should be forced to extremities not fit to be named, and make good the saying,* "That necessity has no law."[c]

Another petition was presented by several poor people, or beggars, in the name of many thousands more; in which the petitioners proposed as a remedy for the public miseries, *That those noble worthies of the house of peers, who concur with the happy votes of the commons, may separate themselves from the rest, and sit and vote as one intire body.* The commons gave thanks for this petition.[d]

The very women were seized with the same rage. A brewer's wife, followed by many thousands of her sex, brought a petition to the house; in which the petitioners expressed their terror of the papists and prelates, and their dread of like massacres, rapes, and outrages, with those which had been committed upon their sex in Ireland. They had been necessitated, they said, to imitate the ex-

---

[z] Rushworth, vol. v. p. 487.   [a] Idem, ibid. p. 462.   [b] Dugdale, p. 87.
[c] Clarendon, vol. ii. p. 412.   [d] Idem, ibid. p. 413.

ample of the woman of Tekoah: And they claimed equal right with the men, of declaring, by petition, their sense of the public cause; because Christ had purchased them at as dear a rate, and in the free enjoyment of Christ consists equally the happiness of both sexes. Pym came to the door of the house; and, having told the female zealots, that their petition was thankfully accepted, and was presented in a seasonable time, he begged that their prayers for the success of the commons might follow their petition. Such low arts of popularity were affected! And by such illiberal cant were the unhappy people incited to civil discord and convulsions!

In the mean time, not only all petitions, which favoured the church or monarchy, from whatever hand they came, were discouraged; but the petitioners were sent for, imprisoned, and prosecuted as delinquents: And this unequal conduct was openly avowed and justified. Whoever desire a change, it was said, must express their sentiments; for how, otherwise, shall they be known? But those who favour the established government in church or state, should not petition; because they already enjoy what they wish for.[e]

The king had possessed a great party in the lower house, as appeared in the vote for the remonstrance; and this party, had every new cause of disgust been carefully avoided, would soon have become the majority; from the odium attending the violent measures, embraced by the popular leaders. A great majority he always possessed in the house of peers, even after the bishops were confined or chased away; and this majority could not have been overcome, but by outrages, which, in the end, would have drawn disgrace and ruin on those who incited them. By the present fury of the people, as by an inundation, were all these obstacles swept away, and every rampart of royal authority laid level with the ground. The victory was pursued with impetuosity by the sagacious commons, who knew the importance of a favourable moment in all popular commotions. The terror of their authority they extended over the whole nation; and all opposition, and even all blame vented in private conversation, were treated as the most atrocious crimes, by these severe inquisitors. Scarcely was it permitted to find fault with the conduct of any particular member, if

[e] Clarendon, vol. ii. p. 449.

CHAPTER LV

he made a figure in the house; and reflections, thrown out on Pym, were at this time treated as breaches of privilege. The populace without doors were ready to execute, from the least hint, the will of their leaders; nor was it safe for any member to approach either house, who pretended to controul or oppose the general torrent. After so undisguised a manner was this violence conducted, that Hollis, in a speech to the peers, desired to know the names of such members as should vote contrary to the sentiments of the commons:[f] And Pym said in the lower house, that the people must not be restrained in the expressions of their just desires.[g]

By the flight, or terror, or despondency of the king's party, an undisputed majority remained every-where to their opponents; and the bills sent up by the commons, which had hitherto stopped with the peers, and would certainly have been rejected, now passed, and were presented for the royal assent. These were, the pressing bill with its preamble, and the bill against the votes of the bishops in parliament. The king's authority was at that time reduced to the lowest ebb. The queen too, being secretly threatened with an impeachment, and finding no resource in her husband's protection, was preparing to retire into Holland. The rage of the people was, on account of her religion, as well as her spirit and activity, universally levelled against her. Usage, the most contumelious, she had hitherto borne with silent indignation. The commons, in their fury against priests, had seized her very confessor; nor would they release him upon her repeated applications. Even a visit of the prince to his mother had been openly complained of, and remonstrances against it had been presented to her.[h] Apprehensive of attacks still more violent, she was desirous of facilitating her escape; and she prevailed with the king to pass these bills, in hopes of appeasing, for a time, the rage of the multitude.[i]

These new concessions, however important, the king immediately found to have no other effect, than had all the preceding ones: They were made the foundation of demands still more exorbitant. From the facility of his disposition, from the weakness of his situation, the commons believed, that he could now refuse them

---

[f] King's Declar. of 12th of August, 1642.   [g] Ibid.   [h] Nalson, vol. ii. p. 512.
[i] Clarendon, vol. ii. p. 428.

nothing. And they regarded the least moment of relaxation, in their invasion of royal authority, as highly impolitic, during the uninterrupted torrent of their successes. The very moment they were informed of these last acquisitions, they affronted the queen, by opening some intercepted letters written to her by lord Digby: They carried up an impeachment against Herbert, attorney-general, for obeying his master's commands in accusing their members.[k] And they prosecuted, with fresh vigour, their plan of the militia, on which they rested all future hopes of an uncontrouled authority.

The commons were sensible, that monarchical government, which, during so many ages, had been established in England, would soon regain some degree of its former dignity, after the present tempest was overblown; nor would all their new-invented limitations be able totally to suppress an authority, to which the nation had ever been accustomed. The sword alone, to which all human ordinances must submit, could guard their acquired power, and fully ensure to them personal safety against the rising indignation of their sovereign. This point, therefore, became the chief object of their aims. A large magazine of arms being placed in the town of Hull, they dispatched thither Sir John Hotham, a gentleman of considerable fortune in the neighbourhood, and of an ancient family; and they gave him the authority of governor. They sent orders to Goring, governor of Portsmouth, to obey no commands but such as he should receive from the parliament. Not content with having obliged the king to displace Lunsford, whom he had appointed governor of the Tower,[l] they never ceased soliciting him, till he had also displaced Sir John Biron, a man of unexceptionable character, and had bestowed that command on Sir John Conyers, in whom alone, they said, they could repose confidence. After making a fruitless attempt, in which the peers refused their concurrence, to give public warning, that the people should put themselves in a posture of defence against the enterprizes of *papists and other ill-affected persons,*[m] they now resolved, by a bold and decisive stroke, to seize at once the whole power of

[k] Rush. vol. v. p. 489. Clarendon, vol. ii. p. 385.   [l] Rush. vol. v. p. 459.
[m] Nalson, vol. ii. p. 850.

CHAPTER LV

the sword, and to confer it entirely on their own creatures and adherents.

The severe votes, passed in the beginning of this parliament, against lieutenants and their deputies, for exercising powers assumed by all their predecessors, had totally disarmed the crown, and had not left in any magistrate military authority, sufficient for the defence and security of the nation. To remedy this inconvenience now appeared necessary. A bill was introduced and passed the two houses, which restored to lieutenants and deputies the same powers, of which the votes of the commons had bereaved them; but at the same time the names of all the lieutenants were inserted in the bill; and these consisted entirely of men, in whom the parliament could confide. And for their conduct, they were accountable, by the express terms of the bill, not to the king, but to the parliament.

The policy pursued by the commons, and which had hitherto succeeded to admiration, was, to astonish the king by the boldness of their enterprizes, to intermingle no sweetness with their severity, to employ expressions no less violent than their pretensions, and to make him sensible in what little estimation they held both his person and his dignity. To a bill so destructive of royal authority, they prefixed, with an insolence seemingly wanton, a preamble equally dishonourable to the personal character of the king. These are the words: "Whereas there has been of late a most dangerous and desperate design upon the house of commons, which we have just cause to believe an effect of the bloody counsels of papists and other ill-affected persons, who have already raised a rebellion in the kingdom of Ireland. And whereas, by reason of many discoveries, we cannot but fear they will proceed, not only to stir up the like rebellions and insurrections in this kingdom of England; but also to back them with forces from abroad, &c."[n]

Here Charles first ventured to put a stop to his concessions; and that not by a refusal, but a delay. When this demand was made; a demand, which, if granted, the commons justly regarded as the last they should ever have occasion to make; he was at Dover, attending the queen and the princess of Orange, in their embarkation.

[n] Rush. vol. v. p. 519.

He replied, that he had not now leisure to consider a matter of so great importance, and must therefore respite his answer till his return.[o] The parliament instantly dispatched another message to him, with solicitations still more importunate. They expressed their great grief on account of his majesty's answer to their just and necessary petition. They represented, that any delay, during dangers and distractions so great and pressing, was not less unsatisfactory and destructive than an absolute denial. They insisted, that it was their duty to see put in execution a measure so necessary for public safety. And they affirmed, that the people, in many counties, had applied to them for that purpose, and, in some places, were, of themselves and by their own authority, providing against those urgent dangers, with which they were threatened.[p]

Even after this insolence, the king durst not venture upon a flat denial. Besides excepting to the preamble, which threw such dishonour upon him, and protesting the innocence of his intentions, when he entered the house of commons; he only desired that the military authority, if it were defective, should first be conferred upon the crown; and he promised to bestow commissions, but such as should be revocable at pleasure, on the same persons whom the parliament had named in the bill.[q] By a former message, he had expressed his wishes, that they would lay before him, in one view, all the concessions, which they deemed requisite for the settlement of the nation. They pretended, that they were exposed to perils so dreadful and imminent, that they had not leisure for such a work.[r] The expedient, proposed by the king, seemed a sufficient remedy during this emergence; and yet maintained the prerogatives of the crown entire and unbroken.

But the intentions of the commons were wide of this purpose, and their panics could be cured by one remedy alone. They instantly replied, that the dangers and distempers of the nation were such as could endure no longer delay; and unless the king speedily complied with their demands, they should be constrained, for the safety of prince and people, to dispose of the militia by the authority of both houses, and were resolved to do it accordingly. They asserted, that those parts of the kingdom, which had, from their

22d Feb.

28th Feb.

1st March.

[o] Rush. vol. v. p. 521.　[p] Idem, ibid.　[q] Idem, ibid.　[r] Idem, ibid. p. 516, 517.

CHAPTER LV

own authority, put themselves in a posture of defence during these prevailing fears and jealousies, had acted suitably to the declarations and directions of both houses, and conformably to the laws of the kingdom. And while they thus menaced the king with their power, they invited him to fix his residence at London, where, they knew, he would be entirely at mercy.[s]

"I am so much amazed at this message," said the king in his prompt reply, "that I know not what to answer. You speak of jealousies and fears! Lay your hands on your hearts, and ask yourselves, whether I may not likewise be disturbed with fears and jealousies: And if so, I assure you, that this message has nothing lessened them.

"As to the militia, I thought so much of it before I gave that answer, and am so much assured, that the answer is agreeable to what in justice or reason you can ask, or I in honour grant, that I shall not alter it in any point.

"For my residence near you, I wish it might be safe and honourable, and that I had no cause to absent myself from Whitehall: Ask yourselves whether I have not.[t]

"What would you have? Have I violated your laws? Have I denied to pass any bill for the ease and security of my subjects? I do not ask what you have done for me.

"Have any of my people been transported with fears and apprehensions? I offer as free and general a pardon as yourselves can devise. All this considered, there is a judgment of heaven upon this nation, if these distractions continue.

"God so deal with me and mine as all my thoughts and intentions are upright for the maintenance of the true protestant profession, and for the observance and preservation of the laws; and I hope God will bless and assist those laws for *my* preservation."[u]

No sooner did the commons despair of obtaining the king's consent to their bill, than they instantly voted, that those who advised his majesty's answer were enemies to the state, and mischievous projectors against the safety of the nation; that this denial is of such dangerous consequence, that, if his majesty persist in it, it will hazard the peace and tranquillity of all his kingdoms, unless

[s] Rushworth, part iii. vol. i. chap. iv. p. 523.   [t] Idem. vol. v. p. 524.
[u] Rushworth, vol. v. p. 532.

some speedy remedy be applied by the wisdom and authority of both houses; and that such of the subjects as have put themselves in a posture of defence against the common danger, have done nothing but what is justifiable, and approved by the house.[w]

Lest the people might be averse to the seconding of all these usurpations, they were plied anew with rumours of danger, with the terrors of invasion, with the dread of English and Irish papists; and the most unaccountable panics were spread throughout the nation. Lord Digby having entered Kingston in a coach and six, attended by a few livery-servants, the intelligence was conveyed to London; and it was immediately voted, that he had appeared in a hostile manner, to the terror and affright of his majesty's subjects, and had levied war against the king and kingdom.[x] Petitions from all quarters loudly demanded of the parliament to put the nation in a posture of defence; and the county of Stafford in particular expressed such dread of an insurrection among the papists, that every man, they said, was constrained to stand upon his guard, not even daring to go to church unarmed.[y]

King arrives at York. That the same violence by which he had so long been oppressed, might not still reach him, and extort his consent to the militia bill, Charles had resolved to remove farther from London: And accordingly, taking the prince of Wales and the duke of York along with him, he arrived, by slow journies, at York, which he determined for some time to make the place of his residence. The distant parts of the kingdom, being removed from that furious vortex of new principles and opinions, which had transported the capital, still retained a sincere regard for the church and monarchy; and the king here found marks of attachment beyond what he had before expected.[z] From all quarters of England, the prime nobility and gentry, either personally, or by messages and letters, expressed their duty towards him; and exhorted him to save himself and them from that ignominious slavery, with which they were threatened. The small interval of time, which had passed since the fatal accusation of the members, had been sufficient to open the eyes of many, and to recover them from the astonishment, with which at first they had been seized. One rash and passionate at-

[w] Ibid. part iii. vol. i. chap. iv. p. 524.   [x] Clarendon. Rush. part iii. vol. i. chap. ii. p. 495.   [y] Dugdale, p. 89.   [z] Warwick, p. 203.

tempt of the king's seemed but a small counterbalance to so many acts of deliberate violence, which had been offered to him, and every branch of the legislature: And, however sweet the sound of liberty, many resolved to adhere to that moderate freedom transmitted them from their ancestors, and now better secured by such important concessions; rather than, by engaging in a giddy search after more independence, run a manifest risk, either of incurring a cruel subjection, or abandoning all law and order.

Charles, finding himself supported by a considerable party in the kingdom, began to speak in a firmer tone, and to retort the accusations of the commons with a vigour, which he had not before exerted. Notwithstanding their remonstrances, and menaces, and insults, he still persisted in refusing their bill; and they proceeded to frame an ordinance, in which, by the authority of the two houses, without the king's consent, they named lieutenants for all the counties, and conferred on them the command of the whole military force, of all the guards, garrisons, and forts of the kingdom. He issued proclamations against this manifest usurpation; and, as he professed a resolution strictly to observe the law himself, so was he determined, he said, to oblige every other person to pay it a like obedience. The name of the king was so essential to all laws, and so familiar in all acts of executive authority, that, the parliament was afraid, had they totally omitted it, that the innovation would be too sensible to the people. In all commands, therefore, which they conferred, they bound the persons to obey the orders of his majesty, signified by both houses of parliament. And, inventing a distinction, hitherto unheard of, between the office and the person of the king; those very forces, which they employed against him, they levied in his name, and by his authority.[a]

It is remarkable how much the topics of argument were now reversed between the parties. The king, while he acknowledged his former error, of employing a plea of necessity, in order to infringe the laws and constitution, warned the parliament not to imitate an example, on which they threw such violent blame; and the parliament, while they cloathed their personal fears or ambition under the appearance of national and imminent danger, made unknowingly an apology for the most exceptionable part of the king's

[a] Rushworth, vol. v. p. 526.

conduct. That the liberties of the people were no longer exposed to any peril from royal authority, so narrowly circumscribed, so exactly defined, so much unsupported by revenue and by military power, might be maintained upon very plausible topics: But that the danger, allowing it to have any existence, was not of that kind; great, urgent, inevitable; which dissolves all law and levels all limitations, seems apparent from the simplest view of these transactions. So obvious indeed was the king's present inability to invade the constitution, that the fears and jealousies, which operated on the people, and pushed them so furiously to arms, were undoubtedly not of a civil, but of a religious nature. The distempered imaginations of men were agitated with a continual dread of popery, with a horror against prelacy, with an antipathy to ceremonies and the liturgy, and with a violent affection for whatever was most opposite to these objects of aversion. The fanatical spirit, let loose, confounded all regard to ease, safety, interest; and dissolved every moral and civil obligation.[b]

Each party was now willing to throw on its antagonist the odium of commencing a civil war; but both of them prepared for an event which they deemed inevitable. To gain the people's favour and good opinion, was the chief point on both sides. Never was there a people less corrupted by vice, and more actuated by principle, than the English during that period: Never were there individuals who possessed more capacity, more courage, more public spirit, more disinterested zeal. The infusion of one ingredient, in too large a proportion, had corrupted all these noble principles, and converted them into the most virulent poison. To determine his choice in the approaching contests, every man hearkened with avidity to the reasons proposed on both sides. The war of the pen preceded that of the sword, and daily sharpened the humours of the opposite parties. Besides private adventurers without number, the king and parliament themselves carried on the controversy, by messages, remonstrances, and declarations; where the nation was really the party, to whom all arguments were addressed. Charles had here a double advantage. Not only his cause was more favourable, as supporting the ancient government in church and state

[b] See note [AA] at the end of the volume.

CHAPTER LV

against the most illegal pretensions: It was also defended with more art and eloquence. Lord Falkland had accepted the office of secretary; a man who adorned the purest virtue with the richest gifts of nature, and the most valuable acquisitions of learning. By him, assisted by the king himself, were the memorials of the royal party chiefly composed. So sensible was Charles of his superiority in this particular, that he took care to disperse every where the papers of the parliament together with his own, that the people might be the more enabled, by comparison, to form a judgment between them: The parliament, while they distributed copies of their own, were anxious to suppress all the king's compositions.[c]

To clear up the principles of the constitution, to mark the boundaries of the powers entrusted by law to the several members, to show what great improvements the whole political system had received from the king's late concessions, to demonstrate his entire confidence in his people, and his reliance on their affections, to point out the ungrateful returns which had been made him, and the enormous encroachments, insults, and indignities, to which he had been exposed; these were the topics, which, with so much justness of reasoning and propriety of expression, were insisted on in the king's declarations and remonstrances.[d]

Though these writings were of consequence, and tended much to reconcile the nation to Charles, it was evident that they would not be decisive, and that keener weapons must determine the controversy. To the ordinance of the parliament concerning the militia, the king opposed his commissions of array. The counties obeyed the one or the other, according as they stood affected. And in many counties, where the people were divided, mobbish combats and skirmishes ensued.[e] The parliament, on this occasion, went so far as to vote, "That when the lords and commons in parliament, which is the supreme court of judicature, shall declare what the law of the land is, to have this not only questioned, but contradicted, is a high breach of their privileges."[f] This was a plain assuming of the whole legislative authority, and exerting it in the most material article, the government of the militia. Upon the

[c] Rushworth, vol. v. p. 751. [d] See note [BB] at the end of the volume.
[e] May, book ii. p. 99. [f] Rushworth, vol. v. p. 534.

same principles they pretended, by a verbal criticism on the tense of a Latin verb, to ravish from the king his negative voice in the legislature.[g]

The magazine of Hull contained the arms of all the forces levied against the Scots; and Sir John Hotham, the governor, though he had accepted of a commission from the parliament, was not thought to be much disaffected to the church and monarchy. Charles, therefore, entertained hopes, that, if he presented himself at Hull before the commencement of hostilities, Hotham, overawed by his presence, would admit him with his retinue; after which he might easily render himself master of the place. But the governor was on his guard. He shut the gates, and refused to receive the king, who desired leave to enter with twenty persons only. Charles immediately, proclaimed him traitor, and complained to the parliament of his disobedience. The parliament avowed and justified the action.[h]

Prepa-rations.

The county of York levied a guard for the king of 600 men: For the kings of England had hitherto lived among their subjects like fathers among their children, and had derived all their security from the dignity of their character, and from the protection of the laws. The two houses, though they had already levied a guard for themselves; had attempted to seize all the military power, all the navy, and all the forts of the kingdom; and had openly employed their authority in every kind of warlike preparations: Yet immediately voted, "That the king, seduced by wicked counsel, intended to make war against his parliament, who, in all their consultations and actions, had proposed no other end, but the care of his kingdoms, and the performance of all duty and loyalty to his person; that this attempt was a breach of the trust reposed in him by his people, contrary to his oath, and tending to a dissolution of the government; and that whoever should assist him in such a war, were traitors by the fundamental laws of the kingdom."[i]

[g] The king, by his coronation oath, promises that he would maintain the laws and customs which the people had chosen, *quas vulgus elegerit:* The parliament pretended, that *elegerit* meant *shall chuse;* and consequently, that the king had no right to refuse any bills which should be presented him. See Rushworth, vol. v. p. 580.   [h] Whitlocke, p. 55. Rushworth, vol. v. p. 565, &c. May, book ii. p. 51.   [i] Whitlocke, p. 57. Rushworth, vol. v. p. 717. Dugdale, p. 93. May, book ii. p. 54.

CHAPTER LV

The armies, which had been every-where raised on pretence of the service in Ireland, were henceforth more openly inlisted by the parliament for their own purposes, and the command of them was given to the earl of Essex. In London no less than four thousand men inlisted in one day.[k] And the parliament voted a declaration, which they required every member to subscribe, that they would live and die with their general.

They issued orders for bringing in loans of money and plate, in order to maintain forces which should defend the king and both houses of parliament: For this stile they still preserved. Within ten days, vast quantities of plate were brought to their treasurers. Hardly were there men enow to receive it, or room sufficient to stow it: And many, with regret, were obliged to carry back their offerings, and wait till the treasures could find leisure to receive them. Such zeal animated the pious partizans of the parliament, especially in the city! The women gave up all the plate and ornaments of their houses, and even their silver thimbles and bodkins, in order to support the *good cause* against the malignants.[l]

10th June.

Meanwhile the splendor of the nobility, with which the king was environed, much eclipsed the appearance at Westminster. Lord-keeper Littleton, after sending the great seal before him, had fled to York. Above forty peers of the first rank attended the king;[m] whilst the house of lords seldom consisted of more than sixteen members. Near the moiety too of the lower house absented themselves from counsels; which they deemed so full of danger. The commons sent up an impeachment against nine peers, for deserting their duty in parliament. Their own members also, who should return to them, they voted not to admit, till satisfied concerning the reason of their absence.

Charles made a declaration to the peers, who attended him, that he expected from them no obedience to any commands which were not warranted by the laws of the land. The peers answered this declaration by a protest, in which they declared their resolution to obey no commands but such as were warranted by that authority.[n] By these deliberate engagements, so worthy of an Eng-

---

[k] Vicar's God in the mount.   [l] Whitlocke, p. 58. Dugdale, p. 96, 99.
[m] May, book ii. p. 59.   [n] Rushworth, vol. v. p. 626, 627. May, book ii. p. 86. Warwick, p. 210.

lish prince and English nobility, they meant to confound the furious and tumultuary resolutions taken by the parliament.

The queen, disposing of the crown-jewels in Holland, had been enabled to purchase a cargo of arms and ammunition. Part of these, after escaping many perils, arrived safely to the king. His preparations were not near so forward as those of the parliament. In order to remove all jealousy, he had resolved, that their usurpations and illegal pretensions should be apparent to the whole world, and thought, that, to recover the confidence of the people, was a point much more material to his interest, than the collecting of any magazines, stores or armies, which might breed apprehensions of violent or illegal counsels. But the urgent necessity of his situation no longer admitted of delay. He now prepared himself for defence. With a spirit, activity, and address, which neither the one party apprehended, nor the other expected, he employed all the advantages which remained to him, and roused up his adherents to arms. The resources of this prince's genius encreased in proportion to his difficulties; and he never appeared greater than when plunged into the deepest perils and distresses. From the mixed character, indeed, of Charles, arose in part the misfortunes, in which England was at this time involved. His political errors, or rather weaknesses, had raised him inveterate enemies: His eminent moral virtues had procured him zealous partizans: And between the hatred of the one, and the affections of the other, was the nation agitated with the most violent convulsions.

That the king might despair of all composition, the parliament sent him the conditions, on which they were willing to come to an agreement. Their demands, contained in nineteen propositions, amounted to a total abolition of monarchical authority. They required, that no man should remain in the council, who was not agreeable to parliament; that no deed of the king's should have validity, unless it passed the council, and was attested under their hand; that all the officers of state and principal judges should be chosen with consent of parliament, and enjoy their offices for life; that none of the royal family should marry without consent of parliament or council; that the laws should be executed against catholics; that the votes of popish lords should be excluded; that the reformation of the liturgy and church-government should have place, according to advice of parliament; that the ordinance,

CHAPTER LV

with regard to the militia, be submitted to; that the justice of parliament pass upon all delinquents; that a general pardon be granted, with such exceptions as should be advised by parliament; that the forts and castles be disposed of by consent of parliament; and that no peer be made but with consent of both houses.[o]

"Should I grant these demands," said the king in reply, "I may be waited on bareheaded; I may have my hand kissed; the title of Majesty may be continued to me; and *The king's authority, signified by both houses,* may still be the stile of your commands; I may have swords and maces carried before me, and please myself with the sight of a crown and scepter (though even these twigs would not long flourish, when the stock upon which they grew was dead): But as to true and real power, I should remain but the outside, but the picture, but the sign of a king."[p] War on any terms was esteemed, by the king and all his counsellors, preferable to so ignominious a peace. Charles accordingly resolved to support his authority by arms. "His towns," he said, "were taken from him, his ships, his arms, his money; but there still remained to him a good cause, and the hearts of his loyal subjects, which, with God's blessing, he doubted not, would recover all the rest." Collecting therefore some forces, he advanced southwards; and at Nottingham he erected his royal standard, the open signal of discord and civil war throughout the kingdom. _25th Aug._

[o] Rushworth, vol. v. p. 722. May, book ii. p. 54.   [p] Rushworth, vol. v. p. 728. Warwick, p. 189.

LVI

Commencement of the civil war –
State of parties – Battle of Edgehill –
Negociation at Oxford – Victories of the royalists
in the west – Battle of Stratton – Of Lansdown –
Of Roundway-down – Death of Hambden –
Bristol taken –Siege of
Gloucester – Battle of Newbury –
Actions in the north of England – Solemn
league and covenant – Arming of
the Scots – State of Ireland

⚜ ⚜ ⚜

1642.
Commence-
ment of the
civil war.

WHEN TWO NAMES, so sacred in the English constitution as those of KING and PARLIAMENT, were placed in opposition; no wonder the people were divided in their choice, and were agitated with most violent animosities and factions.

The nobility, and more considerable gentry, dreading a total confusion of rank from the fury of the populace, inlisted themselves in defence of the monarch, from whom they received, and to whom they communicated their lustre. Animated with the spirit of loyalty, derived from their ancestors, they adhered to the ancient principles of the constitution, and valued themselves on exerting the maxims, as well as inheriting the possessions, of the old English families. And while they passed their time mostly at their country-seats, they were surprised to hear of opinions prevailing,

State of
parties

CHAPTER LVI

with which they had ever been unacquainted, and which implied, not a limitation, but an abolition almost total, of monarchical authority.

The city of London, on the other hand, and most of the great corporation, took part with the parliament, and adopted with zeal those democratical principles, on which the pretensions of that assembly were founded. The government of cities, which even under absolute monarchies, is commonly republican, inclined them to this party: The small hereditary influence, which can be retained over the industrious inhabitants of towns; the natural independence of citizens; and the force of popular currents over those more numerous associations of mankind; all these causes gave, there, authority to the new principles propagated throughout the nation. Many families too, which had lately been enriched by commerce, saw with indignation, that notwithstanding their opulence, they could not raise themselves to a level with the ancient gentry: They therefore adhered to a power, by whose success they hoped to acquire rank and consideration.[q] And the new splendor and glory of the Dutch commonwealth, where liberty so happily supported industry, made the commercial part of the nation desire to see a like form of government established in England.

The genius of the two religions, so closely at this time interwoven with politics, corresponded exactly to these divisions. The presbyterian religion was new, republican, and suited to the genius of the populace: The other had an air of greater show and ornament, was established on ancient authority, and bore an affinity to the kingly and aristocratical parts of the constitution. The devotees of presbytery became of course zealous partizans of the parliament: The friends of the episcopal church valued themselves on defending the rights of monarchy.

Some men also there were of liberal education, who, being either careless or ignorant of those disputes, bandied about by the clergy of both sides, aspired to nothing but an easy enjoyment of life, amidst the jovial entertainment and social intercourse of their companions. All these flocked to the king's standard, where they breathed a freer air, and were exempted from that rigid pre-

[q] Clarendon, vol. iii. p. 4.

ciseness and melancholy austerity, which reigned among the parliamentary party.

Never was a quarrel more unequal than seemed at first that
between the contending parties: Almost every advantage lay
against the royal cause. The king's revenue had been seized, from
the beginning, by the parliament, who issued out to him, from time
to time, small sums for his present subsistence; and as soon as he
withdrew to York, they totally stopped all payments. London and
all the sea-ports, except Newcastle, being in their hands, the customs yielded them a certain and considerable supply of money;
and all contributions, loans, and impositions, were more easily
raised from the cities, which possessed the ready money, and
where men lived under their inspection, than they could be levied
by the king in those open countries, which, after some time, declared for him.

The seamen naturally followed the disposition of the sea-ports,
to which they belonged: And the earl of Northumberland, lord
admiral, having embraced the party of the parliament, had appointed at their desire, the earl of Warwic to be his lieutenant; who
at once established his authority in the fleet, and kept the entire
dominion of the sea in the hands of that assembly.

All the magazines of arms and ammunition were from the first
seized by the parliament; and their fleet intercepted the greater
part of those which were sent by the queen from Holland. The
king was obliged, in order to arm his followers, to borrow the
weapons of the train-bands, under promise of restoring them as
soon as peace should be settled in the kingdom.

The veneration for parliaments was at this time extreme
throughout the nation.[r] The custom of reviling those assemblies
for corruption, as it had no pretence, so was it unknown, during all
former ages. Few or no instances of their encroaching ambition or
selfish claims had hitherto been observed. Men considered the
house of commons, in no other light than as the representatives of
the nation, whose interest was the same with that of the public,
who were the eternal guardians of law and liberty, and whom no
motive, but the necessary defence of the people, could ever engage
in an opposition to the crown. The torrent, therefore, of general

[r] Walker, p. 336.

affection, ran to the parliament. What is the great advantage of popularity; the privilege of affixing epithets fell of course to that party. The king's adherents were the *Wicked* and the *Malignant:* Their adversaries were the *Godly* and the *Well-affected.* And as the force of the cities was more united than that of the country, and at once gave shelter and protection to the parliamentary party, who could easily suppress the royalists in their neighbourhood; almost the whole kingdom, at the commencement of the war, seemed to be in the hands of the parliament.[s]

What alone gave the king some compensation for all the advantages possessed by his adversaries, was, the nature and qualities of his adherents. More bravery and activity were hoped for, from the generous spirit of the nobles and gentry, than from the base disposition of the multitude. And as the men of estates, at their own expence, levied and armed their tenants; besides an attachment to their masters, greater force and courage were to be expected in these rustic troops, than in the vicious and enervated populace of cities.

The neighbouring states of Europe, being engaged in violent wars, little interested themselves in these civil commotions; and this island enjoyed the singular advantage (for such it surely was) of fighting out its own quarrels without the interposition of foreigners. France, from policy, had fomented the first disorders in Scotland; had sent over arms to the Irish rebels; and continued to give countenance to the English parliament: Spain, from bigotry, furnished the Irish with some supplies of money and arms. The prince of Orange, closely allied to the crown, encouraged English officers, who served in the Low Countries, to enlist in the king's army: The Scottish officers, who had been formed in Germany, and in the late commotions, chiefly took part with the parliament.

The contempt, entertained by the parliament, for the king's party, was so great, that it was the chief cause of pushing matters to such extremities against him; and many believed that he never would attempt resistance, but must soon yield to the pretensions, however enormous, of the two houses. Even after his standard was erected, men could not be brought to apprehend the danger of a civil war; nor was it imagined, that he would have the imprudence

[s] Warwick, p. 318.

to enrage his implacable enemies, and render his own condition more desperate, by opposing a force, which was so much superior. The low condition, in which he appeared at Nottingham, confirmed all these hopes. His artillery, though far from numerous, had been left at York, for want of horses to transport it. Besides the trained bands of the county, raised by Sir John Digby, the sheriff, he had not gotten together above three hundred infantry. His cavalry, in which consisted his chief strength, exceeded not eight hundred, and were very ill provided with arms. The forces of the parliament lay at Northampton, within a few days march of him; and consisted of above six thousand men, well armed and well appointed. Had these troops advanced upon him, they must soon have dissipated the small force, which he had assembled. By pursuing him in his retreat, they had so discredited his cause and discouraged his adherents, as to have for ever prevented his collecting an army able to make head against them. But the earl of Essex, the parliamentary general, had not yet received any orders from his masters.[t] What rendered them so backward, after such precipitate steps as they had formerly taken, is not easily explained. It is probable, that, in the extreme distress of his party, consisted the present safety of the king. The parliament hoped, that the royalists, sensible of their feeble condition, and convinced of their slender resources, would disperse of themselves, and leave their adversaries a victory, so much the more complete and secure, as it would be gained without the appearance of force, and without bloodshed. Perhaps too, when it became necessary to make the concluding step, and offer barefaced violence to their sovereign, their scruples and apprehensions, though not sufficient to overcome their resolutions, were able to retard the execution of them.[u]

Sir Jacob Astley, whom the king had appointed major-general of his intended army, told him, that he could not give him assurance but he might be taken out of his bed, if the rebels should make a brisk attempt to that purpose. All the king's attendants were full of well-grounded apprehensions. Some of the lords having desired that a message might be sent to the parliament, with overtures to a treaty; Charles, who well knew, that an accommodation, in his present condition, meant nothing but a total submission, hastily

[t] Clarendon, vol. iii. p. 1, 2. [u] Idem, ibid. p. 18.

broke up the council, lest this proposal should be farther insisted on. But next day, the earl of Southampton, whom no one could suspect of base or timid sentiments, having offered the same advice in council, it was hearkened to with more coolness and deliberation. He urged, that, though such a step would probably encrease the insolence of the parliament; this was so far from being an objection, that such dispositions must necessarily turn to the advantage of the royal cause: That if they refused to treat, which was more probable, the very sound of peace was so popular, that nothing could more disgust the nation than such haughty severity: That if they admitted of a treaty, their proposals, considering their present situation, would be so exorbitant, as to open the eyes of their most partial adherents, and turn the general favour to the king's party: And that, at worst, time might be gained by this expedient, and a delay of the imminent danger, with which the king was at present threatened.[w]

Charles, on assembling the council, had declared against all advances towards an accommodation; and had said, that, having now nothing left him but his honour, this last possession he was resolved steadily to preserve, and rather to perish than yield any farther to the pretensions of his enemies.[x] But by the unanimous desire of the counsellors, he was prevailed on to embrace Southampton's advice. That nobleman, therefore, with Sir John Colepeper and Sir William Uvedale, was dispatched to London, with offers of a treaty.[y] The manner, in which they were received, gave little hopes of success. Southampton was not allowed by the peers to take his seat; but was ordered to deliver his message to the usher, and immediately to depart the city: The commons showed little better disposition towards Colepeper and Uvedale.[z] Both houses replied, that they could admit of no treaty with the king, till he took down his standard, and recalled his proclamations, in which the parliament supposed themselves to be declared traitors. The king, by a second message, denied any such intention against the two houses; but offered to recal these proclamations, provided the parliament agreed to recal theirs, in which his adherents were declared traitors. They desired him in return to dismiss his forces,

[w] Clarendon, vol. iii. p. 7.　　[x] Idem, ibid.　　[y] Rush. vol. v. p. 784.
[z] Clarendon, vol. iii. p. 10.

to reside with his parliament, and to give up delinquents to their justice; that is, abandon himself and his friends to the mercy of his enemies.[a] Both parties flattered themselves, that, by these messages and replies, they had gained the ends, which they proposed.[b] The king believed, that the people were made sufficiently sensible of the parliament's insolence and aversion to peace: The parliament intended by this vigour in their resolutions, to support the vigour of their military operations.

The courage of the parliament was increased, besides their great superiority of force, by two recent events, which had happened in their favour. Goring was governor of Portsmouth, the best fortified town in the kingdom, and, by its situation, of great importance. This man seemed to have rendered himself an implacable enemy to the king, by betraying, probably magnifying, the secret cabals of the army; and the parliament thought, that his fidelity to them might, on that account, be entirely depended on. But the same levity of mind still attended him, and the same disregard to engagements and professions. He took underhand his measures with the court, and declared against the parliament. But, though he had been sufficiently supplied with money, and long before knew his danger; so small was his foresight, that he had left the place entirely destitute of provisions, and, in a few days, he was obliged to surrender to the parliamentary forces.[c]

The marquis of Hertford was a nobleman of the greatest quality and character in the kingdom, and equally with the king, descended, by a female, from Henry VII. During the reign of James, he had attempted, without having obtained the consent of that monarch, to marry Arabella Stuart, a lady nearly related to the crown; and upon discovery of his intentions, had been obliged, for some time, to fly the kingdom. Ever after, he was looked on with an evil eye at court, from which, in a great measure, he withdrew; and living in an independant manner, he addicted himself entirely to literary occupations and amusements. In proportion as the king declined in popularity, Hertford's character flourished with the people; and when this parliament assembled, no nobleman possessed more general favour and authority. By his sagacity, he soon

[a] Rushworth, vol. v. p. 786. Dugdale, p. 102.   [b] Whitlocke, p. 59.
[c] Rushworth, vol. v. p. 683. Whitlocke, p. 60. Clarendon, vol. ii. p. 19.

perceived, that the commons, not content with correcting the abuses of government, were carried, by the natural current of power and popularity, into the opposite extreme, and were committing violations, no less dangerous than the former, upon the English constitution. Immediately he devoted himself to the support of the king's falling authority, and was prevailed with to be governor to the young prince, and reside at court, to which, in the eyes of all men, he gave, by his presence, a new lustre and authority. So high was his character for mildness and humanity, that he still preserved, by means of these popular virtues, the public favour; and every one was sensible of the true motive of his change. Notwithstanding his habits of ease and study, he now exerted himself in raising an army for the king; and being named general of the western counties, where his interest chiefly lay, he began to assemble forces in Somersetshire. By the assistance of lord Seymour, lord Paulet, John Digby, son of the earl of Bristol, Sir Francis Hawley, and others, he had drawn together some appearance of an army; when the parliament, apprehensive of the danger, sent the earl of Bedford, with a considerable force against him. On his approach, Hertford was obliged to retire into Sherborne castle; and, finding that place untenable, he himself passed over into Wales, leaving Sir Ralph Hopton, Sir John Berkeley, Digby, and other officers, with their horse, consisting of about a hundred and twenty, to march into Cornwal, in hopes of finding that county better prepared for their reception.[d]

All the dispersed bodies of the parliamentary army were now ordered to march to Northampton; and the earl of Essex, who had joined them, found the whole amount to 15,000 men.[e] The king, though his camp had been gradually reinforced from all quarters, was sensible that he had no army, which could cope with so formidable a force; and he thought it prudent, by slow marches, to retire to Derby, thence to Shrewsbury, in order to countenance the levies, which his friends were making in those parts. At Wellington, a day's march from Shrewsbury, he made a rendezvous of all his forces, and caused his military orders to be read at the head of every regiment. That he might bind himself by reciprocal ties, he solemnly made the following declaration before his whole army:

[d] Clarendon, vol. vi. p. 2, 3, &c.　　[e] Whitlocke, p. 60.

"I do promise, in the presence of Almighty God, and as I hope for his blessing and protection, that I will, to the utmost of my power, defend and maintain the true reformed protestant religion, established in the church of England, and, by the grace of God, in the same will live and die.

"I desire that the laws may ever be the measure of my government, and that the liberty and property of the subject may be preserved by them with the same care as my own just rights. And if it please God, by his blessing on this army, raised for my necessary defence, to preserve me from the present rebellion; I do solemnly and faithfully promise, in the sight of God, to maintain the just privileges and freedom of parliament, and to govern to the utmost of my power, by the known statutes and customs of the kingdom, and particularly, to observe inviolably the laws, to which I have given my consent this parliament. Meanwhile, if this emergence, and the great necessity, to which I am driven, beget any violation of law, I hope it shall be imputed by God and man to the authors of this war; not to me, who have so earnestly laboured to preserve the peace of the kingdom.

"When I willingly fail in these particulars, I shall expect no aid or relief from man, nor any protection from above: But in this resolution, I hope for the chearful assistance of all good men, and am confident of the blessing of heaven."*f*

Though the concurrence of the church undoubtedly encreased the king's adherents, it may safely be affirmed, that the high monarchical doctrines, so much inculcated by the clergy, had never done him any real service. The bulk of that generous train of nobility and gentry, who now attended the king in his distresses, breathed the spirit of liberty as well as of loyalty: And in the hopes alone of his submitting to a legal and limited government, were they willing in his defence to sacrifice their lives and fortunes.

While the king's army lay at Shrewsbury, and he was employing himself in collecting money, which he received, though in no great quantities, by voluntary contributions, and by the plate of the universities, which was sent him; the news arrived of an action, the first which had happened in these wars, and where he was successful.

On the appearance of commotions in England, the princes

---

f Clarendon, vol. iii. p. 16, 17. Dugdale, p. 104.

CHAPTER LVI

Rupert and Maurice, sons of the unfortunate Palatine, had offered their service to the king; and the former, at that time, commanded a body of horse, which had been sent to Worcester, in order to watch the motions of Essex, who was marching towards that city. No sooner had the prince arrived, than he saw some cavalry of the enemy approaching the gates. Without delay, he briskly attacked them, as they were defiling from a lane, and forming themselves. Colonel Sandys, who led them, and who fought with valour, being mortally wounded, fell from his horse. The whole party was routed, and was pursued above a mile. The prince hearing of Essex's approach, retired to the main body.[g] This rencounter, though in itself of small importance, mightily raised the reputation of the royalists, and acquired to prince Rupert the character of promptitude and courage; qualities, which he eminently displayed during the whole course of the war.

The king, on mustering his army, found it amount to 10,000 men. The earl of Lindesey, who in his youth had sought experience of military service in the Low Countries,[h] was general: Prince Rupert commanded the horse: Sir Jacob Astley, the foot: Sir Arthur Aston, the dragoons: Sir John Heydon, the artillery. Lord Bernard Stuart was at the head of a troop of guards. The estates and revenue of this single troop, according to lord Clarendon's computation, were at least equal to those of all the members, who, at the commencement of war, voted in both houses. Their servants, under the command of Sir William Killigrew, made another troop, and always marched with their masters.[i]

With this army the king left Shrewsbury, resolving to give battle as soon as possible to the army of the parliament, which, he heard, was continually augmenting by supplies from London. In order to bring on an action, he directed his march towards the capital, which, he knew, the enemy would not abandon to him. Essex had now received his instructions. The import of them was, to present a most humble petition to the king, and to rescue him and the royal family from those desperate malignants, who had seized their persons.[k] Two days after the departure of the royalists from Shrewsbury, he left Worcester. Though it be commonly easy in civil wars

15th Oct.

---

[g] Clarendon, vol. iii. p. 25. May, book iii. p. 10.   [h] He was then lord Willoughby.   [i] Clarendon, vol. iii. p. 41. Warwick, p. 231.   [k] Whitlocke, p. 59. Clarendon, vol. iii. p. 27, 28, &c.

to get intelligence, the armies were within six miles of each other, ere either of the generals was acquainted with the approach of his enemy. Shrewsbury and Worcester, the places from which they set out, are not above twenty miles distant; yet had the two armies marched ten days in this mutual ignorance. So much had military skill, during a long peace, decayed in England.[1]

Battle of Edge-hill. 23d of Oct.

The royal army lay near Banbury: That of the parliament, at Keinton, in the county of Warwic. Prince Rupert sent intelligence of the enemy's approach. Tho' the day was far advanced, the king resolved upon the attack: Essex drew up his men to receive him. Sir Faithful Fortescue, who had levied a troop for the Irish wars, had been obliged to serve in the parliamentary army, and was now posted on the left wing, commanded by Ramsay, a Scotchman. No sooner did the king's army approach, than Fortescue, ordering his troop to discharge their pistols in the ground, put himself under the command of prince Rupert. Partly from this incident, partly from the furious shock made upon them by the prince; that whole wing of cavalry immediately fled, and were pursued for two miles. The right wing of the parliament's army had no better success. Chased from their ground with Wilmot and Sir Arthur Aston, they also took to flight. The king's body of reserve, commanded by Sir John Biron, judging, like raw soldiers, that all was over, and impatient to have some share in the action, heedlessly followed the chase, which their left wing had precipitately led them. Sir William Balfour, who commanded Essex's reserve, perceived the advantage: He wheeled about upon the king's infantry, now quite unfurnished of horse; and he made great havoc among them. Lindesey, the general, was mortally wounded, and taken prisoner. His son, endeavouring his rescue, fell likewise into the enemy's hands. Sir Edmund Verney, who carried the king's standard, was killed, and the standard taken; but it was afterwards recovered. In this situation, prince Rupert, on his return, found affairs. Every thing bore the appearance of a defeat, instead of a victory, with which he had hastily flattered himself. Some advised the king to leave the field: But that prince rejected such pusillanimous counsel. The two armies faced each other for some time, and neither of them retained courage sufficient for a new attack. All night they lay under arms; and next morning found themselves in sight of each

[1] Clarendon, vol. iii. p. 44.

other. General, as well as soldier, on both sides, seemed averse to renew the battle. Essex first drew off, and retired to Warwic. The king returned to his former quarters. Five thousand men are said to have been found dead on the field of battle; and the loss of the two armies, as far as we can judge by the opposite accounts, was nearly equal. Such was the event of this first battle, fought at Keinton, or Edge-hill.[m]

Some of Essex's horse, who had been driven off the field in the beginning of the action, flying to a great distance, carried news of a total defeat, and struck a mighty terror into the city and parliament. After a few days, a more just account arrived; and then the parliament pretended to a complete victory.[n] The king also, on his part, was not wanting to display his advantages; though, except the taking of Banbury, a few days after, he had few marks of victory to boast of. He continued his march, and took possession of Oxford, the only town in his dominions, which was altogether at his devotion.

After the royal army was recruited and refreshed; as the weather still continued favourable, it was again put in motion. A party of horse approached to Reading, of which Martin was appointed governor by the parliament. Both governor and garrison were seized with a panic, and fled with precipitation to London. The king, hoping that every thing would yield before him, advanced with his whole army to Reading. The parliament, who, instead of their fond expectations, that Charles would never be able to collect an army, had now the prospect of a civil war, bloody, and of uncertain event; were farther alarmed at the near approach of the royal army, while their own forces lay at a distance. They voted an address for a treaty. The king's nearer approach to Colebroke quickened their advances for peace. Northumberland and Pembroke, with three commoners, presented the address of both houses; in which they besought his majesty to appoint some convenient place where he might reside, till committees could attend him with proposals. The king named Windsor, and desired that their garrison might be removed, and his own troops admitted into that castle.[o]

[m] Clarendon, vol. iii. p. 44, &c. May, book iii. p. 16, &c.   [n] Whitlocke, p. 61. Clarendon, vol. iii. p. 59.   [o] Whitlocke, p. 62. Clarendon, vol. iii. p. 73.

30th Nov.   Meanwhile Essex, advancing by hasty marches, had arrived at London. But neither the presence of his army, nor the precarious hopes of a treaty, retarded the king's approaches. Charles attacked, at Brentford, two regiments quartered there, and, after a sharp action, beat them from that village, and took about 500 prisoners. The parliament had sent orders to forbear all hostilities, and had expected the same from the king; though no stipulations to that purpose had been mentioned by their commissioners. Loud complaints were raised against this attack, as if it had been the most apparent perfidy, and breach of treaty.[p] Inflamed with resentment, as well as anxious for its own safety, the city marched its trained bands in excellent order, and joined the army under Essex. The parliamentary army now amounted to above 24,000 men, and was much superior to that of the king.[q] After both armies had faced each other for some time, Charles drew off and retired to Reading, thence to Oxford.

While the principal armies on both sides were kept in inaction by the winter-season, the king and parliament were employed in real preparations for war, and in seeming advances toward peace. By means of contributions or assessments, levied by the horse, Charles maintained his cavalry: By loans and voluntary presents, sent him from all parts of the kingdom, he supported his infantry: But the supplies were still very unequal to the necessities, under which he laboured.[r] The parliament had much greater resources for money; and had, by consequence, every military preparation in much greater order and abundance. Besides an imposition levied in London, amounting to the five-and-twentieth part of every one's substance, they established on that city a weekly assessment of 10,000 pounds, and another of 23,518, on the rest of the kingdom.[s] And as their authority was at present established in most counties, they levied these taxes with regularity; though they amounted to sums much greater than the nation had formerly paid to the public.

1643.   The king and parliament sent reciprocally their demands; and a treaty commenced, but without any cessation of hostilities, as had at first been proposed. The earl of Northumberland, and four

---

[p] Whitlocke, p. 62. Clarendon, vol. iii. p. 75.   [q] Whitlocke, p. 62.
[r] Clarendon, vol. iii. p. 87.   [s] Clarendon, vol. iii. p. 171.

CHAPTER LVI

members of the lower house, came to Oxford as commissioners.[t] *Negocia-* In this treaty, the king perpetually insisted on the re-establishment *tion at* of the crown in its legal powers, and on the restoration of his *Oxford.* constitutional prerogative:[u] The parliament still required new concessions, and a farther abridgment of regal authority, as a more effectual remedy to their fears and jealousies. Finding the king supported by more forces and a greater party than they had ever looked for, they seemingly abated somewhat of those extravagant conditions, which they had formerly claimed; but their demands were still too high for an equal treaty. Besides other articles, to which a complete victory alone could entitle them, they required the king, in express terms, utterly to abolish episcopacy; a demand, which, before, they had only insinuated: And they required, that all other ecclesiastical controversies should be determined by *their* assembly of divines; that is, in the manner the most repugnant to the inclinations of the king and all his partizans. They insisted, that he should submit to the punishment of his most faithful adherents. And they desired him to acquiesce in their settlement of the militia, and to confer on their adherents the entire power of the sword. In answer to the king's proposal, that his magazines, towns, forts, and ships, should be restored to him, the parliament required, that they should be put into such hands as they could confide in:[w] The nineteen propositions, which they formerly sent to the king, shewed their *inclination* to abolish monarchy: They only asked, at present, the *power* of doing it. And having now, in the eye of the law, been guilty of treason, by levying war against their sovereign; it is evident, that their fears and jealousies must, on that account, have multiplied extremely; and have rendered their personal safety, which they interwove with the safety of the nation, still more incompatible with the authority of the monarch. Though the gentleness and lenity of the king's temper might have ensured them against schemes of future vengeance; they preferred, as is, no doubt, natural, an independent security, accompanied too with sovereign power, to the station of subjects, and that not entirely guarded from all apprehensions of danger.[x]

The conferences went no farther than the first demand on each

---

[t] Whitlocke, p. 64.   [u] Rush. vol. vi. p. 202.   [w] Rushworth, vol. vi. p. 166. Clarendon, vol. iii. p. 119.   [x] See note [CC] at the end of the volume.

side. The parliament, finding that there was no likelihood of coming to any agreement, suddenly recalled their commissioners.

A military enterprize, which they had concerted early in the spring, was immediately undertaken. Reading, the garrison of the king's, which lay nearest to London, was esteemed a place of considerable strength, in that age, when the art of attacking towns was not well understood in Europe, and was totally unknown in England. The earl of Essex sat down before this place with an army of 18,000 men; and carried on the siege by regular approaches. Sir Arthur Aston, the governor, being wounded, colonel Fielding succeeded to the command. In a little time the town was found to be no longer in a condition of defence; and though the king approached, with an intention of obliging Essex to raise the siege, the disposition of the parliamentary army was so strong, as rendered the design impracticable. Fielding, therefore, was contented to yield the town, on condition that he should bring off all the garrison with the honours of war, and deliver up deserters. This last article was thought so ignominious and so prejudicial to the king's interests, that the governor was tried by a council of war, and condemned to lose his life, for consenting to it. His sentence was afterwards remitted by the king.[y]

Essex's army had been fully supplied with all necessaries from London: Even many superfluities and luxuries were sent them by the care of the zealous citizens: Yet the hardships, which they suffered from the siege, during so early a season, had weakened them to such a degree, that they were no longer fit for any new enterprize. And the two armies, for some time, encamped in the neighbourhood of each other, without attempting, on either side, any action of moment.

Besides the military operations between the principal armies, which lay in the centre of England; each county, each town, each family almost, was divided within itself; and the most violent convulsions shook the whole kingdom. Throughout the winter, continual efforts had every-where been made by each party to surmount its antagonist; and the English, rouzed from the lethargy of peace, with eager, though unskilful hands, employed against their fellow-citizens their long-neglected weapons. The furious zeal for

15th April.

27th April.

[y] Rush. vol. vi. p. 265, &c. Clarendon, vol. iii. p. 237, 238, &c.

CHAPTER LVI

liberty and presbyterian discipline, which had hitherto run uncontrouled throughout the nation, now at last excited an equal ardour for monarchy and episcopacy; when the intention of abolishing these ancient modes of government was openly avowed by the parliament. Conventions for neutrality, though, in several counties, they had been entered into, and confirmed by the most solemn oaths, yet, being voted illegal by the two houses, were immediately broken;[z] and the fire of discord was spread into every quarter. The altercation of discourse, the controversies of the pen, but, above all, the declamations of the pulpit, indisposed the minds of men towards each other, and propagated the blind rage of party.[a] Fierce, however, and inflamed as were the dispositions of the English, by a war both civil and religious, that great destroyer of humanity; all the events of this period are less distinguished by atrocious deeds either of treachery or cruelty, than were ever any intestine discords, which had so long a continuance. A circumstance which will be found to reflect great praise on the national character of that people, now so unhappily rouzed to arms.

In the north, lord Fairfax commanded for the parliament, the earl of Newcastle for the king. The latter noblemen began those associations, which were afterwards so much practised in other parts of the kingdom. He united in a league for the king the counties of Northumberland, Cumberland, Westmoreland, and the Bishopric, and engaged, some time after, other counties in the same association. Finding that Fairfax, assisted by Hotham and the garrison of Hull, was making progress in the southern parts of Yorkshire; he advanced with a body of four thousand men, and took possession of York. At Tadcaster, he attacked the forces of the parliament, and dislodged them: But his victory was not decisive. In other rencounters he obtained some inconsiderable advantages. But the chief benefit, which resulted from his enterprizes, was, the establishing of the king's authority in all the northern provinces.

In another part of the kingdom, lord Broke was killed by a shot, while he was taking possession of Litchfield for the parliament.[b]

[z] Clarendon, vol. iii. p. 137, 139.   [a] Dugdale, p. 95.   [b] He had taken possession of Litchfield, and was viewing from a window St. Chad's cathedral, in which a party of the royalists had fortified themselves. He was cased in complete armour, but was shot through the eye by a random-ball. Lord Broke was a zealous puritan; and had formerly said, that he hoped to

After a sharp combat, near Stafford, between the earl of North-ampton and Sir John Gell, the former, who commanded the king's forces, was killed while he fought with great valour; and his forces, discouraged by his death, though they had obtained the advantage in the action, retreated into the town of Stafford.[c]

Sir William Waller began to distinguish himself among the generals of the parliament. Active and indefatigable in his oper-ations, rapid and enterprising; he was fitted by his genius to the nature of the war; which, being managed by raw troops, conducted by unexperienced commanders, afforded success to every bold and sudden undertaking. After taking Winchester and Chichester, he advanced towards Glocester, which was in a manner blockaded by lord Herbert, who had levied considerable forces in Wales for the royal party.[d] While he attacked the Welsh on one side, a sally from Glocester made impression on the other. Herbert was de-feated; five hundred of his men killed on the spot; a thousand taken prisoners; and he himself escaped with some difficulty to Oxford. Hereford, esteemed a strong town, defended by a consid-erable garrison, was surrendered to Waller, from the cowardice of colonel Price, the governor. Tewkesbury underwent the same fate. Worcester refused him admittance; and Waller, without placing any garrisons in his new conquests, retired to Glocester, and he thence joined the army under the earl of Essex.[e]

Victories of the royalists in the west.

But the most memorable actions of valour, during this winter-season, were performed in the west. When Sir Ralph Hopton, with his small troop, retired into Cornwall before the earl of Bedford, that nobleman, despising so inconsiderable a force, abandoned the pursuit, and committed the care of suppressing the royal party to the sheriffs of the county. But the affections of Cornwall were much inclined to the king's service. While Sir Richard Buller and Sir Alexander Carew lay at Launceston, and employed themselves in executing the parliament's ordinance for the militia, a meeting of the county was assembled at Truro; and after Hopton produced

see with his eyes the ruin of all the cathedrals of England. It was a super-stitious remark of the royalists, that he was killed on St. Chad's day by a shot from St. Chad's cathedral, which pierced that very eye by which he hoped to see the ruin of all cathedrals. Dugdale, p. 118. Clarendon, &c.
[c] Whitlocke, p. 66. Rush. vol. vi. p. 152. Clarendon, vol. iii. p. 151.   [d] Rush. vol. vi. p. 92, 100.   [e] Rush. vol. vi. p. 263.

CHAPTER LVI

his commission from the earl of Hertford, the king's general, it was agreed to execute the laws, and to expel these invaders of the county. The train-bands were accordingly levied, Launceston taken, and all Cornwall reduced to peace and to obedience under the king.

It had been usual for the royal party, on the commencement of these disorders, to claim, on all occasions, the strict execution of the laws, which, they knew, were favourable to them; and the parliament, rather than have recourse to the plea of necessity, and avow the transgression of any statute, had also been accustomed to warp the laws, and, by forced constructions, to interpret them in their own favour.*f* But though the king was naturally the gainer by such a method of conducting war, and it was by favour of law that the train-bands were raised in Cornwall; it appeared that those maxims were now prejudicial to the royal party. These troops could not legally, without their own consent, be carried out of the county; and consequently, it was impossible to push into Devonshire, the advantage, which they had obtained. The Cornish royalists, therefore, bethought themselves of levying a force, which might be more serviceable. Sir Bevil Granville, the most beloved man of that country, Sir Ralph Hopton, Sir Nicholas Slanning, Arundel, and Trevannion, undertook, at their own charges, to raise an army for the king; and their great interest in Cornwall soon enabled them to effect their purpose. The parliament, alarmed at this appearance of the royalists, gave a commission to Ruthven, a Scotchman, governor of Plymouth, to march with all the forces of Dorset, Somerset, and Devon, and make an entire conquest of Cornwall. The earl of Stamford followed him, at some distance, with a considerable supply. Ruthven, having entered Cornwall by bridges thrown over the Tamar, hastened to an action; lest Stamford should join him, and obtain the honour of that victory, which he looked for with assurance. The royalists, in like manner, were impatient to bring the affair to a decision, before Ruthven's army should receive so considerable a reinforcement. The battle was fought on Bradoc-down; and the king's forces, though inferior in number, gave a total defeat to their enemies. Ruthven, with a few broken troops, fled to Saltash; and when that

f Clarendon, vol. iii. p. 130.

town was taken, he escaped, with some difficulty, and almost alone, into Plymouth. Stamford retired, and distributed his forces into Plymouth and Exeter.

Notwithstanding these advantages, the extreme want both of money and ammunition, under which the Cornish royalists laboured, obliged them to enter into a convention of neutrality with the parliamentary party in Devonshire; and this neutrality held all the winter-season. In the spring, it was broken by the authority of the two houses; and war recommenced with great appearance of disadvantage to the king's party. Stamford, having assembled a strong body of near seven thousand men, well supplied with money, provisions, and ammunition, advanced upon the royalists, who were not half his number, and were oppressed *Battle of* by every kind of necessity. Despair, joined to the natural gallantry *Stratton.* of these troops, commanded by the prime gentry of the county, *May* made them resolve, by one vigorous effort, to overcome all these *16th.* disadvantages. Stamford being encamped on the top of a high hill near Stratton, they attacked him in four divisions, at five in the morning, having lain all night under arms. One division was commanded by lord Mohun and Sir Ralph Hopton, another by Sir Bevile Granville and Sir John Berkeley, a third by Slanning and Trevannion, a fourth by Basset and Godolphin. In this manner the action began; the king's forces pressing with vigour those four ways up the hill, and their enemies obstinately defending themselves. The fight continued with doubtful success, till word was brought to the chief officers of the Cornish, that their ammunition was spent to less than four barrels of powder. This defect, which they concealed from the soldiers, they resolved to supply by their valour. They agreed to advance without firing till they should reach the top of the hill, and could be on equal ground with the enemy. The courage of the officers was so well seconded by the soldiers, that the royalists began on all sides to gain ground. Major-general Chidley, who commanded the parliamentary army (for Stamford kept at a distance) failed not in his duty; and when he saw his men recoil, he himself advanced with a good stand of pikes, and, piercing into the thickest of the enemy, was at last overpowered by numbers and taken prisoner. His army, upon this disaster, gave ground apace; insomuch that the four parties of the royalists, growing nearer and nearer as they ascended, at length met together upon the plain at the top; where they embraced with great joy, and signalized their victory with loud shouts and mutual congratulations.[g]

After this success, the attention both of king and parliament was turned towards the west, as to a very important scene of action. The king sent thither the marquis of Hertford and prince Maurice with a reinforcement of cavalry; who, having joined the Cornish army, soon over-ran the county of Devon; and advancing into that of Somerset, began to reduce it to obedience. On the other hand, the parliament, having supplied Sir William Waller, in whom they much trusted, with a complete army, dispatched him westwards, in order to check the progress of the royalists. After some skirmishes, the two armies met at Lansdown, near Bath, and fought a pitched battle, with great loss on both sides, but without any decisive event.[h] The gallant Granville was there killed; and Hopton, by the blowing up of some powder, was dangerously hurt. The royalists next attempted to march eastwards, and to join their forces to the king's at Oxford: But Waller hung on their rear, and infested their march till they reached the Devizes. Reinforced by additional troops, which flocked to him from all quarters; he so much surpassed the royalists in number, that they durst no longer continue their march, or expose themselves to the hazard of an action. It was resolved, that Hertford and prince Maurice should proceed with the cavalry; and, having procured a reinforcement from the king, should hasten back to the relief of their friends. Waller was so confident of taking this body of infantry, now abandoned by the horse, that he wrote to the parliament, that their work was done, and that, by the next post, he would inform them of the number and quality of the prisoners. But the king, even before Hertford's arrival, hearing of the great difficulties, to which his western army was reduced, had prepared a considerable body of cavalry, which he immediately dispatched to their succour under the command of lord Wilmot. Waller drew up on Roundway-down, about two miles from the Devizes; and advancing with his cavalry to fight Wilmot, and prevent his conjunction with the Cornish infantry, was received with equal valour by the royalists. After a sharp action he

Battle of Lansdown. 5th July.

Battle of Roundway-down. 13th July.

[g] Rush. vol. vi. p. 267, 273. Clarendon, vol. iii. p. 269, 279. [h] Rush. vol. vi. p. 284. Clarendon, vol. iii. p. 282.

was totally routed, and, flying with a few horse, escaped to Bristol. Wilmot, seizing the enemy's cannon, and having joined his friends, whom he came to relieve, attacked Waller's infantry with redoubled courage, drove them off the field, and routed and dispersed the whole army.[i]

This important victory, following so quick after many other successes, struck great dismay into the parliament, and gave an alarm to their principal army commanded by Essex. Waller exclaimed loudly against that general, for allowing Wilmot to pass him, and proceed without any interruption to the succour of the distressed infantry at the Devizes. But Essex, finding that his army fell continually to decay after the siege of Reading, was resolved to remain upon the defensive; and the weakness of the king, and his want of all military stores, had also restrained the activity of the royal army. No action had happened in that part of England, except one skirmish, which, of itself, was of no great consequence, and was rendered memorable by the death alone of the famous Hambden.

Colonel Urrey, a Scotchman, who served in the parliamentary army, having received some disgust, came to Oxford, and offered his services to the king. In order to prove the sincerity of his conversion, he informed Prince Rupert of the loose disposition of the enemy's quarters, and exhorted him to form some attempt upon them. The Prince, who was entirely fitted for that kind of service, falling suddenly upon the dispersed bodies of Essex's army, routed two regiments of cavalry and one of infantry, and carried his ravages within two miles of the general's quarters. The alarm being given, every one mounted on horseback, in order to pursue the prince, to recover the prisoners, and to repair the disgrace, which the army had sustained. Among the rest, Hambden, who had a regiment of infantry that day at a distance, joined the horse as a volunteer; and overtaking the royalists on Chalgrave field, entered into the thickest of the battle. By the bravery and activity of Rupert, the king's troops were brought off, and a great booty, together with two hundred prisoners, was conveyed to Oxford. But what most pleased the royalists, was, the expectation that some disaster had happened to Hambden, their capital and much-

[i] Rush, vol. vi. p. 285. Clarendon, vol. iii. p. 291.

dreaded enemy. One of the prisoners taken in the action, said, that he was confident Mr. Hambden was hurt: For he saw him, contrary to his usual custom, ride off the field, before the action was finished, his head hanging down, and his hands leaning upon his horse's neck. Next day, the news arrived, that he was shot in the shoulder with a brace of bullets, and the bone broken. Some days after, he died, in exquisite pain, of his wound; nor could his whole party, had their army met with a total overthrow, have been thrown into greater consternation. The king himself so highly valued him, that, either from generosity or policy, he intended to have sent him his own surgeon to assist at his cure.[k]

Death of Hambden.

Many were the virtues and talents of this eminent personage; and his valour during the war, had shone out with a lustre equal to that of the other accomplishments, by which he had ever been distinguished. Affability in conversation; temper, art, and eloquence in debate; penetration and discernment in counsel; industry, vigilance, and enterprize in action; all these praises are unanimously ascribed to him by historians of the most opposite parties. His virtue too and integrity, in all the duties of private life, are allowed to have been beyond exception: We must only be cautious, notwithstanding his generous zeal for liberty, not hastily to ascribe to him the praises of a good citizen. Through all the horrors of civil war, he sought the abolition of monarchy, and subversion of the constitution; an end, which, had it been attainable by peaceful measures, ought carefully to have been avoided by every lover of his country. But whether, in the pursuit of this violent enterprize, he was actuated by private ambition, or by honest prejudices, derived from the former exorbitant powers of royalty, it belongs not to an historian of this age, scarcely even to an intimate friend, positively to determine.[l]

Essex, discouraged by this event, dismayed by the total rout of Waller, was farther informed, that the queen, who landed in Burlington-bay, had arrived at Oxford, and had brought from the north a reinforcement of three thousand foot and fifteen hundred horse. Dislodging from Thame and Aylesbury, where he had hitherto lain, he thought proper to retreat nearer to London, and he

---

[k] Warwick's Memoirs, p. 241. Clarendon, vol. i. p. 264. [l] See note [DD] at the end of the volume.

showed to his friends his broken and disheartened forces, which a few months before he had led into the field in so flourishing a condition. The king, freed from this enemy, sent his army westward under prince Rupert; and, by their conjunction with the Cornish troops, a formidable force, for numbers as well as reputation and valour, was composed. That an enterprize, correspondent to men's expectations, might be undertaken, the prince resolved to lay siege to Bristol, the second town for riches and greatness in the kingdom. Nathaniel Fiennes, son of lord Say, he himself, as well as his father, a great parliamentary leader, was governor, and commanded a garrison of two thousand five hundred foot, and two regiments, one of horse, another of dragoons. The fortifications not being complete or regular, it was resolved by prince Rupert to storm the city; and next morning, with little other provisions, suitable to such a work, besides the courage of the troops, the assault began. The Cornish, in three divisions, attacked the west side, with a resolution which nothing could controul: But though the middle division had already mounted the wall, so great was the disadvantage of the ground, and so brave the defence of the garrison, that in the end the assailants were repulsed with a considerable loss both of officers and soldiers. On the prince's side, the assault was conducted with equal courage, and almost with equal loss, but with better success. One party, led by lord Grandison, was indeed beaten off, and the commander himself mortally wounded: Another, conducted by colonel Bellasis, met with a like fate: but Washington, with a less party, finding a place in the curtain weaker than the rest, broke in, and quickly made room for the horse to follow. By this irruption, however, nothing but the suburbs was yet gained: The entrance into the town was still more difficult: And by the loss already sustained, as well as by the prospect of farther danger, every one was extremely discouraged: When, to the great joy of the army, the city beat a parley. The garrison was allowed to march out with their arms and baggage, leaving their cannon, ammunition, and colours. For this instance of cowardice, Fiennes was afterwards tried by a court-martial, and condemned to lose his head; but the sentence was remitted by the general.[m]

Bristol taken. 25th July.

---

[m] Rushworth, vol. vi. p. 284. Clarendon, vol. iii. p. 293, 294, &c.

CHAPTER LVI

Great complaints were made of violences exercised on the garrison, contrary to the capitulation. An apology was made by the royalists, as if these were a retaliation for some violences, committed on their friends at the surrender of Reading. And under pretence of like retaliations, but really from the extreme animosity of the parties, were such irregularities continued during the whole course of the war."

The loss sustained by the royalists in the assault of Bristol, was considerable. Five hundred excellent soldiers perished. Among those of condition were Grandison, Slanning, Trevannion, and Moyle: Bellasis, Ashley, and Sir John Owen, were wounded: Yet was the success, upon the whole, so considerable as mightily raised the courage of the one party, and depressed that of the other. The king, to show that he was not intoxicated with good fortune, nor aspired to a total victory over the parliament, published a manifesto; in which he renewed the protestation, formerly taken, with great solemnity, at the head of his army, and expressed his firm intention of making peace upon the re-establishment of the constitution. Having joined the camp at Bristol, and sent prince Maurice with a detachment into Devonshire, he deliberated how to employ the remaining forces in an enterprize of moment. Some proposed, and seemingly with reason, to march directly to London; where every thing was in confusion, where the army of the parliament was baffled, weakened, and dismayed, and where, it was hoped, either by an insurrection of the citizens, by victory, or by treaty, a speedy end might be put to the civil disorders. But this undertaking, by reason of the great number and force of the London militia, was thought by many to be attended with considerable difficulties. Glocester, lying within twenty miles, presented an easier, yet a very important conquest. It was the only remaining garrison possessed by the parliament in those parts. Could that city be reduced, the king held the whole course of the Severn under his command; the rich and malcontent counties of the west, having lost all protection from their friends, might be forced to pay high contributions, as an atonement for their disaffection; an open communication could be preserved between Wales and these new

---

" Clarendon, ubi supra, p. 297.

conquests; and half of the kingdom, being entirely freed from the enemy, and thus united into one firm body, might be employed in re-establishing the king's authority throughout the remainder. These were the reasons for embracing that resolution; fatal, as it was ever esteemed, to the royal party.[o]

Siege of Glocester.

The governor of Glocester was one Massey, a soldier of fortune, who, before he engaged with the parliament, had offered his service to the king; and as he was free from the fumes of enthusiasm, by which most of the officers on that side were intoxicated, he would lend an ear, it was presumed, to proposals for accommodation. But Massey was resolute to preserve an entire fidelity to his masters; and though no enthusiast himself, he well knew how to employ to advantage that enthusiastic spirit so prevalent in his city and garrison. The summons to surrender allowed two hours for an answer: But before that time expired, there appeared before the king two citizens, with lean, pale, sharp, and dismal visages: Faces, so strange and uncouth, according to lord Clarendon; figures, so habited and accoutered; as at once moved the most severe countenance to mirth, and the most chearful heart to sadness: It seemed impossible, that such messengers could bring less than a defiance. The men, without any circumstance of duty or good manners, in a pert, shrill, undismayed accent, said, that they brought an answer from the godly city of Glocester: And extremely ready were they, according to the historian, to give insolent and seditious replies to any question; as if their business were chiefly, by provoking the king, to make him violate his own safe conduct. The answer from the city was in these words: "We the inhabitants, magistrates, officers and soldiers, within the garrison of Glocester, unto his Majesty's gracious message, return this humble answer: That we do keep this city, according to our oaths and allegiance, to and for the use of his majesty and his royal posterity: And do accordingly conceive ourselves wholly bound to obey the commands of his majesty signified by both houses of parliament: And are resolved by God's help to keep this city accordingly."[p] After these preliminaries, the siege was resolutely undertaken by the army, and as resolutely sustained by the citizens and garrison.

10th Aug.

---

[o] Whitlocke, p. 69. May, book iii. p. 91.   [p] Rush. vol. vi. p. 287. Clarendon, vol. iii. p. 315. May, book iii. p. 96.

CHAPTER LVI

When intelligence of the siege of Glocester arrived in London, the consternation among the inhabitants was as great as if the enemy were already at their gates. The rapid progress of the royalists threatened the parliament with immediate subjection: The factions and discontents, among themselves, in the city, and throughout the neighbouring counties, prognosticated some dangerous division or insurrection. Those parliamentary leaders, it must be owned, who had introduced such mighty innovations into the English constitution, and who had projected so much greater, had not engaged in an enterprize which exceeded their courage and capacity. Great vigour, from the beginning, as well as wisdom, they had displayed in all their counsels; and a furious, headstrong body, broken loose from the restraint of law, had hitherto been retained in subjection under their authority, and firmly united by zeal and passion, as by the most legal and established government. A small committee, on whom the two houses devolved their power, had directed all their military operations, and had preserved a secrecy in deliberation, and a promptitude in execution, beyond what the king, notwithstanding the advantages possessed by a single leader, had ever been able to attain. Sensible that no jealousy was by their partizans entertained against them, they had on all occasions exerted an authority much more despotic than the royalists, even during the pressing exigencies of war, could with patience endure in their sovereign. Whoever incurred their displeasure, or was exposed to their suspicions, was committed to prison, and prosecuted under the notion of delinquency: After all the old jails were full, many new ones were erected; and even the ships were crowded with the royalists, both gentry and clergy, who languished below decks, and perished in those unhealthy confinements: They imposed taxes, the heaviest, and of the most unusual nature, by an ordinance of the two houses: They voted a commission for sequestrations; and they seized, wherever they had power, the revenues of all the king's party:[q] And knowing that themselves, and all their adherents, were, by resisting the prince, exposed to the penalties of law, they resolved, by a severe admin-

---

[q] The king afterwards copied from this example; but, as the far greater part of the nobility and landed gentry were his friends, he reaped much less profit from this measure.

istration, to overcome these terrors, and to retain the people
in obedience, by penalties of a more immediate execution. In
the beginning of this summer, a combination, formed against
them in London, had obliged them to exert the plenitude of their
authority.

Edmond Waller, the first refiner of English versification, was a
member of the lower house; a man of considerable fortune, and
not more distinguished by his poetical genius than by his parliamentary talents, and by the politeness and elegance of his manners. As full of keen satire and invective in his eloquence, as of
tenderness and panegyric in his poetry, he caught the attention of
his hearers, and exerted the utmost boldness in blaming those
violent counsels, by which the commons were governed. Finding
all opposition within doors to be fruitless, he endeavoured to form
a party without, which might oblige the parliament to accept of
reasonable conditions, and restore peace to the nation. The
charms of his conversation, joined to his character of courage and
integrity had procured him the entire confidence of Northumberland, Conway, and every eminent person of either sex who
resided in London. They opened their breast to him without reserve, and expressed their disapprobation of the furious measures,
pursued by the commons, and their wishes that some expedient
could be found for stopping so impetuous a career. Tomkins,
Waller's brother-in-law, and Chaloner, the intimate friend of
Tomkins, had entertained like sentiments: And as the connexions
of these two gentlemen lay chiefly in the city, they informed
Waller, that the same abhorrence of war prevailed there, among all
men of reason and moderation. Upon reflection, it seemed not
impracticable that a combination might be formed between the
lords and citizens; and, by mutual concert, the illegal taxes be
refused, which the parliament, without the royal assent, imposed
on the people. While this affair was in agitation, and lists were
making of such as they conceived to be well-affected to their design; a servant of Tomkins, who had overheard their discourse,
immediately carried intelligence to Pym. Waller, Tomkins, and
Chaloner were seized, and tried by a court-martial.[r] They were all
three condemned, and the two latter executed on gibbets erected

[r] Rushworth, vol. vi. p. 326. Clarendon, vol. iii. p. 249. 250, &c.

before their own doors. A covenant, as a test, was taken[s] by the lords and commons, and imposed on their army, and on all who lived within their quarters. Besides resolving to amend and reform their lives, the covenanters there vow, that they will never lay down their arms so long as the papists, now in open war against the parliament, shall, by force of arms, be protected from justice; they express their abhorrence of the late conspiracy; and they promise to assist to the utmost the forces raised by both houses, against the forces levied by the king.[t]

Waller, as soon as imprisoned, sensible of the great danger into which he had fallen, was so seized with the dread of death, that all his former spirit deserted him; and he confessed whatever he knew, without sparing his most intimate friends, without regard to the confidence reposed in him, without distinguishing between the negligence of familiar conversation and the schemes of a regular conspiracy. With the most profound dissimulation, he counterfeited such remorse of conscience, that his execution was put off, out of mere christian compassion, till he might recover the use of his understanding. He invited visits from the ruling clergy of all sects; and while he expressed his own penitence, he received their devout exhortations with humility and reverence, as conveying clearer conviction and information than in his life he had ever before attained. Presents too, of which, as well as of flattery, these holy men were not insensible, were distributed among them; as a small retribution for their prayers and ghostly counsel. And by all these artifices, more than from any regard to the beauty of his genius, of which, during that time of furious cant and faction, small account would be made, he prevailed so far as to have his life spared, and a fine of ten thousand pounds accepted in lieu of it.[u]

The severity, exercised against the conspiracy or rather project of Waller, encreased the authority of the parliament, and seemed to ensure them against like attempts for the future. But by the progress of the king's arms, the defeat of Sir William Waller, the taking of Bristol, the siege of Glocester, a cry for peace was renewed, and with more violence than ever. Crowds of women, with

[s] 6th of June. [t] Rush. vol. vi. p. 325. Clarendon, vol. ii. p. 255. [u] Whitlocke, p. 66. Rushworth, vol. vi. p. 330. Clarendon, vol. iii. p. 253, 254, &c.

a petition for that purpose, flocked about the house, and were so clamorous and importunate, that orders were given for dispersing them; and some of the females were killed in the fray.[w] Bedford, Holland, and Conway, had deserted the parliament, and had gone to Oxford; Clare and Lovelace had followed them.[x] Northumberland had retired to his country-seat: Essex himself shewed extreme dissatisfaction, and exhorted the parliament to make peace.[y] The upper house sent down terms of accommodation, more moderate than had hitherto been insisted on. It even passed by a majority among the commons, that these proposals should be transmitted to the king. The zealots took the alarm. A petition against peace was framed in the city, and presented by Pennington, the factious mayor. Multitudes attended him, and renewed all the former menaces against the moderate party.[z] The pulpits thundered, and rumours were spread of twenty thousand Irish, who had landed, and were to cut the throat of every protestant.[a] The majority was again turned to the other side; and all thoughts of pacification being dropped, every preparation was made for resistance, and for the immediate relief of Glocester, on which the parliament was sensible, all their hopes of success in the war did so much depend.

Massey, resolute to make a vigorous defence, and having under his command a city and garrison ambitious of the crown of martyrdom, had hitherto maintained the siege with courage and abilities, and had much retarded the advances of the king's army. By continual sallies, he infested them in their trenches, and gained sudden advantages over them: By disputing every inch of ground, he repressed the vigour and alacrity of their courage, elated by former successes. His garrison, however, was reduced to the last extremity; and he failed not, from time to time, to inform the parliament, that, unless speedily relieved, he should be necessitated, from the extreme want of provisions and ammunition, to open his gates to the enemy.

The parliament, in order to repair their broken condition, and put themselves in a posture of defence, now exerted to the utmost their power and authority. They voted, that an army should be

[w] Rushworth, vol. vi. p. 357.   [x] Whitlocke, p. 67.   [y] Rush. vol. vi. p. 290.
[z] Idem, ibid. p. 356.   [a] Clarendon, vol. iii. p. 320. Rush. vol. vi. p. 588.

levied under Sir William Waller, whom, notwithstanding his misfortunes, they loaded with extraordinary caresses. Having associated in their cause the counties of Hertford, Essex, Cambridge, Norfolk, Suffolk, Lincoln, and Huntingdon, they gave the earl of Manchester a commission to be general of the association, and appointed an army to be levied under his command. But, above all, they were intent that Essex's army on which their whole fortune depended, should be put in a condition of marching against the king. They excited afresh their preachers to furious declamations against the royal cause. They even employed the expedient of pressing, though abolished by a late law, for which they had strenuously contended.[b] And they engaged the city to send four regiments of its militia to the relief of Glocester. All shops, meanwhile, were ordered to be shut; and every man expected, with the utmost anxiety, the event of that important enterprize.[c]

Essex, carrying with him a well-appointed army of 14,000 men, took the road of Bedford and Leicester; and, though inferior in cavalry, yet, by the mere force of conduct and discipline, he passed over those open champaign countries, and defended himself from the enemy's horse, who had advanced to meet him, and who infested him during his whole march. As he approached to Glocester, the king was obliged to raise the siege, and open the way for Essex to enter that city. The necessities of the garrison were extreme. One barrel of powder was their whole stock of ammunition remaining; and their other provisions were in the same proportion. Essex had brought with him military stores; and the neighbouring country abundantly supplied him with victuals of every kind. The inhabitants had carefully concealed all provisions from the king's army, and, pretending to be quite exhausted, had reserved their stores for that cause, which they so much favoured.[d]

The chief difficulty still remained. Essex dreaded a battle with the king's army, on account of its great superiority in cavalry; and he resolved to return, if possible, without running that hazard. He lay five days at Tewkesbury, which was his first stage after leaving Glocester; and he feigned, by some preparations, to point towards Worcester. By a forced march during the night, he reached Cirencester, and obtained the double advantage of passing un-

[b] Rushworth, vol. vi. p. 292.   [c] Idem, ibid.   [d] Clarendon, vol. iii. p. 344.

molested an open country, and of surprising a convoy of provisions, which lay in that town.*' Without delay, he proceeded
towards London; but, when he reached Newbury, he was surprised to find, that the king, by hasty marches, had arrived before
him, and was already possessed of the place.

20th Sept.
Battle of
Newbury.
An action was now unavoidable; and Essex prepared for it with
presence of mind, and not without military conduct. On both sides,
the battle was fought with desperate valour and a steady bravery.
Essex's horse were several times broken by the king's, but his infantry maintained themselves in firm array; and, besides giving a
continued fire, they presented an invincible rampart of pikes
against the furious shock of prince Rupert, and those gallant
troops of gentry, of which the royal cavalry was chiefly composed.
The militia of London especially, though utterly unacquainted
with action, though drawn but a few days before from their ordinary occupations, yet having learned all military exercises, and
being animated with unconquerable zeal for the cause, in which
they were engaged, equalled, on this occasion, what could be expected from the most veteran forces. While the armies were engaged with the utmost ardour, night put an end to the action, and
left the victory undecided. Next morning, Essex proceeded on his
march; and though his rear was once put in some disorder by an
incursion of the king's horse, he reached London in safety, and
received applause for his conduct and success in the whole enterprize. The king followed him on his march; and having taken
possession of Reading, after the earl left it, he there established a
garrison; and straitened, by that means, London and the quarters
of the enemy.*f*

In the battle of Newbury, on the part of the king, besides the
earls of Sunderland and Carnarvon, two noblemen of promising
hopes, was unfortunately slain, to the regret of every lover of
ingenuity and virtue throughout the kingdom, Lucius Cary viscount Falkland, secretary of state. Before assembling the present
parliament, this man, devoted to the pursuits of learning, and to
the society of all the polite and elegant, had enjoyed himself in
every pleasure, which a fine genius, a generous disposition, and an
opulent fortune could afford. Called into public life, he stood

*' Rush. vol. vi. p. 292.   *f* Rush. vol. vi. p. 293. Clarendon, vol. iii. p. 347.

foremost in all attacks on the high prerogatives of the crown; and displayed that masculine eloquence, and undaunted love of liberty, which, from his intimate acquaintance with the sublime spirits of antiquity, he had greedily imbibed. When civil convulsions proceeded to extremities, and it became requisite for him to chuse his side; he tempered the ardour of his zeal, and embraced the defence of those limited powers, which remained to monarchy, and which he deemed necessary for the support of the English constitution. Still anxious, however, for his country, he seems to have dreaded the too prosperous success of his own party as much as of the enemy; and, among his intimate friends, often after a deep silence, and frequent sighs, he would, with a sad accent, re-iterate the word, *Peace.* In excuse for the too free exposing of his person, which seemed unsuitable in a secretary of state, he alledged, that it became him to be more active than other men in all hazardous enterprizes, lest his impatience for peace might bear the imputation of cowardice or pusillanimity. From the commencement of the war, his natural chearfulness and vivacity became clouded; and even his usual attention to dress, required by his birth and station, gave way to a negligence, which was easily observable. On the morning of the battle in which he fell, he had shown some care of adorning his person; and gave for a reason, that the enemy should not find his body in any slovenly, indecent situation. "I am weary," subjoined he, "of the times, and foresee much misery to my country; but believe, that I shall be out of it ere night."[g] This excellent person was but thirty four years of age, when a period was thus put to his life.

The loss sustained on both sides in the battle of Newbury, and the advanced season, obliged the armies to retire into winter-quarters.

In the north, during this summer, the great interest and popularity of the earl, now created marquis of Newcastle, had raised a considerable force for the king; and great hopes of success were entertained from that quarter. There appeared, however, in opposition to him, two men, on whom the event of the war finally depended, and who began about this time to be remarked for their valour and military conduct. These were Sir Thomas Fairfax, son

Actions in the north.

[g] Whitlocke, p. 70. Clarendon, vol. iii. p. 350, 351, &c.

of the lord of that name, and Oliver Cromwel. The former gained a considerable advantage at Wakefield[h] over a detachment of royalists, and took general Goring prisoner: The latter obtained a victory at Gainsborow[i] over a party commanded by the gallant Cavendish, who perished in the action. But both these defeats of the royalists were more than sufficiently compensated by the total rout of lord Fairfax at Atherton moor,[k] and the dispersion of his army. After this victory, Newcastle, with an army of 15,000 men, sat down before Hull. Hotham was no longer governor of this place. That gentleman and his son, partly from a jealousy entertained of lord Fairfax, partly repenting of their engagements against the king, had entered into a correspondence with Newcastle, and had expressed an intention of delivering Hull into his hands. But their conspiracy being detected, they were arrested and sent prisoners to London; where, without any regard to their former services, they fell, both of them, victims to the severity of the parliament.[l]

Newcastle, having carried on the attack of Hull for some time, was beat off by a sally of the garrison,[m] and suffered so much, that he thought proper to raise the siege. About the same time, Manchester, who advanced from the eastern associated countries, having joined Cromwel and young Fairfax, obtained a considerable victory over the royalists at Horn Castle; where the two officers last mentioned gained renown by their conduct and gallantry. And though fortune had thus balanced her favours, the king's party still remained much superior in those parts of England; and had it not been for the garrison of Hull, which kept Yorkshire in awe, a conjunction of the northern forces with the army in the south might have been made, and had probably enabled the king, instead of entering on the unfortunate, perhaps imprudent, enterprize of Glocester, to march directly to London, and put an end to the war.[n]

While the military enterprizes were carried on with vigour in England, and the event became every day more doubtful, both parties cast their eye towards the neighbouring kingdoms, and sought assistance for the finishing of that enterprize, in which

[h] 21st of May.　[i] 31st of July.　[k] 30th of June.　[l] Rush. vol. vi. p. 275. [m] 12th of October.　[n] Warwick, p. 261. Walker, p. 278.

CHAPTER LVI

their own forces experienced such furious opposition. The parliament had recourse to Scotland; the king, to Ireland.

When the Scottish covenanters obtained that end, for which they so earnestly contended, the establishment of presbyterian discipline in their own country, they were not satisfied, but indulged still an ardent passion for propagating, by all methods, that mode of religion in the neighbouring kingdoms. Having flattered themselves, in the fervor of their zeal, that, by supernatural assistances, they should be enabled to carry their triumphant covenant to the gates of Rome itself, it behoved them first to render it prevalent in England, which already showed so great a disposition to receive it. Even in the articles of pacification, they expressed a desire of uniformity in worship with England; and the king, employing general expressions, had approved of this inclination, as pious and laudable. No sooner was there an appearance of a rupture, than the English parliament, in order to allure that nation into a close confederacy, openly declared their wishes of ecclesiastical reformation, and of imitating the example of their northern brethren.[o] When war was actually commenced, the same artifices were used; and the Scots beheld, with the utmost impatience, a scene of action, of which they could not deem themselves indifferent spectators. Should the king, they said, be able, by force of arms, to prevail over the parliament of England, and re-establish his authority in that powerful kingdom, he will undoubtedly retract all those concessions, which, with so many circumstances of violence and indignity, the Scots have extorted from him. Besides a sense of his own interests, and a regard to royal power, which has been entirely annihilated in this country; his very passion for prelacy and for religious ceremonies must lead him to invade a church, which he has ever been taught to regard as antichristian and unlawful. Let us but consider who the persons are that compose the factions, now so furiously engaged in arms. Does not the parliament consist of those very men, who have ever opposed all war with Scotland, who have punished the authors of our oppressions, who have obtained us the redress of every grievance, and who, with many honourable expressions, have conferred on us an ample reward for our brotherly assistance? And is not the court

[o] Rush. vol. vi. p. 390. Clarendon, vol. iii. p. 68.

full of papists, prelates, malignants; all of them zealous enemies to our religious model, and resolute to sacrifice their lives for their idolatrous establishments? Not to mention our own necessary security; can we better express our gratitude to heaven for that pure light, with which we are, above all nations, so eminently distinguished, than by conveying the same divine knowledge to our unhappy neighbours, who are wading through a sea of blood in order to attain it? These were in Scotland the topics of every conversation: With these doctrines the pulpits echoed: And the famous curse of Meroz, that curse so solemnly denounced and re-iterated against neutrality and moderation, resounded from all quarters.[p]

The parliament of England had ever invited the Scots, from the commencement of the civil dissentions, to interpose their mediation, which, they knew, would be so little favourable to the king: And the king, for that very reason, had ever endeavoured, with the least offensive expressions, to decline it.[q] Early this spring, the earl of Loudon, the chancellor, with other commissioners, and attended by Henderson, a popular and intriguing preacher, was sent to the king at Oxford, and renewed the offer of mediation; but with the same success as before. The commissioners were also empowered to press the king on the article of religion, and to recommend to him the Scottish model of ecclesiastic worship and discipline. This was touching Charles in a very tender point: His honour, his conscience, as well as his interest, he believed to be intimately concerned in supporting prelacy and the liturgy.[r] He begged the commissioners, therefore, to remain satisfied with the concessions which he had made to Scotland; and having modelled their own church according to their own principles, to leave their neighbours in the like liberty, and not to intermeddle with affairs, of which they could not be supposed competent judges.[s]

The divines of Oxford, secure, as they imagined, of a victory, by means of their authorities from church-history, their quotations from the fathers, and their spiritual arguments, desired a confer-

[p] Curse ye Meroz, said the angel of the Lord; curse ye bitterly the inhabitants thereof: Because they came not to the help of the Lord, to the help of the Lord against the mighty. Judges, chap. v. ver. 23.   [q] Rush. vol. vi. p. 398.   [r] See note [EE] at the end of the volume.   [s] Rush. vol. vi. p. 462.

ence with Henderson, and undertook, by dint of reasoning, to convert that great apostle of the north: But Henderson, who had ever regarded as impious the least doubt with regard to his own principles, and who knew of a much better way to reduce opponents than by employing any theological topics, absolutely refused all disputation or controversy. The English divines went away, full of admiration at the blind assurance and bigotted prejudices of the man: He, on his part, was moved with equal wonder at their obstinate attachment to such palpable error and delusions.

By the concessions, which the king had granted to Scotland, it became necessary for him to summon a parliament once in three years; and in June of the subsequent year, was fixed the period for the meeting of that assembly. Before that time elapsed, Charles flattered himself, that he should be able, by some decisive advantage, to reduce the English parliament to a reasonable submission, and might then expect with security the meeting of a Scottish parliament. Though earnestly solicited by Loudon to summon presently that great council of the nation, he absolutely refused to give authority to men, who had already excited such dangerous commotions, and who showed still the same disposition to resist and invade his authority. The commissioners, therefore, not being able to prevail in any of their demands, desired the king's passport for London, where they purposed to confer with the English parliament;[t] and being likewise denied this request, they returned with extreme dissatisfaction to Edinburgh.

The office of conservators of the peace was newly erected in Scotland, in order to maintain the confederacy between the two kingdoms; and these, instigated by the clergy, were resolved, since they could not obtain the king's consent, to summon, in his name, but by their own authority, a convention of states; and to bereave their sovereign of this article, the only one which remained, of his prerogative. Under colour of providing for national peace, endangered by the neighbourhood of English armies, was a convention called;[u] an assembly, which, though it meets with less solemnity, has the same authority as a parliament, in raising money and levying forces. Hamilton and his brother the earl of Laneric, who had been sent into Scotland in order to oppose these

[t] Rush. vol. vi. p. 406. [u] 22d of June.

measures, wanted either authority or sincerity; and passively yielded to the torrent. The general assembly of the church met at the same time with the convention; and exercising an authority almost absolute over the whole civil power, made every political consideration yield to their theological zeal and prejudices.

The English parliament was, at that time, fallen into great distress, by the progress of the royal arms; and they gladly sent to Edinburgh commissioners, with ample power, to treat of a nearer union and confederacy with the Scottish nation. The persons employed were the earl of Rutland, Sir William Armyne, Sir Henry Vane the younger, Thomas Hatcher, and Henry Darley, attended by Marshal and Nye, two clergymen of signal authority.[w] In this negociation, the man chiefly trusted was Vane, who, in eloquence, address, capacity, as well as in art and dissimulation, was not surpassed by any one, even during that age, so famous for active *Solemn* talents. By his persuasion was framed at Edinburgh, that SOLEMN *league* LEAGUE AND COVENANT; which effaced all former protestations *and* and vows taken in both kingdoms; and long maintained its credit *covenant.* and authority. In this covenant, the subscribers, besides engaging mutually to defend each other against all opponents, bound themselves to endeavour, without respect of persons, the extirpation of popery and prelacy, superstition, heresy, schism, and profaneness; to maintain the rights and privileges of parliaments, together with the king's authority; and to discover and bring to justice all incendiaries and malignants.[x]

The subscribers of the covenant vowed also to preserve the reformed religion established in the church of Scotland; but by the artifice of Vane no declaration more explicit was made with regard to England and Ireland, than that these kingdoms should be reformed, according to the word of God and the example of the purest churches. The Scottish zealots, when prelacy was abjured, deemed this expression quite free from ambiguity, and regarded their own model as the only one, which corresponded, in any degree, to such a description: But that able politician had other views; and while he employed his great talents in over-reaching the presbyterians, and secretly laughed at their simplicity, he had

[w] Whitlocke, p. 73. Rush. vol. vi. p. 466. Clarendon, vol. iii. p. 300.
[x] Rush. vol. vi. p. 478. Clarendon, vol. iii. p. 373.

blindly devoted himself to the maintenance of systems, still more absurd and more dangerous.

In the English parliament there remained some members, who, though they had been induced, either by private ambition or by zeal for civil liberty, to concur with the majority, still retained an attachment to the hierarchy and to the ancient modes of worship. But in the present danger, which threatened their cause, all scruples were laid aside; and the covenant, by whose means alone they could expect to obtain so considerable a reinforcement as the accession of the Scottish nation, was received without opposition. *Sept. 17.* The parliament therefore, having first subscribed it themselves, ordered it to be received by all who lived under their authority.

Great were the rejoicings among the Scots, that they should be the happy instruments of extending their mode of religion, and dissipating that profound darkness, in which the neighbouring nations were involved. The general assembly applauded this glorious imitation of the piety displayed by their ancestors, who, they said, in three different applications, during the reign of Elizabeth, had endeavoured to engage the English, by persuasion, to lay aside the use of the surplice, tippet, and corner-cap.[y] The convention too, in the height of their zeal, ordered every one to swear to this covenant, under the penalty of confiscation; beside what farther punishment it should please the ensuing parliament to inflict on the refusers, as enemies to God, to the king, and to the kingdom. And being determined, that the sword should carry conviction to all refractory minds, they prepared themselves, with great vigilance and activity, for their military enterprizes. By means of a *Arming* hundred thousand pounds, which they received from England; by *of the* the hopes of good pay and warm quarters; not to mention men's *Scots.* favourable disposition towards the cause; they soon completed their levies. And having added, to their other forces, the troops which they had recalled from Ireland, they were ready, about the end of the year, to enter England, under the command of their old general, the earl of Leven, with an army of above twenty thousand men.[z]

The king, foreseeing this tempest, which was gathering upon him, endeavoured to secure himself by every expedient; and he

[y] Rushworth, vol. vi. p. 388.   [z] Clarendon, vol. iii. p. 383.

cast his eye towards Ireland, in hopes that this kingdom, from which his cause had already received so much prejudice, might at length contribute somewhat towards his protection and security.

State of Ireland. After the commencement of the Irish insurrection, the English parliament, though they undertook the suppression of it, had ever been too much engaged, either in military projects or expeditions at home, to take any effectual step towards finishing that enterprize. They had entered indeed into a contract with the Scots, for sending over an army of ten thousand men into Ireland; and in order to engage that nation in this undertaking, beside giving a promise of pay, they agreed to put Caricfergus into their hands, and to invest their general with an authority quite independent of the English government. These troops, so long as they were allowed to remain, were useful, by diverting the force of the Irish rebels, and protecting in the north the small remnants of the British planters. But except this contract with the Scottish nation, all the other measures of the parliament either were hitherto absolutely insignificant, or tended rather to the prejudice of the protestant cause in Ireland. By continuing their violent persecution, and still more violent menaces against priests and papists, they confirmed the Irish catholics in their rebellion, and cut off all hopes of indulgence and toleration. By disposing beforehand of all the Irish forfeitures to subscribers or adventurers, they rendered all men of property desperate, and seemed to threaten a total extirpation of the natives.[a] And while they thus infused zeal and animosity into the enemy, no measure was pursued, which could tend to support or encourage the protestants, now reduced to the last extremities.

So great is the ascendant, which, from a long course of successes, the English has acquired over the Irish nation, that though the latter, when they receive military discipline among foreigners, are not surpassed by any troops, they have never, in their own country, been able to make any vigorous effort for the defence or recovery of their liberties. In many rencounters, the English, un-

[a] A thousand acres in Ulster were given to every one that subscribed 200 pounds, in Connaught to the subscribers of 350, in Munster for 450, in Leinster for 600.

CHAPTER LVI

der lord More, Sir William St. Leger, Sir Frederic Hamilton, and others, had, though under great disadvantages of situation and numbers, put the Irish to rout, and returned in triumph to Dublin. The rebels raised the siege of Tredah, after an obstinate defence made by the garrison.[b] Ormond had obtained two complete victories, at Kilrush and Ross; and had brought relief to all the forts, which were besieged or blockaded in different parts of the kingdom.[c] But notwithstanding these successes, even the most common necessaries of life were wanting to the victorious armies. The Irish, in their wild rage against the British planters, had laid waste the whole kingdom, and were themselves totally unfit, from their habitual sloth and ignorance, to raise any convenience of human life. During the course of six months, no supplies had come from England; except the fourth part of one small vessel's lading. Dublin, to save itself from starving, had been obliged to send the greater part of its inhabitants to England. The army had little ammunition, scarcely exceeding forty barrels of gun-powder; not even shoes or cloaths; and for want of food the soldiers had been obliged to eat their own horses. And though the distress of the Irish was not much inferior;[d] besides that they were more hardened against such extremities, it was but a melancholy reflection, that the two nations, while they continued their furious animosities, should make desolate that fertile island, which might serve to the subsistence and happiness of both.

The justices and council of Ireland had been engaged chiefly by the interest and authority of Ormond, to fall into an entire dependence on the king. Parsons, Temple, Loftus, and Meredith, who favoured the opposite party, had been removed; and Charles had supplied their place by others, better affected to his service. A committee of the English house of commons, which had been sent over to Ireland, in order to conduct the affairs of that kingdom, had been excluded the council, in obedience to orders transmitted from the king.[e] And these were reasons sufficient, besides the great difficulties, under which they themselves laboured, why the parliament was unwilling to send supplies to an army, which

[b] Rushworth, vol. vi. p. 506.   [c] Idem, ibid. p. 512.   [d] Idem, ibid. p. 555.
[e] Idem, ibid. p. 530. Clarendon, vol. iii. p. 167.

though engaged in a cause much favoured by them, was commanded by their declared enemies. They even intercepted some small succours sent thither by the king.

The king, as he had neither money, arms, ammunition, nor provisions to spare from his own urgent wants, resolved to embrace an expedient, which might at once relieve the necessities of the Irish protestants, and contribute to the advancement of his affairs in England. A truce with the rebels, he thought, would enable his subjects in Ireland to provide for their own support, and would procure him the assistance of the army against the English parliament. But as a treaty with a people, so odious for their barbarities, and still more for their religion, might be represented in invidious colours, and renew all those calumnies, with which he had been loaded; it was necessary to proceed with great caution in conducting that measure. A remonstrance from the army was made to the Irish council, representing their intolerable necessities, and craving permission to leave the kingdom: And if that were refused, *We must have recourse,* they said, *to that first and primary law, with which God has endowed all men; we mean the law of nature, which teaches every creature to preserve itself.*[f] Memorials both to the king and parliament were transmitted by the justices and council, in which their wants and dangers are strongly set forth;[g] and though the general expressions in these memorials might perhaps be suspected of exaggeration, yet from the particular facts mentioned, from the confession of the English parliament itself;[h] and from the very nature of things, it is apparent that the Irish protestants were reduced to great extremities;[i] and it became prudent in the king, if not absolutely necessary, to embrace some expedient, which might secure them, for a time, from the ruin and misery, with which they were threatened.

Accordingly, the king gave orders[k] to Ormond and the justices to conclude, for a year, a cessation of arms with the council of Kilkenny, by whom the Irish were governed, and to leave both

[f] Rushworth, vol. vi. p. 537.   [g] Idem, ibid. p. 538.   [h] Rush. vol. vi. p. 540.
[i] See farther Carte's Ormond, vol. iii. No. 113, 127, 128, 129, 134, 136, 141; 144, 149, 158, 159. All these papers put it past doubt, that the necessities of the English army in Ireland were extreme. See farther, Rush. vol. vi. p. 537. and Dugdale, p. 853, 854.   [k] 7th September, See Rush. vol. vi. p. 537, 544, 547.

CHAPTER LVI

sides in possession of their present advantages. The parliament, whose business it was to find fault with every measure adopted by the opposite party, and who would not lose so fair an opportunity of reproaching the king with his favour to the Irish papists, exclaimed loudly against this cessation. Among other reasons, they insisted upon the divine vengeance, which England might justly dread for tolerating antichristian idolatry, on pretence of civil contracts and political agreements.[l] Religion, though every day employed as the engine of their own ambitious purposes, was supposed too sacred to be yielded up to the temporal interests or safety of kingdoms.

After the cessation, there was little necessity, as well as no means of subsisting the army in Ireland. The king ordered Ormond, who was entirely devoted to him, to send over considerable bodies of it to England. Most of them continued in his service: But a small part having imbibed in Ireland a strong animosity against the catholics, and hearing the king's party universally reproached with popery, soon after deserted to the parliament.

Some Irish catholics came over with these troops, and joined the royal army, where they continued the same cruelties and disorders, to which they had been accustomed.[m] The parliament voted, that no quarter, in any action, should ever be given them: But prince Rupert, by making some reprizals, soon repressed this inhumanity.[n]

[l] Idem, ibid, p. 557.   [m] Whitlocke, p. 78, 103.   [n] Rush. vol. vi. p. 680, 783.

LVII

Invasion of the Scots –
Battle of Marston-moor – Battle of
Cropredy-bridge – Essex's forces disarmed –
Second battle of Newbury – Rise and
character of the Independents – Self-denying
ordinance – Fairfax, Cromwell – Treaty
of Uxbridge – Execution of Laud

🌀 🌀 🌀

1644. THE KING HAD HITHERTO, during the course of the war, obtained many advantages over the parliament, and had raised himself, from that low condition, into which he had first fallen, to be nearly upon an equal footing with his adversaries. Yorkshire, and all the northern counties, were reduced by the marquess of Newcastle; and, excepting Hull, the parliament was master of no garrison in these quarters. In the west, Plymouth alone, having been in vain besieged by prince Maurice, resisted the king's authority: And had it not been for the disappointment in the enterprize of Gloucester, the royal garrisons had reached, without interruption, from one end of the kingdom to the other; and had occupied a greater extent of ground, than those of the parliament. Many of the royalists flattered themselves, that the same vigorous spirit, which had elevated them to the present height of power, would still favour their progress, and obtain them a final victory over their enemies: But those who judged more soundly, observed, that, besides the accession of the whole Scottish nation to the side

428

CHAPTER LVII

of the parliament; the very principle, on which the royal successes had been founded, was every day acquired, more and more, by the opposite party. The king's troops, full of gentry and nobility, had exerted a valour superior to their enemies, and had hitherto been successful in almost every rencounter: But in proportion as the whole nation became warlike, by the continuance of civil discords, this advantage was more equally shared; and superior numbers, it was expected, must at length obtain the victory. The king's troops also, ill paid, and destitute of every necessary, could not possibly be retained in equal discipline with the parliamentary forces, to whom all supplies were furnished from unexhausted stores and treasures.[o] The severity of manners, so much affected by these zealous religionists, assisted their military institutions; and the rigid inflexibility of character, by which the austere reformers of church and state were distinguished, enabled the parliamentary chiefs to restrain their soldiers within stricter rules and more exact order. And while the king's officers indulged themselves even in greater licences, than those to which, during times of peace, they had been accustomed, they were apt, both to neglect their military duty, and to set a pernicious example of disorder, to the soldiers under their command.

At the commencement of the civil war, all Englishmen, who served abroad, were invited over, and treated with extraordinary respect: And most of them, being descended of good families, and by reason of their absence, unacquainted with the new principles, which depressed the dignity of the crown, had inlisted under the royal standard. But it is observable, that, though the military profession requires great genius, and long experience, in the principal commanders, all its subordinate duties may be discharged by ordinary talents, and from superficial practice. Citizens and country-gentlemen soon became excellent officers; and the generals of greatest fame and capacity happened, all of them, to spring up on the side of the parliament. The courtiers and great nobility, in the other party, checked the growth of any extraordinary genius among the subordinate officers; and every man there, as in regular established government, was confined to the station, in which his birth had placed him.

[o] Rush. vol. vi. p. 560.

The king, that he might make preparations, during winter, for the ensuing campaign, summoned to Oxford all the members of either house, who adhered to his interests; and endeavoured to avail himself of the name of parliament, so passionately cherished by the English nation.[p] The house of peers was pretty full; and besides the nobility, employed in different parts of the kingdom, it contained twice as many members as commonly voted at Westminster. The house of commons consisted of about 140; which amounted not to above half of the other house of commons.[q]

So extremely light had government hitherto lain upon the people, that the very name of *excise* was unknown to them; and among the other evils arising from these domestic wars, was the introduction of that impost into England. The parliament at Westminster having voted an excise on beer, wine, and other commodities; those at Oxford imitated the example, and conferred that revenue on the king. And in order to enable him the better to recruit his army, they granted him the sum of 100,000 pounds, to be levied by way of loan upon the subject. The king circulated privy seals, countersigned by the speakers of both houses, requiring the loan of particular sums, from such persons as lived within his quarters.[r] Neither party had as yet got above the pedantry of reproaching their antagonists with these illegal measures.

The Westminster parliament passed a whimsical ordinance, commanding all the inhabitants of London and the neighbourhood, to retrench a meal a week, and to pay the value of it for the support of the public cause.[s] It is easily imagined, that, provided the money were paid, they troubled themselves but little about the execution of their ordinance.

Such was the king's situation, that, in order to restore peace to the nation, he had no occasion to demand any other terms, than the restoring of the laws and constitution; the replacing him in the same rights which had ever been enjoyed by his predecessors; and the re-establishing, on its ancient basis, the whole frame of government, civil as well as ecclesiastical. And that he might facilitate an end, seemingly so desirable, he offered to employ means equally popular, an universal act of oblivion, and a toleration or in-

[p] Rush. vol. vi. p. 559. [q] Idem. p. 566, 574, 575. [r] Rush. vol. vi. p. 590.
[s] Dugdale, p. 119. Rush. vol. vi. p. 748.

CHAPTER LVII

dulgence to tender consciences. Nothing therefore could contribute more to his interests, than every discourse of peace, and every discussion of the conditions, upon which that blessing could be obtained. For this reason, he solicited a treaty, on all occasions, and desired a conference and mutual examination of pretensions, even when he entertained no hopes, that any conclusion could possibly result from it.

For like reasons, the parliament prudently avoided, as much as possible, all advances towards negociation, and were cautious not to expose too easily to censure those high terms, which their apprehensions or their ambition made them previously demand of the king. Though their partizans were blinded with the thickest veil of religious prejudices, they dreaded to bring their pretensions to the test, or lay them open before the whole nation. In opposition to the sacred authority of the laws, to the venerable precedents of many ages, the popular leaders were ashamed to plead nothing but fears and jealousies, which were not avowed by the constitution, and for which, neither the personal character of Charles, so full of virtue, nor his situation, so deprived of all independent authority, seemed to afford any reasonable foundation. Grievances which had been fully redressed; powers, either legal or illegal, which had been entirely renounced; it seemed unpopular, and invidious, and ungrateful, any farther to insist on.

The king, that he might abate the universal veneration, paid to the name of parliament, had issued a declaration, in which he set forth all the tumults, by which himself and his partizans in both houses had been driven from London; and he thence inferred, that the assembly at Westminster was no longer a free parliament, and, till its liberty were restored, was intitled to no authority. As this declaration was an obstacle to all treaty, some contrivance seemed requisite, in order to elude it.

A letter was written, in the foregoing spring, to the earl of Essex, and subscribed by the prince, the duke of York, and forty-three noblemen.[f] They there exhort him to be an instrument of restoring peace, and to promote that happy end with those, by whom he was employed. Essex, though much disgusted with the parliament, though apprehensive of the extremities to which they

[f] Clarendon, vol. iii. p. 442. Rush. vol. vi. p. 566. Whitlocke, p. 77.

were driving, though desirous of any reasonable accommodation; yet was still more resolute to preserve an honourable fidelity to the trust reposed in him. He replied, that, as the paper sent him neither contained any address to the two houses of parliament, nor any acknowledgement of their authority, he could not communicate it to them. Like proposals had been reiterated by the king, during the ensuing campaign, and still met with a like answer from Essex.[u]

In order to make a new trial for a treaty, the king, this spring, sent another letter directed to the lords and commons of parliament assembled at Westminster: But as he also mentioned, in the letter, the lords and commons of parliament assembled at Oxford, and declared, that his scope and intention was to make provision, that all the members of both houses might securely meet in a full and free assembly; the parliament, perceiving the conclusion implied, refused all treaty upon such terms.[w] And the king, who knew what small hopes there were of accommodation, would not abandon the pretensions, which he had assumed; nor acknowledge the two houses, more expressly, for a free parliament.

This winter the famous Pym died; a man as much hated by one party, as respected by the other. At London, he was considered as the victim to national liberty, who had abridged his life by incessant labours for the interests of his country:[x] At Oxford, he was believed to have been struck with an uncommon disease, and to have been consumed with vermin; as a mark of divine vengeance, for his multiplied crimes and treasons. He had been so little studious of improving his private fortune in those civil wars, of which he had been one principal author, that the parliament thought themselves obliged, from gratitude, to pay the debts which he had contracted.[y] We now return to the military operations, which, during the winter, were carried on with vigour in several places, notwithstanding the severity of the season.

The forces, brought from Ireland, were landed at Mostyne in North-Wales; and being put under the command of lord Biron, they besieged and took the castles of Hawarden, Beeston, Acton, and Deddington-house.[z] No place in Cheshire or the neigh-

[u] Clarendon, vol. iii. p. 444. Rush. vol. vi. p. 569, 570. Whitlocke, p. 94. [w] Clarendon, vol. iii. p. 449. Whitlocke, p. 79. [x] Ibid. p. 66. [y] Journ. 13th of February, 1643. [z] Rush. vol. vi. p. 299.

CHAPTER LVII

bourhood now adhered to the parliament, except Nantwich: And to this town Biron laid siege during the depth of winter. Sir Thomas Fairfax, alarmed at so considerable a progress of the royalists, assembled an army of 4000 men in Yorkshire, and having joined Sir William Brereton, was approaching to the camp of the enemy. Biron and his soldiers, elated with successes obtained in Ireland, had entertained the most profound contempt for the parliamentary forces; a disposition, which, if confined to the army, may be regarded as a good presage of victory; but if it extend to the general, is the most probable forerunner of a defeat. Fairfax suddenly attacked the camp of the royalists. The swelling of the river by a thaw divided one part of the army from the other. That part, *25th Jan.* exposed to Fairfax, being beaten from their post, retired into the church of Acton, and were all taken prisoners: The other retreated with precipitation.[a] And thus was dissipated or rendered useless that body of forces, which had been drawn from Ireland; and the parliamentary party revived in those north-west counties of England.

The invasion from Scotland was attended with consequences of *Invasion* much greater importance. The Scots, having summoned in vain *from* the town of Newcastle, which was fortified by the vigilance of Sir *Scotland.* Thomas Glenham, passed the Tyne; and faced the marquess of Newcastle, who lay at Durham with an army of 14000 men.[b] After some military operations, in which that nobleman reduced the enemy to difficulties for forage and provisions, he received intel- *22d Feb.* ligence of a great disaster, which had befallen his forces in Yorkshire. Colonel Bellasis, whom he had left with a considerable body of troops, was totally routed at Selby, by Sir Thomas Fairfax, who *11th* had returned from Cheshire, with his victorious forces.[c] Afraid of *April.* being inclosed between two armies, Newcastle retreated; and Leven having joined Lord Fairfax, they sat down before York, to which the army of the loyalists had retired. But as the parliamentary and Scottish forces were not numerous enough to invest so large a town, divided by a river, they contented themselves with incommoding it by a loose blockade; and affairs remained, for some time, in suspense between these opposite armies.[d]

[a] Ibid. p. 301.   [b] Rush. vol. vi. p. 615.   [c] Idem, ibid. p. 618.   [d] Idem, ibid. p. 620.

During this winter and spring, other parts of the kingdom had also been infested with war. Hopton, having assembled an army of 14000 men, endeavoured to break into Sussex, Kent, and the southern association, which seemed well disposed to receive him. Waller fell upon him at Cherington, and gave him a defeat[e] of considerable importance. In another quarter, siege being laid to Newark by the parliamentary forces, prince Rupert prepared himself for relieving a town of such consequence, which alone preserved the communication open between the king's southern and northern quarters.[f] With a small force, but that animated by his active courage, he broke through the enemy, relieved the town, and totally dissipated that army of the parliament.[g]

But though fortune seemed to have divided her favours between the parties, the king found himself, in the main, a considerable loser by this winter-campaign; and he prognosticated a still worse event from the ensuing summer. The preparations of the parliament were great, and much exceeded the slender resources, of which he was possessed. In the eastern association, they levied fourteen thousand men, under the earl of Manchester, seconded by Cromwell.[h] An army of ten thousand men, under Essex; another of nearly the same force under Waller, were assembled in the neighbourhood of London. The former was destined to oppose the king: The latter was appointed to march into the west, where prince Maurice, with a small army which went continually to decay, was spending his time in vain before Lyme, an inconsiderable town upon the sea-coast. The utmost efforts of the king could not raise above ten thousand men at Oxford; and on their sword chiefly, during the campaign, were these to depend for subsistance.

The queen, terrified with the dangers, which every way environed her, and afraid of being enclosed in Oxford, in the middle of the kingdom, fled to Exeter, where she hoped to be delivered unmolested of the child, with which she was now pregnant, and whence she had the means of an easy escape into France, if pressed by the forces of the enemy. She knew the implacable hatred, which the parliament, on account of her religion and her credit with the king, had all along borne her. Last summer, the commons had sent

---

[e] 29th of March.   [f] Rush. vol. vi. p. 306.   [g] 21st of March.   [h] Rush. vol. vi. p. 621.

CHAPTER LVII

up to the peers an impeachment of high treason against her;
because, in his utmost distresses, she had assisted her husband with
arms and ammunition, which she had bought in Holland.[i] And
had she fallen into their hands, neither her sex, she knew, nor high
station, could protect her against insults at least, if not danger,
from those haughty republicans, who so little affected to conduct
themselves by the maxims of gallantry and politeness.

From the beginning of these dissensions, the parliament, it is
remarkable, had, in all things, assumed an extreme ascendant over
their sovereign, and had displayed a violence and arrogated an
authority, which, on his side, would not have been compatible,
either with his temper or his situation. While he spoke perpetually
of pardoning all *rebels;* they talked of nothing but the punishment
of *delinquents* and *malignants:* While he offered a toleration and
indulgence to tender consciences; they threatened the utter extirpation of prelacy. To his professions of lenity, they opposed
declarations of rigour: And the more the ancient tenor of the laws
inculcated a respectful subordination to the crown, the more careful were they, by their lofty pretensions, to cover that defect, under
which they laboured.

Their great advantages in the north seemed to second their
ambition, and finally to promise them success in their un-
warrantable enterprizes. Manchester, having taken Lincoln, had
united his army to that of Leven and Fairfax; and York was now
closely besieged by their combined forces. That town, though vigorously defended by Newcastle, was reduced to extremity; and the
parliamentary generals, after enduring great losses and fatigues,
flattered themselves, that all their labours would at last be crowned
by this important conquest. On a sudden, they were alarmed by the
approach of prince Rupert. This gallant commander, having vigorously exerted himself in Lancashire and Cheshire, had collected
a considerable army; and joining Sir Charles Lucas, who commanded Newcastle's horse, hastened to the relief of York with an
army of 20,000 men. The Scottish and parliamentary generals
raised the siege, and drawing up on Marston-moor, purposed to
give battle to the royalists. Prince Rupert approached the town by
another quarter, and interposing the river Ouse between him and

[i] Rush. vol. vi. p. 321.

the enemy, safely joined his forces to those of Newcastle. The marquess endeavoured to persuade him, that, having so success-fully effected his purpose, he ought to be content with the present advantages, and leave the enemy, now much diminished by their losses, and discouraged by their ill success, to dissolve by those mutual dissensions, which had begun to take place among them.[k] The prince, whose martial disposition was not sufficiently tem-pered with prudence, nor softened by complaisance, pretending

2d July. positive orders from the king, without deigning to consult with Newcastle, whose merits and services deserved better treatment, immediately issued orders for battle, and led out the army to

Battle of Marston-moor Marston-moor.[l] This action was obstinately disputed between the most numerous armies, that were engaged during the course of these wars; nor were the forces on each side much different in number. Fifty thousand British troops were led to mutual slaugh-ter; and the victory seemed long undecided between them. Prince Rupert, who commanded the right wing of the royalists, was op-posed to Cromwell,[m] who conducted the choice troops of the par-liament, enured to danger under that determined leader, ani-mated by zeal, and confirmed by the most rigid discipline. After a sharp combat, the cavalry of the royalists gave way; and such of the infantry, as stood next them, were likewise borne down, and put to flight. Newcastle's regiment alone, resolute to conquer or to per-ish, obstinately kept their ground, and maintained, by their dead bodies, the same order, in which they had at first been ranged. In the other wing, Sir Thomas Fairfax and Colonel Lambert, with some troops, broke through the royalists; and, transported by the ardour of pursuit, soon reached their victorious friends, engaged also in pursuit of the enemy. But after that tempest was past, Lucas, who commanded the royalists in this wing, restoring order to his broken forces, made a furious attack on the parliamentary cavalry, threw them into disorder, pushed them upon their own infantry, and put that whole wing to rout. When ready to seize on their carriages and baggage, he perceived Cromwell, who was now returned from pursuit of the other wing. Both sides were not a little surprised to find, that they must again renew the combat for

[k] Life of the D. of Newcastle, p. 40.   [l] Clarendon, vol. v. p. 506.   [m] Rush. part 3. vol. ii. p. 633.

that victory, which each of them thought they had already obtained. The front of the battle was now exactly counter-changed; and each army occupied the ground which had been possessed by the enemy at the beginning of the day. This second battle was equally furious and desperate with the first: But after the utmost efforts of courage by both parties, victory wholly turned to the side of the parliament. The prince's train of artillery was taken; and his whole army pushed off the field of battle.[n]

This event was in itself a mighty blow to the king; but proved more fatal in its consequences. The marquess of Newcastle was entirely lost to the royal cause. That nobleman, the ornament of the court and of his order, had been engaged, contrary to the natural bent of his disposition, into these military operations, merely by a high sense of honour and a personal regard to his master. The dangers of war were disregarded by his valour; but its fatigues were oppressive to his natural indolence. Munificent and generous in his expence; polite and elegant in his taste; courteous and humane in his behaviour; he brought a great accession of friends and of credit to the party, which he embraced. But amidst all the hurry of action, his inclinations were secretly drawn to the soft arts of peace, in which he took delight; and the charms of poetry, music, and conversation often stole him from his rougher occupations. He chose Sir William Davenant, an ingenious poet, for his lieutenant-general: The other persons, in whom he placed confidence, were more the instruments of his refined pleasures, than qualified for the business which they undertook: And the severity and application, requisite to the support of discipline, were qualities, in which he was entirely wanting.[o]

When prince Rupert, contrary to his advice, resolved on this battle, and issued all orders without communicating his intentions to him; he took the field, but, he said, merely as a volunteer; and, except by his personal courage, which shone out with lustre, he had no share in the action. Enraged to find, that all his successful labours were rendered abortive by one act of fatal temerity, terrified with the prospect of renewing his pains and fatigue, he resolved no longer to maintain the few resources which remained to

[n] Rush. vol. vi. p. 632. Whitlocke, p. 89.   [o] Clarendon, vol. v. p. 507, 508. See Warwick.

a desperate cause, and thought, that the same regard to honour, which had at first called him to arms, now required him to abandon a party, where he met with such unworthy treatment. Next morning early, he sent word to the prince, that he was instantly to leave the kingdom; and without delay, he went to Scarborough, where he found a vessel, which carried him beyond sea. During the ensuing years, till the restoration, he lived abroad in great necessity, and saw with indifference his opulent fortune sequestered by those who assumed the government of England. He disdained, by submission or composition, to show obeisance to their usurped authority; and the least favourable censors of his merit allowed, that the fidelity and services of a whole life had sufficiently atoned for one rash action, into which his passion had betrayed him.[p]

16th
July.

Prince Rupert, with equal precipitation, drew off the remains of his army, and retired into Lancashire. Glenham, in a few days, was obliged to surrender York; and he marched out his garrison with all the honours of war.[q] Lord Fairfax, remaining in the city, established his government in that whole county, and sent a thousand horse into Lancashire, to join with the parliamentary forces in that quarter, and attend the motions of prince Rupert: The Scottish army marched northwards, in order to join the earl of Calender, who was advancing with ten thousand additional forces;[r] and to reduce the town of Newcastle, which they took by storm: The earl of Manchester, with Cromwel, to whom the fame of this great victory was chiefly ascribed, and who was wounded in the action, returned to the eastern association, in order to recruit his army.[s]

While these events passed in the north, the king's affairs in the south were conducted with more success and greater abilities. Ruthven, a Scotchman, who had been created earl of Brentford, acted, under the king, as general.

The parliament soon compleated their two armies commanded by Essex and Waller. The great zeal of the city facilitated this undertaking. Many speeches were made to the citizens, by the parliamentary leaders, in order to excite their ardour. Hollis, in particular, exhorted them not to spare, on this important occasion,

---

[p] Clarendon, vol. v. p. 511.   [q] Rush. vol. vi. p. 638.   [r] Whitlocke, p. 88.
[s] Rush. vol. vi. p. 641.

either their purses, their persons, or their prayers;[t] and, in general, it must be confessed, they were sufficiently liberal in all these contributions. The two generals had orders to march with their combined armies towards Oxford; and, if the king retired into that city, to lay siege to it, and by one enterprize put a period to the war. The king, leaving a numerous garrison in Oxford, passed with dexterity between the two armies, which had taken Abingdon, and had enclosed him on both sides.[u] He marched towards Worcester; and Waller received orders from Essex to follow him and watch his motions; while he himself marched into the west, in quest of prince Maurice. Waller had approached within two miles of the royal camp, and was only separated from it by the Severn, when he received intelligence, that the king was advanced to Beudly, and had directed his course towards Shrewsbury. In order to prevent him, Waller presently dislodged, and hastened by quick marches to that town, while the king, suddenly returning upon his own footsteps, reached Oxford; and having reinforced his army from that garrison, now in his turn marched out in quest of Waller. The two armies faced each other at Cropredy-bridge near Banbury; but the Charwell ran between them. Next day, the king decamped and marched towards Daventry. Waller ordered a considerable detachment to pass the bridge, with an intention of falling on the rear of the royalists. He was repulsed, routed, and pursued with considerable loss.[w] Stunned and disheartened with this blow, his army decayed and melted away by desertion; and the king thought he might safely leave it, and march westward against Essex. That general, having obliged prince Maurice to raise the siege of Lyme, having taken Weymouth and Taunton, advanced still in his conquests, and met with no equal opposition. The king followed him, and having re-inforced his army from all quarters, appeared in the field with an army superior to the enemy. Essex, retreating into Cornwall, informed the parliament of his danger, and desired them to send an army, which might fall on the king's rear. General Middleton received a commission to execute that service; but came too late. Essex's army, cooped up in a narrow corner at Lestithiel, deprived of all forage and provisions, and seeing no prospect of

Battle of Cropredy-bridge. 29th June.

[t] Rush. vol. vi. p. 662.   [u] 3d of June.   [w] Rush. vol. vi. p. 676. Clarendon, vol. v. p. 497. Sir Ed. Walker, p. 31.

succour, was reduced to the last extremity. The king pressed them on one side; prince Maurice on another; Sir Richard Granville on a third. Essex, Robarts, and some of the principal officers, escaped in a boat to Plymouth: Balfour with his horse passed the king's out-posts, in a thick mist, and got safely to the garrison of his own party. The foot under Skippon were obliged to surrender their arms, artillery, baggage and ammunition; and being conducted to the parliament's quarters, were dismissed. By this advantage, which was much boasted of, the king, besides the honour of the enterprize, obtained what he stood extremely in need of: The parliament, having preserved the men, lost what they could easily repair.[x]

1st Sept.

Essex's forces disarmed.

No sooner did this intelligence reach London, than the committee of the two kingdoms voted thanks to Essex for his fidelity, courage, and conduct; and this method of proceeding, no less politic than magnanimous, was preserved by the parliament throughout the whole course of the war. Equally indulgent to their friends and rigorous to their enemies, they employed, with success, these two powerful engines of reward and punishment, in confirmation of their authority.

That the king might have less reason to exult in the advantages, which he had obtained in the west, the parliament opposed to him very numerous forces. Having armed anew Essex's subdued, but not disheartened troops, they ordered Manchester and Cromwell to march with their recruited forces from the eastern association; and joining their armies to those of Waller and Middleton, as well as of Essex, offer battle to the king. Charles chose his post at Newbury, where the parliamentary armies, under the Earl of Manchester, attacked him with great vigour; and that town was a second time the scene of the bloody animosities of the English. Essex's soldiers, exhorting one another to repair their broken honour, and revenge the disgrace of Lestithiel, made an impetuous assault on the royalists; and having recovered some of their cannon, lost in Cornwall, could not forbear embracing them with tears of joy. Though the king's troops defended themselves with valour, they were overpowered by numbers; and the night came very season-

Second battle of Newbury.

27th Oct.

---

[x] Rush. vol. vi. p. 699, &c. Whitlocke, p. 98. Clarendon, vol. v. p. 524, 525. Sir Edw. Walker, p. 69, 70, &c.

ably to their relief, and prevented a total overthrow. Charles, leaving his baggage and cannon in Dennington-castle, near Newbury, forthwith retreated to Wallingford, and thence to Oxford. There, prince Rupert and the earl of Northampton joined him, with considerable bodies of cavalry. Strengthened by this reinforcement, he ventured to advance towards the enemy, now employed before Dennington-castle.[y] Essex, detained by sickness, had not joined the army, since his misfortune in Cornwall. Manchester, who commanded, though his forces were much superior to those of the king, declined an engagement, and rejected Cromwell's advice, who earnestly pressed him not to neglect so favourable an opportunity of finishing the war. The king's army, by bringing off their cannon from Dennington-castle, in the face of the enemy, seemed to have sufficiently repaired the honour which they had lost at Newbury; and Charles, having the satisfaction to excite, between Manchester and Cromwell, equal animosities with those which formerly took place between Essex and Waller;[z] distributed his army into winter-quarters.

9th Nov.

Those contests among the parliamentary generals, which had distributed their military operations, were renewed in London during the winter-season; and each being supported by his own faction, their mutual reproaches and accusations agitated the whole city and parliament. There had long prevailed, in that party, a secret distinction, which, though the dread of the king's power had hitherto suppressed it, yet, in proportion as the hopes of success became nearer and more immediate, began to discover itself, with high contest and animosity. The Independents, who had, at first, taken shelter and concealed themselves under the wings of the Presbyterians, now evidently appeared a distinct party, and betrayed very different views and pretensions. We must here endeavour to explain the genius of this party, and of its leaders, who henceforth occupy the scene of action.

23d Nov.

During those times, when the enthusiastic spirit met with such honour and encouragement, and was the immediate means of distinction and preferment; it was impossible to set bounds to these holy fervours, or confine, within any natural limits, what was directed towards an infinite and supernatural object. Every man,

Rise and character of the Independents.

[y] Rush. vol. vi. p. 721, &c.   [z] Rush. vol. vii. p. 1.

as prompted by the warmth of his temper, excited by emulation, or supported by his habits of hypocrisy, endeavoured to distinguish himself beyond his fellows, and to arrive at a higher pitch of saintship and perfection. In proportion to its degree of fanaticism, each sect became dangerous and destructive; and as the independents went a note higher than the presbyterians, they could less be restrained within any bounds of temper and moderation. From this distinction, as from a first principle, were derived, by a necessary consequence, all the other differences of these two sects.

The independents rejected all ecclesiastical establishments, and would admit of no spiritual courts, no government among pastors, no interposition of the magistrate in religious concerns, no fixed encouragement annexed to any system of doctrines or opinions. According to their principles, each congregation, united voluntarily and by spiritual ties, composed, within itself, a separate church, and exercised a jurisdiction, but one destitute of temporal sanctions, over its own pastor and its own members. The election alone of the congregation was sufficient to bestow the sacerdotal character; and as all essential distinction was denied between the laity and the clergy, no ceremony, no institution, no vocation, no imposition of hands, was, as in all other churches, supposed requisite to convey a right to holy orders. The enthusiasm of the presbyterians led them to reject the authority of prelates, to throw off the restraint of liturgies, to retrench ceremonies, to limit the riches and authority of the priestly office: The fanaticism of the independents, exalted to a higher pitch, abolished ecclesiastical government, disdained creeds and systems, neglected every ceremony, and confounded all ranks and orders. The soldier, the merchant, the mechanic, indulging the fervors of zeal, and guided by the illapses of the spirit, resigned himself to an inward and superior direction, and was consecrated, in a manner, by an immediate intercourse and communication with heaven.

The catholics, pretending to an infallible guide, had justified, upon that principle, their doctrine and practice of persecution: The presbyterians, imagining that such clear and certain tenets, as they themselves adopted, could be rejected only from a criminal and pertinacious obstinacy, had hitherto gratified, to the full, their bigotted zeal, in a like doctrine and practice: The independents, from the extremity of the same zeal, were led into the milder

CHAPTER LVII

principles of toleration. Their mind, set afloat in the wide sea of inspiration, could confine itself within no certain limits; and the same variations, in which an enthusiast indulged himself, he was apt, by a natural train of thinking, to permit in others. Of all christian sects, this was the first, which, during its prosperity, as well as its adversity, always adopted the principle of toleration; and, it is remarkable, that so reasonable a doctrine owed its origin, not to reasoning, but to the height of extravagance and fanaticism.

Popery and prelacy alone, whose genius seemed to tend towards superstition, were treated by the independents with rigour. The doctrines too of fate or destiny, were deemed by them essential to all religion. In these rigid opinions, the whole sectaries, amidst all their other differences, unanimously concurred.

The political system of the independents kept pace with their religions. Not content with confining, to very narrow limits, the power of the crown, and reducing the king to the rank of first magistrate, which was the project of the presbyterians; this sect, more ardent in the pursuit of liberty, aspired to a total abolition of the monarchy, and even of the aristocracy; and projected an entire equality of rank and order, in a republic, quite free and independent. In consequence of this scheme, they were declared enemies to all proposals for peace, except on such terms as, they knew, it was impossible to obtain; and they adhered to that maxim, which is, in the main, prudent and political, that whoever draws the sword against his sovereign, should throw away the scabbard. By terrifying others with the fear of vengeance from the offended prince, they had engaged greater numbers into the opposition against peace, than had adopted their other principles with regard to government and religion. And the great success, which had already attended the arms of the parliament, and the greater, which was soon expected, confirmed them still further in this obstinacy.

Sir Harry Vane, Oliver Cromwell, Nathaniel Fiennes, and Oliver St. John, the solicitor-general, were regarded as the leaders of the independents. The earl of Essex, disgusted with a war, of which he began to foresee the pernicious consequences, adhered to the presbyterians, and promoted every reasonable plan of accommodation. The earl of Northumberland, fond of his rank and dignity, regarded with horror a scheme, which, if it took place, would confound himself and his family with the lowest in the kingdom. The earls of Warwic, and Denbigh, Sir Philip Stapleton, Sir William Waller, Hollis, Massey, Whitlocke, Mainard, Glyn, had embraced the same sentiments. In the parliament, a considerable majority, and a much greater in the nation, were attached to the presbyterian party; and it was only by cunning and deceit at first, and afterwards by military violence, that the independents could entertain any hopes of success.

The earl of Manchester, provoked at the impeachment, which the king had lodged against him, had long forwarded the war with alacrity; but, being a man of humanity and good principles, the view of public calamities, and the prospect of a total subversion of government, began to moderate his ardor, and inclined him to promote peace on any safe or honourable terms. He was even suspected, in the field, not to have pushed to the utmost against the king the advantages, obtained by the arms of the parliament; and Cromwell, in the public debates, revived the accusation, that this nobleman had wilfully neglected at Dennington-castle a favourable opportunity of finishing the war by a total defeat of the royalists. "I showed him evidently," said Cromwell, "how this success might be obtained; and only desired leave, with my own brigade of horse, to charge the king's army in their retreat; leaving it in the earl's choice, if he thought proper, to remain neuter with the rest of his forces: But, notwithstanding my importunity, he positively refused his consent; and gave no other reason but that, if we met with a defeat, there was an end of our pretensions: We should all be rebels and traitors, and be executed and forfeited by law?"[a]

Manchester, by way of recrimination, informed the parliament, that, at another time, Cromwell, having proposed some scheme, to which it seemed improbable the parliament would agree, he insisted and said, *My lord, if you will stick firm to honest men, you shall find yourself at the head of an army, which shall give law both to king and parliament.* "This discourse," continued Manchester, "made the greater impression on me, because I knew the lieutenant-general to be a man of very deep designs; and he has even ventured to tell me, that it never would be well with England till I were Mr. Montague, and there were ne'er a lord or peer in the kingdom."[b] So full

[a] Clarendon, vol. v. p. 561.   [b] Idem, ibid. p. 562.

CHAPTER LVII

was Cromwell of these republican projects, that, notwithstanding his habits of profound dissimulation, he could not so carefully guard his expressions, but that sometimes his favourite notions would escape him.

These violent dissensions brought matters to extremity, and pushed the independents to the execution of their designs. The present generals, they thought, were more desirous of protracting than finishing the war; and having entertained a scheme for preserving still some balance in the constitution, they were afraid of entirely subduing the king, and reducing him to a condition, where he should not be intitled to ask any concessions. A new model alone of the army could bring compleat victory to the parliament, and free the nation from those calamities, under which it laboured. But how to effect this project was the difficulty. The authority, as well as merits, of Essex was very great with the parliament. Not only he had served them all along with the most exact and scrupulous honour: It was, in some measure, owing to his popularity, that they had ever been enabled to levy an army or make head against the royal cause. Manchester, Warwic, and the other commanders had likewise great credit with the public; nor were there any hopes of prevailing over them, but by laying the plan of an oblique and artificial attack, which would conceal the real purpose of their antagonists. The Scots and Scottish commissioners, jealous of the progress of the independents, were a new obstacle; which, without the utmost art and subtlety, it would be difficult to surmount.[c] The methods, by which this intrigue was conducted, are so singular, and show so fully the genius of the age, that we shall give a detail of them, as they are delivered by lord Clarendon.[d]

A fast, on the last Wednesday of every month, had been ordered by the parliament at the beginning of these commotions; and their preachers, on that day, were careful to keep alive, by their vehement declamations, the popular prejudices entertained against the king, against prelacy, and against popery. The king, that he might combat the parliament with their own weapons, appointed likewise a monthly fast, when the people should be instructed in the duties of loyalty and of submission to the higher

[c] Clarendon, vol. v. p. 562.   [d] Idem, ibid. p. 565.

powers; and he chose the second Friday of every month for the devotion of the royalists.[e] It was now proposed and carried in parliament, by the independents, that a new and more solemn fast should be voted, when they should implore the divine assistance for extricating them from those perplexities, in which they were at present involved. On that day, the preachers, after many political prayers, took care to treat of the reigning divisions in the parliament, and ascribed them entirely to the selfish ends, pursued by the members. In the hands of those members, they said, are lodged all the considerable commands of the army, all the lucrative offices in the civil administration: And while the nation is falling every day into poverty, and groans under an insupportable load of taxes; these men multiply possession on possession, and will, in a little time, be masters of all the wealth of the kingdom. That such persons, who fatten on the calamities of their country, will ever embrace any effectual measure for bringing them to a period, or ensuring final success to the war, cannot reasonably be expected. Lingering expedients alone will be pursued: And operations in the field concurring, in the same pernicious end, with deliberations in the cabinet; civil commotions will, for ever, be perpetuated in the nation. After exaggerating these disorders, the ministers returned to their prayers; and besought the Lord, that he would take his own work into his own hand; and if the instruments, whom he had hitherto employed, were not worthy to bring to a conclusion so glorious a design, that he would inspire others more fit, who might perfect what was begun, and by establishing true religion, put a speedy period to the public miseries.

On the day subsequent to these devout animadversions, when the parliament met, a new spirit appeared in the looks of many. Sir Henry Vane told the commons, that, if ever God appeared to them, it was in the ordinances of yesterday: That, as he was credibly informed by many, who had been present in different congregations, the same lamentations and discourses, which the godly preachers had made before them, had been heard in other churches: That so remarkable a concurrence could proceed only from the immediate operation of the Holy Spirit: That he therefore intreated them, in vindication of their own honour, in consid-

[e] Rushworth, vol. vi. p. 364.

CHAPTER LVII

eration of their duty to God and their country, to lay aside all private ends, and renounce every office, attended with profit or advantage: That the absence of so many members, occupied in different employments, had rendered the house extremely thin, and diminished the authority of their determinations: And that he could not forbear, for his own part, accusing himself as one who enjoyed a gainful office, that of treasurer of the navy; and though he was possessed of it before the civil commotions, and owed it not to the favour of the parliament, yet was he ready to resign it, and to sacrifice, to the welfare of his country, every consideration of private interest and advantage.

Cromwel next acted his part, and commended the preachers for having dealt with them plainly and impartially, and told them of their errors, of which they were so unwilling to be informed. Though they dwelt on many things, he said, on which he had never before reflected: yet, upon revolving them, he could not but confess, that, till there were a perfect reformation in these particulars, nothing which they undertook could possibly prosper. The parliament, no doubt, continued he, had done wisely on the commencement of the war, in engaging several of its members in the most dangerous parts of it; and thereby satisfying the nation, that they intended to share all hazards with the meanest of the people. But affairs are now changed. During the progress of military operations, there have arisen, in the parliamentary armies, many excellent officers, who are qualified for higher commands than they are now possessed of. And though it becomes not men, engaged in such a cause, *to put trust in the arm of flesh,* yet he could assure them, that their troops contained generals, fit to command in any enterprize in Christendom. The army indeed, he was sorry to say it, did not correspond, by its discipline, to the merit of the officers; nor were there any hopes, till the present vices and disorders, which prevail among the soldiers, were repressed by a new model, that their forces would ever be attended with signal success in any undertaking.

In opposition to this reasoning of the independents, many of the presbyterians showed the inconvenience and danger of the projected alteration. Whitlocke, in particular, a man of honour, who loved his country, though, in every change of government, he always adhered to the ruling power, said, that, besides the ingratitude of discarding, and that by fraud and artifice, so many noble persons, to whom the parliament had hitherto owed its chief support; they would find it extremely difficult to supply the place of men, now formed by experience to command and authority: That the rank alone, possessed by such as were members of either house, prevented envy, retained the army in obedience, and gave weight to military orders: That greater confidence might safely be reposed in men of family and fortune, than in mere adventurers, who would be apt to entertain separate views from those which were embraced by the persons, who employed them: That no maxim of policy was more undisputed, than the necessity of preserving an inseparable connexion between the civil and military powers, and of retaining the latter in strict subordination to the former: That the Greeks and Romans, the wisest and most passionate lovers of liberty, had ever entrusted to their senators the command of armies, and had maintained an unconquerable jealousy of all mercenary forces: And that such men alone, whose interests were involved in those of the public, and who possessed a vote in the civil deliberations, would sufficiently respect the authority of parliament, and never could be tempted to turn the sword against those, by whom it was committed to them.[f]

Self-denying ordinance. Notwithstanding these reasonings, a committee was chosen to frame what was called the *Self-denying ordinance,* by which the members of both houses were excluded from all civil and military employments, except a few offices which were specified. This ordinance was the subject of great debate, and, for a long time, rent the parliament and city into factions. But, at last, by the prevalence of envy with some; with others, of false modesty; with a great many, of the republican and independent views; it passed the house of commons, and was sent to the upper house. The peers, though the scheme was, in part, levelled against their order; though all of them were, at bottom, extremely averse to it; though they even ventured once to reject it; yet possessed so little authority, that they durst not persevere in opposing the resolution of the commons; and they thought it better policy, by an unlimited compliance, to ward off that ruin, which they saw approaching.[g] The ordinance, therefore, having passed both houses, Essex, Warwic, Manchester,

[f] Whitlocke, p. 114, 115. Rush. vol. vii. p. 6. [g] Rush. vol. vii. p. 8, 15.

CHAPTER LVII

Denbigh, Waller, Brereton, and many others, resigned their commands, and received the thanks of parliament for their good services. A pension of ten thousand pounds a year was settled on Essex.

It was agreed to recruit the army to 22,000 men; and Sir Thomas Fairfax was appointed general.[h] It is remarkable, that his commission did not run, like that of Essex, in the name of the king and parliament, but in that of the parliament alone: And the article concerning the safety of the king's person was omitted. So much had animosities encreased between the parties.[i] Cromwel, being a member of the lower house, should have been discarded with the others; but this impartiality would have disappointed all the views of those, who had introduced the self-denying ordinance. He was saved by a subtilty, and by that political craft, in which he was so eminent. At the time, when the other officers resigned their commissions, care was taken, that he should be sent with a body of horse, to relieve Taunton, besieged by the royalists. His absence being remarked, orders were dispatched for his immediate attendance in parliament; and the new general was directed to employ some other officer in that service. A ready compliance was feigned; and the very day was named, on which, it was averred, he would take his place in the house. But Fairfax, having appointed a rendezvous of the army, wrote to the parliament, and desired leave to retain, for some days, lieutenant-general Cromwel, whose advice, he said, would be useful, in supplying the place of those officers, who had resigned. Shortly after, he begged, with much earnestness, that they would allow Cromwel to serve that campaign.[k] And thus the independents, though the minority, prevailed by art and cunning over the presbyterians, and bestowed the whole military authority, in appearance, upon Fairfax; in reality, upon Cromwel.

Fairfax was a person equally eminent for courage and for humanity; and though strongly infected with prejudices or principles, derived from religious and party zeal, he seems never, in the course of his public conduct, to have been diverted, by private interest or ambition, from adhering strictly to these principles.

1645.

Fairfax.

[h] Whitlocke, p. 118. Rush. vol. vii. p. 7.   [i] Whitlocke, p. 133.
[k] Clarendon, vol. v. p. 629, 630. Whitlocke, p. 141.

Sincere in his professions; disinterested in his views; open in his conduct; he had formed one of the most shining characters of the age; had not the extreme narrowness of his genius, in every thing but war, and his embarrassed and confused elocution, on every occasion but when he gave orders, diminished the lustre of his merit, and rendered the part, which he acted, even when vested with the supreme command, but secondary and subordinate.

Cromwel. Cromwel, by whose sagacity and insinuation Fairfax was entirely governed, is one of the most eminent and most singular personages, that occurs in history: The strokes of his character are as open and strongly marked, as the schemes of his conduct were, during the time, dark and impenetrable. His extensive capacity enabled him to form the most enlarged projects: His enterprizing genius was not dismayed with the boldest and most dangerous. Carried, by his natural temper, to magnanimity, to grandeur, and to an imperious and domineering policy; he yet knew, when necessary, to employ the most profound dissimulation, the most oblique and refined artifice, the semblance of the greatest moderation and simplicity. A friend to justice, though his public conduct was one continued violation of it; devoted to religion, though he perpetually employed it as the instrument of his ambition; he was engaged in crimes from the prospect of sovereign power, a temptation which is, in general, irresistible to human nature. And by using well that authority, which he had attained by fraud and violence, he has lessened, if not overpowered, our detestation of his enormities, by our admiration of his success and of his genius.

Treaty of Uxbridge. During this important transaction of the self-denying ordinance, the negociations for peace were likewise carried on, though with small hopes of success. The king having sent two messages, one from Evesham,[l] another from Tavistoke,[m] desiring a treaty, the parliament dispatched commissioners to Oxford, with proposals, as high as if they had obtained a compleat victory.[n] The advantages gained during the campaign, and the great distresses of the royalists, had much elevated their hopes; and they were resolved to repose no trust in men, enflamed with the highest animosity against them, and who, were they possessed of power, were fully

[l] 4th of July, 1644. [m] 8th of Sept. 1644. [n] Dugdale, p. 737. Rush. vol. vi. p. 850.

CHAPTER LVII

authorized by law, to punish all their opponents as rebels and traitors.

The king, when he considered the proposals and the disposition of the parliament, could not expect any accommodation, and had no prospect but of war, or of total submission and subjection: Yet, in order to satisfy his own party, who were impatient for peace, he agreed to send the duke of Richmond and earl of Southampton, with an answer to the proposals of the parliament, and at the same time to desire a treaty upon their mutual demands and pretensions.[o] It now became necessary for him to retract his former declaration, that the two houses at Westminster were not a free parliament; and accordingly, he was induced, though with great reluctance, to give them, in his answer, the appellation of the parliament of England.[p] But it appeared afterwards, by a letter, which he wrote to the queen, and of which a copy was taken at Naseby, that he secretly entered an explanatory protest in his council-book; and he pretended, that, though he had *called* them the parliament, he had not thereby *acknowledged* them for such.[q] This subtlety, which has been frequently objected to Charles, is the most noted of those very few instances, from which the enemies of this prince have endeavoured to load him with the imputation of insincerity; and have inferred, that the parliament could repose no confidence in his professions and declarations, not even in his laws and statutes. There is, however, it must be confessed, a difference universally avowed between simply giving to men the appellation, which they assume, and the formal acknowledgement of their title to it; nor is any thing more common and familiar in all public transactions.

The time and place of treaty being settled, sixteen commissioners from the king met at Uxbridge with twelve authorized by   *30th Jan.*

---

[o] Whitlocke, p. 110.   [p] Whitlocke, p. 111. Dugdale, p. 748.   [q] His words are, "As for my calling those at London a parliament, I shall refer thee to Digby for particular satisfaction; this in general: If there had been but two besides myself, of my opinion, I had not done it; and the argument, that prevailed with me was, that the calling did no ways acknowledge them to be a parliament: upon which condition and construction I did it; and no otherwise: and accordingly it is registered in the council books, with the council's unanimous approbation." The king's cabinet opened. Rush, vol. vi. p. 943.

the parliament, attended by the Scottish commissioners. It was agreed, that the Scottish and parliamentary commissioners should give in their demands with regard to three important articles, *religion,* the *militia,* and *Ireland;* and that these should be successively discussed in conference with the king's commissioners.[r] It was soon found impracticable to come to any agreement with regard to any of these articles.

In the summer 1643, while the negociations were carried on with Scotland, the parliament had summoned an assembly at Westminster, consisting of 121 divines and 30 laymen, celebrated in their party for piety and learning. By their advice, alterations were made in the thirty-nine articles, or in the metaphysical doctrines of the church; and, what was of greater importance, the liturgy was entirely abolished, and, in its stead, a new directory for worship was established; by which, suitably to the spirit of the puritans, the utmost liberty, both in praying and preaching, was indulged to the public teachers. By the solemn league and covenant, episcopacy was abjured, as destructive of all true piety; and a national engagement, attended with every circumstance, that could render a promise sacred and obligatory, was entered into with the Scots, never to suffer its re-admission. All these measures showed little spirit of accommodation in the parliament; and the king's commissioners were not surprized to find the establishment of presbytery and the directory positively demanded, together with the subscription of the covenant, both by the king and kingdom.[s]

[r] Whitlocke, p. 121. Dugdale, p. 758.   [s] Such love of contradiction prevailed in the parliament, that they had converted Christmas, which, with the churchmen, was a great festival, into a solemn fast and humiliation; "In order," as they said, "that it might call to remembrance our sins and the sins of our forefathers, who, pretending to celebrate the memory of Christ, have turned this feast into an extreme forgetfulness of him, by giving liberty to carnal and sensual delights." Rush. vol. vi. p. 817. It is remarkable, that, as the parliament abolished all holy days, and severely prohibited all amusement on the sabbath; and even burned, by the hands of the hangman, the king's book of sports; the nation found, that there was no time left for relaxation or diversion. Upon application, therefore, of the servants and apprentices, the parliament appointed the second Tuesday of every month for play and recreation. *Rush.* vol. vii. p. 460. *Whitlocke,* p. 247. But these institutions, they found great difficulty to execute; and the people were resolved to be merry when they themselves pleased, not when the

CHAPTER LVII

Had Charles been of a disposition to neglect all theological controversy; he yet had been obliged, in good policy, to adhere to episcopal jurisdiction, not only because it was favourable to monarchy, but because all his adherents were passionately devoted to it; and to abandon them, in what they regarded as so important an article, was for ever to relinquish their friendship and assistance. But Charles had never attained such enlarged principles. He deemed bishops essential to the very being of a christian church; and he thought himself bound, by more sacred ties, than those of policy, or even of honour, to the support of that order. His concessions therefore, on this head, he judged sufficient, when he agreed, that an indulgence should be given to tender consciences with regard to ceremonies; that the bishops should exercise no act of jurisdiction or ordination, without the consent and counsel of such presbyters as should be chosen by the clergy of each diocese; that they should reside constantly in their diocese, and be bound to preach every Sunday; that pluralities be abolished; that abuses in ecclesiastical courts be redressed; and that a hundred thousand pounds be levied on the bishops' estates and the chapter lands, for payment of debts contracted by the parliament.' These conces-

---

parliament should prescribe it to them. The keeping of Christmas holy-days was long a great mark of malignancy, and, very severely censured by the commons. *Whitlocke*, p. 286. Even minced pyes, which custom had made a Christmas dish among the churchmen, was regarded, during that season, as a profane and superstitious viand by the sectaries; though at other times it agreed very well with their stomachs. In the parliamentary ordinance too, for the observance of the sabbath, they inserted a clause for the taking down of may-poles, which they called a heathenish vanity. Since we are upon this subject, it may not be amiss to mention, that, besides setting apart Sunday for the ordinances, as they called them, the godly had regular meetings on the Thursdays for resolving cases of conscience, and conferring about their progress in grace. What they were chiefly anxious about, was the fixing the precise moment of their conversion or new birth; and whoever could not ascertain so difficult a point of calculation, could not pretend to any title to saintship. The profane scholars at Oxford, after the parliament became masters of that town, gave to the house, in which the zealots assembled, the denomination of *Scruple Shop:* The zealots, in their turn, insulted the scholars and professors; and, intruding into the place of lectures, declaimed against human learning, and challenged the most knowing of them to prove that their calling was from Christ. See Wood's Fasti Oxonienses, p. 740.   ' Dugdale, p. 779, 780.

sions, though considerable, gave no satisfaction to the parliamentary commissioners; and, without abating any thing of their rigour on this head, they proceeded to their demands with regard to the militia.

The king's partizans had all along maintained, that the fears and jealousies of the parliament, after the securities so early and easily given to public liberty, were either feigned or groundless; and that no human institution could be better poized and adjusted, than was now the government of England. By the abolition of the star-chamber and court of high commission, the prerogative, they said, has lost all that coercive power, by which it had formerly suppressed or endangered liberty: By the establishment of triennial parliaments, it can have no leisure to acquire new powers, or guard itself, during any time, from the inspection of that vigilant assembly: By the slender revenue of the crown, no king can ever attain such influence as to procure a repeal of these salutary statutes: And while the prince commands no military force, he will in vain, by violence, attempt an infringement of laws, so clearly defined by means of late disputes, and so passionately cherished by all his subjects. In this situation surely, the nation, governed by so virtuous a monarch, may, for the present, remain in tranquillity, and try, whether it be not possible, by peaceful arts, to elude that danger, with which, it is pretended its liberties are still threatened.

But though the royalists insisted on these plausible topics, before the commencement of war, they were obliged to own, that the progress of civil commotions had somewhat abated the force and evidence of this reasoning. If the power of the militia, said the opposite party, be entrusted to the king, it would not now be difficult for him to abuse that authority. By the rage of intestine discord, his partizans are inflamed into an extreme hatred against their antagonists; and have contracted, no doubt, some prejudices against popular privileges, which, in their apprehension, have been the source of so much disorder. Were the arms of the state, therefore, put entirely into such hands; what public security, it may be demanded, can be given to liberty, or what private security to those, who, in opposition to the letter of the law, have so generously ventured their lives in its defence? In compliance with this apprehension, Charles offered, that the arms of the state should be

CHAPTER LVII

entrusted during three years, to twenty commissioners, who should be named, either by common agreement between him and the parliament, or one half by him, the other by the parliament. And, after the expiration of that term, he insisted, that his consti-tutional authority over the militia should again return to him.[u]

The parliamentary commissioners at first demanded, that the power of the sword should for ever be entrusted to such persons, as the parliament alone should appoint:[w] But afterwards, they relaxed so far, as to require that authority only for seven years; after which it was not to return to the king, but to be settled by bill, or by common agreement between him and his parliament.[x] The king's commissioners asked, Whether jealousies and fears were all on one side, and whether the prince, from such violent attempts and pretensions as he had experienced, had not, at least, as great reason to entertain apprehensions for his authority, as they for their liberty? Whether there were any equity, in securing only one party, and leaving the other, during the space of seven years, entirely at the mercy of their enemies? Whether, if unlimited power were entrusted to the parliament during so long a period, it would not be easy for them to frame the subsequent bill in the manner most agreeable to themselves, and keep for ever posses-sion of the sword, as well as of every article of civil power and jurisdiction?[y]

The truth is, after the commencement of war, it was very diffi-cult, if not impossible, to find security for both parties, especially for that of the parliament. Amidst such violent animosities, power alone could ensure safety; and the power of one side was neces-sarily attended with danger to the other. Few or no instances occur in history of an equal, peaceful, and durable accommodation, that has been concluded between two factions, which had been en-flamed into civil war.

With regard to Ireland, there were no greater hopes of agree-ment between the parties. The parliament demanded, that the truce with the rebels should be declared null; that the manage-ment of the war should be given over entirely to the parliament; and that after the conquest of Ireland, the nomination of the lord

[u] Dugdale, p. 798.   [w] Ibid. p. 791.   [x] Ibid. p. 820.   [y] Dugdale, p. 877.

lieutenant and of the judges, or in other words the sovereignty of that kingdom, should likewise remain in their hands.[z]

What rendered an accommodation more desperate was, that the demands on these three heads, however exorbitant, were acknowledged, by the parliamentary commissioners, to be nothing but preliminaries. After all these were granted, it would be necessary to proceed to the discussion of those other demands, still more exorbitant, which, a little before, had been transmitted to the king at Oxford. Such ignominious terms were there insisted on, that worse could scarcely be demanded, were Charles totally vanquished, a prisoner, and in chains. The king was required to attaint and except from a general pardon, forty of the most considerable of his English subjects, and nineteen of his Scottish, together with all popish recusants in both kingdoms, who had borne arms for him. It was insisted, that forty-eight more, with all the members who had sitten in either house at Oxford, all lawyers and divines who had embraced the king's party, should be rendered incapable of any office, be forbidden the exercise of their profession, be prohibited from coming within the verge of the court, and forfeit the third of their estates to the parliament. It was required, that whoever had borne arms for the king, should forfeit the tenth of their estates, or if that did not suffice, the sixth, for the payment of public debts. As if royal authority were not sufficiently annihilated by such terms, it was demanded, that the court of wards should be abolished; that all the considerable officers of the crown, and all the judges, should be appointed by parliament; and that the right of peace and war should not be exercised without the consent of that assembly.[a] The presbyterians, it must be confessed, after insisting on such conditions, differed only in words from the independents, who required the establishment of a pure republic. When the debates had been carried on to no purpose, during twenty days, among the commissioners, they separated, and returned; those of the king, to Oxford, those of the parliament, to London.

A little before the commencement of this fruitless treaty, a deed was executed by the parliament, which proved their determined resolution to yield nothing, but to proceed in the same violent and

---

[z] Ibid. p. 826, 827.   [a] Rush. vol. vi. p. 850. Dugdale, p. 737.

imperious manner, with which they had, at first, entered on these dangerous enterprizes. Archbishop Laud, the most favoured minister of the king, was brought to the scaffold; and in this instance, the public might see, that popular assemblies, as, by their very number, they are, in a great measure, exempt from the restraint of shame, so when they also overleap the bounds of law, naturally break out into acts of the greatest tyranny and injustice.

Execution of Laud.

From the time, that Laud had been committed, the house of commons, engaged in enterprizes of greater moment, had found no leisure to finish his impeachment; and he had patiently endured so long an imprisonment, without being brought to any trial. After the union with Scotland, the bigotted prejudices of that nation revived the like spirit in England; and the sectaries resolved to gratify their vengeance in the punishment of this prelate, who had so long, by his authority, and by the execution of penal laws, kept their zealous spirit under confinement. He was accused of high treason, in endeavouring to subvert the fundamental laws, and of other high crimes and misdemeanors. The same illegality of an accumulative crime and a constructive evidence, which appeared in the case of Strafford; the same violence and iniquity in conducting the trial, are conspicuous throughout the whole course of this prosecution. The groundless charge of popery, though belied by his whole life and conduct, was continually urged against the prisoner; and every error rendered unpardonable by this imputation, which was supposed to imply the height of all enormities. "This man, my lords," said serjeant Wilde, concluding his long speech against him, "is like Naaman the Syrian; a great man, but a leper."[b]

We shall not enter into a detail of this matter, which, at present, seems to admit of little controversy. It suffices to say, that, after a long trial, and the examination of above a hundred and fifty witnesses, the commons found so little likelihood of obtaining a judicial sentence against Laud, that they were obliged to have recourse to their legislative authority, and to pass an ordinance for taking away the life of this aged prelate. Notwithstanding the low condition, into which the house of peers was fallen, there appeared some intention of rejecting this ordinance; and the popular lead-

[b] Rush. vol. vi. p. 830.

ers were again obliged to apply to the multitude, and to extinguish, by threats of new tumults, the small remains of liberty, possessed by the upper house. Seven peers alone voted in this important question. The rest, either from shame or fear, took care to absent themselves.[c]

Laud, who had behaved during his trial with spirit and vigor of genius, sunk not under the horrors of his execution; but though he had usually professed himself apprehensive of a violent death, he found all his fears to be dissipated before that superior courage, by which he was animated. "No one," said he, "can be more willing to send me out of life, than I am desirous to go." Even upon the scaffold, and during the intervals of his prayers, he was harassed and molested by Sir John Clotworthy, a zealot of the reigning sect, and a great leader in the lower house: This was the time he chose for examining the principles of the dying primate, and trepaning him into a confession, that he trusted, for his salvation, to the merits of good works, not to the death of the Redeemer.[d] Having extricated himself from these theological toils, the archbishop laid his head on the block; and it was severed from the body at one blow.[e] Those religious opinions, for which he suffered, contributed, no doubt, to the courage and constancy of his end. Sincere he undoubtedly was, and however misguided, actuated by pious motives in all his pursuits; and it is to be regretted, that a man of such spirit, who conducted his enterprizes with so much warmth and industry, had not entertained more enlarged views, and embraced principles more favourable to the general happiness of society.

The great and important advantage, which the party gained by Strafford's death, may, in some degree, palliate the iniquity of the sentence pronounced against him: But the execution of this old infirm prelate, who had so long remained an inoffensive prisoner, can be ascribed to nothing but vengeance and bigotry in those severe religionists, by whom the parliament was entirely governed. That he deserved a better fate was not questioned by any reasonable man: The degree of his merit, in other respects, was disputed. Some accused him of recommending slavish doctrines, of promoting persecution, and of encouraging superstition; while others

[c] Warwick, p. 169. [d] Rush. vol. vi. p. 838, 839. [e] 12th of July, 1644.

thought, that his conduct, in these three particulars, would admit of apology and extenuation.

That the *letter* of the law, as much as the most flaming court-sermon, inculcates passive obedience, is apparent: And though the *spirit* of a limited government seems to require, in extraordinary cases, some mitigation of so rigorous a doctrine; it must be confessed, that the preceding genius of the English constitution had rendered a mistake in this particular very natural and excusable. To inflict death at least on those, who depart from the exact line of truth in these nice questions; so far from being favourable to national liberty; savours strongly of the spirit of tyranny and proscription.

Toleration had hitherto been so little the principle of any christian sect, that even the catholics, the remnant of the religion professed by their fore-fathers, could not obtain from the English the least indulgence. This very house of commons, in their famous remonstrance, took care to justify themselves, as from the highest imputation, from any intention to relax the golden reins of discipline, as they called them, or to grant any toleration:[f] And the enemies of the church were so fair from the beginning, as not to lay claim to liberty of conscience, which they called a toleration for foul murder. They openly challenged the superiority, and even menaced the established church with that persecution, which they afterwards exercised against her with such severity. And if the question be considered in the view of policy; though a sect, already formed and advanced, may, with good reason, demand a toleration; what title had the puritans to this indulgence, who were just on the point of separation from the church, and whom, it might be hoped, some wholesome and legal severities would still retain in obedience.[g]

Whatever ridicule, to a philosophical mind, may be thrown on pious ceremonies, it must be confessed, that, during a very religious age, no institutions can be more advantageous to the rude multitude, and tend more to mollify that fierce and gloomy spirit of devotion, to which they are subject. Even the English church, though it had retained a share of popish ceremonies, may justly be thought too naked and unadorned, and still to approach too near

---

[f] Nalson, vol. ii. p. 705.   [g] See note [FF] at the end of the volume.

the abstract and spiritual religion of the puritans. Laud and his associates, by reviving a few primitive institutions of this nature, corrected the error of the first reformers, and presented to the affrightened and astonished mind, some sensible, exterior observances, which might occupy it during its religious exercises, and abate the violence of its disappointed efforts. The thought, no longer bent on that divine and mysterious essence, so superior to the narrow capacities of mankind, was able, by means of the new model of devotion, to relax itself in the contemplation of pictures, postures, vestments, buildings; and all the fine arts, which minister to religion, thereby received additional encouragement. The primate, it is true, conducted this scheme, not with the enlarged sentiments and cool reflection of a legislator, but with the intemperate zeal of a sectary; and by overlooking the circumstances of the times, served rather to enflame that religious fury, which he meant to repress. But this blemish is more to be regarded as a general imputation on the whole age, than any particular failing of Laud's; and it is sufficient for his vindication to observe, that his errors were the most excusable of all those, which prevailed during that zealous period.

LVIII

Montrose's victories – The new model of the army – Battle of Naseby – Surrender of Bristol – The west conquered by Fairfax – Defeat of Montrose – Ecclesiastical affairs – King goes to the Scots at Newark – End of the war – King delivered up by the Scots

WHILE THE KING'S AFFAIRS declined in England, some events happened in Scotland, which seemed to promise him a more prosperous issue of the quarrel.

Before the commencement of these civil disorders, the earl of Montrose, a young nobleman of a distinguished family, returning from his travels, had been introduced to the king, and had made an offer of his services; but by the insinuations of the marquess, afterwards duke of Hamilton, who possessed much of Charles's confidence, he had not been received with that distinction, to which he thought himself justly entitled.[h] Disgusted with this treatment, he had forwarded all the violence of the covenanters; and agreeably to the natural ardour of his genius, he had employed himself, during the first Scottish insurrection, with great zeal as

1645.

Montrose's victories.

[h] Nalson, Intr. p. 63.

461

well as success, in levying and conducting their armies. Being commissioned by the *Tables* to wait upon the king, while the royal army lay at Berwic, he was so gained by the civilities and caresses of that monarch, that he thenceforth devoted himself entirely, though secretly, to his service, and entered into a close correspondence with him. In the second insurrection, a great military command was entrusted to him by the covenanters; and he was the first that passed the Tweed, at the head of their troops, in the invasion of England. He found means, however, soon after to convey a letter to the king: And by the infidelity of some about that prince; Hamilton, as was suspected; a copy of this letter was sent to Leven, the Scottish general. Being accused of treachery, and a correspondence with the enemy; Montrose openly avowed the letter; and asked the generals, if they dared to call their sovereign an enemy: And by this bold and magnanimous behaviour, he escaped the danger of an immediate prosecution. As he was now fully known to be of the royal party, he no longer concealed his principles; and he endeavoured to draw those, who had entertained like sentiments, into a bond of association for his master's service. Though thrown into prison for this enterprize,[i] and detained some time, he was not discouraged; but still continued, by his countenance and protection, to infuse spirit into the distressed royalists. Among other persons of distinction, who united themselves to him, was lord Napier of Merchiston, son of the famous inventor of the logarithms, the person to whom the title of a GREAT MAN is more justly due, than to any other, whom his country ever produced.

There was in Scotland another party, who, professing equal attachment to the king's service, pretended only to differ with Montrose about the means of attaining the same end; and of that party, duke Hamilton was the leader. This nobleman had cause to be extremely devoted to the king, not only by reason of the connexion of blood, which united him to the royal family; but on account of the great confidence and favour, with which he had ever been honoured by his master. Being accused by lord Rae, not

[i] It is not improper to take notice of a mistake committed by Clarendon, much to the disadvantage of this gallant nobleman; that he offered the king, when his majesty was in Scotland, to assassinate Argyle. All the time the king was in Scotland, Montrose was confined to prison. Rush. vol. vi. p. 980.

CHAPTER LVIII

without some appearance or probability, of a conspiracy against the king; Charles was so far from harbouring suspicion against him, that, the very first time Hamilton came to the court, he received him into his bedchamber, and passed alone the night with him.[k] But such was the duke's unhappy fate or conduct, that he escaped not the imputation of treachery to his friend and sovereign; and though he at last sacrificed his life in the king's service, his integrity and sincerity have not been thought by historians entirely free from blemish. Perhaps, (and this is the more probable opinion) the subtilties and refinements of his conduct and his temporizing maxims, though accompanied with good intentions, have been the chief cause of a suspicion, which has never yet been either fully proved or refuted. As much as the bold and vivid spirit of Montrose prompted him to enterprizing measures, as much was the cautious temper of Hamilton inclined to such as were moderate and dilatory. While the former foretold, that the Scottish covenanters were secretly forming an union with the English parliament, and inculcated the necessity of preventing them by some vigorous undertaking; the latter still insisted, that every such attempt would precipitate them into measures, to which, otherwise, they were not, perhaps, inclined. After the Scottish convention was summoned without the king's authority, the former exclaimed, that their intentions were now visible, and that, if some unexpected blow were not struck, to dissipate them, they would arm the whole nation against the king; the latter maintained the possibility of outvoting the disaffected party, and securing, by peaceful means, the allegiance of the kingdom.[l] Unhappily for the royal cause, Hamilton's representations met with more credit from the king and queen, than those of Montrose; and the covenanters were allowed, without interruption, to proceed in all their hostile measures. Montrose then hastened to Oxford; where his invectives against Hamilton's treachery, concurring with the general prepossession, and supported by the unfortunate event of his counsels, were entertained with universal approbation. Influenced by the clamour of his party, more than his own suspicions, Charles, as soon as Hamilton appeared, sent him prisoner to Pendennis cas-

[k] Nalson, vol. ii. p. 683. [l] Clarendon, vol. iii. p. 380, 381. Rush. vol. vi. p. 980. Wishart, cap. 2.

tle in Cornwall. His brother, Laneric, who was also put under confinement, found means to make his escape, and to fly into Scotland.

The king's ears were now open to Montrose's counsels, who proposed none but the boldest and most daring, agreeably to the desperate state of the royal cause in Scotland. Though the whole nation was subjected by the covenanters, though great armies were kept on foot by them, and every place guarded by a vigilant administration; he undertook, by his own credit, and that of the few friends, who remained to the king, to raise such commotions, as would soon oblige the malcontents to recal those forces, which had so sensibly thrown the balance in favour of the parliament.[m] Not discouraged with the defeat at Marston-moor, which rendered it impossible for him to draw any succour from England; he was content to stipulate with the earl of Antrim, a nobleman of Ireland, for some supply of men from that country. And he himself, changing his disguises and passing through many dangers, arrived in Scotland; where he lay concealed in the borders of the Highlands, and secretly prepared the minds of his partizans for attempting some great enterprize.[n]

No sooner were the Irish landed, though not exceeding eleven hundred foot, very ill armed, than Montrose declared himself, and entered upon that scene of action, which has rendered his name so celebrated. About eight hundred of the men of Athole flocked to his standard. Five hundred men more, who had been levied by the covenanters, were persuaded to embrace the royal cause: And with this combined force, he hastened to attack lord Elcho, who lay at Perth with an army of 6000 men, assembled upon the first news of the Irish invasion. Montrose, inferior in number, totally unprovided with horse, ill supplied with arms and ammunition, had nothing to depend on, but the courage, which he himself, by his own example, and the rapidity of his enterprizes, should inspire into his raw soldiers. Having received the fire of the enemy, which was answered chiefly by a volley of stones, he rushed amidst them with his sword drawn, threw them into confusion, pushed his ad-

---

[m] Wishart, cap. 3.   [n] Clarendon, vol. v. p. 618. Rush. vol. vi. p. 982. Wishart, cap. 4.

CHAPTER LVIII

vantage, and obtained a complete victory, with the slaughter of two thousand of the covenanters.[o]

This victory, though it augmented the renown of Montrose, encreased not his power or numbers. The far greater part of the kingdom was extremely attached to the covenant; and such as bore an affection to the royal cause, were terrified by the established authority of the opposite party. Dreading the superior power of Argyle, who, having joined his vassals to a force levied by the public, was approaching with a considerable army; Montrose hastened northwards, in order to rouze again the marquess of Huntley and the Gordons, who, having before hastily taken arms, had been instantly suppressed by the covenanters. He was joined on his march by the earl of Airly, with his two younger sons, Sir Thomas and Sir David Ogilvy: The eldest was, at that time, a prisoner with the enemy. He attacked at Aberdeen the lord Burley, who commanded a force of 2500 men. After a sharp combat, by his undaunted courage, which, in his situation, was true policy, and was also not unaccompanied with military skill, he put the enemy to flight, and in the pursuit did great execution upon them.[p]

But by this second advantage, he obtained not the end, which he expected. The envious nature of Huntley, jealous of Montrose's glory, rendered him averse to join an army, where he himself must be so much eclipsed by the superior merit of the general. Argyle, re-inforced by the earl of Lothian, was behind him with a great army: The militia of the northern counties, Murray, Ross, Caithness, to the number of 5000 men, opposed him in front, and guarded the banks of the Spey, a deep and rapid river. In order to elude these numerous armies, he turned aside into the hills, and saved his weak, but active troops, in Badenoch. After some marches and counter-marches, Argyle came up with him at Faivy-castle. This nobleman's character, though celebrated for political courage and conduct, was very low for military prowess; and after some skirmishes, in which he was worsted, he here allowed Montrose to escape him. By quick marches, through these inaccessible

[o] 1st of September, 1644. Rush. vol. vi. p. 983. Wishart, cap. 5.   [p] 11th of September, 1644. Rush. vol. vi. p. 983. Wishart, cap. 7.

mountains, that general freed himself from the superior forces of the covenanters.

Such was the situation of Montrose, that very good or very ill fortune was equally destructive to him, and diminished his army. After every victory, his soldiers, greedy of spoil, but deeming the smallest acquisition to be unexhausted riches, deserted in great numbers, and went home to secure the treasures, which they had acquired. Tired too, and spent with hasty and long marches, in the depth of winter, through snowy mountains unprovided with every necessary, they fell off, and left their general almost alone with the Irish, who, having no place, to which they could retire, still adhered to him in every fortune.

With these, and some reinforcements of the Atholemen, and Macdonalds whom he had recalled, Montrose fell suddenly upon Argyle's country, and let loose upon it all the rage of war; carrying off the cattle, burning the houses, and putting the inhabitants to the sword. This severity, by which Montrose sullied his victories, was the result of private animosity against the chieftain, as much as of zeal for the public cause. Argyle, collecting three thousand men, marched in quest of the enemy, who had retired with their plunder; and he lay at Innerlochy; supposing himself still at a considerable distance from them. The earl of Seaforth, at the head of the garrison of Inverness, who were veteran soldiers, joined to 5000 new levied troops of the northern counties, pressed the royalists on the other side, and threatened them with inevitable destruction. By a quick and unexpected march, Montrose hastened to Innerlochy, and presented himself in order of battle, before the surprised, but not affrightened, covenanters. Argyle alone, seized with a panic, deserted his army, who still maintained their ground, *2d Feb.* and gave battle to the royalists. After a vigorous resistance, they were defeated, and pursued with great slaughter.[q] And the power of the Campbells (that is Argyle's name) being thus broken; the highlanders, who were in general well-affected to the royal cause, began to join Montrose's camp, in great numbers. Seaforth's army dispersed of itself, at the very terror of his name. And lord Gordon, eldest son of Huntley, having escaped from his uncle Argyle, who had hitherto detained him, now joined Montrose, with no con-

[q] Rush. vol. vi. p. 985. Wishart, cap. 8.

temptible number of his followers, attended by his brother, the earl of Aboine.

The council at Edinburgh, alarmed at Montrose's progress, began to think of a more regular plan of defence, against an enemy, whose repeated victories had rendered him extremely formidable. They sent for Baillie, an officer of reputation, from England; and joining him in command with Urrey, who had again inlisted himself among the king's enemies, they sent them to the field, with a considerable army, against the royalists. Montrose, with a detachment of 800 men, had attacked Dundee, a town extremely zealous for the covenant: And having carried it by assault, had delivered it up to be plundered by his soldiers; when Baillie and Urrey, with their whole force, were unexpectedly upon him.[r] His conduct and presence of mind, in this emergence, appeared conspicuous. Instantly he called off his soldiers from plunder, put them in order, secured his retreat by the most skilful measures; and having marched sixty miles in the face of an enemy much superior, without stopping, or allowing his soldiers the least sleep or refreshment, he at last secured himself in the mountains.

Baillie and Urrey now divided their troops, in order the better to conduct the war against an enemy, who surprised them, as much by the rapidity of his marches, as by the boldness of his enterprizes. Urrey, at the head of 4000 men, met him at Alderne, near Inverness; and, encouraged by the superiority of number (for the covenanters were double the royalists) attacked him in the post which he had chosen. Montrose, having placed his right wing in strong ground, drew the best of his forces to the other, and left no main body between them; a defect which he artfully concealed, by showing a few men through the trees and bushes, with which that ground was covered. That Urrey might have no leisure to perceive the stratagem, he instantly led his left wing to the charge; and, making a furious impression upon the covenanters, drove them off the field, and gained a compleat victory.[s] In this battle, the valour of young Napier, son to the lord of that name, shone out with signal lustre.

Baillie now advanced, in order to revenge Urrey's discom-

[r] Rush. vol. vii. p. 228. Wishart, cap. 9. [s] Rush. vol. vii. p. 229. Wishart, cap. 10.

fiture; but, at Alford, he met, himself, with a like fate.[t] Montrose, weak in cavalry, here lined his troops of horse with infantry; and after putting the enemies' horses to rout, fell with united force upon their foot, who were entirely cut in pieces, though with the loss of the gallant lord Gordon on the part of the royalists.[u] And having thus prevailed in so many battles, which his vigour ever rendered as decisive as they were successful; he summoned together all his friends and partizans, and prepared himself for marching into the southern provinces, in order to put a final period to the power of the covenanters, and dissipate the parliament, which, with great pomp and solemnity, they had summoned to meet at St. Johnstone's.

While the fire was thus kindled in the north of the island, it blazed out with no less fury in the south: The parliamentary and royal armies, as soon as the season would permit, prepared to take the field, in hopes of bringing their important quarrel to a quick decision. The passing of the self-denying ordinance had been protracted by so many debates and intrigues, that the spring was far advanced before it received the sanction of both houses; and it was thought dangerous by many to introduce, so near the time of action, such great innovations into the army. Had not the punctilious principles of Essex engaged him, amidst all the disgusts which he received, to pay implicit obedience to the parliament; this alteration had not been effected without some fatal accident: Since, notwithstanding his prompt resignation of the command, a mutiny was generally apprehended.[w] Fairfax, or more properly speaking, Cromwell under his name, introduced, at last, the *new model* into the army, and threw the troops into a different shape. From the same men, new regiments and new companies, were formed, different officers appointed, and the whole military force put into such hands, as the independents could rely on. Besides members of parliament who were excluded, many officers, unwilling to serve under the new generals, threw up their commissions; and unwarily facilitated the project of putting the army entirely into the hands of that faction.

Though the discipline of the former parliamentary army was

[t] 2d of July. [u] Rush. vol. vii. p. 229. Wishart, cap. 11. [w] Rush. vol. vii. p. 126, 127.

CHAPTER LVIII

not contemptible, a more exact plan was introduced, and rigorously executed, by these new commanders. Valour indeed was very generally diffused over the one party as well as the other, during this period: Discipline also was attained by the forces of the parliament: But the perfection of the military art, in concerting the general plans of action, and the operations of the field, seems still, on both sides, to have been, in a great measure, wanting. Historians at least, perhaps from their own ignorance and inexperience, have not remarked any thing but a headlong impetuous conduct; each party hurrying to a battle, where valour and fortune chiefly determined the success. The great ornament of history, during these reigns, are the civil, not the military transactions.

Never surely was a more singular army assembled, than that which was now set on foot by the parliament. To the greater number of the regiments, chaplains were not appointed: The officers assumed the spiritual duty, and united it with their military functions. During the intervals of action, they occupied themselves in sermons, prayers, exhortations; and the same emulation, there, attended them, which, in the field, is so necessary to support the honour of that profession. Rapturous ecstasies supplied the place of study and reflection; and while the zealous devotees poured out their thoughts in unpremeditated harangues, they mistook that eloquence, which, to their own surprize, as well as that of others, flowed in upon them, for divine illuminations, and for illapses of the Holy Spirit. Wherever they were quartered, they excluded the minister from his pulpit; and, usurping his place, conveyed their sentiments to the audience, with all the authority, which followed their power, their valour, and their military exploits, united to their appearing zeal and fervor. The private soldiers, seized with the same spirit, employed their vacant hours in prayer, in perusing the Holy Scriptures, in ghostly conferences; where they compared the progress of their souls in grace, and mutually stimulated each other to farther advances in the great work of their salvation. When they were marching to battle, the whole field resounded, as well with psalms and spiritual songs adapted to the occasion, as with the instruments of military music;[x] and every man endeavoured to drown the sense of present danger, in the prospect

New model of the army.

[x] Dugdale, p. 7. Rush. vol. vi. p. 281.

of that crown of glory, which was set before him. In so holy a cause, wounds were esteemed meritorious; death, martyrdom; and the hurry and dangers of action, instead of banishing their pious visions, rather served to impress their minds more strongly with them.

The royalists were desirous of throwing a ridicule on this fanaticism of the parliamentary armies, without being sensible how much reason they had to apprehend its dangerous consequences. The forces, assembled by the king at Oxford, in the west, and in other places, were equal, if not superior, in number, to their adversaries; but actuated by a very different spirit. That licence, which had been introduced by want of pay, had risen to a great height among them, and rendered them more formidable to their friends than to their enemies. Prince Rupert, negligent of the people, fond of the soldiery, had indulged the troops in unwarrantable liberties: Wilmot, a man of dissolute manners, had promoted the same spirit of disorder: And the licentious Goring, Gerrard, Sir Richard Granville, now carried it to a great pitch of enormity. In the west especially, where Goring commanded, universal spoil and havoc were committed; and the whole country was laid waste by the rapine of the army. All distinction of parties being in a manner dropped; the most devoted friends of the church and monarchy wished there for such success to the parliamentary forces, as might put an end to these oppressions. The country people, despoiled of their substance, flocked together in several places, armed with clubs and staves; and though they professed an enmity to the soldiers of both parties, their hatred was in most places levelled chiefly against the royalists, from whom they had met with the worst treatment. Many thousands of these tumultuary peasants were assembled in different parts of England; who destroyed all such straggling soldiers as they met with, and much infested the armies.[y]

The disposition of the forces on both sides, was as follows: Part of the Scottish army was employed in taking Pomfret, and other towns in Yorkshire: Part of it besieged Carlisle, valiantly defended by sir Thomas Glenham. Chester, where Biron commanded, had long been blockaded by sir William Brereton; and was reduced to

[y] Rush. vol. vii. p. 52, 61, 62. Whitlocke, p. 130, 131, 133, 135. Clarendon, vol. v. p. 665.

great difficulties. The king, being joined by the princes, Rupert and Maurice, lay at Oxford, with a considerable army, about 15,000 men. Fairfax and Cromwel were posted at Windsor, with the new-modelled army, about 22,000 men. Taunton, in the county of Somerset, defended by Blake, suffered a long siege from Sir Richard Granville, who commanded an army of about 8000 men; and though the defence had been obstinate, the garrison was now reduced to the last extremity. Goring commanded, in the west, an army of nearly the same number.[z]

On opening the campaign, the king formed the project of relieving Chester; Fairfax, that of relieving Taunton. The king was first in motion. When he advanced to Draiton in Shropshire, Biron met him, and brought intelligence, that his approach had raised the siege, and that the parliamentary army had withdrawn. Fairfax, having reached Salisbury in his road westward, received orders from the committee of both kingdoms, appointed for the management of the war, to return and lay siege to Oxford, now exposed by the king's absence. He obeyed, after sending colonel Weldon to the west, with a detachment of 4000 men. On Weldon's approach, Granville, who imagined that Fairfax with his whole army was upon him, raised the siege, and allowed this pertinacious town, now half taken and half burned, to receive relief: But the royalists, being reinforced with 3000 horse under Goring, again advanced to Taunton, and shut up Weldon, with his small army, in that ruinous place.[a]

The king having affected his purpose with regard to Chester, returned southwards; and, in his way, sat down before Leicester, a garrison of the parliament's. Having made a breach in the wall, he stormed the town on all sides; and, after a furious assault, the soldiers entered sword in hand, and committed all those disorders, to which their natural violence, especially when enflamed by resistance, is so much addicted.[b] A great booty was taken and distributed among them: Fifteen hundred prisoners fell into the king's hands. This success, which struck a great terror into the parliamentary party, determined Fairfax to leave Oxford, while he was beginning to approach; and he marched towards the king, with an intention of offering him battle. The king was advancing towards Oxford, in

[z] Rush. vol. vii. p. 18, 19, &c.   [a] Ibid. p. 28.   [b] Clarendon, vol. v. p. 652.

order to raise the siege, which, he apprehended, was now begun; and both armies, ere they were aware, had advanced within six miles of each other. A council of war was called by the king, in order to deliberate concerning the measures, which he should now pursue. On the one hand, it seemed more prudent to delay the combat; because Gerard, who lay in Wales with 3000 men, might be enabled, in a little time, to join the army; and Goring, it was hoped, would soon be master of Taunton, and having put the west in full security, would then unite his forces to those of the king, and give him an incontestible superiority over the enemy. On the other hand, prince Rupert, whose boiling ardour still pushed him on to battle, excited the impatient humour of the nobility and gentry, of which the army was full; and urged the many difficulties, under which the royalists laboured, and from which nothing but a victory could relieve them: The resolution was taken to give battle to Fairfax; and the royal army immediately advanced upon him.

Battle of Naseby.   At Naseby was fought, with forces nearly equal, this decisive and well disputed action, between the king and parliament. The main body of the royalists was commanded by the king himself: The right wing, by prince Rupert; the left, by Sir Marmaduke Langdale. Fairfax, seconded by Skippon, placed himself in the main body of the opposite army: Cromwel, in the right wing: Ireton, Cromwel's son-in-law, in the left. The charge was begun, with his usual celerity and usual success, by prince Rupert. Though Ireton made stout resistance, and even after he was run through the thigh with a pike, still maintained the combat, till he was taken prisoner; yet was that whole wing broken, and pursued with precipitate fury by Rupert: He was even so inconsiderate as to lose time in summoning and attacking the artillery of the enemy, which had been left with a good guard of infantry. The king led on his main body, and displayed in this action, all the conduct of a prudent general, and all the valour of a stout soldier.[c] Fairfax and Skippon encountered him, and well supported that reputation, which they had acquired. Skippon, being dangerously wounded, was desired by Fairfax to leave the field; but declared that he would remain there as long as one man maintained his ground.[d] The infantry of the parliament was broken, and pressed upon by

[c] Whitlocke, p. 146.   [d] Rush. vol. vii. p. 43. Whitlocke, p. 145.

the king; till Fairfax, with great presence of mind, brought up the reserve and renewed the combat. Mean while, Cromwel, having led on his troops to the attack of Langdale, overbore the force of the royalists, and by his prudence improved that advantage, which he had gained by his valour. Having pursued the enemy about a quarter of a mile, and detached some troops to prevent their rallying; he turned back upon the king's infantry, and threw them into the utmost confusion. One regiment alone preserved its order unbroken, though twice desperately assailed by Fairfax: And that general, excited by so steddy a resistance, ordered Doyley, the captain of his life-guard, to give them a third charge in front, while he himself attacked them in rear. The regiment was broken. Fairfax, with his own hands, killed an ensign, and, having seized the colours, gave them to a soldier to keep for him. The soldier afterwards boasting that he had won this trophy, was reproved by Doyley, who had seen the action; *Let him retain that honour,* said Fairfax, *I have to-day acquired enough beside.*[e]

Prince Rupert, sensible too late of his error, left the fruitless attack on the enemy's artillery, and joined the king, whose infantry was now totally discomfited. Charles exhorted this body of cavalry not to despair, and cried aloud to them, *One charge more, and we recover the day.*[f] But the disadvantages, under which they laboured, were too evident; and they could by no means be induced to renew the combat. Charles was obliged to quit the field, and leave the victory to the enemy.[g] The slain, on the side of the parliament, exceeded those of the side of the king: They lost a thousand men; he not above eight hundred. But Fairfax made 500 officers prisoners, and 4000 private men; took all the king's artillery and ammunition; and totally dissipated his infantry: So that scarce any victory could be more complete, than that which he obtained.

Among the other spoils, was seized the king's cabinet, with the copies of his letters to the queen, which the parliament afterwards ordered to be published.[h] They chose, no doubt, such of them as they thought would reflect dishonour on him: Yet upon the whole, the letters are written with delicacy and tenderness, and give an advantageous idea both of the king's genius and morals. A mighty

[e] Whitlocke, p. 145.   [f] Rush. vol. vii. p. 44.   [g] Clarendon, vol. iv. p. 656, 657. Walker, p. 130, 131.   [h] Clarendon, vol. iv. p. 658.

fondness, it is true, and attachment, he expresses to his consort, and often professes that he never would embrace any measures, which she disapproved: But such declarations of civility and confidence are not always to be taken in a full literal sense. And so legitimate an affection, avowed by the laws of God and man, may, perhaps, be excusable towards a woman of beauty and spirit, even though she was a papist.[i]

The Athenians, having intercepted a letter written by their enemy, Philip of Macedon, to his wife, Olympia; so far from being moved by a curiosity of prying into the secrets of that relation, immediately sent the letter to the queen unopened. Philip was not their sovereign; nor were they enflamed with that violent animosity against him, which attends all civil commotions.

After the battle, the king retreated with that body of horse, which remained entire, first to Hereford, then to Abergavenny; and remained some time in Wales, from the vain hope of raising a body of infantry in those harassed and exhausted quarters. Fairfax, having first retaken Leicester, which was surrendered upon articles, began to deliberate concerning his future enterprizes. A letter was brought to him, written by Goring to the king, and unfortunately entrusted to a spy of Fairfax's. Goring there informed the king, that, in three weeks, he hoped to be master of Taunton; after which he would join his majesty with all the forces in the west; and entreated him, in the mean while, to avoid coming to any general action. This letter, which, had it been safely delivered, had probably prevented the battle of Naseby, served now to direct the operations of Fairfax.[k] After leaving a body of 3000 men to Pointz and Rossiter, with orders to attend the king's motions, he

17th June.

---

[i] Hearne has published the following extract from a manuscript work of Sir Simon D'Ewes, who was no mean man in the parliamentary party. "On Thursday the 30th and last day of this instant June 1625, I went to Whitehall, purposely to see the queen, which I did fully all the time she sat at dinner. I perceiv'd her to be a most absolute delicate lady, after I had exactly survey'd all the features of her face, much enliven'd by her radiant and sparkling black eyes. Besides, her deportment among her women was so sweet and humble, and her speech and looks to her other servants so mild and gracious, as I could not abstain from divers deep fetched sighs, to consider, that she wanted the knowledge of the true religion." See Preface to the Chronicle of Dunstable, p. 64.   [k] Rush. vol. vii. p. 49.

marched immediately to the west, with a view of saving Taunton, and suppressing the only considerable force, which now remained to the royalists.

In the beginning of the campaign, Charles, apprehensive of the event, had sent the prince of Wales, then fifteen years of age, to the west, with the title of general, and had given orders, if he were pressed by the enemy, that he should make his escape into a foreign country, and save one part of the royal family from the violence of the parliament. Prince Rupert had thrown himself into Bristol, with an intention of defending that important city. Goring commanded the army before Taunton.

On Fairfax's approach, the siege of Taunton was raised; and the royalists retired to Lamport, an open town in the county of Somerset. Fairfax attacked them in that post, beat them from it, killed about 300 men, and took 1400 prisoners.[l] After this advantage, he sat down before Bridgewater, a town esteemed strong, and of great consequence in that country. When he had entered the outer town by storm, Windham, the governor, who had retired into the inner, immediately capitulated, and delivered up the place to Fairfax. The garrison, to the number of 2600 men, were made prisoners of war. *20th July.*

23d July.

Fairfax, having next taken Bath and Sherborne, resolved to lay siege to Bristol, and made great preparations for an enterprize, which, from the strength of the garrison, and the reputation of prince Rupert, the governor, was deemed of the last importance. But, so precarious in most men is this quality of military courage! a poorer defence was not made by any town, during the whole war: And the general expectations were here extremely disappointed. No sooner had the parliamentary forces entered the lines by storm, than the prince capitulated, and surrendered the city to Fairfax.[m] A few days before, he had written a letter to the king, in which he undertook to defend the place for four months, if no mutiny obliged him to surrender it. Charles, who was forming schemes, and collecting forces, for the relief of Bristol, was astonished at so unexpected an event, which was little less fatal to his cause than the defeat at Naseby.[n] Full of indignation, he instantly

11th Sept.

Surrender of Bristol.

[l] Ibid. vol. vii. p. 55.   [m] Rush. vol. vii. p. 83.   [n] Clarendon, vol. iv. p. 690. Walker, p. 137.

recalled all prince Rupert's commissions, and sent him a pass to go beyond sea.[o]

The king's affairs now went fast to ruin in all quarters. The Scots, having made themselves masters of Carlisle,[p] after an obstinate siege, marched southwards, and laid siege to Hereford; but were obliged to raise it on the king's approach: And this was the last glimpse of success, which attended his arms. Having marched to the relief of Chester, which was a-new besieged by the parliamentary forces under colonel Jones; Pointz attacked his rear, and forced him to give battle. While the fight was continued with great obstinacy, and victory seemed to incline to the royalists; Jones fell upon them from the other side, and put them to rout, with the loss of 600 slain and 1000 prisoners.[q] The king, with the remains of his broken army, fled to Newark, and thence escaped to Oxford, where he shut himself up during the winter season.

24th Sept.

The news, which he received from every quarter, were no less fatal than those events, which passed, where he himself was present. Fairfax and Cromwel, after the surrender of Bristol, having divided their forces, the former marched westwards, in order to complete the conquest of Devonshire and Cornwal; the latter attacked the king's garrisons which lay to the east of Bristol. The Devizes were surrendered to Cromwel; Berkeley castle was taken by storm; Winchester capitulated; Basing-house was entered sword in hand: And all these middle counties of England were, in a little time, reduced to obedience under the parliament.

1646.
The west conquered by Fairfax.

The same rapid and uninterrupted success attended Fairfax. The parliamentary forces, elated by past victories, governed by the most rigid discipline, met with no equal opposition from troops, dismayed by repeated defeats, and corrupted by licentious manners. After beating up the quarters of the royalists at Bovey-Tracy, Fairfax sat down before Dartmouth, and in a few days entered it by storm. Poudram castle being taken by him, and Exeter blockaded on all sides; Hopton, a man of merit, who now commanded the royalists, having advanced to the relief of that town with an army of 8000 men, met with the parliamentary army at Torrington; where he was defeated, all his foot dispersed, and he himself with his horse obliged to retire into Cornwal. Fairfax fol-

18th Jan.

19th Feb.

[o] Clarendon, vol. iv. p. 695. [p] 28th of June. [q] Rush. vol. vii. p. 117.

CHAPTER LVIII

lowed him, and vigorously pursued the victory. Having inclosed the royalists at Truro, he forced the whole army, consisting of 5000 men, chiefly cavalry, to surrender upon terms. The soldiers, delivering up their horses and arms, were allowed to disband, and received twenty shillings a-piece, to carry them to their respective abodes. Such of the officers, as desired it, had passes to retire beyond sea: The others, having promised never more to bear arms, payed compositions to the parliament,[r] and procured their pardon.[s] And thus Fairfax, after taking Exeter, which completed the conquest of the west, marched, with his victorious army, to the centre of the kingdom, and fixed his camp at Newbury. The prince of Wales, in pursuance of the king's orders, retired to Scilly, thence to Jersey; whence he went to Paris; where he joined the queen, who had fled thither from Exeter, at the time the earl of Essex conducted the parliamentary army to the west.

In the other parts of England, Hereford was taken by surprize: Chester surrendered: Lord Digby, who had attempted, with 1200 horse, to break into Scotland and join Montrose, was defeated at Sherburn, in Yorkshire, by colonel Copley; his whole force was dispersed; and he himself was obliged to fly, first to the isle of Man, thence to Ireland. News too arrived that Montrose himself, after some more successes, was at last routed; and this only remaining hope of the royal party finally extinguished.

When Montrose descended into the southern counties, the covenanters, assembling their whole force, met him with a numerous army, and gave him battle, but without success, at Kilsyth.[t] This was the most complete victory that Montrose ever obtained. The royalists put to sword six thousand of their enemies, and left the covenanters no remains of any army in Scotland. The whole kingdom was shaken with these repeated successes of Montrose; and many noblemen, who secretly favoured the royal cause, now declared openly for it, when they saw a force able to support them. The marquess of Douglass, the earls of Annandale and Hartfield, the lords Fleming, Seton, Maderty, Carnegy, with many others, flocked to the royal standard. Edinburgh opened its gates, and

[r] These compositions were different, according to the demerits of the person: But by a vote of the house they could not be under two years rent of the delinquent's estate. Journ. 11th of August 1648. Whitlocke, p. 160.
[s] Rush. vol. vii. p. 108.   [t] 15th August, 1645.

gave liberty to all the prisoners, there detained by the covenanters. Among the rest, was lord Ogilvy, son of Airly, whose family had contributed extremely to the victory, gained at Kilsyth.[u]

David Lesly was detached from the army in England, and marched to the relief of his distressed party in Scotland. Montrose advanced still farther to the south, allured by vain hopes, both of rouzing to arms the earls of Hume, Traquaire, and Roxborough, who had promised to join him; and of obtaining from England some supply of cavalry, in which he was deficient. By the negligence of his scouts, Lesly, at Philip-haugh in the Forrest, surprized his army, much diminished in numbers, from the desertion, of the Highlanders, who had retired to the hills, according to custom, in order to secure their plunder. After a sharp conflict, where Montrose exerted great valour, his forces were routed by Lesly's cavalry:[w] And he himself was obliged to fly with his broken forces into the mountains; where he again prepared himself for new battles and new enterprizes.[x]

Defeat of Montrose.

The covenanters used the victory with rigour. Their prisoners, Sir Robert Spotiswood, secretary of state, and son to the late primate, Sir Philip Nisbet, Sir William Rollo, colonel Nathaniel Gordon, Andrew Guthry, son of the bishop of Murray, William Murray, son of the earl of Tullibardine, were condemned and executed. The sole crime, imputed to the secretary, was his delivering to Montrose the king's commission to be captain-general of Scotland. Lord Ogilvy, who was again taken prisoner, would have undergone the same fate, had not his sister found means to procure his escape, by changing cloaths with him. For this instance of courage and dexterity, she met with harsh usage. The clergy solicited the parliament, that more royalists might be executed; but could not obtain their request.[y]

After all these repeated disasters, which every where befel the royal party, there remained only one body of troops, on which fortune could exercise her rigour. Lord Astley with a small army of 3000 men, chiefly cavalry, marching to Oxford, in order to join the king, was met at Stowe by colonel Morgan, and entirely defeated; himself being taken prisoner. "You have done your work,"

22d March.

[u] Rush. vol. vii. p. 230, 231. Wishart, cap. 13.   [w] 13th of Sept. 1645.
[x] Rush. vol. vii. p. 231.   [y] Guthry's Memoirs. Rush. vol. vii. p. 232.

CHAPTER LVIII

said Astley to the parliamentary officers; "and may now go to play, unless you choose to fall out among yourselves."[z]

The condition of the king, during this whole winter, was, to the last degree, disastrous and melancholy. As the dread of ills is commonly more oppressive than their real presence, perhaps in no period of his life was he more justly the object of compassion: His vigour of mind, which, though it sometimes failed him in acting, never deserted him in his sufferings, was what alone supported him; and he was determined, as he wrote to lord Digby, if he could not live as a king to die like a gentleman; nor should any of his friends, he said, ever have reason to blush for the prince, whom they had so unfortunately served.[a] The murmurs of discontented officers, on the one hand, harassed their unhappy sovereign; while they over-rated those services and sufferings, which, they now saw, must, for ever, go unrewarded.[b] The affectionate duty, on the other hand, of his more generous friends, who respected his misfortunes and his virtues, as much as his dignity, wrung his heart with a new sorrow; when he reflected, that such disinterested attachment would so soon be exposed to the rigour of his implacable enemies. Repeated attempts, which he made for a peaceful and equitable accommodation with the parliament, served to no purpose, but to convince them, that the victory was entirely in their hands. They deigned not to make the least reply to several of his messages, in which he desired a passport for commissioners.[c] At last, after reproaching him with the blood spilt during the war, they told him, that they were preparing bills for him; and his passing them would be the best pledge of his inclination towards peace: In other words, he must yield at discretion.[d] He desired a personal treaty, and offered to come to London, upon receiving a safe conduct for himself and his attendants: They absolutely refused him admittance, and issued orders for the guarding, that

[z] Rush. vol. vii. p. 141. It was the same Astley, who, before he charged at the battle of Edgehill, made this short prayer, *O Lord! thou knowest how busy I must be this day. If I forget thee, do not thou forget me.* And with that rose up, and cry'd, *March on, boys!* Warwic, p. 229. There were certainly much longer prayers said in the parliamentary army; but I doubt, if there was so good a one.   [a] Carte's Ormond, vol. iii. No. 433.   [b] Walker, p. 147.   [c] Rush. vol. vii. p. 215, &c.   [d] Ibid. vol. vii. p. 217, 219. Clarendon, vol. iv. p. 744.

is, the seizing of his person, in case he should attempt to visit them.[e] A new incident, which happened in Ireland, served to enflame the minds of men, and to encrease those calumnies, with which his enemies had so much loaded him, and which he ever regarded as the most grievous part of his misfortunes.

After the cessation with the Irish rebels, the king was desirous of concluding a final peace with them, and obtaining their assistance in England: And he gave authority to Ormond, lord lieutenant, to promise them an abrogation of all the penal laws, enacted against catholics; together with the suspension of Poinings' statute, with regard to some particular bills, which should be agreed on. Lord Herbert, created earl of Glamorgan, (though his patent had not yet passed the seals) having occasion for his private affairs to go to Ireland, the king considered, that this nobleman, being a catholic and allied to the best Irish families, might be of service: He also foresaw, that farther concessions with regard to religion might probably be demanded by the bigotted Irish; and that, as these concessions, however necessary, would give great scandal to the protestant zealots in his three kingdoms, it would be requisite, both to conceal them during some time, and to preserve Ormond's character, by giving private orders to Glamorgan to conclude and sign these articles. But as he had a better opinion of Glamorgan's zeal and affection for his service, than of his capacity, he enjoined him to communicate all his measures to Ormond; and though the final conclusion of the treaty must be executed only in Glamorgan's own name, he was required to be directed, in the steps towards it, by the opinion of the lord lieutenant. Glamorgan, bigotted to his religion, and passionate for the king's service, but guided in these pursuits by no manner of judgment or discretion, secretly, of himself, without any communication with Ormond, concluded a peace with the council of Kilkenny, and agreed in the king's name, that the Irish should enjoy all the churches, of which they had ever been in possession, since the commencement of their insurrection; on condition that they should assist the king in England with a body of ten thousand men. This transaction was discovered by accident. The titular archbishop of Tuam being killed by a sally of the garrison of Sligo, the articles of the treaty were found

[e] Rush. vol. vii. p. 249. Clarendon, vol. iv. p. 741.

among his baggage, and were immediately published every where, and copies of them sent over to the English parliament.*f* The lord lieutenant and lord Digby, foreseeing the clamour which would be raised against the king, committed Glamorgan to prison, charged him with treason for his temerity, and maintained, that he had acted altogether without any authority from his master. The English parliament however neglected not so favourable an opportunity of reviving the old clamour with regard to the king's favour of popery, and accused him of delivering over, in a manner, the whole kingdom of Ireland to that hated sect. The king told them, "That the earl of Glamorgan having made an offer to raise forces in the kingdom of Ireland, and to conduct them into England for his majesty's service, had a commission to that purpose, and to that purpose only, and that he had no commission at all to treat of any thing else, without the privity and direction of the lord lieutenant, much less to capitulate any thing concerning religion, or any property belonging either to church or laity."*g* Though this declaration seems agreeable to truth, it gave no satisfaction to the parliament; and some historians, even at present, when the ancient bigotry is somewhat abated, are desirous of representing this very innocent transaction, in which the king was engaged by the most violent necessity, as a stain on the memory of that unfortunate prince.*h*

Having lost all hope of prevailing over the rigour of the parliament, either by arms or by treaty, the only resource, which remained to the king, was derived from the intestine dissentions, which ran very high among his enemies. Presbyterians and independents, even before their victory was fully compleated, fell into contests about the division of the spoil; and their religious as well as civil disputes agitated the whole kingdom.

The parliament, though they had early abolished episcopal authority, had not, during so long a time, substituted any other spiritual government in its place; and their committees of religion had hitherto assumed the whole ecclesiastical jurisdiction: But they now established, by an ordinance, the presbyterian model in all its forms of *congregational, classical, provincial,* and *national* assemblies. All the inhabitants of each parish were ordered to meet

Ecclesiastical affairs.

f Rush. vol. vii. p. 239.   *g* Birch, p. 119.   *h* See note [GG] at the end of the volume.

and chuse elders, on whom, together with the minister, was bestowed the entire direction of all spiritual concerns within the congregation. A number of neighbouring parishes, commonly between twelve and twenty, formed a classis; and the court, which governed this division, was composed of all the ministers, together with two, three, or four elders chosen from each parish. The provincial assembly retained an inspection over several neighbouring classes, and was composed entirely of clergymen: The national assembly was constituted in the same manner; and its authority extended over the whole kingdom. It is probable, that the tyranny, exercised by the Scotish clergy, had given warning not to allow laymen a place in the provincial or national assemblies; lest the nobility and more considerable gentry, soliciting a seat in these great ecclesiastical courts, should bestow a consideration upon them, and render them, in the eyes of the multitude, a rival to the parliament. In the inferior courts, the mixture of the laity might serve rather to temper the usual zeal of the clergy.[i]

But though the presbyterians, by the establishment of parity among the ecclesiastics, were so far gratified, they were denied satisfaction in several other points, on which they were extremely intent. The assembly of divines had voted presbytery to be of divine right: The parliament refused their assent to that decision.[k] Selden, Whitlocke, and other political reasoners, assisted by the independents, had prevailed in this important deliberation. They thought, that, had the bigotted religionists been able to get their heavenly charter recognized, the presbyters would soon become more dangerous to the magistrate than had ever been the prelatical clergy. These latter, while they claimed to themselves a divine right, admitted to a like origin to civil authority: The former, challenging to their own order a celestial pedigree, derived the legislative power from a source no more dignified than the voluntary association of the people.

Under colour of keeping the sacraments from profanation, the clergy of all christian sects had assumed, what they call the power of the keys, or the right of fulminating excommunication. The example of Scotland was a sufficient lesson for the parliament to use precaution in guarding against so severe a tyranny. They de-

---

[i] Rush. vol. vii. p. 224.   [k] Whitlocke, p. 106. Rush. vol. vii. p. 260, 261.

termined, by a general ordinance, all the cases in which excommunication could be used. They allowed of appeals to parliament from all ecclesiastical courts. And they appointed commissioners in every province to judge of such cases as fell not within their general ordinance.[l] So much civil authority, intermixed with the ecclesiastical, gave disgust to all the zealots.

But nothing was attended with more universal scandal than the propensity of many in the parliament towards a toleration of the protestant sectaries. The presbyterians exclaimed, that this indulgence made the church of Christ resemble Noah's ark, and rendered it a receptacle for all unclean beasts. They insisted, that the least of Christ's truths was superior to all political considerations.[m] They maintained the eternal obligation imposed by the covenant to extirpate heresy and schism. And they menaced all their opponents with the same rigid persecution, under which they themselves had groaned, when held in subjection by the hierarchy.

So great prudence and reserve, in such material points, does great honour to the parliament; and proves, that, notwithstanding the prevalency of bigotry and fanaticism, there were many members, who had more enlarged views, and paid regard to the civil interests of society. These men, uniting themselves to the enthusiasts, whose genius is naturally averse to clerical usurpations, exercised so jealous an authority over the assembly of divines, that they allowed them nothing but the liberty of tendering advice, and would not entrust them even with the power of electing their own chairman or his substitute, or of supplying the vacancies of their own members.

While these disputes were canvassed by theologians, who engaged in their spiritual contests every order of the state; the king, though he entertained hopes of reaping advantage from those divisions, was much at a loss which side it would be most for his interest to comply with. The presbyterians were, by their principles, the least averse to regal authority; but were rigidly bent on the extirpation of prelacy: The independents were resolute to lay the foundation of a republican government; but as they pretended not to erect themselves into a national church, it might be hoped, that, if gratified with a toleration, they would admit the re-

[l] Rush. vol. vii. p. 210.   [m] Rush. vol. vii. p. 308.

establishment of the hierarchy. So great attachment had the king to episcopal jurisdiction, that he was ever inclined to put it in balance even with his own power and kingly office.

But whatever advantage he might hope to reap from the divisions in the parliamentary party, he was apprehensive, lest it should come too late, to save him from the destruction, with which he was instantly threatened. Fairfax was approaching with a powerful and victorious army, and was taking the proper measures for laying siege to Oxford, which must infallibly fall into his hands. To be taken captive, and led in triumph by his insolent enemies, was what Charles justly abhorred; and every insult, if not violence, was to be dreaded, from that enthusiastic soldiery, who hated his person, and despised his dignity. In this desperate extremity, he embraced a measure, which in any other situation, might lie under the imputation of imprudence and indiscretion.

Montreville, the French minister, interested for the king more by the natural sentiments of humanity, than any instructions from his court, which seemed rather to favour the parliament, had solicited the Scottish generals and commissioners, to give protection to their distressed sovereign; and having received many general professions and promises, he had always transmitted these, perhaps with some exaggeration, to the king. From his suggestions, Charles began to entertain thoughts of leaving Oxford, and flying to the Scottish army, which at that time lay before Newark.[n] He considered, that the Scottish nation had been fully gratified in all their demands; and having already, in their own country, annihilated both episcopacy and regal authority, had no farther concessions to exact from him. In all disputes, which had passed about settling the terms of peace, the Scots, he heard, had still adhered to the milder side, and had endeavoured to soften the rigour of the English parliament. Great disgusts also, on other accounts, had taken place between the nations; and the Scots found, that, in proportion as their assistance became less necessary, less value was put upon them. The progress of the independents gave them great alarm; and they were scandalized to hear their beloved covenant spoken of, every day, with less regard and reverence. The refusal of a divine right to presbytery, and the infringing of ecclesiastical

[n] Clarendon, vol. iv. p. 750. vol. v. p. 16.

CHAPTER LVIII

discipline from political considerations, were, to them, the subject
of much offence: And the king hoped, that, in their present disposition, the sight of their native prince, flying to them in this extremity of distress, would rouze every spark of generosity in their
bosom, and procure him their favour and protection.

That he might the better conceal his intentions, orders were
given at every gate in Oxford, for allowing three persons to pass;
and in the night, the king, accompanied by none but Dr. Hudson
and Mr. Ashburnham, went out at that gate, which leads to London. He rode before a portmanteau, and called himself Ashburnham's servant. He passed through Henley, St. Albans, and
came so near to London as Harrow on the Hill. He once entertained thoughts of entering into that city, and of throwing himself
on the mercy of the parliament. But at last, after passing through
many cross roads, he arrived at the Scottish camp before Newark.[o]
The parliament, hearing of his escape from Oxford, issued rigorous orders and threatened with instant death, whoever should
harbour or conceal him.[p]

5th May.

The Scottish generals and commissioners affected great surprize on the appearance of the king: And though they payed him
all the exterior respect due to his dignity, they instantly set a guard
upon him, under colour of protection; and made him in reality a
prisoner. They informed the English parliament of this unexpected incident, and assured them, that they had entered into no
private treaty with the king. They applied to him for orders to
Bellasis, governor of Newark, to surrender that town, now reduced
to extremity; and the orders were instantly obeyed. And hearing,
that the parliament laid claim to the entire disposal of the king's
person, and that the English army was making some motions
towards them; they thought proper to retire northwards, and to fix
their camp at Newcastle.[q]

*King
goes to
the
Scotch
camp at
Newark.*

This measure was very grateful to the king; and he began to
entertain hopes of protection from the Scots. He was particularly
attentive to the behaviour of their preachers, on whom all depended. It was the mode of that age to make the pulpit the scene
of news; and on every great event the whole scripture was ran-

[o] Rush. vol. vii. p. 267.   [p] Whitlocke, p. 209.   [q] Rush. vol. vii. p. 271.
Clarendon, vol. v. p. 23.

sacked by the clergy, for passages applicable to the present occasion. The first minister who preached before the king, chose these words for his text. "And behold all the men of Israel came to the king, and said unto him, Why have our brethren the men of Judah, stolen thee away, and have brought the king and his houshold, and all David's men with him, over Jordan? And all the men of Judah answered the men of Israel, Because the king is near of kin to us; wherefore then be ye angry for this matter? Have we eaten at all of the king's cost? or hath he given us any gift? And the men of Israel answered the men of Judah, and said, We have ten parts in the king, and we have also more right in David than ye: Why then did ye despise us, that our advice should not be first had in bringing back our king? And the words of the men of Judah were fiercer than the words of the men of Israel."[r] But the king soon found, that the happiness chiefly of the allusion had tempted the preacher to employ this text, and that the covenanting zealots were no wise pacified towards him. Another preacher, after reproaching him to his face, with his misgovernment, ordered this psalm to be sung;

> Why dost thou, tyrant, boast thyself
> Thy wicked deeds to praise.

The king stood up, and called for that psalm which begins with these words,

> Have mercy, Lord, on me, I pray;
> For men would me devour:

The good-natured audience, in pity to fallen majesty, showed, for once, greater deference to the king than to the minister, and sung the psalm, which the former had called for.[s]

Charles had very little reason to be pleased with his situation. He not only found himself a prisoner, very strictly guarded: All his friends were kept at a distance; and no intercourse, either by letters or conversation, was allowed him with any one, on whom he

---

[r] 2 Sam. chap. xix. 41, 42, and 43 verses. See Clarendon, vol. v. p. 23, 24.
[s] Whitlocke, p. 234.

could depend, or who was suspected of any attachment towards him. The Scottish generals would enter into no confidence with him; and still treated him with distant ceremony and feigned respect. And every proposal, which they made him, tended farther to his abasement and to his ruin.[t]

They required him to issue orders to Oxford, and all his other garrisons, commanding their surrender to the parliament: And the king, sensible that their resistance was to very little purpose, willingly complied. The terms, given to most of them, were honourable; and Fairfax, as far as it lay in his power, was very exact in observing them. Far from allowing violence; he would not even permit insults or triumph over the unfortunate royalists; and by his generous humanity, so cruel a civil war was ended in appearance, very calmly, between the parties.

Ormond having received like orders, delivered Dublin, and other forts, into the hands of the parliamentary officers. Montrose also, after having experienced still more variety of good and bad fortune, threw down his arms, and retired out of the kingdom.

The marquess of Worcester, a man past eighty-four was the last in England that submitted to the authority of the parliament. He defended Raglan castle to extremity; and opened not its gates till the middle of August. Four years, a few days excepted, were now elapsed, since the king first erected his standard at Nottingham.[u] So long had the British nations, by civil and religious quarrels, been occupied in shedding their own blood, and laying waste their native country.

The parliament and the Scots laid their proposals before the king. They were such as a captive, entirely at mercy, could expect from the most inexorable victor: Yet were they little worse than what were insisted on before the battle of Naseby. The power of the sword, instead of ten, which the king now offered, was demanded for twenty years, together with a right to levy whatever money the parliament should think proper for the support of their armies. The other conditions were, in the main, the same with those which had formerly been offered to the king.[w]

Charles said, that proposals, which introduced such important innovations in the constitution, demanded time for deliberation:

[t] Clarendon, vol. v. p. 30.   [u] Rush. vol. vi. p. 293.   [w] Ibid. p. 309.

The commissioners replied, that he must give his answer in ten days.[x] He desired to reason about the meaning and import of some terms: They informed him, that they had no power of debate; and peremptorily required his consent or refusal. He requested a personal treaty with the parliament: They threatened, that, if he delayed compliance, the parliament would, by their own authority, settle the nation.

What the parliament was most intent upon, was not their treaty with the king, to whom they paid little regard; but that with the Scots. Two important points remained to be settled with that nation; their delivery of the king, and the estimation of their arrears.

The Scots might pretend, that, as Charles was king of Scotland as well as of England, they were intitled to an equal vote in the disposal of his person: And that, in such a case, where the titles are equal, and the subject indivisible, the preference was due to the present possessor. The English maintained, that the king, being in England, was comprehended within the jurisdiction of that kingdom, and could not be disposed of by any foreign nation. A delicate question this, and what surely could not be decided by precedent; since such a situation is not, any where, to be found in history.[y]

As the Scots concurred with the English, in imposing such severe conditions on the king, that, notwithstanding his unfortunate situation, he still refused to accept of them; it is certain, that they did not desire his freedom: Nor could they ever intend to join lenity and rigour together, in so inconsistent a manner. Before the settlement of terms, the administration must be possessed entirely by the parliaments of both kingdoms; and how incompatible that scheme with the liberty of the king, is easily imagined. To carry him a prisoner into Scotland, where few forces could be supported to guard him, was a measure so full of inconvenience and danger, that, even if the English had consented to it, it must have appeared to the Scots themselves altogether uneligible: And how could such a plan be supported in opposition to England, possessed of such numerous and victorious armies, which were, at that time, at least, seemed to be, in entire union with the parliament? The only expedient, it is obvious, which the Scots

[x] Ibid. vol. vii. p. 319.   [y] Rush. vol. vii. p. 339.

could embrace, if they scrupled wholly to abandon the king, was immediately to return, fully and cordially, to their allegiance; and, uniting themselves with the royalists in both kingdoms, endeavour, by force of arms, to reduce the English parliament to more moderate conditions: But besides that this measure was full of extreme hazard; what was it but instantly to combine with their old enemies against their old friends; and in a fit of romantic generosity, overturn what, with so much expence of blood and treasure, they had, during the course of so many years, been so carefully erecting?

But, though all these reflections occurred to the Scottish commissioners, they resolved to prolong the dispute, and to keep the king as a pledge for those arrears, which they claimed from England, and which they were not likely, in the present disposition of that nation, to obtain by any other expedient. The sum, by their account, amounted to near two millions: For they had received little regular pay, since they had entered England. And though the contributions, which they had levied, as well as the price of their living at free quarters, must be deducted; yet still the sum, which they insisted on, was very considerable. After many discussions, it was, at last, agreed, that, in lieu of all demands, they should accept of 400,000 pounds, one half to be paid instantly, another in two subsequent payments. [z]

Great pains were taken by the Scots (and the English complied with their pretended delicacy) to make this estimation and payment of arrears appear a quite different transaction from that for the delivery of the king's person: But common sense requires, that they should be regarded as one and the same. The English, it is evident, had they not been previously assured of receiving the king, would never have parted with so considerable a sum; and, while they weakened themselves, by the same measure have strengthened a people, with whom they must afterwards have so material an interest to discuss.

Thus the Scottish nation underwent, and still undergo (for such grievous stains are not easily wiped off) the reproach of selling their king, and betraying their prince for money. In vain, did they maintain, that this money was, on account of former services,

---

[z] Rush. vol. vii. p. 326. Parl. Hist. vol. xv. p. 236.

undoubtedly their due; that in their present situation, no other measure, without the utmost discretion, or even their apparent ruin, could be embraced; and that, though they delivered their king into the hands of his open enemies, they were themselves as much his open enemies as those to whom they surrendered him, and their common hatred against him had long united the two parties in strict alliance with each other. They were still answered, that they made use of this scandalous expedient for obtaining their wages; and that, after taking arms, without any provocation, against their sovereign, who had ever loved and cherished them, they had deservedly fallen into a situation, from which they could not extricate themselves, without either infamy or imprudence.

The infamy of this bargain had such an influence on the Scottish parliament, that they once voted, that the king should be protected, and his liberty insisted on. But the general assembly interposed, and pronounced, that, as he had refused to take the covenant, which was pressed on him, it became not the godly to concern themselves about his fortunes. After this declaration, it behoved the parliament to retract their vote.[a]

Intelligence concerning the final resolution of the Scottish nation to surrender him, was brought to the king; and he happened, at that very time, to be playing at chess.[b] Such command of temper did he possess, that he continued his game without interruption; and none of the by-standers could perceive, that the letter, which he perused, had brought him news of any consequence. The English commissioners, who, some days after, came to take him under their custody, were admitted to kiss his hands; and he received them with the same grace and chearfulness, as if they had travelled on no other errand, than to pay court to him. The old earl of Pembroke in particular, who was one of them, he congratulated on his strength and vigour, that he was still able, during such a season, to perform so long a journey, in company with so many young people.

1647.
King
delivered
up by
the Scots.

The king, being delivered over by the Scots to the English commissioners, was conducted, under a guard, to Holdenby, in the county of Northampton. On his journey, the whole country flocked to behold him, moved partly by curiosity, partly by com-

[a] Parl. Hist. vol. xv. p. 243, 244.   [b] Burnet's Memoirs of the Hamiltons.

CHAPTER LVIII

passion and affection. If any still retained rancour against him, in his present condition, they passed in silence; while his well-wishers, more generous than prudent, accompanied his march with tears, with acclamations, and with prayers for his safety.[c] That ancient superstition likewise, of desiring the king's touch in scrophulous distempers, seemed to acquire fresh credit among the people, from the general tenderness, which began to prevail for this virtuous and unhappy monarch.

The commissioners rendered his confinement at Holdenby very rigorous; dismissing his ancient servants, debarring him from visits, and cutting off all communication with his friends or family. The parliament, though earnestly applied to by the king, refused to allow his chaplains to attend him; because they had not taken the covenant. The king refused to assist at the service, exercised according to the directory; because he had not, as yet, given his consent to that mode of worship.[d] Such religious zeal prevailed on both sides! And such was the unhappy and distracted condition, to which it had reduced king and people!

During the time, that the king remained in the Scottish army at Newcastle, died the earl of Essex, the discarded, but still powerful and popular general of the parliament. His death, in this conjuncture, was a public misfortune. Fully sensible of the excesses, to which affairs had been carried, and of the worse consequences, which were still to be apprehended, he had resolved to conciliate a peace, and to remedy, as far as possible, all those ills, to which, from mistake, rather than any bad intentions, he had himself so much contributed. The presbyterian, or the moderate party among the commons, found themselves considerably weakened by his death: And the small remains of authority, which still adhered to the house of peers, were, in a manner, wholly extinguished.[e]

[c] Ludlow, Herbert.   [d] Clarendon, vol. v. p. 39. Warwick, p. 298.
[e] Clarendon, vol. v. p. 43.

LIX

Mutiny of the army – The king seized
by Joyce – The army march against the parliament –
The army subdue the parliament – The king
flies to the isle of Wight – Second
civil war – Invasion from Scotland –
The treaty of Newport – The civil war and
invasion repressed – The king seized again
by the army – The house purged –
The king's trial – And execution –
And character

❁ ❁ ❁

1647.	THE DOMINION OF THE PARLIAMENT was of short duration. No sooner had they subdued their sovereign, than their own servants rose against them, and tumbled them from their slippery throne. The sacred boundaries of the laws being once violated, nothing remained to confine the wild projects of zeal and ambition. And every successive revolution became a precedent for that which followed it.

In proportion as the terror of the king's power diminished, the division between independent and presbyterian became every day more apparent; and the neuters found it, at last, requisite to seek shelter in one or the other faction. Many new writs were issued for elections, in the room of members, who had died, or were disqualified by adhering to the king; yet still the presbyterians re-

CHAPTER LIX

tained the superiority among the commons: And all the peers, except Lord Say, were esteemed of that party. The independents, to whom the inferior sectaries adhered, predominated in the army: And the troops of the new model were universally infected with that enthusiastic spirit. To their assistance did the independent party, among the commons, chiefly trust, in their projects for acquiring the ascendant over their antagonists.

Soon after the retreat of the Scots, the presbyterians, seeing every thing reduced to obedience, began to talk of diminishing the army: And, on pretence of easing the public burthens, they levelled a deadly blow at the opposite faction. They purposed to embark a strong detachment, under Skippon and Massey, for the service of Ireland: They openly declared their intention of making a great reduction of the remainder.[f] It was even imagined, that another new model of the army was projected, in order to regain to the presbyterians, that superiority, which they had so imprudently lost by the former.[g]

The army had small inclination to the service of Ireland; a country barbarous, uncultivated, and laid waste by massacres, and civil commotions: They had less inclination to disband, and to renounce that pay, which, having earned it through fatigues and dangers, they now purposed to enjoy in ease and tranquillity. And most of the officers, having risen from the dregs of the people, had no other prospect, if deprived of their commission, than that of returning to languish in their native poverty and obscurity.

These motives of interest acquired additional influence, and became more dangerous to the parliament, from the religious spirit, by which the army was universally actuated. Among the generality of men, educated in regular, civilized societies, the sentiments of shame, duty, honour, have considerable authority, and serve to counterbalance and direct the motives, derived from private advantage: But, by the predominancy of enthusiasm among the parliamentary forces, these salutary principles lost their credit, and were regarded as mere human inventions, yea moral institutions, fitter for heathens than for christians.[h] The saint, resigned

---

[f] Fourteen thousand men were only intended to be kept up; 6000 horse, 6000 foot, and 2000 dragoons. Bates.   [g] Rush. vol. vii. p. 564.   [h] Rush. vol. vi. p. 134.

over to superior guidance, was at full liberty to gratify all his appetites, disguised under the appearance of pious zeal. And, besides the strange corruptions engendered by this spirit, it eluded and loosened all the ties of morality, and gave entire scope, and even sanction, to the selfishness and ambition, which naturally adhere to the human mind.

The military confessors were farther encouraged in disobedience to superiors, by that spiritual pride, to which a mistaken piety is so subject. They were not, they said, mere janizaries; mercenary troops inlisted for hire, and to be disposed of at the will of their paymasters.[i] Religion and liberty were the motives, which had excited them to arms; and they had a superior right to see those blessings, which they had purchased with their blood, ensured to future generations. By the same title, that the presbyterians, in contradistinction to the royalists, had appropriated to themselves the epithet of *godly,* or the *well-affected;*[k] the independents did now, in contradistinction to the presbyterians, assume this magnificent appellation, and arrogate all the ascendant, which naturally belongs to it.

Hearing of parties in the house of commons, and being informed, that the minority were friends to the army, the majority enemies; the troops naturally interested themselves in that dangerous distinction, and were eager to give the superiority to their partizans. Whatever hardships they underwent, though perhaps derived from inevitable necessity, were ascribed to a settled design of oppressing them, and resented as an effect of the animosity and malice of their adversaries.

Notwithstanding the great revenue, which accrued from taxes, assessments, sequestrations, and compositions, considerable arrears were due to the army; and many of the private men, as well as officers, had near a twelvemonth's pay still owing them. The army suspected, that this deficiency was purposely contrived in order to oblige them to live at free quarters; and, by rendering them odious to the country, serve as a pretence for disbanding them. When they saw such members, as were employed in committees and civil offices, accumulate fortunes, they accused them of rapine and public plunder. And, as no plan was pointed out by the

---

[i] Ibid. vol. vii. p. 565.   [k] Ibid. vol. vii. p. 474.

CHAPTER LIX

commons for the payment of arrears, the soldiers dreaded, that, after they should be disbanded or embarked for Ireland, their enemies, who predominated in the two houses, would entirely defraud them of their right, and oppress them with impunity.

On this ground or pretence did the first commotions begin in the army. A petition, addressed to Fairfax the general, was handed about; craving an indemnity, and that ratified by the king, for any illegal actions, of which, during the course of the war, the soldiers might have been guilty; together with satisfaction in arrears, freedom from pressing, relief of widows and maimed soldiers, and pay till disbanded.[l] The commons, aware of what combustible materials the army was composed, were alarmed at this intelligence. Such a combination, they knew, if not checked in its first appearance, must be attended with the most dangerous consequences, and must soon exalt the military above the civil authority. Besides summoning some officers to answer for this attempt, they immediately voted, that the petition tended to introduce mutiny, to put conditions upon the parliament, and to obstruct the relief of Ireland; and they threatened to proceed against the promoters of it, as enemies to the state, and disturbers of public peace.[m] This declaration, which may be deemed violent, especially as the army had some ground for complaint, produced fatal effects. The soldiers lamented, that they were deprived of the privileges of Englishmen; that they were not allowed so much as to represent their grievances; that, while petitions from Essex and other places were openly encouraged against the army, their mouths were stopped; and that they, who were the authors of liberty to the nation, were reduced, by a faction in parliament, to the most grievous servitude.

Mutiny of the army.

March 30.

In this disposition was the army found by Warwic, Dacres, Massey, and other commissioners; who were sent to make them proposals for entering into the service of Ireland.[n] Instead of inlisting, the generality objected to the terms; demanded an indemnity; were clamorous for their arrears: And, though they expressed no dissatisfaction against Skippon, who was appointed commander, they discovered much stronger inclination to serve under Fairfax and Cromwel.[o] Some officers, who were of the pres-

---

[l] Parl. Hist. vol. xv. p. 342.   [m] Parl. Hist. vol. xv. p. 344.   [n] Rush. vol. vii. p. 457.   [o] Ibid. vol. vii. p. 458.

byterian party, having entered into engagements for this service, could prevail on very few of the soldiers to inlist under them. And, as these officers lay all under the grievous reproach of deserting the army, and betraying the interests of their companions; the rest were farther confirmed in that confederacy, which they had secretly formed.[p]

To petition and remonstrate being the most cautious method of conducting a confederacy, an application to parliament was signed by near 200 officers; in which they made their apology with a very imperious air, asserted their right of petitioning, and complained of that imputation thrown upon them by the former declaration of the lower house.[q] The private men likewise of some regiments sent a letter to Skippon; in which, together with insisting on the same topics, they lament, that designs were formed against them and many of the godly party in the kingdom; and declare, that they could not engage for Ireland, till they were satisfied in their expectations, and had their just desires granted.[r] The army, in a word, felt their power, and resolved to be masters.

The parliament too resolved, if possible, to preserve their dominion; but being destitute of power, and not retaining much authority, it was not easy for them to employ any expedient, which could contribute to their purpose. The expedient, which they now made use of, was the worst imaginable. They sent Skippon, Cromwel, Ireton, and Fleetwood, to the head-quarters at Saffron-Weldon in Essex; and empowered them to make offers to the *7th May.* army, and enquire into the cause of its *distempers.* These very generals, at least the three last, were secretly the authors of all the discontents; and failed not to foment those disorders, which they pretended to appease. By their suggestion, a measure was embraced, which, at once, brought matters to extremity, and rendered the mutiny incurable.

In opposition to the parliament at Westminster, a military parliament was formed. Together with a council of the principal officers, which was appointed after the model of the house of peers; a more free representative of the army was composed, by the election of two private men or inferior officers, under the title of agitators, from each troop or company.[s] By this means, both the

---

[p] Ibid. vol. vii. p. 461, 556.   [q] Rush. vol. vii. p. 468.   [r] Idem, ibid. p. 474.
[s] Idem, ibid. p. 485. Clarendon, vol. v. p. 43.

CHAPTER LIX

general humour of that time was gratified, intent on plans of imaginary republics; and an easy method contrived for conducting underhand, and propagating the sedition of the army.

This terrible court, when assembled; having first declared, that they found no *distempers* in the army, but many *grievances,* under which it laboured; immediately voted the offers of the parliament unsatisfactory. Eight weeks' pay alone, they said, was promised; a small part of fifty-six weeks, which they claimed as their due: No visible security was given for the remainder: And having been declared public enemies by the commons, they might hereafter be prosecuted as such, unless the declaration were recalled.[*t*] Before matters came to this height, Cromwel had posted up to London, on pretence of laying before the parliament the rising discontents of the army.

The parliament made one vigorous effort more, to try the force of their authority: They voted, that all the troops, which did not engage for Ireland, should instantly be disbanded in their quarters.[*u*] At the same time, the council of the army ordered a general rendezvous of all the regiments, in order to provide for their common interests. And while they thus prepared themselves for opposition to the parliament, they struck a blow, which at once decided the victory in their favour.

A party of five hundred horse appeared at Holdenby, conducted by one Joyce, who had once been a taylor by profession; but was now advanced to the rank of cornet, and was an active agitator in the army. Without being opposed by the guard, whose affections were all on their side; Joyce came into the king's presence, armed with pistols, and told him, that he must immediately go along with him. *Whither?* said the king. *To the army;* replied Joyce. *By what warrant?* asked the king. Joyce pointed to the soldiers, whom he brought along; tall, handsome, and well accoutred. *Your warrant,* said Charles smiling, *is writ in fair characters, legible without spelling.*[*w*] The parliamentary commissioners came into the room: They asked Joyce, whether he had any orders from the parliament? He said, *No:* From the general? *No:* By what authority he came? He made the same reply as to the king: *They would write,* they said, *to the parliament to know their pleasure. You may do so,* replied

3d June.
The king seized by Joyce.

[*t*] Rush. vol. vii. p. 497, 505. Whitlocke, p. 250.   [*u*] Rush. vol. vii. p. 487.
[*w*] Whitlocke, p. 254. Warwick, p. 299.

Joyce; *but in the mean time the king must immediately go with me.* Resistance was vain. The king, after protracting the time as long as he could, went into his coach; and was safely conducted to the army, who were hastening to their rendezvous at Triplo-Heath near Cambridge. The parliament, informed of this event by their commissioners, were thrown into the utmost consternation.[x]

Fairfax himself was no less surprized at the king's arrival. That bold measure, executed by Joyce, had never been communicated to the general. The orders were entirely verbal; and no body avowed them. And, while every one affected astonishment at the enterprize, Cromwel, by whose counsel it had been directed, arrived from London, and put an end to their deliberations.

This artful and audacious conspirator had conducted himself in the parliament with such profound dissimulation, with such refined hypocrisy, that he had long deceived those, who, being themselves very dextrous practitioners in the same arts, should naturally have entertained the more suspicion against others. At every intelligence of disorders in the army, he was moved to the highest pitch of grief and of anger. He wept bitterly: He lamented the misfortunes of his country: He advised every violent measure for suppressing the mutiny; and by these precipitate counsels, at once seemed to evince his own sincerity, and inflamed those discontents, of which he intended to make advantage. He obtested heaven and earth, that his devoted attachment to the parliament had rendered him so odious in the army, that his life, while among them, was in the utmost danger; and he had very narrowly escaped a conspiracy, formed to assassinate him. But information being brought, that the most active officers and agitators were entirely his creatures, the parliamentary leaders secretly resolved, that, next day, when he should come to the house, an accusation should be entered against him, and he should be sent to the Tower.[y] Cromwel, who, in the conduct of his desperate enterprizes, frequently approached to the very brink of destruction, knew how to make the requisite turn with proper dexterity and boldness. Being informed of this design, he hastened to the camp; where he was received with acclamations, and was instantly invested with the supreme command both of general and army.

[x] Rush. vol. vii. p. 514, 515. Clarendon, vol. v. p. 47.   [y] Clarendon, vol. v. p. 46.

CHAPTER LIX

Fairfax, having neither talents himself for cabal, nor penetration to discover the cabals of others, had given his entire confidence to Cromwel; who, by the best coloured pretences, and by the appearance of an open sincerity and a scrupulous conscience, imposed on the easy nature of this brave and virtuous man. The council of officers and the agitators were moved altogether by Cromwel's direction, and conveyed his will to the whole army. By his profound and artful conduct, he had now attained a situation, where he could cover his enterprizes from public view; and seeming either to obey the commands of his superior officer, or yield to the movements of the soldiers, could secretly pave the way for his future greatness. While the disorders of the army were yet in their infancy, he kept at a distance; lest his counterfeit aversion might throw a damp upon them, or his secret encouragement beget suspicion in the parliament. As soon as they came to maturity, he openly joined the troops; and in the critical moment, struck that important blow of seizing the king's person, and depriving the parliament of any resource of an accommodation with him. Though one vizor fell off, another still remained, to cover his natural countenance. Where delay was requisite, he could employ the most indefatigable patience: Where celerity was necessary, he flew to a decision. And by thus uniting in his person the most opposite talents, he was enabled to combine the most contrary interests in a subserviency to his secret purposes.

The parliament, though at present defenceless, was possessed of many resources; and time might easily enable them to resist that violence, with which they were threatened. Without farther deliberation, therefore, Cromwel advanced the army upon them, and arrived in a few days at St. Albans. *The army march against the parliament.*

Nothing could be more popular, than this hostility, which the army commenced against the parliament. As much as that assembly was once the idol of the nation, as much was it now become the object of general hatred and aversion.

The self-denying ordinance had no longer been put in execution, than till Essex, Manchester, Waller, and the other officers of that party, had resigned their commission: Immediately after, it was laid aside by tacit consent; and the members, sharing all offices of power and profit among them, proceeded with impunity in exercising acts of oppression on the helpless nation. Though the necessity of their situation might serve as an apology for many of their measures, the people, not accustomed to such a species of government, were not disposed to make the requisite allowances.

A small supply of 100,000 pounds a year could never be obtained by former kings from the jealous humour of parliaments; and the English, of all nations in Europe, were the least accustomed to taxes: But this parliament, from the commencement of the war, according to some computations, had levied, in five years, above forty millions;[z] yet were loaded with debts and incumbrances, which, during that age, were regarded as prodigious. If these computations should be thought much exaggerated, as they probably are,[a] the taxes and impositions were certainly far higher than in any former state of the English government; and such popular exaggerations are, at least, a proof of popular discontents.

But the disposal of this money was no less the object of general complaint against the parliament than the levying of it. The sum of 300,000 pounds they openly took, 'tis affirmed,[b] and divided among their own members. The committees, to whom the management of the different branches of revenue was entrusted, never brought in their accounts, and had unlimited power of secreting whatever sums they pleased from the public treasure.[c] These branches were needlessly multiplied, in order to render the revenue more intricate, to share the advantages among greater numbers, and to conceal the frauds, of which they were universally suspected.[d]

The method of keeping accounts, practised in the exchequer, was confessedly the exactest, the most ancient, the best known, and the least liable to fraud. The exchequer was, for that reason, abolished, and the revenue put under the management of a committee, who were subject to no controul.[e]

The excise was an odious tax, formerly unknown to the nation;

[z] Clement Walker's history of the two Juntos, prefixed to his history of independency, p. 8. This is an author of spirit and ingenuity; and being a zealous parliamentarian, his authority is very considerable, notwithstanding the air of satire, which prevails in his writings. This computation, however, seems much too large; especially as the sequestrations, during the time of war, could not be so considerable as afterwards. [a] Yet the same sum precisely is assigned in another book, called Royal Treasury of England, p. 297. [b] Clement Walker's history of independency, p. 3, 166. [c] Ibid. p. 8. [d] Id. Ibid. [e] Clement Walker's history of independency, p. 8.

CHAPTER LIX

and was now extended over provisions and the common necessaries of life. Near one half of the goods and chattels, and at least
one half of the lands, rents, and revenues of the kingdom, had
been sequestered. To great numbers of royalists, all redress from
these sequestrations was refused: To the rest, the remedy could be
obtained only by paying large compositions and subscribing the
covenant, which they abhorred. Besides pitying the ruin and deso-
lation of so many ancient and honourable families; indifferent
spectators could not but blame the hardship of punishing with
such severity, actions, which the law, in its usual and most undisputed interpretation, strictly required of every subject.

The severities, too, exercised against the episcopal clergy, naturally affected the royalists, and even all men of candor, in a
sensible manner. By the most moderate computation,^{f} it appears,
that above one half of the established clergy had been turned out
to beggary and want, for no other crime than their adhering to the
civil and religious principles, in which they had been educated;
and for their attachment to those laws, under whose countenance
they had at first embraced that profession. To renounce episcopacy and the liturgy, and to subscribe the covenant, were the only
terms, which could save them from so rigorous a fate; and if the
least mark of malignancy, as it was called, or affection to the king,
who so entirely loved them, had ever escaped their lips, even this
hard choice was not permitted. The sacred character, which gives
the priesthood such authority over mankind, becoming more venerable from the sufferings, endured, for the sake of principle, by
these distressed royalists, aggravated the general indignation
against their persecutors.

But what excited the most universal complaint was, the unlimited tyranny and despotic rule of the country-committees. During
the war, the discretionary power of these courts was excused, from
the plea of necessity: But the nation was reduced to despair, when
it saw neither end put to their duration, nor bounds to their au-

---

^{f} See John Walker's attempt towards recovering an account of the numbers
and sufferings of the clergy. The parliament pretended to leave the sequestered clergy a fifth of their revenue; but this author makes it sufficiently
appear, that this provision, small as it is, was never regularly paid the
ejected clergy.

thority. These could sequester, fine, imprison, and corporally pun-ish, without law or remedy. They interposed in questions of private property. Under colour of malignancy, they exercised vengeance against their private enemies. To the obnoxious, and sometimes to the innocent, they sold their protection. And instead of one star-chamber, which had been abolished, a great number were anew erected, fortified with better pretences, and armed with more unlimited authority.[g]

Could any thing have increased the indignation against that slavery, into which the nation, from the too eager pursuit of lib-erty, had fallen; it must have been the reflection on the pretences, by which the people had so long been deluded. The sanctified hypocrites, who called their oppressions the spoiling of the Egyp-tians, and their rigid severity the dominion of the Elect, inter-larded all their iniquities with long and fervent prayers, saved themselves from blushing by their pious grimaces, and exercised, in the name of the Lord, all their cruelty on men. An undisguised violence could be forgiven: But such a mockery of the under-standing, such an abuse of religion, were, with men of penetration, objects of peculiar resentment.

The parliament, conscious of their decay in popularity, seeing a formidable armed force advance upon them, were reduced to despair, and found all their resources much inferior to the present necessity. London still retained a strong attachment to presby-terianism; and its militia, which was numerous, and had acquired reputation in the wars, had, by a late ordinance, been put into hands, in whom the parliament could entirely confide. This militia was now called out, and ordered to guard the lines, which had been drawn round the city, in order to secure it against the king. A body of horse was ordered to be instantly levied. Many officers, who had been cashiered by the new model of the army, offered their service to the parliament. An army of 5000 men lay in the north under the command of general Pointz, who was of the presbyterian faction;

[g] Clement Walker's history of independency, p. 5. Hollis gives the same representation, as Walker, of the plundering, oppressions, and tyranny of the parliament: Only, instead of laying the fault on both parties, as Walker does, he ascribes it solely to the independent faction. The presbyterians indeed, being commonly denominated the *moderate* party, would probably be more inoffensive. See Rush. vol. vii. p. 598, and Parl. Hist. vol. xv. p. 230.

but these were too distant to be employed in so urgent a necessity. The forces, destined for Ireland, were quartered in the west; and, though deemed faithful to the parliament, they also lay at a distance. Many inland garrisons were commanded by officers of the same party; but their troops, being so much dispersed, could, at present, be of no manner of service. The Scots were faithful friends and zealous for presbytery and the covenant; but a long time was required, ere they could collect their forces, and march to the assistance of the parliament.

In this situation it was thought more prudent to submit, and by compliance to stop the fury of the enraged army. The declaration, *8th June.* by which the military petitioners had been voted public enemies, was recalled, and erazed from the journal-book.[h] This was the first symptom, which the parliament gave of submission; and the army, hoping, by terror alone, to effect all their purposes, stopped at St. Albans, and entered into negociation with their masters.

Here commenced the encroachments of the military upon the civil authority. The army, in their usurpations on the parliament, copied exactly the model, which the parliament itself had set them, in their recent usurpations on the crown.

Every day, they rose in their demands. If one claim was granted, they had another ready, still more enormous and exorbitant; and were determined never to be satisfied. At first, they pretended only to petition for what concerned themselves as soldiers: Next, they must have a vindication of their character: Then, it was necessary, that their enemies be punished:[i] At last, they claimed a right of modelling the whole government, and settling the nation.[k]

They preserved, in words, all deference and respect to the parliament; but in reality, insulted them and tyrannized over them. That assembly, they pretended not to accuse: It was only evil counsellors, who seduced and betrayed it.

They proceeded so far as to name eleven members, whom, in *16th June.* general terms, they charged with high treason, as enemies to the army and evil counsellors to the parliament. Their names were Hollis, Sir Philip Stapleton, Sir William Lewis, Sir John Clotwor-

---

[h] Rush. vol. vii. p. 503, 547. Clarendon, vol. v. p. 45.   [i] Rush. vol. vii. p. 509.   [k] Ibid. vol. vii. p. 567, 633. Ibid. vol. viii. p. 731.

thy, Sir William Waller, Sir John Maynard, Massey, Glyn, Long, Harley, and Nichols.[l] These were the very leaders of the presbyterian party.

They insisted that these members should immediately be sequestered from parliament, and be thrown into prison.[m] The commons replied, that they could not, upon a general charge, proceed so far.[n] The army observed to them, that the cases of Strafford and Laud were direct precedents for that purpose.[o] At last, the eleven members themselves, not to give occasion for discord, begged leave to retire from the house; and the army, for the present, seemed satisfied with this mark of submission.[p]

Pretending, that the parliament intended to levy war upon them, and to involve the nation again in blood and confusion, they required, that all new levies should be stopped. The parliament complied with this demand.[q]

There being no signs of resistance, the army, in order to save appearances, removed, at the desire of the parliament, to a greater distance from London, and fixed their head quarters at Reading. They carried the king along with them in all their marches.

That prince now found himself in a better situation than at Holdenby, and had attained some greater degree of freedom, as well as of consideration with both parties.

All his friends had access to his presence: His correspondence with the queen was not interrupted: His chaplains were restored to him, and he was allowed the use of the liturgy: His children were once allowed to visit him, and they passed a few days at Caversham, where he then resided.[r] He had not seen the duke of Gloucester, his youngest son, and the princess Elizabeth, since he left London, at the commencement of the civil disorders;[s] nor the duke of York, since he went to the Scottish army before Newark. No private man, unacquainted with the pleasures of a court, and the tumult of a camp, more passionately loved his family, than did this good prince; and such an instance of indulgence in the army was ex-

[l] Rush. vol. vii. p. 570.   [m] Ibid. vol. vii. p. 572.   [n] Ibid. vol. vii. p. 592.
[o] Ibid. vol. vii. p. 594. Whitlocke, p. 259.   [p] Ibid. vol. vii. p. 593, 594.
[q] Rush. vol. vii. p. 572, 574.   [r] Clarendon, vol. i. p. 51, 52, 57.   [s] When the king applied to have his children, the parliament always told him, that they could take as much care at London, both of their bodies and souls, as could be done at Oxford. Parl. Hist. vol. xiii. p. 127.

tremely grateful to him. Cromwel, who was witness to the meeting of the royal family, confessed, that he never had been present at so tender a scene; and he extremely applauded the benignity, which displayed itself in the whole disposition and behaviour of Charles.

That artful politician, as well as the leaders of all parties, payed court to the king; and fortune; notwithstanding all his calamities, seemed again to smile upon him. The parliament, afraid of his forming some accommodation with the army, addressed him in a more respectful style than formerly; and invited him to reside at Richmond, and contribute his assistance to the settlement of the nation. The chief officers treated him with regard, and spake on all occasions of restoring him to his just powers and prerogatives. In the public declarations of the army, the settlement of his revenue and authority was insisted on.[t] The royalists, every where, entertained hopes of the restoration of monarchy; and the favour, which they universally bore to the army, contributed very much to discourage the parliament, and to forward their submission.

The king began to feel of what consequence he was. The more the national confusions encreased, the more was he confident, that all parties would, at length, have recourse to his lawful authority, as the only remedy for the public disorders. *You cannot be without me,* said he, on several occasions: *You cannot settle the nation but by my assistance.* A people without government and without liberty, a parliament without authority, an army without a legal master: Distractions every where, terrors, oppressions, convulsions: From this scene of confusion, which could not long continue, all men, he hoped, would be brought to reflect on that ancient government, under which they and their ancestors had so long enjoyed happiness and tranquillity.

Though Charles kept his ears open to all proposals, and expected to hold the balance between the opposite parties, he entertained more hopes of accommodation with the army. He had experienced the extreme rigour of the parliament. They pretended totally to annihilate his authority: They had confined his person. In both these particulars, the army showed more indulgence.[u] He had a free intercourse with his friends. And in the proposals, which

[t] Rush. vol. vii. p. 590.   [u] Warwick, p. 303. Parl. Hist. vol. xvi. p. 40. Clarendon, vol. v. p. 50.

the council of officers sent for the settlement of the nation, they insisted neither on the abolition of episcopacy, nor of the punishment of the royalists; the two points to which the king had the most extreme reluctance: And they demanded, that a period should be put to the present parliament, the event for which he most ardently longed.

His conjunction too seemed more natural with the generals, than with that usurping assembly, who had so long assumed the entire sovereignty of the state, and who had declared their resolution still to continue masters. By gratifying a few persons with titles and preferments, he might draw over, he hoped, the whole military power, and, in an instant, reinstate himself in his civil authority. To Ireton he offered the lieutenancy of Ireland: To Cromwel, the garter, the title of earl of Essex, and the command of the army. Negociations to this purpose were secretly conducted. Cromwel pretended to hearken to them; and was well pleased to keep the door open for an accommodation, if the course of events should, at any time, render it necessary. And the king, who had no suspicion, that one, born a private gentleman, could entertain the daring ambition of seizing a sceptre, transmitted through a long line of monarchs; indulged hopes, that he would, at last, embrace a measure, which, by all the motives of duty, interest, and safety, seemed to be recommended to him.

While Cromwel allured the king by these expectations, he still continued his scheme of reducing the parliament to subjection, and depriving them of all means of resistance. To gratify the army, the parliament invested Fairfax with the title of general in chief of all the forces in England and Ireland; and entrusted the whole military authority to a person, who, though well inclined to their service, was no longer at his own disposal.

They voted, that the troops, which, in obedience to them, had inlisted for Ireland, and deserted the rebellious army, should be disbanded, or, in other words, be punished for their fidelity. The forces in the north, under Pointz, had already mutinied against their general, and had entered into an association with that body of the army, which was so successfully employed in exalting the military above the civil authority.[w]

That no resource might remain to the parliament, it was de-

[w] Rush. vol. vii. p. 620.

manded, that the militia of London should be changed, the presbyterian commissioners displaced, and the command restored to those, who, during the course of the war, had constantly exercised it. The parliament even complied with so violent a demand, and passed a vote in obedience to the army.[x]

By this unlimited patience, they purposed to temporize under their present difficulties, and they hoped to find a more favourable opportunity for recovering their authority and influence: But the impatience of the city lost them all the advantage of their cautious measures. A petition against the alteration of the militia was carried to Westminster, attended by the apprentices and seditious multitude, who besieged the door of the house of commons; and by their clamour, noise, and violence, obliged them to reverse that vote, which they had passed so lately. When gratified in this pretension, they immediately dispersed, and left the parliament at liberty.[y]

20th July.

No sooner was intelligence of this tumult conveyed to Reading, than the army was put in motion. The two houses being under restraint, they were resolved, they said, to vindicate, against the seditious citizens, the invaded privileges of parliament, and restore that assembly to its just freedom of debate and counsel. In their way to London, they were drawn up on Hounslow-Heath; a formidable body, twenty thousand strong, and determined, without regard to laws or liberty, to pursue whatever measures their generals should dictate to them. Here the most favourable event happened, to quicken and encourage their advance. The speakers of the two houses, Manchester and Lenthal, attended by eight peers, and about sixty commoners, having secretly retired from the city, presented themselves with their maces, and all the ensigns of their dignity; and complaining of the violence put upon them, applied to the army for defence and protection. They were received with shouts and acclamations: Respect was paid to them as to the parliament of England: And the army being provided with so plausible a pretence, which, in all public transactions, is of great consequence, advanced to chastise the rebellious city, and to re-instate the violated parliament.[z]

[x] Rush. vol. vii. p. 629, 632.   [y] Ibid. vol. vii. p. 641, 643. Clarendon, vol. vi. p. 61. Whitlocke, p. 269. Cl. Walker, p. 38.   [z] Rush. vol. viii. p. 750. Clarendon, vol. v. p. 63.

Neither Lenthal nor Manchester were esteemed independents; and such a step in them was unexpected. But they probably foresaw, that the army must, in the end, prevail; and they were willing to pay court in time to that authority, which began to predominate in the nation.

The parliament, forced from their temporizing measures, and obliged to resign, at once, or combat for their liberty and power, prepared themselves with vigour for defence, and determined to resist the violence of the army. The two houses immediately chose new speakers, lord Hunsdon, and Henry Pelham: They renewed their former orders for enlisting troops: They appointed Massey to be commander: They ordered the trained bands to man the lines: And the whole city was in a ferment, and resounded with military preparations.[a]

When any intelligence arrived, that the army stopped or retreated, the shout of *One and all,* ran with alacrity, from street to street, among the citizens: When news came of their advancing, the cry of *Treat and capitulate* was no less loud and vehement.[b] The terror of an universal pillage, and even massacre, had seized the timid inhabitants.

As the army approached, Rainsborow, being sent by the general over the river, presented himself before Southwark, and was gladly received by some soldiers, who were quartered there for its defence, and who were resolved not to separate their interests from those of the army. It behoved then the parliament to submit. The army marched in triumph through the city; but preserved the greatest order, decency, and appearance of humility. They conducted to Westminster the two speakers, who took their seats as if nothing had happened. The eleven impeached members, being accused as authors of the tumult, were expelled; and most of them retired beyond sea: Seven peers were impeached: The mayor, one sheriff, and three aldermen, sent to the Tower: Several citizens and officers of the militia committed to prison: Every deed of the parliament annulled, from the day of the tumult till the return of the speakers: The lines about the city levelled: The militia restored to the independents: Regiments quartered in Whitehall and the Meuse: And the parliament being reduced to a regular formed

6th Aug.

The army subdue the parliament.

---

[a] Rush. vol. vii. p. 646.   [b] Whitlocke, p. 265.

CHAPTER LIX

servitude, a day was appointed of solemn thanksgiving for the restoration of its liberty.[c]

The independent party among the commons exulted in their victory. The whole authority of the nation, they imagined, was now lodged in their hands; and they had a near prospect of moulding the government into that imaginary republic, which had long been the object of their wishes. They had secretly concurred in all encroachments of the military upon the civil power; and they expected, by the terror of the sword, to impose a more perfect system of liberty on the reluctant nation. All parties, the king, the church, the parliament, the presbyterians, had been guilty of errors, since the commencement of these disorders: But it must be confessed, that this delusion of the independents and republicans was, of all others, the most contrary to common sense and the established maxims of policy. Yet were the leaders of that party, Vane, Fiennes, St. John, Martin, the men in England the most celebrated for profound thought and deep contrivance; and by their well-coloured pretences and professions, they had over-reached the whole nation. To deceive such men would argue a superlative capacity in Cromwel; were it not, that, besides the great difference there is between dark, crooked councils and true wisdom, an exorbitant passion for rule and authority will make the most prudent overlook the dangerous consequences of such measures as seem to tend, in any degree, to their own advancement.

The leaders of the army, having established their dominion over the parliament and city, ventured to bring the king to Hampton-Court; and he lived, for some time, in that palace, with an appearance of dignity and freedom. Such equability of temper did he possess, that, during all the variety of fortune, which he underwent, no difference was perceived in his countenance or behaviour; and though a prisoner, in the hands of his most inveterate enemies, he supported, towards all who approached him, the majesty of a monarch; and that, neither with less nor greater state, than he had been accustomed to maintain. His manner, which was not in itself popular nor gracious, now appeared amiable, from its great meekness and equality.

The parliament renewed their applications to him, and

[c] Rush. vol. viii. p. 797, 798, &c.

presented him with the same conditions, which they had offered at Newcastle. The king declined accepting them, and desired the parliament to take the proposals of the army into consideration, and make them the foundation of the public settlement.[d] He still entertained hopes, that his negociations with the generals would be crowned with success; though every thing, in that particular, daily bore a worse aspect. Most historians have thought, that Cromwel never was sincere in his professions; and that, having, by force, rendered himself master of the king's person, and, by fair pretences, acquired the countenance of the royalists, he had employed these advantages to the enslaving of the parliament: And afterwards thought of nothing but the establishment of his own unlimited authority, with which he esteemed the restoration, and even life of the king, altogether incompatible. This opinion, so much warranted by the boundless ambition and profound dissimulation of his character, meets with ready belief; though it is more agreeable to the narrowness of human views, and the darkness of futurity, to suppose, that this daring usurper was guided by events, and did not, as yet, foresee, with any assurance, that unparalleled greatness, which he afterwards attained. Many writers of that age have asserted,[e] that he really intended to make a private bargain with the king; a measure, which carried the most plausible appearance both for his safety and advancement: But that he found insuperable difficulties in reconciling to it the wild humours of the army. The horror and antipathy of these fanatics had, for many years, been artfully fomented against Charles; and though their principles were, on all occasions, easily warped and eluded by private interest, yet was some colouring requisite, and a flat contradiction to all former professions and tenets could not safely be proposed to them. It is certain, at least, that Cromwel made use of this reason, why he admitted rarely of visits from the king's friends, and showed less favour than formerly to the royal cause. The agitators, he said, had rendered him odious to the army, and had represented him as a traitor, who, for the sake of private interest, was ready to betray the cause of God to the great enemy of piety and religion. Desperate projects too, he asserted to be secretly formed, for the murder of the king; and he pretended

[d] Rush. vol. viii. p. 810.   [e] See note [HH] at the end of the volume.

much to dread lest all his authority, and that of the commanding officers, would not be able to restrain these enthusiasts from their bloody purposes.[f]

Intelligence being daily brought to the king of menaces thrown out by the agitators; he began to think of retiring from Hampton-Court, and of putting himself in some place of safety. The guards were doubled upon him: The promiscuous concourse of people restrained: A more jealous care exerted in attending his person: All, under colour of protecting him from danger; but really with a view of making him uneasy in his present situation. These artifices soon produced the intended effect. Charles, who was naturally apt to be swayed by counsel, and who had not then access to any good counsel, took suddenly a resolution of withdrawing himself, though without any concerted, at least, any rational scheme, for the future disposal of his person. Attended only by Sir John Berkeley, Ashburnham, and Leg, he privately left Hampton-Court; and his escape was not discovered, till near an hour after; when those, who entered his chamber, found on the table some letters directed to the parliament, to the general, and to the officer, who had attended him.[g] All night, he travelled through the forest, and arrived next day at Tichfield, a seat of the earl of Southampton's, where the countess dowager resided, as woman of honour, to whom, the king knew, he might safely entrust his person. Before he arrived at this place, he had gone to the sea-coast; and expressed great anxiety, that a ship, which he seemed to look for, had not arrived; and thence, Berkeley and Leg, who were not in the secret, conjectured, that his intention was to transport himself beyond sea.

11th Nov.

The king could not hope to remain long concealed at Tichfield: What measure should next be embraced, was the question. In the neighbourhood lay the isle of Wight, of which Hammond was governor. This man was entirely dependent on Cromwel. At his recommendation he had married a daughter of the famous Hampden, who, during his life-time, had been an intimate friend of Cromwel's, and whose memory was ever respected by him. These circumstances were very unfavourable: Yet because the governor was nephew to Dr. Hammond, the king's favourite chaplain, and

King flies to the isle of Wight.

---

[f] Clarendon, vol. v. p. 76.   [g] Rush. vol. viii. p. 871.

had acquired a good character in the army, it was thought proper to have recourse to him, in the present exigence, when no other rational expedient could be thought of. Ashburnham and Berkeley were dispatched to the island. They had orders not to inform Hammond of the place, where the king was concealed, till they had first obtained a promise from him not to deliver up his majesty, though the parliament and army should require him; but to restore him to his liberty, if he could not protect him. This promise, it is evident; would have been a very slender security: Yet even without exacting it, Ashburnham, imprudently, if not treacherously, brought Hammond to Tichfield; and the king was obliged to put himself in his hands, and to attend him to Carisbroke-castle in the isle of Wight, where, though received with great demonstrations of respect and duty, he was in reality a prisoner.

Lord Clarendon[h] is positive, that the king, when he fled from Hampton-Court, had no intention of going to this island; and indeed all the circumstances of that historian's narrative, which we have here followed, strongly favour this opinion. But there remains a letter of Charles's to the earl of Laneric, secretary of Scotland; in which he plainly intimates, that that measure was voluntarily embraced, and even insinuates, that, if he had thought proper, he might have been in Jersey or any other place of safety.[i] Perhaps, he still confided in the promises of the generals; and flattered himself, that, if he were removed from the fury of the agitators, by which his life was immediately threatened, they would execute what they had so often promised in his favour.

Whatever may be the truth in this matter; for it is impossible fully to ascertain the truth; Charles never took a weaker step, nor one more agreeable to Cromwel and all his enemies. He was now lodged in a place, removed from his partizans, at the disposal of the army, whence it would be very difficult to deliver him, either by force or artifice. And though it was always in the power of Cromwel, whenever he pleased, to have sent him thither; yet such a measure, without the king's consent, would have been very invidious, if not attended with some danger. That the king should voluntarily throw himself into the snare, and thereby gratify his

[h] P. 79, 80, &c.   [i] See note [II] at the end of the volume.

CHAPTER LIX

implacable persecutors, was to them an incident peculiarly fortunate, and proved in the issue very fatal to him.

Cromwel, being now entirely master of the parliament, and free from all anxiety, with regard to the custody of the king's person, applied himself seriously to quell those disorders in the army, which he himself had so artfully raised, and so successfully employed, against both king and parliament. In order to engage the troops into a rebellion against their masters, he had encouraged an arrogant spirit among the inferior officers and private men; and the camp, in many respects, carried more the appearance of civil liberty than of military obedience. The troops themselves were formed into a kind of republic; and the plans of imaginary republics, for the settlement of the state, were, every day, the topics of conversation among these armed legislators. Royalty it was agreed to abolish: Nobility must be set aside: Even all ranks of men be levelled; and an universal equality of property, as well as of power, be introduced among the citizens. The saints, they said, were the salt of the earth: An entire parity had place among the elect: And, by the same rule, that the apostles were exalted from the most ignoble professions, the meanest sentinel, if enlightened by the spirit, was entitled to equal regard with the greatest commander. In order to wean the soldiers from these licentious maxims, Cromwel had issued orders for discontinuing the meetings of the agitators; and he pretended to pay entire obedience to the parliament, whom, being now fully reduced to subjection, he purposed to make, for the future, the instruments of his authority. But the *Levellers,* for so that party in the army was called, having experienced the sweets of dominion, would not so easily be deprived of it. They secretly continued their meetings: They asserted, that their officers, as much as any part of the church or state, needed reformation: Several regiments joined in seditious remonstrances and petitions:[k] Separate rendevouses were concerted: And every thing tended to anarchy and confusion. But this distemper was soon cured by the rough, but dextrous hand of Cromwel. He chose the opportunity of a review, that he might display the greater boldness, and spread the terror the wider. He seized the ring-

[k] Rush. vol. viii. p. 845, 859.

leaders before their companions: Held in the field a council of war: Shot one mutineer instantly: And struck such dread into the rest, that they presently threw down the symbols of sedition, which they had displayed, and thenceforth returned to their wonted discipline and obedience.[l]

Cromwel had great deference for the counsels of Ireton; a man, who, having grafted the soldier on the lawyer, the statesman on the saint, had adopted such principles as were fitted to introduce the severest tyranny, while they seemed to encourage the most unbounded licence, in human society. Fierce in his nature, though probably sincere in his intentions; he purposed by arbitrary power to establish liberty, and, in prosecution of his imagined religious purposes, he thought himself dispensed from all the ordinary rules of morality, by which inferior mortals must allow themselves to be governed. From his suggestion, Cromwel secretly called at Windsor a council of the chief officers, in order to deliberate concerning the settlement of the nation, and the future disposal of the king's person.[m] In this conference, which commenced with devout prayers, poured forth by Cromwel himself and other inspired persons (for the officers of this army received inspiration with their commission,) was first opened the daring and unheard-of counsel, of bringing the king to justice, and of punishing, by a judicial sentence, their sovereign for his pretended tyranny and maladministration. While Charles lived, even though restrained to the closest prison, conspiracies, they knew, and insurrections would never be wanting, in favour of a prince, who was so extremely revered and beloved by his own party, and whom the nation in general began to regard with great affection and compassion. To murder him privately was exposed to the imputation of injustice and cruelty, aggravated by the baseness of such a crime; and every odious epithet of *Traitor* and *Assassin* would, by the general voice of mankind, be undisputably ascribed to the actors in such a villany. Some unexpected procedure must be attempted, which would astonish the world by its novelty, would bear the semblance of justice, and would cover its barbarity by the audaciousness of the enterprize. Striking in with the fanatical notions of the entire equality of mankind, it would ensure the devoted obedience of the

[l] Idem, ibid. p. 875. Clarendon, vol. v. p. 87.   [m] Clarendon, vol. v. p. 92.

army, and serve as a general engagement against the royal family, whom, by their open and united deed, they would so heinously affront and injure."

This measure, therefore, being secretly resolved on, it was requisite, by degrees, to make the parliament adopt it, and to conduct them from violence to violence; till this last act of atrocious iniquity should seem, in a manner, wholly inevitable. The king, in order to remove those fears and jealousies, which were perpetually pleaded as reasons for every invasion of the constitution, had offered, by a message, sent from Carisbroke-castle, to resign, during his own life, the power of the militia and the nomination to all the great offices; provided, that, after his demise, these prerogatives should revert to the crown." But the parliament acted entirely as victors and enemies; and, in all their transactions with him, payed no longer any regard to equity or reason. At the instigation of the independents and army, they neglected this offer, and framed four proposals, which they sent him as preliminaries; and, before they would deign to treat, they demanded his positive assent to all of them. By one, he was required to invest the parliament with the military power for twenty years, together with an authority to levy whatever money should be necessary for exercising it: And even after the twenty years should be elapsed, they reserved a right of resuming the same authority, whenever they should declare the safety of the kingdom to require it. By the second, he was to recall all his proclamations and declarations against the parliament, and acknowledge that assembly to have taken arms in their just and necessary defence. By the third, he was to annul all the acts, and void all the patents of peerage, which had passed the great seal, since it had been carried from London by lord-keeper Littleton; and at the same time, renounce for the future the power of making peers without consent of parliament. By the fourth, he gave the

---

" The following was a favourite text among enthusiasts of that age. "Let the high praises of God be in the mouths of his saints, and a two-fold sword in their hands, to execute vengeance upon the heathen and punishment upon the people; to bind their kings with chains and their nobles with fetters of iron; to execute upon them the judgments written: This honour have all his saints." Psalm cxlix. ver. 6, 7, 8, 9. Hugh Peters, the mad chaplain of Cromwel, preached frequently upon this text.   " Rush. vol. viii. p. 880.

two houses power to adjourn as they thought proper: A demand seemingly of no great importance; but contrived by the independents, that they might be able to remove the parliament to places, where it should remain in perpetual subjection to the army.[p]

1648.   The king regarded the pretension as unusual and exorbitant, that he should make such concessions, while not secure of any settlement; and should blindly trust his enemies for the conditions, which they were afterwards to grant him. He required, therefore, a personal treaty with the parliament, and desired, that all the terms, on both sides, should be adjusted, before any concession, on either sides, should be insisted on. The republican party in the house pretended to take fire at this answer; and openly inveighed, in violent terms, against the person and government of the king; whose name, hitherto, had commonly, in all debates, been mentioned with some degree of reverence. Ireton, seeming to speak the sense of the army, under the appellation of many thousand godly men, who had ventured their lives in defence of the parliament, said, that the king, by denying the four bills, had refused safety and protection to his people; that their obedience to him was but a reciprocal duty for his protection of them; and that, as he had failed on his part, they were freed from all obligations to allegiance, and must settle the nation, without consulting any longer so misguided a prince.[q] Cromwel, after giving an ample character of the valour, good affections, and godliness of the army, subjoined, that it was expected the parliament should guide and defend the kingdom by their own power and resolutions, and not accustom the people any longer to expect safety and government from an obstinate man, whose heart God had hardened; that those, who, at the expence of their blood, had hitherto defended the parliament from so many dangers, would still continue, with fidelity and courage, to protect them against all opposition, in this vigorous measure. "Teach them not," added he, "by your neglecting your own safety and that of the kingdom (in which theirs too is involved) to imagine themselves betrayed, and their interests abandoned to the rage and malice of an irreconcileable enemy, whom, for your sake, they have dared to provoke. Beware, (*and at these words he laid his hands on his sword,*) beware, lest despair cause

[p] Clarendon, vol. v. p. 88.   [q] Cl. Walker, p. 70.

them to seek safety by some other means, than by adhering to you, who know not how to consult your own safety."[r] Such arguments prevailed, though ninety-one members had still the courage to oppose. It was voted, that no more addresses be made to the king, nor any letters or messages be received from him; and that it be treason for any one, without leave of the two houses, to have any intercourse with him. The lords concurred in the same ordinance.[s] *15th Jan.*

By this vote of non-addresses, so it was called, the king was, in reality, dethroned, and the whole constitution formally overthrown. So violent a measure was supported by a declaration of the commons no less violent. The blackest calumnies were there thrown upon the king; such as, even in their famous remonstrance, they thought proper to omit, as incredible and extravagant: The poisoning of his father, the betraying of Rochelle, the contriving of the Irish massacre.[t] By blasting his fame, had that injury been in their power, they formed a very proper prelude to the executing of violence on his person.

No sooner had the king refused his assent to the four bills, than Hammond, by orders from the army, removed all his servants, cut off his correspondence with his friends, and shut him up in close confinement. The king afterwards showed to Sir Philip Warwick, a decrepid old man, who, he said, was employed to kindle his fire, and was the best company he enjoyed, during several months that this rigorous confinement lasted.[u] No amusement was allowed him, nor society, which might relieve his anxious thoughts: To be speedily poisoned or assassinated was the only prospect, which he had, every moment, before his eyes: For he entertained no apprehension of a judicial sentence and execution; an event, of which no history hitherto furnished an example. Meanwhile the parliament was very industrious in publishing, from time to time, the intelligence, which they received from Hammond; how chearful the king was, how pleased with every one that approached him, how satisfied in his present condition:[w] As if the view of such benignity and constancy had not been more proper to inflame, than allay, the general compassion of the people. The great source whence the king derived consolation amidst all his calamities, was un-

[r] Ibid. p. 70.   [s] Rush. vol. viii. p. 965, 967.   [t] Rush. vol. viii. p. 998. Clarendon, vol. v. p. 93.   [u] Warwick, p. 329.   [w] Rush. vol. viii. p. 989.

doubtedly religion; a principle, which, in him, seems to have contained nothing fierce or gloomy, nothing which enraged him against his adversaries, or terrified him with the dismal prospect of futurity. While every thing around him bore a hostile aspect; while friends, family, relations, whom he passionately loved, were placed at a distance, and unable to serve him; he reposed himself with confidence in the arms of that being, who penetrates and sustains all nature, and whose severities, if received with piety and resignation, he regarded as the surest pledges of unexhausted favour.

Second civil war. The parliament and army, meanwhile, enjoyed not, in tranquility, that power, which they had obtained with so much violence and injustice. Combinations and conspiracies, they were sensible, were every where forming around them; and Scotland, whence the king's cause had received the first fatal disaster, seemed now to promise it support and assistance.

Before the surrender of the king's person at Newcastle, and much more, since that event, the subjects of discontent had been daily multiplying between the two kingdoms. The independents, who began to prevail, took all occasions of mortifying the Scots, whom the presbyterians looked on with the greatest affection and veneration. When the Scottish commissioners, who, joined to a committee of English lords and commons, had managed the war, were ready to depart, it was proposed in parliament to give them thanks for their civilities and good offices. The independents insisted, that the words, *Good offices,* should be struck out; and thus the whole brotherly friendship and intimate alliance with the Scots resolved itself into an acknowledgment of their being well-bred gentlemen.

The advance of the army to London, the subjection of the parliament, the seizing of the king at Holdenby, his confinement in Carisbroke-castle, were so many blows, sensibly felt by that nation; as threatening the final overthrow of presbytery, to which they were so passionately devoted. The covenant was profanely called, in the house of commons, an almanac out of date,[x] and that impiety, though complained of, had passed uncensured. Instead of being able to determine and establish orthodoxy by the sword and by penal statutes, they saw the sectarian army, who were abso-

---

[x] Cl. Walker, p. 80.

lute masters, claim an unbounded liberty of conscience, which the presbyterians regarded with the utmost abhorrence. All the violences, put on the king, they loudly blamed, as repugnant to the covenant, by which they stood engaged to defend his royal person. And those very actions, of which they themselves had been guilty, they denominated treason and rebellion, when executed by an opposite party.

The earls of Loudon, Lauderdale, and Laneric, who were sent to London, protested against the four bills; as containing too great a diminution of the king's civil power, and providing no security for religion. They complained, that, notwithstanding this protestation, the bills were still insisted on; contrary to the solemn league, and to the treaty between the two nations. And when they accompanied the English commissioners to the isle of Wight, they secretly formed a treaty with the king, for arming Scotland in his favour.[y]

Three parties, at that time, prevailed in Scotland: The *Royalists,* who insisted upon the restoration of the king's authority, without any regard to religious sects or tenets: Of these Montrose, though absent, was regarded as the head. The *Rigid presbyterians,* who hated the king, even more than they abhorred toleration; and who determined to give him no assistance, till he should subscribe the covenant: These were governed by Argyle. The *Moderate presbyterians,* who endeavoured to reconcile the interests of religion and of the crown, and hoped, by supporting the presbyterian party in England, to suppress the sectarian army, and to re-instate the parliament, as well as the king, in their just freedom and authority: The two brothers, Hamilton and Laneric, were leaders of this party.

Invasion from Scotland.

When Pendennis castle was surrendered to the parliamentary army, Hamilton, who then obtained his liberty, returned into Scotland; and being generously determined to remember ancient favours, more than recent injuries, he immediately embraced, with zeal and success, the protection of the royal cause. He obtained a vote from the Scottish parliament to arm 40,000 men in support of the king's authority, and to call over a considerable body under Monro, who commanded the Scottish forces in Ulster. And though

[y] Clarendon, vol. v. p. 101.

he openly protested, that the covenant was the foundation of all his measures, he secretly entered into correspondence with the English royalists, Sir Marmaduke Langdale and Sir Philip Musgrave, who had levied considerable forces in the north of England.

The general assembly, who sat at the same time, and was guided by Argyle, dreaded the consequence of these measures, and foresaw, that the opposite party, if successful, would effect the restoration of monarchy, without the establishment of presbytery, in England. To join the king before he had subscribed the covenant, was, in their eyes, to restore him to his honour before Christ had obtained his;[z] and they thundered out anathemas against every one, who payed obedience to the parliament. Two supreme independent judicatures were erected in the kingdom; one threatening the people with damnation and eternal torments, the other with imprisonment, banishment, and military execution. The people were distracted in their choice; and the armament of Hamilton's party, though seconded by all the civil power, went on but slowly. The royalists he would not, as yet, allow to join him, lest he might give offence to the ecclesiastical party; though he secretly promised them trust and preferment, as soon as his army should advance into England.

While the Scots were making preparations for the invasion of England, every part of that kingdom was agitated with tumults, insurrections, conspiracies, discontents. It is seldom, that the people gain any thing by revolutions in government; because the new settlement, jealous and insecure, must commonly be supported with more expence and severity than the old: But on no occasion was the truth of this maxim more sensibly felt, than in the present situation of England. Complaints against the oppression of ship-money, against the tyranny of the star-chamber, had rouzed the people to arms: And having gained a complete victory over the crown, they found themselves loaded with a multiplicity of taxes, formerly unknown; and scarcely an appearance of law and liberty remained in the administration. The presbyterians, who had chiefly supported the war, were enraged to find the prize, just when it seemed within their reach, snatched by violence from them. The royalists, disappointed in their expectations, by the

[z] Whitlocke, p. 305.

CHAPTER LIX

cruel treatment which the king now received from the army, were strongly animated to restore him to liberty, and to recover the advantages, which they had unfortunately lost. All orders of men were inflamed with indignation at seeing the military prevail over the civil power, and king and parliament at once reduced to subjection by a mercenary army. Many persons of family and distinction had, from the beginning of the war, adhered to the parliament: But all these were, by the new party, deprived of authority; and every office was entrusted to the most ignoble part of the nation. A base populace exalted above their superiors: Hypocrites exercising iniquity under the vizor of religion: These circumstances promised not much liberty or lenity to the people; and these were now found united, in the same usurped and illegal administration.

Though the whole nation seemed to combine in their hatred of military tyranny, the ends which the several parties pursued, were so different, that little concert was observed in their insurrections. Langhorne, Poyer, and Powel, presbyterian officers, who commanded bodies of troops in Wales, were the first that declared themselves; and they drew together a considerable army in those parts, which were extremely devoted to the royal cause. An insurrection was raised in Kent by young Hales and the earl of Norwich. Lord Capel, Sir Charles Lucas, Sir George Lisle, excited commotions in Essex. The earl of Holland, who had several times changed sides, since the commencement of the civil wars, endeavoured to assemble forces in Surrey. Pomfret castle in Yorkshire was surprized by Morrice. Langdale and Musgrave were in arms, and masters of Berwic and Carlisle in the north.

What seemed the most dangerous circumstance; the general spirit of discontent had seized the fleet. Seventeen ships, lying in the mouth of the river, declared for the king; and putting Rainsborow, their admiral, ashore, sailed over to Holland, where the prince of Wales took the command of them.[a]

The English royalists exclaimed loudly against Hamilton's delays, which they attributed to a refined policy in the Scots; as if their intentions were, that all the king's party should first be suppressed, and the victory remain solely to the presbyterians. Hamilton, with better reason, complained of the precipitate humour of

[a] Clarendon, vol. v. p. 137.

the English royalists, who, by their ill-timed insurrections, forced him to march his army, before his levies were completed, or his preparations in any forwardness.

No commotions, beyond a tumult of the apprentices, which was soon suppressed, were raised in London: The terror of the army kept the citizens in subjection. The parliament was so over-awed, that they declared the Scots to be enemies, and all who joined them, traitors. Ninety members, however, of the lower house had the courage to dissent from this vote.

Cromwel and the military council prepared themselves with vigour and conduct for defence. The establishment of the army was, at this time, 26,000 men; but by inlisting supernumeraries, the regiments were greatly augmented, and commonly consisted of more than double their stated complement.[b] Colonel Horton first attacked the revolted troops in Wales, and gave them a considerable defeat. The remnants of the vanquished threw themselves into Pembroke, and were there closely besieged, and soon after taken, by Cromwel. Lambert was opposed to Langdale and Musgrave in the north, and gained advantages over them. Sir Michael Livesey defeated the earl of Holland at Kingston, and pursuing his victory, took him prisoner at St. Neots. Fairfax, having routed the Kentish royalists at Maidstone, followed the broken army: And when they joined the royalists of Essex, and threw themselves into Colchester; he laid siege to that place, which defended itself to the last extremity. A new fleet was manned, and sent out under the command of Warwic, to oppose the revolted ships, of which the prince had taken the command.

While the forces were employed in all quarters, the parliament regained its liberty, and began to act with its wonted courage and spirit. The members, who had withdrawn, from terror of the army, returned; and infusing boldness into their companions, restored to the presbyterian party the ascendant, which it had formerly lost. The eleven impeached members were recalled, and the vote, by which they were expelled, was reversed. The vote too of non-addresses was repealed; and commissioners, five peers and ten commoners, were sent to Newport in the isle of Wight, in order to

[b] Whitlocke, p. 284.

treat with the king.[c] He was allowed to summon several of his friends and old counsellors, that he might have their advice in this important transaction.[d] The theologians on both sides, armed with their syllogisms and quotations, attended as auxiliaries.[e] By them, the flame had first been raised; and their appearance was but a bad prognostic of its extinction. Any other instruments seemed better adapted for a treaty of pacification.

When the king presented himself to this company, a great and sensible alteration was remarked in his aspect, from what it appeared the year before, when he resided at Hampton Court. The moment his servants had been removed, he had laid aside all care of his person, and had allowed his beard and hair to grow, and to hang dishevelled and neglected. His hair was become almost entirely gray; either from the decline of years, or from that load of sorrows, under which he laboured, and which, though borne with constancy, preyed inwardly on his sensible and tender mind. His friends beheld with compassion, and perhaps even his enemies, that *grey and discrowned head;* as he himself terms it, in a copy of verses, which the truth of the sentiment, rather than any elegance of expression, renders very pathetic.[f] Having in vain endeavoured by courage to defend his throne from his armed adversaries, it now behoved him, by reasoning and persuasion, to save some fragments of it from these peaceful, and no less implacable negotiators.

18th Sept. Treaty of Newport.

The vigour of the king's mind, notwithstanding the seeming decline of his body, here appeared unbroken and undecayed. The parliamentary commissioners would allow none of his council to be present, and refused to enter into reasoning with any but himself. He alone, during the transactions of two months, was obliged to maintain the argument against fifteen men of the greatest parts and capacity in both houses; and no advantage was ever obtained over him.[g] This was the scene, above all others, in which he was qualified to excel. A quick conception, a cultivated understanding, a chaste elocution, a dignified manner; by these accomplishments

[c] Clarendon, vol. v. p. 180. Sir Edward Walker's perfect Copies, p. 6. [d] Ibid. p. 8. [e] Ibid. p. 8, 38. [f] Burnet's Memoirs of Hamilton. [g] Herbert's Memoirs, p. 72.

he triumphed in all discussions of cool and temperate reasoning. *The king is much changed,* said the earl of Salisbury to Sir Philip Warwic: *He is extremely improved of late. No,* replied Sir Philip; *he was always so: But you are now at last sensible of it.*[h] Sir Henry Vane, discoursing with his fellow commissioners, drew an argument from the king's uncommon abilities, why the terms of pacification must be rendered more strict and rigid.[i] But Charles's capacity shone not equally in action as in reasoning.

The first point, insisted on by the parliamentary commissioners, was the king's recalling all his proclamations and declarations against the parliament, and the acknowledging, that they had taken arms in their own defence. He frankly offered the former concession; but long scrupled the latter. The falsehood, as well as indignity of that acknowledgement, begat in his breast an extreme reluctance against it. The king had, no doubt, in some particulars of moment, invaded, from a seeming necessity, the privileges of his people: But having renounced all claim to these usurped powers, having confessed his errors, and having repaired every breach in the constitution, and even erected new ramparts, in order to secure it; he could no longer, at the commencement of the war, be represented as the aggressor. However it might be pretended, that the former display of his arbitrary inclinations, or rather his monarchical principles, rendered an offensive or preventive war in the parliament prudent and reasonable; it could never, in any propriety of speech, make it be termed a defensive one. But the parliament, sensible, that the letter of the law condemned them as rebels and traitors, deemed this point absolutely necessary for their future security: And the king, finding, that peace could be obtained on no other terms, at last yielded to it. He only entered a protest, which was admitted; that no concession, made by him, should be valid, unless the whole treaty of pacification were concluded.[k]

He agreed, that the parliament should retain, during the term of twenty years, the power over the militia and army, and that of levying what money they pleased for their support. He even yielded to them the right of resuming, at any time afterwards, this

[h] Warwick, p. 324.   [i] Clarendon, Sir Edward Walker, p. 319.   [k] Walker, p. 11, 12, 24.

CHAPTER LIX

authority, whenever they should declare such a resumption necessary for public safety. In effect, the important power of the sword
was for ever ravished from him and his successors.[l]

He agreed, that all the great offices, during twenty years,
should be filled by both houses of parliament.[m] He relinquished to
them the entire government of Ireland, and the conduct of the war
there.[n] He renounced the power of the wards, and accepted of
100,000 pounds a year in lieu of it.[o] He acknowledged the validity
of their great seal, and gave up his own.[p] He abandoned the power
of creating peers without consent of parliament. And he agreed,
that all the debts, contracted in order to support the war against
him, should be paid by the people.

So great were the alterations, made on the English constitution
by this treaty, that the king said, not without reason, that he had
been more an enemy to his people by these concessions, could he
have prevented them, than by any other action of his life.

Of all the demands of the parliament, Charles refused only two.
Though he relinquished almost every power of the crown, he
would neither give up his friends to punishment, nor desert what
he esteemed his religious duty. The severe repentance, which he
had undergone, for abandoning Strafford, had, no doubt, confirmed him in the resolution never again to be guilty of a like error.
His long solitude and severe afflictions had contributed to rivet
him the more in those religious principles, which had ever a considerable influence over him. His desire, however, of finishing an
accommodation induced him to go as far in both these particulars,
as he thought any wise consistent with his duty.

The estates of the royalists being, at that time, almost entirely
under sequestration, Charles, who could give them no protection,
consented, that they should pay such compositions, as they and the
parliament could agree on; and only begged, that they might be
made as moderate as possible. He had not the disposal of offices;
and it seemed but a small sacrifice to consent, that a certain number of his friends should be rendered incapable of public employments.[q] But when the parliament demanded a bill of attainder and
banishment against seven persons, the marquess of Newcastle,

[l] Ibid. p. 51.   [m] Ibid. p. 78.   [n] Ibid. p. 45.   [o] Walker, p. 69, 77.   [p] Ibid.
p. 56, 68.   [q] Walker, p. 61.

lord Digby, lord Biron, Sir Marmaduke Langdale, Sir Richard Granville, Sir Francis Doddington, and judge Jenkins, the king absolutely refused compliance: Their banishment for a limited time he was willing to agree to.[r]

Religion was the fatal point about which the differences had arisen; and of all others, it was the least susceptible of composition or moderation between the contending parties. The parliament insisted on the establishment of presbytery, the sale of the chapter lands, the abolition of all forms of prayer, and strict laws against catholics. The king offered to retrench every thing, which he did not esteem of apostolical institution: He was willing to abolish archbishops, deans, prebends, canons: He offered, that the chapter lands should be let at low leases during ninety-nine years: He consented, that the present church government should continue during three years.[s] After that time, he required not, that any thing should be restored to bishops but the power of ordination, and even that power to be exercised by advice of the presbyters.[t] If the parliament, upon the expiration of that period, still insisted on their demand, all other branches of episcopal jurisdiction were abolished, and a new form of church government must, by common consent, be established. The book of common prayer he was willing to renounce, but required the liberty of using some other liturgy in his own chapel:[u] A demand, which, though seemingly reasonable, was positively refused by the parliament.

In the dispute on these articles, one is not surprised, that two of the parliamentary theologians should tell the king, *That if he did not consent to the utter abolition of episcopacy, he would be damned.* But it is not without some indignation, that we read the following vote of the lords and commons. "The houses, out of their detestation to that abominable idolatry used in the mass, do declare, that they cannot admit of, or consent unto, any such indulgence in any law, as is desired by his majesty for exempting the queen and her family from the penalties to be enacted against the exercise of the mass."[w] The treaty of marriage, the regard to the queen's sex and high station, even common humanity; all considerations were undervalued, in comparison of their bigotted prejudices.[x]

---

[r] Ibid. p. 91, 93.   [s] Ibid. p. 29, 35, 49.   [t] Ibid. p. 65.   [u] Ibid. p. 75, 82. Rush. vol. viii. p. 1323.   [w] Walker, p. 71.   [x] See note [JJ] at the end of the volume.

CHAPTER LIX

It was evidently the interest, both of king and parliament, to finish their treaty with all expedition; and endeavour, by their combined force, to resist, if possible, the usurping fury of the army. It seemed even the interest of the parliament, to leave, in the king's hand, a considerable share of authority, by which he might be enabled to protect them and himself, from so dangerous an enemy. But the terms, on which they insisted, were so rigorous, that the king, fearing no worse from the most implacable enemies, was in no haste to come to a conclusion. And so great was the bigotry on both sides, that they were willing to sacrifice the greatest civil interests, rather than relinquish the most minute of their theological contentions. From these causes, assisted by the artifice of the independents, the treaty was spun out to such a length, that the invasions and insurrections were every where subdued; and the army had leisure to execute their violent and sanguinary purposes.

Hamilton, having entered England with a numerous, though undisciplined, army, durst not unite his forces with those of Langdale; because the English royalists had refused to take the covenant; and the Scottish presbyterians, though engaged for the king, refused to join them on any other terms. The two armies marched together though at some distance; nor could even the approach of the parliamentary army under Cromwel, oblige the covenanters to consult their own safety, by a close union with the royalists. When principles are so absurd and so destructive of human society, it may safely be averred, that, the more sincere and the more disinterested they are, they only become the more ridiculous and more odious. *Civil war and invasion repressed.*

Cromwel feared not to oppose 8000 men, to the numerous armies of 20,000, commanded by Hamilton and Langdale. He attacked the latter by surprize, near Preston in Lancashire;[y] and, though the royalists made a brave resistance, yet, not being succoured in time by their confederates, they were almost entirely cut in pieces. Hamilton was next attacked, put to rout, and pursued to Utoxeter, where he surrendered himself prisoner. Cromwel followed his advantage; and marching into Scotland with a considerable body, joined Argyle, who was also in arms; and having suppressed Laneric, Monro, and other moderate presby-

[y] 17th of August.

terians, he placed the power entirely in the hands of the violent party. The ecclesiastical authority, exalted above the civil, exercised the severest vengeance on all who had a share in Hamilton's engagement, as it was called; nor could any of that party recover trust, or even live in safety, but by doing solemn and public penance for taking arms, by authority of parliament, in defence of their lawful sovereign.

The chancellor, Loudon, who had, at first, countenanced Hamilton's enterprize, being terrified with the menaces of the clergy, had, some time before, gone over to the other party; and he now, openly in the church, though invested with the highest civil character in the kingdom, did penance for his obedience to the parliament, which he termed a *carnal self-seeking*. He accompanied his penance with so many tears, and such pathetical addresses to the people for their prayers in this his uttermost sorrow and distress, that an universal weeping and lamentation took place among the deluded audience.[z]

The loan of great sums of money, often to the ruin of families, was exacted from all such as lay under any suspicion of favouring the king's party, though their conduct had been ever so inoffensive. This was a device, fallen upon by the ruling party, in order, as they said, to reach *Heart Malignants*.[a] Never, in this island, was known a more severe and arbitrary government, than was generally exercised, by the patrons of liberty in both kingdoms.

The siege of Colchester terminated in a manner no less unfortunate than Hamilton's engagement, for the royal cause. After suffering the utmost extremities of famine, after feeding on the vilest aliments; the garrison desired, at last, to capitulate. Fairfax required them to surrender at discretion; and he gave such an explanation to these terms, as to reserve to himself power, if he pleased, to put them all instantly to the sword. The officers endeavoured, though in vain, to persuade the soldiers, by making a vigorous sally, to break through, at least, to sell their lives as dear as possible. They were obliged[b] to accept of the conditions offered; and Fairfax, instigated by Ireton, to whom Cromwel, in his absence, had consigned over the government of the passive general, seized Sir Charles Lucas and Sir George Lisle, and resolved to

[z] Whitlocke, p. 360.   [a] Guthrey.   [b] 18th of August.

CHAPTER LIX

make them instant sacrifices to military justice. This unusual severity was loudly exclaimed against by all the prisoners. Lord Capel,
fearless of danger, reproached Ireton with it; and challenged him,
as they were all engaged in the same honourable cause, to exercise
the same impartial vengeance on all of them. Lucas was first shot,
and he himself, gave orders to fire, with the same alacrity, as if he
had commanded a platoon of his own soldiers. Lisle instantly ran
and kissed the dead body, then chearfully presented himself to a
like fate. Thinking that the soldiers, destined for his execution,
stood at too great a distance, he called to them to come nearer: One
of them replied, *I'll warrant you, Sir, we'll hit you:* He answered
smiling, *Friends, I have been nearer you when you have missed me.* Thus
perished this generous spirit, not less beloved for his modesty and
humanity, than esteemed for his courage and military conduct.

Soon after, a gentleman appearing in the king's presence,
cloathed in mourning for Sir Charles Lucas; that humane prince,
suddenly recollecting the hard fate of his friends, paid them a
tribute, which none of his own unparalleled misfortunes ever extorted from him: He dissolved into a flood of tears.[c]

By these multiplied successes of the army, they had subdued all
their enemies; and none remained but the helpless king and parliament, to oppose their violent measures. From Cromwel's suggestion, a remonstrance was drawn by the council of general officers, and sent to the parliament. They there complain of the treaty
with the king; demand his punishment for the blood spilt during
the war; require a dissolution of the present parliament, and a
more equal representative for the future; and assert, that, though
servants, they are entitled to represent these important points to
their masters, who are themselves no better than servants and
trustees of the people. At the same time, they advanced with the
army to Windsor, and sent colonel Eure to seize the king's person
at Newport, and convey him to Hurst castle in the neighbourhood,
where he was detained in strict confinement.

*The king
seized again
by the army.*

This measure being foreseen some time before, the king was
exhorted to make his escape, which was conceived to be very easy:
But having given his word to the parliament not to attempt the
recovery of his liberty during the treaty, and three weeks after; he

[c] Whitlocke.

would not, by any persuasion, be induced to hazard the reproach of violating that promise. In vain was it urged, that a promise, given to the parliament, could no longer be binding; since they could no longer afford him protection from violence, threatened him by other persons, to whom he was bound by no tye or engagement. The king would indulge no refinements of casuistry, however plausible, in such delicate subjects; and was resolved, that, what depredations soever fortune should commit upon him, she never should bereave him of his honour.[d]

The parliament lost not courage, notwithstanding the danger, with which they were so nearly menaced. Tho' without any plan for resisting military usurpations, they resolved to withstand them to the uttermost; and rather to bring on a violent and visible subversion of government, than lend their authority to those illegal and sanguinary measures, which were projected. They set aside the remonstrance of the army, without deigning to answer it; they voted the seizing of the king's person, to be without their consent, and sent a message to the general, to know by what authority that enterprize had been executed; and they issued orders, that the army should advance no nearer to London.

Hollis, the present leader of the presbyterians, was a man of unconquerable intrepidity; and many others of that party seconded his magnanimous spirit. It was proposed by them, that the generals, and principal officers should, for their disobedience and usurpations, be proclaimed traitors by the parliament.

But the parliament was dealing with men, who would not be frightened by words, nor retarded by any scrupulous delicacy. The generals, under the name of Fairfax, (for he still allowed them to employ his name) marched the army to London, and placing guards in Whitehall, the Meuse, St. James's, Durham-house, Covent-garden, and Palace-yard, surrounded the parliament with their hostile armaments.

Decemb. 6.
The house
purged.

The parliament, destitute of all hopes of prevailing retained, however, courage to resist. They attempted, in the face of the army, to close their treaty with the king; and, though they had formerly voted his concessions with regard to the church and delinquents to be unsatisfactory, they now took into consideration the final resolution with regard to the whole. After a violent debate

---

[d] Col. Cooke's Memoirs, p. 174. Rush. vol. viii. p. 1347.

of three days, it was carried by a majority of 129 against 83, in the house of commons, that the king's concessions were a foundation for the houses to proceed upon in the settlement of the kingdom.

Next day, when the commons were to meet, colonel Pride, formerly a drayman, had environed the house with two regiments; and, directed by lord Grey of Groby, he seized in the passage forty-one members of the presbyterian party, and sent them to a low room, which passed by the appelation of *hell;* whence they were afterwards carried to several inns. Above 160 members more were excluded; and none were allowed to enter but the most furious and most determined of the independents; and these exceeded not the number of fifty or sixty. This invasion of the parliament commonly passed under the name of *colonel Pride's purge;* so much disposed was the nation to make merry with the dethroning of those members, who had violently arrogated the whole authority of government, and deprived the king of his legal prerogatives.

The subsequent proceedings of the parliament, if this diminutive assembly deserve that honourable name, retain not the least appearance of law, equity, or freedom. They instantly reversed the former vote, and declared the king's concessions unsatisfactory. They determined, that no member, absent at this last vote, should be received, till he subscribed it, as agreeable to his judgment. They renewed their former vote of non-addresses. And they committed to prison, Sir William Waller, Sir John Clotworthy, the generals Massey, Brown, Copley, and other leaders of the presbyterians. These men, by their credit and authority, which was then very high, had, at the commencement of the war, supported the parliament; and thereby prepared the way for the greatness of the present leaders, who, at that time, were of small account in the nation.

The secluded members having published a paper, containing a narrative of the violence, which had been exercised upon them, and a protestation, that all acts were void, which, from that time, had been transacted in the house of commons; the remaining members encountered it with a declaration, in which they pronounced it false, scandalous, seditious, and tending to the destruction of the visible and fundamental government of the kingdom.

These sudden and violent revolutions held the whole nation in terror and astonishment. Every man dreaded to be trampled under foot, in the contention between those mighty powers, which disputed for the sovereignty of the state. Many began to withdraw their effects beyond sea: Foreigners scrupled to give any credit to a people, so torn by domestic faction, and oppressed by military usurpation: Even the internal commerce of the kingdom began to stagnate: And in order to remedy these growing evils, the generals, in the name of the army, published a declaration, in which they expressed their resolution of supporting law and justice.[e]

The more to quiet the minds of men, the council of officers took into consideration, a scheme called *The agreement of the people;* being the plan of a republic, to be substituted in the place of that government, which they had so violently pulled in pieces. Many parts of this scheme, for correcting the inequalities of the representative, are plausible; had the nation been disposed to receive it, or had the army intended to impose it. Other parts are too perfect for human nature, and favour strongly of that fanatical spirit, so prevalent throughout the kingdom.

The height of all iniquity and fanatical extravagance yet remained; the public trial and execution of their sovereign. To this period was every measure precipitated by the zealous independents. The parliamentary leaders of that party had intended, that the army, themselves, should execute that daring enterprize; and they deemed so irregular and lawless a deed, best fitted to such irregular and lawless instruments.[f] But the generals were too wise, to load themselves singly with the infamy, which, they knew, must attend an action, so shocking to the general sentiments of mankind. The parliament, they were resolved, should share with them the reproach of a measure, which was thought requisite for the advancement of their common ends of safety and ambition. In the house of commons, therefore, a committee was appointed to bring in a charge against the king. On their report a vote passed, declaring it a treason in a king, to levy war against his parliament, and appointing a HIGH COURT OF JUSTICE to try Charles for this new invented treason. This vote was sent up to the house of peers.

The house of peers, during the civil wars, had, all along, been of small account; but it had lately, since the king's fall, become totally contemptible; and very few members would submit to the mortification of attending it. It happened, that day, to be fuller

[e] Rush. vol. viii. p. 1364.   [f] Whitlocke.

than usual, and they were assembled to the number of sixteen. Without one dissenting voice, and almost without deliberation, they instantly rejected the vote of the lower house, and adjourned themselves for ten days; hoping that this delay would be able to retard the furious career of the commons.

The commons were not to be stopped by so small an obstacle. *1649.* Having first established a principle, which is noble in itself, and seems specious, but is belied by all history and experience, *That the people are the origin of all just power;* they next declared, that the commons of England, assembled in parliament, being chosen by the people, and representing them, are the supreme authority of the nation, and that whatever is enacted and declared to be law by the commons, hath the force of law, without the consent of king or house of peers. The ordinance for the trial of Charles Stuart, king *January 4.* of England, so they called him, was again read and unanimously assented to.

In proportion to the enormity of the violences and usurpations, were augmented the pretences of sanctity, among those regicides. "Should any one have voluntarily proposed," said Cromwel in the house, "to bring the king to punishment, I should have regarded him as the greatest traitor; but, since providence and necessity have cast us upon it, I will pray to God for a blessing on your counsels; though I am not prepared to give you any advice on this important occasion. Even I myself," subjoined he, "when I was lately offering up petitions for his majesty's restoration, felt my tongue cleave to the roof of my mouth, and considered this preternatural movement as the answer which heaven, having rejected the king, had sent to my supplications."

A woman of Hertfordshire, illuminated by prophetical visions, desired admittance into the military council, and communicated to the officers a revelation, which assured them, that their measures were consecrated from above, and ratified by a heavenly sanction. This intelligence gave them great comfort, and much confirmed them in their present resolutions.[g]

Colonel Harrison, the son of a butcher, and the most furious enthusiast in the army, was sent with a strong party to conduct the king to London. At Windsor, Hamilton, who was there detained a

[g] Whitlocke, p. 360.

prisoner, was admitted into the king's presence; and falling on his knees, passionately exclaimed, *My dear master!—I have indeed been so to you,* replied Charles, embracing him. No farther intercourse was allowed between them. The king was instantly hurried away. Hamilton long followed him with his eyes, all suffused in tears, and prognosticated, that, in this short salutation, he had given the last adieu to his sovereign and his friend.

Charles himself was assured, that the period of his life was now approaching; but notwithstanding all the preparations, which were making, and the intelligence, which he received, he could not, even yet, believe, that his enemies really meant to conclude their violences by a public trial and execution. A private assassination he every moment looked for; and though Harrison assured him, that his apprehensions were entirely groundless, it was by that catastrophe, so frequent with dethroned princes, that he expected to terminate his life. In appearance, as well as in reality, the king was now dethroned. All the exterior symbols of sovereignty were withdrawn, and his attendants had orders to serve him without ceremony. At first, he was shocked with instances of rudeness and familiarity, to which he had been so little accustomed. *Nothing so contemptible as a despised prince!* was the reflection, which they suggested to him. But he soon reconciled his mind to this, as he had done to his other calamities.

All the circumstances of the trial were now adjusted; and the high court of justice fully constituted. It consisted of 133 persons, as named by the commons; but there scarcely ever sate above 70: So difficult was it, notwithstanding the blindness of prejudice, and the allurements of interest, to engage men of any name or character in that criminal measure. Cromwel, Ireton, Harrison, and the chief officers of the army, most of them of mean birth, were members, together with some of the lower house and some citizens of London. The twelve judges were at first appointed in the number: But as they had affirmed, that it was contrary to all the ideas of English law to try the king for treason, by whose authority all accusations for treason must necessarily be conducted; their names, as well as those of some peers, were afterwards struck out. Bradshaw, a lawyer, was chosen president. Coke was appointed solicitor for the people of England. Dorislaus, Steele, and Aske, were named assistants. The court sat in Westminster-hall.

CHAPTER LIX

It is remarkable, that, in calling over the court, when the crier pronounced the name of Fairfax, which had been inserted in the number, a voice came from one of the spectators, and cried, *He has more wit than to be here.* When the charge was read against the king, *In the name of the people of England;* the same voice exclaimed, *Not a tenth part of them.* Axtel the officer, who guarded the court, giving orders to fire into the box, whence these insolent speeches came; it was discovered, that lady Fairfax was there, and that it was she who had had the courage to utter them. She was a person of noble extraction, daughter of Horace lord Vere of Tilbury; but being seduced by the violence of the times, she had long seconded her husband's zeal against the royal cause, and was now, as well as he, struck with abhorrence at the fatal and unexpected consequence of all his boasted victories.

The pomp, the dignity, the ceremony of this transaction, corresponded to the greatest conception, that is suggested in the annals of human kind; the delegates of a great people sitting in judgment upon their supreme magistrate, and trying him for his misgovernment and breach of trust. The solicitor, in the name of the commons, represented, that Charles Stuart, being admitted king of England, and *entrusted* with a limited power; yet nevertheless, from a wicked design to erect an unlimited and tyrannical government, had traiterously and maliciously levied war against the present parliament, and the people, whom they represented, and was therefore impeached as a tyrant, traitor, murderer, and a public and implacable enemy to the commonwealth. After the charge was finished, the president directed his discourse to the king, and told him, that the court expected his answer. *The king's trial.*

The king, though long detained a prisoner, and now produced as a criminal, sustained, by his magnanimous courage, the majesty of a monarch. With great temper and dignity, he declined the authority of the court, and refused to submit himself to their jurisdiction. He represented, that, having been engaged in treaty with his two houses of parliament, and having finished almost every article, he had expected to be brought to his capital in another manner, and ere this time, to have been restored to his power, dignity, revenue, as well as to his personal liberty: That he could not now perceive any appearance of the upper house, so essential a member of the constitution; and had learned, that even the commons, whose authority was pretended, were subdued by lawless force, and were bereaved of their liberty: That he himself was their NATIVE HEREDITARY KING; nor was the whole authority of the state, though free and united, intitled to try him, who derived his dignity from the Supreme Majesty of Heaven: That, admitting those extravagant principles, which levelled all orders of men, the court could plead no power, delegated by the people; unless the consent of every individual, down to the meanest and most ignorant peasant, had been previously asked and obtained: That he acknowledged, without scruple, that he had a *trust* committed to him, and one most sacred and inviolable; he was entrusted with the liberties of his people, and would not now betray them, by recognizing a power, founded on the most atrocious violence and usurpation: That having taken arms, and frequently exposed his life, in defence of public liberty, of the constitution, of the fundamental laws of the kingdom, he was willing, in this last and most solemn scene, to seal with his blood those precious rights, for which, though in vain, he had so long contended: That those, who arrogated a title to sit as his judges, were born his subjects, and born subjects to those laws, which determined, *That the king can do no wrong:* That he was not reduced to the necessity of sheltering himself under this general maxim, which guards every English monarch, even the least deserving; but was able, by the most satisfactory reasons, to justify those measures, in which he had been engaged: That, to the whole world, and even to them, his pretended judges, he was desirous, if called upon in another manner, to prove the integrity of his conduct, and assert the justice of those defensive arms, to which, unwillingly and unfortunately, he had had recourse: But that, in order to preserve a uniformity of conduct, he must at present, forego the apology of his innocence; lest, by ratifying an authority, no better founded than that of robbers and pyrates, he be justly branded as the betrayer, instead of being applauded as the martyr, of the constitution.

The president, in order to support the majesty of the people, and maintain the superiority of his court above the prisoner, still inculcated, that he must not decline the authority of his judges; that they over-ruled his objections; that they were delegated by the people, the only source of every lawful power; and that kings themselves acted but in trust from that community, which had

CHAPTER LIX

invested this high court of justice with its jurisdiction. Even according to those principles, which, in his present situation, he was perhaps obliged to adopt, his behaviour, in general, will appear not a little harsh and barbarous; but when we consider him as a subject, and one too of no high character, addressing himself to his unfortunate sovereign, his style will be esteemed, to the last degree, audacious and insolent.

Three times was Charles produced before the court, and as often declined their jurisdiction. On the fourth, the judges having examined some witnesses, by whom it was proved, that the king had appeared in arms against the forces commissioned by the parliament, they pronounced sentence against him. He seemed very anxious, at this time, to be admitted to a conference with the two houses; and it was supposed, that he intended to resign the crown to his son: But the court refused compliance, and considered that request as nothing but a delay of justice.

27th Jan.

It is confessed, that the king's behaviour, during this last scene of his life, does honour to his memory; and that, in all appearances before his judges, he never forgot his part, either as a prince or as a man. Firm and intrepid, he maintained, in each reply, the utmost perspicuity and justness both of thought and expression: Mild and equable, he rose into no passion at that unusual authority, which was assumed over him. His soul, without effort or affectation, seemed only to remain in the situation familiar to it, and to look down with contempt on all the efforts of human malice and iniquity. The soldiers, instigated by their superiors, were brought, though with difficulty, to cry aloud for justice: *Poor souls!* said the king to one of his attendants; *for a little money they would do as much against their commanders.* [h] Some of them were permitted to go the utmost length of brutal insolence, and to spit in his face, as he was conducted along the passage to the court. To excite a sentiment of piety was the only effect, which this inhuman insult was able to produce upon him.

The people, though under the rod of lawless, unlimited power, could not forbear, with the most ardent prayers, pouring forth their wishes for his preservation; and, in his present distress, they avowed *him,* by their generous tears, for their monarch, whom, in

[h] Rush. vol. viii. p. 1425.

their misguided fury, they had before so violently rejected. The king was softened at this moving scene, and expressed his gratitude for their dutiful affection. One soldier too, seized by contagious sympathy, demanded from heaven a blessing on oppressed and fallen majesty: His officer, overhearing the prayer, beat him to the ground in the king's presence. *The punishment, methinks, exceeds the offence:* This was the reflection which Charles formed on that occasion.[i]

As soon as the intention of trying the king was known in foreign countries, so enormous an action was exclaimed against by the general voice of reason and humanity; and all men, under whatever form of government they were born, rejected this example, as the utmost effort of undisguised usurpation, and the most heinous insult on law and justice. The French ambassador, by orders from his court, interposed in the king's behalf: The Dutch employed their good offices: The Scots exclaimed and protested against the violence: The queen, the prince, wrote pathetic letters to the parliament. All solicitations were found fruitless with men whose resolutions were fixed and irrevocable.

Four of Charles's friends, persons of virtue and dignity, Richmond, Hertford, Southampton, Lindesey, applied to the commons. They represented, that they were the king's counsellors, and had concurred, by their advice, in all those measures, which were now imputed as crimes to their royal master: That, in the eye of the law, and according to the dictates of common reason, they alone were guilty, and were alone exposed to censure for every blameable action of the prince: And that they now presented themselves, in order to save, by their own punishment, that precious life, which it became the commons themselves, and every subject, with the utmost hazard, to protect and defend.[k] Such a generous effort tended to their honour; but contributed nothing towards the king's safety.

The people remained in that silence and astonishment, which all great passions, when they have not an opportunity of exerting themselves, naturally produce in the human mind. The soldiers, being incessantly plied with prayers, sermons, and exhortations, were wrought up to a degree of fury, and imagined, that in the acts

[i] Warwick, p. 339.   [k] Perinchef, p. 85. Lloyde, p. 319.

of the most extreme disloyalty towards their prince, consisted their greatest merit in the eye of heaven.[l]

Three days were allowed the king between his sentence and his execution. This interval he passed with great tranquillity, chiefly in reading and devotion. All his family, that remained in England, were allowed access to him. It consisted only of the princess Elizabeth and the duke of Glocester; for the duke of York had made his escape. Glocester was little more than an infant: The princess, notwithstanding her tender years, shewed an advanced judgment; and the calamities of her family had made a deep impression upon her. After many pious consolations and advices, the king gave her in charge to tell the queen, that, during the whole course of his life, he had never once, even in thought, failed in his fidelity towards her; and that his conjugal tenderness and his life should have an equal duration.

To the young duke too, he could not forbear giving some advice, in order to season his mind with early principles of loyalty and obedience towards his brother, who was so soon to be his sovereign. Holding him on his knee, he said, "Now they will cut off thy father's head." At these words, the child looked very stedfastly upon him. "Mark! child, what I say: They will cut off my head! and perhaps make thee a king: But mark what I say: Thou must not be a king, as long as thy brothers, Charles and James, are alive. They will cut off thy brothers' heads, when they can catch them! And thy head too they will cut off at last! Therefore I charge thee, do not be made a king by them!" The duke, sighing, replied, "I will be torn in pieces first!" So determined an answer, from one of such tender years, filled the king's eyes with tears of joy and admiration.

Every night, during this interval, the king slept sound as usual; though the noise of workmen, employed in framing the scaffold, and other preparations for his execution, continually resounded in his ears.[m] The morning of the fatal day, he rose early; and calling Herbert, one of his attendants, he bade him employ more than usual care in dressing him, and preparing him for so great and joyful a solemnity. Bishop Juxon, a man endowed with the same *30th Jan.* mild and steady virtues, by which the king himself was so much

[l] Burnet's History of his own Times. [m] Clement Walker's history of independency.

distinguished, assisted him in his devotions, and paid the last melancholy duties to his friend and sovereign.

And execution. The street before Whitehall was the place destined for the execution: For it was intended, by choosing that very place, in sight of his own palace, to display more evidently the triumph of popular justice over royal majesty. When the king came upon the scaffold, he found it so surrounded with soldiers, that he could not expect to be heard by any of the people: He addressed, therefore, his discourse to the few persons who were about him; particularly colonel Tomlinson, to whose care he had lately been committed, and upon whom, as upon many others, his amiable deportment had wrought an entire conversion. He justified his own innocence in the late fatal wars, and observed, that he had not taken arms, till after the parliament had inlisted forces; nor had he any other object in his warlike operations, than to preserve that authority entire, which his predecessors had transmitted to him. He threw not, however, the blame upon the parliament; but was more inclined to think, that ill instruments had interposed, and raised in them fears and jealousies with regard to his intentions. Though innocent towards his people, he acknowledged the equity of his execution in the eyes of his Maker; and observed, that, an unjust sentence, which he had suffered to take effect, was now punished by an unjust sentence upon himself. He forgave all his enemies, even the chief instruments of his death; but exhorted them and the whole nation to return to the ways of peace, by paying obedience to their lawful sovereign, his son and successor. When he was preparing himself for the block, bishop Juxon called to him: "There is, Sir, but one stage more, which, though turbulent and troublesome, is yet a very short one. Consider, it will soon carry you a great way; it will carry you from earth to heaven; and there you shall find, to your great joy, the prize, to which you hasten, a crown of glory." "I go," replied the king, "from a corruptible to an incorruptible crown; where no disturbance can have place." At one blow was his head severed from his body. A man in a vizor performed the office of executioner: Another, in a like disguise, held up to the spectators, the head, streaming with blood, and cried aloud, *This is the head of a traitor!*

It is impossible to describe the grief, indignation, and astonishment, which took place, not only among the spectators, who were overwhelmed with a flood of sorrow, but throughout the whole nation, as soon as the report of this fatal execution was conveyed to them. Never monarch, in the full triumph of success and victory, was more dear to his people, than his misfortunes and magnanimity, his patience and piety, had rendered this unhappy prince. In proportion to their former delusions, which had animated them against him, was the violence of their return to duty and affection; while each reproached himself, either with active disloyalty towards him, or with too indolent defence of his oppressed cause. On weaker minds, the effect of these complicated passions was prodigious. Women are said to have cast forth the untimely fruit of their womb: Others fell into convulsions, or sunk into such a melancholy as attended them to their grave: Nay some, unmindful of themselves, as though they could not, or would not survive their beloved prince, it is reported, suddenly fell down dead. The very pulpits were bedewed with unsuborned tears; those pulpits, which had formerly thundered out the most violent imprecations and anathemas against him. And all men united in their detestation of those hypocritical parricides, who, by sanctified pretences, had so long disguised their treasons, and in this last act of iniquity, had thrown an indelible stain upon the nation.

A fresh instance of hypocrisy was displayed the very day of the king's death. The generous Fairfax, not content with being absent from the trial, had used all the interest, which he yet retained, to prevent the execution of the fatal sentence; and had ever employed persuasion with his own regiment, though none else should follow him, to rescue the king from his disloyal murderers. Cromwel and Ireton, informed of this intention, endeavoured to convince him, that the Lord had rejected the king; and they exhorted him to seek by prayer some direction from heaven on this important occasion: But they concealed from him that they had already signed the warrant for the execution. Harrison was the person appointed to join in prayer with the unwary general. By agreement, he prolonged his doleful cant, till intelligence arrived, that the fatal blow was struck. He then rose from his knees, and insisted with Fairfax, that this event was a miraculous and providential answer, which heaven had sent to their devout supplications.[n]

It being remarked, that the king, the moment before he stretched out his neck to the executioner, had said to Juxon, with a very earnest accent, the single word, REMEMBER; great mysteries were supposed to be concealed under that expression; and the generals vehemently insisted with the prelate, that he should inform them of the king's meaning. Juxon told them, that the king, having frequently charged him to inculcate on his son the forgiveness of his murderers, had taken this opportunity, in the last moment of his life, when his commands, he supposed, would be regarded as sacred and inviolable, to re-iterate that desire; and that his mild spirit thus terminated its present course, by an act of benevolence towards his greatest enemies.

The character of this prince, as that of most men, if not of all men, was mixed; but his virtues predominated extremely above his vices, or, more properly speaking, his imperfections: For scarce any of his faults rose to that pitch as to merit the appellation of vices. To consider him in the most favourable light, it may be affirmed, that his dignity was free from pride, his humanity from weakness, his bravery from rashness, his temperance from austerity, his frugality from avarice: All these virtues, in him, maintained their proper bounds, and merited unreserved praise. To speak the most harshly of him, we may affirm, that many of his good qualities were attended with some latent frailty, which, though seemingly inconsiderable, was able, when seconded by the extreme malevolence of his fortune, to disappoint them of all their influence: His beneficent disposition was clouded by a manner not very gracious; his virtue was tinctured with superstition; his good sense was disfigured by a deference to persons of a capacity inferior to his own; and his moderate temper exempted him not from hasty and precipitate resolutions. He deserves the epithet of a good, rather than of a great man; and was more fitted to rule in a regular established government, than either to give way to the encroachments of a popular assembly, or finally to subdue their pretensions. He wanted suppleness and dexterity sufficient for the first measure: He was not endowed with the vigour requisite for

[n] Herbert, p. 135.

the second. Had he been born an absolute prince, his humanity and good sense had rendered his reign happy and his memory precious: Had the limitations on prerogative been, in his time, quite fixed and certain, his integrity had made him regard, as sacred, the boundaries of the constitution. Unhappily, his fate threw him into a period, when the precedents of many former reigns favoured strongly of arbitrary power, and the genius of the people ran violently towards liberty. And if his political prudence was not sufficient to extricate him from so perilous a situation, he may be excused; since, even after the event, when it is commonly easy to correct all errors, one is at a loss to determine what conduct, in his circumstances, could have maintained the authority of the crown, and preserved the peace of the nation. Exposed, without revenue, without arms, to the assault of furious, implacable, and bigotted factions, it was never permitted him, but with the most fatal consequences, to commit the smallest mistake; a condition too rigorous to be imposed on the greatest human capacity.

Some historians have rashly questioned the good faith of this prince: But, for this reproach, the most malignant scrutiny of his conduct, which, in every circumstance, is now thoroughly known, affords not any reasonable foundation. On the contrary, if we consider the extreme difficulties, to which he was so frequently reduced, and compare the sincerity of his professions and declarations; we shall avow, that probity and honour ought justly to be numbered among his most shining qualities. In every treaty, those concessions, which, he thought, he could not, in conscience, maintain, he never could, by any motive or persuasion, be induced to make. And though some violations of the petition of right may perhaps be imputed to him; these are more to be ascribed to the necessity of his situation, and to the lofty ideas of royal prerogative, which, from former established precedents, he had imbibed, than to any failure in the integrity of his principles.[o]

This prince was of a comely presence; of a sweet, but melancholy aspect. His face was regular, handsome, and well complexioned; his body strong, healthy, and justly proportioned; and being of a middle stature, he was capable of enduring the greatest fatigues. He excelled in horsemanship and other exercises; and he

[o] See note [KK] at the end of the volume.

possessed all the exterior, as well as many of the essential qualities, which form an accomplished prince.

The tragical death of Charles begat a question, whether the people, in any case, were intitled to judge and to punish their sovereign; and most men, regarding chiefly the atrocious usurpation of the pretended judges, and the merit of the virtuous prince who suffered, were inclined to condemn the republican principle, as highly seditious and extravagant: But there still were a few, who, abstracting from the particular circumstances of this case, were able to consider the question in general, and were inclined to moderate, not contradict, the prevailing sentiment. Such might have been their reasoning. If ever, on any occasion, it were laudable to conceal truth from the populace; it must be confessed, that the doctrine of resistance affords such an example; and that all speculative reasoners ought to observe, with regard to this principle, the same cautious silence, which the laws, in every species of government, have ever prescribed to themselves. Government is instituted, in order to restrain the fury and injustice of the people; and being always founded on opinion, not on force, it is dangerous to weaken, by these speculations, the reverence, which the multitude owe to authority, and to instruct them beforehand, that the case can ever happen, when they may be freed from their duty of allegiance. Or should it be found impossible to restrain the licence of human disquisitions, it must be acknowledged, that the doctrine of obedience ought alone to be *inculcated,* and that the exceptions, which are rare, ought seldom or never to be mentioned in popular reasonings and discourses. Nor is there any danger, that mankind, by this prudent reserve, should universally degenerate into a state of abject servitude. When the exception really occurs, even though it be not previously expected and descanted on, it must, from its very nature, be so obvious and undisputed, as to remove all doubt, and overpower the restraint, however great, imposed by teaching the general doctrine of obedience. But between resisting a prince and dethroning him, there is a wide interval; and the abuses of power, which can warrant the latter violence, are greater and more enormous, than those which will justify the former. History, however, supplies us with examples even of this kind; and the reality of the supposition, though, for the future, it ought ever to be little looked for, must, by all candid enquirers, be acknowledged in the past. But between dethroning a prince and punishing him, there is another very wide interval; and it were not strange, if even men of the most enlarged thought should question, whether human nature could ever, in any monarch, reach that height of depravity, as to warrant, in revolted subjects, this last act of extraordinary jurisdiction. That illusion, if it be an illusion, which teaches us to pay a sacred regard to the persons of princes, is so salutary, that to dissipate it by the formal trial and punishment of a sovereign, will have more pernicious effects upon the people, than the example of justice can be supposed to have a beneficial influence upon princes, by checking their career of tyranny. It is dangerous also, by these examples, to reduce princes to despair, or bring matters to such extremities against persons endowed with great power, as to leave them no resource, but in the most violent and most sanguinary counsels. This general position being established, it must, however, be observed, that no reader, almost of any party or principle, was ever shocked, when he read, in ancient history, that the Roman senate voted Nero, their absolute sovereign, to be a public enemy, and, even without trial, condemned him to the severest and most ignominious punishment; a punishment, from which the meanest Roman citizen, was, by the laws, exempted. The crimes of that bloody tyrant are so enormous, that they break through all rules; and extort a confession, that such a dethroned prince is no longer superior to his people, and can no longer plead, in his own defence, laws, which were established for conducting the ordinary course of administration. But when we pass from the case of Nero to that of Charles, the great disproportion, or rather total contrariety, of character immediately strikes us; and we stand astonished, that, among a civilized people, so much virtue could ever meet with so fatal a catastrophe. History, the great mistress of wisdom, furnishes examples of all kinds; and every prudential, as well as moral precept, may be authorized by those events, which her enlarged mirror is able to present to us. From the memorable revolutions, which passed in England during this period, we may naturally deduce the same useful lesson, which Charles himself, in his later years, inferred; that it is dangerous for princes, even from the appearance of necessity, to assume more authority, than the laws have allowed them. But, it must be confessed, that these events furnish us with another instruction, no less natural, and no less useful, concerning the madness of the people, the furies of fanaticism, and the danger of mercenary armies.

6th Feb. In order to close this part of British history, it is also necessary to relate the dissolution of the monarchy in England: That event soon followed upon the death of the monarch. When the peers met, on the day appointed in their adjournment, they entered upon business, and sent down some votes to the commons, of which the latter deigned not to take the least notice. In a few days, the lower house passed a vote, that they would make no more addresses to the house of peers, nor receive any from them; and that that house was useless and dangerous, and was therefore to be abolished. A like vote passed with regard to the monarchy; and it is remarkable, that Martin, a zealous republican, in the debate on this question, confessed, that, if they desired a king, the last was as proper as any gentleman in England.[p] The commons ordered a new great seal to be engraved, on which that assembly was represented, with this legend, ON THE FIRST YEAR OF FREEDOM, BY GOD'S BLESSING, RESTORED, 1648. The forms of all public business were changed, from the king's name, to that of the keepers of the liberties of England.[q] And it was declared high treason to proclaim, or any otherwise acknowledge Charles Stuart, commonly called prince of Wales.

The commons intended, it is said, to bind the princess Elizabeth apprentice to a button-maker: The duke of Glocester was to be taught some other mechanical employment. But the former soon died; of grief, as is supposed, for her father's tragical end: The latter was, by Cromwel, sent beyond sea.

The king's statue, in the Exchange, was thrown down; and on the pedestal these words were inscribed: EXIT TYRANNUS, REGUM ULTIMUS: *The tyrant is gone, the last of the kings.*

Duke Hamilton was tried by a new high court of justice, as earl of Cambridge in England; and condemned for treason. This sentence, which was certainly hard, but which ought to save his memory from all imputations of treachery to his master, was exe-

---

[p] Walker's history of independency, part 2.   [q] The court of King's Bench was called the court of Public Bench. So cautious on this head were some of the republicans, that, it is pretended, in reciting the Lord's prayer, they would not say *thy kingdom come,* but always *thy commonwealth come.*

CHAPTER LIX

cuted on a scaffold, erected before Westminster-hall. Lord Capel underwent the same fate. Both these noblemen had escaped from prison, but were afterwards discovered and taken. To all the solicitations of their friends for pardon, the generals and parliamentary leaders still replied, that it was certainly the intention of providence they should suffer; since it had permitted them to fall into the hands of their enemies, after they had once recovered their liberty.

The earl of Holland lost his life by a like sentence. Though of a polite and courtly behaviour, he died lamented by no party. His ingratitude to the king, and his frequent changing of sides, were regarded as great stains on his memory. The earl of Norwich and Sir John Owen, being condemned by the same court, were pardoned by the commons.

The king left six children; three males, Charles, born in 1630, James, duke of York, born in 1633, Henry duke of Glocester, born in 1641; and three females, Mary princess of Orange, born in 1631, Elizabeth, born 1635, and Henrietta, afterwards duchess of Orleans, born at Exeter 1644.

The archbishops of Canterbury in this reign were Abbot and Laud: The lord keepers, Williams, bishop of Lincoln, lord Coventry, lord Finch, lord Littleton, and Sir Richard Lane; the high admirals, the duke of Buckingham and the earl of Northumberland; the treasurers, the earl of Marlborough, the earl of Portland, Juxon, bishop of London, and lord Cottington; the secretaries of state, lord Conway, Sir Albertus Moreton, Coke, Sir Henry Vane, lord Falkland, lord Digby, and Sir Edward Nicholas.

It may be expected, that we should here mention the *Icon Basiliké,* a work published in the king's name a few days after his execution. It seems almost impossible, in the controverted parts of history, to say any thing which will satisfy the zealots of both parties: But with regard to the genuineness of that production, it is not easy for an historian to fix any opinion, which will be entirely to his own satisfaction. The proofs brought to evince, that this work is or is not the king's, are so convincing, that, if an impartial reader peruse any one side apart,[r] he will think it impossible, that

---

[r] See on the one hand, Toland's Amyntor, and on the other, Wagstaffe's vindication of the royal martyr, with Young's addition. We may remark,

arguments could be produced, sufficient to counter-balance so strong an evidence: And when he compares both sides, he will be some time at a loss to fix any determination. Should an absolute suspence of judgment be found difficult or disagreeable in so interesting a question, I must confess, that I much incline to give the preference to the arguments of the royalists. The testimonies, which prove that performance to be the king's, are more numerous, certain, and direct, than those on the other side. This is the case, even if we consider the external evidence: But when we weigh the internal, derived from the style and composition, there is no manner of comparison. These meditations resemble, in elegance, purity, neatness, and simplicity, the genius of those performances, which we know with certainty to have flowed from the royal pen: But are so unlike the bombast, perplexed, rhetorical, and corrupt style of Dr. Gauden, to whom they are ascribed, that no human testimony seems sufficient to convince us, that he was the author. Yet all the evidences, which would rob the king of that honour, tend to prove, that Dr. Gauden had the merit of writing so fine a performance, and the infamy of imposing it on the world for the king's.

It is not easy to conceive the general compassion excited towards the king, by the publishing, at so critical a juncture, a work so full of piety, meekness, and humanity. Many have not scrupled to ascribe to that book the subsequent restoration of the royal family. Milton compares its effects to those which were wrought on the tumultuous Romans by Anthony's reading to them the will of Caesar. The *Icon* passed through fifty editions in a twelvemonth; and independent of the great interest taken in it by the nation, as the supposed production of their murdered sovereign, it must be acknowledged the best prose composition, which, at the time of its publication, was to be found in the English language.

---

that lord Clarendon's total silence with regard to this subject, in so full a history, composed in vindication of the king's measures and character, forms a presumption on Toland's side, and a presumption of which that author was ignorant; the works of the noble historian not being then published. Bishop Burnet's testimony too must be allowed of some weight against the *Icon*.

NOTES TO THE
FIFTH VOLUME

NOTE [A], p. 17

Sir Charles Cornwallis the king's ambassador at Madrid, when pressed by the duke of Lerma to enter into a league with Spain, said to that minister; *though his majesty was an* absolute *king, and therefore not bound to give an account to any, of his actions; yet that so gracious and regardful a prince he was of the love and contentment of his own subjects, as I assured myself he would not think it fit to do any thing of so great consequence without acquainting them with his intentions.* Winwood, vol. ii. p. 222. Sir Walter Raleigh has this passage in the preface to his History of the World. *Philip II. by strong hand and main force, attempted to make himself not only an* absolute *monarch* over the Netherlands, *like unto the kings and monarchs of England and France, but Turk like, to tread under his feet all their natural and fundamental laws, privileges and ancient rights.* We meet with this passage in Sir John Davis's question concerning impositions, p. 161. "Thus we see by this comparison, that the king of England doth lay but his little finger upon his subjects, when other princes and states do lay their heavy loins upon their people: What is the reason of this difference? From whence cometh it? assuredly not from a different power or prerogative? For the king of England is as absolute a monarch as any emperor or king in the world, and hath as many prerogatives, incident to his crown." Coke, in Cawdry's case, says, "That by the ancient laws of this realm, England is an *absolute* empire and monarchy; and that the king is furnished with plenary and entire power, prerogative, and jurisdiction, and is supreme governor over all persons within this realm." Spencer, speaking of some grants of the English kings to the Irish corporations, says, "All which, though at the time of their first grant they were tolerable, and perhaps reasonable, yet now are most unreasonable and inconvenient. But all these will easily be cut off, with the superior power of her majesty's prerogative, against which her own grants are not to be pleaded or enforced." State of Ireland, p. 1537. edit. 1706. The same author in p. 1660, proposes a plan for the civilization of Ireland; that the queen should create a provost marshal in every county, who might ride about with eight or ten followers in search of stragglers and vagabonds: The first time he catches any, he may punish them more lightly, by the stocks; the second time, by whipping; but the third time, he may hang them, without trial or process, on the first bough: And he thinks, that this authority may more safely be entrusted to the provost marshal than to the sheriff: Because the latter magistrate, having a profit by the escheats of felons, may be tempted to hang innocent persons. Here a real absolute, or rather despotic power is pointed out; and we may infer from all these passages, either that the word *absolute* bore a different sense from what it does at present, or that men's ideas of the English, as well as Irish government were then different. This latter inference seems juster. The word, being derived from the French, bore always the same sense as in that language. An absolute monarchy in Charles I.'s answer to the nineteen propositions is opposed to a limited; and the king of England is acknowledged not to be absolute. So much had matters changed even before the civil war. In Sir John Fortescue's treatise of absolute and limited monarchy, a book written in the reign of Edward the IVth, the word *absolute* is taken in the same sense as at present; and the government of England is also said not to be absolute. They were the princes of the house of Tudor chiefly, who introduced that administration, which had the appearance of absolute government. The princes before them were restrained by the barons; as those after them by the house of commons. The people had, properly speaking, little liberty in either of these ancient governments, but least, in the more ancient.

NOTE [B], p. 18

Even this parliament, which shewed so much spirit and good-sense in the affair of Goodwin, made a strange concession to the crown, in their fourth session. Toby Mathews, a member, had been banished by order of the council upon direction from his majesty. The parliament not only acquiesced in this arbitrary proceeding, but issued writs for a new election. Such novices were they, as yet, in the principles of Liberty! See Journ. 14 Feb. 1609. Mathews was banished by the king, on account of his change of religion to popery. The king had an indulgence to those who had been educated catholics; but could not bear the new converts. It was probably the animosity of the commons against the papists, which made them acquiesce in this precedent, without reflecting on the consequences! The jealousy of Liberty, though rouzed, was not yet thoroughly enlightened.

NOTE [C], p. 19

At that time, men of genius and of enlarged minds had adopted the principles of liberty, which were, as yet, pretty much unknown to the generality of the people. Sir Matthew Hales has published a remonstrance against the king's conduct towards the parliament during this session. The remonstrance is drawn with great force of reasoning and spirit of liberty; and was the production of Sir Francis Bacon and Sir Edwin Sandys, two men of the greatest parts and knowledge in England. It is drawn in the name of the commons; but as there is no hint of it in the journals, we must conclude,

NOTES TO THE FIFTH VOLUME

either that the authors, sensible that the strain of the piece was much beyond the principles of the age, had not ventured to present it to the house, or that it had been, for that reason, rejected. The dignity and authority of the commons are strongly insisted upon in this remonstrance; and it is there said, that their submission to the ill treatment, which they received during the latter part of Elizabeth's reign, had proceeded from their tenderness towards her age and her sex. But the authors are mistaken in these facts: For the house received and submitted to as bad treatment in the beginning and middle of that reign. The government was equally arbitrary in Mary's reign, in Edward's, in Harry the eighth and seventh's. And the farther we go back into history, though there might be more of a certain irregular kind of liberty among the barons, the commons were still of less authority.

NOTE [D], p. 23

This parliament passed an act of recognition of the king's title in the most ample terms. They recognized and acknowledged, that immediately upon the dissolution and decease of Elizabeth, late queen of England, the imperial crown thereof did, by inherent birthright and lawful and undoubted succession, descend and come to his most excellent majesty, as being lineally, justly, and lawfully next and sole heir of the blood royal of this realm. 1 James I. cap. 1. The puritans, though then prevalent, did not think proper to dispute this great constitutional point. In the recognition of queen Elizabeth the parliament declares, that the queen's highness is, and in very deed and of most mere right ought to be, by the laws of God and by the laws and statutes of this realm, our most lawful and rightful sovereign, liege lady and queen, &c. It appears then, that, if king James's *divine right* be not mentioned by parliament, the omission came merely from chance; and because that phrase did not occur to the compiler of the recognition; his title being plainly the same with that of his predecessor, who was allowed to have a divine right.

NOTE [E], p. 30

Some historians have imagined, that the king had secret intelligence of the conspiracy, and that the letter to Monteagle was written by his direction, in order to obtain the praise of penetration in discovering the plot. But the known facts refute this supposition. That letter, being commonly talked of, might naturally have given an alarm to the conspirators, and made them contrive their escape. The visit of the lord chamberlain ought to have had the same effect. In short, it appears, that no body was arrested or enquired after, for some days, till Fawkes discovered the names of the conspirators. We may infer, however, from a letter in Winwood's Memorials, vol. ii. p. 171. that Salisbury's sagacity led the king in his conjectures, and that the minister, like an artful courtier, gave his master the praise of the whole discovery.

NOTE [F], p. 42

We find the king's answer in Winwood's Memorials, vol. iii. p. 193. 2d edit. "To the third and fourth (namely, that it might be lawful to arrest the king's servants without leave, and that no man should be inforced to lend money, nor to give a reason why he would not) his majesty sent us an answer, that because we brought precedents of antiquity to strengthen those demands, he allowed not of any precedents drawn from the time of usurping or decaying princes, or people too bold and wanton; that he desired not to govern in that commonwealth, where subjects should be assured of all things, and hope for nothing. It was one thing *submittere principatum legibus;* and another thing *submittere principatum subditis.* That he would not leave to posterity such a mark of weakness upon his reign; and therefore his conclusion was, *non placet petitio, non placet exemplum:* Yet with this mitigation, that in matters of loans he would refuse no reasonable excuse, nor should my lord chamberlain deny the arresting of any of his majesty's servants, if just cause was shown." The parliament, however, acknowledged at this time with thankfulness to the king, that he allowed disputes and inquiries about his prerogative, much beyond what had been indulged by any of his predecessors. *Parliament. Hist.* vol. v. p. 230. This very sessions, he expressly gave them leave to produce all their grievances, without exception.

NOTE [G], p. 45

It may not be unworthy of observation, that James, in a book called *The true Laws of free Monarchies,* which he published a little before his accession to the crown of England, affirmed, "That a good king, although he be above the law, will subject and frame his actions thereto, for example's sake to his subjects, and of his own free will, but not as subject or bound thereto." In another passage, "According to the fundamental law already alleged, we daily see, that in the parliament (which is nothing else but the head-court of the king and his vassals) the laws are but craved by his subjects, and only made by him at their rogation, and with their advice. For albeit the king *make daily* statutes and ordinances, enjoining such pains thereto as he thinks meet, without any advice of parliament or estates; yet it lies in the power of no parliament to make any kind of law or statute, without his sceptre be to it, for giving it the force of a law." *King James's Works,* p. 202. It is not to be supposed, that, at such a critical juncture, James had so little sense as, directly, in so material a point, to have openly shocked what were the universal established principles of that age: On the contrary, we are told by historians, that nothing tended more to facilitate his accession, than the good opinion entertained of him by the English, on account of his learned and judicious writings. The question, however, with regard to the royal power was, at this time, become a very dangerous point; and without employing ambiguous, insignificant terms, which determined nothing, it was impossible to please both king and parliament. Dr. Cowell, who had magnified the prerogative in words too intelligible, fell this session under the indignation of the commons. *Parliament. Hist.* vol. v. p. 221. The king

NOTES TO THE FIFTH VOLUME

himself, after all his magnificent boasts, was obliged to make his escape through a distinction, which he framed between a king *in abstracto* and a king *in concreto:* An abstract king, he said, had all power; but a concrete king was bound to observe the laws of the country, which he governed. *King James's Works,* p. 533. But, how bound? By conscience only? Or might his subjects resist him and defend their privileges? This he thought not fit to explain. And so difficult is it to explain that point, that, to this day, whatever liberties may be used by private enquirers, the laws have, very prudently, thought proper to maintain a total silence with regard to it.

NOTE [H], p. 59

Parl. Hist. vol. v. p. 290. So little fixed at this time were the rules of parliament, that the commons complained to the peers of a speech made in the upper house by the bishop of Lincoln; which it belonged only to that house to censure, and which the other could not regularly be supposed to be acquainted with. These at least are the rules established since the parliament became a real seat of power, and scene of business. Neither the king must take notice of what passes in either house, nor either house of what passes in the other, till regularly informed of it. The commons, in their famous protestation 1621, fixed this rule with regard to the king, though at present they would not bind themselves by it. But as liberty was yet new, those maxims, which guard and regulate it, were unknown and unpractised.

NOTE [I], p. 78

Some of the facts in this narrative, which seem to condemn Raleigh, are taken from the king's declaration, which being published by authority, when the facts were recent, being extracted from examinations before the privy council, and subscribed by six privy counsellors, among whom was Abbot archbishop of Canterbury, a prelate no wise complaisant to the court, must be allowed to have great weight, or rather to be of undoubted credit. Yet the most material facts are confirmed either by the nature and reason of the thing, or by Sir Walter's own apology and his letters. The king's declaration is in the Harleyan miscellany, Vol. 3, No. 2.

1. There seems to be an improbability, that the Spaniards, who knew nothing of Raleigh's pretended mine, should have built a town, in so wide a coast, within three miles of it. The chances are extremely against such a supposition: And it is more natural to think, that the view of plundering the town led him thither, than that of working a mine. 2. No such mine is there found to this day. 3. Raleigh in fact found no mine, and in fact he plundered and burned a Spanish town. Is it not more probable, therefore, that the latter was his intention? How can the secrets of his breast be rendered so visible as to counterpoise certain facts? 4. He confesses, in his letter to lord Carew, that, though he knew it, yet he concealed from the king the settlement of the Spaniards on that coast. Does not this fact alone render him sufficiently criminal? 5. His commission impowers him only to settle on

a coast possessed by savage and barbarous inhabitants. Was it not the most evident breach of orders to disembark on a coast possessed by Spaniards? 6. His orders to Keymis, when he sent him up the river, are contained in his own apology, and from them it appears, that he knew (what was unavoidable) that the Spaniards would resist, and would oppose the English landing and taking possession of the country. His intentions, therefore were hostile from the beginning. 7. Without provocation, and even when at a distance, he gave Keymis orders to dislodge the Spaniards from their own town. Could any enterprize be more hostile? And considering the Spaniards as allies to the nation, could any enterprize be more criminal? Was he not the aggressor, even though it should be true that the Spaniards fired upon his men at landing? It is said, he killed three or four hundred of them. Is that so light a matter? 8. In his letter to the king, and in his apology, he grounds his defence on former hostilities exercised by the Spaniards against other companies of Englishmen. These are accounted for by the ambiguity of the treaty between the nations. And it is plain, that though these might possibly be reasons for the king's declaring war against that nation, they could never intitle Raleigh to declare war, and, without any commission, or contrary to his commission, to invade the Spanish settlements. He pretends indeed that peace was never made with Spain in the Indies: A most absurd notion! The chief hurt which the Spaniards could receive from England was in the Indies; and they never would have made peace at all, if hostilities had been still to be continued on these settlements. By secret agreement, the English were still allowed to support the Dutch even after the treaty of peace. If they had also been allowed to invade the Spanish settlements, the treaty had been a full peace to England, while the Spaniards were still exposed to the full effects of war. 9. If the claim to the property of that country, as first discoverers, was good, in opposition to present settlement, as Raleigh pretends; why was it not laid before the king with all its circumstances, and submitted to his judgment? 10. Raleigh's force is acknowledged by himself to have been insufficient to support him in the possession of St. Thomas against the power of which Spain was master on that coast; yet it was sufficient, as he owns, to take by surprize and plunder twenty towns. It was not therefore his design to settle, but to plunder. By these confessions, which I have here brought together, he plainly betrays himself. 11. Why did he not stay and work his mine, as at first he projected? He apprehended that the Spaniards would be upon him with a greater force. But before he left England, he knew that this must be the case, if he invaded any part of the Spanish colonies. His intention therefore never was to settle, but only to plunder. 12. He acknowledges that he knew neither the depth nor riches of the mine, but only that there was some ore there. Would he have ventured all his fortune and credit on so precarious a foundation? 13. Would the other adventurers, if made acquainted with this, have risqued every thing to attend him? Ought a fleet to have been equipped for an experiment? Was there not plainly an imposture in the management of this affair? 14. He says to Keymis, in his orders,

NOTES TO THE FIFTH VOLUME

Bring but a basket-full of ore, and it will satisfy the king, that my project was not imaginary. This was easily done from the Spanish mines; and he seems to have been chiefly displeased at Keymis for not attempting it. Such a view was a premeditated apology to cover his cheat. 15. The king in his declaration imputes it to Raleigh, that as soon as he was at sea, he immediately fell into such uncertain and doubtful talk of his mine, and said, that it would be sufficient if he brought home a basket-full of ore. From the circumstance last mentioned, it appears that this imputation was not without reason. 16. There are many other circumstances of great weight in the king's declaration; that Raleigh, when he fell down to Plymouth, took no pioneers with him, which he always declared to be his intention; that he was no wise provided with instruments for working a mine, but had a sufficient stock of warlike stores; that young Raleigh, in attacking the Spaniards, employed the words, which, in the narration, I have put in his mouth; that the mine was moveable, and shifted as he saw convenient: Not to mention many other public facts which prove him to have been highly criminal against his companions as well as his country. Howel in his letters says, that there lived in London, in 1645, an officer, a man of honour, who asserted, that he heard young Raleigh speak these words, vol. ii. letter 63. That was a time when there was no interest in maintaining such a fact. 17. Raleigh's account of his first voyage to Guiana proves him to have been a man capable of the most extravagant credulity or most impudent imposture. So ridiculous are the stories which he tells of the Inca's chimerical empire in the midst of Guiana; the rich city of El Dorado, or Manao, two days journey in length, and shining with gold and silver; the old Peruvian prophecies in favour of the English, who, he says, were expresly named as the deliverers of that country, long before any European had ever touched there; the Amazons or republic of women; and in general, the vast and incredible riches which he saw on that continent, where nobody has yet found any treasures. This whole narrative is a proof that he was extremely defective either in solid understanding, or morals, or both. No man's character indeed seems ever to have been carried to such extremes as Raleigh's, by the opposite passions of envy and pity. In the former part of his life, when he was active and lived in the world, and was probably best known, he was the object of universal hatred and detestation throughout England; in the latter part, when shut up in prison, he became, much more unreasonably, the object of great love and admiration.

As to the circumstances of the narrative, that Raleigh's pardon was refused him, that his former sentence was purposely kept in force against him, and that he went out under these express conditions, they may be supported by the following authorities. 1. The king's word and that of six privy-counsellors, who affirm it for fact. 2. The nature of the thing. If no suspicion had been entertained of his intentions, a pardon would never have been refused to a man, to whom authority was entrusted. 3. The words of the commission itself, where he is simply stiled Sir Walter Raleigh, and not *faithful and well beloved*, according to the usual and never-failing stile on such occasions. 4. In all the letters which he wrote home to Sir Ralph Winwood and to his own wife, he always considers himself as a person unpardoned and liable to the law. He seems indeed, immediately upon the failure of his enterprize, to have become desperate, and to have expected the fate which he met with.

It is pretended, that the king gave intelligence to the Spaniards of Raleigh's project; as if he had needed to lay a plot for destroying a man, whose life had been fourteen years, and still was, in his power. The Spaniards wanted no other intelligence to be on their guard, than the known and public fact of Raleigh's armament. And there was no reason why the king should conceal from them the project of a settlement, which Raleigh pretended, and the king believed, to be entirely innocent.

The king's chief blame seems to have lain in his negligence, in allowing Raleigh to depart without a more exact scrutiny: But for this he apologizes, by saying, that sureties were required for the good behaviour of Raleigh and all his associates in the enterprize, but that they gave in bonds for each other: A cheat which was not perceived till they had failed, and which encreased the suspicion of bad intentions.

Perhaps the king ought also to have granted Raleigh a pardon for his old treason, and to have tried him anew for his new offences. His punishment in that case would not only have been just, but conducted in a just and unexceptionable manner. But we are told that a ridiculous opinion at that time prevailed in the nation (and it is plainly supposed by Sir Walter in his apology) that, by treaty, war was allowed with the Spaniards in the Indies, though peace was made in Europe: And while that notion took place, no jury would have found Raleigh guilty. So that had not the king punished him upon the old sentence, the Spaniards would have had a just cause of complaint against the king, sufficient to have produced a war, at least to have destroyed all cordiality between the nations.

This explication I thought necessary, in order to clear up the story of Raleigh; which, though very obvious, is generally mistaken in so gross a manner, that I scarcely know its parallel in the English history.

NOTE [J], p. 85

This parliament is remarkable for being the epoch, in which were first regularly formed, though without acquiring these denominations, the parties of court and country; parties, which have ever since continued, and which, while they oft threaten the total dissolution of the government, are the real causes of its permanent life and vigour. In the ancient feudal constitution, of which the English partook with other European nations, there was a mixture, not of authority and liberty, which we have since enjoyed in this island, and which now subsist uniformly together; but of authority and anarchy, which perpetually shocked with each other, and which took place alternately, according as circumstances were more or less favourable to either of them. A parliament composed of barbarians, summoned from their fields and forests, uninstructed by study, conversation,

NOTES TO THE FIFTH VOLUME

or travel; ignorant of their own laws and history, and unacquainted with the situation of all foreign nations; a parliament called precariously by the king, and dissolved at his pleasure; sitting a few days, debating a few points prepared for them, and whose members were impatient to return to their own castles, where alone they were great, and to the chace, which was their favourite amusement. Such a parliament was very little fitted to enter into a discussion of all the questions of government, and to share, in a regular manner, the legal administration. The name, the authority of the king alone appeared, in the common course of government; in extraordinary emergencies, he assumed, with still better reason, the sole direction; the imperfect and unformed laws left, in every thing, a latitude of interpretation; and when the ends, pursued by the monarch, were, in general, agreeable to his subjects, little scruple or jealousy was entertained with regard to the regularity of the means. During the reign of an able, fortunate, or popular prince, no member of either house, much less of the lower, durst think of entering into a formed party, in opposition to the court; since the dissolution of the parliament, must, in a few days, leave him unprotected, to the vengeance of his sovereign, and to those stretches of prerogative, which were then so easily made, in order to punish an obnoxious subject. During an unpopular and weak reign, the current commonly ran so strong against the monarch, that none durst inlist themselves in the court-party; or if the prince was able to engage any considerable barons on his side, the question was decided with arms in the field, not by debates or arguments in a senate or assembly. And upon the whole, the chief circumstance, which, during ancient times, retained the prince in any legal form of administration, was, that the sword, by the nature of the feudal tenures, remained still in the hands of his subjects; and this irregular and dangerous check had much more influence than the regular and methodical limits of the laws and constitution. As the nation could not be compelled, it was necessary that every public measure of consequence, particularly that of levying new taxes, should seem to be adopted by common consent and approbation.

The princes of the house of Tudor, partly by the vigour of their administration, partly by the concurrence of favourable circumstances, had been able to establish a more regular system of government; but they drew the constitution so near to despotism, as diminished extremely the authority of the parliament. The senate became, in a great degree, the organ of royal will and pleasure: Opposition would have been regarded as a species of rebellion: And even religion, the most dangerous article in which innovations could be introduced, had admitted, in the course of a few years, four several alterations, from the authority alone of the sovereign. The parliament was not then the road to honour and preferment: The talents of popular intrigue and eloquence were uncultivated and unknown: And though that assembly still preserved authority, and retained the privilege of making laws and bestowing public money, the members acquired not, upon that account, either with prince or people, much more weight and consideration. What powers were necessary for conducting the machine of government, the king was accustomed, of himself, to assume. His own revenues supplied him with money sufficient for his ordinary expences. And when extraordinary emergencies occurred, the prince needed not to solicit votes in parliament, either for making laws or imposing taxes, both of which were now become requisite for public interest and preservation.

The security of individuals, so necessary to the liberty of popular councils, was totally unknown in that age. And as no despotic princes, scarcely even the eastern tyrants, rule entirely without the concurrence of some assemblies, which supply both advice and authority; little, but a mercenary force, seems then to have been wanting towards the establishment of a simple monarchy in England. The militia, though more favourable to regal authority, than the feudal institutions, was much inferior, in this respect, to disciplined armies; and if it did not preserve liberty to the people, it preserved, at least, the power, if ever the inclination should arise, of recovering it.

But so low, at that time, ran the inclination towards liberty, that Elizabeth, the last of that arbitrary line, herself no less arbitrary, was yet the most renowned and most popular of all the sovereigns, that had filled the throne of England. It was natural for James to take the government as he found it, and to pursue her measures, which he heard so much applauded; nor did his penetration extend so far as to discover, that neither his circumstances nor his character could support so extensive an authority. His narrow revenues and little frugality began now to render him dependent on his people, even in the ordinary course of administration. Their encreasing knowledge discovered to them that advantage, which they had obtained; and made them sensible of the inestimable value of civil liberty. And as he possessed too little dignity to command respect, and too much good-nature to impress fear, a new spirit discovered itself every day in the parliament; and a party, watchful of a free constitution, was regularly formed in the house of commons.

But notwithstanding these advantages acquired to liberty, so extensive was royal authority, and so firmly established in all its parts, that it is probable the patriots of that age would have despaired of ever resisting it, had they not been stimulated by religious motives, which inspire a courage unsurmountable by any human obstacle.

The same alliance, which has ever prevailed between kingly power and ecclesiastical authority, was now fully established in England; and while the prince assisted the clergy in suppressing schismatics and innovators, the clergy, in return, inculcated the doctrine of an unreserved submission and obedience to the civil magistrate. The genius of the church of England, so kindly to monarchy, forwarded the confederacy; its submission to episcopal jurisdiction; its attachment to ceremonies, to order, and to a decent pomp and splendor of worship; and in a word, its affinity to the same superstition of the catholics, rather than to the wild fanaticism of the puritans.

On the other hand, opposition to the church, and the persecutions under which they laboured, were sufficient to throw the puritans into the country party, and to beget political principles little favourable to the high pretensions of the sovereign. The spirit too of enthusiasm; bold, daring, and uncontrouled; strongly disposed their minds to adopt republican tenets; and inclined them to arrogate, in their actions and conduct, the same liberty, which they assumed, in their rapturous flights and ecstasies. Ever since the first origin of that sect, through the whole reign of Elizabeth as well as of James, puritanical principles had been understood in a double sense, and expressed the opinions favourable both to political and to ecclesiastical liberty. And as the court, in order to discredit all parliamentary opposition, affixed the denomination of puritans to its antagonists; the religious puritans willingly adopted this idea, which was so advantageous to them, and which confounded their cause with that of the patriots or country party. Thus were the civil and ecclesiastical factions regularly formed; and the humour of the nation, during that age, running strongly towards fanatical extravagancies, the spirit of civil liberty gradually revived from its lethargy, and by means of its religious associate, from which it reaped more advantage than honour, it secretly enlarged its dominion over the greater part of the kingdom.

This Note was in the first editions a part of the text; but the author omitted it, in order to avoid, as much as possible, the style of dissertation in the body of his history. The passage however, contains views so important, that, he thought it might be admitted as a note.

NOTE [K], p. 92

This protestation is so remarkable, that it may not be improper to give it in its own words. "The commons now assembled in parliament, being justly occasioned thereunto, concerning sundry liberties, franchises, and privileges, of parliament, amongst others here mentioned, do make this protestation following; That the liberties, franchises, and jurisdictions of parliament are the ancient and undoubted birth right and inheritance of the subjects of England; and that the urgent and arduous affairs concerning the king, state, and defence of the realm and of the church of England; and the maintenance and making of laws, and redress of mischiefs and grievances, which daily happen within this realm, are proper subjects and matter of council and debate in parliament; and that in the handling and proceeding of those businesses, every member of the house of parliament hath, and, of right, ought to have, freedom of speech to propound, treat, reason, and bring to conclusion the same; and that the commons in parliament have like liberty and freedom to treat of these matters, in such order as in their judgment shall seem fittest, and that every member of the said house hath like freedom from all impeachment, imprisonment, and molestation (other than by censure of the house itself) for or concerning any speaking, reasoning, or declaring of any matter or matters touching the parliament or parliament-business. And that if any of the said members be complained of and questioned for any thing done or said in parliament, the same is to be shown to the king by the advice and assent of all the commons assem-

HISTORY OF ENGLAND

bled in parliament, before the king give credence to any private information." Franklyn, p. 65. Rushworth, vol. i. p. 53. Kennet, p. 747. Coke, p. 77.

NOTE [L] p. 112

The moment the prince embarked at St. Andero's, he said, to those about
him, that it was folly in the Spaniards to use him so ill, and allow him to
depart: A proof that the duke had made him believe they were insincere in
the affair of the marriage and the Palatinate: For, as to his reception, in
other respects, it had been altogether unexceptionable. Besides, had not
the prince believed the Spaniards to be insincere, he had no reason to
quarrel with them, though Buckingham had. It appears, therefore, that
Charles himself must have been deceived. The multiplied delays of the
dispensation, though they arose from accident, afforded Buckingham a
plausible pretext for charging the Spaniards with insincerity.

NOTE [M], p. 113

Among other particulars, he mentions a sum of 80,000 pounds borrowed
from the king of Denmark. In a former speech to the parliament, he told
them, that he had expended 500,000 pounds in the cause of the Palatine,
besides the voluntary contribution given him by the people. See Franklyn,
p. 50. But what is more extraordinary, the treasurer, in order to show his
own good services, boasts to the parliament, that by his contrivance, 60,000
pounds had been saved in the article of exchange in the sums remitted to
the Palatine. This seems a great sum, nor is it easy to conceive whence the
king could procure such vast sums as would require a sum so considerable
to be paid in exchange. From the whole, however, it appears, that the king
had been far from neglecting the interests of his daughter and son-in-law,
and had even gone far beyond what his narrow revenue could afford.

NOTE [N], p. 114

How little this principle had prevailed, during any former period of the
English government, particularly during the last reign, which was certainly
not so perfect a model of liberty as most writers would represent it, will
easily appear from many passages in the history of that reign. But the ideas
of men were much changed, during about twenty years of a gentle and
peaceful administration. The commons, though James, of himself, had
recalled all patents of monopolies, were not contented without a law against
them, and a declaratory law too; which was gaining a great point, and
establishing principles very favourable to liberty: But they were extremely
grateful, when Elizabeth, upon petition (after having once refused their
requests) recalled a few of the most oppressive patents; and employed some
soothing expressions towards them.

The parliament had surely reason, when they confessed, in the seventh
of James, that he allowed them more freedom of debate, than ever was
indulged by any of his predecessors. His indulgence in this particular,
joined to his easy temper, was probably one cause of the great power

assumed by the commons. Monsieur de la Boderie, in his dispatches, vol. i. p. 449. mentions the liberty of speech in the house of commons as a new practice.

NOTE [O], p. 119

Rymer, tom. xviii. p. 224. 'Tis certain that the young prince of Wales, afterwards Charles II. had protestant governors from his early infancy; first the earl of Newcastle, then the Marquis of Hertford. The king, in his memorial to foreign churches after the commencement of the civil wars, insists on his care in educating his children in the protestant religion, as a proof that he was no-wise inclined to the catholic. Rushworth, vol. v. p. 752. It can scarcely, therefore, be questioned, but this article, which has so odd an appearance, was inserted only to amuse the pope, and was never intended by either party to be executed.

NOTE [P], p. 127

"Monarchies," according to Sir Walter Raleigh, "are of two sorts touching their power or authority, *viz.* 1. Entire, where the whole power of ordering all state matters, both in peace and war, doth, by law and custom, appertain to the prince, as in the English kingdom; where the prince hath the power to make laws, league and war; to create magistrates; to pardon life; of appeal, &c. Though, to give a contentment to the other degrees, they have a suffrage in making laws, yet ever subject to the prince's pleasure and negative will.—2. Limited or restrained, that hath no full power in all the points and matters of state, as the military king that hath not the sovereignty in time of peace, as the making of laws, &c. But in war only, as the Polonian king. *Maxims of State.*" And a little after, "In every just state, some part of the government is, or ought to be, imparted to the people, as in a kingdom, a voice and suffrage in making laws; and sometimes also of levying of arms (if the charge be great, and the prince forced to borrow help of his subjects) the matter rightly may be propounded to a parliament, that the tax may *seem* to have proceeded from themselves. So consultations and some proceedings in judicial matters may, in part, be referred to them. The reason, lest, seeing themselves to be in no number nor of reckoning, they mislike the state or government." This way of reasoning differs little from that of king James, who considered the privileges of the parliament as matters of grace and indulgence, more than of inheritance. It is remarkable that Raleigh was thought to lean towards the puritanical party, notwithstanding these positions. But ideas of government change much in different times.

Raleigh's sentiments on this head are still more openly expressed, in his *Prerogative of parliaments,* a work not published till after his death. It is a dialogue between a courtier or counsellor and a country justice of peace, who represents the patriot party, and defends the highest notions of liberty, which the principles of that age would bear. Here is a passage of it: "*Counsellor.* That which is done by the king, with the advice of his private or privy council, is done by the king's absolute power. *Justice.* And by whose power is it done in parliament but by the king's absolute power? Mistake it not, my lord: The three estates do but advise as the privy council doth; which advice, if the king embrace, it becomes the king's own act in the one, and the king's law in the other, &c. "

The earl of Clare, in a private letter to his son-in-law Sir Thomas Wentworth, afterwards earl of Strafford, thus expresses himself, "We live under a prerogative government, "where book law submits to *lex loquens.* " He spoke from his own, and all his ancestors' experience. There was no single instance of power, which a king of England might not, at that time, exert, on pretence of necessity or expediency: The continuance alone or frequent repetition of arbitrary administration might prove dangerous, for want of force to support it. It is remarkable that this letter of the earl of Clare was written in the first year of Charles's reign; and consequently must be meant of the general genius of the government, not the spirit or temper of the monarch. See Strafford's letters, vol. i. p. 32. From another letter in the same collection, vol. i. p. 10. it appears that the council sometimes assumed the power of forbidding persons disagreeable to the court, to stand in the elections. This authority they could exert in some instances; but we are not thence to infer, that they could shut the door of that house to every one who was not acceptable to them. The genius of the ancient government reposed more trust in the king, than to entertain any such suspicion, and it allowed scattered instances, of such a kind as would have been totally destructive of the constitution, had they been continued without interruption.

I have not met with any English writer in that age, who speaks of England as a limited monarchy, but as an absolute one, where the people have many privileges. That is no contradiction. In all European monarchies, the people have privileges; but whether dependant or independant on the will of the monarch, is a question, that, in most governments, it is better to forbear. Surely that question was not determined, before the age of James. The rising spirit of the parliament, together with that king's love of general, speculative principles, brought it from its obscurity, and made it be commonly canvassed. The strongest testimony, that I remember from a writer of James's age, in favour of English liberty, is in cardinal Bentivoglio, a foreigner, who mentions the English government as similar to that of the low-country provinces under their princes, rather than to that of France or Spain. Englishmen were not so sensible that their prince was limited, because they were sensible, that no individual had any security against a stretch of prerogative: But foreigners, by comparison, could perceive, that these stretches were, at that time, from custom or other causes, less frequent in England than in other monarchies. Philip de Comines too remarked the English constitution to be more popular, in his time, than that of France. But in a paper written by a patriot in 1627, it is remarked that the freedom of speech in parliament had been lost in England, since the days of Comines. See Franklyn, p. 238. Here is a stanza of Malherbe's Ode to Mary de Medicis, the queen-regent, written in 1614.

Entre les rois a qui cet age
Doit son principal ornement,
Ceux de la Tamise et du Tage
Font louer leur gouvernement:
Mais en de si calmes provinces,
Ou le peuple adore les princes,
Et met au gré le plus haut
L'honneur du sceptre legitime,
Scauroit-on excuser le crime
De ne regner pas comme il faut.

The English, as well as the Spaniards, are here pointed out as much more obedient subjects than the French, and much more tractable and submissive to their princes. Though this passage be taken from a poet, every man of judgment will allow its authority to be decisive. The character of a national government cannot be unknown in Europe; though it changes sometimes very suddenly. Machiavel, in his Dissertations on Livy, says repeatedly, that France was the most legal and most popular monarchy then in Europe.

NOTE [Q], p. 127

Passive obedience is expressly and zealously inculcated in the homilies, composed and published by authority, in the reign of queen Elizabeth. The convocation, which met in the very first year of the king's reign, voted as high monarchical principles as are contained in the decrees of the university of Oxford, during the rule of the tories. These principles, so far from being deemed a novelty, introduced by James's influence, passed so smoothly, that no historian has taken notice of them: They were never the subject of controversy, or dispute, or discourse; and it is only by means of bishop Overall's Convocation-book, printed near seventy years after, that we are acquainted with them. Would James, who was so cautious, and even timid, have ventured to begin his reign with a bold stroke, which would have given just ground of jealousy to his subjects? It appears, from that monarch's Basilicon Doron, written while he was in Scotland, that the republican ideas of the origin of power from the people were, at that time, esteemed puritanical novelties. The patriarchal scheme, it is remarkable, is inculcated in those votes of the convocation preserved by Overall; nor was Filmer the first inventor of those absurd notions.

NOTE [R], p. 142

That of the honest historian Stowe seems not to have been of this number. "The great blessings of God," says he, "through increase of wealth in the common subjects of this land, especially upon the citizens of London; such within men's memory, and chiefly within these few years of peace, that, except there were now due mention of some sort made thereof, it would in time to come be held incredible, &c." In another place, "Amongst the manifold tokens and signs of the infinite blessings of Almighty God bestowed upon this kingdom, by the wondrous and merciful establishing of peace within ourselves, and the full benefit of concord with all christian nations and others: Of all which graces let no man dare to presume he can speak too much; whereof in truth there can never be enough said, neither was there ever any people less considerate and less thankful than at this time, being not willing to endure the memory of their present happiness, as well as in the universal increase of commerce and traffic throughout the kingdom, great building of royal ships and by private merchants, the re-peopling of cities, towns, and villages, beside the discernable and sudden increase of fair and costly buildings, as well within the city of London as the suburbs thereof, especially within these twelve years, &c. "

NOTE [S], p. 170

By a speech of Sir Simon D'Ewes, in the first year of the long parliament, it clearly appears, that the nation never had, even to that time, been rightly informed concerning the transactions of the Spanish negociation; and still believed the court of Madrid to have been altogether insincere in their professions. What reason, upon that supposition, had they to blame either the prince or Buckingham for their conduct, or for the narrative delivered to the parliament? This is a capital fact, and ought to be well attended to. D'Ewes's speech is in Nalson, vol. ii. p. 368. No author or historian of that age mentions the discovery of Buckingham's impostures as a cause of disgust in the parliament. Whitlocke, p. 1, only says, that the commons began to suspect, *that it had been spleen in Buckingham,* not zeal for public good, *which had induced him to break the Spanish match:* A clear proof that his falsehood was not suspected. Wilson, p. 780, says, that Buckingham lost his popularity after Bristol arrived, not because that nobleman discovered to the world the falsehood of his narrative, but because he proved that Buck-ingham, while in Spain, had professed himself a papist; which is false, and which was never said by Bristol. In all the debates which remain, not the least hint is ever given, that any falsehood was suspected in the narrative. I shall farther add, that even if the parliament had discovered the deceit in Buckingham's narrative, this ought not to have altered their political mea-sures, or made them refuse supply to the king. They had supposed it practicable to wrest the Palatinate by arms from the house of Austria; they had represented it as prudent to expend the blood and treasure of the nation in such an enterprize; they had believed that the king of Spain never had any sincere intention of restoring that principality. It is certain that he had not now any such intention: And though there was reason to suspect, that this alteration in his views had proceeded from the ill conduct of Buckingham, yet past errors could not be retrieved; and the nation was undoubtedly in the same situation, which the parliament had ever sup-posed, when they so much harassed their sovereign, by their impatient, importunate, and even undutiful solicitations. To which we may add, that Charles himself was certainly deceived by Buckingham, when he corrobo-rated his favourite's narrative by his testimony. Party historians are somewhat inconsistent in their representations of these transactions: They represent the Spaniards as totally insincere, that they may reproach James with credulity in being so long deceived by them: They represent them as sincere, that they may reproach the king, the prince, and the duke, with falsehood in their narrative to the parliament. The truth is, they were insincere at first; but the reasons, proceeding from bigotry, were not suspected by James, and were at last overcome. They became sincere; but the prince, deceived by the many unavoidable causes of delay, believed that they were still deceiving him.

NOTE [T], p. 197

This petition is of so great importance, that we shall here give it at length. Humbly shew unto our sovereign lord the king, the lords spiritual and temporal, and commons, in parliament assembled. That, whereas it is declared and enacted, by a statute made in the time of the reign of king Edward I. commonly called *Statutum de tallagio non concedendo,* that no tallage or aid shall be levied by the king or his heirs in this realm, without the good will and assent of the archbishops, bishops, earls, barons, knights, burgesses, and other the freemen of the commonalty of this realm: And, by authority of parliament holden in the five and twentieth year of the reign of king Edward III. it is declared and enacted, That, from thenceforth, no person shall be compelled to make any loans to the king against his will, because such loans were against reason, and the franchise of the land: And, by other laws of this realm, it is provided, that none should be charged by any charge or imposition called a benevolence, or by such like charge: By which the statutes before mentioned, and other the good laws and statutes of this realm, your subjects have inherited this freedom, that they should not be compelled to contribute to any tax, tallage, aid, or other like charge, not set by common consent in parliament.

II. Yet nevertheless, of late divers commissions directed to sundry commissioners in several counties, with instructions, have issued; by means whereof your people have been in divers places assembled, and required to lend certain sums of money unto your majesty, and many of them, upon their refusal so to do, have had an oath administered unto them not warrantable by the laws or statutes of this realm, and have been constrained to become bound to make appearance and give attendance before your privy council, and in other places, and others of them, have been therefore imprisoned, confined, and sundry other ways molested and disquieted: And divers other charges have been laid and levied upon your people, in several counties, by lord-lieutenants, deputy-lieutenants, commissioners for musters, justices of peace, and others, by command or direction from your majesty, or your privy council, against the laws and free customs of this realm.

III. And whereas also, by the statute called *The great charter of the liberties of England,* it is declared and enacted, That no freeman may be taken or imprisoned, or be disseized of his freehold or liberties, or his free customs, or be outlawed or exiled, or in any manner destroyed, but by the lawful judgment of his peers, or by the law of the land.

IV. And, in the eight and twentieth year of the reign of king Edward III. it was declared and enacted, by authority of parliament, That no man, of what estate or condition that he be, should be put out of his land or tenements; nor taken, nor imprisoned, nor disherited, nor put to death, without being brought to answer by due process of law.

V. Nevertheless, against the tenor of the said statutes, and other the good laws and statutes of your realm to that end provided, divers of your subjects have of late been imprisoned without any cause shewed: And, when, for their deliverance, they were brought before justice, by your majesty's writs of *Habeas Corpus,* there to undergo and receive as the court should order, and their keepers commanded to certify the causes of their detainer, no cause was certified, but that they were detained by your majesty's special command, signified by the lords of your privy council, and yet were returned back to several prisons, without being charged with any thing to which they might make answer according to the law.

VI. And whereas of late great companies of soldiers and mariners have been dispersed into divers counties of the realm, and the inhabitants, against their wills, have been compelled to receive them into their houses, and there to suffer them to sojourn, against the laws and customs of this realm, and to the great grievance and vexation of the people.

VII. And whereas also, by authority of parliament, in the five and twentieth year of the reign of king Edward III. it is declared and enacted, That no man should be fore-judged of life or limb against the form of the *Great charter,* and law of the land: And, by the said *Great charter,* and other the laws and statutes of this your realm, no man ought to be judged to death but by the laws established in this your realm, either by the customs of the same realm, or by acts of parliament: And whereas no offender, of what kind soever, is exempted from the proceedings to be used, and punishments to be inflicted by the laws and statutes of this your realm: Nevertheless, of late divers commissions, under your majesty's great seal, have issued forth, by which certain persons have been assigned and appointed commissioners, with power and authority to proceed within the land, according to the justice of martial law, against such soldiers and mariners, or other dissolute persons joining with them, as should commit any murther, robbery, felony, mutiny, or other outrage or misdemeanour whatsoever, and by such summary course and order as is agreeable to martial law, and as is used in armies in time of war, to proceed to the trial and condemnation of such offenders, and them to cause to be executed and put to death according to the law martial.

VIII. By pretext whereof some of your majesty's subjects have been, by some of the said commissioners, put to death, when and where, if, by the laws and statutes of the land, they had deserved death, by the same laws and statutes also they might, and by no other ought, to have been judged and executed.

NOTES TO THE FIFTH VOLUME

IX. And also sundry grievous offenders, by colour thereof claiming an exemption, have escaped the punishments due to them by the laws and statutes of this your realm, by reason that divers of your officers and ministers of justice have unjustly refused or forborn to proceed against such offenders, according to the same laws and statutes, upon pretence that the said offenders were punishable only by martial law, and by authority of such commissions as aforesaid: Which commissions, and all other of like nature, are wholly and directly contrary to the said laws and statutes of this your realm.

X. They do therefore humbly pray your most excellent majesty, That no man hereafter be compelled to make or yield any gift, loan, benevolence, tax, or such like charge, without common consent, by act of parliament: And that none be called to make answer, or take such oath, or to give attendance, or be confined or otherways molested or disquieted concerning the same, or for refusal thereof: And that no freeman, in any such manner as is before-mentioned, be imprisoned or detained: And that your majesty would be pleased to remove the said soldiers and mariners, and that people may not be so burthened in time to come; and that the aforesaid commissions, for proceeding by martial law, may be revoked and annulled: And that hereafter no commissions of like nature may issue forth, to any person or persons whatsoever, to be executed as aforesaid, lest, by colour of them, any of your majesty's subjects be destroyed, or put to death, contrary to the laws and franchise of the land.

XI. All which they most humbly pray of your most excellent majesty, as their rights and liberties, according to the laws and statutes of this realm: And that your majesty would also vouchsafe to declare, That the awards, doings, and proceedings to the prejudice of your people, in any of the premisses, shall not be drawn hereafter into consequence or example: And that your majesty would be also graciously pleased, for the further comfort and safety of your people, to declare your royal will and pleasure, that in the things aforesaid, all your officers and ministers shall serve you according to the laws and statutes of this realm, as they tender the honour of your majesty, and the prosperity of this kingdom. *Stat. 17 Car. cap. 14.*

NOTE [U], p. 208

The reason assigned by Sir Philip Warwick, p. 2. for this unusual measure of the commons, is, that they intended to deprive the crown of the prerogative, which it had assumed, of varying the rates of the impositions, and at the same time were resolved to cut off the new rates fixed by James. These were considerable diminutions both of revenue and prerogative; and whether they would have there stopped, considering their present disposition, may be much doubted. The king, it seems, and the lords, were resolved not to trust them; nor to render a revenue once precarious, which perhaps they might never afterwards be able to get re-established on the old footing.

NOTE [V], p. 236

Here is a passage of Sir John Davis's question concerning impositions, p. 131. "This power of laying on arbitrarily new impositions being a prerogative in point of government, as well as in point of profit, it cannot be restrained or bound by act of parliament; it cannot be limited by any certain or fixt rule of law, no more than the course of a pilot upon the sea, who must turn the helm or bear higher or lower sail, according to the wind or weather; and therefore it may be properly said, that the king's prerogative in this point, is as strong as *Samson;* it cannot be bound: For though an act of parliament be made to restrain it, and the king doth give his consent unto it, as *Samson* was bound with his own consent, yet if the *Philistines* come; that is, if any just or important occasion do arise, it cannot hold or restrain the prerogative; it will be as thread, and broken as easy as the bonds of *Samson* —The king's prerogatives are the sun-beams of the crown, and as inseparable from it as the sun-beams from the sun: The king's crown must be taken from him; *Samson's* hair must be cut out, before his courage can be any jot abated. Hence it is that neither the king's act nor any act of parliament can give away his prerogative.

NOTE [W], p. 278

We shall here make use of the liberty, allowed in a note, to expatiate a little on the present subject. It must be confessed, that the king in this declaration touched upon that circumstance in the English constitution, which it is most difficult, or rather altogether impossible, to regulate by laws, and which must be governed by certain delicate ideas of propriety and decency, rather than by any exact rule or prescription. To deny the parliament all right of remonstrating against what they esteem grievances, were to reduce that assembly to a total insignificancy, and to deprive the people of every advantage, which they could reap from popular councils. To complain of the parliament's employing the power of taxation, as the means of extorting concessions from their sovereign, were to expect, that they would entirely disarm themselves, and renounce the sole expedient, provided by the constitution, for enduring to the kingdom a just and legal administration. In different periods of English story, there occur instances of their remonstrating with their princes in the freest manner, and sometimes of their refusing supply when disgusted with any circumstance of public conduct. 'Tis, however, certain, that this power, though essential to parliaments, may easily be abused, as well by the frequency and minuteness of their remonstrances, as by their intrusion into every part of the king's counsels and determinations. Under colour of advice, they may give disguised orders; and in complaining of grievances, they may draw to themselves every power of government. Whatever measure is embraced, without consulting them, may be pronounced an oppression of the people; and till corrected, they may refuse the most necessary supplies to their indigent sovereign. From the very nature of this parliamentary liberty, it is evident, that it must be left unbounded by law: For who can foretell, how frequently grievances may occur, or what part of administration may be affected by them? From the nature too of the human frame, it may be expected, that this liberty would be exerted in its full extent, and no branch of authority be allowed to remain unmolested in the hands of the prince: For will the weak limitations of respect and decorum be sufficient to restrain human ambition, which so frequently breaks through all the prescriptions of law and justice?

But, here it is observable, that the wisdom of the English constitution, or rather the concurrence of accidents, has provided, in different periods, certain irregular checks to this privilege of parliament, and thereby maintained, in some tolerable measure, the dignity and authority of the crown.

In the ancient constitution, before the beginning of the seventeenth century, the meetings of parliament were precarious and were not frequent. The sessions were short; and the members had no leisure, either to get acquainted with each other, or with public business. The ignorance of the age made men more submissive to that authority which governed them. And above all, the large demesnes of the crown, with the small expence of government during that period, rendered the prince almost independent, and taught the parliament to preserve great submission and duty towards him.

In our present constitution, many accidents, which have rendered governments, every where, as well as in Great Britain, much more burthensome than formerly, have thrown into the hands of the crown the disposal of a large revenue, and have enabled the king, by the private interest and ambition of the members, to restrain the public interest and ambition of the body. While the opposition (for we must still have an opposition, open or disguised) endeavours to draw every branch of administration under the cognizance of parliament, the courtiers reserve a part to the disposal of the crown; and the royal prerogative, though deprived of its ancient powers, still maintains a due weight in the balance of the constitution.

It was the fate of the house of Stuart to govern England at a period, when the former source of authority was already much diminished, and before the latter began to show in any tolerable abundance. Without a regular and fixed foundation, the throne perpetually tottered; and the prince sat upon it anxiously and precariously. Every expedient, used by James and Charles, in order to support their dignity, we have seen, attended with sensible inconveniences. The majesty of the crown, derived from ancient powers and prerogatives, procured respect; and checked the approaches of insolent intruders: But it begat in the king so high an idea of his own rank and station, as made him incapable of stooping to popular courses, or submitting, in any degree, to the controul of parliament. The alliance with the hierarchy strengthened law by the sanction of religion: But it enraged the puritanical party, and exposed the prince to the attacks of enemies, numerous, violent, and implacable. The memory too of these two kings, from like causes, has been attended, in some degree, with the same infelicity, which pursued them during the whole course of their lives.

Though it must be confessed, that their skill in government was not proportioned to the extreme delicacy of their situation; a sufficient indulgence has not been given them, and all the blame, by several historians, has been unjustly thrown on *their* side. Their violations of law, particularly those of Charles, are, in some few instances, transgressions of a plain limit, which was marked out to royal authority. But the encroachments of the commons, though, in the beginning, less positive and determinate, are no less discernible by good judges, and were equally capable of destroying the just balance of the constitution. While they exercised the powers, transmitted to them, in a manner more independent, and less compliant, than had ever before been practised; the kings were, perhaps imprudently, but, as they imagined, from necessity, tempted to assume powers, which had scarcely ever been exercised, or had been exercised in a different manner, by the crown. And from the shock of these opposite pretensions, together with religious controversy, arose all the factions, convulsions, and disorders, which attended that period.

This Note was, in the first editions, a part of the text.

NOTE [X], p. 324

Mr. Carte, in his life of the duke of Ormond, has given us some evidence to prove, that this letter was intirely a forgery of the popular leaders, in order to induce the king to sacrifice Strafford. He tells us, that Strafford said so to his son, the night before his execution. But there are some reasons, why I adhere to the common way of telling this story. 1. The account of the forgery comes through several hands, and from men of characters not fully known to the public. A circumstance which weakens every evidence. It is a hearsay of a hearsay. 2. It seems impossible, but young Lord Strafford must inform the king, who would not have failed to trace the forgery, and expose his enemies to their merited infamy. 3. It is not to be conceived but Clarendon and Whitlocke, not to mention others, must have heard of the matter. 4. Sir George Ratcliffe, in his life of Strafford, tells the story the same way that Clarendon and Whitlocke do. Would he also, who was Strafford's intimate friend, never have heard of the forgery? It is remarkable, that his life is dedicated or addressed to young Strafford. Would not he have put Sir George right in so material and interesting a fact?

NOTE [Y], p. 325

What made this bill appear of less consequence was, that the parliament voted tonnage and poundage for no longer a period than two months: And as that branch was more than half of the revenue, and the government could not possibly subsist without it; it seemed indirectly in the power of the parliament to continue themselves as long as they pleased. This indeed was true in the ordinary administration of government: But on the approaches towards a civil war, which was not then foreseen, it had been of great consequence to the king to have reserved the right of dissolution, and to have endured any extremity rather than allow the continuance of the parliament.

NOTE [Z], p. 349

It is now so universally allowed, notwithstanding some muttering to the contrary, that the king had no hand in the Irish rebellion, that it will be superfluous to insist on a point which seems so clear. I shall only suggest a very few arguments, among an infinite number which occur. (1) Ought the affirmation of perfidious, infamous rebels ever to have passed for any authority? (2) Nobody can tell us what the words of the pretended commission were. That commission which we find in Rushworth, vol. v. p. 400, and in Milton's Works, Toland's edition, is plainly an imposture; because it pretends to be dated in October 1641, yet mentions facts which happened not till some months after. It appears that the Irish rebels, observing some inconsistence in their first forgery, were obliged to forge this commission anew, yet could not render it coherent or probable. (3) Nothing could be more obviously pernicious to the king's cause than the Irish rebellion; because it increased his necessities, and rendered him still more dependent on the parliament, who had before sufficiently shown on what terms they would assist him. (4) The instant the king heard of the rebellion, which was a very few days after its commencement, he wrote to the parliament, and gave over to them the management of the war. Had he built any projects on that rebellion, would he not have waited some time, to see how they would succeed? Would he presently have adopted a measure which was evidently so hurtful to his authority? (5) What can be imagined to be the king's projects? To raise the Irish to arms, I suppose, and bring them over to England for his assistance. But is it not plain, that the king never intended to raise war in England? Had that been his intention, would he have rendered the parliament perpetual? Does it not appear, by the whole train of events, that the parliament forced him into the war? (6) The king conveyed to the justices intelligence which ought to have prevented the rebellion. (7) The Irish catholics, in all their future transactions with the king, where they endeavour to excuse their insurrection, never had the assurance to plead his commission. Even amongst themselves they dropped that pretext. It appears that Sir Phelim Oneale, chiefly, and he only at first, promoted that imposture. See Carte's Ormond, vol. iii. No. 100, 111, 112, 114, 115, 121, 132, 137. (8) Oneale himself confessed the imposture on his trial and at his execution. See Nalson, vol. ii. p. 528. Maguire, at his execution, made a like confession. (9) It is ridiculous to mention the justification which Charles II. gave to the marquis of Antrim, as if he had acted by his father's commission. Antrim had no hand in the first rebellion and the massacre. He joined not the rebels till two years after: It was with the king's consent; and he did important service, in sending over a body of men to Montrose.

HISTORY OF ENGLAND

NOTE [AA], p. 380

The great courage and conduct, displayed by many of the popular leaders, have commonly inclined men to do them, in one respect, more honour than they deserve, and to suppose, that, like able politicians, they employed pretences which they secretly despised, in order to serve their selfish purposes. It is, however, probable, if not certain, that they were, generally speaking, the dupes of their own zeal. Hypocrisy, quite pure and free from fanaticism, is perhaps, except among men fixed in a determined philosophical scepticism, then unknown, as rare as fanaticism entirely purged from all mixture of hypocrisy. So congenial to the human mind are religious sentiments, that it is impossible to counterfeit long these holy fervours, without feeling some share of the assumed warmth. And, on the other hand, so precarious and temporary, from the frailty of human nature, is the operation of these spiritual views, that the religious ecstasies, if constantly employed, must often be counterfeit, and must be warped by those more familiar motives of interest and ambition, which insensibly gain upon the mind. This indeed seems the key to most of the celebrated characters of that age. Equally full of fraud and of ardour, these pious patriots talked perpetually of seeking the Lord, yet still pursued their own purposes; and have left a memorable lesson to posterity, how delusive, how destructive, that principle is by which they were animated.

With regard to the people, we can entertain no doubt, that the controversy was, on their part, entirely theological. The generality of the nation could never have flown out into such fury, in order to obtain new privileges and acquire greater liberty than they and their ancestors had ever been acquainted with. Their fathers had been entirely satisfied with the government of Elizabeth: Why should they have been thrown into such extreme rage against Charles, who, from the beginning of his reign, wished only to maintain such a government? And why not, at least, compound matters with him, when, by all his laws, it appeared, that he had agreed to depart from it? Especially, as he had put it entirely out of his power to retract that resolution. It is in vain, therefore, to dignify this civil war and the parliamentary authors of it, by supposing it to have any other considerable foundation than theological zeal, that great and noted source of animosity among men. The royalists also were very commonly zealots; but as they were, at the same time, maintaining the established constitution, in state as well as church, they had an object, which was natural, and which might produce the greatest passion, even without any considerable mixture of theological fervour. *The former part of this note was, in the first editions, a part of the text.*

NOTE [BB], p. 381

In some of these declarations, supposed to be penned by Lord Falkland, is found the first regular definition of the constitution, according to our present ideas of it, that occurs in any English composition; at least any published by authority. The three species of government, monarchical, aristocratical, and democratical, are there plainly distinguished, and the English government is expressly said to be none of them pure, but all of them mixed and tempered together. This stile, though the sense of it was implied in many institutions, no former king of England would have used, and no subject would have been permitted to use. Banks and the crown-lawyers against Hambden, in the case of ship-money, insist plainly and openly on the king's absolute and sovereign power: And the opposite lawyers do not deny it: They only assert, that the subjects have also a fundamental property in their goods, and that no part of them can be taken but by their own consent in parliament. But that the parliament was instituted to check and controul the king, and share the supreme power, would, in all former times, have been esteemed very blunt and indiscreet, if not illegal, language. We need not be surprised that governments should long continue, though the boundaries of authority, in their several branches, be implicit, confused, and undetermined. This is the case all over the world. Who can draw an exact line between the spiritual and temporal powers in catholic states? What code ascertained the precise authority of the Roman senate, in every occurrence? Perhaps the English is the first mixed government, where the authority of every part has been very accurately defined: And yet there still remain many very important questions between the two houses, that, by common consent, are buried in a discreet silence. The king's power is, indeed, more exactly limited; but this period, of which we now treat, is the time at which that accuracy commenced. And it appears from Warwick and Hobbes, that many royalists blamed this philosophical precision in the king's penman, and thought that the veil was very imprudently drawn off the mysteries of government. It is certain, that liberty reaped mighty advantages from these controversies and enquiries; and the royal authority itself became more secure, within those provinces which were assigned to it. *Since the first publication of this history, the sequel of Lord Clarendon has been published; where that nobleman asserts, that he himself was the author of most of these remonstrances and memorials of the king.*

NOTE [CC], p. 399

Whitlocke, who was one of the commissioners, says, p. 65, "In this treaty, the king manifested his great parts and abilities, strength of reason and quickness of apprehension, with much patience in hearing what was objected against him; wherein he allowed all freedom, and would himself sum up the arguments, and give a most clear judgment upon them. His unhappiness was, that he had a better opinion of others judgments than of his own, though they were weaker than his own; and of this the parliament commissioners had experience to their great trouble. They were often waiting on the king, and debating some points of the treaty with him, until midnight, before they could come to a conclusion. Upon one of the most material points, they pressed his majesty with their reasons and best arguments they could use to grant what they desired. The king said, he was fully satisfied, and promised to give them his answer in writing according to their desire; but because it was then past midnight, and too late to put it into writing, he would have it drawn up next morning (when he commanded them to wait on him again) and then he would give them an answer in writing, as it was now agreed upon. But next morning the king told them, that he had altered his mind: And some of his friends, of whom the commissioners enquired, told them; that after they were gone, and even his council retired, some of his bed-chamber never left pressing and persuading him till they prevailed on him to change his former resolutions." It is difficult, however, to conceive that any negociation could have succeeded between the king and parliament, while the latter insisted, as they did all along, on a total submission to all their demands; and challenged the whole power, which they professedly intended to employ, to the punishment of all the king's friends.

NOTE [DD], p. 407

The author is sensible, that some blame may be thrown upon him, on account of this last clause in Mr. Hambden's character; as if he were willing to entertain a suspicion of bad intentions, where the actions were praiseworthy. But the author's meaning is directly contrary: He esteems the last actions of Mr. Hambden's life to have been very blameable; though, as they were derived from good motives only pushed to an extreme, there is room left to believe, that the intentions of that patriot, as well as of many of his party, were laudable. Had the preceding administration of the king, which we are apt to call arbitrary, proceeded from ambition, and an unjust desire of encroaching on the ancient liberties of the people, there would have been less reason for giving him any trust, or leaving in his hands a considerable share of that power which he had so much abused. But if his conduct was derived in a great measure from necessity, and from a natural desire of defending that prerogative which was transmitted to him from his ancestors, and which his parliaments were visibly encroaching on; there is no reason why he may not be esteemed a very virtuous prince, and entirely worthy of trust from his people. The attempt, therefore, of totally annihilating monarchical power, was a very blameable extreme; especially as it was attended with the danger, to say the least, of a civil war, which, besides the numberless ills inseparable from it, exposed liberty to much greater perils than it could have incurred under the now limited authority of the king. But as these points could not be supposed so clear during the time as they are, or may be, at present; there are great reasons of alleviation for men who were heated by the controversy, or engaged in the action. And it is remarkable, that even at present, (such is the force of party prejudices,) there are few people who have coolness enough to see these matters in a proper light, and are convinced that the parliament could prudently have stopped in their pretensions. They still plead the violations of liberty attempted by the king, after granting the petition of right; without consid-

575

ering the extreme harsh treatment, which he met with, after making that
great concession, and the impossibility of supporting government by the
revenue then settled on the crown. The worst of it is, that there was a great
tang of enthusiasm in the conduct of the parliamentary leaders, which,
though it might render their conduct sincere, will not much enhance their
character with posterity. And though Hambden was, perhaps, less infected
with this spirit than many of his associates, he appears not to have been
altogether free from it. His intended migration to America, where he could
only propose the advantage of enjoying puritanical prayers and sermons,
will be allowed a proof of the prevalence of this spirit in him.

NOTE [EE], p. 420

In a letter of the king to the queen, preserved in the British Musæum, and
published by Mrs. Macaulay, vol. iv. p. 420, he says, that unless religion was
preserved, the militia (being not as in France a formed powerful strength)
would be of little use to the crown; and that if the pulpits had not obedience, which would never be, if presbyterian government was absolutely
established, the king would have but small comfort of the militia. This
reasoning shows the king's good sense, and proves, that his attachment to
episcopacy, though partly founded on religious principles, was also, in his
situation, derived from the soundest views of civil policy. In reality, it was
easy for the king to perceive, by the necessary connexion between trifles
and important matters, and by the connexion maintained at that time
between religion and politics, that, when he was contending for the surplice, he was, in effect, fighting for his crown and even for his head. Few
of the popular party could perceive this connexion. Most of them were
carried headlong by fanaticism; as might be expected in the ignorant multitude. Few even of the leaders seem to have had more enlarged views.

NOTE [FF], p. 459

That Laud's severity was not extreme, appears from this fact, that he caused
the acts or records of the high commission court to be searched, and found
that there had been fewer suspensions, deprivations, and other punishments, by three, during the seven years of his time, than in any seven
years of his predecessor Abbot; who was notwithstanding in great esteem
with the house of commons. *Troubles and trials of Laud,* p. 164. But Abbot
was little attached to the court, and was also a puritan in doctrine, and bore
a mortal hatred to the papists. Not to mention, that the mutinous spirit was
rising higher in the time of Laud, and would less bear controul. The
maxims, however, of his administration were the same that had ever prevailed in England, and that had place in every other European nation,
except Holland, which studied chiefly the interests of commerce, and
France, which was fettered by edicts and treaties. To have changed them
for the modern maxims of toleration, how reasonable soever, would have
been deemed a very bold and dangerous enterprize. It is a principle advanced by president Montesquieu, that, where the magistrate is satisfied

with the established religion, he ought to repress the first attempts towards innovation, and only grant a toleration to sects that are diffused and established. See l'Esprit des Loix, liv. 25. chap. 10. According to this principle, Laud's indulgence to the catholics, and severity to the puritans, would admit of apology. I own, however, that it is very questionable, whether persecution can in any case be justifyed: But, at the same time, it would be hard to give that appellation to Laud's conduct, who only enforced the act of uniformity, and expelled the clergymen that accepted of benefices, and yet refused to observe the ceremonies, which they previously knew to be enjoined by law. He never refused them separate places of worship; because they themselves would have esteemed it impious to demand them, and no less impious to allow them.

NOTE [GG], p. 481

Dr. Birch has written a treatise on this subject. It is not my business to oppose any facts contained in that gentleman's performance. I shall only produce arguments, which prove that Glamorgan, when he received his private commission, had injunctions from the king to act altogether in concert with Ormond. (1.) It seems to be implied in the very words of the commission. Glamorgan is empowered and authorised to treat and conclude with the confederate Roman catholics in Ireland. "If upon necessity any *(articles)* be condescended unto, wherein the king's lieutenant cannot so well be seen in, as not fit for us at present publickly to own." Here no articles are mentioned, which are not fit to be communicated to Ormond, but only not fit for him and the king publicly to be seen in, and to avow. (2.) The king's protestation to Ormond, ought, both on account of that prince's character, and the reasons he assigns, to have the greatest weight. The words are these, "Ormond, I cannot but add to my long letter, that, upon the word of a christian, I never intended Glamorgan should treat any thing without your approbation, much less without your knowledge. For besides the injury to you, I was always diffident of his judgment (though I could not think him so extremely weak as now to my cost I have found); which you may easily perceive in a postscript of a letter of mine to you." Carte, vol. ii. App. xxiii. It is impossible, that any man of honour, however he might dissemble with his enemies, would assert a falsehood in so solemn a manner to his best friend, especially where that person must have had opportunities of knowing the truth. The letter, whose postscript is mentioned by the king, is to be found in Carte, vol. ii. App. xiii. (3.) As the king had really so low an opinion of Glamorgan's understanding, it is very unlikely that he would trust him with the sole management of so important and delicate a treaty. And if he had intended, that Glamorgan's negociation should have been independant of Ormond, he would never have told the latter nobleman of it, nor have put him on his guard against Glamorgan's imprudence. That the king judged aright of this nobleman's character, appears from his *century of arts or scantling of inventions,* which is a ridiculous compound of lies, chimeras and impossibilities, and shows what might be expected from such a man. (4.) Mr. Carte has published a whole series of the king's correspondence with Ormond from the time that Glamorgan came into Ireland; and it is evident that Charles all along considers the lord lieutenant as the person who was conducting the negociations with the Irish. The 31st of July 1645, after the battle of Naseby, being reduced to great straits, he writes earnestly to Ormond to conclude a peace upon certain conditions mentioned, much inferior to those granted by Glamorgan; and to come over himself with all the Irish he could engage in his service. Carte, vol. iii. No. 400. This would have been a great absurdity, if he had already fixed a different canal, by which, on very different conditions, he purposed to establish a peace. On the 22d of October, as his distresses multiply, he somewhat enlarges the conditions, though they still fall short of Glamorgan's: A new absurdity! See Carte, vol. iii. p. 411. (5.) But what is equivalent to a demonstration, that Glamorgan was conscious, that he had no powers to conclude a treaty on these terms, or without consulting the lord lieutenant, and did not even expect, that the king would ratify the articles, is the defeazance which he gave to the Irish council at the time of signing the treaty. "The earl of Glamorgan does no way intend hereby to oblige his majesty other than he himself shall please, after he has received these 10,000 men as a pledge and testimony of the said Roman catholics' loyalty and fidelity to his majesty; yet he promises faithfully, upon his word and honour, not to acquaint his majesty with this defeazance, till he had endeavoured, as far as in him lay, to induce his majesty to the granting of the particulars in the said articles: But that done, the said commissioners discharge the said earl of Glamorgan, both in honour and conscience, of any farther engagement to them therein; though his majesty should not be pleased to grant the said particulars in the articles mentioned; the said earl having given them assurance, upon his word, honour, and voluntary oath, that he would never, to any person whatsoever, discover this defeazance in the interim without their consents." Dr. Birch, p. 96. All Glamorgan's view was to get troops for the king's service without hurting his own honour or his master's. The wonder only is, why the Irish accepted of a treaty, which bound no body, and which the very person, who concludes it, seems to confess he does not expect to be ratified. They probably hoped, that the king would, from their services, be more easily induced to ratify a treaty which was concluded, than to consent to its conclusion. (6.) I might add, that the lord lieutenant's concurrence in the treaty was the more requisite; because without it the treaty could not be carried into execution by Glamorgan, nor the Irish troops be transported into England: And even with Ormond's concurrence, it clearly appears, that a treaty, so ruinous to the protestant religion in Ireland, could not be executed in opposition to the zealous protestants in that kingdom. No one can doubt of this truth, who peruses Ormond's correspondence in Mr. Carte. The king was sufficiently apprised of this difficulty. It appears indeed to be the only reason why Ormond objected to the granting of high terms to the Irish catholics.

Dr. Birch, in p. 360, has published a letter of the king's to Glamorgan, where he says, "Howbeit I know you cannot be but confident of my making good all instructions and promises to you and the nuncio." But it is to be remarked that this letter is dated in April 5, 1646; after there had been a new negociation entered into between Glamorgan and the Irish, and after a provisional treaty had even been concluded between them. See Dr. Birch, p. 179. The king's assurances, therefore, can plainly relate only to this recent transaction. The old treaty had long been disavowed by the king, and supposed by all parties to be annulled.

NOTE [HH], p. 510

Salmonet, Ludlow, Hollis, &c. all these, especially the last, being the declared inveterate enemies of Cromwel, are the more to be credited, when they advance any fact, which may serve to apologize for his violent and criminal conduct. There prevails a story, that Cromwel intercepted a letter written to the queen, where the king said, that he would first raise and then destroy Cromwel. But, besides that this conduct seems to contradict the character of the king, it is, on other accounts, totally unworthy of credit. It is first told by Roger Coke, a very passionate and foolish historian, who wrote too so late as king William's reign; and even he mentions it only as a mere rumor or hearsay, without any known foundation. In the Memoirs of lord Broghill, we meet with another story of an intercepted letter which deserves some more attention, and agrees very well with the narration here given. It is thus related by Mr. Maurice, chaplain to Roger, earl of Orrery. "Lord Orrery, in the time of his greatness with Cromwel, just after he had so seasonably relieved him in his great distress at Clonmell, riding out of Youghall one day with him and Ireton, they fell into discourse about the king's death. Cromwel thereupon said more than once, that if the king had followed his own judgment, and had been attended by none but trusty servants, he had fooled them all; and that once they had a mind to have closed with him, but, upon something that happened, fell off from that design. Orrery finding them in good humour, and being alone with them, asked, if he might presume to desire to know, why they would once have closed with his majesty, and why they did not. Cromwel very freely told him, he would satisfy him in both his queries. The reason (says he) why we would have closed with the king was this: We found that the Scotch and presbyterians began to be more powerful than we, and were likely to agree with him, and leave us in the lurch. For this reason we thought it best to prevent them by offering first to come in upon reasonable conditions: But whilst our thoughts were taken up with this subject, there came a letter to us from one of our spies, who was of the king's bed-chamber, acquainting us, that our final doom was decreed that very day; that he could not possibly learn what it was, but we might discover it, if we could but intercept a letter sent from the king to the queen, wherein he informed her of his resolution; that this letter was sown up in the skirt of a saddle, and the bearer of it would come with the saddle upon his head, about ten of the clock that night to the Blue Boar in Holborn, where he was to take horse for Dover. The messenger knew nothing of the letter in the saddle, though some in Dover did. We were at Windsor (said Cromwel) when we received this letter, and immediately upon the receipt of it, Ireton and I resolved to take one trusty fellow with us, and go in troopers habits to that inn. We did so; and leaving our man at the gate of the inn (which had a wicket only open to let persons in and out), to watch and give us notice when any man came in with a saddle, we went into a drinking-stall. We there continued, drinking cans of beer, till about ten of the clock, when our sentinel at the gate gave us notice, that the man with the saddle was come. We rose up presently, and just as the man was leading out his horse saddled we came up to him with drawn swords, and told him we were to search all that went in and out there; but as he looked like an honest man, we would only search his saddle, and so dismiss him. The saddle was ungirt; we carried it into the stall, where we had been drinking, and ripping open one of the skirts, we found the letter we wanted. Having thus got it into our hands, we delivered the man (whom we had left with our centinel) his saddle, told him he was an honest fellow, and bid him go about his business; which he did; pursuing his journey without more ado, and ignorant of the harm he had suffered. We found in the letter, that his majesty acquainted the queen, that he was courted by both factions, the Scotch presbyterians and the army; and that those which bade the fairest for him should have him: But yet he thought he should close with the Scots sooner than with the other. Upon this we returned to Windsor; and finding we were not like to have good terms from the king, we from that time vowed his destruction." "This relation suiting well enough with other passages and circumstances at this time, I have inserted to gratify the reader's curiosity." Carte's Ormond, vol. ii. p. 12.

NOTE [II], p. 512

These are the words: "Laneric; I wonder to hear (if that be true) that some of my friends say, that my going to Jersey would have much more furthered my personal treaty, than my coming hither, for which, as I see no colour of reason, so I had not been here, if I had thought that fancy true, or had not been secured of a personal treaty; of which I neither do, nor I hope will repent: For I am daily more and more satisfied with the governor, and find these islanders very good, peaceable and quiet people. This encouragement I have thought not unfit for you to receive, hoping at least it may do good upon others, though needless to you." Burnet's Memoirs of Hamilton, p. 326. See also Rushworth, part 4, vol. ii. p. 941. All the writers of that age, except Clarendon, represent the king's going to the isle of Wight as voluntary and intended. Perhaps the king thought it little for his credit, to be trepanned into this measure, and was more willing to take it on himself as entirely voluntary. Perhaps, he thought it would encourage his friends, if they thought him in a situation, which was not disagreeable to him.

NOTE [JJ], p. 526

The king composed a letter to the prince, in which he related the whole course of this transaction, and accompanied his narrative with several wise, as well as pathetical reflections and advices. The words with which he concluded the letter, are remarkable. "By what hath been said, you see how long I have laboured in the search of peace: Do not you be disheartened to tread in the same steps. Use all worthy means to restore yourself to your rights, but prefer the way of peace: Show the greatness of your mind, rather to conquer your enemies by pardoning, than by punishing. If you saw how unmanly and unchristian the implacable disposition is in our ill-wishers, you would avoid that spirit. Censure me not for having parted with so much of our right: The price was great; but the commodity was, security to us, peace to my people. And I am confident, that another parliament would remember, how useful a king's power is to a people's liberty; of how much power I divested myself, that I and they might meet once again in a parliamentary way, in order to agree the bounds of prince and people. Give belief to my experience, never to affect more greatness or prerogative, than what is really and intrinsically for the good of the subjects, not the satisfaction of favourites. If you thus use it, you will never want means to be a father to all, and a bountiful prince to any, whom you incline to be extraordinarily gracious to. You may perceive, that all men entrust their treasure, where it returns them interest; and if a prince, like the sea, receive and repay all the fresh streams, which the rivers entrust with him, they will not grudge, but pride themselves, to make up an ocean. These considerations may make you as great a prince as your father is a low one; and your state may be so much the more established, as mine hath been shaken. For our subjects have learned, I dare say, that victories over their princes, are but triumphs over themselves, and so, will more unwillingly hearken to changes hereafter. The English nation are a sober people, however, at present, infatuated. I know not but this may be the last time, I may speak to you or the world publicly. I am sensible into what hands I am fallen; and yet, I bless God, I have those inward refreshments, which the malice of my enemies cannot perturb. I have learned to be busy myself, by retiring into myself; and therefore can the better digest whatever befals me, not doubting, but God's providence will restrain our enemies power, and turn their fierceness into his praise. To conclude, if God give you success, use it humbly, and be ever far from revenge. If he restore you to your right on hard conditions, whatever you promise, keep. These men, who have violated laws, which they were bound to preserve, will find their triumphs full of trouble. But do not you think any thing in the world worth attaining, by foul and unjust means."

NOTE [KK], p. 543

The imputation of insincerity on Charles I. like most party clamours, is difficult to be removed; though it may not here be improper to say something with regard to it. I shall first remark, that this imputation seems to be of a later growth than his own age; and that even his enemies, though they loaded him with many calumnies, did not insist on this accusation. Ludlow, I think, is almost the only parliamentarian, who imputes that vice to him; and how passionate a writer he is, must be obvious to every one. Neither Clarendon nor any other of the royalists ever justify him from insincerity; as not supposing that he had ever been accused of it. In the second place, his deportment and character in common life was free from that vice: He was reserved, distant, stately; cold in his address, plain in his discourse, inflexible in his principles; wide of the caressing, insinuating manners of his son; or the professing, talkative humour of his father. The imputation of insincerity must be grounded on some of his public actions, which we are therefore in the third place to examine. The following are the only instances, which I find cited to confirm that accusation. (1.) His vouching Buckingham's narrative of the transactions in Spain. But it is evident that Charles himself was deceived: Why otherwise did he quarrel with Spain? The following is a passage of a letter from lord Kensington, ambassador in France, to the duke of Buckingham, Cabbala, p. 318. "But his highness (the prince) had observed as great a weakness and folly as that, in that after they (the Spaniards) had used him so ill, they would suffer him to depart, which was one of the first speeches he uttered after he came into the ship: But did he say so? said the queen (of France). Yes, madam, I will assure you, quoth I, from the witness of mine own ears. She smiled and replied, Indeed I heard he was used ill. So he was, answered I, but not in his entertainment; for that was as splendid as that country could afford it; but in their frivolous delays, and in the unreasonable conditions which they propounded and pressed, upon the advantage they had of his princely person." (2.) Bishop Burnet, in his history of the house of Hamilton, p. 154, has preserved a letter of the king's to the Scottish bishops, in which he desires them not to be present at the parliament, where they would be forced to ratify the abolition of their own order: "For," adds the king, "we do hereby assure you, that it shall be still one of our chiefest studies how to rectify and establish the government of that church aright, and to repair your losses, which we desire you to be most confident of." And in another place, "You may rest secure, that though perhaps we may give way for the present to that which will be prejudicial both to the church and our own government: yet we shall not leave thinking in time how to remedy both." But does the king say, that he will arbitrarily revoke his concessions? Does not candor require us rather to suppose, that he hoped his authority would so far recover as to enable him to obtain the national consent to re-establish episcopacy, which he believed so material a part of religion as well as of government? It is not easy indeed to think how he could hope to effect this purpose in any other way than his father had taken, that is, by consent of parliament. (3.) There is a passage in lord Clarendon, where it is said, that the king assented the more easily to the bill, which excluded the bishops from the house of peers; because he thought, that that law, being enacted by force, could not be valid. But the king certainly reasoned right in that conclusion. Three-fourths of the temporal peers were at that time banished by the violence of the populace: Twelve bishops were unjustly thrown into the Tower by the commons: Great numbers of the commons themselves were kept away by fear or violence: The king himself was chased from London. If all this be not force, there is no such thing. But this scruple of the king's affects only the bishop's bill, and that against pressing. The other constitutional laws had passed without the least appearance of violence, as did indeed all the bills passed during the first year, except Strafford's attainder, which could not be recalled. The parliament, therefore, even if they had known the king's sentiments in this particular, could not, on that account, have had any just foundation of jealousy. (4.) The king's letter intercepted at Naseby, has been the source of much clamour. We have spoken of it already in chap. lviii. Nothing is more usual in all public transactions than such distinctions. After the death of Charles II. of Spain, king William's ambassadors gave the duke of Anjou the title of king of Spain: Yet at that very time king William was secretly forming alliances to dethrone him: And soon after he refused him that title, and insisted (as he had reason) that he had not acknowledged his right. Yet king William justly passes for a very sincere prince; and this transaction is not regarded as any objection to his character in that particular. In all the negociations at the peace of Ryswic, the French ambassadors always addressed king William as king of England; yet it was made an express article of the treaty, that the French king should acknowledge him as such. Such a palpable difference is there between giving a title to a prince, and positively recognizing his right to it. I may add, that Charles when he inserted that protestation in the council-books before his council, surely thought he had reason to justify his conduct. There were too many men of honour in that company to avow a palpable cheat. To which we may subjoin, that, if men were as much disposed to judge of this prince's actions with candor as severity, this precaution of entering a protest in his council-books might rather pass for a proof of scrupulous honour; lest he should afterwards be reproached with breach of his word, when he should think proper again to declare the assembly at Westminster no parliament. (5.) The denying of his commission to Glamorgan is another instance which has been cited. This matter has been already treated in a note to chap. lviii. That transaction was entirely innocent. Even if the king had given a commission to Glamorgan to conclude that treaty, and had ratified it, will any reasonable man, in our age, think it strange, that, in order to save his own life, his crown, his family, his friends, and his party, he should make a treaty with papists, and grant them very large concessions for their religion. (6.) There is another of the king's intercepted letters to the queen commonly mentioned; where, it is pretended, he talked of raising and then destroying Cromwel: But that story stands on no manner of foundation, as we have observed in a preceding note to this chapter. In a word, the parliament, after the commencement of their violences, and still more, after beginning the civil war, had

NOTES TO THE FIFTH VOLUME

reason for their scruples and jealousies, founded on the very nature of their situation, and on the general propensity of the human mind; not on any fault of the king's character; who was candid, sincere, upright; as much as any man, whom we meet with in history. Perhaps, it would be difficult to find another character so unexceptionable in this particular.

As to the other circumstances of Charles's character, chiefly exclaimed against, namely his arbitrary principles in government, one may venture to assert, that the greatest enemies of this prince will not find, in the long line of his predecessors, from the conquest to his time, any one king, except perhaps his father, whose administration was not more arbitrary and less legal, or whose conduct could have been recommended to him, by the popular party themselves, as a model, in this particular, for his government. Nor is it sufficient to say, that example and precedent can never authorize vices: Examples and precedents, uniform and ancient, can surely fix the nature of any constitution, and the limits of any form of government. There is indeed no other principle by which those land-marks or boundaries can be settled.

What a paradox in human affairs, that Henry VIII. should have been almost adored in his life-time and his memory be respected: While Charles I. should, by the same people, at no greater distance than a century, have been led to a public and ignominious execution, and his name be ever after pursued by falsehood and by obloquy! Even at present, an historian, who, prompted by his courageous generosity, should venture, though from the most authentic and undisputed facts, to vindicate the fame of that prince, would be sure to meet with such treatment, as would discourage even the boldest from so dangerous, however splendid an enterprize.

END OF THE FIFTH VOLUME